# The Palgrave Handbook of Humanitarian Logistics and Supply Chain Management

Gyöngyi Kovács • Karen Spens • Mohammad Moshtari
Editors

# The Palgrave Handbook of Humanitarian Logistics and Supply Chain Management

palgrave
macmillan

*Editors*
Gyöngyi Kovács
Hanken School of Economics
Helsinki, Finland

Karen Spens
Hanken School of Economics
Helsinki, Finland

Mohammad Moshtari
Hanken School of Economics
Helsinki, Finland

ISBN 978-1-137-59098-5          ISBN 978-1-137-59099-2 (eBook)
https://doi.org/10.1057/978-1-137-59099-2

Library of Congress Control Number: 2017941623

Cover illustration: Brain light / Alamy Stock Photo

Printed on acid-free paper

This Palgrave Macmillan imprint is published by Springer Nature
The registered company is Macmillan Publishers Ltd.
The registered company address is: The Campus, 4 Crinan Street, London, N1 9XW, United Kingdom

# Acknowledgements

## Handbook Reviewers:

| | |
|---|---|
| Afshin Mansoori | Brunel University |
| Alain Vaillancourt | Jönköping University |
| Alessandra Cozzolino | Sapienza University of Rome |
| Ali Torabi | University of Tehran |
| Altay Nezih | Driehaus College of Business |
| Amir Masoumi | Manhattan College |
| Andréa Cynthia Santos Duhamel | University of Technology of Troyes |
| Aris Matopoulos | Aston University |
| Arni Halldorsson | Chalmers University of Technology |
| Bartel Van de Walle | Delft University of Technology |
| Brito Jr Irineu | University of São Paulo |
| Carolien de Blok | University of Groningen |
| Cécile L'Hermitte | University of Tasmania |
| Charles Mbohwa | University of Johannesburg |
| David Grant | Hull University Business School |
| Diego Vega | NEOMA Business School |
| Erica Gralla | George Washington University |
| Gloria Cecilia Urrea Castano | University of Lugano |
| Graham Heaslip | Galway Mayo Institute of Technology |
| Hella Abidi | FOM University of Applied Sciences |
| Hlekiwe Kachali | Hanken School of Economics |
| Hossein Baharmand | University of Agder |
| Ioanna Falagara Sigala | Vienna University of Economics and Business |

| | |
|---|---|
| Isabell Storsjö | Hanken School of Economics |
| Jaime Andrés Castañeda | Universidad del Rosario |
| Karthik Sankaranarayanan | University of Ontario Institute of Technology |
| Kirstin Scholten | University of Groningen |
| Laura Laguna Salvadó | University of Toulouse – Mines Albi |
| Lijo John | Indian Institute of Management Kozhikode |
| Linda Annala | Hanken School of Economics |
| Mahed Maddah | Florida International University |
| Marc Goerigk | Lancaster University Management School |
| Maria Besiou | Kühne Logistics University |
| Maria Ehrnström | Hanken School of Economics |
| Mark Goh | National University of Singapore |
| Mark Wilson | Lincoln University |
| Matthieu Lauras | University of Toulouse – Mines Albi |
| Minchul Sohn | Hanken School of Economics |
| Natalie Simpson | State University of New York at Buffalo |
| Paul Larson | University of Manitoba |
| Pervaiz Akhtar | University of Hull |
| Peter Tatham | Griffith University |
| Prashant Barsing | Indian Institute of Management |
| Rolando Tomasini | UNOPS |
| Ruth Banomyong | Thammasat University |
| Sabari Prasanna | Hanken School of Economics |
| Sebastian Villa Betancur | University of Lugano |
| Simonov Kusi-Sarpong | Dalian University of Technology |
| Stephen Pettit | Cardiff University |
| Suhaiza Zailani | University of Malaya |
| Susanna Meriläinen | Hanken School of Economics |
| Tariq Syed | Lahore University of Management Sciences |
| Tina Comes | University of Agder |
| Tina Wakolbinger | Vienna University of Economics and Business |
| Tunca Tabaklar | University of Agder |
| Yasmine Hassan | KTH Royal Institute of Technology in Stockholm |
| Yewondwossen Tesfaye Gemechu | Hanken School of Economics |

# Contents

## Part VI   Conceptual, Future

# Notes on Contributers

**Natalie Simpson** is Associate Professor of Operations Management and Strategy at the University at Buffalo (SUNY) and a member of the UB Institute for Sustainable Transportation and Logistics. Natalie received an MBA and PhD from the University of Florida, and her research interests are emergency services and emergent networks.

**Zhasmina Tacheva** is a doctoral student in Supply Chains and Operations Management at the University at Buffalo (SUNY). Her research interests include sustainable supply chains and socially responsible logistics in emerging democracies and post-conflict regions. She has worked on dangerous goods and air freight-forwarding projects in Bulgaria and Poland.

**Ta-Wei (Daniel) Kao** is Assistant Professor in Operations Management at the University of Michigan-Dearborn. He received his MBA from National Cheng Kung University and PhD from the University at Buffalo (SUNY). His research appears in *EJOR*, the *Journal of Business and Industrial Marketing*, and *Computers in Human Behavior*.

**Yasmine Sabri** is a PhD candidate of Erasmus Mundus European Doctorate in Industrial Management. Currently she is working on finalising her PhD dissertation on supply chain configuration, in the School of Management, Politecnico di Milano, Italy, and Department of Industrial Economics and Management, KTH-Royal Institute of Technology, Sweden.

Yasmine holds an MSc in Production Engineering and Management from KTH-Royal Institute of Technology. Prior to embarking on her PhD research journey, she spent six years as a working professional, which laid the foundation to build a portfolio of diverse experience, with involvement in various operations management and business development projects in Egypt, UK, Sweden, and Italy.

**Karthik Sankaranarayanan** is Assistant Professor of Operations Management at the University of Ontario Institute of Technology, Canada. His research encompasses the study of complex adaptive systems using agent-based modeling, experimental design and other computational tools.

**Jaime Andrés Castañeda** is Principal Professor at the Del Rosario University's School of Management, Colombia, where he teaches supply chain and operations management topics at both undergraduate and graduate levels. He conducts research on behavioral issues in supply chain and operations management, including humanitarian logistics and supply chain management.

**Sebastian Villa** is Assistant Professor in the School of Management at the University of Los Andes and a visiting researcher at the University of Texas at Dallas. His research focuses in understanding the dynamics and behavioral biases that affects coordination in multi-level supply chains.

**Pervaiz Akhtar** is Senior Lecturer (Associate Professor), Program Director of the MSc Analytics/Data Science Division and Program Leader for BSc Logistics and Supply Chain Management at Hull University Business School, UK. Pervaiz has also worked for leading non-profit and for-profit organizations at senior levels (operations/logistics/project manager) and published in top-ranked journals.

**Minchul Sohn** is researcher at Hanken School of economics and HUMLOG Institute in Helsinki, Finland. His research area includes humanitarian supply chain in both relief and development, strategic decisions on logistics preparedness, climate risk in supply chain, and agriculture supply chain.

**Diego Vega** is Assistant Professor of Logistics and Supply Chain Management at the Neoma Business School (Reims, France) and Researcher at the CRET-LOG research centre (Aix-Marseille University). He is an Industrial Engineer and holds a PhD in management sciences:

specialty on logistics from the Aix-Marseille University. His research interests include humanitarian logistics and supply chain management, temporary organizations, and competence-based strategic management. Assistant Professor Diego Vega is the corresponding author and can be contacted at: diego.vega@neoma-bs.fr

**Mark M.J. Wilson** specialises in supply chain management and has over 23 years industry and defence experience in the fields of logistics, strategic supply chain management and operations at both tactical and senior managerial levels. Currently, Mark is researching humanitarian logistics, complex adaptive systems, network theory, supply chain governance and collaboration. Mark has published in national and international journals Mark can be contacted at: mark.wilson@lincoln.ac.nz

**Muhammad Umar** is a PhD scholar and also working as a research assistant in Lincoln University, New Zealand. He is doing his research in the supply chain discipline with special emphasis on resilience of food chains in disaster prone areas. He can be contacted at: Muhammad.umar@lincolnuni.ac.nz

**Jeff Heyl's** expertise resides in business management, economics and operations management. Jeff's specific research interests are quality management and measurement in both manufacturing and service environments, procurement systems and practices, supply chain management, and managing process change for complex systems. He can be contacted at: Jeff.heyl@lincoln.ac.nz

**Jihee Kim** is a PhD student in Logistics and Operations Management at Cardiff Business School, Cardiff University. She studied MA in Management with a higher degree at Durham University in the 2009–2010 academic year. She had worked in several organisations such as Korean National Assembly, Samsung, LG, and Korean Air. Her research is being funded by the **Economic and Social Research Council** (ESRC). Her research interests involve: cooperation, coordination, collaboration, supply chain integration, and partnerships in humanitarian and disaster relief supply chain management. In particular, she seeks to apply the key assumptions of Business-SCM and determine the suitability for the analysis of Humanitarian-SCM.

**Stephen Pettit** is Reader in Logistics and Operations Management at Cardiff Business School. In 1993 he was awarded a PhD from the University of Wales and he has worked at Cardiff Business School since 2000. He has been involved in a range of transport-related research projects, notably a ground-breaking project for the Department of Transport analysing the UK economy's requirements for people with seafaring experience. This work highlighted important issues relating to the decline in the number of UK seafaring officers. Subsequently, he has been involved in a range of transport-related research projects for EU DGTREN including the 'Economic Value of Shipping to the UK Economy'; an 'Analysis of the Cost Structure of the main TEN Ports'; and 'Work Organisation in Ports'. His most recent work has focused on Humanitarian Aid Logistics and Supply Chain Management. An initial project was funded by the Chartered Institute of Logistics and Transport through their Seedcorn Grant scheme and was co-researched with Anthony Beresford. This work has been extended through collaboration with Cranfield University in the Cardiff-Cranfield Humanitarian Logistics Initiative. Stephen has written a large number of journal papers, conference papers and reports primarily on port development, port policy and the logistics of humanitarian aid delivery.

**Irina Harris** is Lecturer in Logistics and Operations Modelling at Cardiff Business School, Cardiff University. Irina's background is Computer Science and her PhD focused on multi-objective optimisation for strategic and tactical network design from economic and environmental perspectives as part of the Green Logistics project. She has gained extensive knowledge of logistics modelling, transportation and optimisation through a partnership with industry and other academic partners. Irina's research interests range from logistics networks and operations modelling to collaborative partnerships and sustainable supply chains with the focus on data analysis and evaluating trade-offs related to different objectives. Her recent work also includes application of Information Systems/Technology in business/logistics environment.

**Anthony Beresford** is Professor of Logistics and Transport in the Cardiff Business School, Cardiff University, UK. He graduated with a BA in Geography from Manchester University and was subsequently awarded his PhD in Environmental Sciences at the University of East Anglia in 1982; his research was focused on climate change in East Africa. He has subsequently travelled widely in an advisory capacity within the ports, transport and humanitarian fields in Europe, Africa, Australasia and North America. He has been involved in a broad range of transport-related research and consultancy projects including: transport rehabilitation, aid distribution and trade facilitation for UNCTAD and, for example, for the Rwandan

Government. His cost model for Multimodal Transport has been widely used by UNESCAP Corridors in Southeast Asia, Africa and elsewhere. He has also advised both the United Kingdom and Welsh Governments on road transport and port policy options.

**Qing Lu** is Assistant Professor in Department of Logistics Management, Izmir University of Economics, Turkey. His interests include supply chain strategy, supply chain security and governance, humanitarian logistics, and supply chain sustainability. He obtained a PhD from the National University of Singapore (NUS) in 2006.

**Mark Goh** is Director for Industry Research at The Logistics Institute-Asia Pacific (TLIAP), and a faculty at the NUS Business School. His current interests are in supply chain strategy, performance measurement, and MCDM. He holds a PhD from the University of Adelaide.

**Robert de Souza** is Executive Director of TLIAP. He received his PhD, MSc and BSc Honors in the United Kingdom.

**Rameshwar Dubey** is Associate Professor with Symbiosis International University currently, on sabbatical leave at the South University of Science and Technology of China. He is also associated with various institutions of repute as a visiting scholar including DePaul University, University of Massachusetts at Dartmouth and Anhui University of Finance and Economics, China. Rameshwar is an Associate Editor for the *Global Journal of Flexible Systems Management* (Springer) and *International Journal of Innovation Science* (Emerald). He has edited over eight special issues and published over 70 papers.

**Nezih Altay** is Associate Professor at the Driehaus College of Business of DePaul University. His research specializes in disruption management and humanitarian supply chains. He has published his research in leading academic journals and presented in national and international arenas. He also co-edited two books: *Service Parts Management: Demand Forecasting and Inventory Control* (2011) and *Advances in Managing Humanitarian Operations* (2016), both published by Springer. He currently serves as the Co-Editor-in-Chief of the *Journal of Humanitarian Logistics & Supply Chain Management*, and Senior Editor of Disaster Management section of *Production and Operations Management*.

**Alessandra Cozzolino** is Researcher and Assistant Professor of Business Market Management at the Sapienza University of Rome, Faculty of Economics, Department of Management. She holds a PhD in Management and Finance. Her research interests focus on supply chain management, humanitarian logistics, and logistics service providers' strategies in sustainability innovation. She is corresponding author and can be contacted at: alessandra.cozzolino@uniroma1.it.

**Ewa Wankowicz** is PhD Candidate in Management, Banking and Commodity Sciences at the Sapienza University of Rome, Faculty of Economics, Department of Management. Her research interests are related to logistics, sustainable supply chain management and business model innovation.

**Enrico Massaroni** is Full Professor of Supply Chain Management and Planning and Strategic Management at the Sapienza University of Rome, Faculty of Economics, Department of Management. His research interests include logistics and supply chain management, production and operations management.

**Kirstin Scholten** is Assistant Professor in Supply Chain Management at the University of Groningen, the Netherlands. She conducts empirical, qualitatively based research around the area of supply chain risk and resilience management in different contexts (e.g. food, public sector, disaster/ humanitarian aid management). Her research has been published in several books and journals, including *Supply Chain Management: An International Journal* (SCMIJ), the *International Journal of Operations & Production Management* (IJOPM), and the *International Journal of Physical Distribution & Logistics Management* (IJPDLM).

**Carolien de Blok** is Assistant Professor in Supply Chain Management at the University of Groningen, the Netherlands. She conducts qualitative research in a variety of public contexts (e.g. health care, justice, refugee networks) and in that mainly focuses on the design and management of chains and networks. Her research has been published in several books and journals, including *Journal of Operations Management* (JOM), the *International Journal of Operations & Production Management* (IJOPM), and the *International Journal of Production Economics* (IJPE).

**Robbin-Jan Haar** graduated in the summer of 2016 in Supply Chain Management at the University of Groningen on the topic of service supply chain flexibility in the European refugee crisis. In his studies, he was energized by courses that allowed for creativity and out-of-the-box solutions, which also partly explains his choice for graduating on the subject of the European refugee crisis. He is currently employed as a Risk Consultant at Deloitte in Amsterdam.

**Graham Heaslip** is Professor of Logistics and Head of School at Galway Mayo Institute of Technology (GMIT), Ireland. Prior to joining GMIT, Graham was Associate Professor of Logistics at UNSW, Australia where he was the course director of the MSc in Logistics. Graham completed his PhD studies in the area of Civil Military Cooperation / Coordination at the Logistics Institute, University of Hull, for which he was awarded the James Cooper Memorial Cup for best PhD in Logistics and Supply Chain Management by the Chartered Institute of Logistics and Transport. Prior to entering academia Graham spent fourteen years working in the Irish Defence Forces both at home and abroad in a variety of logistical appointments, as well as spending time seconded to Humanitarian agencies in a logistical capacity. Graham's research interests are broadly in the intersections between global logistics/supply chain management, humanitarian logistics and organisational management development.

**Alain Vaillancourt**, Ph. D., is Acting Assistant Professor at Jönköping International Business School, Researcher at the Centre of Logistics and Supply Chain Management and affiliated to the Humanitarian Logistics and Supply Chain Research Institute in Helsinki Finland. His research area specializes in humanitarian logistics and supply chains with publications on disaster policies, logistics competencies and a thesis on material consolidation. Alain Vaillancourt also has practical field experience in humanitarian logistics with NGOs and UN agencies both working on delivering executive trainings and working as a logistic manager.

**Gyöngyi Kovács** is Erkko Professor in Humanitarian Logistics at Hanken School of Economics, Finland. She is a founding Editor-in-Chief of a leading journal and is on the editorial board of several others. She has published extensively in the area of humanitarian logistics and supply chain management and is currently supervising a number of doctoral dissertations in these fields. She led the Humanitarian Logistics and Supply Chain Research

Institute (HUMLOG Institute), Hanken School of Economics since its establishment in 2008 until 2014.

**Syed Tariq** is a doctoral student in Suleman Dawood School of Business at Lahore University of Management Sciences. His primary research interests include operations research, disaster relief logistics, coordination during disaster response phase, and multimodal logistics. (Tel.: +92 3335 2353468, E-mail address: 14080009@lums.edu.pk)

**Muhammad Naiman Jalil** (PhD-Management, Rotterdam School of Management, Erasmus University) is Associate Professor at the Lahore University of Management Sciences. His research interests include operations management, supply chain management, revenue management, after sales service, closed loop supply chain management and humanitarian logistics. (Tel.: +92 300 9839813, E-mail address: muhammad.jalil@lums.edu.pk)

**Muhammad Adeel Zaffar** (PhD-Information Technology, University of North Carolina at Charlotte) is Assistant Professor at the Lahore University of Management Sciences. His research interests include the development of decision support systems, agent-based computational economics, and network location models in the context of disaster response and recovery systems. (Tel.: +92 303 4440257, E-mail address: adeel.zaffar@lums.edu.pk)

**Laura Laguna Salvadó** is a PhD student at the Industrial Engineering Department of the University of Toulouse – Mines Albi, France. She has collaborated with *Medecins Sans Frontieres* in the Brussels HQs. Laura's research is focused in improving the performance of the organisations through Humanitarian Supply Chain Management, collaboration and decision support systems. Tina Comes and Matthieu Lauras support her work.

**Matthieu Lauras** is Associate Professor at the Industrial Engineering Department of the University of Toulouse – Mines Albi, France; Affiliate Professor at Toulouse Business School, France; and co-founder of the Agilea consulting and training company. During the last decade, he has published number of papers in journals and international conferences on the field of decision support systems for commercial supply chains and humanitarian supply chains.

**Tina Comes** is Full Professor in the Department of ICT, University of Agder, Norway, and Deputy Director of the Centre for Integrated

Emergency Management. Tina holds a position as Senior Researcher at the Smart Instrumentation Group with Teknova AS. Her research aims at supporting decision-making and risk management in complex, dynamic and uncertain situations. Tina is author of more than 70 papers published in international journals and conferences, and she has been actively promoting the topic of decision support in disaster management.

**Frederick Bénaben** is currently Associate Professor of Information Systems at the Industrial Engineering Department of the University of Toulouse – Mines Albi, France. He is the head of the Interoperability of Organizations team. He has participated in many European and national projects, in the field of Crisis Management, ICT, interoperability of IS and Collaborative networks of organizations. He has more than 100 publications in journals and international conferences proceedings.

**Marc Goerigk** is 50th Anniversary Lecturer in the Department of Management Science at Lancaster University. He completed his PhD in applied mathematics at the University of Göttingen in 2012, and worked as a Post-Doc at University of Kaiserslautern. His research interests include disaster management, robust optimization, and transportation problems. Email: m.goerigk@lancaster.ac.uk

**Horst W. Hamacher** obtained his PhD in 1980 at the University of Cologne. He was Assistant and Associate Professor at the University of Florida. Since 1988 he holds the chair for management mathematics at the University of Kaiserslautern. He received the Julius von Haast Fellowship Award and the GOR Science Award. Email: hamacher@mathematik.uni-kl.de

**Sebastian Schmitt** studied computer science at the University of Kaiserslautern and worked as a consultant for a local software company. After managing software projects at the technical side, he left the industry in 2012 to start looking at software from different perspectives as a research assistant at the University of Kaiserslautern. Email: schmitt@mathematik. uni-kl.de

**Andréa Cynthia Santos** obtained her PhD in Computer Science at the PUC-Rio in 2006, Brazil. She is Associate Professor at the Technological University of Troyes, France, and a member of the Charles Delaunay Institut, Optimization and Industrial Systems team. She led the "Optimizing logistics for large scale disasters project" (OLIC) project, funded by the *"Conseil Supérieur de la Formation et de la Recherche Stratégiques"* (CSFRS), France. The OLIC project focused on logistics after major earthquakes and was dedicated, among other problems, to the rehabilitation of urban networks and accessibility issues. She has already participated in several multidisciplinary projects and the methods developed in her scientific research are part of some decision-making systems. She has published eighteen articles in reputed international reviews, and made more than sixty communications in national and international conferences. She also received a team award in a mathematical challenge proposed by the French association of mathematical games *"Fédération Française des Jeux Mathématiques"* (FFJM) and the French mathematics calculus society SA *"Société de Calcul Mathématique"* in 2012. Her research is dedicated to OR/OM problems, especially combinatorial optimization problems in transportation and network design, with applications for humanitarian logistics and urban transportation.

**Dorit Schumann-Bölsche** is Full Professor for Logistics and Vice President at the German Jordanian University in Jordan. In her research she focuses on humanitarian logistics and SCM. She completed her PhD at the Goethe-University Frankfurt, worked as a consultant and started her position as a professor for logistics at the University of Fulda.

**Cécile L'Hermitte** Australian Maritime College, University of Tasmania (Cecile.LHermitte@utas.edu.au)

After having worked 10 years in the banking industry as a specialist of international business, both in France and in Germany, Cécile L'Hermitte completed an MBA in maritime and logistics management and undertook research work in humanitarian logistics. Having just completed her doctoral research project at the Australian Maritime College/University of Tasmania, she is planning to return to the industry and to work in the field of humanitarian logistics. Her research explored the concept of organizational capacity building and the critical role played by an organization's systems, structure and culture in supporting agility in humanitarian logistics operations.

**Marcus Bowles** The Centre for Regional & Rural Futures, Deakin University (mbowles@workingfutures.com.au)

Marcus Bowles is an expert on organizational design and capability development. He holds visiting/adjunct professorial appointments with Australian universities and conducts extensive research into leadership and the design of agile organizations. As the Director of The Institute for Working Futures, Marcus mixes academic with professional expertise drawing on his positive track record and experience that includes over 200 engagements by ASX top 50 companies, international Forbes 500 companies, peak professional, industry and government bodies, as well as global research and education institutions. He is also an entrepreneur having won international awards for breakthrough applications in learning, assessment and capability management.

**Peter Tatham** Department of International Business and Asian Studies, Griffith University (p.tatham@griffith.edu.au)

Following his retirement from the (UK) Royal Navy in 2004, Peter Tatham joined Cranfield University and completed his doctoral thesis which investigated the role of shared values within UK military supply networks. This work received the 2010 Emerald/EFMD prize for the year's best logistics/supply network management-related PhD. Peter joined Griffith University in July 2010 where he teaches and researches in humanitarian supply chain management. He is the Asian and Australasian Editor of the Journal of Humanitarian Logistics and Supply Chain Management, and a member of the Editorial Board of the International Journal of Physical Distribution and Logistics Management.

**Ben Brooks** Australian Maritime College, University of Tasmania (Benjamin.Brooks@utas.edu.au)

Benjamin Brooks is a maritime and emergency management human factors researcher in the National Centre for Ports and Shipping at the Australian Maritime College, University of Tasmania. Ben has 20 years of experience as a researcher and safety consultant. He currently works on research in areas such as innovation in high-risk environments, system design, safety culture, decision-making, and the measurement of human performance. He works with a range of stakeholders including regulators, private companies, pilotage organizations, port authorities, and emergency management agencies.

**Rolando M. Tomasini** is Head of Global Outreach at UNOPS. In this role he leads the collaboration with strategic partners across the organization. This includes partnerships with the private sector, academia and NGOs, and due diligence on the latter actors. At UNOPS, he has held several roles in procurement, policy and partnerships. Prior to joining UNOPS, he managed the supplier risk team at a leading multinational for strategic suppliers and served as a procurement consultant to implement category management and cost modelling tools. He also designed and rolled out global corporate procurement academies for seven fast-moving consumer goods (FMCG) and industrial leading multinationals.

At the onset of his career, he contributed to the establishment of a research group at INSEAD on humanitarian logistics. This led him to conduct field research through secondments to all the UN emergency agencies and produce a collection of award winning case studies, chapters and books on emergency supply chain and humanitarian logistics. He holds a Specialized Master in International Procurement, MCIPS and a PhD in Supply Chain on public private partnerships. His commitment to research keeps him engaged in multiple projects and lecturing at business schools and corporate academies in Spanish, French and English.

**Lijo John** is currently a Researcher in the Quantitative Methods and Operations Management area at Indian Institute of Management Kozhikode (IIMK). Prior to joining IIMK, he did his B. Tech in Mechanical (Production) Engineering from University of Kerala. Subsequently he joined for M. Tech in Industrial Engineering and Management at National Institute of Technology Calicut. His current research interest includes supply chain management, humanitarian logistics and sustainable supply chains. He has published papers in various peer-reviewed international journals and has presented his research in various international conferences in India and abroad. He has also contributed to books on his research topic.

**Richard Oloruntoba**, PhD, is Senior Lecturer in Logistics, Operations and Supply Chain Management. Richard's expertise is humanitarian operations and humanitarian logistics. His research program focuses mainly on the interface of logistics for humanitarian aid delivery and distribution, humanitarian supply chains, and management of the aid and service supply chains for responding to and managing crises, conflicts and disasters. Richard has undertaken several international and national projects resulting in over 40 refereed articles including 16 in leading logistics, operations, disaster and supply chain management journals, 4 refereed book chapters, and several other research and media publications primarily on the topic of humanitarian operations and humanitarian logistics.

**Eija Meriläinen** is Researcher at HUMLOG Institute at Hanken School of Economics. She studies how top-down disaster relief can support the recovery that emerges from within the disaster struck community. The focus of her research is on post-disaster reconstruction with respect to in/formality of settlements. The common nominators of her research are natural, sudden onset disasters and the involvement of local actors in disaster relief. In 2015 Meriläinen studied the aftermath of the Valparaíso fire of 2014 and before that the reconstruction of the 2010/2011 Christchurch earthquakes. Prior to embarking on an academic career she worked in supply chain management functions within the fast-moving consumer goods industry.

# List of Figures

# List of Tables

# Introduction to the Handbook

## Introduction

Disaster trends show an increase in the impact of natural disasters, not to speak of man-made crises. At the time of finalizing this anthology, the disaster in the spotlight is Hurricane Matthew (2016), which is one of the larger hurricanes in the annual hurricane season, and which is mirrored with cyclone seasons in the Pacific, floods in Pakistan, and for years, erratic weather conditions in the Sahel. Adding to the demand of humanitarian aid are the various insurgencies and wars around the world leading to humanitarian crises in those regions, and refugee fluxes outside. In the spotlight are the wars in Syria, Iraq and Yemen, but there are many others that can be labelled the "forgotten disasters" in the world, whether in the Central African Republic or South Sudan. Other disasters trigger one another, as in the cascading events of Fukushima from earthquake to tsunami to a nuclear disaster in 2011. In parallel to natural disasters and wars are pandemic outbreaks – primarily cholera, yellow fever or ebola. Already since the Indian Ocean Tsunami 2004, the role of logistics has been highlighted in the support of disaster relief. Therefore, research within humanitarian logistics has increased particularly during the last decade.

This led to the establishment of the *Journal of Humanitarian Logistics and Supply Chain Management,* which now in 2016 is in its sixth volume. But also other journals have shown interest in this field. There have been over 15 special issues in international peer-reviewed journals that were dedicated to humanitarian logistics and/or humanitarian operations since 2009. In addition, universities across the world initiated teaching courses or running training programmes on humanitarian logistics. There are also more and more comprehensive literature reviews published in the field.

That said, humanitarian logistics, humanitarian operations and supply chain management literature has faced substantial criticism over the years for its lack of empirical studies. Conducting research in humanitarian logistics has its specific challenges, especially in terms of *finding research questions that are relevant to the field* and hence can contribute back to the development of humanitarian logistics at large. Further challenges relate to the *use of appropriate methods*, due to the combination of a lack of access to data, the need to develop robust field research and to capture the interest of humanitarians who would be willing to contribute with their knowledge and expertise.

This handbook, therefore, assembles a variety of research questions and types of studies in humanitarian logistics, and focuses on research methods as a cross-cutting theme. The aim of the book is to provide an overview of the state of the art of humanitarian logistics research, but also to help researchers identifying when and how to apply certain research methods. We have therefore asked authors to be very honest in their descriptions of their *challenges and opportunities of conducting research* in this field, describe their struggles with particular methods and also to give advice in how to overcome these struggles. Thereby, this book allows us researchers to share our knowledge and experience on teaching and research, to figure out further avenues for future research and to guide junior researchers conducting research projects within humanitarian logistics and supply chain management.

## An Overview of the Handbook

This handbook covers a variety of current topics in humanitarian logistics and supply chain management practice, from the use of logistics emergency teams of commercial logistics service providers in humanitarian logistics, to the evacuation of cities in light of a natural disaster, to managing a sudden influx of refugees. Even larger is the conceptual variation, which ranges from a strong focus on various aspects of (supply chain) collaboration to other strategic questions of supply chain configuration, to very functional focus areas in logistics. There are chapters that focus on process alignment, the support of information and communication technology, and also chapters that question the current system of humanitarian aid. Reflecting also trends in practice, resilience is much discussed, both from the perspective of the supply chain and also the community. But as we set out with methods as a cross-cutting theme, the book is also structured around those.

The handbook starts with a number of chapters in Section 1 that focus on research methods that are not (yet) commonly used in humanitarian logistics literature and outline the use and usability of these methods. These include social network analysis (SNA), action research and clinical inquiry, as well as behavioural operations experiments. The first chapter reviews SNA in the context of supply chains outlining SNA concepts and metrics, and elaborates on the potential of SNA in the context of humanitarian logistics. Next chapter explores the appropriateness of deploying collaborative research approaches in humanitarian logistics and supply chains management (i.e. action research, and clinical inquiry). The chapter examines how to ensure the rigour, relevance and reflectiveness, while adopting two collaborative approaches. The third chapter reviews the steps within behavioural experiments, simulation and agent-based modelling. In addition, it introduces the (potential) applications of the three methods within the humanitarian logistics and supply chain management.

Section 2 continues with a focus on empirical research, whether quantitative or qualitative. Responding to the trend in various journals to ask for mixed methods, or multi-method approaches, the first chapter in this section is dedicated to these including also their potential shortcomings, aptly calling them the "dreadful biases and heavenly combinations of mixed methods". The other chapters in the section elucidate the use of field research and case studies more in detail – for example, a case study on Médecins Sans Frontières, or one on resilience in the food supply chain.

Section 3 combines various chapters on the topic of collaboration and shows the use of different methods on researching similar topics. There are case studies on supply chain integration and on learning agility from humanitarian organizations through cross-sectoral partnerships, as well as a survey on the topic of swift trust – which is a useful concept to understand the way humanitarians work together, in contrast to habitual trust that is more typical in commercial settings – and the use of interpretive structural modelling to tease out the drivers of coordination. Each of these chapters argue for their choice of research methods as appropriate to answer their research questions.

Section 4 moves on to a variety of topics in humanitarian logistics. The section starts with an interview study focusing on demand variability in the asylum seeking process. Next, a systematic literature review is combined with a pilot study in the area of developing humanitarian logistics skills and competencies. This is followed by field research on the topic of governance in service triads – which is also an interesting application of agency theory. The section ends with case studies on planning multimodality in disaster relief.

Section 5 is a combination of chapters that all develop a tool that is then applied to the humanitarian setting. Two chapters develop decision support systems – one to structure humanitarian logistics knowledge, the other more focused on urban evacuation. The next chapter concentrates on the topic of accessibility after an earthquake. Access to beneficiaries, and their own accessibility of aid, remain important topics in the area of humanitarian supply chains overall. Finally, the topic of agility is taken up once again in the development of a diagnostic tool for organizational agility. Both this and the chapter on agility in Section 3 pay tribute to humanitarian organizations, and humanitarian supply chains often being attributed the label of being "most agile", which is why they are much in focus in research and practice alike when wanting to learn about agility.

Section 6 finishes the book with an outlook to the future. While most of these chapters are conceptual in nature, they take up important topics that bear the potential to systemically change how we view and organize humanitarian supply chains. The section commences with an outlook to how the UN Global Compact and more recently, Agenda 2030 and the Sustainable Development Goals are shaping cross-sectoral partnerships. The next chapter provides an overview of trends and considerations in the use of research methods in empirical studies in humanitarian supply chain management. This is followed by a conceptual suggestion of four main groups of theories in humanitarian logistics; and last but not the least, the section includes a chapter focusing on a change in perspective from humanitarian aid towards community resilience.

## A Final Comment on the Use of This Handbook

This handbook is of course an anthology, and as such, there may be discrepancies in the use of terminology, or in the understanding of terms across chapters. While there are more commonly adopted definitions in the field – starting with the list of definitions in the United Nations International Strategy for Disaster Reduction (UN/ISDR) terminology – there are also differences between (a) the practitioner and the researcher understanding of certain terms, starting with what "logistics", "operation" versus "supply chain" would encompass in this area; (b) the understanding of the same terms across various organizations; and (c) their understanding dependent on the background discipline, or stream of discipline, a scholar attributes herself or himself to. Humanitarian logistics is and remains a field in which various interests cross-sect, whether these stem from disaster management versus public health versus development research, or logistics versus purchasing versus operations views on supply chain management. We have not attempted to resolve such differences, rather, the book is a kaleidoscope of extant research in humanitarian logistics.

We have asked contributors to send us their current work, and to be brutally honest with any challenges in research methods. The handbook thus provides a current overview on what is going on in research, but is also meant to be of use when designing a study, to be able to watch out for potential pitfalls and problems, and to thereby improve the quality of research in this field in future. Do, however, not criticize the studies presented here for their shortcomings – authors are, after all, very honest and self-reflective here to help the next generation of researchers on their way. We rather invite you to learn from their challenges, and hope that the handbook can thereby contribute to elevating the field of humanitarian logistics and supply chain management overall.

# Part I

## Innovative Methods - not that Much Used Yet

# 1

# Social Network Analysis in the Context of Humanitarian Logistics

Natalie Simpson, Zhasmina Tacheva
and Ta-Wei (Daniel) Kao

## Introduction

Increased attention to the adaptive and emergent properties of whole networks has been posited as vital to the future development of supply chain management (SCM) (Pathak et al. 2007), a perspective that is particularly critical to the humanitarian sector. Humanitarian operations are uniquely challenged to serve uncertain yet urgent demand in highly dynamic environments, where success relies on coordination within supply chains otherwise heavily influenced by circumstance. Advancing the field of humanitarian logistics depends in part on better understanding of why this process is more successful in some instances when compared to others, but this in turn depends upon an ability to capture and study complex and changing logistical relationships. One branch of emerging supply chain research employs social network analysis (SNA) to quantify complex supply networks, enabling holistic assessments of network structure to be empirically related to outcomes such as profitability and risk (Borgatti and Li 2009; Galaskiewicz 2011; Kim et al. 2011; Bellamy et al. 2014). As a

N. Simpson (✉) · Z. Tacheva
University at Buffalo (SUNY), Buffalo, New York, USA
e-mail: nsimpson@buffalo.edu; zhasmina@buffalo.edu

T.-W. (Daniel) Kao
University of Michigan-Dearborn, Dearborn, Michigan, USA
e-mail: taweikao@umich.edu

© The Author(s) 2018                                                                                        **3**
G. Kovács et al. (eds.), *The Palgrave Handbook of Humanitarian Logistics and Supply Chain Management*, https://doi.org/10.1057/978-1-137-59099-2_1

methodology, SNA provides a new lens through which to study dynamic logistical networks in search for the antecedents of success in this context. In light of this potential, the objective of this chapter is to provide a state-of-the-art briefing on SNA, blending literature review with SNA tutorial, to ultimately argue humanitarian logistics as best positioned to lead network research in SCM.

SNA provides a methodology and related metrics for mapping relationships between members of a group, characterizing the individual entities as nodes connected by ties to create networks (Borgatti and Foster 2003). Many aspects of humanitarian relief are amenable to this approach, as demonstrated by our first example, a network of developmental assistance between nations pictured in Fig. 1.1. Here, ties represent recent official development assistance of at least 100 million US$ between nodes that represent OECD Development Assistance Committee (DAC) members and recipient countries. These nodes have been arranged such that recipients with similar sets of benefactors are grouped closer, reducing visual noise and demonstrating one powerful feature of this methodology, the visualization of data (Basole and Bellamy 2014). Rendering major donation data as a network highlights the politicized over-tones of such relationships (Day 2014), as regional clusters can be seen where main donors have geographical or historical ties, such as Australia's aid to Papua New Guinea, Timor-Leste, and the Solomon Islands, or France's support of Guinea and Cameroon. This visualization also highlights the complexity of Japan in the lower left quadrant, a DAC member providing aid to developing countries such as Vietnam and Myanmar while simultaneously receiving funds from countries such as Thailand and Malaysia, reflecting the fact that Japan has traditionally been a top donor to Southeast Asia, likewise making it a top creditor in the region.

In the following section, we begin with a brief chronological survey of SNA and supply chain-related literature, starting from SNA's early socio-logical origins and concluding with a discussion of recent humanitarian logistics research featuring this methodology. This is followed by tutorial discussion and demonstration of common SNA concepts and metrics appear-ing within that body of literature. This aspect of briefing is organized into two sections, starting with the node-level focus of Part III and proceeding to the whole network focus of Part IV. Throughout the discussion, content is demonstrated with humanitarian sector data, creating a series of illustrations that starts with Fig. 1.1. The purpose of this diverse set of examples is not to pursue any particular research hypothesis within the confines of this chapter, but rather to transform the abstract into the concrete, a powerful mechanism in any tutorial-style communication (Morrison et al. 2004).

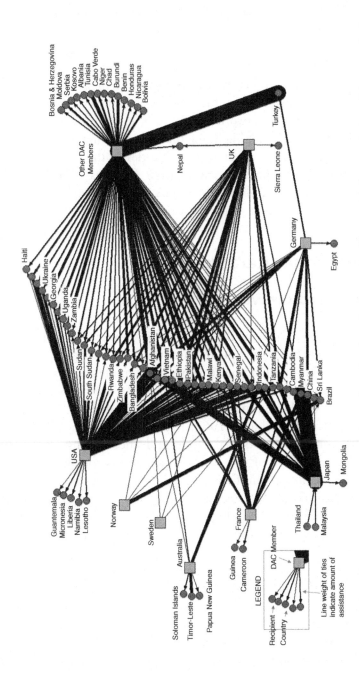

**Fig. 1.1** Net 2013 official development assistance (ODA) of at least 100 million USD between Development Assistance Committee (DAC) members of the Organisation for Economic Co-operation and Development (OECD) and recipient countries

Furthermore, the illustrations have been prepared with a range of software tools to simultaneously serve as a gallery of technical options readily available to interested researchers. Consistent with an overarching goal of promoting research interest in the application of SNA to humanitarian logistics, the details required for obtaining both the example data and the software used in any chapter example are provided in an Appendix at the end of this discussion. The literature drawn into the first four sections then "sets the stage" for Part V, where we employ network visualization to clarify how the existing literature relates to itself, highlighting the fact that not only does SNA methodology offer multiple research opportunities in the context of humanitarian logistics, it is humanitarian logistics that may bridge a divide between the truly "social" applications of SNA and a growing body of related but "nonsocial" investigations of complex networks.

# A Review of the Literature

## SNA: Origins and Growth

Current interest in SNA in the context of supply chain research is arguably one branch of its uptake into multiple disciplines (Borgatti et al. 2009). However, sociologists have been modeling groups as networks of individuals for well over a century. SNA's sociological foundations rely heavily on the seminal work of Georg Simmel (1955) and others (e.g., Kadushin 1966; Milgram 1967; Merton 1968), who first brought focus to the concept of a social circle and the ensuing dynamics of affiliation. The influence of this work spread across sociology and organizational science just as the field of graph theory was likewise gaining prominence, creating an intersection that would become the genesis of SNA. In this initial period, Granovetter (1973) introduced the theory of weak ties, postulating that the stronger the tie between two actors, the more likely their social worlds would overlap, and that aside from strong connections, weak ties can exist between communities, particularly important to the linking of macro- and micro-levels of society. Coleman (1988) proposed the term social capital as a resource derived from an actor's pattern of links, value that is distinct from financial, physical, or human capital. Coleman (1988) offered this concept as a theoretical reconciliation between the socialized and the rational, self-interested lenses of sociology and economics, respectively, and further emphasized the public good aspect of social capital, describing closure as its main facilitating function. Burt (1987, 1992, 2000) problematized this theory, arguing social cohesion as weaker than structural equivalence in the social contagion process (Burt 1987), tie weakness as correlating to rather than causing value derived from bridging ties (Burt 1992), and the function of closure as at best complementing the value of brokering structural holes (Burt 2000) within a network of actors.

Using the constructs of graph theory to quantify complex affiliations among individuals, SNA evolved into an established field of research in the social sciences by the 1980s, with related network analysis diffusing into disciplines such as biology and physics starting from 1990s (Borgatti et al. 2009). In recent years, SNA research has been galvanized by the groundbreaking work of Barabási and Albert (1999), which provided a new perspective on network generation in many real-life scenarios, including the World Wide Web. Podolny (2001) took an in-depth look at market networks, uncovering two alternative models: one interpreting ties as conduits for resources, and another in which they serve as prisms through which actors are evaluated by potential partners on the basis of their market relations. Podolny (2001) also distinguished between egocentric and altercentric uncertainty and demonstrated that structural holes are helpful in resolving the former, whereas status can help alleviate the latter. Concurrently, the creation of the UCINET software platform as described in Borgatti et al. (2002) enabled convenient empirical testing of previous theory from works such as Granovetter (1973) and Burt (1992). Another factor accelerating growth in SNA-related research in this time period was the simultaneous advent of online social media platforms such as Twitter, LinkedIn, and Facebook, applications now so ubiquitous in daily life and such a ready source of SNA data that they have attained a misnomer status for the field of social networks as a whole.

## SNA: Supply Chain Literature

Similar to SNA, SCM emerged as a distinct area of research in the 1980s, although early investigations often modeled a supply chain as the interorganizational equivalent of the older concept of a bill of materials. In a recent review, Bellamy and Basole (2013) identify De Toni and Nassimbeni (1995) as among the earliest to adopt the broader network analytic lens in a comparative study of two manufacturing sectors. Thadakamalla et al. (2004) demonstrate the relative robustness of certain SNA-related network archetypes in military supply simulations, being among the earliest to relate the role of network structure to supply chain resilience. Network-oriented supply chain research grew dramatically during this time period (Bellamy and Basole 2013), culminating in supply chains being argued as complex adaptive systems, or the emergent result of deliberate design and circumstance (Choi et al. 2001; Surana et al. 2005; Pathak et al. 2007). As organizations within a supply chain can be readily characterized as actors in a network, the potential of SNA as a new research methodology was recognized in this interval. SNA's introduction to supply chain research began with hypothesis development, largely focused on the intrinsic value of network structure to a firm (Choi and Krause 2006; Autry and Griffis 2008), potential interpretations of common SNA metrics (Borgatti and Li 2009), and proposals of structural archetypes (Choi and Wu 2009). Extending the framework of Podolny (2001) discussed earlier, Borgatti and Halgin (2011) describe two contrasting interpretations of network ties as a flow model versus a bond or coordination model, and suggest that the latter may be marked by the concept of virtual capitalization, or the transfer of capabilities of nodes to each other without the need for a node to actually assume the formal function. This contribution to broader SNA theory is especially amenable to supply chain networks where, rather than taking on the abilities of upstream suppliers through vertical integration, a firm may establish bonds with those suppliers enabling it to behave as if it had those capabilities. Further, SCM/SNA theory development continues into the present, such as Pathak et al. (2014)'s theory of "co-opetition" (the simultaneity of cooperation and competition) in supply networks and Yan et al. (2015)'s theory of the "nexus supplier."

Despite the intensive work on the theoretical foundation of supply network analysis, relatively few empirical studies of these hypotheses are available to date (Pathak et al. 2014), and those outcomes investigated in the available literature vary widely. Among the earliest investigations relating supply network structure and some aspect of organizational performance are Echols and Tsai (2005)'s examination of the role of network embeddedness in product and process niches and Grewal et al. (2006)'s investigation of embeddedness in the success of open-source projects. Carter et al. (2007) investigate an intra-organizational social network to identify a relationship between the centrality of individuals and their respective influence over informal projects in the context of logistics. Schilling and Phelps (2007) examine how the structural characteristics of industry alliances relate to the number of patents generated, identifying a positive relationship between patents and the alliance network's average clustering coefficient and reach, two metrics which will be discussed in Part III and IV, while Phelps (2010) finds similar results in a longitudinal study in a similar industry setting. Dong et al. (2015) find relationships between a distributor's opportunistic behavior and the structural characteristics of the supply network of which the distributor is a member. Carnovale and Yeniyurt (2014) investigate the relationship between network structure and the selection of joint venture partners in manufacturing and confirm the role of network structure in innovation (measured by patents) in a similar setting (Carnovale and Yeniyurt 2015). Keeping in the stream of better understanding how connections form between firms, Ravindran et al. (2015) relate network structure to the duration of contracts awarded in IT outsourcing.

Although the benefits of applying an SNA framework to the study of complex logistical flows have long been recognized, empirical research with this particular focus lags the study of collaboration and related behaviors within and between firms. In primarily descriptive studies, Kim et al. (2011) demonstrate the application of node-level SNA measures to authentic supply networks in the automotive industry, while Mizgier et al. (2013) examine the utility of SNA metrics in detecting bottleneck elements in complex supply structures. Bellamy et al. (2014) investigate a network that represents the union of logistical supply relationships with industry alliances similar to Schilling and Phelps (2007), finding that patent generation at the node level is similarly related to node-level measures of network structure. Basole and Bellamy (2014) explore the power of network visualization in assessment of risk, while Kim et al. (2015) use simulation to demonstrate how risk and resilience relate to network structure.

## SNA: Humanitarian Logistics and Supply Chain Management

Given the relative dearth of empirical supply chain studies employing SNA methodology, it is not surprising that very little of what is available addresses humanitarian logistics, as this research area did not gain widespread recognition until relatively recently (Kovács and Spens 2009). Early SNA-related studies include Houghton et al. (2006) and Simpson and Hancock (2009), in analysis of communication patterns during emergency response simulations. Haase (2010) applies SNA metrics in evaluation of the Indonesian response network emerging after the Sumatran earthquake and tsunami. Jahre and Jensen (2010) draw on SNA conceptually in examining logistical clustering in the provision of humanitarian relief, although this theory-building paper did not cite any aspect of SNA specifically. Similarly, clustering and its algorithms are at the heart of ongoing efforts to harness social media in mapping emergent events, such as the Twitter-based methodology of Yin et al. (2012). Closer to the logistics of humanitarian relief, Day et al. (2012) discuss the potential of social/structural capital model in advancing research in disaster relief, an approach reflected in Álvarez and Serrato's (2013) analysis of communication between disaster management organizations throughout the disaster life cycle, mapping humanitarian relief actors in Mexico, Panama, and Chile. Day (2014) highlights the salience of the complex adaptive network paradigm to humanitarian supply chains in particular, building on the earlier arguments of Choi et al. (2001) and Pathak et al. (2007) for the supply chain domain as a whole. Most recently, Urrea et al. (2016) examine how interactions among humanitarian actors are related to performance in response, first in a network-level comparison of two large-scale humanitarian operations, and then in a node-level analysis of over 700 ongoing developmental projects.

In summary, it should be noted that the bulk of the work in organizational science which preceded SNA-related supply chain research can be broadly described as the research of structural capital (Borgatti and Foster 2003), in which a node is assumed to naturally exploit its position in the network for maximum gain, and some patterns of connectivity are more beneficial to others in this regard. Interestingly, most of the supply chain literature that followed has kept within that conceptual framework, which is why closer examination of the SNA metrics used begins with a focus on the properties of nodes.

## Describing, Measuring, and Interpreting Nodes

From its beginnings, graph theory has been described as " . . . a terminological jungle, in which any newcomer may plant a tree" (Barnes 1972; Easley and Kleinberg 2010). SNA appears to have inherited this trait from its parent discipline, as some concepts are established under multiple names, with several similar metrics embedded in the literature. Even within the definition of a network as a set of nodes and ties, the reader should be aware that nodes may also be referred to as actors or vertices, ties likewise called edges, all in forming networks also referred to as graphs. Returning to the previous nomenclature, this section provides a brief tutorial of common descriptors and measures of nodes in particular, relating them, where possible, to applications in existing supply chain research. This focus on nodes reflects a fundamental axiom of most SNA research to date: a node's position in its network is a partial determinant of its opportunities and constraints, and thus a factor in some aspect of the node's performance (Borgatti et al. 2009). While it is not difficult to visualize the equivalent in humanitarian settings, such as the performance of a particular nongovernmental organization (NGO) being related to the pattern of collaborative connections surrounding it, it should be noted that this underlying axiom is being favored over exploration of hypotheses concerning the nature of networks as a whole. In Part IV, we will cover examples of terminology and metrics for the latter context, and return to this important distinction in Part V.

To initiate this discussion, Fig. 1.2 provides a second network modeled on humanitarian data, which is introduced here to illustrate structural characteristics that contrast with Fig. 1.1. Where Fig. 1.1 illustrates major streams of developmental assistance between country-level donors and recipients, Fig. 1.2 illustrates concurrent ground-level presence of specific NGOs supporting food security within a local area of a specific country. Unlike Fig. 1.1, all nodes in Fig. 1.2 have the same role in the humanitarian operation, with graph ties indicating when nodes are co-supporters of at least one county within the country of Liberia, assisting the population in close geographic proximity to one another. Figure 1.2 provides an example of the distinction between a directed (Fig. 1.1) and an undirected network (Fig. 1.2), an important feature in that other nomenclature can vary between the two circumstances. Figure 1.2 graph edges indicating co-support of a local population are unweighted relationships, whereas the varying line widths of Fig. 1.1 indicate weighted relationships between donors and recipients, communicating both flow and magnitude of support. Furthermore, the higher level of interconnectedness among Fig. 1.2 nodes provides a useful backdrop for the discussion of quantification of such states, through the application of measurement of degree and distance.

## Degree and Distance

Table 1.1 provides descriptions and potential interpretations of node-level concepts common to supply chain research, including the measurement of degree and distance. In Fig. 1.2, nodes representing NGOs are scaled according to their degree, or the number of other NGOs to which they are tied in the Liberian food security graph. The degree of a node is often assumed to measure some aspect of the node's ability to coordinate or influence others, as apparent in the UN's World Food Program (WFP) domination of all other nodes in this regard. Table 1.2 provides a sample of node-level metrics calculated across Fig. 1.2 NGOs, and WFP's degree of 14 indicates that it operates in the presence of all other NGOs in the larger 15-node graph, suggesting that the organization is well placed to serve as a broker or facilitator between any of the otherwise unconnected NGOs. Another concept critical to the calculation of more specialized SNA measures is that of geodesic

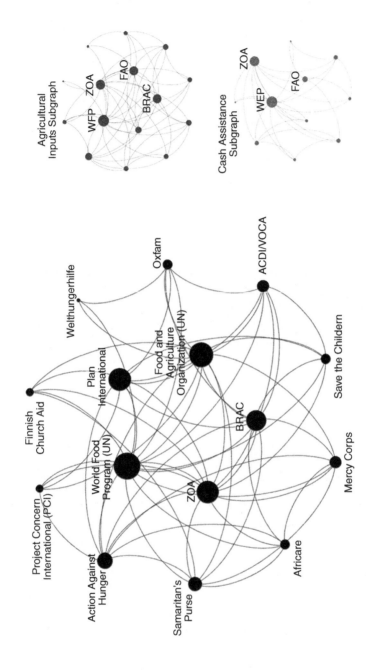

**Fig. 1.2** NGOs simultaneously present in at least one of 15 counties in support of food security in Liberia during 2015. Nodes are scaled to reflect SNA metric 'degree', or number of edges connecting to NGOs in this network

**Table 1.1** Descriptive SNA metrics for individual nodes

| SNA metric | Description | Discussion |
|---|---|---|
| **Degree, in-Degree and out-Degree** | Number of ties connecting a node to its network. In directed networks, in-degree + out-degree = degree (Freeman 1979). A *pendant* is a node with a degree value of 1. | Degree measures visibility, influence, and potential as coordinator. Out-degree quantifies "demand load" and indicates the role of allocator (Kim et al. 2011, Marsden 2002). In-degree expresses "supply load" or complexity of inbound material flow (Yan et al. 2015, Kim et al. 2011). |
| **Geodesic distance** | Shortest path between a node and another node, in terms of the total number of ties traveled. | Also known as "distance" between two nodes (Easley and Kleinberg 2010). While multiple paths between node pairs may exist, there is only one distance in this sense; confusion may arise when considering areas such as information diffusion, where metrics monitor all paths between nodes (e.g., Stephenson and Zelen 1989). |
| **Betweenness centrality** | The betweenness of node C is the proportion of all shortest paths between nodes A and B that include C, summed across all possible node pairs A and B (Freeman 1977). Can be normalized by dividing by $(N-1)(N-2)$ in the case of directed networks, or ½ $(N-1)(N-2)$ for undirected networks, where $N$ = number of nodes in network. | When calculated on an undirected network, this measure is called symmetric betweenness and is assumed to detect "key players" and potential "gate keepers" in network (Borgatti and Li 2009). When calculated on a directed network, this measure is referred to as directed betweenness, helpful in revealing "hubs" who may mediate and control material flow (Yan et al. 2015, Kim et al. 2011). |

*(continued)*

**Table 1.1** (continued)

| SNA metric | Description | Discussion |
|---|---|---|
| **Eigenvector centrality** | For a given node $i$, vector element $x_i$ from the vector of positive values $\mathbf{x}$ which solves $A\mathbf{x} = \lambda\mathbf{x}$, where $A$ is a binary matrix indicating node connectedness within network, and $\lambda$ a constant (Bonacich 1972). | Higher eigenvector centrality ($x_i$) indicates node $i$ is likely connected to other nodes which are highly connected, interpreted as indicating influence and ready access to information (Yan et al. 2015). |
| **Closeness centrality** | Sum of geodesic distances to all other nodes; or the inverse of same sum; also stated as $N - 1$ divided by that sum (Freeman 1979), where $N$ = number of nodes in network. | The simple sum of geodesic distances also referred to as *farness*. Closeness centrality may measure access to information or risk of disruption (Borgatti and Li 2009; Kim et al. 2011). |
| **Reach** | The number of nodes a node can reach in $k$ or fewer steps (Carnovale et al. 2016). | A firm's network reach may measure how far a node can send or receive information in the network (Gu et al. 2012). |
| **Eccentricity** | The number of links a node requires to connect to the farthest node. | Average eccentricity has been used in network vulnerability studies to measure the global impact of node or link removal (Shimbel 1953). |
| **Clustering Coefficient** | Ratio of number of ties among a node's immediate neighbors to the total number of such ties possible. If $D_i$ is the degree of node $i$ and $T_i$ is the number of ties among its neighbors, its clustering coefficient is calculated by $(2 \times T_i)/[D_i \times (D_i - 1)]$ (Watts and Strogatz 1998). | Clustering coefficient captures the small-world nature inherent in several real-world networks. In the presence of disruptions, the robustness of the supply network is negatively associated with its clustering coefficient (Nair and Vidal 2011). |

**Table 1.2** Comparative statistics for individual nodes in Fig. 1.2 network

| Node | Degree | Symmetric betweenness | Eigenvector centrality | Closeness* centrality | Eccentricity | Clustering coefficient |
|---|---|---|---|---|---|---|
| ACDI/VOCA | 7 | 0.40 | 0.23 | 0.67 | 2 | 0.43 |
| Action Against Hunger | 9 | 1.82 | 0.27 | 0.74 | 2 | 0.38 |
| Africare | 6 | 0.00 | 0.19 | 0.64 | 2 | 0.50 |
| BRAC | 11 | 4.67 | 0.32 | 0.82 | 2 | 0.32 |
| Finnish Church Aid | 2 | 0.17 | 0.18 | 0.61 | 2 | 0.50 |
| Food and Agriculture Organization | 11 | 10.85 | 0.34 | 0.93 | 2 | 0.29 |
| Mercy Corps | 7 | 0.17 | 0.22 | 0.67 | 2 | 0.45 |
| OXFAM | 5 | 1.00 | 0.18 | 0.64 | 2 | 0.40 |
| Project Concern International (PCI) | 8 | 3.57 | 0.36 | 0.78 | 2 | 0.41 |
| Plan International | 5 | 0.00 | 0.18 | 0.61 | 2 | 0.50 |
| Samaritan's Purse | 6 | 1.15 | 0.24 | 0.70 | 2 | 0.50 |
| Save the Children | 6 | 0.00 | 0.21 | 0.64 | 2 | 0.50 |
| Welthungerhilfe | 3 | 0.00 | 0.10 | 0.56 | 2 | 0.50 |
| World Food Program (WFP) | 14 | 14.10 | 0.36 | 1.00 | 1 | 0.23 |
| ZOA | 12 | 6.12 | 0.33 | 0.88 | 2 | 0.28 |

*Freeman's normalization: Sum of geodesic distances to all other nodes, divided into N − 1, where N = 15 is the number of nodes in the network

distance, or the length of the shortest path between two nodes, stated in terms of the number of intervening ties. In the case of Fig. 1.2, the distance between the WFP and all other NGOs is 1, and thus the distance between any NGO and any other NGO in that same network is no more than 2.

As a measurement, degree relates to the broader concept of node centrality, initially defined in Freeman (1977) and (1979), and widely assumed to model some aspect of a node's interaction and influence over other nodes in the network (see, e.g., Borgatti 2005; Marsden 2002). However, SNA literature provides multiple cautionary notes concerning attribution and causality. For instance, in the context of logistics, Carter and colleagues (2007) warn against the widely accepted notion that being connected to highly connected others is beneficial to the focal node, citing an opposing scenario of benefits gained by leveraging connections to partners with lower degree indicators. From the outset of SNA's research history, seminal works such as Burt (1987) and (1992) demonstrate how the quantification of known connections is not a process that confirms activities such as collaboration are taking place. As an example, the high centrality of the WFP in Fig. 1.2 does not directly indicate collaborative activities with the remaining NGOs, as this is not supported by the underlying data on financial expenditures. Indeed, although the NGOs sharing edges in Fig. 1.2 are supporting food security to the same tightly defined regions of Liberia, one or more of them may be doing so through third-party intermediaries, which negates the likelihood of any on-the-ground contact and conferral between their respective personnel. However, Fig. 1.2 could be interpreted as a visualization of the potential for collaboration between NGOs, if only at a strategic level, by clarifying their co-support of local populations, or as an informal test of network resiliency, in that it reveals how each Liberian county is supported by more than one NGO, and it is the WFP in particular that could be called upon to increase support if one of the other NGOs should fail for any reason.

## Centrality Metrics

While centrality measures should be interpreted with caution, they remain the most widely studied SNA metrics to date (Borgatti 2005), and thus Tables 1.1 and 1.2 continue with definition and demonstration of the most common measures, in support of the present discussion. A node's *betweenness* centrality, typically assumed to represent its potential for power as an intermediary (Borgatti and Li 2009), states the frequency of which that node is an intermediate component of the shortest paths to other nodes. Caution should be exercised when comparing betweenness values across studies, as various derivatives of this observation exist. Betweenness calculated across the paths of an undirected graph such as Fig. 1.2 is known as symmetric betweenness, whereas the same measurement in the context of a directed graph is directed betweenness. Figure 1.1, the network of major flows of developmental assistance between nations, provides an interesting example of this distinction, in that the only nation with directed betweenness greater than zero is Japan, indicating that nation is both a donor and a recipient in that year. Symmetric betweenness can be calculated for directed networks by ignoring the directionality of the ties; in the context of Fig. 1.1, the recipient nation with the highest symmetric betweenness is Afghanistan, located near the center of the network, signaling its high degree of connectedness across all the donors pictured. Finally, like many SNA measures, betweenness may be stated in its simple form or it may be normalized. In Table 1.2, symmetric betweenness is reported in a simple form, where the highest value associated with the WFP is another testimony to its centrality in this network. In contrast, closeness centrality for the same NGOs is reported in a normalized form in Table 1.2, as this transformation is helpful when comparing metrics across different networks.

Eigenvector centrality (Bonacich 1972) captures both the node's centrality and the centrality of other nodes in its neighborhood, on the assumption that connecting to highly connected others is itself a form of influence. Closeness centrality (Freeman 1979) is a statement of the total distance from a node to every other node in the network, and has been variously interpreted as monitoring "good" and "bad" conditions within supply chain networks, as it could indicate accessibility and/or risk (Borgatti and Li 2009; Kim et al. 2011). In summary, it should be noted that all Table 1.1 metrics that tally paths between nodes define those paths in terms of geodesic distance, or the shortest path between two nodes. However, alternative measures that assess all possible pathways are also available from the literature, on the argument that information may not always flow across the shortest path, and thus all pathways must be recognized when characterizing the potential for such (Stephenson and Zelen 1989). These adaptations are featured in some supply chain studies, such as "information centrality" in the case of Bellamy et al. (2014), and preservation of this information concerning multiple redundant paths has been suggested as critical to modeling supply chain resilience (Day 2014).

## Other Measures

Similar to issues of centrality, each node in a network can be evaluated for reach and eccentricity, as described in Table 1.1, both being measures of the node's potential for and/or exposure to diffusion of some issue from other nodes. Finally, one of the best known metrics outside of centrality-oriented measures is the clustering coefficient, which expresses the degree to which a node's neighbors are connected to one another. This metric is also similar to evaluating the embeddedness of a tie, or the number of neighbors that nodes at each end of a tie have in common (Easley and Kleinberg 2010). Ironically, despite the visual groupings that suggest donor nations' political interests, all countries in Fig. 1.1 possess a clustering coefficient score of zero, as the alternative would require donor nations (or recipient counties) to provide developmental support to one another, highly unlikely in the context of this network. In contrast, Table 1.2 provides the clustering coefficients of the 15 NGOs in Fig. 1.2 network, where these values represent the proportion of time that the NGO's co-supporters of food security in Liberia are in fact acquainted with one another in that same sense. Clustering coefficients are of particular significance in their role in the typology of whole networks, discussed next.

## Describing, Measuring, and Interpreting Whole Networks

Of the typologies and measures to characterize whole networks, one foundational concept particularly relevant to humanitarian logistics is the condition of multiplexity. While the larger network in Fig. 1.2 represents NGOs sharing roles in food security in counties across Liberia, these roles can be readily separated into food assistance, cash assistance, agricultural inputs, and training, with most links in the larger network representing more than one category. To calculate node-level metrics, these roles must either be aggregated as pictured on the left, or broken out into separate subgraphs, such as the two smaller networks on the right. In either case, the particular mix and the simultaneity of certain roles might be one of the more relevant factors in the field. The larger graph in Fig. 1.2 is said to be a multiplex network, while each of its insets, as well as the entirety of Fig. 1.1, is uniplex in nature. Multiple simultaneous and interdependent networks of tangible resources, information, and money are typical of humanitarian supply chains (Day 2014), although multiplex network modeling is not common in current supply chain research. In contrast, the biosciences make ample use of multiplex networks in the study of genome engineering and neuronal dependencies (Wang et al. 2009).

Figure 1.3 displays another uniplex network, in which ties in both the main graph and the inset graph illustrate cash assistance from private sector organizations in response to the 2014 Ebola crisis in West Africa. The relationship between the pair of networks within Fig. 1.3 demonstrates the concept of an ego network, to be discussed later in this section, and provides an additional context for discussion of how unlike networks can be measured relative to one another, beginning with the simple descriptive statistics at the top of Table 1.3. Figure 1.3 differs from Fig. 1.1 not only in the scope of support (specific nation versus international) and commitment (specific incident versus annual), but also in the nature of the donors, as the entities pictured in Fig. 1.3 are predominantly for-profit organizations, typically assisting through a governmental or NGO intermediary. This structural feature of Fig. 1.3 is common to public/private humanitarian networks (Kovács and Spens 2007), and choices of intermediary create distinct cohorts of donors clarified by the network visualization. For-profit organizations are noted for maintaining their intrinsic focus on profit during humanitarian response (van Wassenhove 2006), although this does not imply that such organizations intend to profit from the disaster, but more likely from building stronger relationships with the intermediaries that define their cohorts.

## Whole Networks Metrics

Networks may be compared with size, or simple counts of the total number of nodes and ties in each. Table 1.4 provides several measures corresponding to the example networks here, beginning with these two descriptive statistics. Another reading of size is a network's radius and diameter, which query the eccentricities of all nodes, discussed earlier, for the minimum and maximum values present. One of the most common metrics for comparison of whole networks is density, which relates the numbers of nodes and ties in a statement of how many ties are present relative to the total number of ties possible in that network. As Table 1.4 shows, Fig. 1.2 is both the smallest and densest of the examples, whereas the financial support networks in Figs. 1.1 and 1.3 have densities similar to those reported by Urrea et al. (2016) in examining the network response to the 2010 Haiti earthquake and 2013 Typhoon Haiyan emergencies.

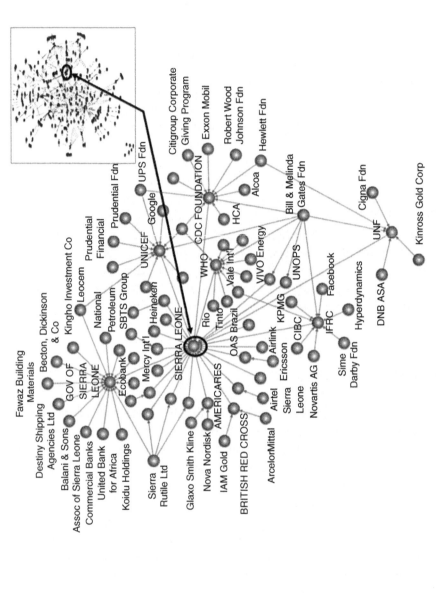

**Fig. 1.3** Two-step ego network of Sierra Leone with respect to inset network, representing all private sector cash contributions supporting the humanitarian response to the 2014 Ebola crisis in West Africa

Table 1.3 Descriptive SNA metrics for whole networks

| SNA metric | Description | Discussion |
|---|---|---|
| **Radius, diameter** | Radius is the minimum eccentricity (see Table 1.1) among all nodes in the network. Diameter is the maximum of same. | A node is central if its eccentricity is the same as the radius of the network. The set of central nodes in the network is the center of the network. If the radius of the network is the same as the diameter of the network, then the network is self-centered and all nodes belong to the center (Yamaguchi 2002). |
| **Density** | Ratio of the actual number of ties in a network ($T$) to the total number of ties possible among the $N$ nodes in that network. Depending on the type of network graph type, density is defined as $T/[N \times (N-1)]$ (directed) or $(2 \times T)/[N \times (N-1)]$ (undirected). | Dense networks facilitate flows of information and effective sanctions, and function as "closed" system, where trust, shared norms, and common behavioral patterns develop more easily (Gnyawali and Madhavan 2001). |
| **Ego network** | A network defined by a single node (the ego) as itself and all nodes (alters) with which it has a direct connection. Includes ties between the ego and alters and any ties between alters. An ego network is often a subgraph of a larger network. | Supply networks have been modeled as ego networks, defined by the set of all firms with a direct supply relationship to a focal firm (Borgatti and Li 2009). |
| **n-Step ego network** | An ego network includes alters along paths up to $n$ in length. A one-step ego network is described above. | Firm's two-step ego network has a first-order network made up of an actor's ties to its exchange partners and a second-order network made up of an actor's exchange partners' ties to their trading partners (Uzzi 1996, 1997). |
| **Small-world network** | Network characterized by the simultaneous conditions of low average geodesic distance and high average clustering coefficient across all its nodes (see Table 1.1). | From the perspective of robustness to failures, small-world networks have similar responses to both random and targeted attacks due to the similarity in their degree distribution (Thadakamalla et al. 2004). |

(continued)

**Table 1.3** (continued)

| SNA metric | Description | Discussion |
|---|---|---|
| **Scale-free network** | Network characterized by the degree (see Table 1.1) distribution of its nodes, specifically a power law distribution where the probability of a single node having a degree of $D$ is approximated by $D^{-\lambda}$. | Examples include the World Wide Web (Albert et al. 2000), the Internet (Faloutsos et al. 1999), or metabolic networks (Jeong et al. 2000). Scale-free networks are highly robust to random failures but are sensitive to targeted attacks (Nair and Vidal 2011). |
| **Network centralization** | While centrality is a property of individual nodes, network centralization measures the centrality of the most central node with respect to the centralities of all other nodes. | Highlights the variation across a network in a node-level centrality score such as degree or betweenness. Ranges from 0 to 1, with lower scores signifying a more decentralized network of nodes with similar centrality (Freeman 1979). |

**Table 1.4** Comparative statistics for networks appearing in Figs. 1.1 and 1.3

|  | Figure 1.1 | Figure 1.2 Main network | Figure 1.3 Sierra Leone ego network | Figure 1.3 Complete network (inset) |
|---|---|---|---|---|
| Nodes | 85 | 15 | 82 | 328 |
| Ties | 184 | 62 | 97 | 491 |
| Network diameter (undirected) | 5 | 2 | 4 | 6 |
| Network density (directed) | 2.58% | – | 1.46% | 0.46% |
| Network density (undirected) | 5.15% | 59.05% | 2.92% | 0.92% |
| Average path length (directed) | 1.51 | – | 1.37 | 1.46 |
| Average path length (undirected) | 2.51 | 1.25 | 3.14 | 3.71 |
| Average closeness | 0.41 | 0.81 | 0.33 | 0.29 |
| Average degree | 4.33 | 8.13 | 2.37 | 2.99 |
| Average normalized degree | 0.05 | 0.58 | 0.03 | 0.01 |
| Degree centralization | 66.65% | 48.35% | 27.38% | 26.16% |
| Betweenness centralization | 1.56% | 13.15% | 0.21% | 0.06% |
| Ave. clustering coefficient | 0.00 | 0.41 | 0.00 | 0.03 |

Urrea et al. (2016) revealed that the Haiti network was larger with nearly twice as many ties, but Haiyan's one was denser and considered to be more successful by survey respondents.

## Aggregating Node-Level Metrics

In some studies, whole networks are evaluated based on some aggregate statement of their node-level metrics, such as average degree or average closeness. As an example, Schilling and Phelps (2007) provide network-level adaptations of the node-level measures of clustering and reach described in Table 1.1, and then demonstrate how higher values for both at the network level are associated with higher knowledge creation (as measured by patent generation) in industry alliances. In contrast, Urrea et al. (2016) compare centralization metrics calculated from the degree, closeness, betweenness, and eigenvector centralities of the nodes Haiti and Typhoon Haiyan response networks. Centralization requires the difference between a network's maximum observation and each node's individual value be summed across the network, and then stated in terms of its proportion of the maximum possible. This provides a value that partially expresses the tendency of the network's component nodes to vary on that dimension, such as the extreme disparity concerning degree centrality visible in Fig. 1.1.

## Network Typology

The potential of organizing whole network structures into insightful categories was recognized early in SNA research, starting in work such as Bavelas (1948) and Leavitt (1951). However, this work focused on very small networks, connected in patterns such as circles and linear chains. While these patterns remain relevant today, there exist remarkably few equivalent categories for typifying larger, complex networks. Table 1.3 provides brief descriptions of the best known categories available, beginning with an ego network, or a network that defined by a focal node (the ego) and all its connections. Figure 1.3 contrasts the ego network of the country of Sierra Leone with the broader network of all private sector support to the 2014 Ebola response in West Africa (inset). Ego networks are often the context in SNA literature, particularly social capital studies, as the balance of the whole network is assumed unimportant to research questions concerning the ego (Borgatti and Li 2009). This approach can be found in supply chain-related research as well, such as Carnovale and Yeniyurt (2014)'s investigation of joint venture formation.

Another well-recognized network type is the small-world network (Watts and Strogatz 1998; Watts 1999), marked by short path lengths and high clustering coefficients. The result is a graph in which a node is connected to a subset of neighbors but never far from any other member of the network, a pattern that has been related to contexts ranging from cliques among people to protein networks (Bork et al. 2004). Logically, the potential of the small-world phenomenon to shed light on supply chain relationships has been voiced as well (Galaskiewicz 2011), particularly the hypothesized relationship between its characteristic high clustering and resultant supply chain resilience (Nair and Vidal 2011; Day 2014). Table 1.4 reveals that only one of the four networks evaluated here, the NGOs of Fig. 1.2, fits the description of a small world. Returning to the definition provided in Table 1.1, high clustering within a larger group is detected by tallying triangular formations, where two actors with a common acquaintance have closed the structural hole between themselves and created a triad. These patterns have been hypothesized to enhance collaboration and innovation when actors are whole organizations as opposed to individual people (Choi and Wu 2009; Bellamy et al. 2014), although empirical studies have returned mixed results (Phelps 2010). Recently, Urrea et al. (2016) present empirical evidence of humanitarian relief and development programs following a small-world structure, with indications that when it comes to relief responses, the presence of structural holes may do more harm than good. Interestingly, the small-world network of Fig. 1.2 does represent at least the potential for collaboration among NGOs supporting food security in Liberia, but the network ties of Figs. 1.1 and 1.3 represent literal flow, and herein lies the problem. Even when interpreted as undirected networks, logistical systems are unlikely to exhibit small-world phenomenon because its requirement of high clustering requires organizations of the same tier to be supplying one another in addition to some downstream tier, a less common pattern in reality. Rather, Figs. 1.1 and 1.3, like many logistical flow systems, fit the description of a scale-free network (Albert et al. 2000), a network largely defined by the distribution of the degree centrality of its nodes, in which a few nodes with very high degree values create a network of interconnected hub-and-spokes patterns.

# The Potential of SNA in the Context of Humanitarian Logistics

Our previous literature review and related tutorials reveal very little SNA-related humanitarian research to date. Moving forward, we believe this methodology has untapped potential to advance knowledge across three areas, the first being its ability to support humanitarian logistics research in leadership of certain areas within the broader domain of SCM.

## Leading Research in Supply Chain Coordination and Emergence

Humanitarian supply chains are already recognized as having "unique" configurations relative to their steady-state peers (Kovács and Spens 2009; Melnyk et al. 2014; Tatham and Spens 2011), but we argue that this uniqueness embodies their potential for leading the broader discipline in:

- **Bringing more focus to coordination mechanisms.** Although humanitarian logistics and disaster response are relatively new research areas, a troublesome gap between scholarship and practice has shadowed this literature from the outset (Boin et al. 2010; Janssen et al. 2010; Pettit and Beresford 2009; Altay and Green 2006). This may be due in part to a well-meaning assumption that humanitarian logistics would benefit from the frameworks of steady-state commercial supply chains, yet many of these frameworks have shown themselves inadequate in a humanitarian context (Day 2014). Balcik et al. (2010) identify only a subset of known supply chain coordination practices that are either observed in the practice of humanitarian logistics or could be argued as promising opportunities for larger NGOs. This is critical in that it is coordination that is undisputed as a factor central to successful response (Boin et al. 2010; Janssen et al. 2010), yet it is coordination that isn't always evident in response to large-scale events (Boin et al. 2010; Altay and Green 2006; Kovács and Spens 2009).

- **Highlighting the significance of ad hoc and emergent networks.** Not surprisingly, steady-state supply chain coordination mechanisms that Balcik et al. (2010) do indicate as applicable to humanitarian response are exclusively decentralized mechanisms, as there is generally a natural absence of central planning in this high uncertainty environment with multiple autonomous participants. Furthermore, many participants self-initiate in responding to the wake of disaster, creating a network that owes less to deliberate design as it does to the phenomenon known as convergence (Day et al. 2012). To date, we lack an underlying body of theory explaining why this process is more successful in some cases versus others (Boin et al. 2010), answers that could prove vital to improving rapid response and resilience throughout the broader domain of SCM.

- **Building knowledge of supply chain life cycles.** Supply chains of all descriptions experience life cycle changes, yet this dynamic dimension of supply chain design is rarely addressed in existing literature (Melnyk et al. 2014). Humanitarian supply chains navigate these transitions vividly and relatively rapidly, having been framed into readily observable life cycle stages from the outset of research in this area (van Wassenhove 2006; Kovács and Spens 2007). Nonetheless, opportunity to better understand when and how to evolve supply chains in this context remains largely unexplored (Day et al. 2012), reflecting the state of the broader domain. Mapping and monitoring the evolution of emergent humanitarian response systems may be critical to a better understanding of their life cycle processes (Day 2014), which would also inform the larger supply chain community.

Each of these research areas relates directly to network structure, suggesting multiple opportunities for SNA-related research. However, the potential of SNA in the context of humanitarian logistics is not confined to advancing the understanding of supply chain coordination and emergence. In addition, this same combination has the ability to mitigate an emerging dilemma in supply network analysis itself, as discussed next.

## Bridging the Gap Between Social Capital and Whole Network Research Streams

Humanitarian logistics may lead to evolving network analysis on behalf of the entire supply chain domain, evidence of which is embedded in this chapter. In clarification, Fig. 1.4 illustrates the scholarly references cited in this chapter as nodes in a network, with the instances in which these

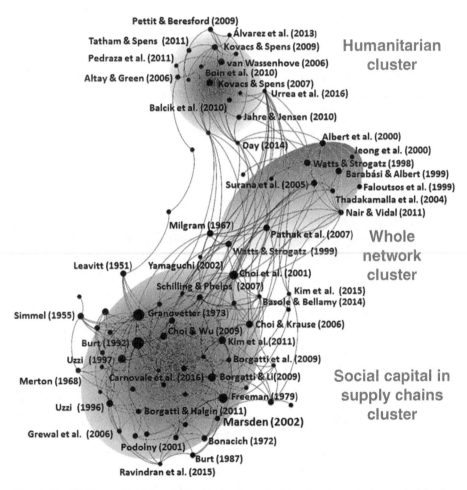

**Fig. 1.4** Citation network of literature discussed in chapter, nodes scaled by in-degree centrality, or the number of citations from within this group

references cite one another as ties (see Appendix for details on network generation). This visualization reveals that, despite calls for greater research focus on the dynamics of whole supply networks (Singhal and Singhal 2012), most of the existing application of SNA to supply chain problems follows SNA's earlier focus on the node-level dynamics of social capital (Borgatti and Foster 2003), clustering tightly around the initial work of Granovetter (1973) and Burt (1992) at the bottom of Fig. 1.4. In contrast, the smaller cluster representing work in whole network typology is largely devoid of supply chain-related studies, with exceptions such as Surana et al. (2005) and Nair and Vidal (2011) drawn to its southern half. Indeed, even as interest in the holistic study of supply networks grows, the broader domain of SCM appears to struggle with this paradigm. In a recent effort to evolve the theory of supply chains, Carter et al. (2015) return to the theme of a supply chain as a complex, adaptive network, but further hypothesize that this system is always defined relative to a particular agent or product, and is further bounded by the focal agent's visible horizon. This latter condition effectively specifies that supply chains are one-step ego networks, which in turn implies that the problems of SCM are confined to subgraphs of larger networks and measurable at the node level.

At the upper left in Fig. 1.4 is the "Humanitarian Cluster", consisting of references drawn into this discussion to provide the conditions specific to humanitarian logistics. A small collection of further references such as Urrea et al. (2016) and Day (2014), the existing intersection of SNA and humanitarian logistics, is logically tied to the core of the humanitarian cluster on the left, but intriguingly displays no collective affiliation with the node level versus the whole network clusters on the right. Rather, even early work in this area has necessarily drawn from both conceptualizations, suggesting that research in humanitarian logistics may lead the way in reconciling both the paucity of research focused on whole supply chains and the relationship between these findings and node-level research in the same context. Indeed, network analysis in the context of humanitarian operations may assist in mediating an even broader epistemological bifurcation in current network research. On one side of this methodological divide are those disciplines employing the sociological foundations of SNA in conjunction with its underlying metrics, the bulk of supply chain-related publications in Fig. 1.4 falling here. On the other side of network theory, however, are investigators in fields such as physics, biology, computer science, and engineering, who often apply a more intricate ontological structure of network theory to their scientific inquiry, rarely informed by the principles of sociality. Star constellations, gene compositions, and cloud computing services are among the many objects of what is usually whole network analysis (Borgatti et al. 2009), prompting the recent creation of new network concepts, metrics, and software platforms.

In our opinion, one of the greatest challenges SNA currently faces is, at its heart, a logistical one – finding a common language for disparate fields of scholarship to communicate their findings to each other, to map the opportunities for exchange of network analysis insights between them. Unless such coordination efforts are taken seriously, each discipline pursuing new opportunities suggested by SNA is at risk of reinventing the proverbial wheel. Current lack of dialogue between the "social" and "nonsocial" sides of network analysis has created a proliferation of variants on those metrics described in Tables 1.1 and 1.2, and there does not yet exist consensus as to which best characterize supply chains. Social network scholars have cautioned against the use of SNA methodology in the context of supply networks unless adequate attention is given to the social component of network relationships (Borgatti and Li 2009; Galaskiewicz 2011). However, examples discussed here and elsewhere highlight the dilemma that behavior among people is not likely to translate directly into interactions between whole organizations within a supply chain (Pathak et al. 2007). The efficient and effective logistical flow of relief to disaster victims has been posited as a defining element of success in humanitarian response and recovery (van Wassenhove 2006), and the central cost driver of response (Tatham and Pettit 2010). Any network pursuing these goals is just as likely to be shaped by the circumstances of the response, a distinctly nonsocial influence, as by collaborative design, rendering humanitarian logistics a rare application in which both branches of network analysis are simultaneously relevant. In the near term, humanitarian researchers should use caution when selecting models and metrics, in that those best known to social science might not be optimal for the particular study at hand. In the long term, research in humanitarian logistics is well positioned to evolve the whole of network analysis forward as it serves as a conduit for reconciling its currently divergent streams.

## Facing the Challenge of Missing Data

Like all empirical analysis, SNA research struggles with the issues of sampling and measurement error, and the evolution of computational resources enabling researchers to work with ever larger networks has exacerbated these difficulties. Granovetter (1976) offers one of the earliest discussions of efficient network sampling strategies for estimating density scores of very large populations. However, despite advances in network sampling theory, the effects of incomplete social network data on network statistics have not been sufficiently examined (Kossinets 2006). Network data incompleteness most commonly stems from inaccurate boundary specification (missing actors or affiliations), survey nonresponse, or inappropriate study design, inadvertently leading to biased estimates of network-level statistics (Kossinets 2006). Wang et al. (2012) expand this measurement error typology by adding the phenomenon of spurious data, as well as false aggregation and disaggregation of nodes. Wang and colleagues (2012) found that networks with low average clustering and less positively skewed degree distributions, or random-like networks as opposed to small worlds, are generally more resistant to measurement error, but the effect of important network properties such as network size on error robustness pends further investigation. Network sampling problems become all the more acute given the highly dynamic and complex nature of humanitarian networks, marked by rapid change in network structure, unexpected node and affiliation activation or decay, and multiple interaction contexts. Logically, it is important to recognize the potential for, and near inevitability of, estimation errors when presenting SNA results in humanitarian logistics research, both when it comes to survey- and secondary-data collection processes. However, given our incomplete understanding of how missing data and related problems affect SNA measures in general, its uptake into humanitarian logistics can be thought of as an opportunity to confront these long-standing gaps in knowledge, ideally narrowing them with improved methodology which strengthens SNA's utility to users across multiple domains.

## Conclusions

The paradigm of a complex, adaptive network evokes a logistical system composed of semiautonomous entities, whose interactions and outcomes are heavily influenced by a dynamic environment. Humanitarian response certainly fits this quintessential description, and strongly embodies the underexplored subject of supply chain life cycle management. SNA offers promising research opportunities addressing these challenging areas, although this review identified few studies in the context of humanitarian logistics to date. This is not surprising in that uptake of network analysis in work on humanitarian problems is in its formative stage at the time of this survey, our motivation behind structuring a portion of this chapter as a quick tutorial for interested readers. Humanitarian logistics ultimately depends on the successful formation and coordination of rapidly evolving ad hoc supply networks, and better understanding of the antecedents of this success may be revealed in the capture and quantification of observed responses. The tools of SNA are well suited to these tasks, poised to support further search for this critical insight.

However, while SNA offers promise in advancing humanitarian logistics research, our literature survey likewise suggests that humanitarian logistics can assist in the further development of SNA, both in the context of supply chains and across other domains. In surveying SNA-related supply chain research, we find the majority of existing studies frame this problem in terms of social or structural capital, which confines inquiry to issues surrounding each entity's immediate connections to a larger network. While this approach is not without its own merits, a focus on structural capital is not synonymous with a holistic view of supply networks. Furthermore, one important insight from recognition of supply chains as complex adaptive networks is that of the finite nature of organizational intentionality: no matter how purposeful a supply chain design might be, it is perpetually shaped and reshaped by both inter- and intra-organizational factors beyond managerial purview. Node-level analyses of supply networks identify beneficial patterns of connection at the firm level; suggesting such insights are for use in supply chain design decisions implies these connections are primarily the result of managerial control, again moving away from the original complex network paradigm. In contrast, even the small body of humanitarian supply chain research available so far appears to break from the broader domain's concentration on social/structural capital, building instead from the full spectrum of node-level to whole-network analysis. Currently, holistic study of networks has received the most attention from researchers outside of the social sciences, as overall SNA-inspired research activity divides into social network analysis versus "purely" network analysis streams. Humanitarian logistics is uniquely positioned to take a leadership role in a reconciliation of these two important but diverging research efforts. Humanitarian logistics ultimately combines complex networks shaped by external forces, similar to the dynamics of problems from the "hard" sciences, with vital activities simultaneously and heavily dependent on human interaction and collaboration. Better understanding of the emergent result of these two sides of humanitarian response can both strengthen capabilities in times of disaster and further evolve the state of the art in network analysis itself.

# Appendix: Source Information for Example Networks, as of 1 May 2016

Software Used in the Generation of Network Diagrams

- **UCINET/Netdraw.** More information about and downloads of *Ucinet* and its graphical module Netdraw are found at http://sites.google.com/ site/ucinetsoftware/home and http://analytictech.com For additional discussion, see Borgatti et al. (2002).
- **Gephi.** More information about and downloads of Gephi are found at **gephi.org**. For additional discussion, see Bastian et al. (2009).
- **Cytoscape.** More information about and downloads of Cytoscape are found at **cytoscape.org**. For additional discussion, see Smoot et al. (2011).

Data Sources Used in the Generation of Figures

- **Figure 1.1.** The data illustrated in this figure was obtained through the World Bank's open data repository at **data.worldbank.org**. The data specific to Figure 1.1 is available at **wdi.worldbank.org/table/6.12** at the time of this writing. This is supplemental online table 6.12 to the publication *World Development Indicators* 2015 (World Bank 2015).
- **Figure 1.2.** The data illustrated in this figure was obtained through OCHA's Humanitarian Data Exchange (HDX), an open data repository site at **data.hdx.rwlabs.org**. The data specific to Figure 1.2 is a "3 W" or "Who-What-Where" file uploaded to the Exchange and updated by the Food Security Cluster, coled by the United Nation's FOA and WFP. The exact data used in the creation of Figure 1.2 was accessed at **data.hdx.rwlabs.org/dataset/0d9869d9-ce3c-43c9-932b-9c27c7c64552/resource/43a5784f-7b42-4ced-addb-4de3b685bc2a/download/liberia-food-security-3w-2015.csv**. An interactive dashboard is available at takavarasha.github.io/Liberia-Food-Security-3 W.
- **Figure 1.3.** The data illustrated in this figure was also obtained through HDX (see Figure 1.2). The data specific to Fig. 1.3 was uploaded and updated by OCHA's Private Sector Section and was accessed through **data.hdx.rwlabs.org/dataset/financial-tracking-of-private-sector-contributions-ebola-2014.**
- **Figure 1.4.** The data was assembled as an "edge" file for processing by Gephi, in which each citation of each paper in the chapter references was examined to determine if it were also a member of the chapter reference list. If the condition was "yes," then a directed edge was appended to Fig. 1.4

edge file, indicating a directed tie from the chapter reference to the cited chapter reference. Pictured in Fig. 1.4 is the largest connected component of the group, containing all 364 cross-citations and 85 of the original 93 references, the remaining 9 being unconnected isolates largely composed of references to technical material used in the generation of other figures. The Force Atlas layout algorithm was used with repulsion set arbitrarily high, to compel similarly interconnected references to cluster.

# References

Albert, Réka, Hawoong Jeong, and Albert-László Barabási. "Error and attack tolerance of complex networks." *Nature* 406, no. 6794 (2000): 378–382.

Altay, Nezih, and Walter G. Green. "OR/MS research in disaster operations management." *European Journal of Operational Research* 175, no. 1 (2006): 475–493.

Álvarez, Humberto R. A., and Marco Serrato. "Social network analysis for humanitarian logistics operations in Latin America." In *IIE Annual Conference. Proceedings*, p. 3835. Institute of Industrial Engineers-Publisher, 2013.

Autry, Chad W., and Stanley E. Griffis. "Supply chain capital: The impact of structural and relational linkages on firm execution and innovation." *Journal of Business Logistics* 29, no. 1 (2008): 157–173.

Balcik, Burcu, Benita M. Beamon, Caroline C. Krejci, Kyle M. Muramatsu, and Magaly Ramirez. "Coordination in humanitarian relief chains: Practices, challenges and opportunities." *International Journal of Production Economics* 126, no. 1 (2010): 22–34.

Barabási, Albert-László, and Réka Albert. "Emergence of scaling in random networks." *Science* 286, no. 5439 (1999): 509–512.

Barnes, John Arundel. *Social networks*. Vol. 26. Reading, MA: Addison-Wesley Publishing Company, 1972.

Basole, Rahul C., and Marcus A. Bellamy. "Visual analysis of supply network risks: Insights from the electronics industry." *Decision Support Systems* 67 (2014): 109–120.

Bastian, Mathieu, Sebastien Heymann, and Mathieu Jacomy. "Gephi: An open source software for exploring and manipulating networks." *International AAAI Conference on Weblogs and Social Media* 8 (2009): 361–362.

Bavelas, Alex. "A mathematical model for group structures." *Human Organization* 7, no. 3 (1948): 16–30.

Bellamy, Marcus A., and Rahul C. Basole. "Network analysis of supply chain systems: A systematic review and future research." *Systems Engineering* 16, no. 2 (2013): 235–249.

Bellamy, Marcus A., Soumen Ghosh, and Manpreet Hora. "The influence of supply network structure on firm innovation." *Journal of Operations Management* 32, no. 6 (2014): 357–373.

Boin, Arjen, Peter Kelle, and D. Clay Whybark. "Resilient supply chains for extreme situations: Outlining a new field of study." *International Journal of Production Economics* 126, no. 1 (2010): 1–6.

Bonacich, Phillip. "Factoring and weighting approaches to status scores and clique identification." *Journal of Mathematical Sociology* 2, no. 1 (1972): 113–120.

Borgatti, Stephen P. "Centrality and network flow." *Social Networks* 27, no. 1 (2005): 55–71.

Borgatti, Stephen P., and Pacey C. Foster. "The network paradigm in organizational research: A review and typology." *Journal of management* 29, no. 6 (2003): 991–1013.

Borgatti, Stephen P., and Daniel S. Halgin. "On network theory." *Organization Science* 22, no. 5 (2011): 1168–1181.

Borgatti, Stephen P., and Xun Li. "On social network analysis in a supply chain context." *Journal of Supply Chain Management* 45, no. 2 (2009): 5–22.

Borgatti, Stephen P., Martin G. Everett, and Linton C. Freeman. "Ucinet for Windows: Software for social network analysis." Harvard, MA: Analytic Technologies, 2002.

Borgatti, Stephen P., Ajay Mehra, Daniel J. Brass, and Giuseppe Labianca. "Network analysis in the social sciences." *Science* 323, no. 5916 (2009): 892–895.

Bork, Peer, Lars J. Jensen, Christian von Mering, Arun K. Ramani, Insuk Lee, and Edward M. Marcotte. "Protein interaction networks from yeast to human." *Current Opinion in Structural Biology* 14, no. 3 (2004): 292–299.

Burt, Ronald S. "Social contagion and innovation: Cohesion versus structural equivalence." *American Journal of Sociology* (1987): 1287–1335.

Burt, Ronald S. *Structural holes: The social structure of competition*. Cambridge: Harvard University Press, 1992.

Burt, Ronald S. "The network structure of social capital." *Research in Organizational Behavior* 22 (2000): 345–423.

Carnovale, Steven, and Sengun Yeniyurt. "The role of ego networks in manufacturing joint venture formations." *Journal of Supply Chain Management* 50, no. 2 (2014): 1–17.

Carnovale, Steven, and Sengun Yeniyurt. "The role of ego network structure in facilitating ego network innovations." *Journal of Supply Chain Management* 51, no. 2 (2015): 22–46.

Carnovale, Steven, Dale S. Rogers, and Sengun Yeniyurt. "Bridging structural holes in global manufacturing equity based partnerships: A network analysis of domestic vs. international joint venture formations." *Journal of Purchasing and Supply Management* 22, no. 1 (2016): 7–17.

Carter, Craig R., Lisa M. Ellram, and Wendy Tate. "The use of social network analysis in logistics research." *Journal of Business Logistics* 28, no. 1 (2007): 137–168.

Carter, Craig R., Dale S. Rogers, and Thomas Y. Choi. "Toward the theory of the supply chain." *Journal of Supply Chain Management* 51, no. 2 (2015): 89–97.

Choi, Thomas Y., and Daniel R. Krause. "The supply base and its complexity: Implications for transaction costs, risks, responsiveness, and innovation." *Journal of Operations Management* 24, no. 5 (2006): 637–652.

Choi, Thomas Y., and Zhaohui Wu. "Triads in supply networks: Theorizing buyer–supplier–supplier relationships." *Journal of Supply Chain Management* 45, no. 1 (2009): 8–25.

Choi, Thomas Y., Kevin J. Dooley, and Manus Rungtusanatham. "Supply networks and complex adaptive systems: Control versus emergence." *Journal of Operations management* 19, no. 3 (2001): 351–366.

Coleman, James S. "Social capital in the creation of human capital." *American Journal of Sociology* (1988): S95–S120.

Day, Jamison M. "Fostering emergent resilience: The complex adaptive supply network of disaster relief." *International Journal of Production Research* 52, no. 7 (2014): 1970–1988.

Day, Jamison M., Steven A. Melnyk, Paul D. Larson, Edward W. Davis, and D. Clay Whybark. "Humanitarian and disaster relief supply chains: A matter of life and death." *Journal of Supply Chain Management* 48, no. 2 (2012): 21–36.

De Toni, A., and Guido Nassimbeni. "Supply networks: Genesis, stability and logistics implications. A comparative analysis of two districts." *Omega* 23, no. 4 (1995): 403–418.

Dong, Maggie Chuoyan, Zhiqiang Liu, Yimin Yu, and Jin-Hui Zheng. "Opportunism in distribution networks: The role of network embeddedness and dependence." *Production and Operations Management* 24, no. 10 (2015): 1657–1670.

Easley, David, and Jon Kleinberg. *Networks, crowds, and markets: Reasoning about a highly connected world.* New York: Cambridge University Press, 2010.

Echols, Ann, and Wenpin Tsai. "Niche and performance: The moderating role of network embeddedness." *Strategic Management Journal* 26, no. 3 (2005): 219–238.

Faloutsos, Michalis, Petros Faloutsos, and Christos Faloutsos. "On power-law relationships of the internet topology." In *ACM SIGCOMM Computer Communication Review*, vol. 29, no. 4, pp. 251–262. ACM, 1999.

Freeman, Linton C. "A set of measures of centrality based on betweenness." *Sociometry* (1977): 35–41.

Freeman, Linton C. "Centrality in social networks conceptual clarification." *Social Networks* 1, no. 3 (1979): 215–239.

Galaskiewicz, Joseph. "Studying supply chains from a social network perspective." *Journal of Supply Chain Management* 47, no. 1 (2011): 4–8.

Gnyawali, Devi R., and Ravindranath Madhavan. "Cooperative networks and competitive dynamics: A structural embeddedness perspective." *Academy of Management Review* 26, no. 3 (2001): 431–445.

Granovetter, Mark S. "The strength of weak ties." *American Journal of Sociology* (1973): 1360–1380.

Granovetter, Mark S. "Network sampling: Some first steps." *American Journal of Sociology* 81, no. 6 (1976): 1287–1303.

Grewal, Rajdeep, Gary L. Lilien, and Girish Mallapragada. "Location, location, location: How network embeddedness affects project success in open source systems." *Management Science* 52, no. 7 (2006): 1043–1056.

Gu, Zuguang, Jialin Liu, Kunming Cao, Junfeng Zhang, and Jin Wang. "Centrality-based pathway enrichment: A systematic approach for finding significant pathways dominated by key genes." *BMC Systems Biology* 6, no. 1 (2012).

Haase, Thomas W. "International disaster resilience: Preparing for transnational disaster." In *Designing Resilience: Preparing for Extreme Events*, edited by Comfort, Louise K., Boin Arjen, and Demchak Chris C., 220–243. Pittsburgh: University of Pittsburgh Press, 2010.

Houghton, Robert J., Chris Baber, Richard McMaster, Neville A. Stanton, Paul Salmon, Rebecca Stewart, and Guy Walker. "Command and control in emergency services operations: A social network analysis." *Ergonomics* 49, no. 12–13 (2006): 1204–1225.

Jahre, Marianne, and Leif-Magnus Jensen. "Coordination in humanitarian logistics through clusters." *International Journal of Physical Distribution and Logistics Management* 40, no. 8/9 (2010): 657–674.

Janssen, Marijn, Jinkyu Lee, Nitesh Bharosa, and Anthony Cresswell. "Advances in multi-agency disaster management: Key elements in disaster research." *Information Systems Frontiers* 12, no. 1 (2010): 1–7.

Jeong, Hawoong, Bálint Tombor, Réka Albert, Zoltan N. Oltvai, and A-L. Barabási. "The large-scale organization of metabolic networks." *Nature* 407, no. 6804 (2000): 651–654.

Kadushin, Charles. "The friends and supporters of psychotherapy: On social circles in urban life." *American Sociological Review* 31, no. 6 (1966): 786–802.

Kim, Yusoon, Thomas Y. Choi, Tingting Yan, and Kevin Dooley. "Structural investigation of supply networks: A social network analysis approach." *Journal of Operations Management* 29, no. 3 (2011): 194–211.

Kim, Yusoon, Yi-Su Chen, and Kevin Linderman. "Supply network disruption and resilience: A network structural perspective." *Journal of Operations Management* 33 (2015): 43–59.

Kossinets, Gueorgi. "Effects of missing data in social networks." *Social Networks* 28, no. 3 (2006): 247–268.

Kovács, Gyöngyi, and Karen Spens. "Humanitarian logistics in disaster relief operations." *International Journal of Physical Distribution and Logistics Management* 37, no. 2 (2007): 99–114.

Kovács, Gyöngyi, and Karen Spens. "Identifying challenges in humanitarian logistics." *International Journal of Physical Distribution and Logistics Management* 39, no. 6 (2009): 506–528.

Leavitt, Harold J. "Some effects of certain communication patterns on group performance." *The Journal of Abnormal and Social Psychology* 46, no. 1 (1951): 38–50.

Marsden, Peter V. "Egocentric and sociocentric measures of network centrality." *Social Networks* 24, no. 4 (2002): 407–422.

Melnyk, Steven A., Ram Narasimhan, and Hugo A. DeCampos. "Supply chain design: Issues, challenges, frameworks and solutions." *International Journal of Production Research* 52, no. 7 (2014): 1887–1896.

Merton, Robert King. *Social Theory and Social Structure.* New York: The Free Press, a division of Simon and Schuster Inc., 1968.

Milgram, Stanley. "The small world problem." *Psychology Today* 2, no. 1 (1967): 60–67.

Mizgier, Kamil J., Matthias P. Jüttner, and Stephan M. Wagner. "Bottleneck identification in supply chain networks." *International Journal of Production Research* 51, no. 5 (2013): 1477–1490.

Morrison, Gary R., Steven M. Ross, Jerrold E. Kemp, and Howard Kalman. *Designing effective instruction.* Hoboken: John Wiley and Sons, 2004.

Nair, Anand, and José M. Vidal. "Supply network topology and robustness against disruptions–an investigation using multi-agent model." *International Journal of Production Research* 49, no. 5 (2011): 1391–1404.

Pathak, Surya D., Jamison M. Day, Anand Nair, William J. Sawaya, and M. Murat Kristal. "Complexity and adaptivity in supply networks: Building supply network theory using a complex adaptive systems perspective." *Decision Sciences* 38, no. 4 (2007): 547–580.

Pathak, Surya D., Zhaohui Wu, and David Johnston. "Toward a structural view of co-opetition in supply networks." *Journal of Operations Management* 32, no. 5 (2014): 254–267.

Pettit, Stephen, and Anthony Beresford. "Critical success factors in the context of humanitarian aid supply chains." *International Journal of Physical Distribution and Logistics Management* 39, no. 6 (2009): 450–468.

Phelps, Corey C. "A longitudinal study of the influence of alliance network structure and composition on firm exploratory innovation." *Academy of Management Journal* 53, no. 4 (2010): 890–913.

Podolny, Joel M. "Networks as the pipes and prisms of the market." *American Journal of Sociology* 107, no. 1 (2001): 33–60.

Ravindran, Kiron, Anjana Susarla, Deepa Mani, and Vijay Gurbaxani. "Social capital, reputation and contract duration in buyer-supplier networks for information technology outsourcing." *Information Systems Research* 26, no. 2 (2015): 379–397.

Schilling, Melissa A., and Corey C. Phelps. "Interfirm collaboration networks: The impact of large-scale network structure on firm innovation." *Management Science* 53, no. 7 (2007): 1113–1126.

Shimbel, Alfonso. "Structural parameters of communication networks." *The Bulletin of Mathematical Biophysics* 15, no. 4 (1953): 501–507.

Simmel, George. *Conflict and the web of group affiliations.* New York: The Free Press, 1955.

Simpson, Natalie C., and Philip G. Hancock. "The incident commander's problem: Resource allocation in the context of emergency response." *International Journal of Services Sciences* 2, no. 2 (2009): 102–124.

Singhal, Kalyan, and Jaya Singhal. "Imperatives of the science of operations and supply-chain management." *Journal of Operations Management* 30, no. 3 (2012): 237–244.

Smoot, Michael E., Keiichiro Ono, Johannes Ruscheinski, Peng-Liang Wang, and Trey Ideker. "Cytoscape 2.8: New features for data integration and network visualization." *Bioinformatics* 27, no. 3 (2011): 431–432.

Stephenson, Karen, and Marvin Zelen. "Rethinking centrality: Methods and examples." *Social Networks* 11, no. 1 (1989): 1–37.

Surana, Amit, Soundar Kumara, Mark Greaves, and Usha Nandini Raghavan. "Supply-chain networks: A complex adaptive systems perspective." *International Journal of Production Research* 43, no. 20 (2005): 4235–4265.

Tatham, Peter H., and Stephen J. Pettit. "Transforming humanitarian logistics: The journey to supply network management." *International Journal of Physical Distribution and Logistics Management* 40, no. 8/9 (2010): 609–622.

Tatham, Peter, and Karen Spens. "Towards a humanitarian logistics knowledge management system." *Disaster Prevention and Management: An International Journal* 20, no. 1 (2011): 6–26.

Thadakamaila, H. P., Usha Nandini Raghavan, Soundar Kumara, and Réka Albert. "Survivability of multiagent-based supply networks: A topological perspective." *IEEE Intelligent Systems* 19, no. 5 (2004): 24–31.

Urrea, Gloria, Sebastián Villa, and Paulo Gonçalves. "Exploratory analyses of relief and development operations using social networks." *Socio-Economic Planning Sciences* (2016). In Press. http://dx.doi.org/10.1016/j.seps.2016.05.001.

Uzzi, Brian. "The sources and consequences of embeddedness for the economic performance of organizations: The network effect." *American Sociological Review* 61, no. 4 (1996): 674–698.

Uzzi, Brian. "Social structure and competition in interfirm networks: The paradox of embeddedness." *Administrative Science Quarterly* 42, no. 1 (1997): 35–67.

Van Wassenhove, Luk N. "Humanitarian aid logistics: Supply chain management in high gear." *Journal of the Operational Research Society* 57, no. 5 (2006): 475–489.

Wang, Harris H., Farren J. Isaacs, Peter A. Carr, Zachary Z. Sun, George Xu, Craig R. Forest, and George M. Church. "Programming cells by multiplex genome engineering and accelerated evolution." *Nature* 460, no. 7257 (2009): 894–898.

Wang, Dan J., Xiaolin Shi, Daniel A. McFarland, and Jure Leskovec. "Measurement error in network data: A re-classification." *Social Networks* 34, no. 4 (2012): 396–409.

Watts, Duncan J. "Networks, dynamics, and the small-world phenomenon 1." *American Journal of Sociology* 105, no. 2 (1999): 493–527.

Watts, Duncan J., and Steven H. Strogatz. "Collective dynamics of 'small-world' networks." *Nature* 393, no. 6684 (1998): 440–442.

World Bank. "World Development Indicators 2015." Washington, DC: World Bank, 2015. doi:10.1596/978-1-4648-0440-3. License: Creative Commons Attribution CC BY 3.0 IGO.

Yamaguchi, Kazuo. "The structural and behavioral characteristics of the smallest-world phenomenon: Minimum distance networks." *Social Networks* 24, no. 2 (2002): 161–182.

Yan, Tingting, Thomas Y. Choi, Yusoon Kim, and Yang Yang. "A theory of the nexus supplier: A critical supplier from a network perspective." *Journal of Supply Chain Management* 51, no. 1 (2015): 52–66.

Yin, Jie, Andrew Lampert, Mark Cameron, Bella Robinson, and Robert Power. "Using social media to enhance emergency situation awareness." *IEEE Intelligent Systems* 27, no. 6 (2012): 52–59.

# 2

# Deploying Collaborative Management Research Approaches in Humanitarian Supply Chains: An Overview and Research Agenda

Yasmine Sabri

## Introduction

Humanitarian supply chains often involve complex networks of interconnected global organisations, operating in harsh and uncertain conditions
caused by natural as well as man-made disasters (Day et al. 2012). Unlike
the commercial ones, the humanitarian supply chains are expected to add
value to an ultimate beneficiary from the affected communities, not to a
customer in the traditional sense (Blanco and Goentzel 2006).

Despite the utter benefits of humanitarian supply chains in mitigating the
implications of disastrous circumstances, they started to gain research attention just recently (Christopher and Tatham 2014). For instance, the findings
of Kovács and Spens (2011) report that humanitarian logistics and supply
chain management scholarly publications were doubled from the year 2005
onwards, following the Indian Ocean Tsunami disaster. Albeit the attention
of researchers in the majority of these publications is on improving preparedness and response (Leiras et al. 2014), lack of coordination and collaboration
between the different stakeholders is still identified as one of the main
challenges faced by the management of humanitarian supply chains
(Vaillancourt 2016; Kovács and Spens 2011). Lack of collaboration was

Y. Sabri (✉)
Department of Management, Economics and Industrial Engineering, Politecnico di
Milano, Milano, Italy
e-mail: yasminesabri.hassan@polimi.it

© The Author(s) 2018
G. Kovács et al. (eds.), *The Palgrave Handbook of Humanitarian Logistics
and Supply Chain Management*, https://doi.org/10.1057/978-1-137-59099-2_2

**41**

observed in sudden-onset natural disasters, for instance subsequent to the aftermath of the Indian Ocean earthquake in 2004 (Telford et al. 2006; Jayasuriya and McCawley 2008). Similarly, it is noted in slow-onset man-made disasters, as recent armed conflicts left unprecedented numbers of displaced populations in need of humanitarian support (UN 2016).

Successful management, of humanitarian supply chains, requires a methodological approach that integrates the roles of the various stakeholders. However, the extant research in humanitarian supply chain domain is often criticised for lacking relevance (Jahre et al. 2015). Thus, the research community would benefit from examining whether the currently adopted methodological approaches enable the generation of relevant knowledge. Relevance should be established in practice, but also to the taxpayers, who mostly fund research activities in universities. In light of the findings attested in Kunz and Reiner (2012), humanitarian supply chain management scholarly publications usually follow two main methodologies: simulation and modelling, and case study. Thus, the question concerning the appropriateness of these methodological approaches, in addressing the challenges faced in humanitarian supply chain research, still holds.

In this chapter, the adoption of collaborative management research is examined as a methodological approach that could contribute in enhancing the collaboration and the engagement of humanitarian actors, as well as to mitigate the shortcomings of the fragmentation of stakeholders' efforts.

Collaborative management research emerged to lessen the diversion between theoretically generated knowledge and real-world events (Gibbons et al. 1994). It is founded on establishing a platform of inter-disciplinary collaboration and continuous inquiry between the involved stakeholders (Pasmore et al. 2007). Hence it enables researchers and practitioners to jointly participate on fulfilling end beneficiaries' (the affected communities') needs. Arguably, it allows for an environment of continuous improvement and increased preparedness to real-world events (Brydon-Miller et al. 2003). However, collaborative management research is always facing a strong critique regarding its scientific nature and implementation challenges. Due to the researcher's great involvement in the practitioner system, there are claims of bias in data analyses. Collaboration between stakeholders might not be so easy to establish, as it requires high levels of trust and agreement on the research project's aim and scope. Furthermore, in some instances there could be attempts from practitioners to influence data analysis and the final output of the project. Further, collaborative research projects need good management of expectations so as to decrease the gap between what the researchers and what the practitioners are expecting as an outcome from the research project.

Shani et al. (2004) identify eight approaches for collaborative management research: action research, field research and different types of inquiries. This chapter specifically focuses on action research and clinical inquiry, as their research process demonstrates higher reliability (Shani et al. 2004).

The aim of this chapter is to expand our conceptual understanding on the different research approaches in generating knowledge in humanitarian logistics and supply chain management. The chapter extends Coughlan and Coghlan's (2002) framework and builds on the findings of Schein (2006) and Näslund et al. (2010), to develop a collaborative research framework suited for the humanitarian logistics and supply chain management domain, as well as highlighting the challenges of adopting these approaches.

# Humanitarian Logistics and Supply Chain Management

## The Idiosyncrasy of Humanitarian Supply Chains

Evidently, the humanitarian empirical scene is currently experiencing an increasing, and repetitive, number of natural and man-made disasters. This critical situation contributes in developing disruptions and results in the displacement of a large number of the affected populations. In a 2016 United Nations report, the number of displaced victims has mounted up to 43 million uprooted victims with humanitarian needs (UN 2016). These unprecedented developments call for developing suitable mitigation frameworks, as well as strengthening the collaboration between the different stakeholders. To address the implications of this critical situation, the international community and representatives from various stakeholders inaugurated the first ever World Humanitarian Summit (WHS) that was held in Istanbul in 2016. The summit brought together the humanitarian actors, decision and policy makers, and concluded with recommendations on making an impact on people's lives not only to deliver aid but also to end the need (WHS Chair's Summary report 2016).

As the magnitude, intensity and frequency of disasters are on increasing trend (UN 2016), the implications of these disasters emphasise the importance of the supply chain functions. Humanitarian actors are responsible to ensure an efficient and effective flow of goods, information and services, with the minimum possible latency between affected locations and providers (Kunz and Riner 2012). Humanitarian supply chains are networks of entities representing multiple stakeholders, starting from donors and ending with the end beneficiaries (affected communities). The stakeholders are linked through flows of information and donations. The humanitarian affected location could embrace these organisations: UN organisations, non-governmental organisations, local authorities, military and the media (Van Wassenhove 2006).

Within the domain of humanitarian supply chain, it is likely to borrow from commercial supply chains literature and research frameworks (Kovács and Spen 2007). The humanitarian supply chain is itself a type of commercial supply chains, but has different settings, due to its different characteristics. Blanco and Goentzel (2006) highlight the main differences between commercial (corporate or for-profit) supply chain and humanitarian supply chain, as demonstrated in Fig. 2.1. The significant difference is the absence of a customer in the humanitarian supply chain, instead there is a beneficiary from the affected communities. The flow of material (physical flow) in commercial supply chain is forward flow from suppliers to customers while in humanitarian supply chains it is forward and also downward flow from donors. Another significant characteristic, according to Blanco and Goentzel (2006), is

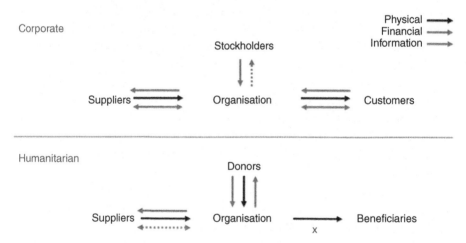

**Fig. 2.1** Differences between corporate and humanitarian supply chains (*source*: Blanco and Goentzel 2006)

the lack of information flow between humanitarian organisations and the affected communities, which we hope to overcome through employing collaborative research approaches.

## Do Humanitarian Supply Chains Need Different Methodological Approaches?

The challenges faced in managing humanitarian supply chains significantly differ from the commercial ones, mainly due to the high uncertainty of demand and supply (Van Wassenhove 2006), and lack of coordination (Jahre et al. 2015). This leads to propose that different problems would need to be (methodologically) approached differently. Furthermore, the efforts in advancing supply chain management discipline might be hindered if the research community keeps addressing the peculiar issues of humanitarian supply chains, with the same approaches used in other research fields (Näslund 2002; Näslund et al. 2010).

In the humanitarian arena, thousands of donations are usually directed to the affected locations. However, the aid and relief processes are not always as effective as expected, which calls for enhancing the integration and the inclusion of all the involved humanitarian actors (Christopher and Tatham 2014). Furthermore, in light of the earlier discussion in section "The Idiosyncrasy of Humanitarian Supply Chains", the peculiar nature of the humanitarian supply chains entails attaining the highest possible levels of collaboration and coordination between the different stakeholders, to achieve greater effectiveness. Balcik et al. (2010) analyse the collaboration practices in humanitarian supply chains; they conclude that coordination mechanisms increase the supply chain's efficiency and performance. Further, Altay (2008) stresses that achieving success, in managing humanitarian logistics and supply chains, depends on establishing effective communication, coordination and collaboration among the chain members. However, it seems challenging to implement coordination schemes. Van Wassenhove (2006) reports on the following challenges: the complicated operating conditions, safety and security concerns, high staff turnover, uncertainty of demand and supply, time pressure, large number of stakeholders and the role of media.

So, do the currently adopted research approaches respond to all these challenges? In the subsequent section, collaborative management research approaches are discussed as means to improve humanitarian supply chains management and to ensure that the field is producing relevant knowledge.

# Collaborative Management Research

## Rationale Behind Collaborative Management Research

Mohrman and Lawler (2011) identify how research could close the gap between practice and theory development. Research should respond to three rationales: instrumental, value based and epistemological, depicted in Fig. 2.2. First is the instrumental rationale. Access to high-quality data is usually ensured when researchers have closer links with practitioners, thus research has to be interesting to practice in the first place. Furthermore, acknowledge that the research process involves multiple actors, not just university based. The engagement and integration between these actors need appropriate methodological approaches that demonstrate higher flexibility and dynamism. This leads to a co-production of knowledge (they refer to this notion as mode 2 knowledge).

Second, value-based rationales relate to value of the topics to be discussed to be relevant to practice, as well as the value of enhancing the position of universities. The authors suggest that organisational innovation is vastly performed in practice compared to academia, and the later has become the position of *playing catch-up* instead of being in a leading position.

Third, epistemologically, organisations do not exist independent from their context. This context sensitivity has to be reflected in the research approach. Furthermore, the global market settings are forcing organisations to constantly change, which should be reflected in the research process.

Mohrman and Lawler (2011) also identify the barriers for the co-production of knowledge between researchers and practitioners, which are mainly related to the institutional barriers facing researchers due to the rules of their

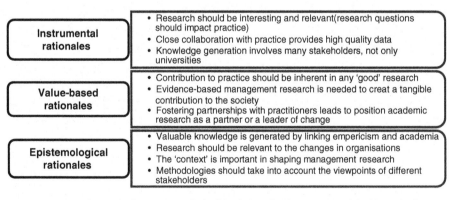

**Fig. 2.2** Overview on the rationale behind developing actionable knowledge

universities, as well as the challenges that will face the *publishability* of such research, due to strict journal rules as well as the journal's expectations of the methodological rigour.

## The Evolution of Collaborative Management Research

Collaborative management research approaches emerged in response to the perpetual debate between positivistic and interpretivistic stances towards science and knowledge production (Müller 2005). The aim of collaborative research approaches is to address the concerns, of both academics and practitioners, regarding the development of organisational research and knowledge generation (Starkey and Madan 2001). A collaborative management research process involves two parties or more. At least one of them represents practitioners. It involves mutual framing of the research agenda and the research questions, a co-design of action plans, as well as co-evaluation of the outcomes (Shani et al. 2012). Its nucleus is to incorporate action with collaboration in order to generate relevant and actionable knowledge (Pasmore et al. 2007). The collaborative research approach doesn't only help organisations to transform, but it also allows researchers to reflect on their own experiences, which might guide them to a positive personal change (Brydon-Miller et al. 2003).

Collaborative management research serves as an enactment of mode 2 knowledge production, in which it simultaneously engages application with academia-based knowledge. It is a trans-disciplinary approach towards integrating empiricism with theoretical approaches (Gibbons et al. 1994; MacLean et al. 2002). The main outcome of a collaborative research process is the so-called actionable knowledge that is theoretically grounded as well as relevant to practice. Co-generation (between researchers and practitioners) of actionable knowledge is assumed to offer a greater rate of progress in addressing organisational challenges, when compared with knowledge developed separately by researchers *or* practitioners (Pasmore et al. 2007).

Canterino et al. (2016) suggest that, in a collaborative research process, the co-production of knowledge is achieved through establishing conversational inquiries between researchers and practitioners, then collaboratively developing and implementing action plans. The process is not linear as it involves cycles of co-evaluation of the outcomes, and it has sequential phases of planning, intervention, taking action, then reflection. This will eventually lead to transformation.

Eight collaborative research approaches are identified in Shani et al. (2004), namely action science, appreciative inquiry, clinical inquiry, developmental action inquiry, intervention research, participatory inquiry/action research, table tennis research and action research.

How could one differentiate between different collaborative research approaches. This chapter adopts Schein's (2006) framework, as depicted in Fig. 2.3, in differentiating the research process of different collaborative approaches. The criteria in Schein's (2006) framework rests on three main dimensions: (1) who is initiating the research process, (2) the extent of researcher's involvement into the system, (3) the extent of practitioner's involvement into the research process.

After a thorough consideration of the criteria provided in prior literature, the scope of this chapter specifically focuses on (1) action research and (2) clinical inquiry. The definitions of both approaches coincide with the understanding of collaborative research which incorporates intervention, inquiry and action to co-generate knowledge (Coghlan 2011; Coghlan and Coughlan 2008). The two approaches are selected due to their limited-to-moderate extent in manipulating the surrounding environment (Shani et al. 2004). This enhances the consistency of their research process and increases the trust in their research outcomes. They also entail high researcher *and* practitioner involvement in the research process (Schein 2006), which will help in better analyses of the data and co-generation of relevant knowledge.

Furthermore, the selection is motivated by building on the line of thinking that the adoption of action research and clinical inquiry in a supply chain context will help in theory building (Coughlan and Coghlan 2002; Schein 2006), and that they will boost the dissemination of research results and knowledge to practice (Starkey and Madan 2001). The two approaches are suitable for the humanitarian context as they focus on achieving a positive change (transformation), thus they can contribute in transforming and improving the current state of humanitarian logistics and supply chains management domain.

## Action Research – An Overview

Action research emerged in response to the criticism of the isolation of the research processes and variables from real-world practices, as well as the absence of researchers and their reflections from the field (Müller 2005). Action research is centred on researcher involvement and participation in the research process, thus it helps researchers to learn from their own experiences

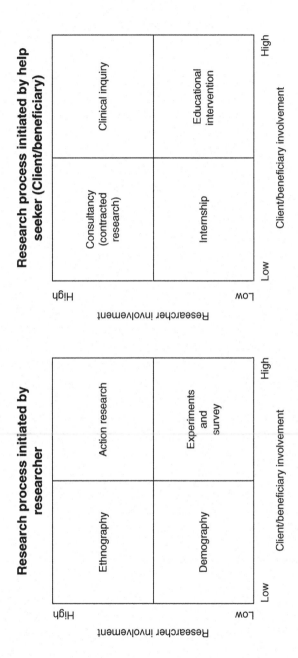

**Fig. 2.3** Research processes based on Schein's (2006) framework

through continuous reflection (Brydon-Miller et al. 2003). Coghlan (2011) stresses that action is an antecedent of learning, and performing action research relies on establishing a conversational questioning process with the concerned stakeholders. By doing so, this will lead to achieving positive change and transformation. In principle, action research is based on researchers spending a significant time in the field (e.g. in an organisation) (Näslund 2002).

Action research is viewed by Shani et al. (2004) as a hybrid approach between cooperative inquiry processes and action science. They propose a definition for action research as " . . . [an] inquiry embedded in partnership between researchers and practitioners to address an organisational issue and produce scientific knowledge . . . " and it is viewed by Bradbury (2013) as " . . . Action Research is not a method, but an orientation to inquiry, with many schools, theories and practices. " These definitions suggest that action research is not a methodology of its own; rather, it is a participatory approach to inquiry, and to the research process at large. Hence, it could be employed within the empirical settings of, for instance, a case study (see, e.g., McManners 2016).

According to Müller's (2005) study, there are three main differences between action research and traditional approaches to social science research: (1) developing stronger cooperation between academia and practitioners, (2) identifying new sources of information and (3) offering new alternative strategies for scientific knowledge production, which would eventually lead to co-production of actionable knowledge. Coughlan and Coghlan (2002) refer to action research as " . . . a paradigm that requires its own quality criteria"; therefore, its rigour cannot be judged through the same criteria of positivistic methodological approaches.

Action research is considered the most applied collaborative approach. It is applied in various research domains such as education research (e.g. Balakrishnan and Claiborne 2016), public management research (e.g. Rasheli 2016) and organisational studies (e.g. Canterino et al. 2016). Action research in supply chain management domain is further analysed in section "Collaborative Research Approaches in Supply Chain Literature – An Overview".

## Clinical Inquiry – An Overview

The clinical inquiry approach hinges on developing knowledge from "inside out", meaning that researchers would be invited to offer help to an organisation as a helper or a consultant. The settings of clinical inquiry provide researchers with a full and complete access to the organisations and their systems. Thus, it enables researchers to make better judgements. Adopting clinical inquiry approach is argued by Schein (2006) to contribute significantly to theory building, as it enables researchers to gain access to a massive body of critical information. The researchers, most probably, wouldn't have secured access to this body of information, if they were perceived as "outsiders" to the system. It is viewed by Coghlan (2009) as " ... the most fruitful way" to understand *and* change organisations.

In the empirical settings of a clinical inquiry research process, research is initiated from real-world needs of a "client" or a beneficiary. The process evolves around whose needs drive the research: the client or the researcher. In other words, does the research stem from practical application or it stems from theoretical perspective (Shani et al. 2004). Clinical inquiry is considered as a help to the beneficiary, and that is why it should involve top-management commitment to the research process. Yet, in the clinical inquiry approach, the research focus shouldn't rely solely on data gathering as a problem-solving technique. Rather first to understand the problem and to scrutinise its context, in order to design a suitable intervention process and to achieve the "treatment" sought after. Thus, adopting clinical inquiry suggests approaching organisational phenomenon with offering a solution (or treatment) as an end goal of the research process (Coghlan 2009). In Schein's (1995) view, action research is an extension to clinical inquiry, in which he argues that there is greater involvement into the client/beneficiary system. Clinical inquiry is mainly applied not only in nursing research but also in organisational research (e.g. Stebbins and Shani 2009) and environmental management research (e.g. Picketts et al. 2016).

## Collaborative Research Approaches in Supply Chain Literature – An Overview

Birkie et al. (2013) investigated the adoption of collaborative research approaches in supply chain literature. Their findings denote a very low level of adoption. For instance, out of all the scholarly publications in supply chain and operations management journals from 2004 to 2012, only 65 papers used collaborative research approaches, and *Journal of Supply Chain Management* topping the list with 9 published articles. A few studies, in humanitarian logistics and supply chain management, attempt to explore novel methodologies so as to increase the preparedness and effectiveness of the aid operations.

Jahre et al. (2015) report on their empirical study in Turkey, Haiti and Ivory Coast, in collaboration with the IFRC (International Federation of Red Crescent and Red Cross Societies) who is an important actor in the humanitarian arena. Their study is implemented on three phases and collectively represents an action research approach. Tomasini and Wassenhove (2009) provide empirical evidences on how adopting collaboration methodologies can significantly reduce costs and increase responses and preparedness of humanitarian chains, which positively overcomes the uncertainty in this peculiar kind of chains. It is worth noting that Tomasini and Wassenhove (2009) did not identify collaborative research as a research approach, rather identified it as coordination scheme. Chandes and Paché (2010) adopt an organisational perspective to improve the performance of the actors in humanitarian chains. Their main recommendation was to form a virtual coalition structure to incorporate all the actors and to improve the collective action in disasters, and similar to Tomasini and Wassenhove (2009) study, they do not identify their intervention as a form of collaborative research.

Within the supply chain research stream, there are numerous studies using collaborative research approaches and explicitly referring to action research. Touboulic and Walker (2016) explore how action research could be employed to enhance engagement and in transforming sustainable supply chain management research. Eltantawy et al. (2015) employ action research in enhancing three echelon supply chain coordination and achieving a superior performance. Seuring (2011) advocates for using mixed methodologies in order to propose a sustainable supply chain strategy; one of them was action research, as well as Taggart et al. (2014) use action research approach for management of construction rework supply chain in the UK. Liu et al. (2016) stress how academic–practitioner collaboration would enrich supply chain management research and knowledge creation. A few studies focus on how the utilisation of action research leads to a more accurate forecasting values, which also leads to having a more accurate input into the supply chain decision making (Caniato et al. 2011). Within the operations management research, some studies (e.g. Farooq and O'Brien 2015) use action research approach to develop a technology-selection framework. The authors in this study advocate for triangulation of methodologies (i.e. combining action research with other methodologies) in order to overcome any validity issue. In their study they embed action research approach in a case study methodology. It is worth noting that their view on collaborative research is limited to the involvement of the researcher, yet they did not provide deeper analyses of the role of action researcher in their study.

In view of the above discussion, a few studies in the field of humanitarian logistics and supply chain management research are performing, to some extent, a form or another of collaborative research, yet, it is not explicitly stated that the research is collaborative. The reason might be due to some concerns on the rigour and validity issues (e.g. Farooq and O'Brien 2015) or might be related to adhering to the mainstream of following a more traditional research methodology.

# Methodological Quality Assessment

## Ensuring Rigour, Relevance and Reflectiveness

The rigour-relevance-reflectiveness criteria emphasise that the data gathering and data analysis steps should adhere to the scholarly quality assurance instruments (Canterino et al. 2016), though trying to find meaning and interpretation of the data is performed collaboratively by members of the research team. Yet the underlying theoretical underpinnings should exist beforehand, and should be clearly stated at the beginning of the collaborative research project. Research would also benefit from triangulation of methodologies and/or of investigators (Näslund et al. 2010); in addition, collaborative research project should be data driven, and demonstrates methodological consistency of its process. This section builds on Pasmore et al.'s (2007) recommendations and illustrates the criteria for ensuring quality in collaborative research approaches, depicted in Fig. 2.4.

Criteria for rigour includes greater researcher involvement, cross-checking and reviewing the research process with other external researchers, ensuring deeper understanding of the phenomena, respecting the research process context, laying the epistemological foundations for hypothesis testing and

| Rigor | Reflectiveness | Relevance |
|---|---|---|
| • **Understanding of underlying mechanisms of phenomena'** "how things work"<br><br>• Researchers to **be involved in the research process**; not just observing<br><br>• **Hypothesis testing** and **research reproducibility**, highlighting the role of "context"<br><br>• **Objective review** with other scientists<br><br>• Analysis and **deeper interpretation for Causality**<br><br>• To be **publishable**<br><br>• The use of **mixed methodologies** to verify results | • To achieve **social impact** and **theoretical significance**<br><br>• Greater knowledge of **other scientists work**<br><br>• **Longitudinal studies**<br><br>• Collaboration with other researchers<br><br>• Creating a **community of scientists** to **share ideas** and **evaluate preliminary results**<br><br>• **Applicable research analyses** over longer period of time and within multiple settings | • To achieve **practical significance** against costs incurred in conducting research<br><br>• Has **impact on organisation's performance** (or the practitioner system)<br><br>• Having a **realistic view on the resources constraints (money+time)** against findings<br><br>• Avoiding **oversimplification** or **overcomplicating** |

**Fig. 2.4** Criteria for ensuring rigour, relevance and reflectiveness in CMR approaches

ensuring research reproducibility, and to produce publishable research. Ensuring reflectiveness criteria include developing a research process that achieves social impact and possesses a theoretical significance. It encourages collaboration with scientists from other disciplines (inter- and trans-disciplinary research), to share ideas with a larger community of researchers and to be able to generate analyses that hold over longer period of time. Ensuring relevance criteria stress a need to achieve practical significance so as to impact organisations' (or practitioners' systems) performances, to establish a realistic view on what are the research constraints in terms of time and money, to avoid oversimplification/over-complication of the phenomenon and to design a research process that generates applicable analyses within various contexts.

Furthermore, detailed and measurable indicators for investigating how collaborative research could be assessed in terms of scientific rigour, relevance and reflectiveness are proposed in Fig. 2.5. The proposed indicators embrace some of the attributes proposed previously in Birkie's et al. (2013) study. The indicators suggest that in order to ensure reflectiveness, the research should have social and historical impact. It should involve its surrounding community and to ensure to replicability. For the relevance dimension, the research should emerge from the need of an end beneficiary (or practitioner/client), which represents real-world needs and events. The research should have clear implication on performance. It should demonstrate applicability and re-applicability in practice, should be teachable, interesting and has true significance.

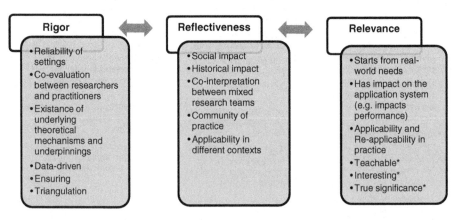

**Fig. 2.5** Indicators for assessing rigour, relevance and reflectiveness in CMR projects

*These indicators were identified in Birkie et al. (2013) as attributes with "subjective judgement"

## Methodological Limitations

Collaborative research approaches often face the challenge of demonstrating and establishing validity and rigour (Näslund 2002; Näslund et al. 2010). They face scepticism concerning their scientific nature. The sceptic views and arguments should be seriously considered before embarking on a collaborative research project.

The main methodological rigour limitations are related to how collaborative approaches might allow for data manipulation. The research question is not clear from the beginning, thus, the research path is continuously changing, and the research process is quite fuzzy. Moreover, in some instances researchers become client centred and they fail to draw a line between the research nature and the client requirements, or to question clients' practices (Argyris 1987). Other studies (e.g. McTaggart 1994) view action research as a common sense, rather than a scientific method. Furthermore, it is worth taking into consideration the coordination challenges identified by Kieser and Leiner (2012). They put forward intriguing questions on the feasibility of strong coordination between researchers and practitioners in collaborative research projects. They highlight the possible communication issues as well as the perpetual issue of rigour-relevance gap, which is often overlooked by most collaborative researchers. Furthermore, collaborative approaches always face the critique that the definitions and the boundaries between the different methodologies are not very clear to management researchers. Moreover, the findings are very context sensitive, and the analyses that result from collaborative research approaches should be always interpreted with respect to its context, thus hindering generalisability (Touboulic and Walker 2016). Among the challenges of collaborative research is the lack of scientific language and rigour among practitioners, as well as lack of managers' involvement in the research design.

# Deploying Collaborative Research Approaches in Humanitarian Supply Chains

## Collaboration in Action

Collaboration between organisations is extensively considered in prior literature (for a comprehensive review, check Phillips et al. 2000). The existing studies provided guidance and frameworks on establishing collaborative inter-organisational relationships (e.g. Ring and Van de ven 1994). There are many commonalities between these studies and the proposed collaborative framework presented hereinafter. There is agreement on the importance of collaboration, on establishing a common strategy and common decision making. However, there are inherent differences. For instance, in collaborative management research process, the researcher has no power or authority to drive change. The research cannot enforce transformation. Collaborative research approaches engage communities and universities in the transformation. While in other inter-organisational collaboration frameworks, collaboration is managed in between cooperative organisations that might be collaborating and competing in the same time. It is important to reflect the essence of deploying collaborative research approaches, as they encourage researchers to opt for a research strategy that accommodates the viewpoint of different collaborating and cooperating stakeholders, in a systematic and scientific way.

Collaboration shouldn't be viewed as a magical solution to all organisational problems. There are studies that highlight if the inter-organisational collaboration is not generating a balanced mutual benefit to all the stakeholders, then relationships might deteriorate slowly (Anderson and Jap 2005). This "dark side" of collaboration is also demonstrated in Villena et al. (2011). In which they find that when the extent of collaboration is stretched to a deeper level, this harms the inter-organisational relationships between buyers and suppliers.

## A Collaborative Framework for Humanitarian Supply Chain Management Research

A framework developed for employing collaborative research approaches in humanitarian and supply chain management research is developed hereinafter.

The collaborative research process, as depicted in Fig. 2.6, could start by an initiation meeting between the research project stakeholders (or a researcher and a practitioner in the minimalistic form) to agree on the project scope and aim. This would be followed by forming the project team and scheduling regular team meetings. The team jointly develops the research rules and the strategy for their collaborative project. The different stakeholders are highly encouraged to get involved in forming the preliminary research question, which will be evolving during the whole process. After deciding on the unit(s) of analysis, data gathering process starts.

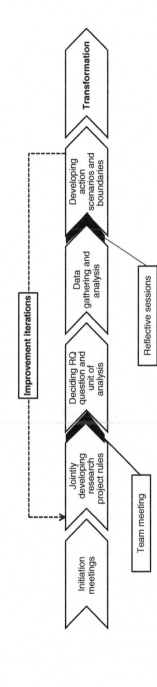

**Fig. 2.6**  A collaborative research project process

Afterwards, this would be followed by conducting reflective sessions which offer the research team an opportunity to co-reflect on the findings and on the initial analyses. Then intervention scenarios for change should be developed and implemented to achieve the desired transformation. The iterative cyclical nature is critical to collaborative research. The research process is not linear, as transformation cannot be achieved from a one-shot linear process.

A proposed framework, depicted in Fig. 2.7, is developed for deploying collaborative management research approaches in humanitarian and supply chain management research. This framework builds on the propositions of Coughlan and Coghlan (2002), who presented one of the most quoted frameworks for systematically establishing a collaborative approach in supply chain and operations management research. The framework embraces the recommendations of Shani et al. (2004), Müller (2005), Schein (2006) and Näslund et al. (2010), which were discussed earlier in section "Collaborative Management Research".

The framework starts with a **First Step**, which involves understanding the context and the purpose of the research. This includes understanding the rationale behind the research project and the social, economic, political and technical implications of the research. In this step, it is important for the management of the involved stakeholders to show commitment to the research project. Issues of mistrust should be cleared, and a detailed project scope will be co-identified. The research design and tools for data gathering will be agreed upon, and the preliminary research question will be co-identified. Also, since the research concerns humanitarian needs, then privacy (e.g. non-disclosure agreements) of sensitive data, as well as the possible ethical issues should also be clarified beforehand. In this step, the research team will be formed from individuals representing all the involved stakeholders, highly preferable to include representatives from the affected communities.

**Second Step** is data gathering. It is done through the continuous involvement of the researcher in the practitioner system, thus data could be collected in a formal setting, such as researchers attending a meeting or interviewing the subject or through surveys, as well as in an informal setting such as over field trips. Data could be collected in a soft qualitative form (e.g. observations, interviews, meetings) or hard quantitative data (e.g. financial, statistics). Since the research process is collaborative, therefore data could be gathered from the different sources and from all the involved stakeholders, which will contribute in enriching the content to be analysed afterwards. In collaborative research, inquiries are made by the researcher in a conversational manner, and data gathering is usually performed while the researcher is

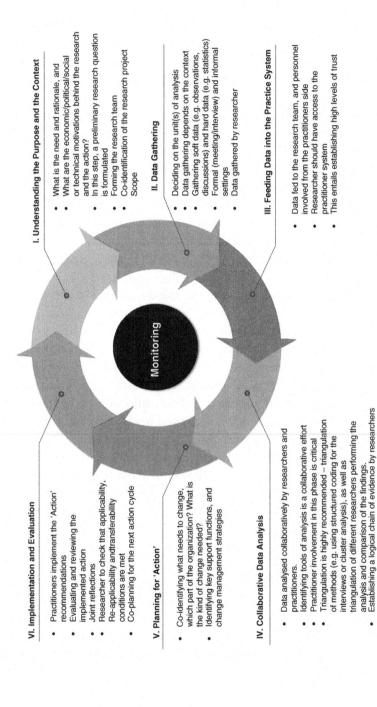

**I. Understanding the Purpose and the Context**

- What is the need and rationale, and
- What are the economic/political/social or technical motivations behind the research and the action?
- In this step, a preliminary research question is formulated
- Forming the research team
- Co-identification of the research project
- Scope

**II. Data Gathering**

- Deciding on the unit(s) of analysis
- Data gathering depends on the context
- Gathering soft data (e.g. observations, discussions) and hard data (e.g. statistics)
- Formal (meeting/interview) and informal settings
- Data gathered by researcher

**III. Feeding Data into the Practice System**

- Data fed to the research team, and personnel involved from the practitioners side
- Researcher should have access to the practitioner system
- This entails establishing high levels of trust

**VI. Implementation and Evaluation**

- Practitioners implement the 'Action' recommendations
- Evaluating and reviewing the implemented action
- Joint reflections
- Researcher to check that applicability, Re-applicability andtransferability conditions are met
- Co-planning for the next action cycle

**V. Planning for 'Action'**

- Co-identifying what needs to change, which part of the organization? What is the kind of change needed?
- Identifying key support functions, and change management strategies

**IV. Collaborative Data Analysis**

- Data analysed collaboratively by researchers and practitioners.
- Identifying tools of analysis is a collaborative effort
- Practitioner involvement in this phase is critical
- Triangulation is highly recommended – triangulation of methods (e.g. using structured coding for the interviews or cluster analysis), as well as triangulation of different researchers performing the analysis and comparison of the findings.
- Establishing a logical chain of evidence by researchers

**Fig. 2.7** Deploying collaborative approach in humanitarian logistics and supply chain management research – based on Shani et al. (2004), Coughlan and Coghlan (2002), Müller (2005), Schein (2006) and Näslund et al. (2010)

spending a significant period of time interacting with the main actors in the field, including representatives from the affected communities. To ensure rigour, data should be gathered by researchers. In the case of interviews, the regular recording of interviews/meetings and transcription could be followed. In case of questionnaires or surveys, regular survey instruments should be employed and designed by researchers, and then consulted with the research team.

**Third Step** is how researchers "feed" the data back to the practitioners. It is concerned with the inclusion of the different stakeholders in making sense of the research findings. Researcher collects all the bits and pieces of the gathered data, from different stakeholders, and then prepares them for further discussion with the research team. This could be done through preparing instruments (e.g. documents/initial coding or themes) containing the data and presenting it to the research project team. To ensure rigour, researchers should have a complete access to the practitioners' systems (organisations) and to data sources (individuals, reports, insights), which entails attaining highest level of trust and collaboration.

**Fourth Step** is collaboratively analysing the data. Prior to this step, it is also critical for the practitioners to be involved in the research process, which will enable them to receive a minimal level of training on the research tools and methods so that they can help in sense-making of the data. To ensure rigour, researchers are advised to opt for triangulation of methodologies, as well as triangulation of the investigators. Triangulation entails using mixed methods approach in data collection and analysis. For instance, each research cycle could be dedicated to collect qualitative and/or quantitative data. Each cycle could also be dedicated to a different methodology; for instance, a cycle for structured interviews, and a second cycle for survey. It is also very convenient to use structured coding, or cluster analysis, when analysing qualitative interview data. Näslund et al. (2010) advise to establish a chain of logical evidences in that stage so as to ensure trust in the findings analysis.

The **Fifth Step** is to co-plan for action. Based on the analyses, a co-identification of what needs to be changed is decided upon by the research team, as well as the plan for intervention and for change management. The research team identifies which part of the system that needs change, what are the key supporting functions for change and who would be involved from the stakeholders' teams. This step could involve discussions, meetings with top management representatives and reflective sessions between the research project team members.

The **Sixth Step** is dedicated for implementation and evaluation. In the implementation phase, the action plan is executed by practitioners, then researchers evaluate the outcomes of the action process. This will be followed by joint reflections from both researchers and practitioners on the implemented process advantages as well as its shortcomings. Meanwhile, researchers are encouraged to check the rigour of the analyses through checking the research process reproducibility, documentation. The research team would jointly identify improvement opportunities in the executed action plan. Then would implement the new plan to ensure a continuous improvement process towards the transformation.

The collaborative research process is continuously monitored in all its stages by the involved stakeholders; monitoring is a meta-step in this framework. It is important to highlight that collaborative research is cyclical. Each cycle could have a different objective (or research question). The research process continues till the treatment (transformation) is reached, and then the project concludes.

## Expected Implications

Deploying collaborative research approaches would impact different humanitarian logistics and supply chain operations and functions. This adoption might have implications on the management of logistics, stakeholders, post-disaster, donor and donations, as well as the affected location (communities). Hereinafter, each implication and their relation to the humanitarian activity are summarised in Table 2.1.

In the area of logistics management, the implementation would mainly help in mitigating demand and supply uncertainty implications (typically, in slow-onset disasters). The inclusion of the entire value chain's stakeholders would lead to better coordination and to lessen any the potential impacts of unpredictability. Collaborative research approaches would also lead to enhancing trust among different stakeholders. This would help in a seamless stakeholder's management. Furthermore, it might lead to a better management of the affected location through enhancing the communication with the affected communities. The donations management area would benefit from improving the forecasting values. There is also a great potential in developing demand-sensing practices and skills, due to the inclusion of the affected communities in the research process. Collaborative research approaches would arguably lead to enhancing the preparedness and responsiveness of the stakeholders, which will contribute in better post-disaster management.

**Table 2.1** Expected implications of applying collaborative research approaches in humanitarian supply chains

| Humanitarian activity | Implication of collaborative research adoption |
| --- | --- |
| Logistics management | Contributes in mitigating the impact of demand uncertainty in slow-onset disasters. Provides deeper involvement for researchers in the deployment process as well as in the allocation of resources. |
| Stakeholders management | Contributes in establishing high levels of trust among different stakeholders, which helps in planning for long-term strategic agreements and partnerships. When all the stakeholders are involved in a collaborative research project, they feel more accountable and get in touch with the process. |
| Post-disaster management | Collaborative research focuses on achieving positive change and transformation. Thus, it contributes in increasing back-office preparedness and front-office response to disasters and post-disaster events, leading to improving the performance of different stakeholders. |
| Donations and donors management | Collaborative research starts from the needs of the end beneficiaries; thus, it yields a better analysis on the end-to-end humanitarian chain which also contributes in improving forecasting values and better demand sensing. |
| Affected location management | Overcoming issues of communication and lack of coordination of different stakeholders. Collaborative research projects engage trans-disciplinary teams from different stakeholders; thus, it guarantees a better top-management involvement. |

## Implementation Challenges

Considering the peculiarities of humanitarian supply chains, achieving collaboration between multiple stakeholders could be a difficult task. Some reflections on the various challenges in opting for collaborative research approaches are presented in the following section.

When initiating a collaborative project, these challenges should be considered, in addition to the methodological limitations highlighted earlier in section "Methodological Limitations". The challenges can be pertained to the initiation of the project, collaboration, data gathering and analyses, and challenges in continuing the project cycles. Furthermore, collaborative research approaches might not be suited to every stage of a humanitarian disaster, especially during a sudden-onset disaster.

## Project Initiation Challenges

The main challenges in initiating a collaborative research project are trust issues. There is a paradox of whether we employ collaborative research to enhance trust and collaboration, or that trust should be established beforehand, so that the project can be initiated. Trust issues could lead to scepticism from practitioners to invest time and effort in a long-term project that they can't grasp its immediate benefits on their businesses on the short term. Moreover, even if the trust and the will are established, there could be some budget constraints that do not allow different stakeholders to take part in the project.

A further main challenge in this phase is managing the expectations of the stakeholders. Thus, a clear explanation of the scope and aim of the research project should be co-identified beforehand the implementation. The project scope should also be clearly communicated to the affected communities, beforehand the implementation. In addition, it is utterly important to identify the team members, and clearly specifying their roles, and the range of their intervention during the different phases of the research project. By doing so, researchers would avoid any potential influence that might hinder the rigour of the research findings and analyses.

## Collaboration Challenges

Almost all studies, employing collaborative research approaches, report on how achieving collaborations in their research projects was a complex process. There could be many challenges pertained to resistance to participation from some of the stakeholders. The resistance stems from mistrust in the worthiness of the project, or scepticism in the project's ability to really drive positive transformation. Resistance to participate could be either on the intra-organisational level, so there could be personnel who are not willing to contribute to be sources of data. It could be also manifested on the inter-organisational level, when there is no cooperation in sharing experiences and knowledge among the stakeholders.

Collaboration challenges can also stem from factors beyond the research team control, such as language or cultural barriers.

## Data Gathering and Analysis Challenges

These challenges can happen mainly due to the inclination of some of the stakeholders' top management to control the data gathering process, through controlling certain sources of data, or to influence the process of data analyses.

Further challenges are due to the lack of the scientific approach towards data analyses and knowledge generation, especially on the practitioners' side. Therefore, a basic training session could be helpful to explain the overall scientific approach. This awareness could also be done during the project meetings.

**Project Continuation Challenges**

The cyclical nature of collaborative research might ignite some disagreements between the stakeholders. The iterative cycles can be time consuming, and practitioners might need to see solutions that can be implemented on a faster pace. The multiple research cycles also require top management commitment, to take part in all the cycles, and also to implement the action plans. Obviously, the researcher here is not in the position to take the decision, and researchers alone don't have authority to force the change. Furthermore, resistance to change is almost an embedded characteristic in many organisations and in human relations. Thus, it is important to deliver awareness session among the stakeholders' personnel and the affected communities. This inclusive approach is essential in sustaining the success and the transformation, of any collaborative research project.

# Conclusion

The aim of this chapter is not to undermine the significant contribution of traditional management research approaches, but to challenge the prevalent understanding of knowledge production in humanitarian supply chain domain. It is about time to question what humanitarian logistics and supply chain management research is addressing. Are the topics discussed, in the scholarly publications, stem from practical issues? Do they reflect the needs of those involved in real-world humanitarian situations? Is the research community willing to embrace evidence-based management research so as to develop relevant and actionable knowledge, instead of focusing on producing university-centred knowledge? The recent first WHS urged all the involved stakeholders to consider its recommendations as a point of departure "to act" (WHS Chair's Summary report 2016). It is now the responsibility of researchers to lessen the relevance gap. Researchers are expected to craft scholarly production that can be communicated seamlessly to all humanitarian stakeholders, thus contributing in ending the need loop.

The chapter develops a comprehensive framework for deploying collaborative research approaches, while addressing the rigour, reflectiveness and relevance issues. The main motivation behind deploying collaborative approaches is to achieve transformation and a positive change. The transformation is achieved through successive and iterative research cycles.

The analyses in this chapter capture how the adoption of collaborative research approaches would result in significant implications on the performance of humanitarian supply chains. The main areas with highest improvement potential are in logistics, stakeholders' management, location management, post-disaster management and donation management. In particular, deploying collaborative research approaches can impact the degree of collaboration and interaction between different stakeholders. It also helps in enhancing trust between different humanitarian actors. The greater involvement of researchers helps in engaging their reflections in the research process. Furthermore, the significant time spent by researchers in the field would yield to mitigating any communication issues.

Researchers must consider the various methodological limitations and implementation challenges that face any collaborative research process. The implementation challenge lies in clearing any mistrust issues. Collaboration is a complex process, and in many instances there will be resistance to participate or to implement change in the stakeholders' teams or within the affected communities. Disagreement might emerge from discussions on forming the research team, deciding on its mission and scope, or in specifying the roles of the different team members. Further challenges are also pertained to the expectations of the research team. Practitioners' expectations might direct them to try to control the data gathering or to influence data analysis. In addition, practitioners might not be willing to collaborate in long-term research project that they cannot foresee its immediate impact on their business or operations.

Methodologically, although the research should start from a real-world need, researchers are expected to have a full understanding of the phenomena's theoretical underpinnings, before their intervention. Data gathering and data analyses should be performed with respect to the scientific quality assurance instruments, to ensure research applicability and reproducibility. To ensure rigour, any potential influence on the analyses should be completely avoided. Sharing the research project ideas and findings with other research teams might be of help to ensure rigour, relevance and reflectiveness of the collaborative research project.

The limitation of the analyses provided in this chapter should be acknowledged. The expected implementation implications provided in section "Deploying Collaborative Research Approaches in Humanitarian Supply Chains" need further empirical verification. As it is now, it is crafted based on the literature analysis as well as the author's reflections. Furthermore, the chapter considered only two collaborative approaches; however, there might be great potential in addressing in the future additional collaborative approaches, or other methodological approaches that ensure relevance and rigour. By doing so, research would benefit from drawing more comprehensive inferences. Obviously collaborative research approaches do not suite all the stages in humanitarian disasters. Perhaps, they better fit slow-onset disasters or management of humanitarian supply chains in long-term conflicts. However, engaging the stakeholders in collaborative projects might be helpful in developing certain skills and capabilities that enable them to react better in sudden-onset disasters.

Avenues for future research include empirically examining the proposed collaborative framework and investigating how its implementation would address the different stakeholders' needs. Moreover, to create knowledge on whether collaborative management research approaches affects humanitarian supply chains efficiency, effectiveness and preparedness.

# References

Altay, N. (2008). *Issues in disaster relief logistics. Large-scale disasters: Prediction, control, and mitigation* (pp. 120–146). Cambridge, UK: Cambridge University Press.

Anderson, J. C., & Jap, S. D. (2005). The dark side of close relationships. *MIT Sloan Management Review*, 46(3), 75–82.

Argyris, C. (1987). Reasoning, action strategies, and defensive routines: The case of OD practitioners. In Woodman, R. A. & Pasmore, A. A. (Eds.), *Research in organizational change and development*. Volume 1, Greenwich: JAI Press.

Balakrishnan, V., & Claiborne, L. (2016). Participatory action research in culturally complex societies: Opportunities and challenges. *Educational Action Research*, 1–18.

Balcik, B., Beamon, B. M., Krejci, C., Muramatsu, K. M., & Ramirez, M. (2010). Coordination in humanitarian relief chains: Practices, challenges and opportunities. *International Journal of Production Economics*, 126(1), 22–34.

Beamon, B. M. (1998). Supply chain design and analysis: Models and methods. *International Journal of Production Economics*, 55(3), 281–294.

Birkie, S. E., Shani, A.B. (Rami), Trucco, P. (2013). How collaborative is empirical research in supply chain risk management: Review and perspective. 20th European Operations Management Association (EurOMA) conference, 7–13 June 2013, Dublin, Ireland.

Blanco, E. E., & Goentzel, J. (2006). Humanitarian supply chains: A review. Presentation given at the *17th Annual Conference of the Production and Operations Management Society*, MIT Centre of Transportation & Logistics.

Bradbury, H. (2013). Action Research: The journal's purpose, vision and mission, Re-enchanting knowledge creation for a flourishing world. *Action Research*, 11(1), 3–7.

Brydon-Miller, M., Greenwood, D., & Maguire, P. (2003). Why action research? *Action Research*, 1(1), 9–28.

Caniato, F., Kalchschmidt, M., & Ronchi, S. (2011). Integrating quantitative and qualitative forecasting approaches: Organizational learning in an action research case. *Journal of the Operational Research Society*, 62(3), 413–424.

Canterino, F., Shani, A. B. R., Coghlan, D., & Brunelli, M. S. (2016). Collaborative management research as a modality of action research learning from a Merger-Based Study. *The Journal of Applied Behavioral Science*, 52(2), 157–186.

Chandes, J., & Paché, G. (2010). Investigating humanitarian logistics issues: From operations management to strategic action. *Journal of Manufacturing Technology Management*, 21(3), 320–340.

Christopher, M., & Tatham, P. (Eds.). (2014). *Humanitarian logistics: Meeting the challenge of preparing for and responding to disasters*. 2nd Ed. London: Kogan Page Publishers.

Coghlan, D. (2009). Toward a philosophy of clinical inquiry/research. *Journal of Applied Behavioral Science*, 45(1), 106–121.

Coghlan, D. (2011). Action research: Exploring perspectives on a philosophy of practical knowing. *Academy of Management Annals*, 5(1), 53–87.

Coghlan, D., & Coughlan, P. (2008). Action learning and Action Research (ALAR): A methodological integration in an inter-organizational setting. *Systemic Practice and Action Research*, 21(2), 97–104.

Coughlan, P., & Coghlan, D. (2002). Action research for operations management. *International Journal of Operations & Production Management*, 22(2), 220–240.

Day, J. M., Melnyk, S. A., Larson, P. D., Davis, E. W., & Whybark, D. C. (2012). Humanitarian and disaster relief supply chains: A matter of life and death. *Journal of Supply Chain Management*, 48(2), 21–36.

Eltantawy, R., Paulraj, A., Giunipero, L., Naslund, D., & Thute, A. A. (2015). Towards supply chain coordination and productivity in a three echelon supply chain: Action research study. *International Journal of Operations & Production Management*, 35(6), 895–924.

Farooq, S., & O'Brien, C. (2015). An action research methodology for manufacturing technology selection: A supply chain perspective. *Production Planning & Control*, 26(6), 467–488.

Gibbons, M., Limoges, C., Nowotny, H., Schwartzman, S., Scott, P., & Trow, M. (1994). *The new production of knowledge: The dynamics of science and research in contemporary societies*. London: Sage.

Jahre, M., Ergun, O., & Goentzel, J. (2015). One size fits all? Using standard global tools in humanitarian logistics. *Procedia Engineering*, 107, 18–26.

Jayasuriya, S., & McCawley, P. (2008). Reconstruction after a major disaster: Lessons from the post-Tsunami experience in Indonesia, Sri Lanka, and Thailand, *ADBI working paper series*, No. 125

Kieser, A., & Leiner, L. (2012). Collaborate with practitioners: But beware of collaborative research. *Journal of Management Inquiry*, 21(1), 14–28.

Kovács, G., & Spens, K. M. (2007). Humanitarian logistics in disaster relief operations. *International Journal of Physical Distribution & Logistics Management*, 37(2), 99–114.

Kovács, G., & Spens, K. M. (2011). Trends and developments in humanitarian logistics – a Gap Analysis. *International Journal of Physical Distribution & Logistics Management*, 41(1), 32–45.

Kunz, N., & Reiner, G. (2012). A meta-analysis of humanitarian logistics research. *Journal of Humanitarian Logistics and Supply Chain Management*, 2(2), 116–147.

Leiras, A., de Brito Jr, I., Queiroz Peres, E., Rejane Bertazzo, T., & Tsugunobu Yoshida Yoshizaki, H. (2014). Literature review of humanitarian logistics research: Trends and challenges. *Journal of Humanitarian Logistics and Supply Chain Management*, 4(1), 95–130.

Liu, X., Wu, Y. C. J., & Goh, M. (2016). Collaborative academic–industry SCM research and knowledge building. *International Journal of Logistics Research and Applications*, 19(1), 19–40.

MacLean, D., Macintosh, R. & Grant, S. (2002), Mode 2 Management Research. *British Journal of Management*, 13(3), 189–207.

McManners, P. (2016). The action research case study approach: A methodology for complex challenges such as sustainability in aviation. *Action Research*, 14(2), 201–216.

McTaggart, R. (1994). Participatory action research: Issues in theory and practice. *Educational Action Research*, 2(3), 313–337.

Mohrman, S. A., & Lawler, E. E. III. (2011). Research for theory and practice: Framing the challenge. In Mohrman, S., & Lawler, E. (Eds.), *Useful research: Advancing theory and practice* (pp. 9–33). San Francisco, CA: Berrett-Koehler Publisher, Inc.

Müller, M. (2005). Action research in supply chain management—An introduction. In Kotzab, H., Seuring, S., Müller, M., & Reiner, G. (Eds.), *Research methodologies in supply chain management* (pp. 349–364). Heidelberg, Germany: Physica-Verlag.

Näslund, D. (2002). Logistics needs qualitative research-especially action research. *International Journal of Physical Distribution & Logistics Management*, 32(5), 321–333.

Näslund, D., Kale, R., & Paulraj, A. (2010). Action research in supply chain management—a framework for relevant and rigorous research. *Journal of Business Logistics*, 31(2), 331–355.

Pasmore, W. A. et al. (2007). The promise of collaborative management research. In Shani, A. B. (Rami), Mohrman, S., Pasmore, W. A., Stymne, B., & Adler, N. (Eds.), *Handbook of collaborative management research* (pp. 7–31). Thousand Oaks, CA: Sage.

Picketts, I. M., Andrey, J., Matthews, L., Déry, S. J., & Tighe, S. (2016). Climate change adaptation strategies for transportation infrastructure in Prince George, Canada. *Regional Environmental Change*, 16(4), 1109–1120.

Phillips, N., Lawrence, T. B., & Hardy, C. (2000). Inter-organizational collaboration and the dynamics of institutional fields. *Journal of Management Studies*, 37(1).

Rasheli, G. A. (2016). Action research in procurement management; evidence from selected lower local government authorities in Tanzania. *Action Research*, 0(0), 1–13.

Ring, P. S., & Van de Ven, A. H. (1994). Developmental processes of cooperative interorganizational relationships. *Academy of Management Review*, 19(1), 90–118.

Schein, E. H. (1995). Process consultation, action research and clinical inquiry: Are they the same? *Journal of Managerial Psychology*, 10(6), 14–19.

Schein, Edgar H. (2006). Clinical inquiry/research. In Reason, P., & Bradbury, H. (Eds.), *Handbook of action research*, Paperback Edition. London: Sage.

Seuring, S. (2011). Supply chain management for sustainable products–insights from research applying mixed methodologies. *Business Strategy and the Environment*, 20(7), 471–484.

Shani, A. B. (Rami), David, A., & Willson, C. (2004). Collaborative research: Alternative roadmaps. In Adler, N., Shani, A. B. (Rami), & Styhre, A. (Eds.), *Collaborative research in organizations: Foundations for learning, change and theoretical development* (pp. 83–100). Thousand Oaks, CA: Sage.

Shani, A. B. (Rami), Coghlan, D., & Cirella, S. (2012). Collaborative management research and action research: More than meets the eye? *International Journal of Action Research*, 8(1), 46–67.

Starkey, K., & Madan, P. (2001). Bridging the relevance gap: Aligning stakeholders in the future of management research. *British Journal of Management*, 12(s1), S3–S26.

Stebbins, M. W., & Shani, A. R. (2009). Clinical inquiry and reflective design in a secrecy-based organization. *The Journal of Applied Behavioral Science*, 45(1), 59–89.

Taggart, M., Koskela, L., & Rooke, J. (2014). The role of the supply chain in the elimination and reduction of construction rework and defects: An action research approach. *Construction Management and Economics*, 32(7–8), 829–842.

Telford, J., Cosgrave, J., & Houghton, R. (2006). *Joint evaluation of the international response to the Indian Ocean tsunami: Synthesis Report*. London, UK: Tsunami Evaluation Coalition.

Tomasini, R. M., & Van Wassenhove, L. N. (2009). From preparedness to partnerships: Case study research on humanitarian logistics. *International Transactions in Operational Research*, 16(5), 549–559.

Touboulic, A., & Walker, H. (2016). A relational, transformative and engaged approach to sustainable supply chain management: The potential of action research. *Human Relations*, 69(2), 301–343.

United Nations. (2016). Retrieved 15 May 2016, from Overview of forced displacement Website http://goo.gl/VuZ3wk.

Vaillancourt, A. (2016). A theoretical framework for consolidation in humanitarian logistics. *Journal of Humanitarian Logistics and Supply Chain Management*, 6(1), 2–23.

Van Wassenhove, L. N. (2006). Humanitarian aid logistics: Supply chain management in high gear. *Journal of the Operational Research Society*, 57(5), 475–489

Villena, V. H., Revilla, E., & Choi, T. Y. (2011). The dark side of buyer–supplier relationships: A social capital perspective. *Journal of Operations Management*, 29(6), 561–576.

WHS Chair's Summary report. (2016). Retrieved 27 May 2016, from World Humanitarian Summit website https://goo.gl/PZkDvh.

# 3

# Future Research in Humanitarian Operations: A Behavioral Operations Perspective

Karthik Sankaranarayanan, Jaime Andrés Castañeda
and Sebastián Villa

## Introduction

Behavioral operations have established itself as a mature field of research in operations and supply chain management. Since almost all operational contexts contain people (e.g., managers, employees and customers) who are prone to decision-making errors that can negatively impact performance, behavioral operations can inform models and frameworks in operations management to account for such shortcomings.

Research in behavioral operations has explored a variety of issues that stem from the field's knowledge base. This knowledge base includes cognitive psychology, social and group psychology, and system dynamics and systems thinking. Cognitive psychology studies how individuals' cognitive limitations impact their decision making. Social and group psychology deals with the complications that multiple actors bring to group and individual decision

K. Sankaranarayanan (✉)
University of Ontario Institute of Technology, Oshawa, Canada
e-mail: Karthik.Sankaranarayanan@uoit.ca

J.A. Castañeda
Universidad del Rosario, Bogotá, Colombia
e-mail: jaime.castaneda@urosario.edu.co

S. Villa
University of Los Andes, Bogotá, Colombia
e-mail: s.villab@uniandes.edu.co

© The Author(s) 2018

**71**

G. Kovács et al. (eds.), *The Palgrave Handbook of Humanitarian Logistics and Supply Chain Management*, https://doi.org/10.1057/978-1-137-59099-2_3

making. Finally, system dynamics and systems thinking study how a system's structure and feedback mechanisms affect decision making. All of these have the potential to affect the extent to which individuals and groups are prone to biases and use heuristics.

Scholars in behavioral operations have conducted studies in a broad range of areas, such as how cognitive biases affect inventory systems, how social preferences affect supply chain performance, how team attributes affect team's operational performance and how a supply chain structure affects its performance, among others. However, while individuals and groups in humanitarian operations are also prone to biases and use heuristics, the literature in behavioral operations studying such contexts is still scant. For instance, relief workers work under significant time pressure, must meet diverse goals from several stakeholders (e.g., media, donors and beneficiaries) and operate with significant demand and supply uncertainty under a novel and challenging supply chain and hierarchical structure. In addition, the functioning, features and dynamics of humanitarian operations are in many cases different from those of commercial operations, for which insights generated from Behavioral Operations Management (BOM) cannot be directly generalized.

The lack of behavioral research in humanitarian operations and the potential for improvement in decision making provides a strong motivation to devote more behavioral OM research to this area. This chapter explores the application of different methodological tools used in behavioral operations to study behavior in humanitarian logistics and supply chain management (HLSCM). We describe each tool, review the literature and highlight the challenges that the typical characteristics of humanitarian operations impose on these tools and the overall process of conducting behavioral research in the area itself. Specifically, the chapter explores the use of behavioral experiments, system dynamics and agent-based modeling (ABM) as methodologies to understand decision making in humanitarian operations.

# Behavioral Experiments

## Method

Behavioral experiments are controlled tests of decision making. They can be classified as an empirical method since they rely on the observation of behavior and on the analysis of data (Siemsen 2011). Hence, their

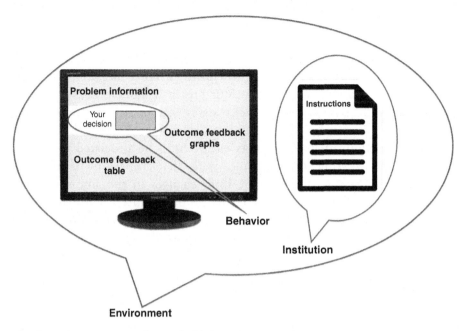

**Fig. 3.1** Components of a typical laboratory experiment

primary purpose is to test and refine existing theory. They are also used to generate observations that can lead to new theory and test institutional designs (Katok 2010).

Behavioral experiments draw on experimental economics, which defines three key components of every experiment: environment, institution and behavior (Smith 1976, 1982). The environment is a set of initial circumstances that cannot be altered by the participants or the institutions within which they interact (e.g., environmental parameters, available information, etc.). The institution refers to the rules or procedures that govern behavior in the experiment. This institution is defined by the experimental instructions given to participants. The behavior refers to the observed decisions of participants, which are interpreted as function of the environment and the institution (Smith 1994). Figure 3.1 illustrates the components of a behavioral experiment run in a laboratory (lab).

The relative advantage of experiments is control. When running an experiment, it is of the greatest importance that one is able to state that, as between a number of treatments, individual characteristics either do or do not differ in a specified way. Such control is achieved by using two mechanisms: induced valuation and randomization.

## Induced Valuation

This mechanism refers to the use of a reward structure to induce prescribed monetary value on the actions of participants, making individual interests irrelevant. This concept depends on four precepts: monotonicity, saliency, dominance and privacy. Monotonicity states that participants will always prefer more of a reward medium than less. Saliency states that the amount of the reward medium that participants receive must be associated with their actions in the experiment. Dominance states that changes in participants' utility during the experiment come from changes in the amount of the reward medium. Privacy is closely related to dominance. Dominance may be lost if participants hold interpersonal utility considerations. Privacy then states that participants are given information such that they cannot estimate the amount of the reward medium that the other participants receive (Smith 1976, 1982).

A number of practical guidelines concerning the precepts are provided in Hey (1996):

- One way to induce monotonicity is to use financial incentives. The average payment should be larger than the average opportunity cost of participants. A good approximation to the average opportunity cost is the hourly wage of the subject pool used for the experiment.
- The participants that better meet the precepts of saliency and dominance are those with low opportunity costs and steep learning curves (e.g., undergraduate students).
- The environment and institution should be as simple as possible to promote saliency. It is convenient to run manipulation checks.
- The frame of the experiment should be as abstract as possible to promote dominance. A neutral language could avoid leading participants and make the experimental results more generalizable.

The precepts are not intended to be necessary conditions. A valid experiment may be built that nevertheless violates some or all of the precepts. For example, financial incentives are not strictly monotonic since increasing the reward medium does not necessarily increase the performance of participants. They only have to perceive that the reward medium is sufficient (Morton and Williams 2010). Dominance could be lessened by adding a cover story related to the research question under investigation, increasing external validity (Katok 2010). The precepts provide general guidelines concerning the control of individual interests.

They may be implemented in various ways and may require adjustments depending on the context and the particular research question one wants to answer (Guala 2005).

## Randomization

When designing an experiment, we are interested in the effect of focus variables but not in the effect of individual characteristics. Focus variables should be systematically manipulated between treatments, while individual characteristics should be held constant across treatments so that any treatment effects cannot be attributed to these characteristics or to the interaction effect between the focus variables and the characteristics. Randomization refers to the random assignment of participants to treatments to avoid any systematic composition of participants in the treatments (Katok 2010). That is, it randomizes individual characteristics such that they do not correlate with the treatments, avoiding or sidestepping the problem of confounding (Siemsen 2011).

The intuition behind induced valuation and randomization is that researchers can choose any relationship between participants' actions and the reward medium as long as they can explain this relationship to the participants (saliency) and they are motivated by the reward medium (monotonicity) and not by other influences (dominance, privacy and randomization).

## Behavioral Experiments in HLSCM

Behavioral experiments in HLSCM have addressed issues related to donations, planning, and development.

## Donations

Experiments on donations fall within the purpose of theory testing. Experiments typically test analytical models, offering the possibility of comparing participants' decisions against benchmarks. However, experiments on donations lack analytical benchmarks. Instead, they build on existing conceptual or theoretical models and devise designs that allow testing these models.

Donations have been studied under several lenses. For example, some studies focus on social norms and identity (e.g., Shang et al. 2008; Croson et al. 2010) and others on identifiable victims (e.g., Small and Loewenstein 2003; Kogut and Ritov 2005). We review experiments stating that the aid is allocated to humanitarian crises or disasters. Evangelidis and Van den Bergh (2013) test whether the number of fatalities drives the allocation of financial aid to disasters compared with the number of survivors, the actual beneficiaries of the aid. They initially test the hypothesis with empirical data and find support for it. They then devise three experiments with the aim of testing the robustness of these results. Participants were given reference material with information about a disaster, including the amount of money donated, and then had to indicate the amount of money they thought should be donated to victims of a similar disaster that was described in a cover story. Experiment 1 is divided into three studies: study one offers a definition of the number of people killed and affected, study 2 makes the affected people's needs concrete and study 3 makes the affected people's needs more salient. They observe that the number of fatalities drives financial aid regardless of attribute definition and the concreteness and saliency of the need. Experiment 2 manipulates the validity of the attribute, priming the validity of affected people, whereas experiment 3 manipulates the reliability of the attribute, enhancing the reliability of affected people. Only experiment 2 was successful in increasing the sensitivity to people in need.

Huber et al. (2011) test the immediacy bias in the allocation of financial aid. The bias refers to the influence in behavior that immediate emotions have. They devise four experiments to test it. Experiment 1 manipulates when participants make allocations, assigning whether they allocate the money after viewing four videos each describing one crisis in an African country or after viewing each of the videos. Participants had to allocate $95 between the crises and were told that one participant's allocation would be randomly selected and donated to Doctors without Borders. They observe that participants allocated a disproportionate fraction of aid to whichever crisis happened to be experience immediately, supporting the operation of the bias. Experiment 2 shows only two videos and manipulates the time at which participants are asked to select a crisis about which to write a letter to be sent to their state senator, assigning whether they select the crisis after viewing the videos or one day after. They observe that participants chose to write a letter to whichever crisis they happened to learn about second, supporting the operation of the bias; in addition, the one-day delay diminished its effect. Experiment 3 builds on the baseline treatment of experiment 2 and manipulates whether participants are forewarned about the immediacy bias. They observe that participants chose to write a letter to whichever crisis they happened to learn about second, supporting the operation of the bias; however, forewarning did not diminish its effect.

The "identified victim" effect refers to the excessive allocation of resources toward identifiable as compared to statistical victims (Small and Loewenstein 2003). For example, Small et al. (2007) test how deliberating about donation decisions impacts the "identified victim" effect when donating money to Save the Children to help alleviate the food crisis in Southern Africa and Ethiopia. The amount participants could donate came from the $5 fee awarded from participation. They devise four experiments to that end. Experiment 1 manipulates whether participants are forewarned about the "identified victim" effect. They observe the effect; in addition, forewarning diminished the effect for identifiable victims. Experiment 2 manipulates the frame of the forewarning, replacing the frame *more to identifiable victims* for *less to statistical victims*. They observe no framing effects. Experiment 3 manipulates whether in the identifiable victim condition participants receive also information about statistical victims. They observe a larger amount of donations when information about identifiable victims is accompanied by information about statistical victims. Experiment 4 manipulates the way of thinking, priming participants with either a calculation-based or a feeling-based mode of thought. They observe that the calculation-based mode of thought diminished the effect; however, the feeling-based mode of thought did not increase donations to statistical victims.

Finally, Kogut and Ritov (2007) explore the role of a perceived shared social group in the "identified victim" effect when donating money to help fund the continued work of an Israeli rescue team after the Southeast Asia tsunami. Experiment 1[1] manipulates the amount of beneficiaries being served, whether the beneficiaries are identifiable or statistical victims and whether the beneficiaries share the participants' social group. They observe a singularity effect of identified victims in the shared social group condition only, that is, the willingness to help a single identified individual is greater than willingness to help a group of identified individuals only when the individual shares the participants' social group.

---

[1] Kogut and Ritov (2007) ran two more experiments. As the tasks are not about allocating aid to humanitarian crises or disasters, they are not reviewed.

## Planning

Here, three experiments fall within the purpose of theory testing, whereas the remaining one is used to generate observations that can lead to new theory.

Gonçalves and Castañeda (2016) explore whether humanitarian practitioners are prone to the same systematic biases that impact inventory decisions when deciding how many emergency supplies to preposition in preparation to emergencies. Experiment 1 manipulates how costly and urgent the supplies are and asked 20 participants to choose prepositioning quantities for 30 rounds or emergencies. Given the low number of participants, half the participants played a low cost-high critical task and a high-cost low-critical task and the other half a high cost-high critical task and a low cost-low critical task. That is, each participant played two treatments; order-of-presentation effects were controlled. They observe the operation of the well-known pull-to-center and demand chasing biases. Experiment 2 manipulates the salience of urgent supplies by bundling them with nonurgent ones in a portfolio to validate the behavioral nuances observed in experiment 1. They observe similar behavioral patterns that lead to an increased availability of urgent supplies.

Similar to donations experiments, Gralla et al.'s (2015) analysis lacks analytical benchmarks. Instead, they build on insights from theories of learning from simulations to analyze a simulated training exercise and draw lessons to the refinement and development of future trainings. They analyze the Logistics Response Team (LRT) training, World Food Program (WFP)'s 1-week simulated emergency response exercise to train humanitarian logisticians from multiple agencies to work as an interagency logistics team responding to emergencies. Despite being designed by a small number of experienced emergency responders, Gralla et al.'s (2015) analysis reveal that the simulation considers many features of retention, generalization and teamwork, aspects emphasized by the literature on strategies for emergency response training (Ford and Schmidt 2000). In a similar vein, Muhren and Van de Walle (2009) build on insights from sense making to analyze the TRIPLEX exercise, the International Humanitarian Partnership's simulation exercise to strengthen preparedness and response. The authors describe how participants handle ambiguity and equivocality, and discuss how information systems can support participants when handling these problems in the needs assessment process.

Finally, Gralla et al. (2016) is the only experiment that works on generating observations that can lead to new theory. They focus on the transportation planning part of the LRT training to generate theory on how people formulate and solve problems in a humanitarian response setting. They observe that the transportation planning problem is solved through greedy search and formulated through sense making, with an interplay between search and formulation in which the greedy search enables updates to the problem formulation and sense making directs and limits the search process.

## Development

The only experiment in this area is about theory testing in a nontraditional context. Castañeda et al. (2016) explore whether supply chain contracts can be utilized to overcome operational constraints in the Ugandan crop storage supply chain. Building on Becker-Peth et al.'s (2013) framework, the experiment manipulates the frame of the supply chain contract and asks both business managers from the sector and students from a local university to choose purchasing quantities of raw materials. They observe chronic underordering among managers and students and buyback and salvage contracts. However, a contract customization designed to counter under-ordering leads to better results, especially for managers in the buyback contract condition.

## Issues and Opportunities with Behavioral Experiments

Behavioral experiments have received multiple critiques, especially with respect to methodological aspects. Here we review some of these critiques and the particular challenges HLSCM brings to the method.

## Design

Experiments require at least two treatments: a baseline treatment and a comparison treatment. An experiment with only one treatment is more a demonstration than an experiment. However, demonstrations can be very influential and informative (Katok 2010). Excluding the training simulations in Gralla and colleagues and Muhren and Van de Walle, all experiments reviewed in this chapter have at least two treatments. Yet, Gralla et al.'s (2015) experiment is very informative since it provides a rather controlled demonstration of strategies for emergency response training, while Muhren and Van de Walle's (2009) study offers insights about the use of information systems in needs assessment. Gralla et al.'s (2016) study is noteworthy also since it is the only study reviewed here that generates observations for new theory. Given that theories in HLSCM are not as developed as theories in commercial LSCM, one-treatment experiments are a tool to demonstrate theories in HLSCM. Similarly, their relative control makes them a tool to generate HLSCM theory. However, as the field becomes more mature, one-treatment experiments will contribute less to its development.

Gralla and colleagues' and Muhren and Van de Walle's studies highlight the challenges that experiments with high external validity bring to design. As the simulated setting becomes closer to reality, it is more difficult to manipulate variables and thus design treatments, not to mention the already inherent difficulty in replicating many aspects of relief assistance in a lab experiment. In this regard, field experiments in the form of randomized controlled trials can give researches a chance to implement HLSCM experiments with such high demands for context (Banerjee and Duflo 2011). For example, one could test the effect of an electronic beneficiary identification mechanism on the performance of aid distribution by comparing it with a similar emergency response where traditional paper-based identification is used. If a behavioral experiment is impractical, one could make some additional behavioral analyses by using secondary data to build models, test hypotheses and understand people's behavior. For example, one could identify emergency responses with similar characteristics except in the variable or intervention of interest and then explore differences in behavior between these responses. This requires a good matching as an alternative to randomization.

## Randomization

Randomization is achieved when there is a simultaneous random assignment of treatments and participants comply with their assignment (Morton and Williams 2010). While the very same nature of experiments makes noncompliance rare, simultaneity in random assignment is often difficult to achieve since researches may not have large laboratories to run multiple treatments. Many times participants are thus randomly assigned to treatments not simultaneously but over time. To circumvent this issue to the greatest extent possible, treatments should be run the same day or approximate time. When this is not possible, a great advantage of using undergraduate students as a subject pool is that it is likely homogeneous in possibly confounding factors, increasing the ability to compare effects of different treatments run over time (Morton and Williams 2010).

Most papers reviewed here present a pseudo-randomization approach. For example, they randomly assign half the participants to a treatment (Evangelidis and Van den Bergh 2013; Small et al. 2007; Castañeda et al. 2016; Gonçalves and Castañeda 2016). The proportion of participants assigned to a treatment should be a byproduct of the random assignment itself. Some of them do not specify the assignment approach followed for some of their studies (Evangelidis and Van den Bergh 2013; Small et al. 2007). Finally, experiments that have more than one study used the same subject pool across studies. The only exception is Evangelidis and Van den Bergh (2013), who used undergraduate students and Amazon's Mechanical Turk.

Humanitarian practitioners could be spread around the globe at any given time due to the uncertain nature of relief assistance, making simultaneity in random assignment difficult to achieve if a behavioral experiment has to be run with them. If the research question makes the use of a sample of participants from the sector a must and simultaneity in random assignment is not possible, then researches should aim to use the same subject pool of participants over time. The use of different subject pools is still an option since confounding unobservable factors that vary over time can be controlled ex post by using regression control methods (Morton and Williams 2010); however, the former approach provides a cleaner test.

## Context and Participants

Experiments are often criticized for their lack of context and the use of undergraduate students as their sample of participants. While one should take great care in balancing the need for context (Katok 2010), decisions in HLSCM have particular characteristics that make them different from typical decisions in commercial LSCM (Holguín-Veras et al. 2012; Day et al. 2012). This is relevant since operational contexts do matter (Kremer et al. 2010). In this regard, the experiments reviewed in this chapter tend to have cover stories related to HLSCM, increasing their external validity. However, this comes at the expense of generalization. That is, insights generated in HLSCM experiments are difficult to apply in other settings. Ideally, one should run a new experiment to explore whether insights from an HLSCM experiment apply in a different setting and vice versa. Gonçalves and Castañeda (2016) and Castañeda et al. (2016) are good examples of this approach since they tested whether theory from commercial LSCM apply in HLSCM settings. External validity comes also at the expense of control. For example, the simulations in Gralla et al. (2015, 2016) and Muhrens and Van de Walle (2009) are rich in context, but with a rather limited control, leaving more room for confounding factors to play a role compared with traditional behavioral experiments.

The criticisms against the use of undergraduate students also fall within the realm of context. Although we have mentioned some of the advantages of using undergraduate students as the sample of participants (e.g., they meet induced valuation precepts easier and are more homogeneous in possibly confounding factors than other types of participants), clearly they are not professionals. Although a number of experiments in commercial LSCM have shown no systematic differences between students and professionals (e.g., Bolton et al. 2012; Moritz et al. 2013; Croson and Donohue 2006), that question is yet to be answered in HLSCM. Hence, experiments on HLSCM with students may lack external validity. Experiments on donations were all run with students; however, students are also potential donors. In Small et al. (2007) the donations came from the actual money students were awarded for participation, improving further in context. Experiments on planning and development were all run with practitioners, leaving little if any room for criticisms in this aspect.

While having access to a pool of undergraduate students is relatively easy, having access to a pool of humanitarian practitioners over time is rather difficult. An alternative is to run experiments when different practitioners gather together outside their day-to-day responsibilities. Currently there are several training and educational programs targeted specifically to humanitarian practitioners. Gonçalves and Castañeda (2016), Gralla et al. (2015, 2016) and Muhren and Van de Walle (2009) took advantage of this and ran their experiments with practitioners enrolled in these programs. When the number of humanitarian practitioners available to participate in an experiment is small, one could run the experiment also with primed students. Priming techniques could be used to activate an HLSCM mind-set in students. Priming techniques are diverse but all serve the same purpose: a mind-set is possessed or activated in one context, and then its effects are explored in contexts unrelated to the source or activation of the mind-set (Smith and Galinsky 2010).

In general, context criticisms can be addressed by either framing the experiment according to what is relevant about the setting or recruiting more relevant participants if one believes that the underlying psychological mechanisms require it (Siemsen 2011).

## Incentives

The use of financial incentives in experiments has been the subject of many debates. Economists presume that participants will work with more motivation if they earn more money for better performance, while psychologists believe that intrinsic motivation is usually high enough to produce steady effort (Camerer and Hogarth 1999). Some psychologists argue also that when money is contingent on performance in an experiment, the intrinsic motivation is replaced by extrinsic motivation and performance will be negatively affected (Morton and Williams 2010). While more money may induce more effort, effort does not always improve performance (Camerer and Hogarth 1999); financially motivated participants could perform suboptimal behaviors with more enthusiasm (Arkes 1991).

The issue of intrinsic versus extrinsic motivation is relevant for this chapter. The socially motivated nature of relief assistance is more often than not aligned with the reason why people decide to work in relief assistance, providing a powerful intrinsic motivator. Providing financial incentives for performance in socially motivated tasks can crowd out intrinsic motivation, hurting performance itself (Perry et al. 2006; Osterloh and Frey 2002). Hence, rewarding participants financially for performance in HLSCM experiments may not be advisable, especially if the goal of the experiment is directly aligned with saving lives and/or alleviating suffering. Gralla et al. (2015, 2016) and Muhren and Van de Walle (2009) did not provide incentives for performance since participants enroll in trainings because they want to improve their skills. Gonçalves and Castañeda (2016) did not provide incentives either. Although the benchmark they used is related to cost minimization, they included a proxy for relief objectives (e.g., Mete and Zabinsky 2010; Rawls and Turnquist 2010, 2012). Nevertheless, they left the use of incentives as an open issue, which is relevant due to potential dissonance between cost and service level (Moritz 2010).

On the other hand, Castañeda et al. (2016) did provide financial incentives, although not contingent on performance; they awarded participants a fixed fee for participation. The experiments on donations report mixed rewarding mechanisms. Evangelidis and Van den Bergh (2013) offered course credit and money as incentives. Huber et al. (2011) offered course credit, Small et al. (2007) a fixed fee and Kogut and Ritov (2007) did not offer any incentive.

The effect of incentives is still an empirical question (Camerer and Hogarth 1999). We recommend to follow a *do-it-both-ways* approach (Hertwig and Ortmann 2001), that is, run experiments with and without incentives. This would generate a database that would eventually enable researches to make informed decisions about incentive mechanisms for experiments in HLSCM (Hertwig and Ortmann 2001; Camerer and Hogarth 1999). In this regard, the use of sizeable financial incentives is most convenient (Brase 2009; Heyman and Ariely 2004). Financial incentives not only induce more effort but reduce variability in the data (Morton and Williams 2010; Camerer and Hogarth 1999; Smith and Walker 1993). However, the amount of financial incentives should not be contingent on performance as explained earlier. A fixed fee larger than the average opportunity cost of participants is a practical guideline (Hey 1996; Morton and Williams 2010).

### Infrastructure and Logistics

Most experiments are run using a computer interface. Computer interfaces are convenient and efficient in collecting data (Katok 2010). There are several platforms such as z-Tree and Forio Business Simulations to implement experiments with relative ease. Occasionally, however, securing a computer lab is not possible. Running experiments with humanitarian practitioners or the HLSCM stakeholders of interest may entail traveling to locations where laboratory infrastructure and the associated logistics are not available or adequate enough. In those cases, careful design and participation measures should be taken to secure the quality of the data collected. In Castañeda et al. (2016), the available infrastructure and logistics not only led to an implementation on paper but also informed the design and procedure of their experiment. Collaborations with international and local organizations were vital to address many of the infrastructure and logistics challenges.

Finally, the experiments in Gralla et al. (2015, 2016) and Muhren and Van de Walle (2009) show clearly a trade-off between external validity and infrastructure and logistics requirements: as the need for external validity increases so does the need for infrastructure and logistics. Collaborations with related organizations and local partners are vital to design and run experiments with high demands for external validity.

# System Dynamics

## Method

System dynamics is a methodology that provides decision makers with the appropriate tools to analyze the future intended and unintended consequences (short and long term) of today's decisions. The methodology has its foundation in the *systems thinking* approach, which considers the interdependence among structures, that is, that "everything is connected to everything else" (Sterman 2001). Systems thinking increases our ability to understand the complexities of the real-world dynamics.

System dynamics provides a systemic perspective of a problem, allowing a proper identification and leverage of the driving forces that avoid policy resistance and align short-term outcomes with long-term benefits (Sterman 2000). Policy resistance arises because our mental models are limited to understand the complexity of real systems. In our decision-making process, we use the limited and imperfect information we perceive from the real world as an input and apply heuristics to this information to adjust our decisions (Forrester 1958, 1961). This course of action is known as the single-loop learning process.

The single-loop learning process does not lead to a significant adjustment of people's beliefs about the sequential flow of causes and effects that explain how a system behaves. To adjust our mental models, we need to incorporate a double-loop learning in our decision-making processes (Argyris 1985). In a double-loop learning process, the feedback information about the real world does not only alter our decisions within the context of existing frames and decision rules, but also feeds back to alter our mental models. As our mental models change, we adjust the structure of our systems, creating different decision rules and new strategies. This way, even when the same information is processed, it is now interpreted by a different decision rule. Changing the structure of the systems then alters the behavior. The implementation of systems thinking by the use of a double-loop learning process leads to a holistic, long-term dynamic view of the world that generates a continuous redesign of our policies and institutions.

## Dynamic Complexity

As conscious and intelligent as people are, the dynamic complexity of the real world overcomes our mental capabilities. Dynamic complexity refers to the difficulty for the human mind to identify long-term cause-and-effect relations. This complexity does not only reduce the learning speed within the double-loop learning process but also reduces the learning gained on each cycle, even when we find the time to reflect on our actions. Dynamic complexity can be found even in systems with a simple structure (Arango et al. 2012; Gonçalves and Villa 2016; Villa et al. 2015). The most important factors that reflect this complexity and constrain people's learning are feedbacks, delays, nonlinearities, and stocks and flows (Sterman 2001).

- *Feedbacks:* The complexity arises due to the fact that systems do not follow the open-loop perspective of humans, which usually explains outcomes as the result of a series of uncontrollable events (Sterman 2001). In fact, real-world systems react to our own decisions.
- *Delays:* Complexity is given also by the separation in time between causes and effects, preventing people from identifying the actual connection among them. Delays are an important source of instability and oscillation, which complicates the processes to control systems such as inventories.
- *Nonlinearities:* Sometimes, systems' behavior is difficult to predict because the relationship between cause and effect are not always proportional. The magnitude of the effect might be a nonlinear function of environmental factors such as capacity availability or separation over time.
- *Stocks and flows:* These characteristics determine the actual system dynamics over time. Stocks refer to accumulations or state variables, while flows provide information about how stocks change over time.

When all these factors interact with one another, they create counterintuitive behaviors and instabilities that increase the tendency of the system to oscillate. These instabilities highlight the complexity of controlling different subsystems with a proper balance between long- and short-term decisions. However, despite systems complexity, humans rely on simple open-loop (event-oriented) mental models to make decisions. System dynamics enables decision makers to use causal maps to represent the interactions among the main variables in a system, which allows the integration of the double-loop learning for the evaluation of the interactions among variables and their long-term consequences.

## Modeling Process

The simulation process enhances the evaluation of strategies that could improve system performance (Sterman 2000). In general, the process of modeling used in system dynamic can be summarized as follows: initially, problem articulation is required, where decision makers need to clearly and precisely define the boundaries of the specific problem that they would like to study. Then, a causal diagram is created using the key variables. The *causal diagram* allows the identification of the important relationships and feedback loops that govern the system (Forrester 1961; Richardson and Pugh 1983). A deeper look of the variables that describe the causal diagram allows the identification of the important stocks and flows that characterize the state of the system and its changes over time. Then, by incorporating actual constraints, the important delays, nonlinearities and the information available, it would be possible to formulate a mathematical simulation model. Finally, a *stock-and-flow diagram* representing the mathematical model allows simulating the dynamic behavior of the system. Although this is a model, its behavior should be qualitatively similar to the real-world system, which will allow decision makers to evaluate the impact of multiple policies and strategies and their intended and unintended implications over time.

It is important to highlight that in many real applications is not possible to get reliable data to formulate and run a mathematical model. In these cases, the modeling process requires the use of blending systems dynamics approaches, which consists on the integration of the typical causal modeling of system dynamics with soft OR methods. This blending systems dynamics approach is based on the technique of "group model building" (Vennix 1996). The main idea is to use stakeholders' perspectives to create a causal conceptualization of the mechanisms and trade-offs that determines the observed dynamics of the system (Besiou and Van Wassenhove 2015). The process used to build the causal map requires an iterative process that lead to the identification of the problem, the current policies and finally the (un-) intended effects (Lane et al. 2016). This iterative process facilitates both thinking about the whole as well as the parts, and the application of double-loop learning by the creation of global consensus. This continuous sharing of both thoughts and feelings about the problem continues until the stakeholders are able to say "Yes, this picture is what we see happening" (van den Belt 2004; Lane et al. 2016). In this way, this piece of systems thinking creates confidence in the sector about the model and it can be accepted as a plausible explanation of the observed behavior. Therefore, it can be used as a tool that gives validity and coherence to the modelers' final recommendations.

## System Dynamics and Behavioral Experiments

Multiple controlled behavioral experiments with underlying system dynamics models have been conducted to capture the behavioral factors that affect performance (e.g., Arango et al. 2013; Donohue and Croson 2002). These studies highlight that the mental models people use to guide their decisions are dynamically deficient (Sterman 2000). People generally do not understand stocks and flows nor the associated delays between action and response. In fact, many of these experiments show that people use reactive and erroneous heuristics based on an event-based, open-loop view of causality, ignoring systems structure and feedback processes (Arango et al. 2012).

Beyond the individual behavior, system dynamics investigates the effects of behavioral regularities at the system level and designs ways to improve real operations. Traditional system dynamics considers that the structure of the system leads to its behavior (Sterman 2000). Therefore, different people placed in the same system structure tend to show the same behavioral patterns. For instance, system dynamics research suggests that decision makers perform poorly in environments with significant feedback delays (Sterman 1989a, b), feedback complexity (Diehl and Sterman 1995; Sterman 1989a) and changing conditions (Kleinmuntz and Thomas 1987). Moreover, this behavior remains suboptimal even when the decision maker has the opportunity to identify and correct errors (Einhorn and Hogarth 1981). Consequently, system dynamics models incorporate boundedly rational individual decisions (Simon 1955) as well as heuristics and biases (Tversky and Kahneman 1974).

Indeed, behavioral studies in commercial LSCM show that humans display a low performance in systems with dynamic complexity, even when the level of this complexity is low. The strong influence of human bounded rationality in understanding feedback and their effects are due to two basic and related deficiencies in our mental maps (Sterman 2000; Bendoly et al. 2010). First, our mental maps embody a simplified representation of the actual causal structure of systems: misperception of feedback structure. Second, even if we understand the structure of the system, we are unable to infer how the system will behave over time: misperception of feedback dynamics (Bendoly et al. 2010; Gonçalves and Villa 2016).

## System Dynamics in HLSCM

During humanitarian operations, organizations must supply the right goods and services, at the right place and time, to the right people, while properly utilizing resources (Chomilier et al. 2000; Samii 2008). However, this appropriate provision is not an easy task for any humanitarian organization due to the large number of actors, time pressures, feedback loops, resource constraints and uncertainties in the system. Humanitarian organizations use different types of programs (relief, recovery, and development) to properly respond to different humanitarian needs. Relief programs are short-term activities focused on providing assistance to immediate damages caused by disasters. Recovery programs take care of the post-emergency needs of the affected population (Beamon and Balcik 2008; Samii 2008). Development programs focus on the medium- and long-term development and sustainability of humans (Beamon and Balcik 2008). Therefore, being able to manage these complex environments and achieve good performance during these programs is in the most interest of humanitarian organizations (Urrea et al. 2016). However, despite system dynamics methodology has been widely used for more than 50 years for improving operations in the private sector, applications to capture dynamics of and improve humanitarian operations are more recent (Gonçalves 2008; Besiou et al. 2010). System dynamics studies in HLSCM have addressed issues related to long-term versus short-term development, fleet and transportation management, and competition and coordination.

## Long-Term Versus Short-Term Development

The myopic and open-loop vision of organizations may lower overall system performance and duplications of efforts, posing important challenges in planning and implementing further logistics in humanitarian operations (Dolinskaya et al. 2011; George 2003; Kaatrud et al. 2003; Tomasini 2012; Wakolbinger and Toyasaki 2011). Therefore, finding a proper balance between long-term and short-term operations is in the most interest of humanitarian organizations.

Trying to address this issue, Gonçalves (2008, 2011) was the first to develop a formal system dynamics model that quantifies the trade-off that exists between providing relief assistance and building capacity in humanitarian organizations. His simulation model analyzes the importance of a proper balance between short-term and long-term needs, showing that organizations focusing on the needs of affected people in the short term make local communities more vulnerable to the long-term threats. He highlights the importance of controlling stress in the field as a complementary strategy for reducing staff turnover and keeping organizational capacity. Humanitarian organizations failing to hold the experience gained in their operations may lead to no lasting relief and recovery strategies. However, if humanitarian organizations can retain a large fraction of the lessons learned in the field, they will improve both short- and long-term organizational performance.

Similarly, Abosuliman (2014) builds on Gonçalves (2008)'s model to create a disaggregated model capable of managing real-time information that enable decision makers to improve humanitarian response. This disaggregated model provides detailed information about the effects of different strategies when responding to typical operational problems related with floods in Jeddah, Saudi Arabia. The model can assist the decision-making process among actors, leading to a better understanding of the outputs that could evolve under different scenarios and the consequences of decisions to frequent problems. To properly estimate and evaluate the model, Abosuliman collected information (both quantitative and qualitative) about the dynamics of the organizational capabilities during the 2009–2011 floods at Jeddah. He incorporates donations, human resources and training to identify the strategies that improve short-term recovery and rebuild proper infrastructure for the long term.

Voyer et al. (2015) use system dynamics to understand the dynamics of operational factors that affect food security during humanitarian operations. The authors created a system dynamics model including factors such as donations, community needs, food supply and warehousing. Their simulations show that (1) one of the most critical factors involved in food supply was warehousing management, which is often a source of waste and inefficiencies due to misperception of the supply line and delays, and (2) the best performance (lowest waste) was obtained by leveraging donations through proper delivery and warehousing processes. Voyer and colleagues propose a number of policy recommendations to improve the overall system performance. These recommendations include the reduction of the time to build/repair infrastructure and implementing a continuous review process for inventory and supply management.

Finally, Lane et al. (2016) develop a system dynamic model to make an examination of child protection activities in England. They build on the concepts of blending system dynamics to incorporate stakeholders' perspectives on the creation and evaluation of long-term strategies. Initially, based on stakeholders' experience, authors create a causal diagram that reflects the main interactions and effects that lead to the observed dynamics. Then, they evaluate impact of past policies that identify some unintended consequences. Authors conclude that due to the rigidity of the child protection system, staff were not able to use their work expertise and professionalism to assess child's needs. This situation led to frequent program delays and staff dissatisfaction, which led to a general reduction of program performance.

## Vehicle Fleet and Transportation Management

Transportation is an expensive and critical operation in humanitarian response (Dispartite 2007). Its importance varies depending on the type of crisis: relief or development (Pedraza-Martinez et al. 2011). For relief operations, the focus is on optimizing the response time to an uncertain demand during the first hours after the crisis occurs, while for development operations, the focus is more on cost-efficiency. In this way, the importance and proper management of transportation and vehicle fleet operations depend on the duration, urgency of the crisis and the uncertainty of the demand (Pedraza-Martinez et al. 2010).

The first system dynamics study in this area is the one by Besiou et al. (2010). They use a case-based research to determine the effectiveness of system dynamics in fleet management. They describe three different humanitarian applications to show how system dynamics can be used to deal with the uncertainties, multiple actors and time pressures that characterize the complexities of the humanitarian sector and avoid making decisions based just on intuition (open loop). They present a parsimonious model where they differentiate among three different vehicle fleet management systems: centralized, hybrid and decentralized. Their results show how a proper creation of feedback loops enable the estimation of accurate fleet capacity to satisfy programs' needs.

Later, Besiou et al. (2014) made a deeper quantitative and qualitative analysis of the effect of centralized, decentralized and hybrid models in the fleet management problem for development and relief operations. They analyze these models' efficiency and equity taking as references four different organizations: International Committee of the Red Cross (ICRC), International Federation of the Red Cross and Red Crescent (IFRC), World Food Programme (WFP) and World Vision International (WVI). They show that for development programs a decentralized model is more suitable due to the short lead times, while for relief operations both the hybrid and decentralized models are suitable. Finally, building on a real application in the humanitarian sector (2011), they highlight the importance of accounting for the fact that the donations organizations work with are usually earmarked. Donors play a fundamental role because they are the ones who provide the resources that organizations use to run their relief and development programs. Donors can be, for instance, individual philanthropists, private companies or governments, following their own priorities and agendas according to their interests. The authors analyze the effect of reducing earmarked donations as an alternative of organizations to move toward a decentralized feet model, concluding that the efficiency of this policy is affected by the number of donors, the lead times and the level of applicability (local vs international).

Similarly, Cruz-Cantillo (2014) created a system dynamics model to study the transportation of relief supplies integrated with GIS information (location of distribution centers, shelters, points of distribution and kitchens' facilities). The model was calibrated using actual data gathered during

Hurricane George. They show how a proper forecast, hazard analysis and the evaluation of routes that cause more delays during distribution allow organizations to have a better plan for managing inventory, dispatching and transportation operations in the aftermath of this type of events.

Finally, Peng et al. (2014) evaluated a system dynamics model to deliver emergency supply that considers environmental factors, dynamic road condition information and delay in information transfer during a post-seismic situation. The results show the importance of considering road condition, road capacity and the in-transit volume to evaluate the actual lead time in the humanitarian response and create strategies that can improve system performance.

## Competition and Coordination

One additional challenge that humanitarian organizations face is the competition for scarce resources. This competition gives organizations little incentive to work together, hampering coordination and reducing overall performance. For instance, organizations may duplicate efforts during the response or hide important information to their counterparts if they believe that this will hinder them from attracting media and donor attention (Kent 1987; Stephenson 2005). The coordination problem can also be created by the high number and diversity of actors such as donors, humanitarian organizations, military, government, beneficiaries and media (Balcik et al. 2010; Besiou et al. 2010; Dolinskaya et al. 2011; van Wassenhove 2006), who have different sizes, authority, structures and interests. However, when a disaster strikes, there is an urgency of having a coordinated effort (Tomasini 2012; Leiras et al. 2014) because this can improve the delivery of aid.

To evaluate coordination of resources during a response to unconventional emergencies, Wang et al. (2012) created a system dynamics model that incorporates demand and supply trends into the feedback loops to get a holistic view of a coordination process. In addition, they evaluated the effectiveness of the model using a numerical example of the rice supply chain in Wenchuan, China, during an earthquake. Their results highlight the importance of work force during the first hours after the earthquake and how the use of transportation schedules and information sharing may improve humanitarian response.

On the other hand, Ni et al. (2015) developed a system dynamics model for two competitive organizations. They argue that a proper preparedness strategy should be implemented to improve effectiveness and efficiency during relief operations. Their model analyzes the effect of strategic decisions (such as prepositioning stocks) of two organizations, one supplier, donors and beneficiaries on the overall relief performance. They tested the model under different values to evaluate the qualitative results of the outcomes. Main results highlight the importance of prepositioning materials and reducing lead times as driving forces for increasing sustainability of organizations.

## Issues and Opportunities with System Dynamics

System dynamics, as a modeling tool, has received multiple critiques with respect to its usefulness. The areas most subject to criticisms are modeling, validation and calibration, and implementation. We review these areas and some considerations particular to HLSCM.

### Modeling

One of the main issues in applying system dynamics is determining the system boundary conditions and decision variables. The idea that the model should not be as simple that it does not represent the problem, nor as difficult that it becomes intractable is one of the main challenges that system dynamics modelers face. The issue comes together with the fact that mode-lers are usually misinformed about the specific objectives and limitations of the methodology, applying the methodology incorrectly (Barlas 2007; Forrester 2007). A proper system dynamics model should be created to parsimoniously model a specific problem and not a system, because model-ing the system will obscure the definition of the limits of the model and, therefore, its applicability (Sterman 2000). A good system dynamics model should capture the main feedback structures involved in the problem under study; if we have problems where exogenous influences drive the system and there are no clear feedback structures, system dynamics should not be applied (Barlas 2007).

These challenges for creating a proper system dynamics model for a specific problem are even higher if we decide to apply them in the humani-tarian sector where limited research has been done and there is limited information about the specific structures and causalities that drive the main dynamics in the sector. Therefore, a higher attention and understanding of the problem is required. As an alternative to deal with the lack of data and with the fact that humanitarian operations are characterized by interaction of multiple stakeholders with conflicting agendas and interconnected trade-offs, soft methodologies are required. We need to create models that provide insights into the most important dynamics in these challenging operations. In this case, we need to take advantage of the "group model building" technique proposed by the blending systems dynamics approach (Vennix 1996). A proper use of this approach should capture both short-term and long-term effects by accounting for the interconnections and the implications for decision makers (van Wassenhove and Besiou 2013). However, it should be clear that while these models remain valuable, we need to understand where, when and how to use them (Besiou and Van Wassenhove 2015; Lane et al. 2016).

## Validation and Calibration

A second aspect of criticism is related with the validation and calibration of the model. On one hand, validation refers mostly to identifying the internal structure of the system and verifying that the system behavior and patterns are accurate (Barlas 1996). Creating a model that properly captures the main feedback loops of one problem is not an easy task. Also, two different modelers could arrive to two different models for the same problem. The challenge then moves toward creating the proper model with the proper size that explains the system behavior using the correct causalities. The process of validation can be divided into two parts: internal and external. The internal validation establishes the validity of the structure (cause-effect relationship) of the model, where different tests (e.g., dimensional consistency test, structure confirmation, extreme condition test) can be used (Forrester and Senge 1980; Richardson and Pugh 1983). The external validity establishes the behavioral validity of the system (Barlas 1996; Forrester and Senge 1980).

On the other hand, during a calibration process, modelers use different statistical analyses for estimating the specific set of parameters that minimize the deviation of the created model from the actual behavior of one specific problem. These estimations can later be used as a tool for learning and scenario analysis. However, getting the data from the real world is usually a difficult task, especially in the humanitarian sector. This lack of data availability poses some challenges for validating both the structure and the behavior of a system.

For the case where blending system dynamics approach is required, in addition to the group validation, researchers should complement this group model with additional literature review and surveys that allow the identification and validation of the most important subsystems likely to drive behavior of the system as a whole. Then, modelers should take advantage of the group modeling for validating the dynamics of the critical subsystems of the global complex problem. Based on the creation of an acceptable causal diagram and the identification of potential consequences, researcher may be able to design strategies that lead to a reduction of unintended consequences. These design and validation processes should verify if the recommendations resulting from the modeling analysis are valid and robust (Besiou and Van Wassenhove 2015).

## Implementation

System dynamics is a flexible tool that allows the integration and evaluation of soft (qualitative) and hard variables (quantitative). Having a well-defined system dynamics model may lead to the (free) evaluation of policies that later could be implemented/avoided in the real word. In humanitarian operations, this methodology is just starting and there is an open door for many more applications that can generate good research outputs and positive impact in real |operations. However, having an impact in humanitarian operations requires a cautious interaction with the humanitarian organizations in sharing with them the specific results and potential policies that mitigate low performances in their organizations. Applying some specific policies and strategies in commercial LSCM is usually easier than doing so in HLSCM due to the high political issues and conflict of interests that are involved in the humanitarian sector. Therefore, researchers should find the way to convince organizations that the use of a system dynamics model may help them understand their problems and improve their operations, without claiming that there is lack of transparency or efficiency in their processes.

We believe that good models can be used in real applications even in the humanitarian sector. A proper system dynamics involving qualitative approach with multiple stakeholders will help modelers to validate the model and then build on it to define scenarios, evaluate alternatives and create new policies. In fact, quantitative (Besiou et al. 2014) and blended (Lane et al. 2016) system dynamics models have been used to informed strategic decisions for real operations.

We encourage readers to develop, evaluate and validate system dynamics models that involve operational factors (warehousing, transportation, forecasting, etc.) together with social preferences (coordination, accountability, trust, reciprocity, etc.) and then evaluate their expected and unexpected consequences in the short and long term.

# Agent-Based Modeling

## Method

Agent-based modeling and multi-agent simulation are terms used to describe a modeling approach that studies individual agents' interactions and how these interactions affect the system as a whole. In this section we will use the acronym ABM to address both ABM (and agent-based models) and multi-agent systems. ABM is being widely used in businesses to aid decision making and also as a research methodology in the study of complex adaptive systems (CAS). It encompasses the concepts of complex systems, game theory, sociology, evolutionary computation and artificial intelligence, and blends them together to solve practical issues. Agent-based models help us understand the micro-macro behavior of complex systems, that is, to see how micro features (individuals in a population coded with certain behavioral rules) result in complex macro behavior (i.e., a key notion that a simple behavioral rule can lead to complex system behavior) (Sankaranarayanan 2011, 2014). Since the 1990s, ABM has been used to solve and/or understand a variety of problems that include predicting the spread of epidemics, population dynamics and agent behavior in stock markets and traffic congestion, and to study consumer behavior in marketing.

### Defining an Agent

There is no accepted formal definition for an agent and many researchers have their own view points on what characterizes an agent (Macal and North 2006). Bonabeau (2002) considers an independent entity (e.g., software module, individual, etc.) to be an agent that can have either primitive capabilities or adaptive intelligence. Casti (1997) proposes the idea that agents should have a set of rules governing environmental interactions, and another set of rules that defines its adaptability. Mellouli et al. (2003) point to the adaptive and learning nature that should be present in an entity to qualify being called an agent. The basic idea that comes out of these discussions is that an agent should be proactive, that is, it should interact with the environment in which it dwells. One possible definition of an agent could be: "Agents are boundedly rational individuals acting towards a goal using simple decision-making rules and experiencing learning, adaptation and reproduction."

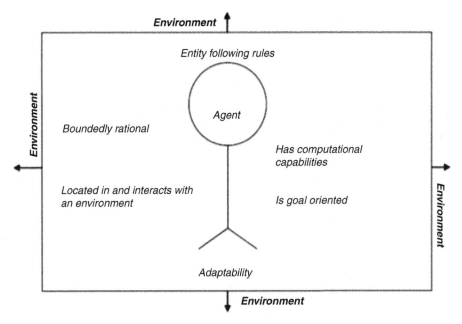

**Fig. 3.2**  An agent (Source: Sankaranarayanan 2011)

An agent, as shown in Fig. 3.2, can be characterized as follows:

- Can be identified, that is, an individual with attributes and rules governing its behavior.
- Dwells in an environment and interacts with other agents in this environment. The environment provides a boundary for all agents, that is, rules of existence along with an objective to achieve.
- Adaptable, that is, ability to learn. Flexible enough to modify rules as elucidated earlier with the aim of achieving its objective.
- Has an objective so that it can compare its behavior relative to this objective.

## ABM Foundations

The idea of ABM and simulation can be traced to the 1940s when von Neumann (Heims et al. 1984) proposed the theoretical concept of a machine that reproduced itself. This idea was extended by Ulam who proposed a grid framework containing cells, which led to cellular automata (CA)

(Gutowitz 1991; Wolfram 2002). Conway's "Game of Life" used a two-dimensional CA and by applying a simple set of rules created a virtual world (Gardner 1970). Schelling, by using coins and graph paper, showed how collective behavior results when individuals interact following simple rules (Schelling 1971). Axelrod's prisoners' (Axelrod 1997) dilemma uses a game-theoretical approach to ABM and Reynolds' flocking model paved the way for the first biological ABM. Even though there were these noteworthy contributions toward the idea of an agent-based framework, this idea did not take off due to computational limitations.

The availability of computational hardware in the 1990s led to the development of various ABM software. During this period a wide gamut of literature was published, providing insights into the use of the ABM framework. Epstein and Axtell (Epstein et al. 1996) in their "Sugarscape" ABM explore social processes like pollution, reproduction, migrations, etc. Gilbert and Troitzsch (2005) in their book *Simulation for the Social Scientist* explain the use of computational models in social sciences and how to choose models for specific social problems. Holland (1992, 2001), considered to be a pioneer in the field of CAS, popularized genetic algorithms that use ideas from genetics and natural selection. Holland and Miller (1991) discuss how artificial agents can be used in economics theory and Miller and Page (2007) provide a clear idea of CAS which are considered to be a building block for ABMs. Agent-based models, which are rule-based adaptive agents interacting in dynamic environments, have strong roots in CAS. CAS look into the emergence of complex behavior when individual components interact. Examples of CAS include stock markets, ant colonies, social networks, political systems and neural systems to name a few (Miller and Page 2007). Agent-based models adopt a bottom-up approach toward modeling, deviating from the system dynamics methodology.

Agent-based models thus span a wide area of topics and are becoming popular among both the academic community and the business world. In academics, it serves as an exploratory tool, and large-scale decision support models help to answer real-world policy issues. North and Macal (2007) use EMCAS (Electricity Market Complex Adaptive System) as an example of a practical application of ABMs. EMCAS is an ABM that is used to study restructured electricity markets and deregulation. The traditional modeling frameworks (e.g., models of economic markets) require a lot of assumptions in order to solve the problems analytically, thus not providing a realistic view. The widespread adoption of ABM confirms the need for a different approach towards capturing complexities observed in the real world.

## ABM in HLSCM

The 2004 Indian Ocean tsunami, 2005 hurricane Katrina and the 2010 earthquake in Haiti showed the complexity of relief operations as well as the limitations of our logistical strategies. Both natural disasters and manmade disasters (e.g., The Syrian crisis) (Bilbao-Osorio et al. 2013) are increasing; hence, it is of paramount importance to rethink our current HLSCM policies. This includes the complex decision-making processes that result from the interaction of multiple agencies (both government and nongovernment) involved in relief, which often lead to imperfect information sharing and lack of preparedness, affecting the quality of aid delivery. Bui et al. (2000) mention that the quality of aid delivery can be affected also by multiple factors such as negotiating style of agencies, impact of scarce resources that need to be distributed, nature of aid and so on. Aid delivery is thus a complex system where multiple actors interact within an environment with time constraints and high levels of uncertainty. ABM is thus well suited for this because it helps to capture the complexity observed in humanitarian operations.

### Collaboration, Coordination and Cooperation

We begin this section by emphasizing the importance of collaboration, coordination and cooperation in supply chains in general and then show how ABMs can be applied to study them in HLSCM. We understand that supply chain management is a core competency of an organization, which deals with the efficient management of the various stakeholders in the supply chain (Oliveira et al. 2016). Choi et al. (2001) make a valid point by calling the supply network (supplier ↔ customer) as a CAS (Miller and Page 2007) and that managers who control this network need to balance between control and giving a free hand to the multiple entities within the supply network. Sterman (2015) talk about the dynamics of supply chains and raises the question whether the dynamics observed are the consequences of operational or behavioral causes. Supply chain management has moved from an arm's length approach to an integrated partnership approach (Albino et al. 2007) wherein stakeholders form strategic partnerships and share both risks and benefits. The beer simulation game (Sterman 1989a) showed the need for information sharing and cooperation within a supply chain. Bendoly et al. (2010) emphasize the need to explore the interaction of human behavior and operational activities in order to understand its impact on performance. The field of behavioral operations management (Bendoly et al. 2015) thus talks about the complexities and dynamics observed in supply chains and the need to incorporate human factors in the operational context.

Albino et al. (2006, 2007) use ABM to study cooperation and innovation in industrial districts (IDs). IDs can be defined as a cluster (Porter 1998) of firms that interact to create a product or service. The authors (Albino et al. 2006) posit that IDs are like CAS and the innovation processes within IDs can be modeled using ABM which can in turn help improve their capabilities and stay competitive. Albino et al. ( 2007) also use ABM to study cooperation within IDs, that is, how cooperation between firms can help balance supplier production capacity utilization and at the same time minimize customer unsatisfied demand.

Ortuno et al. (2013) while talking about humanitarian decision support tools describe the complex and cumbersome nature of collaborations in disaster management. In this context Menth and Stamm (2015) use ABM to study a facility location problem (FLP). The authors study the FLP by using data collected from the 2015 Nepal earthquake. They show the need to improve coordination among various aid agencies to not only efficiently locate its facilities, that is, preposition inventories, but also for equity in the distribution of aid. Menth and Stamm show how ABMs can capture the complexities observed and help improve coordination efforts (i.e., when over 400 aid organizations are involved in relief work). Rubel (2014) uses ABM as a tool to study fleet allocation issues in humanitarian relief operations. The author uses ABM to analyze the effects of resource allocation when dealing with resource constraints. The study shows how ABM provides flexibility when compared with traditional models such as linear programming and dynamic linear programming. Altay and Pal (2014) study and apply ABM on the United Nations cluster approach to disaster management. They show through multiple agent-based models that if clusters are utilized properly would aid in better information flow in turn resulting in effective response to disasters. Clusters were created to ensure coordinated actions since information exchange makes coordination a difficult endeavor. Altay and Patel show through their simulation that if managed efficiently information diffuses faster, which leads to a better humanitarian response.

## Decision Support System

Oliveira et al. (2016) through a systematic literature review show the complexities that one can observe in a supply chain and voice the need for the use of computational modeling and simulation as a decision support tool for managers. In this context, many researches have used ABMs to addresses such complexity. Julka et al. (2002) emphasize the need for decision support systems and propose an agent-based supply chain management framework. The authors then apply this framework to a refinery and show how this decision support system aids in understanding the effects of policy changes, external environment and more on the overall refinery business (Julka et al. 2002). Forget et al. (2009) study supply chain planning and use ABM as a simulation methodology for a lumber supply chain. In a similar vein, Garcia-Flores and Wang (2002) use ABM as a management support system for a chemical supply chain. Amini et al. (2012) use ABM to study the interaction between new product diffusion and supply chain production-sales policies. Chaturvedi et al. (2014) discuss the need of coordination and cooperation within the food supply chain and use ABM as a tool to provide a decision support system for food defense training and analysis. Fiedrich and Burghardt (2007) elucidate the advantages of agent technology and how it could be used as a tool to support decision making.

Disaster or humanitarian operations involve time constraints, high levels of uncertainty and collaboration among multiple agencies. Ortuno et al. (2013) classify agencies involved in disaster aid as (1) local – first response from local authorities; (2) national – federal governments, army, etc. fall under this category; and finally (3) international – international governments and international agencies such as UN, WHO, etc. fall under this category and come into picture when national capacity does not suffice. In this context, Ortuno et al. (2013) discuss decision aid systems and give Humanitarian Logistics Software (HLS) and HELIOS (an open source IT solution for humanitarian supply chain named after a Greek god) as examples of humanitarian decision aid tools that were developed at the Fritz Institute in collaboration with the IFRC. These tools show how agent-based technology can be used to provide organizations with real time data to improve humanitarian relief operations.

## Optimization

Barbati et al. (2012) and Bruzzone (2005) show how ABM can be used as an optimization tool for applications such as scheduling, supply chain planning, distributed logistics, transportation networks and so on. Balcik et al. (2008) use optimization to solve last mile distribution problem, that is, the final stage of humanitarian relief where resources are distributed from local distribution centers to disaster regions. The authors conclude by saying that there is a huge potential for intelligent transportation systems to carry out last mile distribution. This is a classic application of ABM as an optimization tool as shown by Rubel (2014) who use ABM to understand fleet allocation in humanitarian operations under resource constraints. The author shows how ABM of this problem provides better flexibility than traditional optimization approaches.

ABM has thus been used to study the dynamics observed in the supply chain and applied to various industries. Oliveira et al. (2016) in their systematic literature review add that ABM addresses the limitations of discrete event simulation (Siebers et al. 2010; Banks et al. 2004), in that it captures the dynamics and complexities one can observe in a supply chain.

Thus all of the above-mentioned papers bring in the behavioral perspective in humanitarian supply chains and how ABM can help understand these dynamics.

## Issues and Opportunities with ABM

Here we illustrate the challenges researchers might face while using ABM as a methodology and some considerations particular to HLSCM.

### Modeling and Implementation

Other than the above-mentioned papers, ABM has not been extensively used in HLSCM. The previous sections elucidated the use and permeation of ABM as a framework to study supply chain management issues and how it is used in the context of HLSCM. As clearly seen from literature (Oliveira et al. 2016), ABM has not been adopted as a methodology but it is gaining traction. The advent of behavioral operations (Bendoly et al. 2010) and the influence of psychological and behavioral factors of decision making on operational performances make ABM an apt framework to understand the complex dynamics researchers observe in HLSCM. Strengths of ABM include modularity, decentralization (i.e., stand-alone, does not need continuous direction) and ability to capture complexity. It is also suitable when we are looking at heterogeneous (Bonabeau 2002; Samuelson and Macal 2006) intelligent entities, for example, organizations within a humanitarian supply chain who learn and adapt based on the needs of the environment.

One of the main challenges with ABM in the context of humanitarian operations is whether to model a system or consider a specific problem. Modeling a system is a tedious and cumbersome process which involves both computational infrastructure and programmers who understand the various stakeholders in humanitarian operations. HLS and HELIOS (Ortuño et al. 2013) are examples of decision support systems in HLSCM, which involve multiple organizations and huge investments. For researchers entering the ABM world it is recommended that they address specific problems within HLSCM like Rubel (2014) and build confidence in the use of ABM for HLSCM issues. This should be the first step as ABM in HLSCM is a nascent field and not much literature or information is available. For example, Zheng et al. (2013) look into the application of ABM in transportation problems, that is, traffic control and management based on real-time traffic data, route choice behaviors and so on. This will be a good starting point for researchers trying to address transportation or last mile distribution problems in humanitarian logistics.

Researchers should give careful thought on the use of ABM as it is a bottom-up approach, that is, local knowledge governs the actions of agents; hence, global optimal results are difficult to achieve, thus the need to carefully understand the problem before venturing into modeling and implementation of humanitarian operations. If the goal is to optimize a system parameter within humanitarian operations, then ABM will not be an apt tool for such a problem but should be used in tandem with other methodological approaches to validate the agent-based model.

## Validation and Verification

As with any modeling framework, ABM is not devoid of limitations. Simulation of complex systems requires computational power and even more so when considering complex actors within a supply chain. Defining complex characteristics and coming up with decision rules when considering human factors will be challenging and often requires behavioral data which in many cases are difficult to obtain. Also, another limitation is the validation of such models especially if they are used to predict behavior. The lack of behavioral data and the sensitivity of such data especially in humanitarian operations are major challenges in the validation and verification of ABMs. Experimental methods can be used in tandem with ABM to validate and verify the results of such models (Sankaranarayanan 2011). It is very difficult to validate an ABM if it is used to predict behavior of an untested system. Calibration is also difficult because the influence of individual behavior on the overall behavior of the system is not completely understood.

ABM has its pros and cons but has started making its presence known and can thus be used to study emergent behaviors in complex humanitarian supply chains. It can also help in building decision support tools for policy makers and decision makers to analyze and calibrate various situations.

# Summary of Findings and Directions for Future Research

Van Wassenhove (2006) in his 2005 Blackett memorial lecture define logistics in the context of humanitarian operations as "the processes and systems involved in mobilizing people, resources, skills and knowledge to help vulnerable people affected by disaster." He emphasizes the fact that logistics is a major factor in humanitarian relief and the need for collaboration between private sector as well as operations researchers. The author concludes by saying that operations researchers can help in the design of processes, manage risks, measure performance, standardize processes as well as efficiently coordinate relief operations.

This chapter is a starting point to bridge this gap and explores the application of three methodological tools, that is, behavioral experiments, system dynamics and ABM, to study behavior observed in HLSCM. Through an elaborated literature review on all three methodologies we provide readers not only with a quick review of the methods but also with what to consider when using these tools to understand the complex dynamics observed in HLSCM. We believe that this chapter will help scholars who are entering the field of HLSCM understand the intricacies of the field as well as how to use these tools in tandem to build confidence in their models.

## Behavioral Experiments

The surveyed works suggest that behavioral experiments are more suitable to study decision problems that happen away from the operations taking place in the field during the response phase of a disaster. This is not surprising since the conditions during a disaster response are difficult to simulate in the controlled environment where behavioral experiments take place.

Donation experiments show that framing and recency effects matter a great deal when individuals face aid allocation-related problems. The controlled nature of behavioral experiments could help test also how media framing (Tierney et al. 2006) affects donation behavior. Impression management is likely to play a role as well (Elsbach 2003), and behavioral experiments could help test how impression management and its combination with media framing affect donation behavior. Behavioral experiments could help test also issues related with material convergence (Holguín-Veras et al. 2014). For example, strategies that aim to change donor behavior to mitigate the negative impact of material convergence could be tested with behavioral experiments.

Gralla and colleagues' and Muhren and Van de Walle's studies are noteworthy, given their high degrees of external validity compared with the other studies reviewed here. Strictly speaking, they lack some elements of formal experimentation like randomization since they are one-treatment experiments. However, they could still be seen as experiments since they simulate an emergency scenario and observe how participants respond to it, much like any supply chain management experiment where researches simulate a supply chain and observe how participants make decisions in the simulation. Similar exercises simulating disasters of different types and magnitudes could generate insights to improve and customize emergency training programs.

The remaining experiments on planning and development show that individuals facing HLSCM problems are prone to systematic decision-making biases. Prepositioning frameworks are gaining attention (e.g., Balcik and Beamon 2008; Campbell and Jones 2011; Rawls and Turnquist 2012) and behavioral experiments could help systematically test how the different environmental factors included in these frameworks affect prepositioning decisions. For example, one could design a behavioral experiment to explore how Campbell and Jones (2011)'s destruction risk factor impacts prepositioning decisions. Behavioral supply chain contracts studies are also gaining attention in recent years (e.g., Katok and Wu 2009; Wu and Chen 2014). Work in development could use these studies as an anchor and start testing how different contracting mechanisms can leverage local markets. For example, they could test which contracting mechanisms are more effective and how contextual factors such as preferences associated with culture and/or the environment (e.g., levels of trust in developing economies may be low due to poor governance structures) impinge on the effectiveness of those mechanisms.

## System Dynamics

The surveyed works suggest system dynamics is a methodology that is especially useful when we have competing objectives or dynamics. This method enables the identification of poor system responses as well as the identification of the feedback dynamics that lead to such a poor response. Understanding the feedback dynamics allows evaluation of alternative policies and the creation of a coherent recommendations for change.

For example, one of the most interesting application is the humanitarian sectors focus on the relationship between the long-term versus short-term dynamics. Results highlight the importance of creating a proper set of strategies that lead to a good balance between short-term and long-term needs. Because a myopic vision of the problem together with rigid policies may lead to duplication of efforts affecting the future development of system, making local communities more vulnerable to short-term inefficiencies and long-term threats.

Similarly, the fleet management studies show that one of the main challenges is to decide among three different vehicle fleet management systems (centralized, hybrid and decentralized) to properly satisfy the needs (short response time or cost efficiency) of either relief or development programs. General results show that identifying the feedback loops and expected delays enable the estimation of accurate fleet capacity to satisfy programs' needs.

Finally, the direct trade-off between competition and coordination poses an additional challenge to humanitarian organizations. Main results obtained by analyzing the feedback dynamics during relief operations highlight the importance of pre-stablishing partnerships that able a fast and coordinated response, especially during the first hours after a crisis.

Therefore, this methodology will be suitable to identify the main unintended consequences and formulate feasible policies for situations where decision makers face confronting or competing objectives. In the humanitarian sector, we see additional applications that might be important to evaluate. For example, (i) understanding the dynamics of providing in-kind versus cash support to program beneficiaries, (ii) understanding donors' perceived benefits when they support either development or relief programs in an environment where media attention may affect the overall dynamics and (iii) the evaluation of the trade-off between earmarked and non-earmarked funding in both relief and development programs.

## Agent-Based Modeling

Section "ABM in HLSCM" summarized the literature that utilizes ABM as a methodology to study and further humanitarian operations. A key theme that emerges out of this literature review is that humanitarian relief efforts include complex decision-making processes which involve multiple actors. This thought process is well echoed by Muggy and Stamm (2014), wherein they talk about the decentralized nature of humanitarian operations and how it acts as a hurdle to provide relief. Muggy and Stamm emphasize the need to integrate game-theoretical concepts to humanitarian operations in order to better understand strategies with respect to collaboration, coordination and cooperation. The authors provide an extensive literature review on the applications of game-theoretical concepts in humanitarian relief operations.

ABM which can include game-theoretical strategies to understand emergence of collective behavior from individual decision making is a good choice to study complexities and dynamics observed in humanitarian operations. Albino et al. (2006) use ABM in IDs (cluster of firms) to study cooperation and show how it can improve capacity utilization and minimize customer unsatisfied demand. Menth and Stamm (2015) use ABM to show the need to improve coordination among aid agencies by using data collected from the 2015 Nepal earthquake. Oliveira et al. (2016) and Ortuno et al. (2013) along with describing the complexity observed in a supply chain emphasize the need to use computational models as decision support tools. Julka et al. (2002b) propose and apply such an ABM framework to a refinery and show its usefulness in understanding effects of policy changes, environmental factors and so on.

ABM can be combined with other concepts. For example, game-theoretical concepts can be used in agent-based models to study how individual decision making in terms of information sharing (information is valuable in humanitarian operations and one who has access to this information has a strategic advantage) can affect relief work. Also, experimental methods can be used to validate and verify agent-based models as shown by Sankaranarayanan (2011, 2014). Laite et al. (2016) use experimental data to train a neural network in order to understand behavioral aspects in service channels. This work is based on ABM wherein the authors try to understand service channel system behavior based on individual choices made by subjects who participated in a controlled experiment.

The main challenges practitioners and researchers encounter in the context of humanitarian operations include unreliable transportation, poor communication infrastructure, decentralized network, that is, multiple agencies making decisions to optimize own objectives with local information, etc. All of these can be modeled using ABM to visualize humanitarian relief networks, strategies that would help provide relief with the above-mentioned constraints and decision support tools for all agencies involved to collaborate and coordinate humanitarian operations. Section "ABM in HLSCM" shows the current literature, avenues to improve and how ABM could be used as one of the tools to improve our understanding of the complexities and dynamics one observes when dealing with humanitarian efforts.

# References

Abosuliman, Shougi Suliman Hassn. 2014. "A System Dynamics & Emergency Logistics Model for Post-Disaster Relief Operations." Melbourne, Victoria: RMIT University.

Albino, Vito, Nunzia Carbonara, and Ilaria Giannoccaro. 2006. "Innovation in industrial districts: An agent-based simulation model." *International Journal of Production Economics* 104 (1): 30–45.

Albino, Vito, Nunzia Carbonara, and Ilaria Giannoccaro. 2007. "Supply Chain Cooperation in Industrial Districts: A Simulation Analysis." *European Journal of Operational Research* 177 (1): 261–280.

Altay, N., and R. Pal. 2014. "Information Diffusion Among Agents: Implications for Humanitarian Operations." *Production and Operations Management* 23 (6): 1015–1027.

Amini, Mehdi, Tina Wakolbinger, Michael Racer, and Mohammad G. Nejad. 2012. "Alternative Supply Chain Production–Sales Policies for New Product Diffusion: An Agent-Based Modeling and Simulation Approach." *European Journal of Operational Research* 216 (2): 301–311.

Arango, S., J. A. Castañeda, and Y. Olaya. 2012. "Laboratory Experiments in the System Dynamics Field." *System Dynamics Review* 28 (1): 94–106.

Arango, S., J. A. Castañeda, and E. R. Larsen. 2013. "Mothballing in Power Markets: An Experimental Study." *Energy Economics* 36 (Elsevier B.V.): 125–134.

Argyris, C. 1985. *Strategy, Change and Defensive Routines.* New York, NY: Harper Business.

Arkes, H. 1991. "Cost and Benefits of Judgment Errors: Implications for Debiasing." *Psychological Bulletin* 110 (3): 486–498.

Axelrod, Robert M. 1997. *The Complexity of Cooperation: Agent-Based Models of Competition and Collaboration.* Princeton, NJ: Princeton University Press.

Balcik, B., and B. M. Beamon. 2008. "Facility Location in Humanitarian Relief." *International Journal of Logistics: Research and Applications* 11 (2): 101–121.

Balcik, Burcu, Benita M. Beamon., Caroline C. Krejci., Kyle M. Muramatsu., and Magaly Ramirez. 2010. "Coordination in Humanitarian Relief Chains: Practices, Challenges and Opportunities." *International Journal of Production Economics* 126 (1): 22–34.

Banerjee, A. V., and E. Duflo. 2011. *Poor Economics: Barefoot Hedge-Fund Managers, DIY Doctors and the Surprising Truth About Life on Less than $1 a Day.* New York, NY: Penguin Books.

Banks, J., J. S. Carson, B. L. Nelson, and D. M. Nicol. 2004. *Discrete-Event System Simulation*. 4 ed. Upper Saddle: Prentice-Hall.

Barbati, M., G. Bruno, and A. Genovese. 2012. "Applications of Agent-Based Models for Optimization Problems: A Literature Review." *Expert Systems with Applications* 39 (5): 6020–6028.

Barlas, Yaman. 1996. "Formal Aspects of Model Validity and Validation in System Dynamics." *System Dynamics Review* 12 (3): 183–210.

Barlas, Yaman. 2007. "Leverage Points to March 'upward from the Aimless Plateau.'" *System Dynamics Review* 23 (4): 469–473.

Beamon, Benita. M., and Burcu Balcik. 2008. "Performance Measurement in Humanitarian Relief Chains." *International Journal of Public Sector Management* 21 (1): 4–25.

Becker-Peth, M., E. Katok, and U. W. Thonemann. 2013. "Designing Buyback Contracts for Irrational But Predictable Newsvendors." *Management Science* 59 (8): 1800–1816.

Bendoly, E., R. Croson, P. Gonçalves, and K. Schultz. 2010. "Bodies of Knowledge for Research in Behavioral Operations." *Production and Operations Management* 19 (4): 434–452.

Bendoly, Elliot, Wout van Wezel, and Daniel G. Bachrach. 2015. *The Handbook of Behavioral Operations Management: Social and Psychological Dynamics in Production and Service Settings*. Oxford University Press, New York, NY.

Besiou, M., and L. N. Van Wassenhove. 2015. "Addressing the Challenge of Modeling for Decision-Making in Socially Responsible Operations." *Production and Operations Management* 24 (9): 1390–1401.

Besiou, M., O. Stapleton, and L. N. van Wassenhove. 2010. "Exploring the Known and the Unknown: Future Possibilities of System Dynamics for Humanitarian Operations." *INSEAD Working Paper 2010/74/TOM/ISIC*.

Besiou, M., A. Pedraza-Martinez, and L. N. van Wassenhove. 2014. "Vehicle Supply Chains in Humanitarian Operations: Decentralization, Operational Mix, and Earmarked Funding." *Production and Operations Management* 23 (11): 1950–1965.

Bilbao-Osorio, Beñat, Soumitra Dutta, and Bruno Lanvin. 2013. The global information technology report 2013.

Bolton, G. E., A. Ockenfels, and U. W. Thonemann. 2012. "Managers and Students as Newsvendors." *Management Science* 58(12): 2225–2233.

Bonabeau, E. 2002. "Agent-Based Modeling: Methods and Techniques for Simulating Human Systems." *Proceedings of the National Academy of Sciences of the United States of America* 99: 7280–7287.

Brase, G. L. 2009. "How Different Types of Participant Payments Alter Task Performance." *Judgment and Decision Making* 4(5): 419–428.

Bruzzone, A. G. 2005. "Agent Directed HLA Simulation for Complex Supply Chain Modeling." *Simulation* 81 (9): 647–655.

Bui, Tung, Sungwon Cho, Siva Sankaran, and Michael Sovereign. 2000. "A Framework for Designing a Global Information Network for Multinational Humanitarian Assistance/Disaster Relief." *Information Systems Frontiers* 1 (4): 427–442.

Camerer, C. F., and R. M. Hogarth. 1999. "The Effects of Financial Incentives in Experiments: A Review and Capital-Labor Production Framework." *Journal of Risk and Uncertainty* 19(1–3): 7–42.

Campbell, A. M., and P. C. Jones. 2011. "Prepositioning Supplies in Preparation for Disasters." *European Journal of Operational Research* 209(2): 156–165.

Castañeda, J. A., M. E. Brennan, and J. Goentzel. 2016. Supply Chain Contract Design for a Newsvendor Problem in a Developing Economy. Working paper, MIT, Cambridge, MA.

Casti, John L. 1997. *Would-Be Worlds: How Simulation Is Changing the Frontiers of Science*. New York; Chichester: Wiley.

Chaturvedi, Alok, Brian Armstrong, and Rashmi Chaturvedi. 2014. "Securing the Food Supply Chain: Understanding Complex Interdependence Through Agent-Based Simulation." *Health and Technology* 4 (2): 159–169.

Choi, T. Y., K. J. Dooley, and M. Rungtusanatham. 2001. "Supply Networks and Complex Adaptive Systems: Control Versus Emergence." *Journal of Operations Management* 19 (3): 351–366.

Chomilier, Bernard, Ramina Samii, and L. N. van Wassenhove. 2000. "The Central Role of Supply Chain Management at IFRC." *Forced Mitigation Review* 18 (1): 15–16.

Croson, R., and K. L. Donohue. 2006. "Behavioral Causes of the Bullwhip Effect and the Observed Value of Inventory Information." *Management Science* 52(3): 323–336.

Croson, R. T. A., F. Handy, and J. Shang. 2010. "Gendered Giving: The Influence of Social Norms on the Donation Behavior of Men and Women." *International Journal of Nonprofit and Voluntary Sector Marketing* 15(2): 199–213.

Cruz-Cantillo, Yesenia. 2014. "A System Dynamics Approach to Humanitarian Logistics and the Transportation of Relief Supplies." *International Journal of System Dynamics Applications* 3 (3): 96–126.

Day, J. M., S. A. Melnyk, P. D. Larson, E. W. Davis, and D. C. Whybark. 2012. "Humanitarian and Disaster Relief Supply Chains: A Matter of Life and Death." *Journal of Supply Chain Management* 48(2): 21–36.

Diehl, E., and J. D. Sterman. 1995. "Effects of Feedback Complexity on Dynamic Decision Making." *Organizational Behavior and Human Decision Processes* 62 (2): 198–215.

Dispartite, D. 2007. "The Postmans Parallel." *Car Nation* 1: 22–27.

Dolinskaya, Irina S., Zhenyu Edwin Shi, Karen R. Smilowitz, and Michael Ross. 2011. "Decentralized Approaches to Logistics Coordination in Humanitarian Relief." In *The 2011 Industrial Engineering Research Conference*. Reno, Nev.

Donohue, K. L., and R. Croson. 2002. "Experimental Economics and Supply-Chain Management." *Interfaces* 32 (5): 74–82.

Einhorn, H. J., and R. M. Hogarth. 1981. "Behavioral Decision Theory: Processes of Judgement and Choice." *Annual Review of Psychology* 32 (1): 53–88.

Elsbach, K. D. 2003. "Organizational Perception Management." In *Research in Organizational Behavior*, edited by R. M. Kramer, B. M. Staw, 297–332. Greenwich, CT: JAI Press.

Epstein, Joshua M., Robert L. Axtell, and Brookings Institution. 1996. *Growing Artificial Societies: Social Science from the Bottom Up; A Product of the 2050 Project, a Collaborative Effort of the Brookings Institution, the Santa Fe Institute, and the World Resources Institute*. Washington, DC: Brookings Institute Press

Evangelidis, I., and B. Van den Bergh. 2013. "The Number of Fatalities Drives Disaster Aid: Increasing Sensitivity to People in Need." *Psychological Science* 24(11): 2226–2234.

Fiedrich, Frank, and Paul Burghardt. 2007. "Agent-Based Systems for Disaster Management." *Communications of the ACM* 50 (3): 41.

Ford, J. K., and A. M. Schmidt. 2000. "Emergency Response Training: Strategies for Enhancing Real-World Performance." *Journal of Hazardous Materials* 75(2–3): 195–215.

Forget, Pascal, Sophie D'Amours, Jean-Marc Frayret, and Jonathan Gaudreault. 2009. "Study of the Performance of Multi-behaviour Agents for Supply Chain Planning." *Computers in Industry* 60 (9): 698–708.

Forrester, J. W. 1958. "Industrial Dynamics – A Major Breakthrough for Decision Makers." *Harvard Business Review* 36 (4): 37–66.

Forrester, J. W. 1961. *Industrial Dynamics*. Cambridge, Massachusetts: MIT Press.

Forrester, J. W. 2007. "System Dynamics – The Next Fifty Years." *System Dynamics Review* 23 (2/3): 359–370. doi:10.1002/sdr.

Forrester, J. W., and Peter Senge. 1980. "Test for Building Confidence in System Dynamic Models." *TIMS Studies in the Management Sciences* 14 (1): 209–228.

García-Flores, Rodolfo, and Xue Zhong Wang. 2002. "A Multi-agent System for Chemical Supply Chain Simulation and Management Support." *OR Spectrum* 24 (3): 343–370.

Gardner, Martin. 1970. "Mathematical Games: The Fantastic Combinations of John Conway's New Solitaire Game 'Life'." *Scientific American* 223 (4): 120–123.

George, A. 2003. "Using Accountability to Improve Reproductive Health Care." *Reproductive Health Matters* 11 (21): 161–170.

Gilbert, G. Nigel, and Klaus G. Troitzsch. 2005. *Simulation for the Social Scientist*. Vol. 2nd. New York; Maidenhead, England: Open University Press.

Gonçalves, P. 2008. "System Dynamics Modeling of Humanitarian Relief Operations." *MIT Sloan School Working Paper 4704-08*.

Gonçalves, P. 2011. "Balancing Provision of Relief and Recovery with Capacity Building in Humanitarian Operations." *Operations Management Research* 4 (1–2): 39–50.

Gonçalves, P., and J. A. Castañeda. 2016. Stockpiling Supplies for Disaster Response: An Experimental Analysis of Prepositioning Biases. Working paper, Università della Svizzera italiana (USI, Lugano), Lugano, Switzerland.

Gonçalves, P., and S. Villa. 2016. "Implications of Misperception of Feedback on Behavior in Operations." In *Behavioural Operational Research: Theory, Methodology and Practice*, edited by M. Kunc, J. Malpass, and L. White. London, UK: Palgrave Publishers.

Gralla, E. L., J. Goentzel, and B. Chomilier. 2015. "Case Study of a Humanitarian Logistics Simulation Exercise and Insights for Training Design." *Journal of Humanitarian Logistics and Supply Chain Management* 5(1): 113–138.

Gralla, E. L., J. Goentzel, and C. Fine 2016. "Problem Formulation and Solution Mechanisms: A Behavioral Study of Humanitarian Transportation Planning." *Production and Operations Management* 25(1): 22–35.

Guala, F. 2005. *The Methodology of Experimental Economics*. Cambridge: Cambridge University Press.

Gutowitz, Howard. 1991. *Cellular Automata: Theory and Experiment*. 1. MIT Press ed. Cambridge, Mass.: MIT Press.

Heims, Steve, John von Neumann, and Norbert Wiener. 1984. *John von Neumann and Norbert Wiener: From Mathematics to the Technologies of Life and Death*. 2. printing. ed. Cambridge, Mass.: MIT Press.

Hertwig, R., and A. Ortmann. 2001. "Experimental Practices in Economics: A Methodological Challenge for Psychologists?" *Behavioral and Brain Sciences* 24(3): 383–403.

Hey, J. D. 1996. *Experimentos en Economía*. México, D.F.: Fondo de Cultura Económica.

Heyman, J., and D. Ariely. 2004. "Effort for Payment: A Tale of Two Markets." *Psychological Science*, 15(11): 787–793.

Holguín-Veras, J., M. Jaller, L. N. van Wassenhove, N. Pérez, and T. Wachtendorf. 2012. "On the Unique Features of Post-Disaster Humanitarian Logistics." *Journal of Operations Management* 30(7–8): 494–506.

Holguín-Veras, J., M. Jaller, L. Van Wassenhove, N. Pérez, and T. Wachtendorf. 2014. "Material Convergence: Important and Understudied Disaster Phenomenon." *Natural Hazards Review* 15(1): 1–12.

Holland, J. H. 1992. "Genetic Algorithms." *Scientific American* 267 (1): 66–72.

Holland, J. H., and J. H. Miller. 1991. "Artificial Adaptive Agents in Economic-Theory." *American Economic Review* 81 (2): 365–370.

Holland, John H. 2001. *Adaptation in Natural and Artificial Systems: An Introductory Analysis with Applications to Biology, Control, and Artificial Intelligence*. 6. printing. ed. Cambridge: MIT Press.

Huber, M., L. Van Boven, A. P. McGraw, and L. Johnson-Graham. 2011. "Whom to Help? Immediacy Bias in Judgments and Decisions About Humanitarian Aid." *Organizational Behavior and Human Decision Processes* 115(2): 283–293.

Julka, Nirupam, Rajagopalan Srinivasan, and I. Karimi. 2002a. "Agent-Based Supply Chain Management—1: Framework." *Computers & Chemical Engineering* 26 (12): 1755–1769.

Julka, Nirupam, I. Karimi, and Rajagopalan Srinivasan. 2002b. "Agent-Based Supply Chain Management—2: A Refinery Application." *Computers & Chemical Engineering* 26 (12): 1771–1781.

Kaatrud, David B., Ramina Samii, and L. N. van Wassenhove. 2003. "UN Joint Logistics Centre: A Coordinated Response to Common Humanitarian Logistics Concerns." *Forced Migration Review* 18 (1): 11–18.

Katok, E. 2010. "Using Laboratory Experiments to Build Better Operations Management Models." *Foundations and Trends in Technology, Information and Operations Management* 5(1): 1–84.

Katok, E., and D. Y. Wu. 2009. "Contracting in Supply Chains: A Laboratory Investigation." *Management Science* 55(12): 1953–1968.

Kent, R. C. 1987. *Anatomy of disaster relief: The international network in action.* London, UK: Pinter.

Kleinmuntz, D., and J. Thomas. 1987. "The value of action and inference in dynamic decision making". *Organizational Behavior and Human Decision Processes* 39 (3): 341–364.

Kogut, T., and I. Ritov. 2005. "The 'Identified Victim' Effect: An Identified Group, or Just a Single Individual?" *Journal of Behavioral Decision Making* 18(3): 157–167.

Kogut, T., and I. Ritov. 2007. "'One of Us': Outstanding Willingness to Help Save a Single Identified Compatriot." *Organizational Behavior and Human Decision Processes* 104(2): 150–157.

Kremer, M., S. Minner, and L. N. van Wassenhove. 2010. "Do Random Errors Explain Newsvendor Behavior?" *Manufacturing & Service Operations Management* 12(4): 673–681.

Laite, Ralph, Nataliya Portman, and Karthik Sankaranarayanan. 2016. "Behavioral Analysis of Agent Based Service Channel Design Using Neural Networks." Forthcoming in the *Proceedings of the* 2016 Winter *Simulation Conference.*

Lane, David C., Eileen Munro, and Elke Husemann. 2016. "Blending Systems Thinking Approaches for Organisational Analysis: Reviewing Child Protection in England." *European Journal of Operational Research* 251 (2): 613–623.

Leiras, A., I. de Brito Jr., E. Queiroz, T. Rejane, and H. T. Yoshida. 2014. "Literature Review of Humanitarian Logistics Research: Trends and Challenges." *Journal of Humanitarian Logistics and Supply Chain Management* 4 (1): 95–130.

Macal, C. M., and M. J. North. 2006. "Tutorial on Agent-Based Modeling and Simulation Part 2: How to Model with Agents." *Proceedings of the* 2006 Winter *Simulation Conference, Vols 1–5*: 73–83.

Macal, C. M., and M. J. North. 2007. "Agent-Based Modeling and Simulation: Desktop ABMS." *Proceedings of the* 2007 Winter *Simulation Conference, Vols 1–5*: 83–94.

Mellouli, S., B. Moulin, and G. Mineau. 2003. "Laying Down the Foundations of an Agent Modelling Methodology for Fault-Tolerant Multi-agent Systems." *Engineering Societies in the Agents World Iv* 3071: 275–293.

Menth, Megan, and Jessica L. Heier Stamm. 2015. "An Agent-Based Modeling Approach to Improve Coordination Between Humanitarian Relief Providers." 2015 Winter Simulation Conference (WSC).

Mete, H. O., and Z. B. Zabinsky. 2010. "Stochastic Optimization of Medical Supply Location and Distribution in Disaster Management." *International Journal of Production Economics* 126 (1): 76–84.

Miller, John H., and Scott E. Page. 2007. *Complex Adaptive Systems: An Introduction to Computational Models of Social Life.* Princeton, NJ: Princeton University Press.

Moritz, B. B. 2010. *Cognition and Heterogeneity in Supply Chain Planning: A Study of Inventory Decision Making.* Ph.D. Dissertation, Carlson School of Management, University of Minnesota, Minneapolis, MN.

Moritz, B. B., A. V. Hill, and K. L. Donohue 2013. "Individual Differences in the Newsvendor Problem: Behavior and Cognitive Reflection." *Journal of Operations Management* 31(1–2): 72–85.

Morton, R. B., and K. C. Williams 2010. *Experimental Political Science and the Study of Causality: From Nature to the Lab.* Cambridge, U.K.: Cambridge University Press.

Muggy, Luke, L. Heier Stamm, Jessica. 2014. "Game theory applications in humanitarian operations: a review." *Journal of Humanitarian Logistics and Supply Chain Management* 4 (1): 4–23.

Muhren, W. J., and B. A. Van de Walle 2009. Sensemaking and Information Management in Humanitarian Disaster Response: Observations from the TRIPLEX Exercise. Paper presented at *6th International ISCRAM Conference on Information Systems for Crisis Response and Management*, Gothenburg, Sweden.

Ni, C., R. De Souza, Q. Lu, and M. Goh. 2015. "Emergency Preparedness of Humanitarian Organizations: A System Dynamics Approach." In *Humanitarian Logistics and Sustainability*, edited by M. Klumpp, S. de Leeuw, A. Regattieri, and R. De Souza, First.

Oliveira, J. B., R. S. Lima, and J. A. B. Montevechi. 2016. "Perspectives and Relationships in Supply Chain Simulation: A Systematic Literature Review." *Simulation Modelling Practice and Theory* 62: 166–191.

Ortuño, M. T., P. Cristóbal, J. M. Ferrer, F. J. Martín-Campo, S. Muñoz, G. Tirado, and B. Vitoriano. 2013. "Decision Aid Models and Systems for Humanitarian Logistics." *A Survey* 7: 17–44.

Osterloh, M., and B. S. Frey. 2002. "Does Pay for Performance Really Motivate Employees?" In *Business Performance Measurement: Theory and Practice*, edited by A. Neely, 107–122. Cambridge: Cambridge University Press.

Pedraza-Martinez, A., S. Hasija, and L. N. van Wassenhove. 2010. "An Operational Mechanism Design for Fleet Management Coordination in Humanitarian Operations." *INSEAD Working Paper 2010/87/TOM/ISIC.*

Pedraza-Martinez, A., O. Stapleton, and L. N. van Wassenhove. 2011. "Field Vehicle Fleet Management in Humanitarian Operations: A Case-Based Approach." *Journal of Operations Management* 29 (1): 401–421.

Peng, Min, Yi Peng, and Hong Chen. 2014. "Post-Seismic Supply Chain Risk Management: A System Dynamics Disruption Analysis Approach for Inventory and Logistics Planning." *Computers and Operations Research* 42 (Elsevier): 14–24.

Perry, J. L., D. Mesch, and L. Paalberg. 2006. "Motivating Employees in a New Governance Era: The Performance Paradigm Revisited." *Public Administration Review* 66(4): 505–514.

Porter, Michael E. 1998. "Cluster and the New Economics of Competition." *Harvard Business Review* 76 (6): 77–90.

Rawls, C. G., and M. A. Turnquist. 2010. "Pre-Positioning of Emergency Supplies for Disaster Response." *Transportation Research Part B* 44(4): 521–534.

Rawls, C. G., and M. A. Turnquist. 2012. "Pre-Positioning and Dynamic Delivery Planning for Short-Term Response Following a Natural Disaster." *Socio-Economic Planning Sciences* 46(1): 46–54.

Richardson, G. P., and A. Pugh. 1983. *Introduction to System Dynamics Modeling with DYNAMO*. Cambridge, MA: MIT Press.

Rubel, Das. 2014. "Advancement on Uncertainty Modeling in Humanitarian Logistics for Earthquake Response." *Doctoral Dissertation of Transport Studies Unit, Tokyo Institute of Technology, TSU-DC2014-007*.

Samii, Ramina. 2008. "Leveraging Logistics Partnerships: Lessons from Humanitarian Organizations." Erasmus University of Rotterdam. http://repub.eur.nl/pub/14519/.

Samuelson, D. A., and C. M. Macal. 2006. "Agent-Based Simulation Comes of Age." *ORMS Today* 33 (4): 34–38.

Sankaranarayanan, Karthik. 2011. "Study on Behavioral Patterns in Queuing." Università della Svizzera italiana.

Sankaranarayanan, K., Delgado, C., van Ackere, A. et al. 2014. "The micro-dynamics of queuing: understanding the formation of queues." *Journal of Simulation* 8 (4): 304–313.

Schelling, Thomas C. 1971. "Dynamic Models of Segregation." *Journal of Mathematical Sociology* 1 (2): 143–186.

Shang, J., A. Reed II, R. T. A. Croson. 2008. "Identity Congruency Effects on Donations." *Journal of Marketing Research* 45(3): 351–361.

Siebers, Peer-Olaf, Charles M. Macal, Jeremy Garnett, D. Buxton, and Michael Pidd. 2010. "Discrete-Event Simulation Is Dead, Long Live Agent-Based Simulation!" *Journal of Simulation* 4 (3): 204–210.

Siemsen, E. 2011. "The Usefulness of Behavioral Laboratory Experiments in Supply Chain Management Research." *Journal of Supply Chain Management* 47(3): 17–18.

Simon, Herbert Alexander. 1955. "A Behavioral Model of Rational Choice." *The Quarterly Journal of Economics* 69 (1): 99–118.

Small, D. A., Loewenstein, G. 2003. "Helping *a* Victim or Helping the Victim: Altruism and Identifiability." *Journal of Risk and Uncertainty* 26(1): 5–16.

Small, D. A., G. Loewenstein, and P. Slovic. 2007. "Sympathy and Callousness: The Impact of Deliberative Thought on Donations to Identifiable and Statistical Victims." *Organizational Behavior and Human Decision Processes* 102(2): 143–153.

Smith, V. L. 1976. "Experimental Economics: Induced Value Theory." *American Economic Review* 66(2): 274–279.

Smith, V. L. 1982. "Microeconomic Systems as an Experimental Science." *American Economic Review* 72(5): 923–955.

Smith, V. L. 1994. "Economics in the Laboratory." *Journal of Economic Perspectives* 8(1): 113–131.

Smith, V. L., and J. M. Walker. 1993. "Monetary Rewards and Decision Cost in Experimental Economics." *Economic Inquiry* 31 (2): 245–261.

Smith, P. K., and A. D. Galinsky. 2010. "The Nonconscious Nature of Power: Cues and Consequences." *Social and Personality Psychology Compass* 4 (10): 918–938.

Stephenson, M. 2005. "Making humanitarian relief networks more effective: operational coordination, trust and sensemaking." *Disasters* 29 (4): 337–350.

Sterman, J. D. 1989a. "Misperceptions of Feedback in Dynamic Decision Making." *Organizational Behavior and Human Decision Processes* 43 (3): 301–335.

Sterman, J. D. 1989b. "Modeling Managerial Behavior: Misperceptions of Feedback in a Dynamic Decision Making Experiment." *Management Science* 35 (3): 321–339.

Sterman, J. D. 2000. *Business Dynamics: Systems Thinking* and *Modeling for a Complex World*. Chicago, Illinois: Irwin-McGraw Hill.

Sterman, J. D. 2001. "System Dynamics Modeling: Tools for Learning in a Complex World." *California Management Review* 43 (4): 8–25.

Sterman, John. 2015. "Booms, Busts, and Beer: Understanding the Dynamics of Supply Chains." In *The Handbook of Behavioral Operations Management: Social and Psychological Dynamics in Production and Service Settings*, edited by Elliot Bendoly, Wout van Wezel and Daniel G. Bachrach. Oxford University Press.

Tierney, K., C. Bevc, and E. Kuligowski. 2006. "Metaphors Matter: Disaster Myths, Media Frames, and Their Consequences in Hurricane Katrina." *Annals of the American Academy of Political and Social Science* 604(1): 57–81.

Tomasini, R. 2012. "Humanitarian Partnerships – Drivers, Facilitators, and Components: The Case of Non-food Item Distribution in Sudan." In *Relief Supply Chain Management for Disasters: Humanitarian Aid and Emergency Logistics*, edited by G. Kovács and K. Spens, 1st ed., 16–30. Hershey PA 17033, USA: IGI Global.

Tversky, A., and Daniel Kahneman. 1974. "Judgment under Uncertainty: Heuristics and Biases." *Science (New York, N.Y.)* 185 (4157): 1124–1131.

Urrea, G., S. Villa, and P. Gonçalves. 2016. "Exploratory Analyses of Relief and Development Ops Using Social Networks." *Socio-Economic Planning Science* 56 (1): 27–39.

van den Belt, M. 2004. *Mediated Modeling: A System Dynamics Approach to Environmental Consensus Building*. Washington DC: Island Pre.

van Wassenhove, L. N. 2006. "Humanitarian Aid Logistics: Supply Chain Management in High Gear." *Journal of the Operational Research Society* 57 (1): 475–489.

van Wassenhove, L. N., and M. Besiou. 2013. "Complex Problems with Multiple Stakeholders: How to Bridge the Gap Between Reality and OR/MS?" *Business Economics* 83 (1): 87–97.

Vennix, J. A. 1996. *Group Model-Building: Facilitating Team Learning Using System Dynamics*. Chichester: Wiley.

Villa, S., P. Gonçalves, and S. Arango. 2015. "Exploring Retailers' Ordering Decisions Under Delays." *System Dynamics Review* 31 (1): 1–27.

Voyer, J., M. Dean, and C. Pickles. 2015. "Understanding Humanitarian Supply Chain Logistics with System Dynamics Modeling." Portland, ME.

Wakolbinger, T., and F. Toyasaki. 2011. "Impacts of Funding Systems on Humanitarian Operations." In *Humanitarian Logistics. Meeting the Challenge of Preparing For and Responding to Disasters*, edited by M. G. Christopher and P. H. Tatham, 41–56. London: Kogan Page Limited.

Wang, Xuping, Qi Wang, and Mingtian Chen. 2012. "System Dynamics Model of Unconventional Emergency Resource Coordination System." In *Proceedings of the* 2012 5th International Joint Conference on Computational Sciences and Optimization, CSO *2012*, 271–275.

Wolfram, Stephen. 2002. *Cellular Automata and Complexity: Collected Papers*. [Nachdr.] ed. Boulder, Co: Westview-Press.

Wu, D. Y., and K.-Y. Chen. 2014. "Supply Chain Contract Design: Impact of Bounded Rationality and Individual Heterogeneity." *Production and Operations Management* 23(2): 253–268.

Zheng, Hong, Young-Jun Son, Yi-Chang Chiu, Larry Head, Yiheng Feng, Hui Xi, Sojung Kim, and Mark Hickman. 2013. "A Primer for Agent-Based Simulation and Modeling in Transportation Applications." Technical Report of the U.S. Department of Transportation, (No. FHWA-HRT-13-054).

# Part II

## More Established Empirical Methods

# 4

# Challenges and Opportunities for Humanitarian Researchers: Dreadful Biases and Heavenly Combinations of Mixed Methods

Pervaiz Akhtar

## Introduction

This chapter first presents the nature of humanitarian operations with three different scenarios. It then links them with mixed methods; case studies coupled with analytic hierarchy/network processes; surveys combined with in-depth interviews, experimental designs and machine learning techniques. It argues that these choices and combinations influence the quality of humanitarian research that is linked with result-oriented research designs and effective data collection choices, leading to convincing and valid findings to resolve realistic problems. Although these heavenly qualitative and quantitative research combinations work well together, several challenges arise from the objective-oriented research designs, nature of humanitarian operations and analytical complications. Particularly, the dealing with statistical complications (e.g., endogeneity issues and urban legends) and maintaining data quality can be very challenging to reach a valid conclusion that can lead toward unbiased estimates for the effective decision making and problem solving in humanitarian operations. Publication biases (e.g., network biases), a bitter truth of academic domains, are also illustrated with a case taken from the special issue handled by senior academics (i.e., professors) and published

P. Akhtar (✉)
Management Systems, Faculty of Business, Law and Politics, Hull, United Kingdom
e-mail: Pervaiz.Akhtar@hull.ac.uk

© The Author(s) 2018                                                                                    **121**
G. Kovács et al. (eds.), *The Palgrave Handbook of Humanitarian Logistics and Supply Chain Management*, https://doi.org/10.1057/978-1-137-59099-2_4

by the *Journal of Business Research (JBR)*. The chapter finally summarizes the heavenly combinations of mixed methods and suggests pragmatic actions against dreadful biases. The structure of this chapter is presented in Fig. 4.1.

Upon completing this chapter, readers should be able to:

• Understand the links between the nature of humanitarian operations and mix methods.
• Explain what a case study research method is, and analyze when case studies and methodological combinations (analytic hierarchy/network processes) are appropriate for humanitarian researchers.
• Discuss what a survey research method is, and answer why a survey research method should be coupled with in-depth interviews.
• Critically examine how statistical complications/biases can affect findings and publications, leading toward misleading conclusions and invalid results.
• Understand the availability of other methodological choices for humanitarian researchers.

## Nature of Humanitarian Operations

Humanitarian operations are different due to the varying severity of disasters and diverse recipients' needs. Some disasters cause losses of lives, shortages of basic needs (e.g., food and water) and damages (e.g., hospitals and schools). For instance, in 2008, more than 67,000 people lost their lives in China due to an earthquake. The Cyclone Nargis in Myanmar killed approximately 78,000 people and 100,000 people passed away in the South Asian Earthquake that also ruined almost 80% of the infrastructure in Pakistani-administrated Kashmir, particularly in the capital (Muzaffarabad). The Tsunami in Tokyo cost millions to re-build the damaged infrastructure (Akhtar et al. 2012). The time to rebuild such areas can take from days to decades. For example, the damaged infrastructure caused by the 2005 South Asian Earthquake has still not been rebuilt. Many children in cities (e.g., Rawalakot and Bagh) and villages (e.g., Kohukot and Ali Sojal) take their school classes underneath trees because of the damaged school buildings. This is directly linked with the politicians and government administrators who failed to provide required resources to rebuild the essential infrastructure. The sort of time scales, political complications, levels of severity,

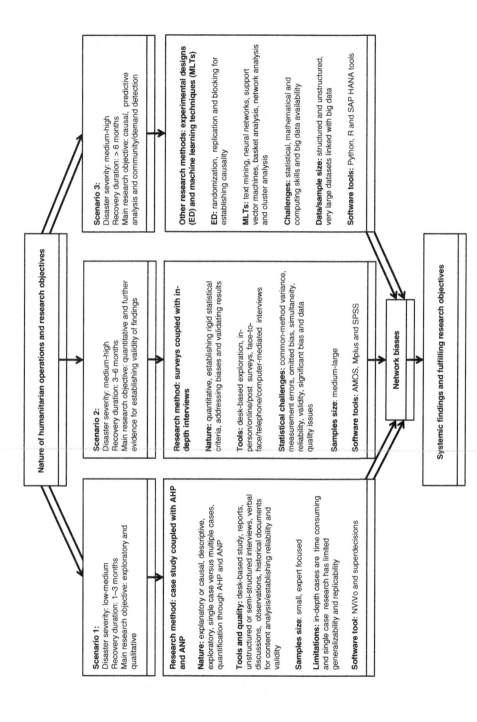

**Fig. 4.1**  Humanitarian operations and mixed-method choices

different recipients' need and relevant research objectives require a variety of research methods that can well fit with different humanitarian scenarios highlighted in Fig. 4.1. As the book focuses on research designs and methods, the nature of humanitarian operations is narrated briefly and the more space in this chapter is devoted to mixed methods and their heavenly combinations, relevant statistical complications, data quality issues and biases that challenge modern methodologists.

## Mixed Methods and Motivation

Mixed-methods and their combinations are linked with the idea of triangulation in which the concept of "multiple operationalism" is applied, following the rules of multi-method research and multiple measures (Boring 1953; Campbell and Fiske 1959; Webb et al. 1966). The term triangulation is used for triangulated methods in which researchers combine different methodologies at various stages (Denzin 1973):

- Data triangulation from a variety of sources (e.g., primary and secondary data).
- Investigator triangulation by using different researchers (e.g., combining a team of researchers from business schools and computing).
- Theory triangulation by applying multiple theories (e.g., integrating different theories from humanitarian and commercial operations).
- Methodological triangulation by employing more than one method (e.g., interviews and surveys – qualitative and quantitative).

The combination of qualitative and quantitative characteristics is at the heart of mixed methods. This combination can occur at any stage of a research cycle (e.g., research design, data collection and analytical stages). Supporting this view, Johnson et al. (2007) collected 19 definitions of mixed methods from the leading methodologists. The majority of them (15 out of 19) agreed that "qualitative and quantitative research is what is mixed" (p. 118). "Mixed methods research involves the use of more than one approach or method of design, data collection or data analysis within a single program of study, with integration of the different approaches or methods occurring during the program of study, and not just at its concluding point" (p. 119). It is not limited to a combination of qualitative and quantitative methods only.

Broadly speaking, it can be any combination of different approaches, methods, data collection techniques and a variety of complementary analyses.

Additionally, Tashakkori and Teddlie (2006) and Johnson et al. (2007) mentioned a number of reasons for applying mixed methods. The primary reason is labeled as a "bottom-up" approach in which research objectives/questions drive the choice of combinations to apply mixed methods. Other reasons include better understanding, breadth, depth, validity, internal consistency and generalization.

However, firstly, the contemporary challenges or reasons of combinations for the specific content (e.g., humanitarian operations) have not been explored (Kaewkitipong et al. 2016). Secondly, the editors/reviewers from top-ranked journals (e.g., *Journal of Operations Management, MIS Quarterly, Journal of Business Studies* and *European Operations Research*) require researchers to integrate mixed methods, so the better validity of results can be established. Finally, advancements in analytical techniques (Abdallah et al. 2015; Antonakis et al. 2014; Benitez et al. 2016), contemporary biases and modern datasets (Papadopoulos et al. 2016; Pham et al. 2016) need different suitable combinations of mix methods. These reasons are thus the key motivation for this chapter.

## Case Study Research Coupled with Analytic Hierarchy Process and Analytic Network Process

A case study research method, being part of qualitative research, generally investigates "how," "what" and "why" questions with a specific focus on events, disasters, persons, groups, communities and organizations. These questions help to explore how/why a disaster occurred and what were the key reasons. This type of research can also help to answer other questions. For example, which organizations did respond to a disaster immediately? Which organizations did support them? Where did they operate effectively? This method is further helpful when humanitarian researchers have little knowledge about the situation or have no control over events. Additional benefits of a case study research method include using of multiple sources such as reports, unstructured/semi-structured interviews, verbal discussions, observations and historical documents that can help to triangulate data (Ellram 1996; Yin 2013). As not much research has been done in humanitarian operations, the case study method being an exploratory tool can be useful to explore humanitarian domains. This is also a practical approach for those humanitarian researchers who are not well equipped with quantitative skills (Akhtar et al. 2012; Kaewkitipong et al. 2016).

The case study method as a tool of exploratory research is a pivotal source to scrutinize emerging practices that help to develop theories in humanitarian operations management. The meaningful and triangulated data produced from case studies on humanitarian practices enables researchers to get insights from the complex mechanisms of inter-relationships, rich real life experiences and processes linked with specific uncertain humanitarian environments. The information and data obtained from such mechanisms are not used for theory building or testing only, it also provides insights assisting to deal with future disasters effectively. Case study methods in fact provide a systematical-methodological procedure that integrates a variety of tools (desk-based exploration, interviews, content analysis and observations) to get insights for better future practices. Also, in case study research, investigators have more flexibility in terms of adopting additional research questions or objectives due to new information and insights obtained from empirical processes.

Yin (2013) provided three types of case study methods: (1) explanatory or causal (2) descriptive and (3) exploratory. The first type uses existing theories to explain and understand an underlying phenomenon related to how- and why-type questions. The second type focuses on the descriptive nature of processes and practices, dealing with many- and how much-type questions. The third category deals with exploratory research questions; what can we learn by studying a specific disaster? What are the key effective ways to support earthquake victims?

Deciding the type of research questions is probably the most important decision, followed by the choice of selecting a single case study versus multiple case studies (Yin 2013). The single case study research approach is acceptable if the phenomenon represents a unique case or the researcher is unable to access suitable research participants. For instance, the Tsunami in Japan was a unique case. Similarly, conducting a case study from war zones can be difficult and researchers cannot access all areas, so accessibility can be an issue to conduct multiple cases based on those areas that can create high risk for researchers or targeted population is resided in an area where accessibility is almost impossible. Researchers often categorize such difficulties as case study limitations. Additionally, in-depth case studies are very time consuming. With limited generalizability and replicability, researchers' personal subjective feeling may create a personal-feeling bias that is also part of limitations (McLeod 2008).

Geographical limitations, time and financial constraints can hinder researchers to choose multiple cases. However, if multiple case studies are utilized, it is important to decide the appropriate number of cases. The numbers basically depend on the content of a research area or topics and how in-depth analyses are conducted. Some researchers (e.g., Eisenhardt 1989) believe that there are no particular principles for numbers. Generally, researchers recommend two to ten case studies (Eisenhardt 1989; Ellram 1996; Yin 2013). Researchers should select multiple case studies if they have a choice, time and resources because multiple case studies could lead toward replication and generalization. However, it could be very difficult to conduct multiple case studies in humanitarian operations as such operations are unique and are considered in the rare category. Thus, any numbers from one to four should be acceptable, particularly when multiple organizations are involved in a case study. Such cases can be benefited from in-depth analyses, for which some software tools can be very helpful (e.g., NVivo). An example of such case study was conducted by Akhtar et al. (2012) in which they investigated seven different organizations, working together under the leadership of an umbrella organization.

Humanitarian case study research often uses purposive sampling that helps to (a) select a single case versus multiple cases (b) decide suitable population samples (c) choose those sample members who meet the study requirements and (d) receive relevant information contributing to research objectives (Akhtar et al. 2012; Hunt 2009; Kabra and Ramesh, 2016). The purposive sampling is divided in various categories, as shown in Fig. 4.2. Interested readers can further consult Palinkas et al. (2015) and Siegle (2016) for more information.

It is also important to take various steps to triangulate the research documents that can improve data quality by ensuring the reliability and validity of case study findings. In case study research, the main data is basically collected through interviews and related data quality issues are discussed in the interview section of this chapter.

Case study research coupled with the analytic hierarchy process (AHP) and analytic network process (ANP) can be a heavenly combination to address humanitarian problems. The AHP, introduced by Saaty, helps to solve complex decision problems and compares the importance of each underlying construct and the relative impact of items on the overall solution or chosen alternatives (Saaty 1987). The ANP, which is a general form of the AHP, integrates feedback loops and interdependencies among criteria, attributes and alternatives (Saaty and Vargas 2013). These methods provide a more accurate approach to model and quantify the solution, thus, they are

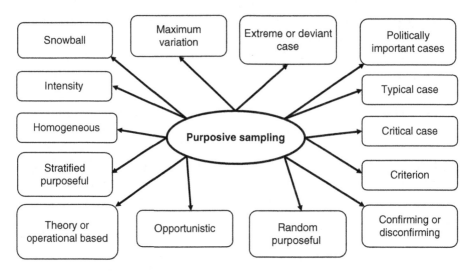

**Fig. 4.2** Types of purposive sampling

able to compliment case study research. In fact, these methods combine both qualitative and quantitative research and have many industrial applications such as supply chain management (Laura Meade and Sarkis, 1998), agile manufacturing (Meade and Sarkis 1999), agility, lean and leagile (Agarwal et al. 2006), logistics (Jharkharia and Shankar 2007), total quality management (Bayazit and Karpak 2007), green supplier selection/development (Dou et al. 2014; Hashemi et al. 2015) and risk management (Mogre et al. 2016) among others. It is unfortunate to see that these methods have not made their way to humanitarian operations despite having similar problems (e.g., agility, risk management, supply chain and logistics coordination) we face in humanitarian domains.

Considering the similarities among problems, time constraints in humanitarian operations (e.g., 1–3 months), ability to integrate both qualitative and quantitative aspects, lack of availability of humanitarian experts, small sample sizes (Agarwal et al. 2006; Jharkharia and Shankar 2007) and no rigid statistical criteria, the combination of case study research with AHP and ANP can be a practical and an effective approach to address humanitarian problems. However, the key challenge for humanitarian researchers is to learn these methods as they are based on mathematical principles. Thanks to Prof. Saaty, who provided a free software tool (www.superdecisions.com) that simplifies AHP and ANP applications. Additionally, the relevant references mentioned in this section can help humanitarian researchers to apply these methods effectively.

# Survey Research, Statistical Biases, Data Quality and Coupling with In-Depth Interviews

This section mainly discusses a survey research method. It also provides the reasons why surveys alone are not enough to produce convincing conclusions and useful insights for addressing real problems. Furthering, the survey analysis and systematical statistical estimates are more complex and can be very challenging for humanitarian researchers, particularly for those who do not have a degree in statistics. The statistical complications (common-method variance [CMV], measurement error, omitted variables/selections and simultaneity) are linked with effective survey designs, which are also discussed.

A survey research method, being part of quantitative research, is related to statistical facts and the estimation of inter-relationships of underlying constructs that are built by theorizing specific relationships, called a deductive approach (Neuman 2005). In other words, this approach consists of hypotheses, theory formulations, preliminary data collections, data investigations and deduction of results (Sekaran and Bougie 2010). The purpose is to develop systematic measures using appropriate statistical tools, so the valid results can be replicated (Kline 2015; Neuman 2005).

Survey research studies are often based on cross sectional data such as data collected from different countries, firms, regions and individuals. Nowadays, some prestigious journals explicitly discourage authors from submitting research papers that are solely based on cross-sectional surveys and do not follow proper statistical procedures. In such research papers, researchers hypothesize that $X$ has a relationship with $Y$ and conclude that the underlying relationship between the constructs ($X$ and $Y$) is supported simply because they have seen that the cross-sectional correlations based on $p$-values have been accepted for too long. This is no longer accepted by some prestigious journals if endogeneity issues are not addressed systematically. For example, the editor from a prestigious journal of operations management said that "our decision as editors is no longer to accept such submission, and our decision is in line with the major management journals today." It is thus time for humanitarian researchers to rethink which research methods they should use to conduct valid and publishable research. Some journals encourage to use a combination of qualitative (case studies and interviews) and quantitative methods (surveys, experimental research and machine learning methods), called a mixed method or digital mixed method (Creswell 2013; O'Halloran et al. 2016). The digital mixed method is mainly used for big data analytics in which qualitative data is transferred into quantitative data (O'Halloran et al. 2016).

## Effective Survey Designs and Endogeneity Biases

Research reveals that (e.g., Antonakis et al. 2010; Hamilton and Nickerson 2003) approximately 90% of the papers published in the selected premier journals have not systematically addressed endogeneity biases. Consequently, "at least 66% and up to 90% of design and estimation conditions make the claims invalid" (Antonakis et al. 2010, p. 1086). Despite recent methodological advances and the extant literature in econometrics and psychology domains, many social science disciplines, including humanitarian domains, are largely estimating inconsistent estimates because of not addressing endogeneity biases systematically. This section thus provides the theoretical and procedural treatments as well as highlights resources to deal with endogeneity biases; CMV, measurement errors, omitted variables or selections and simultaneity.

### CMV Bias

Statistical analyses can be significantly affected by survey designs. A badly designed survey can create a CMV bias, which attributes to the effectiveness of measurement methods. Richardson et al. (2009, p. 4) defined the CMV as "systematic error variance shared among variables measured with and introduced as a function of the same method and/or source." For instance, the familiarity of respondents with the specific type of mediums (e.g., electronic surveys or in-person surveys) can influence the results compared to those respondents who are not familiar with such types. If such biases exist, the inter-correlations can be inflated or deflated (Williams and Brown 1994). They can also affect the amounts of variance explained by the constructs. For example, Podsakoff et al. (2003) found that the difference between the amounts of variance accounted was 24% when the CMV bias was controlled (i.e., 35%) versus when it was not controlled (i.e., 11%).

Such bias can be problematic as it connects with the sources of measurement errors that may arise from common-ratter effects (Malhotra et al. 2006; Podsakoff et al. 2003), which come when researchers collect data from similar respondents. For example, this can be the case when someone collects data only from humanitarian program managers (top management) and does not collect data from relevant logistics managers/data analysts (middle-level management). Additionally, the common-measurement content-related issues can be problematic (Malhotra et al. 2006; Podsakoff et al. 2003). For instance, many researchers use a single medium (e.g., electronic surveys) that could create biased results. Time scales and locations are also categorized in common-measurement-related biases. The sources of measurement errors can also come from the common-item context or item characteristics (Malhotra et al. 2006; Podsakoff et al. 2003). Jargons, double-barreled questions and unfamiliar words for humanitarian participants are examples of the common-item context bias. In addition to this, scale types, response formats and the general content can also create the sources of measurement errors (Malhotra et al. 2006; Podsakoff et al. 2003).

So what should be done theoretically and statistically to deal with CMV biases? Although CMV biases might not be eliminated completely, a series of steps can be taken to minimize them. Theoretically, researchers can design a survey consisting of systematical measures (items) to form the constructs. Tourangeau et al. (2000) advised that systematical measures avoid unfamiliar words, jargons and double-barreled questions. Technical words should also be defined for survey respondents, so they can understand the content of the survey before completing it. It is also advisable to keep sentences and questions simple and concise. This does not only save respondents' time but also increases response rates and the accuracy of their judgment. Complex sentences can distract the pattern of judgments. Measures further should be specific to the research objectives. Adding (many) negatively worded measures can also destruct the respondents' pattern of responding and can create a source of biases (Podsakoff et al. 2003). Thus, avoiding negatively worded questions can reduce the bias. Similarly, grouping items in different construct items can distract the flow of respondent answering the questions and can be more time consuming as well, although some researchers suggest that the questions/items should be grouped with different construct items (i.e., not in the conceptual dimensions). Also, to avoid a single-informant bias, researchers should collect data from multiple participants; humanitarian program managers, country directors, operations managers and frontline workers in the same domains.

The statistical approaches to control the CMV bias have different advantages and disadvantages (Malhotra et al. 2006; Podsakoff et al. 2003). There are few well-known methods to statistically deal with the CMV bias, although some of them have been highly criticized. An exploratory factor analysis (EFA) is often used to form constructs, reduce the dimensions of measures with the assumption that the presence of CMV bias is indicated by the emergence of either a single factor or a general factor accounting for the majority of covariance among measures. During this process, analysts can produce factors (based on eigenvalues greater than 1 and scree plot observations) and see whether a multiple-factor solution provides the greater variance than a single-factor solution. Podsakoff et al. (2003) stated that Harman's single-factor test as a diagnostic technique, which "actually does nothing to statistically control for (or partial out) method effects" (Podsakoff et al. 2003, p. 889). Further, they argue that the emergence of multiple factors does not indicate the absence of the CMV bias and recommend not to use this test alone (Sharma et al. 2009). Additionally, it is noticed that negatively worded items often have low loadings during EFA. Consequently, such items are deleted.

The marker variable technique (using an unrelated variable), proposed by Lindell and Whitney (2001), can be a good alternative to assess the CMV bias. The small correlations used in this technique provide a reasonable proxy (see Lindell and Whitney 2001 for further details). The latent factor technique can also investigate the CMV bias (see Malhotra et al. 2006 for further details).

## Measurement Errors

It is a universal fact that the theoretical constructs of interest cannot be measured with precision, resulting in as measurement errors that are common in research. Consequently, the estimates can be inconsistent and the errors affect other involved variables as well (Antonakis et al. 2010; Antonakis et al. 2014; DeShon 1998).

However, some methods such as structural equation modeling with maximum likelihood estimates (software tools are AMOS and Mplus) correct for the "biasing effects of random measurement errors" (Frone et al. 1994, p. 573) or "successfully correct for the small amount of measurement errors in the items" (DeShon 1998, p. 417), researchers still need to control the measurement errors if they employ a single indicator approach, that is parceling using multi-item scales (DeShon 1998). The process is followed by constraining the relevant random error variance equal to the product of the variance multiply by one minus the reliability (i.e., alpha). The relevant loadings (i.e., standard deviation * square-root of alpha) for the parcels are also fixed (Antonakis et al. 2014; Bollen 1989; DeShon 1998). By controlling such errors, the empirical analysis shows that there could be two types of effects: (1) minor changes in the significance levels (i.e., differences in $t$-values) and (2) the difference between the amounts of variance accounted is up to 9% when measurement errors are controlled versus when they are not controlled, indicating the importance of correcting measurement errors and following the methodological rigor.

## Omitted Biases and Simultaneity

Omitted biases can have various forms (see for details; Antonakis et al. 2010; Antonakis et al. 2014). One possibility of this can be when researchers test the validity of an underlying construct without including other important variables/constructs. For instance, researchers measuring the operational performance of humanitarian organizations without including their social performance can introduce the omitted bias. In this regard, researchers should consider "theory, theory and more theory" (Antonakis et al. 2014; Antonakis and Dietz 2011, p. 218). They should also apply multiple dimensions of a construct, even the second- and third-order constructs. For example, to measure operational performance in humanitarian operations, researchers can use service agility, the fair distribution of relief goods, product quality, receivers' satisfaction and trust, the cooperation with local community and reduction of corruption in relief operations. These second-order constructs can be measured by using various items/questions and collectively some of these constructs can form third-order constructs that can be more complicated. It is thus important to build such constructs carefully based on extensive theory and they should be refined systematically by applying appropriate statistical techniques and effective survey designs. Additionally, the two-stage least squares (2SLS) estimations and instrumental variables can be used for the robustness check (see Antonakis et al. 2010; Bowblis and McHone 2013).

The problem of simultaneity can occur when two variables simultaneously affect each other and have reciprocal feedback loops, creating non-recursive models. Although this problem is easy to understand, it is complicated to resolve statistically; especially when a study involves multiple constructs. Some researchers suggest resolving such problems using instrumental variables. However, finding instrumental variables for various constructs is not easy, sometimes even it is impossible (Antonakis et al. 2010, 2014). The fundamental problem for such models is the identification of models because of numerous complications such as not having sufficient data, high correlations of instrumental variables and deficient order and rank conditions (Bentler and Chou 1987; Martens and Haase 2006).

Researchers should at least acknowledge and statistically test alternative models. For example, receivers' satisfaction can build trust. Alternatively, receivers' trust can contribute to satisfaction. They should also use strong theoretical arguments to build the bidirectional hypotheses. The interested readers should consult other methodological studies (e.g., Bentler and Chou 1987; Martens and Haase 2006) on how to test reciprocal feedback loops and model identification issues that are more complicated topics and are beyond the scope of this chapter.

## Significant Bias and Data Quality

Beside endogeneity biases, it is a general trend that researchers and journal editors prefer to publish studies with significant results. This is problematic, particularly when data quality has not been investigated systematically and significant results are produced. Additionally, it is not fair to consider that studies with significant results are superior to those studies that have null results, which is also highlighted by some researchers (e.g., Easterbrook et al. 1991; Franco et al. 2014). Unfortunately, studies with statistically significant results are likely to be more easily published compared to studies with null results. Recent research shows that 62% studies with strongly significant results made into journals compared to 21% studies with null results (Franco et al. 2014).

It is a fact that many reviewers and editors are not statisticians or mathematicians in social sciences, which makes it difficult to see the links between the importance of data quality, appropriate analytical tools and significant results. Some reviewers, particularly in special issues, also provide misleading suggestions such as applying of partial least square rather than traditional structural equation modeling because sample sizes are small, even for a sample size of 240 plus. An example of such comments has been received from the special issue on big data and analytics (Big Data and Analytics in Technology Organizational Resource Management 2016) called by *JBR*. This is particularly worrying when special issues are handled by emails (again the same example from the *JBR*) rather than their original system and the guest editors select incompetent reviewers from their own networks (again the same example from the *JBR*). This does not only create network-biased publications but often quality is compromised and publications come from specific academic networks due to their politically motivated systems (Bias 2016). A detailed example of network biases is presented in the network bias section.

Outliers or strongly correlated cases are linked with statistical significance (i.e., $p < 0.05$), which should not be used alone to justify publications. Only few strongly related cases can change insignificant (even negative significant results) results to positive significant results (or vice versa few outliers can change significant results into insignificant results). To demonstrate this point, a real dataset consisting of three variables and 170 cases collected from humanitarian managers were used. The three variables were: managers' quantitative skills, the meeting frequency and operational performance. When the regression analyses were conducted based on 170 cases, the first independent variable (managers' quantitative skills) was significant at $p < 0.05$ and the second independent variable (meeting frequency) showed a negative insignificant relationship. After a closer investigation by using scatter plots, a cluster of four strong positive cases (strongly positively related) were found problematic and they were affecting the relationship between the meeting frequency and operational performance, the new analysis based on 166 cases showed the negative significant results ($p < 0.05$). Thus, it is not only about outliers but few strongly related cases can also change results significantly. Researchers should consider the robustness of analysis and journal editors should ask for exploratory characteristics as well, rather than just accepting $p$-values. They should also make $t$-values compulsory, which can further show a better picture of the relationships among the underlying constructs.

Additionally, various tools are used to check data quality. Traditionally, reliability and validity are used to check data/item/construct quality. The reliability is measured by employing three commonly used guidelines that aim to reduce errors and produce consistent results: (a) Cronbach's alpha > 0.7 (b) construct reliability > 0.7 (c) average variance extracted (AVE) > 0.5 (Byrne 2013; Kline 2015). The validity refers to "the accuracy of a measure or the extent to which a score truthfully represents a concept" (Zikmund et al. 2012, p. 303). The types of commonly used validity are content validity (i.e., conceptuality that clarifies the concepts used in a study) and construct validity, which is measured by convergent validity (measuring how valid the results are) and discriminant validity (how strongly the constructs are related). The convergent validity is measured by scrutinizing the loadings of underlying items (>0.50 and significant). This means the items share more variance with their respective underlying constructs (Sekaran and Bougie 2010). In addition to the loadings, the AVE is used for this type of validity. The discriminant validity is measured by the correlation between two factors (<0.85) (Kline 2015). It is also measured by assessing whether the average variance explained by each pair of constructs is greater than the square of the correction between the constructs (Sekaran and Bougie 2010). Also, the descriptive measures such as the mean closer to median, skewness less than 2 and kurtosis less than 5 should be used to check the quality of data distributions (Byrne 2013).

Although data analysts can provide evidence about the psychometric properties of datasets by investigating the above reviewed measures, some of these "urban legends" (the cut-off criteria) have recently been criticized. For example, Lance et al. (2006) unambiguously debunk the "0.70 rule." Interested humanitarian survey researchers should further consult recent methodological advances on these issues (e.g. Cortina 2002; Lance 2011; Lance et al. 2006).

## Coupling Survey Methods with In-Depth Interviews

Surveys alone are not sufficient to draw reasonable conclusions. The analyses produced from surveys show the correlation between underlying constructs but they do not tell you what the reasons are behind the relationships/problems and how we can address them. Thus, coupling surveys with interviews can help to find out specific reasons and examples, leading toward logical and rational solutions. Also, survey results can be validated using in-depth interviews.

Interviews are generally categorized based on, structured interview questions (closed-ended questions), semi-structured questions (a combination of open-ended and closed-ended questions) and unstructured interview questions (open-ended interview questions). Interviews can be conducted via a face-to-face mode, using telephones and modern computer-mediated applications (e.g., Skype, Viber, WhatsApp and GoToMeeting) (Mann 2016); the choice of selection depends on the nature of underlying research objectives (Robson and McCartan 2016). The advantages and disadvantage of these modes are listed in Table 4.1.

Like quantitative analyses, establishing reliability and validity for interview data is also crucial. These quality measures are established by checking whether the questions asked can provide the same findings when they are used in other situations or used by other researchers. Developing effective findings from interview data also depends on reducing biases and errors by using multiple tools; repeating the same questions, consulting documents, observations, interview notes, using the same language for all interview participants, fully understanding the questions and study content, carefully using interview transcripts and matching them with interview notes and not unnecessarily interrupting interviewees. Additionally, it is also important to replicate interview findings (Ellram 1996; Saunders 2011).

An in-depth content analysis method can be very useful to analyze a large set of interviews (e.g., greater than 500), relative transcripts (e.g., 20, 000 pages) and massive documents/communication (e.g., video, images, observations, interview transcripts). Such analyses contain both qualitative and quantitative steps that advocate common research criteria (Elo et al. 2014; Mayring 2000; Ohm 2016), it particularly shares the

Table 4.1 Advantages and disadvantages of interview modes

| Collection modes | Advantages | Disadvantages |
|---|---|---|
| Face-to-face interviews | Question clarification<br>Using nonverbal cues<br>Visual aids to clarify points<br>Rich data | Time consuming<br>Costly when wide geographic regions are included<br>Respondents' confidentiality risk<br>Interviewers need training<br>Personal bias |
| Telephone interviews | Less costly<br>Time efficient compared to face-to-face interviews<br>Wide geographical areas can be accessed | Respondents prefer short interviews<br>No visual help<br>Data not very rich like face-to-face interviews<br>International calls can be expensive |
| Computer-mediated interviews | Less costly than other two forms<br>Global coverage as long as internet is available<br>Convenient for both interviewers and interviewees<br>Notes can be easily made<br>Text/typing can help to clarify points<br>Interviewers and interviewees can see each other<br>Time efficient compared to other two forms | Cannot be done without internet<br>Technical skills may be required<br>Risk of losing responds due to technical faults<br>Bad voice quality can lead toward misunderstanding |

characteristics mentioned in the case study section of this chapter. Considering the space and already existing extensive research on qualitative content (Elo et al. 2014; Graneheim and Lundman 2004; Mayring 2000) and quantitative content (Riff et al. 2014; Riffe et al. 2005; Rourke and Anderson 2004) analyses, interested readers are suggested to consult such sources for further details.

# Network Biases and Related Issues

Network biases and related issues are demonstrated by using the special issue (Bias 2016) that was handled by Prof. Irani (Brunel University London, UK) and Prof. Love (Curtin University, Australia), and the editor-in-chief was

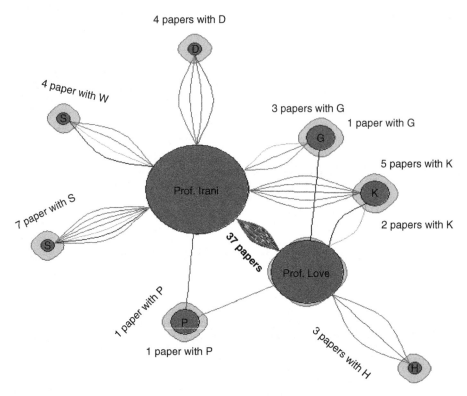

**Fig. 4.3**  An example of network biases

also affiliated with the same Australian University. How they have created the network bias is presented in Fig. 4.3.

The nodes represent two guest editors (Prof. Irani and Prof. Love) and their co-authors. The letters (D, G, H, K, P, S and W) are the initials of the last name of these authors whose papers were published in the special issue and the lines show the number of papers these authors already published with the guest editors before the special issue published in 2016 (JBRSI 2016). For example, Prof. Irani published seven papers with the author S (before this special issue). The acceptance rate for these authors is almost certain when they have such networks and sometime editors accept more than one paper from the same author, as it was the case for the author G here. On top, the guest editor (Prof. Irani) has two of his own papers in this special issue, which clearly demonstrates the conflict of interest. The raw data (i.e., publication recodes) for Fig. 4.3 is publicly available on the following resources: Irani (2016), Love (2016) and JBRSI (2016).

If required, a CSV file can also be requested through this email: pervaiz_khan972@hotmail.com

A reviewer mentioned that he was bypassed for one of the papers submitted by the author H[1] and the guest editors directly accepted his/her paper, despite the author having been given a major revision in May 2016. The guest editors did not even consult the reviewer and the reviewer only found out when he saw the publication (JBRSI 2016) in August 2016. It was a big surprise to see that supper-quick publication in two months without acting on the recommended revision. If a proper review procedure was followed to produce high quality of research, it could have taken longer more than a year. Additionally, the guest editors did not share the feedback/comments/decision (e.g., rejected/major revision/accepted) provided by the other reviewer – if that paper was sent to two reviewers. When investigated, it was found that the author H was a colleague/friend of Prof. Love and they already published three papers together in 2015 before this acceptance (Love 2016), as also can be observed in Fig. 4.3. Again, this shows a clear case of network-biased publications.

The network-biased citation is another issue that can be demonstrated through this special issue. The authors cited the literature in a circumstantial way and cluttered references to accommodate the guest editors' papers (an obvious purpose is to increase citations and h-indices of colleagues and friends). These cited papers have nothing to do with big data and analytics, the papers were not even highlighted in the special issue call (Bias 2016). Examples of this bias can be observed from the following authors' papers: G, K and S. Readers can observe these papers in the special issue (JBRSI 2016). This questions publishers and academic institutions whether h-indices and citations achieved through a bias approach should be counted or not. Also, the extant referencing style is dubious. Cluttering references frequently compromises the quality of literature reviews and insights that can be extracted from individual studies.

Another form of network bias comes in when authors frequently publish their studies in one/two journals based on their professional or personal links. Examples of such bias can be found on many university websites. This hinders interdisciplinary research as well as creates obstacles for early-/mid-career researchers who do not have such networks and they certainly struggle to publish their bright ideas and innovative research.

---

[1] The paper was originally titled "The Exploring the Role of Business Analytics Capabilities in Creating Business Value in Healthcare Industries: A Resource-Based View Perspective" – published with a changed title "Exploring the Path to Big Data Analytics Success in Healthcare"

## Other Choices

Although the focus of this chapter is on case studies, surveys, their combinations, statistical complications and biases, the chapter also provides an overview of other options/resources that humanitarian researchers should consider as well. Both case study and survey research methods cannot establish causal relationships between two underlying constructs or variables. An experimental research method is a very powerful research approach to establish such relationships. An experiment is defined "as a test or series of runs in which purposeful changes are made to input variables of a process or system so that we may observe and identify the reasons for changes that may be observed in the output response" (Montgomery 2013, p. 1). Montgomery (2013) provided three principles of experiment designs: (1) randomization (2) replication and (3) blocking. The randomization refers to the process of selecting participants randomly, means using chance methods rather than by choice methods such as random tables and randomly generated numbers from computers. The purpose of randomization is to reduce or eliminate biases. The replication is the repetition of an experiment in the same conditions. The purpose is to estimate the variability associated with the underlying phenomenon (i.e., the source of variability between runs and within runs), and replications also provide information about the reliability of conclusions drawn from experiments. The blocking is a technique to arrange experiment units in blocks (groups), which are similar to each other. Montgomery (2013) further provided the following guidelines for designing a good experiment:

- Recognition and problem statements
- Selection of response variables
- Choice of factors, levels and ranges
- Choice of experimental designs
- Performance of experiments
- Statistical analysis of data
- Conclusions and recommendations

Experimental designs involve various complicated factors and they cannot be covered in one chapter or section, there are many books available on this topic. Interested humanitarian readers should consider them (e.g., Campbell and Stanley 2015; Montgomery 2013).

Nowadays, humanitarian operations are inundated with data and information, which can be scrutinized using various machine learning techniques such as text mining/topic mining (i.e., a family of content analysis), neural networks, support vector machines, basket analysis, network analysis and clustering. If reasonable data is available, these techniques can be used for predictive analysis that can help to predict recipients' demand in affected areas. These techniques (e.g., network analysis) can also detect more affected areas or people who have been mostly affected. Additionally, many free (e.g., R packages, Python) and commercial software tools (e.g., SAP HANA functionalities) are available to apply these techniques effectively. However, applying these techniques can be challenging as they require technical skills and a deeper understanding of statistical tools and mathematical algorithms. As these techniques and software tools are very complicated and the purpose here is to provide the awareness of these tools, interested readers should consult other sources (e.g., Danneman and Heimann 2014; Lantz 2015; Lewis et al. 2013).

## Summary and Concluding Remarks

Humanitarian research requires the diverse and complementary combinations of qualitative and quantitative research methods, depending on the nature of humanitarian disasters. Some humanitarian disasters are categorized as a small and medium sized and exploring them (e.g., how, what, where and why questions) using a case study method could be useful. The lack of availability of humanitarian experts is the main reason that case studies should be applied for small- and medium-sized disasters. Also, the recovery time is shorter for such disasters and case studies are less time consuming compared to surveys. To integrate the advantages of quantitative methods, case studies should be coupled with the AHP and ANP as these methods emphasize quality (e.g., experts) rather than quantity (e.g., sample sizes).

Although a survey research method coupled with in-depth interviews can be an effective choice for medium- and large-sized humanitarian disasters, statistical complications/biases (e.g., CMV, measurement error, omitted bias, simultaneity, reliability, validity, significant bias and data quality issues) throw many challenges and require specialized expertise in statistics and computing to deal with modern software tools that effectively handle these complications/biases. Such methods, however, cannot establish causality, thus the experimental design is a better choice to dealing with those humanitarian problems that require establishing causalities among underlying variables/constructs. Other machine learning techniques and contemporary methods (text mining, neural networks, support vector machines, basket analysis, cluster analysis and network analysis) can also be useful for structured and unstructured data that can be used for predictive analytics or to detect affected areas.

These modern methods (e.g., text mining and network analysis) can also be used to detect corporate corruption. Network biases in research are examples of such corruption that does not only hinder the quality of research but is a barrier for innovation and bright ideas. The research subject to network biases (e.g., Bias 2016) is not only invalid, it is also poisonous to build on such research. It is thus important for policy makers (e.g., journal editors, publishers, universities, ranking bodies and the ministry of education) to take the responsibility to resolve these issues. For examples, it is the responsibility of the editor-in-chief/publisher to restrict the guest editors/their colleagues and friends to publish in the same issue in which the guest editors make the final recommendations. There should be a law to punish (e.g., fines, ban to publish in the journals, restrictions from work and prison sentences even) such academics who are subject to these unethical research practices. Additionally, universities and ranking bodies can stop crediting their research. The role of reviewers to detect the citation bias is important; they should explicitly highlight those editors' studies that are not relevant and are cluttered with other references. These practical steps will not only retain the quality of research but are also important to provide the equal rights for researchers.

# References

Abdallah, W., Goergen, M., & O'Sullivan, N. (2015). Endogeneity: How failure to correct for it can cause wrong inferences and some remedies. *British Journal of Management, 26*(4), 791–804.

Agarwal, A., Shankar, R., & Tiwari, M. (2006). Modeling the metrics of lean, agile and leagile supply chain: An ANP-based approach. *European Journal of Operational Research, 173*(1), 211–225.

Akhtar, P., Marr, N., & Garnevska, E. (2012). Coordination in humanitarian relief chains: Chain coordinators. *Journal of Humanitarian Logistics and Supply Chain Management, 2*(1), 85–103.

Antonakis, J., & Dietz, J. (2011). More on testing for validity instead of looking for it. *Personality and Individual Differences, 50*(3), 418–421.

Antonakis, J., Bendahan, S., Jacquart, P., & Lalive, R. (2010). On making causal claims: A review and recommendations. *The Leadership Quarterly, 21*(6), 1086–1120.

Antonakis, J., Bendahan, S., Jacquart, P., & Lalive, R. (2014). Causality and endogeneity: Problems and solutions. In D. V. Day (Ed.), *The Oxford Handbook of Leadership and Organizations* (93–117). New York: Oxford University Press.

Bayazit, O., & Karpak, B. (2007). An analytical network process-based framework for successful total quality management (TQM): An assessment of Turkish manufacturing industry readiness. *International Journal of Production Economics, 105*(1), 79–96.

Benitez, J., Henseler, J., & Roldán, J. (2016). How to address endogeneity in partial least squares path modeling, http://aisel.aisnet.org/amcis2016/AsiaPac/Presentations/6/.

Bentler, P. M., & Chou, C.-P. (1987). Practical issues in structural modeling. *Sociological Methods & Research, 16*(1), 78–117.

Bias, N. (2016). Special issue on big data and analytics in technology and organizational resource management. Available at: http://mailman11.u.washington.edu/pipermail/egov-list/2015/000577.html. Assessed 30 August 2016.

Bollen, K. A. (1989). *Structural equations with latent variables.* NY, USA: John Wiley & Sons.

Boring, E. G. (1953). The role of theory in experimental psychology. *The American Journal of Psychology, 66*(2), 169–184.

Bowblis, J. R., & McHone, H. S. (2013). An instrumental variables approach to post-acute care nursing home quality: Is there a dime's worth of evidence that continuing care retirement communities provide higher quality? *Journal of Health Economics, 32*(5), 980–996.

Byrne, B. M. (2013). *Structural equation modeling with AMOS: Basic concepts, applications, and programming.* NY, USA: Routledge.

Campbell, D. T., & Fiske, D. W. (1959). Convergent and discriminant validation by the multitrait-multimethod matrix. *Psychological Bulletin, 56*(2), 81.

Campbell, D. T., & Stanley, J. C. (2015). *Experimental and quasi-experimental designs for research.* NJ, USA: Ravenio Books.

Cortina, J. M. (2002). Big things have small beginnings: An assortment of "minor" methodological misunderstandings. *Journal of Management, 28*(3), 339–362.

Creswell, J. W. (2013). *Research design: Qualitative, quantitative, and mixed methods approaches.* London, UK: Sage Publications.

Danneman, N., & Heimann, R. (2014). *Social media mining with R.* Birmingham, UK: Packt Publishing Ltd.

Denzin, N. K. (1973). *The research act: A theoretical introduction to sociological methods.* Transaction Publishers.

DeShon, R. P. (1998). A cautionary note on measurement error corrections in structural equation models. *Psychological Methods, 3*(4), 412–423.

Dou, Y., Zhu, Q., & Sarkis, J. (2014). Evaluating green supplier development programs with a grey-analytical network process-based methodology. *European Journal of Operational Research, 233*(2), 420–431.

Easterbrook, P. J., Gopalan, R., Berlin, J., & Matthews, D. R. (1991). Publication bias in clinical research. *The Lancet, 337*(8746), 867–872.

Eisenhardt, K. M. (1989). Building theories from case study research. *Academy of Management Review, 14*(4), 532–550.

Ellram, L. M. (1996). The use of the case study method in logistics research. *Journal of Business Logistics, 17*(2), 93.

Elo, S., Kääriäinen, M., Kanste, O., Pölkki, T., Utriainen, K., & Kyngäs, H. (2014). Qualitative content analysis. *Sage Open, 4*(1), 2158244014522633.

Franco, A., Malhotra, N., & Simonovits, G. (2014). Publication bias in the social sciences: Unlocking the file drawer. *Science, 345*(6203), 1502–1505.

Frone, M. R., Russell, M., & Cooper, M. L. (1994). Relationship between job and family satisfaction: Causal or noncausal covariation? *Journal of Management, 20*(3), 565–579.

Graneheim, U. H., & Lundman, B. (2004). Qualitative content analysis in nursing research: Concepts, procedures and measures to achieve trustworthiness. *Nurse Education Today, 24*(2), 105–112.

Hamilton, B. H., & Nickerson, J. A. (2003). Correcting for endogeneity in strategic management research. *Strategic Organization, 1*(1), 51–78.

Hashemi, S. H., Karimi, A., & Tavana, M. (2015). An integrated green supplier selection approach with analytic network process and improved Grey relational analysis. *International Journal of Production Economics, 159*(2015), 178–191.

Hunt, M. R. (2009). Moral experience of Canadian healthcare professionals in humanitarian work. *Prehospital and Disaster Medicine, 24*(06), 518–524.

Irani, Z. (2016). Available at: http://www.brunel.ac.uk/people/zahir-irani. Assessed 30 August 2016.

JBRSI. (2016). Available at: http://www.sciencedirect.com/science/journal/aip/01482963. Retrieved 30 August 2016.

Jharkharia, S., & Shankar, R. (2007). Selection of logistics service provider: An analytic network process (ANP) approach. *Omega, 35*(3), 274–289.

Johnson, R. B., Onwuegbuzie, A. J., & Turner, L. A. (2007). Toward a definition of mixed methods research. *Journal of Mixed Methods Research, 1*(2), 112–133.

Kabra, G., & Ramesh, A. (2016). Exploring the challenges in implementation of information technology in humanitarian Relief Organisations in India: A qualitative study. In *Managing humanitarian logistics* (pp. 105–113), Springer Proceedings in Business and Economics.

Kaewkitipong, L., Chen, C. C., & Ractham, P. (2016). A community-based approach to sharing knowledge before, during, and after crisis events: A case study from Thailand. *Computers in Human Behavior, 54*, 653–666.

Kline, R. B. (2015). *Principles and practice of structural equation modeling*. NY, USA: Guilford Publications.

Lance, C. E. (2011). More statistical and methodological myths and urban legends. *Organizational Research Methods, 14*(2), 279–286.

Lance, C. E., Butts, M. M., & Michels, L. C. (2006). The sources of four commonly reported cutoff criteria what did they really say? *Organizational Research Methods, 9*(2), 202–220.

Lantz, B. (2015). *Machine learning with R*. Packt Publishing Ltd.

Lewis, S. C., Zamith, R., & Hermida, A. (2013). Content analysis in an era of big data: A hybrid approach to computational and manual methods. *Journal of Broadcasting & Electronic Media, 57*(1), 34–52.

Lindell, M. K., & Whitney, D. J. (2001). Accounting for common method variance in cross-sectional research designs. *Journal of Applied Psychology, 86*(1), 114–121.

Love, P. (2016). Available at: http://oasisapps.curtin.edu.au/staff/profile/view/P. Love. Retrieved30 August 2016.

Malhotra, N. K., Kim, S. S., & Patil, A. (2006). Common method variance in IS research: A comparison of alternative approaches and a reanalysis of past research. *Management Science, 52*(12), 1865–1883.

Mann, S. (2016). Research interviews: Modes and types. In *The research interview* (pp. 86–113), Palgrave Macmillan, UK.

Martens, M. P., & Haase, R. F. (2006). Advanced applications of structural equation modeling in counseling psychology research. *The Counseling Psychologist, 34*(6), 878–911.

Mayring, P. (2000). *Qualitative content analysis [28 paragraphs]. Forum Qualitative Sozialforshung.* Paper presented at the Forum: Qualitative Social Research [On-line Journal].

McLeod, S. (2008). Case study method. *Retrieved from* www.simplypsychology.org/case-study.html.

Meade, L., & Sarkis, J. (1998). Strategic analysis of logistics and supply chain management systems using the analytical network process. *Transportation Research Part E: Logistics and Transportation Review, 34*(3), 201–215.

Meade, L., & Sarkis, J. (1999). Analyzing organizational project alternatives for agile manufacturing processes: An analytical network approach. *International Journal of Production Research, 37*(2), 241–261.

Mogre, R., & D'Amico, F. (2016). A Decision Framework to Mitigate Supply Chain Risks: An Application in the Offshore-Wind Industry. *IEEE Transactions on Engineering Management, 63*(3), 316–325.

Montgomery, D. C. (2013). *Design and analysis of experiments.* North Carolina, USA: Wiley.

Neuman, W. L. (2005). *Social research methods: Quantitative and qualitative approaches* (Vol. 13). Allyn and Bacon Boston.

O'Halloran, K., Tan, S., Pham, S., Bateman, J., & Vande Moere, A. (2016). A digital mixed methods research design: Integrating multimodal analysis with data mining and information visualization for big data analytics, 1–20, DOI: 10.1177/1558689816651015.

Ohm, J. (2016). *Multimedia content analysis,* Berlin, Germany: Springer.

Palinkas, L. A., Horwitz, S. M., Green, C. A., Wisdom, J. P., Duan, N., & Hoagwood, K. (2015). Purposeful sampling for qualitative data collection and analysis in mixed method implementation research. *Administration and Policy in Mental Health and Mental Health Services Research, 42*(5), 533–544.

Papadopoulos, T., Gunasekaran, A., Dubey, R., Altay, N., Childe, S. J., & Fosso-Wamba, S. (2016). The role of big data in explaining disaster resilience in supply chains for sustainability. *Journal of Cleaner Production, 142*(2), 1108–1118.

Pham, P. N., Vinck, P., Marchesi, B., Johnson, D., Dixon, P. J., & Sikkink, K. (2016). Evaluating transitional justice: The role of multi-level mixed methods datasets and the Colombia reparation program for War Victims. *Transitional Justice Review, 1*(4), 60–94.

Podsakoff, P. M., MacKenzie, S. B., Lee, J.-Y., & Podsakoff, N. P. (2003). Common method biases in behavioral research: A critical review of the literature and recommended remedies. *Journal of Applied Psychology, 88*(5), 879–903.

Richardson, H. A., Simmering, M. J., & Sturman, M. C. (2009). A tale of three perspectives: Examining post hoc statistical techniques for detection and correction of common method variance. *Organizational Research Methods, 12*(4), 762–800.

Riffe, D., Lacy, S., & Fico, F. G. (2005). *Analyzing media messages: Using quantitative content analysis in research.* Mahwah, NJ: Lawrence Earlbaum Associates Inc.

Riff, D., Lacy, S., & Fico, F. (2014). *Analyzing media messages: Using quantitative content analysis in research.* NY, USA: Routledge.

Robson, Colin, and Kieran McCartan. *Real world research.* London, UK: John Wiley & Sons, 2016.

Rourke, L., & Anderson, T. (2004). Validity in quantitative content analysis. *Educational Technology Research and Development, 52*(1), 5–18.

Saaty, R. W. (1987). The analytic hierarchy process—what it is and how it is used. *Mathematical Modelling, 9*(3), 161–176.

Saaty, T. L., & Vargas, L. G. (2013). *Decision making with the analytic network process: Economic, political, social and technological applications with benefits, opportunities, costs and risks* (Vol. 195). Springer Science & Business Media. NY, USA: Springer.

Saunders, M. N. (2011). *Research methods for business students, 5/e.* England: Pearson Education Ltd.

Sekaran, U., & Bougie, R. (2010). *Research method for business, a skill building approach.* Singapore: John Wiley & Sons Inc.

Sharma, R., Yetton, P., & Crawford, J. (2009). Estimating the effect of common method variance: The method—Method pair technique with an Illustration from TAM Research. *MIS Quarterly, 33*(3), 473–490.

Siegle, D. (2016). Purposive sampling. Available at: http://researchbasics.education.uconn.edu/purposive-sampling/. Assessed 25 August 2016.

Tashakkori, A., & Teddlie, C. (2006). *Validity issues in mixed methods research: Calling for an integrative framework.* Paper presented at the annual meeting of the American Educational Research Association, San Francisco.

Tourangeau, R., Rips, L. J., & Rasinski, K. (2000). *The psychology of survey response.* Cambridge, England: Cambridge University Press.

Webb, E. J., Campbell, D. T., Schwartz, R. D., & Sechrest, L. (1966). *Unobtrusive measures: Nonreactive research in the social sciences* (Vol. 111). USA: Rand McNally Chicago.

Williams, L. J., & Brown, B. K. (1994). Method variance in organizational behavior and human resources research: Effects on correlations, path coefficients, and hypothesis testing. *Organizational Behavior and Human Decision Processes, 57*(2), 185–209.

Yin, R. K. (2013). *Case study research: Design and methods.* USA: Sage Publications.

Zikmund, W., Babin, B., Carr, J., & Griffin, M. (2012). *Business research methods.* USA: Cengage Learning.

# 5

# So Much of Research Is Context: Fieldwork Experience in Humanitarian Logistics

Minchul Sohn

## Introduction

For the last decade, humanitarian operations and supply chain management (HOSCM) research has received much attention together with several climatic extremes, complex crisis, and various global agendas discussed in the field of humanitarian, disaster risk reduction, and climate change adaptation. However, despite the growing attention from many scholars, arguably HOSCM still remains on the 'nascent' level (Edmondson and McManus 2007) as an emerging and interdisciplinary research arena in terms of the state of prior theory and research (Jahre et al. 2009). Consequently, there have been calls for the development of theory as well as research propositions in HOSCM to better understand and study the subject (Jahre et al. 2009; Jensen and Hertz 2016; Kovács and Spens 2011a; Tabaklar et al. 2015).

Field-based research has been suggested as an effort to advance theoretical contribution in supply chain management (Meredith 1998). DeHoratius and Rabinovich (2011) claim that field research is critical to the 'development of scientific knowledge' and for the deeper 'understanding of the operating phenomenon' that would advance supply chain management theory. This is particularly true when it comes to study supply chain management in a humanitarian context, where contextual specificities are crucial

M. Sohn (✉)
Hanken School of Economics, HUMLOG Institute, Helsinki, Finland
e-mail: minchul.sohn@hanken.fi

© The Author(s) 2018

**149**

G. Kovács et al. (eds.), *The Palgrave Handbook of Humanitarian Logistics and Supply Chain Management*, https://doi.org/10.1057/978-1-137-59099-2_5

elements to be considered in designing and managing supply chain for humanitarian/development assistance (Jahre 2010; Pedraza-Martinez et al. 2013). In other words, more field research is required in order to develop research further based on ideas, phenomenon, and contextual specificities of the humanitarian world and to realise empirical, evidence-based, and practice-near research domain (Holguín-Veras et al. 2014; Jahre and Heigh 2008; Kovács and Spens 2011a).

Whilst there are studies relatively more focused on research design and the process of field research with particular emphasis on philosophical aspects, e.g. 'methodological fit' (Alvesson and Kärreman 2007; Edmondson and McManus 2007), the current chapter will focus on fieldwork experience and fieldwork as a method to conduct first-hand data collection of qualitative or quantitative empirical materials for the purpose of achieving a detailed understanding of the context and practice. Yet again, what this chapter will discuss is inherently related to abductive research process, in other words, empirical material as a result of completed or ongoing fieldwork iteratively interact with research ideas, problems, and questions.

First, the chapter aims to review HLSCM literature based on empirical materials collected in field sites to identify how previous studies conducted field research in different circumstances. It will examine the benefits and challenges of conducting field research, as well as relevant activities the previous studies have created during the course of field research.

Second, the chapter aims to provide HLSCM researchers with 'practical' insights concerning important considerations in the design and conduct of field research. Similar to Jahre (2010), which is to the author's knowledge, the first personal account that provides highly relevant insights into conducting field research, this chapter will present the author's field research experience of studying disaster logistics preparedness in Zambia. As the compelling story of Jahre that would encourage other researchers to 'get out there', the author also believes that the current chapter can provide good insights to research students and early career researchers.

The chapter is organised as follows. First, the definition of field research will be delineated drawing on literature that discusses the methodological aspects of field research from sociology and management studies. Next, to address the first aim, fieldwork experiences in HLSCM literature are reviewed. In doing so, article selection process, descriptive analysis, and the findings of the content analysis are presented, respectively. Lastly, the second aim of the chapter is addressed through the author's personal account.

# Defining Field Research

*What is field research?* The term field research can be used very broadly in various ways, such as fieldwork, case study, or ethnography with a slightly different emphasis given to the work by researchers[1] (Burgess 2002). While Burgess (2002) defines 'field' as a circumscribed area of study in social research, it may not necessarily exist as a bounded entity as it is 'brought into being by social actors who collectively engage in their production' (Atkinson 2014). Consequently, field research incorporates an observational approach involving a relationship between the researcher and the research subject (Burgess 2002), driven by 'intrinsic curiosity' about distinctive lives and actions (Atkinson 2014).

In the arena of operations and supply chain management (OSCM), field research is considered as a methodology to understand the phenomena with the attributes, causes, and effects adhered to a process-oriented approach (Meredith 1998), rather than normative model/theory research, suggesting what and how things should be done based on idealised decision models (DeHoratius and Rabinovich 2011; Swamidass 1991).

Field research is often accompanied with interpretative procedures as the understanding of the phenomenon can only be made through the researcher's perceptual framework and be meaningful within that framework of assumptions specified by the researcher (Meredith 1998). Therefore, field research is not merely the adoption of a systematic and objective research technique but involves complex interaction between the research problem, subject, and researcher (Burgess 2002).

Schatzman and Strauss (1973) characterise a field researcher as '*a methodological pragmatist*' striving to clarify and understand the events of interest. Field research relies on primary data collection methods from real organisations in natural settings, considering temporal and contemporary aspects of the phenomenon being investigated (Meredith 1998; DeHoratius and Rabinovich 2011; Edmondson and McManus 2007; Scandura and Williams 2000). Sources of empirical materials can be both qualitative and quantitative, such as 'financial data, interviews, memoranda, business plans, organization charts, tools and other physical artefacts, questionnaires, and observations of […] (human) actions and interactions' (Meredith 1998).

---

[1] For more detailed discussion on historical roots and the science tradition of fieldwork, see Adler and Adler 1987; McCall 2006.

Therefore, activities, such as interviews, observations, demographic survey, or participations, in the environment of the phenomenon under study are essential to collect empirical materials while other forms of data gathering (e.g. desktop survey, interviews via telephone/teleconference, or even controlled laboratory experiments) can be incorporated to support field research.

In this regard, this chapter defines field research as:

Research conducted based on first-hand knowledge and empirical materials – qualitative and/or quantitative – obtained in the field sites for the purpose of achieving a detailed understanding of the context and practice.

In addition, this chapter adapts the term 'fieldwork' to particularise activities that unfold in the field and defined as:

A set of activities which are exploratory in nature in order to obtain first-hand knowledge and empirical materials in field sites.

Although separate definitions are given, the two terms are used interchangeably in this chapter in the context of conveying the main objective of two terminologies, which is the exploration of the phenomenon under study.

Also, it should be clear that the above definitions are narrower than suggested in the traditional field research literature, for example, Schatzman and Strauss (1973) use field research as an umbrella term for different activities that make a situation more understandable. Instead, this chapter's definitions intend to underline the 'being' in the field sites to scrutinise humanitarian contextual specifics of field research in HOSCM. As the chapter's aim is to appreciate more about field research in HOSCM, the focus should be the 'experience-based fieldwork' (Borneman and Hammoudi 2009).

# Fieldwork Experience

Shaffir and Stebbins (1990) describe that fieldwork is 'usually inconvenient, to say the least, sometimes physically uncomfortable, frequently embarrassing, and, to a degree, always tense' (p.1). They further characterise fieldwork as being 'fraught regularly with feelings of uncertainty and anxiety (...and) accompanied by an intense concern with whether the research is conducted and managed properly' (p. 2).

Such experiences are typical for field research although it may not usually be reported in such ways. It is almost unavailable through other forms of scientific research methods, which may have strict procedures to follow or a controllable environment with certain assumptions of reality. Field research is an intervention of other people's daily life and thoughts, where one should navigate without clear rules and signals (Schatzman and Strauss 1973).

Borneman and Hammoudi (2009) claim that fieldwork is a planned but dynamic encounter with people. In other words, many encounters are 'unintentional and accidental. Both planned and accidental encounters unfold under unpredictable conditions that nonetheless can result in fortunate outcomes…(through) on going relationships that intensify and multiply over time, resulting in knowledge that develops incrementally with the uneven accumulation of insights – a process that entails constant revision of what one has learned' (p.270). Critical aspects of field research are the 'constant revision' of 'accumulation of insights'. During the course of the research process, although it hardly is a linear process, researchers constantly doubt and learn from the ongoing experience of fieldwork full of unpredictable components.

While research 'encounters' can take place in various forms, such as reading written texts or screening films, Borneman and Hammoudi (2009) argue that the researcher's presence in the field is pre-conditional to explore the dynamics of connected episodes. Furthermore, they underline that fieldwork is not solely mapping of a place or personhood but it is an engagement of 'being there', also 'distancing' enough to be open to enrich understanding (Borneman and Hammoudi 2009).

It is important for researchers to recognise on-the-ground experience and expertise when conducting HOSCM research. Pedraza-Martinez et al. (2013) shared an anecdotal but very meaningful story as below:

> Following our first presentation at the Fleet Forum Annual Conference of 2007, the Fleet Forum Coordinator told our research team: 'the problem is that you look at us from an ivory tower. You should leave your ivory tower and go to the field to understand the way we work'. Another practitioner added: 'you do not understand our context'. Other practitioners repeatedly asked: 'have you been to the field?' Both the lack of trust of practitioners and of literature relevant to our subject motivated us to include field trips in our research project. (p.S58)

This highlights the fundamental importance of using fieldworks to ensure that the research is relevant in HOSCM.

Many studies in humanitarian logistics have pointed out the difference between commercial logistics and humanitarian contexts. Humanitarian contextual particularities were identified and enhanced our understanding of humanitarian logistics, yet many were made at a general and abstract level, such as unpredictable demand and supply, level of urgency, chaotic environment, and deprived resources. Holguín-Veras et al. (2014) claim that 'a major issue that hampers research, development, and implementation of more effective PD-HL (post disaster humanitarian logistics) systems is that the realities of actual operations are poorly understood' (p.87); particularly, the transient and dynamic nature of the activities. Although Holguín-Veras et al. (2014) specified the context of post disaster, arguably fieldwork is a great opportunity for a researcher to characterise and collect data through access to real people on the ground as well as observing actual operations. Only a handful of publications discussed humanitarian logistics based on direct observation, in other words 'research community has only scratched the surface of the subject' (Holguín-Veras et al. 2014).

# Fieldwork Experience in HOSCM: A Literature Review

The first aim of the chapter, to identify how previous HOSCM literature conducted field research, will be addressed in this section. For the last few years, there have been several calls from the major journal outlets for empirical research in the field of humanitarian logistics and operations management, including a call for a special issue in the *Journal of Operations* (2014)[2] and *European Journal of Operational Research* (2016).[3] Fieldwork may not be the only empirical methodology that these special issues call for, however it is the sine qua non of the studies that are 'well-grounded in practical foundation' and 'explore (new) humanitarian problems using rigorous case study research'. In this regard, content analysis of relevant literature will be discussed below.

## Article Selection

Four major databases were used, including Emerald, Science Direct, Taylor and Francis, and Wiley to identify relevant studies in HOSCM. The keywords search was used mainly for the initial stage and then delimited the literature thereafter. The keywords used were: 'humanitarian logistics',

---

[2] Special issue on Empirically Grounded Research in Humanitarian Operations Management.
[3] Special issue on OR Applied to Humanitarian Operations.

'humanitarian supply chain', 'disaster logistics', and 'disaster supply chain'. These keywords were chosen to adequately filter the research related to logistics and supply chain management related to pre/post disaster management, humanitarian assistance, and disaster risk reduction. However, it is possible that this search may miss some relevant studies. The article selection process is shown in Fig. 5.1.

The initial search identified 556 articles in total. After reviewing the titles and abstracts to exclude irrelevant articles, conference papers, and editorials, the number was reduced to 262. Subsequently, literature review papers and conceptual studies were excluded after reviewing the contents, reducing the number of papers to 193. More in-depth reading of the contents was conducted in order to sort out papers that used secondary data, 'case studies' mainly for the validation of operations research (OR) algorithms, computational simulations, and numerical experiments. Some OR studies, which belong to axiomatic domain of OR, are often conceptualised based on optimal solutions focusing on mathematical correctness whereas empirical OR studies start from problems of context and situations (Bertrand and Fransoo 2002; Galindo and Batta 2013). Thus, particularly for the OR studies, this chapter focuses on empirical OR studies that are based on field research to decide relevant parameters and assumptions that are convincingly grounded in reality for defining problems and building models. These studies largely use first-hand knowledge and empirical materials rather than historical data of past cases or secondary documents. After this stage, 98 articles remained.

Lastly, studies that conducted fieldworks in the field sites were selected based on two criteria. First, 'being there', in other words, studies based on remote interviews, questionnaire survey, or Delphi method were excluded. Second, interest in a particular empirical setting or 'scene' rather than general system characteristics.

This process excluded some studies that were not clear in reporting and describing their methodology regarding data collection. Such studies without specification of empirical methods tend not to focus on the 'scene' or contextual settings but rather prioritise gathering required functional data and information to synthesise models, concepts, or frameworks at a systems level. These articles are excluded as the chapter's overriding focus is on field research and experience. However, there are a few exceptions. Some papers were included even though no specification was provided about methodologies related to field research: if the paper clearly indicated field visits, if the paper's fieldworks could be traced from the other publications, or if the paper contained research problems and models that are heavily empirically grounded. The four-stage selection process resulted in 55 articles for further analysis.

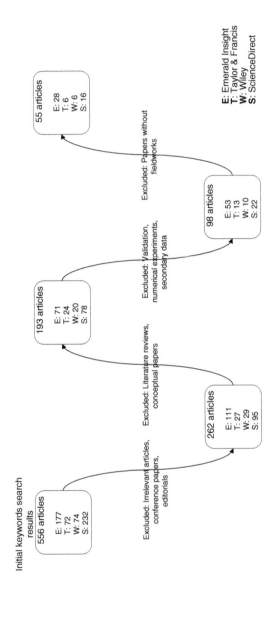

Initial keywords search results

**556 articles**
E: 177
T: 72
W: 74
S: 232

Excluded: Irrelevant articles, conference papers, editorials

**262 articles**
E: 111
T: 27
W: 29
S: 95

Excluded: Literature reviews, conceptual papers

**193 articles**
E: 71
T: 24
W: 20
S: 78

Excluded: Validation, numerical experiments, secondary data

**98 articles**
E: 53
T: 13
W: 10
S: 22

Excluded: Papers without fieldworks

**55 articles**
E: 28
T: 6
W: 6
S: 16

**E:** Emerald Insight
**T:** Taylor & Francis
**W:** Wiley
**S:** ScienceDirect

**Fig. 5.1**  Article selection process

# Fieldwork Experience in HOSCM: Findings from the Review

The analysis of literature about the fieldwork experience is discussed in four sections as below. These four categories were developed through a series of questions during the analysis of the final list of articles such as: why did they conduct fieldwork, how did they organise it and what did they actually do, and what were the benefits and challenges? It should be noted that some articles provided a detailed description of their methodologies including fieldwork, while others only briefly mentioned their fieldwork or field visit.

* Motivations for conducting fieldwork
* Challenges for conducting fieldwork
* Activities in fieldwork
* Reflection on lack of field research

Under each heading, selected excerpts from the literature are shown in Tables 5.1–5.3 to bring in a live voice of fieldwork experience from the literature.

## Motivation for Conducting Fieldworks

As researchers consider their aims and objectives in the design of their research strategies, they determine relevant and necessary methodologies that are aligned to their research strategies. Not all empirical studies conduct fieldworks, as manifested during the process of article selection. The particular motivation for conducting fieldworks can be for close observation, improved contextuality, and as a preparatory step.

### Close Observation

Fieldwork enables researchers to make close observations of the subject and phenomenon under investigation. Being close to the field has several benefits. First, it gives a great opportunity for exploratory studies to investigate under-studied areas, producing in-depth textual data, including interviews, field notes and other data sources. Researchers can explore first-hand information and 'unheralded' aspects of reality, its complexity, dynamics, and real problems. As Holguín-Veras et al. (2014) asserted, research development of HOSCM can be facilitated through a thorough under-standing of the reality of actual operations. Research with actual experience in the field can reveal the specific mechanism by which things are organised in practice.

Second, the participative nature of research will be enjoyed in the field. For example, a researcher may participate in the daily decision-making process, routines of different operations, and some may engage in action research (Chandes and Paché 2010; Jahre et al. 2012). In addition, many studies have indicated that informal discussions become possible, not only with the arranged interviewees but also with others, such as the locals, working staff, government officials, or participants in exercises. The associa-tion with the local environment while staying in the field is an important aspect of field research in that a researcher can achieve a wide variety of evidence-based insights, increasing the credibility (Pedraza-Martinez et al. 2013).

Third, the instantaneous nature of disaster management research can be captured through fieldwork. Researchers who were in the field underlined the opportunities to obtain on-the-spot knowledge and understanding (Coles et al. 2012; Holguín-Veras et al. 2014; Holguín-Veras et al. 2012; Perry 2007). The immediate perceptions from the crucial initial phases by both humanitarian workers and researchers are inherently ephemeral (Holguín-Veras et al. 2014). Fieldwork provide researchers with distinct impressions based on the direct observation of the impact of disasters on the infrastructure, community, and people, whilst being available to interview individuals involved in the chaotic initial stage (Holguín-Veras et al. 2014). For example, field visits to Haiti right after the earthquake allowed the gathering of information that would characterise humanitarian logistics with an immediate impact and to capture subtler dynamics between agencies in the field (Coles et al. 2012; Holguín-Veras et al. 2012).

## Increased Contextualisation

Fieldwork allows theoretical concepts and frameworks to be contextualised and understood in empirical settings. Conceptualisation of humanitarian logistics is often based on typical supply chain strategic traits manifested dependent on pre/post disaster events or one or more of phases within the disaster cycle. Such conceptualisation may provide a better understanding of the logistical processes required in disaster management and critical success factors. However, it is also important to remember that contextualisation through empirical research is required to further develop the concepts to be more relevant and rigorous to humanitarian world. Particularly, fieldwork is essential to perform a research investigation spatially and temporally, for all disasters do have diverse and dynamic patterns (IPCC 2012). Many case studies of HOSCM are centred on particular disaster events (e.g. South Asian Tsunami, Haiti earthquake) or organisational operations of disaster logistics in some localities. These studies provide rich contextual information provided that they are empirically well grounded. Fieldwork can supplement the inadequacy of other data collection techniques (Akhtar et al. 2012) or enhance the existing secondary data to investigate a particular context (Jahre et al. 2012). Contextualisation can be also made in a deductive way from corroborating theory in a particular context (Ketokivi and Choi 2014), preferably in the field being away from the ivory tower (Pedraza-Martinez et al. 2013). In other words, pre-defined prepositions and theoretical concepts can be contextualised through fieldwork and be demonstrated with empirical materials (Kunz and Gold 2015; L'Hermitte et al. 2016).

## Preparatory Step

Fieldwork provides useful and firm ground for further research objectives as a preparatory stage during the research project. Researchers can be more familiarised with the setting through the interviews and observations of the initial stage, in which development and revision of the interview guide, hypothesis, and propositions can be facilitated (Jensen and Hertz 2016; Kabra and Ramesh 2015). Formal and informal discussions provide opportunities to define relevant problems emerging from the field and to gain access to internal documents and other knowledge to broaden the understanding of the context (Cao et al. 2016; Jahre and Heigh 2008; Jensen and Hertz 2016; Kunz et al. 2015). In development of mathematical models, simulation, and decision support systems, such a preparatory step is appropriate in order for better empirically grounded research. Many studies explained that they identified important parameters and assumptions for incorporation into their model via interviews and observations during their fieldwork. Discussion with end-users and on-site inspections were essential to confirm the feasibility of the assumptions embedded in the decision model (Hadiguna et al. 2014). Beamon and Kotleba (2006) noted that mode of transportation, discrete intervals of demand, and other attributes of contextual elements that contribute to unpredictability in the relief supply chain were identified and used for their model development. Input data were collected, and better understanding of locality could be realised (Green et al. 2013). Furthermore, collaboration between researchers and practitioners in the field could shape the simulation model to become based on real organisations (Beamon and Kotleba 2006; Ergun et al. 2014; Saputra et al. 2015) (Table 5.1).

**Table 5.1** Motivation and benefits of conducting fieldworks – selected excerpts from the literature

| Close observation | | Excerpt from the literature |
|---|---|---|
| | | 1. Explorative nature |
| | Thompson (2015) | 'Although time consuming, this research approach (field research) was chosen primarily because the disaster management literature on the region is small. The research strategy therefore relies upon the collection of rich textual data that could then be explored inductively' |
| | Holguín-Veras et al. (2012) | 'The authors' field work identified, in contrast to these difficulties (as reported in the media), a number of unheralded relief operations that were able to deliver relief aid [...] this paper is to identify the factors that explain these contrasting performances' |
| | Gralla et al. (2015) | (Fieldworks can) 'capture the extensive knowledge and experience that went into (training) development' |
| | Jensen (2012) | (To explore) 'actual experience in the field, [...] how the cluster system has worked in practice' |
| | | 2. Participative nature |
| | Rietjens et al. (2014) | 'possibility to participate in several meetings [...]In addition to the formal interviews and participatory observation, many informal conversation took place through which information was gathered' |
| | Coles et al. (2012) | 'Meeting agency representatives in person and conducting interviews in the field helped to increase research credibility, diversify the types of data shared, and increase the volume of information collected.' |
| | Pedraza Martinez et al. (2011) | 'Although collected on a less formal basis, this data was recorded and stored using the same rigorous procedures outlined below' |

Table 5.1  (continued)

| | | 3. Instantaneous nature |
|---|---|---|
| | Holguín-Veras et al. (2012) | 'This paper have looked into the real-life performance of humanitarian logistics [...] (have collected) field data so soon after the event' |
| | Holguín-Veras et al. (2014) | 'if (researchers) are not allowed to observe the operations, the opportunity to characterise and collect data about the initial stages gets increasingly difficult' |
| Increased contextualisation | L'Hermitte et al. (2016) | 'our study is motivated by the need to understand a research phenomenon that has only been delineated conceptually' |
| | Rancourt et al. (2015) | 'Not having spent time in the field would have resulted in a misconception of the problem, and some important realities would not have been identified' |
| Preparatory step | Jensen and Hertz (2016) | 'to obtain an understanding of what questions were most pertinent to the field' |

## Challenges for Conducting Fieldwork

As Jahre (2010) documented in her personal fieldwork experience, undertaking fieldwork in HOSCM is a challenging process. Most of the reviewed studies have not presented in detail the challenges of fieldwork; however, several important traits were evident. Rancourt et al. (2015) remarked that the difficult task was more about defining the research problem and carrying out field data collection rather than developing algorithmic solutions.

It has been observed that often field sites are located in remote areas, hence difficult to access (Jahre et al. 2012; Pedraza Martinez et al. 2011). Meeting with interviewees and stakeholders is not a simple task due to the geographical distance (Beamon and Kotleba 2006). Not only the physical access but getting permission from the organisations and other research subjects was challenging. Kunz et al. (2015) referred to making good contacts in their longitudinal study as a particularly difficult process, unless organisations were partnered or co-involved in the project they would not have a strong willingness to collaborate.

Security was another important challenge; for example, researchers were not allowed to go out of the military camp, thus limiting their direct contact with people outside the camp. Instead, researchers could participate meetings within the camp where people from the outside were invited by the military reconstruction team (Rietjens et al. 2014).

**Table 5.2** Challenges and impediments of conducting fieldworks – selected excerpts from the literature

|  |  | Excerpt from the literature |
|---|---|---|
| Remoteness | Jahre et al. (2012) | 'The field context was challenging, with 5,000 km at a speed of 30 km per hour on dirt roads, wearing bulletproof vests, and helmets' |
|  | Pedraza Martinez et al. (2011) | 'we travelled approximately 750 km by road, over the course of a 2 days round trip to observe field fleet in action' |
| Security | Rietjens et al. (2014) | 'The security situation made it impossible for the research team to leave the camp' |
| Real-life complexity | Holguín-Veras et al. (2014) | 'At some point it is no longer possible to document the operations as memories fade, data are lost, and the ability to identify and find the individuals involved evaporates' |
| Local constraints | Soneye (2014) | 'The administration was […] with limited challenges (although) the enumerators were residing in the communities, could speak the local language and had adequate communication skills […]' |

Other challenges include the dynamics and urgencies embedded in disaster studies (Oloruntoba 2013; Thévenaz and Resodihardjo 2010). Given that the limited and chaotic time in the aftermath of the disaster, examining real life complexity is highly challenging (Holguín-Veras et al. 2014). Also, there is some restraint related to a particular locality where languages and cultural issues can be difficult. In some cases, the purpose of the research can be misconstrued politically and information is unattainable or sharing it becomes impossible (Soneye 2014) (Table 5.2).

## Activities in Fieldwork

In addition to the benefits and challenges related to fieldwork, the findings from content analysis include several purposeful activities that the studies have created. These purposeful activities could be a good point of reference for those who have conducted fieldwork to reflect on or for those who are planning HOSCM fieldwork.

Many studies have a host organisation or organisations who are in collaboration in terms of conducting research in the field. These organisations are located in the field and play a crucial supporting role for researchers, such as opening the way for access to the site, identifying the main stakeholders and contacts to interview, and providing real data (Beamon and Balcik 2008; Coles et al. 2012; Jahre et al. 2012; Kretschmer et al. 2014; Rancourt et al. 2015; Rietjens et al. 2014). There are some common concerns in disaster management field that it is unsafe or unhelpful for people other than first responders to enter the field. Coles et al. (2012) described how they overcome such concerns with the pivotal support from the host organisation in Haiti who provided researchers with the legitimate role of coordinating logistics operations in the aftermath of the disaster. When it comes to close collaboration, some research projects involve active interaction between theory and practice, thus, develop into a form of action research or co-authoring a paper about the detailed investigation of the organisation's system (Kunz et al. 2015; Mohanty and Chakravarty 2013; Saputra et al. 2015).

Studies have highlighted that maintaining a good rapport with interviewees and other practitioners is important in field research. Committed field visits could increase the mutual trust between researchers and practitioners, demonstrating the researchers' commitment to understanding the context (Pedraza Martinez et al. 2011). This could be appreciated by interviewees who would trust the researchers more, providing more detailed accounts and even, some contentious topics. Such credibility could be realised through getting help from a local venerated person, such as a pastor, working in the field when building relationship with local agencies (Coles et al. 2012).

When planning fieldwork for a particular disaster or a particular organisation as a case, relevant secondary data has been collected alongside the fieldwork. Depending on the research subject, pre-examining the information related to the field cannot always be possible. However, Holguín-Veras et al. (2014, 2012) have created a 'timeline' of relevant incidents related to the case disaster through different sources of media and organisations involved in disaster management. Such efforts could help researchers to better understand how things evolve in the field and continue during their time in the field.

Data collection during the fieldwork can be overwhelming if careful measures are not made. An intensive field visit can cause some unexpected process and also create an overwhelming mass of unanalysed data. Such issues can be a large burden for a researcher. Thus, it is wise to briefly reflect on the research process as well as the collected empirical materials. Researchers have noted that interview questionnaires were constantly updated as interviews progressed and discussion about preliminary findings with practitioners helped them to confirm and re-organise the research process (Jahre et al. 2012; Kunz et al. 2015). Also, it is worth referring to some of the structured approaches to adeptly handle the volume of data in the field. Pedraza Martinez et al. (2011) have carried out a series of activities for data collection

**Table 5.3** Activities in conducting fieldworks – selected excerpts from the literature

| | | Excerpt from the literature |
|---|---|---|
| Host/partnered organisation | Coles et al. (2012) | 'A pastor (from the partnered organisation) travelled with the researcher for the first week [...] to assist the researcher in establishing credibility and connecting with (other) agencies' |
| Action research | Chandes and Paché (2010) | 'One of the author [...] has been involved in the management of logistical humanitarian operations. Taking full advantage of his status as an internal participant observer [...]' |
| Planning | Holguín-Veras et al. (2014) | '(to facilitate understanding of the complex response) develop timelines of the key events, and a basic script that describes how the response evolved' |
| Ethical approval | Ibegbunam and McGill (2012) | 'The ethical approval request included the following documentation: detailed application form, participant information sheet, informed consent form, interview instrument and approved research proposal.' |

and storage in the field including daily debriefings, sharing field notes and impressions, revising and updating the interview guide, compiling detailed interview notes, and application to the theoretical framework.

Lastly, studies underlined the importance of establishing ethical guidelines for research concerning population affected by disasters and other impoverishment (Ibegbunam and McGill 2012; Oloruntoba 2013). Ethical approvals were required both internally and externally, the researcher's own institutions and local health research authority, respectively. To secure the approvals, Ibegbunam and McGill (2012) noted that they had to inform and complete the relevant documentation that underpin the research in great detail and even obtain certificates from online ethics courses. Pre-arrangement of such approvals is important so as not to delay the fieldwork process (Table 5.3).

## Reflection – Why the Lack of Fieldwork?

This chapter reviewed previous studies with fieldwork and presented the benefits, challenges, and practical activities for fieldwork. Holguín-Veras et al. (2014) claimed that 'field research [...] is key to develop new paradigms of PD-HL able to deal with the real life complexity of the operations.' Field research is essential to provide evidence-based insights and to better plan the future response in practice. Although field research will not be the only way to attain such benefits, relevant and rigorous research is largely attributed to findings, knowledge, and experience from field research and will be even better when complemented by other types of methodologies.

Although previously pointed out as in Kovács and Spens (2009), Kovács and Spens (2011b), and Kunz and Reiner (2012), empirical research is still required as well as studies based on fieldwork to enhance the contextuality and relevance to the real-life situation.

There are a number of factors for the lack of empirical/field-based research. It was observed that some fieldwork, particularly for logistics research in the post-disaster response, was initiated in a short period of time as emergency fieldworkers are rapidly deployed in response to the unexpected onset of a disaster, e.g. Holguín-Veras et al. (2012). It could be that many researchers are not in a position to make such an immediate field visit. In addition, security issues discourage and constrain researchers from going into the field. A review of studies delivering humanitarian aid in a highly insecure environment revealed limited academic engagement (Schreter and Harmer 2013). Field visits also require dedicated time. Indeed, researchers may not be motivated to perform fieldwork but also may prefer or be required to use their research grant for quantitative studies rather than 'soft data' from fieldwork. Moreover, field-based research may be difficult to get published (Borgström 2012). The chapter also highlighted that the importance of fieldwork experience is not widely shared in the literature with a few exceptions, such as Jahre (2010) and Pedraza-Martinez et al. (2013), who reflected on their field experience. This may be due to a number of factors including limited space in journal publications for detailed descriptions about field research, a tendency to report the research process overly formalised as linear and concise, and an interest in generic system levels.

Therefore, this chapter is an exceptional opportunity to engage in an in depth discussion about field research. To add further to previous fieldwork accounts in HOSCM literature; and to complement the limited formal outlet to describe fieldwork experience, the next section will elaborate the author's field experience based on a case study conducted in Zambia.

## Field Research in Zambia

The author's field research experience is based on the case study of disaster preparedness logistics in Zambia. As aforementioned, the focus is to deliver some practical insights through the author's confessional tale. For this reason, the current section is organised in a successive sequential manner as often appears in traditional fieldwork textbooks. However, such linear conceptualisation is more of a heuristic device rather than what and how actual engagements unfolded during the field research (Gubrium 1990). Most of the author's engagements and encounters in the field were constantly rearranged and renegotiated throughout the course of the field research.

## Gaining Entry

The author's field research was a part of a large two-year research project. The overall purpose of the project was to strengthen the societies' resilience to climate hazards and to enhance the climate change adaptation research in Zambia. The author's field research focused particularly on the use of weather information and early warning systems for humanitarian supply chains.

It must be noted that being within the large project, the author's fieldwork process has been largely facilitated by its pre-determined scope of the subject and geographical range. Other researchers might have different starting point than the author. Also, the Zambia Meteorological Department (ZMD) as a partner of the project could host the author during the field visit. Preparation for the field visits was realised based on secondary sources and communication with the ZMD.

Some of prominent actors in the field were identified through desk research. About three weeks before the field visit, the author contacted them via email to arrange meetings and reminders were sent after two weeks. However, many interviews were arranged in the field via telephone and interviewees were identified through snowball sampling.

In general, gaining access to the government and public sector was difficult. These institutions tend to have a rather hierarchical bureaucracy, in which official requests are strictly required, preferably from the higher hierarchical level of the requested side. The author managed to get assistance from the ZMD, hence, official letters written by the chief of the ZMD were sent to authorities concerned, which played a crucial role for entry to the government authorities. However, this was very time consuming, that being so, many encounters with the government authorities were at the end of the field visit period. Considering that some information gained from one actor can be very used for the others, the process of official requests could have been made ahead of time, particularly if the stay in the field is limited.

One useful tool to convince interviewees to participate was the one-page document, which was sent together with the interview invitation email. The one-page explains the project and purpose of the interview in brief. During the interviews, many interviewees mentioned what they already understood from the one-page. Otherwise, the author handed it out on site for their perusal.

## Getting Organised

As the author became engaged and more adapted into the field, the methods had to be reassessed, reflecting and improving on what had been done. After each interview, the author made a brief summary before updating the interview guide. The initial interviews were decisive to alter the initial focus of disaster response to disaster preparedness.

Also, the author closely studied the map of Zambia, particularly the southern province which often experiences droughts and floods. Interviewees often mentioned place names in their accounts of a disaster or some issues related to weather variability. It was crucial to recognise such place names and their location on the map so that the author could comprehend the context and to prompt related questions.

An accidental meeting with one of the initial interviewees over lunch led to an informal conversation about general topics but he also provided a detailed picture of Zambia disaster management, his thoughts on the system, and other weather-related issues. From then, the author took the opportunity to invite interviewees to lunch as it was culturally acceptable in Zambia, according to a local colleague.

## Maintaining Relationships

The author's fieldwork experience consisted of many 'short-term encounters' (Gurney 1990). It involved intensive interviewing of different managers in governmental, non-governmental, United Nations, and private sector organisations. Engaging in short-term encounters meant that the researcher's intrusion into the settings of the research subjects was relatively brief in comparison to long-term field research (Gurney 1990). Consequently, participants were less reluctant to accept the author's interview invitation. On the other hand, the author had to cope with the anxiety of not getting 'good' and 'enough' information from each short-term encounter. During the interviews, although most were about an hour-long, different impressions are made which will influence rapport, trust, and other expectations between the researcher and the participant. Hence, the author has to play different roles. Beyond the control of the author, the author's image was perceived by the research subjects as a logistics expert, meteorologist, research student, or sometimes a sort of programme evaluator. Rather than providing them with a 'correct' image of the author, if it ever exists, the author had to role-play depending on the contingencies to enable subjects to put down their guard and to help conversation flow. Shaffir (1990) described such role-playing as 'the tactic of self-presentation' and this never became static during the author's fieldwork.

Similar to role-playing, the research partnership with the ZMD should not be overlooked. The involvement of the ZMD hugely supported the project and the author's fieldwork, yet at the same time, it had repercussions for the research subjects' attitudes. For example, although the interviews were confidential, subjects were rather hazy about the quality of weather information or hesitant towards being critical of the early warning systems. The author's tactic was to establish, naturally during the conversation, the rather clear division between the researcher and the government's role, as well as highlighting the importance of end-users' viewpoint from the subjects' perspective.

## Reflection – Coming Back from the Field

Although this chapter is based on the author's field experience in Zambia, fieldwork is not necessarily associated with visits to exotic or unfamiliar parts of the world. As can be seen from the example of (Burgess 2002), fieldwork can be conducted at 'home', such as in local schools or neighbourhoods. Nonetheless, the intensive nature of the fieldwork experience, regardless of the location or the duration, will be transformative and will be followed by a pronounced change in one's routine. Thus, it is useful to ask questions before 'leaving' the field, as Cupples and Kindon (2003) have suggested:

> How am I going to manage my data? Do I need time for transcribing and data analysis before writing can commence? What should I include and what should I leave out? Is a return visit to the field possible, if necessary?

Other relevant questions that the author asked were:

Are there any materials that I did not obtain that I could go back and find? How should I close or maintain the relationship with the people I met in the field? Where would I start with my data and what should I prioritise?

The author believes that these questions and thinking about the scenario are worth considering before vivid field impressions fade away. They will also be helpful in providing a new perspective on the field by 'zooming out' from the data while remaining physically in the field.

Analysis and writing following fieldwork is extremely challenging. The author's case was no exception, as the author had to digest a vast amount of messy data. Interviews, field notes, organisational reports, and other relevant secondary data were reviewed and analysed. Soon after the field visit, the author was required to compile a report on the project. The report consisted of preliminary findings from the field that were mainly based on the author's memories and field notes. While the output was worthwhile, the author would like to point out that there are some risks of being bound by a few initial thoughts.

Fieldwork is an ongoing process that includes the analysis and writing stages. One would never consider 'writing it up' as a disparate and unproblematic activity (Berg and Mansvelt 2000). The author spent several months reading the data and other materials to analyse and find meanings. The author's interest was disaster preparedness as a practice and related decision making, but a concrete theoretical approach was not determined prior to the fieldwork. Hence, constructing a theoretical perspective was another challenging process, and many of the author's attempts were reconsidered and refined.

In addition, the author often sensed that the data were incomplete. This is completely natural, although such feelings can cause anxiety and discourage one from analysis and writing. The author is convinced that a firm belief in a common axiom 'writing is a way of knowing' will help to overcome any writing blocks or obstructions. Small field notes, photos, or local newspapers can sometimes be very useful in the analysis and representation of data.

## Conclusion

Despite the fact that many studies have argued for considering humanitarian specificities when studying HOSCM, there is still a need for HOSCM research based on fieldwork. This chapter offered some practical insight for those who have conducted fieldwork to reflect on or for those who are planning HOSCM fieldwork. HOSCM literature was reviewed to identify the benefits and challenges of conducting field research, as well as relevant activities that previous studies have undertaken during the fieldwork. In addition, the author also reflected on his previous fieldwork experience. Reports of field research in the literature are often constrained by editorial policy and restricted to a formal report on methodological accounts, limiting more detailed dialogue on the fieldwork experience and actual implementation. Together with the literature review, the author's personal experience was intended to underline the practical aspects and to provide some guidance on the actual implementation of fieldwork.

Despite the importance of field research, there are some acknowledged pitfalls in conducting field research, particularly in the area of HOSCM. Lee-Treweek and Linkogle (2002) contended that the nature of field research or qualitative inquiry may pose a potential danger and unexpected threat to researchers. They identified four key areas of danger in the field: physical, emotional, ethical, and professional. These risks are highly relevant to the context of HOSCM field research, particularly those set in disaster affected and humanitarian crisis areas. Physically, field researchers need to ensure their own safety as well as the safety of others. Emotionally, it is important to develop coping strategies for the unexpected effects on researchers after their field experience. In some post disaster environments and complex disasters, researchers may experience feelings of frustration, powerlessness, and emotional deprivation. Ethically, it is critical to have ethical responsibility for the management of the research project, protecting participants within ethical guidelines, e.g. research on vulnerable population or humanitarian aid in an unstable regime. Professionally, researchers may be confronted with the consequences of being in the minority by challenging the existing 'occupational dynamics' of the discipline or by pursuing the 'unfashionable' topics and methodologies. Indeed, this is in fact an inevitable aspect of the subject field of OSCM, although the boundaries of acceptable methodology in this field have certainly changed.

Apart from such areas of 'danger', what may seem like practical and mundane activities will occupy an enormous portion of researcher's time and effort in conducting field research. These mundane, practical issues should not be regarded as trivial but require careful planning and preparation well in advance (Barrett and Cason 2010; Stiffman 2009). In other words, fieldwork requires researchers to consider 'a host of issues that are simultaneously pragmatic, ethical, and scientific' during the course of field research (Stiffman 2009).

Many have called for well-grounded empirical research in HOSCM and indeed studies have been carried out to acquire theoretical and practical insight. Not all empirical research in HOSCM requires field research. However, if we aim to take account of contextuality and to be deeply involved in the episodes of practice, fieldwork will be very useful and have a profound effect on researchers. The close interaction, including conversation, observation, or participation, with research subjects can provide detailed dynamics of their pursuits, e.g. thoughts, commitments, motives, and other associated rationalisation (Dodge and Geis 2006). On the other hand, fieldwork should not be romanticised. There is no one right way or easy way of conducting field research yet recognising the meaningful contingencies will be critical in every fieldwork experience.

# Appendix 1

## Recommended Reading for Fieldwork Experience

Most of the books in the list below are referred to in the main text; however, a short introduction is presented here.

Borneman and Hammoudi (2009)

Eight essays of reflective writing on their fieldwork experience from an anthropologists' point of view. This book critically reviews 'textualism' while underlining fieldwork encounters 'in which experiential insights are arrived', particularly in interlocution.

Burgess (2002)

A good introductory book for a researcher looking to explore how to conduct field research. As this book is a sort of 'how-to' book, it is helpful in designing research strategies. This book contains suggested readings in each chapter. The author of this book exemplifies his own field experiences of a contemporary school setting in which he said researchers have 'come home' to study.

Johnson (1978)

An author's reflection on his own field experience, providing a detailed description. The critical appraisal of several field research text books are interesting to read.

Schatzman and Strauss (1973)

A classics field research text book that describes a hypothetical setting of a researcher involved in field research. Although the book is dated, it is read easily. Selectable reading of each chapter can be made with ease depending on the reader's interest.

# References

Adler, Patricia, and Peter Adler. 1987. *Membership Roles in Field Research*. 2455 Teller Road, Thousand Oaks California 91320 USA: SAGE Publications, Inc.

Akhtar, P., N. E. Marr, and E. V. Garnevska. 2012. 'Coordination in Humanitarian Relief Chains: Chain Coordinators'. *Journal of Humanitarian Logistics and Supply Chain Management* 2 (1): 85–103. doi:10.1108/20426741211226019.

Alvesson, Mats, and Dan Kärreman. 2007. 'Constructing Mystery: Empirical Matters in Theory Development'. *Academy of Management Review* 32 (4): 1265–81. doi:10.5465/AMR.2007.26586822.

Atkinson, Paul. 2014. *For Ethnography*. London: SAGE.

Barrett, Christopher B., and Jeffrey Cason. 2010. *Overseas Research II: A Practical Guide*. Abingdon, Oxon: Routledge.

Beamon, Benita M., and Burcu Balcik. 2008. 'Performance Measurement in Humanitarian Relief Chains'. *International Journal of Public Sector Management* 21 (1): 4–25. doi:10.1108/09513550810846087.

Beamon, Benita M., and Stephen A. Kotleba. 2006. 'Inventory Management Support Systems for Emergency Humanitarian Relief Operations in South Sudan'. *The International Journal of Logistics Management* 17 (2): 187–212. doi:10.1108/09574090610689952.

Berg, Lawrence, and Juliana Mansvelt. 2000. 'Writing In, Speaking Out: Communicating Qualitative Research Findings'. In *Qualitative Research Methods in Human Geography*, edited by Iain Hay. Melbourne: Oxford University Press.

Bertrand, J.Will M., and Jan C. Fransoo. 2002. 'Operations Management Research Methodologies Using Quantitative Modeling'. *International Journal of Operations & Production Management* 22 (2): 241–64. doi:10.1108/01443570210414338.

Borgström, Benedikte. 2012. 'Towards a Methodology for Studying Supply Chain Practice'. *International Journal of Physical Distribution & Logistics Management* 42 (8/9): 843–62. doi:10.1108/09600031211269785.

Borneman, John, and Abdellah Hammoudi. 2009. *Being There: The Fieldwork Encounter and the Making of Truth*. London: University of California Press.

Burgess, Robert G. 2002. *In the Field: An Introduction to Field Research*. London: Routledge.

Cao, Wenwei, Melih Çelik, Özlem Ergun, Julie Swann, and Nadia Viljoen. 2016. 'Challenges in Service Network Expansion: An Application in Donated Breastmilk Banking in South Africa'. *Socio-Economic Planning Sciences*, Location Analysis for Public Sector Decision-Making in Uncertain Times, 53 (March): 33–48. doi:10.1016/j.seps.2015.10.006.

Chandes, Jérôme, and Gilles Paché. 2010. 'Investigating Humanitarian Logistics Issues: From Operations Management to Strategic Action'. *Journal of*

*Manufacturing Technology Management* 21 (3): 320–40. doi:10.1108/17410381011024313.

Coles, John B., Jun Zhuang, and Justin Yates. 2012. 'Case Study in Disaster Relief: A Descriptive Analysis of Agency Partnerships in the Aftermath of the January 12th, 2010 Haitian Earthquake'. *Socio-Economic Planning Sciences*, Special Issue: Disaster Planning and Logistics: Part 1, 46 (1): 67–77. doi:10.1016/j.seps.2011.08.002.

Cupples, Julie, and Sara Kindon. 2003. 'Returning to University and Writing the Field'. In *Development Fieldwork*, edited by Regina Scheyvens and Donovan Storey, 217–32. 6 Bonhill Street, London England EC2A 4PU United Kingdom: SAGE Publications Ltd.

DeHoratius, Nicole, and Elliot Rabinovich. 2011. 'Field Research in Operations and Supply Chain Management'. *Journal of Operations Management*, Special Issue on Field Research in Operations and Supply Chain Management, 29 (5): 371–75. doi:10.1016/j.jom.2010.12.007.

Dodge, Mary, and Gilbert Geis. 2006. 'Fieldwork with the Elite: Interviewing White-Collar Criminals'. In *The SAGE Handbook of Fieldwork*, edited by Dick Hobbs and Richard Wright, 80–91. 1 Oliver's Yard, 55 City Road, London EC1Y 1SP United Kingdom: SAGE Publications Ltd.

Edmondson, Amy C., and Stacy E. McManus. 2007. 'Methodological Fit in Management Field Research'. *Academy of Management Review* 32 (4): 1246–64. doi:10.5465/AMR.2007.26586086.

Ergun, Özlem, Luyi Gui, Jessica L. Heier Stamm, Pinar Keskinocak, and Julie Swann. 2014. 'Improving Humanitarian Operations through Technology-Enabled Collaboration'. *Production and Operations Management* 23 (6): 1002–14. doi:10.1111/poms.12107.

Galindo, Gina, and Rajan Batta. 2013. 'Review of Recent Developments in OR/MS Research in Disaster Operations Management'. *European Journal of Operational Research* 230 (2): 201–11. doi:10.1016/j.ejor.2013.01.039.

Gralla, Erica, Jarrod Goentzel, and Bernard Chomilier. 2015. 'Case Study of a Humanitarian Logistics Simulation Exercise and Insights for Training Design'. *Journal of Humanitarian Logistics and Supply Chain Management* 5 (1): 113–38. doi:10.1108/JHLSCM-01-2014-0001.

Green, Jennifer L., Olivier L. de Weck, and Pablo Suarez. 2013. 'Evaluating the Economic Sustainability of Sanitation Logistics in Senegal'. *Journal of Humanitarian Logistics and Supply Chain Management* 3 (1): 7–21. doi:10.1108/20426741311328484.

Gubrium, Jaber. 1990. 'Recognizing and Analyzing Local Cultures'. In *Experiencing Fieldwork: An Inside View of Qualitative Research*, edited by William Shaffir and Robert A. Stebbins, 131–42. SAGE Publications.

Gurney, Joan Neff. 1990. 'Female Researchers in Male-Dominated Settings: Implications for Short-Term Versus Long-Term Research'. In *Experiencing*

*Fieldwork: An Inside View of Qualitative Research*, edited by William Shaffir and Robert A. Stebbins, 53–61. SAGE Publications.

Hadiguna, Rika Ampuh, Insannul Kamil, Azalika Delati, and Richard Reed. 2014. 'Implementing a Web-Based Decision Support System for Disaster Logistics: A Case Study of an Evacuation Location Assessment for Indonesia'. *International Journal of Disaster Risk Reduction* 9 (September): 38–47. doi:10.1016/j.ijdrr.2014.02.004.

Holguín-Veras, José, Miguel Jaller, and Tricia Wachtendorf. 2012. 'Comparative Performance of Alternative Humanitarian Logistic Structures after the Port-Au-Prince Earthquake: ACEs, PIEs, and CANs'. *Transportation Research Part A: Policy and Practice* 46 (10): 1623–40. doi:10.1016/j.tra.2012.08.002.

Holguín-Veras, José, Eiichi Taniguchi, Miguel Jaller, Felipe Aros-Vera, Frederico Ferreira, and Russell G. Thompson. 2014. 'The Tohoku Disasters: Chief Lessons Concerning the Post Disaster Humanitarian Logistics Response and Policy Implications'. *Transportation Research Part A: Policy and Practice* 69 (November): 86–104. doi:10.1016/j.tra.2014.08.003.

Ibegbunam, Innocent, and Deborah McGill. 2012. 'Health Commodities Management System: Priorities and Challenges'. *Journal of Humanitarian Logistics and Supply Chain Management* 2 (2): 161–82. doi:10.1108/20426741211260741.

IPCC. 2012. Managing the Risks of Extreme Events and Disasters to Advance Climate Change Adaptation. A Special Report of Working Groups I and II of the Intergovernmental Panel on Climate Change [Field, C.B., V. Barros, T.F. Stocker, D. Qin, D.J. Dokken, K.L. Ebi, M.D. Mastrandrea, K.J. Mach, G.-K. Plattner, S.K. Allen, M. Tignor, and P.M. Midgley (eds.)]. Cambridge University Press, Cambridge, UK, and New York, NY, USA, 582 pp.

Jahre, Marianne. 2010. 'Field Logistics and Logistics in the Field: Undertaking a Mission or Performing Research in Humanitarian Logistics'. *Supply Chain Forum: An International Journal* 11 (3): 54–62. doi:10.1080/16258312.2010.11517240.

Jahre, Marianne, and Ian Heigh. 2008. 'Does the Current Constraints in Funding Promote Failure in Humanitarian Supply Chains?' *Supply Chain Forum: An International Journal* 9 (2): 44–54. doi:10.1080/16258312.2008.11517198.

Jahre, Marianne, Leif-Magnus Jensen, and Tore Listou. 2009. 'Theory Development in Humanitarian Logistics: A Framework and Three Cases'. *Management Research News* 32 (11): 1008–23. doi:10.1108/01409170910998255.

Jahre, Marianne, Luc Dumoulin, Langdon B. Greenhalgh, Claudia Hudspeth, Phillips Limlim, and Anna Spindler. 2012. 'Improving Health in Developing Countries: Reducing Complexity of Drug Supply Chains'. *Journal of Humanitarian Logistics and Supply Chain Management* 2 (1): 54–84. doi:10.1108/20426741211226000.

Jensen, Leif-Magnus. 2012. 'Humanitarian Cluster Leads: Lessons from 4PLs'. *Journal of Humanitarian Logistics and Supply Chain Management* 2 (2): 148–60. doi:10.1108/20426741211260732.

Jensen, Leif-Magnus, and Susanne Hertz. 2016. 'The Coordination Roles of Relief Organisations in Humanitarian Logistics'. *International Journal of Logistics Research and Applications* 0 (0): 1–21. doi:10.1080/13675567.2015.1124845.

Johnson, John M. 1978. *Doing Field Research*. Free Press.

Kabra, Gaurav, and A. Ramesh. 2015. 'An Empirical Investigation of the Enablers in Humanitarian Supply Chain Management in India: A Case Study'. *Journal of Advances in Management Research* 12 (1): 30–42. doi:10.1108/JAMR-01-2014-0005.

Ketokivi, Mikko, and Thomas Choi. 2014. 'Renaissance of Case Research as a Scientific Method'. *Journal of Operations Management* 32 (5): 232–40. doi:10.1016/j.jom.2014.03.004.

Kovács, Gyöngyi, and Karen Spens. 2009. 'Identifying Challenges in Humanitarian Logistics'. *International Journal of Physical Distribution & Logistics Management* 39 (6): 506–28. doi:10.1108/09600030910985848.

Kovács, Gyöngyi, and Karen M. Spens. 2011a. 'Trends and Developments in Humanitarian Logistics – a Gap Analysis'. *International Journal of Physical Distribution & Logistics Management* 41 (1): 32–45. doi:10.1108/09600031111101411.

Kovács, Gyöngyi, and Karen M. Spens. 2011b. 'The Journal of Humanitarian Logistics and Supply Chain Management: First Reflections'. *Journal of Humanitarian Logistics and Supply Chain Management* 1 (2): 108–13. doi:10.1108/20426741111158403.

Kretschmer, Andreas, Stefan Spinler, and Luk N. Van Wassenhove. 2014. 'A School Feeding Supply Chain Framework: Critical Factors for Sustainable Program Design'. *Production and Operations Management* 23 (6): 990–1001. doi:10.1111/poms.12109.

Kunz, Nathan, and Stefan Gold. 2015. 'Sustainable Humanitarian Supply Chain Management – Exploring New Theory'. *International Journal of Logistics Research and Applications* 0 (0): 1–20. doi:10.1080/13675567.2015.1103845.

Kunz, Nathan, and Gerald Reiner. 2012. 'A Meta-Analysis of Humanitarian Logistics Research'. *Journal of Humanitarian Logistics and Supply Chain Management* 2 (2): 116–47. doi:10.1108/20426741211260723.

Kunz, Nathan, Luk N. Van Wassenhove, Rob McConnell, and Ketil Hov. 2015. 'Centralized Vehicle Leasing in Humanitarian Fleet Management: The UNHCR Case'. *Journal of Humanitarian Logistics and Supply Chain Management* 5 (3): 387–404. doi:10.1108/JHLSCM-07-2015-0034.

Lee-Treweek, Geraldine, and Stephanie Linkogle. 2002. *Danger in the Field: Ethics and Risk in Social Research*. London: Routledge.

L'Hermitte, Cécile, Peter Tatham, Marcus Bowles, and Ben Brooks. 2016. 'Developing Organisational Capabilities to Support Agility in Humanitarian Logistics: An Exploratory Study'. *Journal of Humanitarian Logistics and Supply Chain Management* 6 (1): 72–99. doi:10.1108/JHLSCM-02-2015-0006.

McCall, George J. 2006. 'The Fieldwork Tradition'. In *The SAGE Handbook of Fieldwork*, edited by Dick Hobbs and Richard Wright, 2–20. London United Kingdom: SAGE Publications Ltd.

Meredith, Jack. 1998. 'Building Operations Management Theory through Case and Field Research'. *Journal of Operations Management* 16 (4): 441–54. doi:10.1016/S0272-6963(98)00023-0.

Mohanty, Amarendranath, and Nayan Chakravarty. 2013. 'An Epidemiological Study of Common Drugs in the Health Supply Chain: Where Does the Compass Point?' *Journal of Humanitarian Logistics and Supply Chain Management* 3 (1): 52–64. doi:10.1108/20426741311328510.

Oloruntoba, Richard. 2013. 'Plans Never Go according to Plan: An Empirical Analysis of Challenges to Plans during the 2009 Victoria Bushfires'. *Technological Forecasting and Social Change*, Planning and Foresight Methodologies in Emergency Preparedness and Management, 80 (9): 1674–1702. doi:10.1016/j.techfore.2012.12.002.

Pedraza Martinez, Alfonso J., Orla Stapleton, and Luk N. Van Wassenhove. 2011. 'Field Vehicle Fleet Management in Humanitarian Operations: A Case-Based Approach'. *Journal of Operations Management*, Special Issue on Field Research in Operations and Supply Chain Management, 29 (5): 404–21. doi:10.1016/j.jom.2010.11.013.

Pedraza-Martinez, Alfonso J., Orla Stapleton, and Luk N. Van Wassenhove. 2013. 'On the Use of Evidence in Humanitarian Logistics Research'. *Disasters* 37 (July): S51–67. doi:10.1111/disa.12012.

Perry, Marcia. 2007. 'Natural Disaster Management Planning: A Study of Logistics Managers Responding to the Tsunami'. *International Journal of Physical Distribution & Logistics Management* 37 (5): 409–33. doi:10.1108/09600030710758455.

Rancourt, Marie-Ève, Jean-François Cordeau, Gilbert Laporte, and Ben Watkins. 2015. 'Tactical Network Planning for Food Aid Distribution in Kenya'. *Computers & Operations Research* 56 (April): 68–83. doi:10.1016/j.cor.2014.10.018.

Rietjens, Sebastiaan, John Goedee, Stijn Van Sommeren, and Joseph Soeters. 2014. 'Meeting Needs: Value Chain Collaboration in Stabilisation and Reconstruction Operations'. *Journal of Humanitarian Logistics and Supply Chain Management* 4 (1): 43–59. doi:10.1108/JHLSCM-10-2012-0029.

Saputra, Tezar Yuliansyah, Olaf Pots, Karin S. de Smidt-Destombes, and Sander de Leeuw. 2015. 'The Impact of Mean Time Between Disasters on Inventory Pre-Positioning Strategy'. *Disaster Prevention and Management: An International Journal* 24 (1): 115–31. doi:10.1108/DPM-11-2013-0197.

Scandura, Terri A., and Ethlyn A. Williams. 2000. 'Research Methodology In Management: Current Practices, Trends, And Implications For Future Research'. *Academy of Management Journal* 43 (6): 1248–64. doi:10.2307/1556348.

Schatzman, Leonard, and Anselm Leonard Strauss. 1973. *Field Research: Strategies for a Natural Sociology*. Prentice Hall PTR.

Schreter, L., and A. Harmer. 2013. 'Delivering Aid in Highly Insecure Environments. A Critical Review of the Literature, 2007–2012', February. http://r4d.dfid.gov.uk/Output/192476/Default.aspx.

Shaffir, William. 1990. 'Managing a Convincing Self-Presentation: Some Personal Reflections on Entering the Field'. In *Experiencing Fieldwork: An Inside View of Qualitative Research*, edited by William Shaffir and Robert A. Stebbins. London: SAGE Publications.

Shaffir, William, and Robert A. Stebbins. 1990. *Experiencing Fieldwork: An Inside View of Qualitative Research*. London: SAGE Publications.

Soneye, Alabi. 2014. 'An Overview of Humanitarian Relief Supply Chains for Victims of Perennial Flood Disasters in Lagos, Nigeria (2010–2012)'. *Journal of Humanitarian Logistics and Supply Chain Management* 4 (2): 179–97. doi:10.1108/JHLSCM-01-2014-0004.

Stiffman, Arlene Rubin. 2009. *The Field Research Survival Guide*. New York: Oxford University Press.

Swamidass, Paul M. 1991. 'Empirical Science: New Frontier in Operations Management Research'. *Academy of Management Review* 16 (4): 793–814. doi:10.5465/AMR.1991.4279634.

Tabaklar, Tunca, Árni Halldórsson, Gyöngyi Kovács, and Karen Spens. 2015. 'Borrowing Theories in Humanitarian Supply Chain Management'. *Journal of Humanitarian Logistics and Supply Chain Management* 5 (3): 281–99. doi:10.1108/JHLSCM-07-2015-0029.

Thévenaz, Céline, and Sandra L. Resodihardjo. 2010. 'All the Best Laid Plans… conditions Impeding Proper Emergency Response'. *International Journal of Production Economics*, Improving Disaster Supply Chain Management – Key supply chain factors for humanitarian relief, 126 (1): 7–21. doi:10.1016/j.ijpe.2009.09.009.

Thompson, Denise D.P. 2015. 'Disaster Logistics in Small Island Developing States: Caribbean Perspective'. *Disaster Prevention and Management: An International Journal* 24 (2): 166–84. doi:10.1108/DPM-09-2014-0187.

# 6

# Conducting In-Depth Case Studies in Humanitarian Logistics: The Case of MSF

Diego Vega

## Introduction

At the core of every research effort, as stated by Halldorsson and Aastrup (2003), lies the notion of methodological soundness and rigor. Since the recognition of logistics as a scientific discipline in the late 1960s, research has been strongly influenced by business disciplines from marketing, management and even engineering (Stock 1997). Different methods have been used in logistics research going from mathematical modeling and simulation to survey research or from case studies to interview methods (Mentzer and Kahn 1995). For several years, most empirical research on logistics and supply chain management has used quantitative methods, such as simulations and model building as well as statistical testing of survey data (Ellram 1996). Although logistics as a discipline is experiencing a movement toward more qualitative methods (Halldorsson and Aastrup 2003), in relatively new and still unexplored fields like humanitarian logistics, 'modeling and simulation constitute the most often used methodology' (Kunz and Reiner 2012, p. 37), perhaps due to unique characteristics of the humanitarian context (cf. Beamon 2004; Oloruntuba and Gray 2006). What is interesting here is that those same reasons should foster the use of qualitative methods as these – and in particular case studies – are preferred when the goal is to

D. Vega (✉)
NEOMA Business School, Reims, France
e-mail: diego.vega@neoma-bs.fr

© The Author(s) 2018
G. Kovács et al. (eds.), *The Palgrave Handbook of Humanitarian Logistics and Supply Chain Management*, https://doi.org/10.1057/978-1-137-59099-2_6

explain, explore or describe a topic of interest, because it provides depth and insight into a little known phenomenon (Ellram 1996, p. 97).

In humanitarian logistics, a small but important number of contributions have used this method. Kunz and Reiner (2012) state that from a sample of 174 articles published in this area as for 2011, only 23% used case studies. Some of these include Beamon and Kotleba's (2006) study on relief efforts in Sudan, Walker and Harland's (2008) study on e-procurement in the United Nations, Jahre and Jensen's (2010) study on coordination, and Schulz and Blecken's (2010) study on horizontal coordination, without mentioning INSEAD's Humanitarian Research Group case studies (cf. Tomasini and van Wassenhove 2009). Nevertheless none of these provide a detailed guideline for the use of case study research or what were the key challenges when conducting case studies in humanitarian logistics. The purpose of this chapter is not to explain when or why case studies can be used to investigate a phenomenon within the humanitarian logistics arena. It is neither about the case itself or the findings that resulted from it.[1] Rather, this chapter aims to (1) describe how this method was used to explore what logistics competencies and capabilities at an organizational level, contribute to the success of the emergency relief operations of an international humanitarian organization, and (2) to reflect on the overall process after a few years of finished, aiming to share the knowledge and experience gained from conducting it. The chapter is structured as follows: First, some methodological considerations are addressed, followed by the case study design where both data collection analysis processes are described before explaining how research quality was ensured. The chapter concludes with a schema that summarizes the overall case study process, and some reflections and recommendations for further research.

## Methodological Considerations

Prior to the conception of the case study, a number of methodological choices were made as a result of a deep analysis on how the chosen phenomenon could be studied. For instance, the characteristics of the context in which the phenomenon is found, and the degree of implication needed as a researcher to be able to describe and understand the phenomenon (Gioia and

---

[1] For a thorough description of the actual case study, please refer to Vega (2016).

Pitre 1990) pointed toward an interpretative paradigm. Moreover, the purpose of the research in exploring a new phenomenon and suggesting hypothesis or propositions led the research to be developed under an abductive reasoning process (Kovács and Spens 2005). Finally, a qualitative methodology (Miles and Huberman 1994) and the case study method (Yin 2009) were selected in accordance with the choice of research paradigm. Case study research was chosen based on different criteria found in the logistics/operations management literature. First, the exploratory nature of the study, and also the type of research question ('what') pointed toward different methods such as in-depth case study or a longitudinal study (Hanfield and Melnyk 1998), case study, experiment, grounded theory, participant observation, ethnography and case survey (Ellram 1996), or case study and action research (Meredith et al. 1989). Based on these suitable research methods, case study is raised as a relevant research method given that 'it provides depth and insight into a little known phenomenon' (Ellram 1996, p. 97), which is the case of organizational logistics competences for humanitarian relief.

## Designing the Case Study

When it comes to the design of the case study, Yin (2009) presents four types of case study based on two criteria: the number of cases and the number of units of analysis (see Fig. 6.1). The author explains that each type of study includes the desire to analyze the conditions of the context in which the case is studied, which is represented in the figure by a dotted line showing that the barrier between the case and the context is not likely to not clear. The four types are (1) the single case study (holistic), (2) the single case study (embedded), (3) the multiple case study (holistic), and (4) the multiple case study (embedded).

The unique case studies (types 1 and 2) are to be adopted when the phenomenon meets one or more of the following conditions:

* The case represents a critical case and can test a well-formulated theory. Here, the case study is used to determine whether the theoretical propositions are correct or, if any, there are other alternative explanations that may be relevant.
* The case is an extreme or unique case where the probability of finding a similar case is very low. Here, the case study documents the characteristics of the case and determines the nature of the existence of such a case.

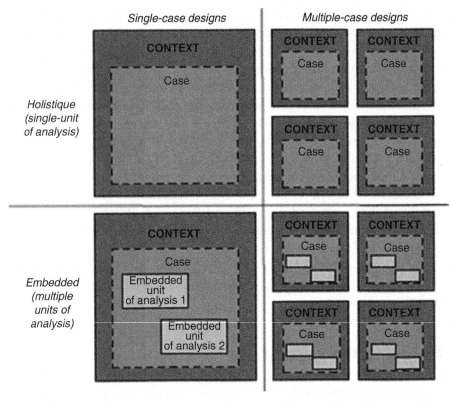

**Fig. 6.1** Basic types of design for case studies. Adapted from Yin (2009)

- The case is a typical or representative case and is a 'project' typical among others. The results of this case study are to be informative of supposed experiences of a person or organization average.
- The case is a revelatory event and allows the researcher to observe and analyze a phenomenon that was previously inaccessible. This is longitudinal where such a case is examined in two or more periods in time.

On the other side, the multiple case studies (types 3 and 4) are appropriate when seeking to replicate the study. For multiple case studies, different cases must be carefully chosen in order to (a) predict similar results (literal replication) or (b) predict contrasting results for predictable reasons (theoretical replication). The simplest case is to select a number of cases, two or more, supposed to be literal replications. The other option is to run a large number of theoretical replications. The second criterion, the number of units of analysis, allows the researcher to choose between holistic or embedded. The holistic approach is one that focuses on the global nature of an organization and can be used when no sublogical unit was identified or when the underlying theory is holistic in nature. Conversely, the embedded approach addresses not only the organization but also one or more subunits. In most cases, the study of units in an organization offers opportunities for an extensive analysis, which increases the depth at which the study is done and therefore the quality of results. Based on these two criteria (number of cases and number of units of analysis), some decisions were made and explained as follows.

## Single Versus Multiple

When studying logistics competencies and capabilities of international humanitarian organizations, there is the possibility of choosing either single or multiple case study designs. However, as each organization has its own history, its own structure, its own objectives, and sometimes a specific activity around which the organization is built, it is possible to consider each nongovernmental organizations (NGOs) as a unique case because the possibility of finding another NGO with same characteristics from another remains very low. Nevertheless, the relief context calls for representativeness in order to better understand this phenomenon at large. Therefore, the decision was to conduct an in-depth case study with a single international humanitarian organization specializing in emergencies, but also performing operations under the development umbrella. This selection covers thus the uniqueness of the type of organization, but also represents the selective group of major international humanitarian organizations. The second criterion relates to the number of units of analysis.

## Holistic Versus Embedded

As previously presented, this research focused on international humanitarian organizations specialized in response to emergencies. Here, the enquiry was about its logistics competence to respond to various disasters worldwide. However, the organization as a whole is not chosen as the only unit of analysis. In order to explore competencies and capabilities, it is necessary to see the resources 'in action,' and the mobilization of some of them will depend on the type of operation. Although there are similarities, each relief operation can be qualified as unique due to the circumstances in which it is developed, and therefore, the competencies and capabilities used can vary from one to another. This justifies the choice of an embedded rather than holistic approach, defining each operation as a unit of analysis, and allowing the identification of the competencies and capabilities deployed in relation to the organization as a whole and the success achieved.

## Conducting the Case Study

Taking into consideration the type of organization chosen for the purpose of the study, an important number of international humanitarian organizations were identified as possible subjects of study. Some of these include the International Federation of the Red Cross, Médecins Sans Frontières (MSF), and the World Food Programme. Of all, the only organization specialized mainly in emergency is MSF, with more than 40 years of expertise in providing medical assistance to populations whose life or health is threatened, mainly due to armed conflicts, but also epidemics, pandemics, natural disasters, or exclusion of care. It was appointed as 2015 the #1 NGO worldwide based on Global Geneva's ranking and is also one of the few NGOs to have received the Nobel Prize in recognition of its pioneering humanitarian work on several continents. For these characteristics, MSF was chosen as the case for this study.

In order to get in contact with the organization, the team began looking for ways to approach them, mainly through the researchers' professional network. The first contact was established by mail in April 2010 after a first approach on late January that was oversaw due to the response to the Haiti 2010 earthquake. At that point, a research protocol had been established and sent to the organization, to which they responded with an invitation to discuss the case in their logistics facility (MSF *Logistique*) in Bordeaux, France. The first exploratory interview took place in May with the head of production at MSF *Logistique*, followed by a meeting with the Deputy General Manager, the Supply Chain Manager and the Head of Human Resources on June. During that meeting, the organization agreed in participating on the research and some final ideas were introduced in the first version of the research protocol, thanks to the feedback given from the MSF *Logistique* staff. A first research agreement was finally signed on August 2010 for a period of 1 year, and then extended 1 more year. During that period, the organization gave the main researcher full access to the documentation from the intranet of both MSF *Logistique* and MSF France in order to conduct a first document analysis prior to the data collection.

## Data Collection

In the case study method, the interview is one of the main sources of information (Voss et al. 2002). In general, there are three types of interviews (Yin 2009): Open or depth, semi-structured or focused, and investigation or directive. In the open type, the researcher can investigate the facts/circumstances of a phenomenon and ask an opinion on an event. This type of interview is conducted in a prolonged period of time, where the interviewee becomes an 'informant' rather than a 'respondent.' On the other hand, in the semi-structured type the interview remains open and is approached as a conversation, but the interviewer should follow a specific number of questions based on the research protocol. Finally, the directive interview is closer to a survey, and each interviewee can be considered as a unit of analysis. For this research, the data consist mainly from 27 semistructured interviews, among which 23 were conducted with the staff of MSF *Logistique*, and 4 with the logistics department of MSF France between November 23, 2010, and February 3, 2012. For this, an interview guide was built from the results of the literature review on logistics competencies and capabilities. To track the type of approach chosen in terms of units of analysis, each interviewee was asked to relate the answers to his field experiences and give specific examples of how these experiences relate to the question. To facilitate management of data, interviews were recorded with the permission of each interviewee and stored in electronic format (.mp3).

When planning the interviews, the question of the sample becomes a factor important to ensure the quality of the study. In quantitative research, the main goal is to find a representative sample or a small collection of units or cases from a larger collection or a reference population (Neuman 2007), through probabilistic techniques. However, in qualitative research the sample is rarely determined in advance due to the limited knowledge of the population from which the sample is. The case or the units are discovered progressively through various nonprobabilistic techniques (Ibid.). A method widely used in logistics and operations management research is theoretical sampling, a process by which the researcher jointly collects, codes, and analyzes the data and then decides what type of data to collect and where to find it (Manuj and Mentzer 2008). In this process, the choice of informants, events, and interactions should be determined by a conceptual issue and not by a representative of the question (Miles and Huberman 1994). In accordance with methodological choices presented, the main type of sampling used in this study was theoretical. However, other types of sampling were also used. An initial 'quota sampling' (Ibid.) was established in cooperation with MSF

*Logistique*'s Head of Human Resources to find a representative of each one of the professions found in the organization. Next, a 'snowball sampling' was developed with the staff of MSF *Logistique*, which enabled us to expand the base sample according to the results of each of the interviews. Several references were made to the logistics department at MSF's headquarter in Paris, France. Finally, a sequential sampling allowed us to reach 'theoretical saturation' (Manuj and Mentzer 2008) at interview no. 21, made with a pharmacist belonging to MSF *Logistique*, from which no new information was found. The remaining interviews (MSF France included) allowed to corroborate the results found and eliminate the possibility of bias due to important number of interviewees belonging to MSF *Logistique*.[2] The different choice of type of sampling during this study and the overall data collection address the three main points to consider when making a case study, namely identify which activities, processes, events, times, locations, and partners must be sampled; keep a theoretical goal; and develop the study in iterative and progressive manner (Miles and Huberman 1994).

In order to overcome the bias in interviews on human subjects and improve the stability and reliability of results (Ellram 1996), data triangulation (Voss et al. 2002) was used, including the analysis of internal documentation (guidelines, minutes of meetings, job profiles, missions report, activity reports, etc.), direct observation (debriefings, meetings, and visits to the logistics facilities in Bordeaux), and participant observation through the participation on a logistics training (Preparation First Logistics Departure – PPDL 2011), in the data analysis. The process of interaction with the field is explained in Fig. 6.2.

## Data Processing

Before beginning the analysis of the collected data, a processing phase data is needed. Qualitative data exist in the form of photographs, written words, phrases, symbols, and diagrams that describe or represent individuals, actions, or events (Neuman 2007). In case studies, these data are, for the most part, notes written by hand or typed, recordings of interviews, and other events from the field (Miles and Huberman 1994). In all cases, the most basic unit in which data can be found is the word. However, notes and specially recorded interviews must be treated in order to analyze them. This

---

[2] The logistics facility is considered as a branch of the French section and the perspective from this facility can vary from that of the staff from the headquarters.

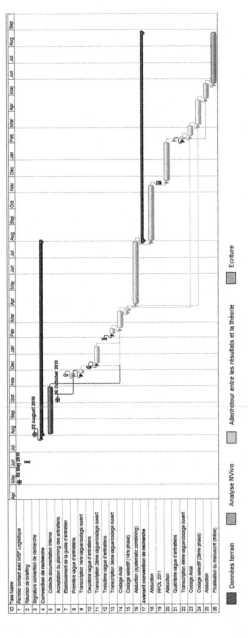

**Fig. 6.2** Interaction between the field and the desk research

process is known as transcription and several techniques can be used depending on the purpose of research. Transcription is a selective process in which sounds and images are translated or processed (in full or partially) into text (Davidson 2009). As stated by Cook (1990), instead of being a problem, the selectivity in the transcript must be understood as theoretical and practical necessity. It gives the researcher the possibility to choose the amount of information with regard to the objectives and provides a clear track of the interview to properly judge its content. According to Ochs (1979, p. 44), 'a more selective transcription is a more useful transcription.' Several authors proposed different approaches for transcription and the degree of selectivity. Bucholtz (2000) considers that the transcript is a continuum between a naturalized approach, where the characteristics of the speech outweigh oral and denaturalized approach, where the characteristics of oral such as 'ums' and 'ers' are preserved. The interviews conducted during the data collection phase were transcribed in a selective manner soon after their recording in order not to lose the elements related to the context in which the interview took place. From the speech of the interviewee, the segments that responded directly to the question of the guide or allowed to extract the relevant elements to our research were selected. Thus, the examples and experiences were transcribed to be analyzed in search of evidence that could support or deepen the subject. These transcripts were stored in electronic format and later treated with audio enhancer software to be subsequently analyzed using qualitative data analysis software.

## Instrumentation

Nowadays, data analysis in most qualitative research is done using Computer Aided Qualitative Data Analysis Software (CAQDAS) as AQUAD, ATLAS. ti, MAXQDA, NUD*IST, or NVivo, among others. These software allow researchers to write or transcribe field notes, to edit (correct, extend and revise) field notes, to code (attach tags or keywords) segments of text for further retrieval, to store data, to search and retrieve text segments for their inspection, to link different segments of data, to perform content analysis (frequency, location, or sequence counting of words or sentences), to map the data, and to display the data, among other possibilities (Miles and Huberman 1994). Most programs are similar to one another and facilitate the execution of the same analysis; however, each CAQDAS has its own features (Leech and Onwuegbuzie 2011). One of the most used software especially among young researchers is NVivo (Dean and Sharp 2006), a

CAQDAS developed by QSR International. The main features of this program are the abilities to organize and analyze literature reviews, to conduct second-hand data analysis, and to record, collect, analyze, and report data (ibid). Moreover, NVivo offers an important number of qualitative data analysis types. Leech and Onwuegbuzie (2011) outline seven types of qualitative data analysis, that is, constant comparison analysis, classical content analysis, keyword-in-context, word count, domain analysis, taxonomic analysis, and componential analysis, that can be performed by the program. Nevertheless, when conducting qualitative research, the researcher is the main tool for analysis (Denzin and Lincoln 2005). Based on these characteristics, the data analysis was performed using NVivo 8, and depending on the goal of the query, some of the data analysis types previously mentioned were performed and are described in the following section.

## Data Analysis

During the study, the researcher identifies a significant number of procedures, causes, characteristics, or mechanisms that are inside of evidence, which will then be examined for similarities, differences, and/or patterns that structure the information collected (Neuman 2007). For this, a conceptualization of data must be done, allowing to organize and make sense of the information collected. This process, also called coding, is to organize raw data into conceptual categories to create themes or concepts and to reduce the amount of data to analyze. The codes are labels for assigning units of meaning to the information compiled during the study (Miles and Huberman 1994). Generally, the codes are attached to 'pieces' of different sizes (words, phrases, sentences, or paragraphs) related directly or indirectly to a certain framework. However, 'what is important is not the words themselves but their meaning' (Ibid., p. 56).

The coding process consists of several phases or stages. Several authors (cf. Ellram 1996; Miles and Huberman 1994; Neuman 2007; Strauss and Corbin 1990) propose two main levels of analysis, namely open and axial. During the first phase (open coding), data is organized by 'pieces' and categorized in order to find, extract, and gather information easily with respect to a particular research question, a hypothesis, or a theme. For this, it is suggested to create a 'starting list' of provisional codes (descriptive and exploratory), after the questions, assumptions, issues, or variables of interest that result from the desk research. For this case, the information gathered in the interviews and documentation was organized into three main themes: competence, success, and the emergency. These three groups correspond to the three key concepts of our research question 'What are the organizational logistics competencies to ensure the success emergency relief operations?' For each theme, a code was created. The three codes were introduced in NVivo in the form of *free nodes*, independent nodes used in the early coding when there is no hierarchical structure defined (QSR 2008). The recorded interviews were imported to the software in the folder 'Documentation \Interviews' and transcribed using the NVivo transcription tool. As the interview was transcribed, a first coding was done to gather information in each of the free nodes created. A second encoding step was then performed to conceptualize and develop categories in the data. The first free nodes then created *tree nodes*, nodes that are organized in a hierarchical structure, from a general category at the top – *parent nodes* – to other specific categories – *child nodes* (QSR 2008). For instance, to structure the node 'competence,' a first structure of codes was created based on the results from the desk research on logistics competences and capabilities. During the analysis, a large number of child nodes emerged and have been classified in the corresponding tree node (see Table 6.1). Other nodes without apparent category were kept as free nodes to be analyzed in the axial coding.

As explained previously, this research uses a data triangulation technique. For this, the different. pdf or. doc files were imported in NVivo 8 under the

Table 6.1 Aggregated starting node list (extract)

| |
|---|
| – Competence |
| Definition |
| + Nature |
| – MSF Competences |
| + MSF Logistics Competences |
| – Emergency |
| + Typology |
| + Criteria |
| – Success |
| – Definition |
| MSF |
| MSF Logistique |
| – Criteria |
| MSF |
| MSF Logistique |
| Key Activity |

folder 'Documentation\MSF' and 'Documentation\MSF Logistique' depending on the source. Other types of files such as videos, photographs, or even audio interviews were imported into software subfolders 'Video,' 'Audio,' and 'Pictures.' In the case of videos and audio files (e.g., meetings, discussions, etc.), the recordings were coded into relevant nodes and in the case photographs, descriptive notes were created and then encoded in the corresponding nodes. When analyzing written material (guidelines, reports, debriefings, etc.), different query tools were used to optimize the treatment of this large amount of information. For instance, based on the starting list, a 'text search query' was performed using the stemmed search option, that is, the word's root, in order to find the different variations of a word. Then, a 'word frequency query' was used to determine the significance of terms/concepts used in this research with regard to the documentation used during the analysis.

During the second phase of coding (axial), the main goal is to create an explanatory code that will identify themes, patterns, and emerging explanations. This step helps the researcher to reduce a large amount of data in a smaller number of analytical units and allows the creation of a cognitive map. The process also allows the identification of relationships between the different codes, but can also raise issues that will suggest dropping some subjects or considering other more thoroughly (Neuman 2007). Then, an additional coding (selective) is performed, where central categories of the analysis are selected, related to other categories, validated or developed into new categories (Ellram 1996). A final step of 'memoing,' a theorization in written form of the ideas that come to mind of the researcher during the data collection or the coding in connection with codes and their relationships is advised, as it is considered as one of the most useful and powerful tools for making sense of the information (Miles and Huberman 1994). Following the open coding where nodes of categories were created, an axial coding process was performed (see Table 6.2). Based on the results from the interviews and the written, graphic, and media documentation gathered during the study, the first structure of nodes was developed following the relationships found between the different responses of the interviewees. Several nodes that were created as free nodes were combined, renamed, and integrated as child nodes into the tree nodes. Finally, subcategories were identified and developed during the last stage of selective coding (see Table 6.3).

**Table 6.2** Axial coding node list

| Name | Created On |
|------|-----------|
| MSF Competences | 30/11/2010 11:58 |
| Medical | 20/12/2010 11:36 |
| Logistics | 20/12/2010 11:37 |
| Human Resources - Administration | 20/12/2010 11:38 |
| Emergency Response | 12/01/2011 16:14 |
| Questioning | 20/12/2010 11:45 |
| Commitment | 20/12/2010 11:54 |
| Analysis | 20/12/2010 12:04 |
| Understanding | 27/06/2011 08:06 |
| Needs assessment | 01/07/2011 07:24 |
| Volunteering | 20/12/2010 11:43 |
| Training | 20/12/2010 11:48 |
| Human skills | 29/12/2010 18:29 |
| MSF Logistique Competences | 20/12/2010 12:15 |
| Technical | 29/12/2010 16:17 |
| Responsiveness | 20/12/2010 12:38 |
| Adaptation | 20/12/2010 12:35 |
| Commitment - Motivation | 03/01/2011 10:45 |
| Analysis | 03/01/2011 16:25 |
| Relationship | 03/01/2011 11:51 |
| Flexibility | 03/01/2011 11:53 |
| Professionnalisation - specialisation | 10/01/2011 16:15 |
| Supply Chain - Global vision | 20/12/2010 12:17 |
| Team Work | 03/01/2011 14:01 |
| Organizational | 20/12/2010 12:34 |
| Forecasting - Anticipation - Planification | 12/01/2011 07:51 |
| Information sharing | 20/12/2010 12:41 |
| Competence versatility | 03/01/2011 15:07 |
| Management | 10/01/2011 16:59 |
| Improvisation | 27/06/2011 08:25 |
| Operations Department | 20/12/2010 12:29 |
| Priorisation | 30/06/2011 09:32 |
| Product know ledge | 07/07/2011 08:43 |
| Understanding | 11/01/2011 17:03 |
| Key Activity | 29/12/2010 17:11 |
| Logistics | 29/12/2010 17:12 |
| Whole | 29/12/2010 18:36 |
| Medical | 29/12/2010 17:01 |
| Exploratory missions | 21/06/2011 09:15 |
| Fund-raising | 18/01/2011 14:34 |
| Emergency Typology | 29/12/2010 16:46 |
| Scale | 29/12/2010 16:33 |
| Type of products | 29/12/2010 16:46 |
| Nature | 03/01/2011 14:34 |
| Location - country - environement | 03/01/2011 12:05 |
| Access | 18/04/2011 18:37 |
| Duration | 21/06/2011 07:50 |

**Table 6.2** (continued)

| Name | Created On |
| --- | --- |
| Multiplicity of acteurs (mediatisation) | 23/06/2011 19:24 |
| Difference betwen daily and emergency | 30/11/2010 11:59 |
| Organisation | 29/12/2010 16:29 |
| Speed | 29/12/2010 16:35 |
| Time | 29/12/2010 16:43 |
| Planification | 03/01/2011 15:54 |
| Priorisation | 18/01/2011 07:22 |
| Information | 29/12/2010 16:36 |
| Motivation | 01/07/2011 08:37 |
| Success | 30/11/2010 12:00 |
| Criteria | 29/12/2010 17:54 |
| MSF Log | 29/12/2010 17:51 |
| MSF | 29/12/2010 17:50 |
| Nature of competence | 22/12/2010 18:23 |
| Technical | 29/12/2010 15:19 |
| Experience | 03/01/2011 15:30 |
| Position - profession | 22/12/2010 18:26 |
| Human | 29/12/2010 17:14 |
| Know-how | 22/12/2010 18:23 |

## Research Quality

Whether quantitative or qualitative, research is supposed to present a number of logical statements and therefore it is possible to judge its quality compared to logical tests (Yin 2009). Two concepts are measured with these tests: reliability and validity. Reliability means consistency or credibility, and suggests that the same phenomenon repeats or is reproduced in identical or very similar conditions (Neuman 2007). Validity, however, suggests the authenticity and addresses the 'match' between the way the researcher conceptualized the idea and its measurement (Ibid.). Several criteria are proposed to measure the quality of case studies. Ellram (1996) offers four criteria, namely conceptual validity, internal validity, external validity and reliability. These four criteria are described by Yin (2009) as follows:

- Construct validity: identifies the correct operational measures for concepts that are studied;
- Internal validity: seeks to establish a causal relationship in which some conditions are expected to bring in other conditions;
- External validity: defines the area in which the study results can be generalized;

**Table 6.3** Selective coding list

| Name | Modified On |
| --- | --- |
| MSF Competences | 25/05/2012 13:21 |
| Analysis | 22/05/2012 08:57 |
| Volunteering | 20/12/2010 11:44 |
| Fund-raising | 22/05/2012 09:38 |
| Commitment | 22/05/2012 08:41 |
| Training | 20/12/2010 11:49 |
| Human skills | 29/12/2010 18:29 |
| Logistics | 22/05/2012 09:00 |
| Understanding | 27/06/2011 08:10 |
| Medical | 22/05/2012 08:58 |
|   Field | 22/05/2012 10:08 |
|   HR | 22/05/2012 10:03 |
|   Healthcare | 22/05/2012 10:07 |
|   Emergency | 22/05/2012 09:59 |
| Exploratory Mission | 22/05/2012 09:38 |
| Questioning | 19/05/2012 10:01 |
| Emergency Response | 24/05/2012 10:56 |
| Human Resources - Admin. | 23/06/2011 08:49 |
| Logistics Competences MSF | 30/05/2012 08:15 |
| Adaptability | 01/06/2012 10:24 |
| Internal Communication | 30/05/2012 08:34 |
| Flexibility | 29/05/2012 16:29 |
|   HR Flexibility | 30/05/2012 08:11 |
| Improvisation | 29/05/2012 16:29 |
| Integration | 30/05/2012 08:11 |
| Organisation | 29/05/2012 16:29 |
| Management | 29/05/2012 16:29 |
| Motivation | 30/05/2012 08:23 |
| Information Sharing | 29/05/2012 16:29 |
| Competence versitality | 29/05/2012 16:29 |
| Prioisation | 31/05/2012 22:14 |
| Professionnalisation | 30/05/2012 08:15 |
| Reponsiveness | 30/05/2012 08:18 |
| Technical | 01/06/2012 15:07 |
|   Purchasing - technical | 29/05/2012 16:07 |
|   Procurement | 29/05/2012 16:27 |
|   Forecasting - Anticipation - Planification | 29/05/2012 16:29 |
|   Supplier relationship | 29/05/2012 16:29 |
| Freight - Transportation | 30/05/2012 08:03 |
| Information systems | 29/05/2012 10:34 |
| Logistics support | 30/05/2012 08:02 |
| Operations Dep. | 19/05/2012 08:16 |
|   Demand analysis | 30/05/2012 08:07 |
| Production | 29/05/2012 16:17 |
| Inventory management | 29/05/2012 10:38 |

- Reliability: demonstrates that the tasks performed during the study, such as collecting data, can be repeated with the same results.

Guba and Lincoln (1989) propose an alternative criterion to measure the quality of a research: the trustworthiness, which aims to support the idea that the research results 'are worth of attention' (p. 290). The trustworthiness is constituted by four dimensions parallel to those described earlier, that are presented referring to Halldorsson and Aastrup (2003), and we will explain how they have been achieved in our research.

- Credibility: Assuming that the reality comes from the respondents and their context, credibility is determined by the 'match' between the respondents' construction and the interpretation of the researcher of those constructions. Then, a credible research is often inaccurate in terms of boundaries, but rich on significance and depth of the phenomenon studied.
- Transferability: This dimension concerns the extent to which research is able to make statements about the world. However, unlike the external validity, transferability considers that the applicability of the results is subject to the context.
- Dependability: Concerns data stability over time. This dimension is similar to that of reliability, but focuses on the traceability of the decision-making process instead of replicating results.
- Confirmability: Seeks to certify that the findings, interpretations, and recommendations represent the results of research and not the bias from the researcher, the objective being to demonstrate how the results can be confirmed through the data.

Guba and Lincoln (1989) propose a number of techniques that can be performed in qualitative research to achieve the dimensions they propose to ensure the quality of research. For the first dimension, the 'extended engagement' and 'persistent observation' techniques were used. The first technique involves spending enough time to observe several aspects of the context, discuss, and build relationships with several members of the organization to develop trust. This was achieved through a research agreement signed between *MSF Logistique* and the CRET-LOG Research Center for a 1-year term contract renewable once. The second technique aims to identify the most relevant elements with respect to the phenomenon studied. During the study period, discussion with members of the organization permitted to identify some relevant points for the investigation and to go further with the case study. This was the case of the participation to the PPDL training, a 1-week training that puts in real situation future MSF logisticians, which provided the idea of 'field' research. In addition to 'data triangulation,' 'peer debreifing' technique was used to avoid bias. This was achieved through the presentation of preliminary results in several research workshops organized by CRET-LOG, as well as other international academic workshops and conferences where the advancement of research was discussed. To ensure transferability, the technique used is that of the 'dense description,' which aims to describe a phenomenon in sufficient detail for a person that can begin to assess the extent to which the conclusions reached are transferable in other contexts, situations, or people. For both dependability and confirmability dimensions, the authors propose an external researcher to examine the process and the results of the research. This was achieved through the examination of the doctoral thesis in which this case study was included.

## Findings

The results from the case study showed that over the past 30 years, MSF has achieved what can be considered as a logistics competence, gaining international recognition in this area, at an equally high level as their medical expertise. This competence is considered as 'the first point that will achieve the success of a good response to an emergency...we could even deliver the material without having a medical team in the field and give it to doctors not belonging to MSF' (Head of Production Department). However, this goal cannot be achieved without the help of other areas of expertise. The study showed that, as well as medical and logistics skills, other competences are also important for the management of humanitarian relief operations. These competences include integration, adaptability, responsiveness, and technical logistics capabilities such as purchasing and procurement, supplier management and stock management, among others.

## Reflections and Recommendations

Case study research has been wrongly defined as a hardly generalizable research method (cf. Flyvbjerg 2006), and this can be partly true if the criteria to judge are based on the size of the sample. However, as stated by Siggelkow (2007), case study research is about finding a 'talking pig,' that is a

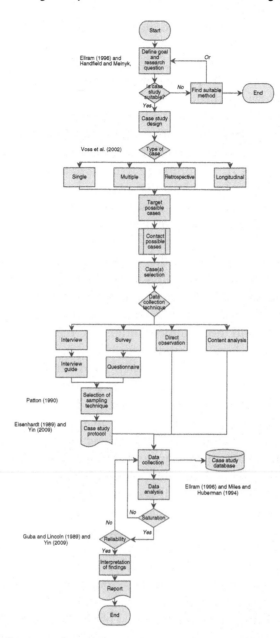

**Fig. 6.3** Overall case study process

case that 'derives its excitement and justification through little more than the description of a particular phenomenon' (p. 20). Although the case presented above is not a talking pig *per se,* the conceptual argument constituted a strong contribution to the partner organization, as it 'shape[d] their [...] thinking and allow[ed] them to see the world in a slightly different light' (p. 23). In light of this, and without any attempt of generalization, it is possible to reflect on the overall process and propose a framework to which academics and practitioners can relate when conducting or being part of a case study (see Fig. 6.3). The proposed framework highlights the main steps to follow, as well as the decisions that need to be considered through the overall process of a case study. It also relates to influential works that provide researchers a reference point where they can find methodological basis.

When conducting research in the humanitarian context, it results paramount to contribute in a tangible way to the work of humanitarians in better delivering the aid, and this is probably the reason for the important amount of quantitative research on humanitarian logistics. However, a more conceptual and deep understanding of the phenomenon is also required and this is where case study research can have a great contribution. One important aspect to consider when conducting case studies is the access to data, and this is particularly true for the humanitarian context. It constitutes probably the biggest barrier for the use of this method in humanitarian logistics, given that units of analysis are in most cases temporary and difficult to attain due to the characteristics of the environment (e.g., responding to an emergency), and thus, the researcher relies in some cases on secondary data. A possible solution is to conduct the study in a more controlled environment such as the headquarters or a logistics facility, and base the study on the representation or perception of a given phenomenon. Nevertheless, in the case of studying an emergency response, to rely on the interviewee's perception can be risky as it represents only one part of what is occurring on the field, unless the phenomenon under study is the headquarters' response to an emergency from a managerial perspective. A remarkable example of conducting a case study on emergency response within a 'controllable' environment is that of Gralla et al. (2016), where the main researcher 'observed the actions and conversations of teams participating in [a] training exercise' (p. 26), seeking to investigate the problem formulation and solving mechanisms in rapidly evolving emergency situations.

For the case presented in this chapter, access was facilitated by the team's network but it was not granted either. Different solutions, such as mailing and phone calls, to get in touch with the organization were put in place and after a few months, one of these went through. Looking back at the entire process, it is now clear that the most important thing and probably the reason why the organization accepted to be part of the research project was the concept behind the study and the way it was presented (i.e., the research protocol) to the steering committee during the first meeting. Therefore, a great effort must be put in building a strong case study protocol, aiming to foresee and anticipate the questions and reactions of that first contact that will ensure the proper development of the entire study.

Another critical issue of case study research is the main data, that is the interviews, and how much can the researcher get from them. Apart from building a coherent and logical interview guide, the researcher conducting a study on humanitarian logistics must pay attention on the language or *jargon* used in this specific environment, as in most cases concepts are too abstract, and thus, the communication with the interviewee is blurred by definitions that do not mean the same for both academics and practitioners. While performing the first interviews with the MSF staff, it became clear that the concept of competence differed from the academic definition, and thus, it was necessary to readjust the interview guide to create a common definition that was used as a basis for the rest of the interview. This is just an example of many situations in which the academic perspective of the humanitarian context can differ significantly from that of those working on the field and it is important, for both the researcher and the interviewee that the terms used and the perspective of humanitarian logistics is comparable. This is only possible through a long and deep interaction with the context and it is of great benefit for the output of the study.

As stated in the introduction of this chapter, its purpose is to show how case study research method was applied through a case conducted with MSF France, and to reflect on the overall process. Some of the limits are those related to the critics that the case study method has received, such as generalization, contextualization, theory development, verification, and so on. Nevertheless, over the past years case study research has become a strong method used in numerous disciplines and criticisms have been revisited (see Flyvbjerg 2006). Future use of the case study research method should continue to challenge the many possibilities that the method has to offer, considering, for instance, the use of secondary data to understand a phenomenon that occurred and infer what happened and try to propose a better solution for future cases.

**Acknowledgments** The author would like to acknowledge Bruno Delouche, Philippe Cachet, David Vicqery, and the staff from MSF Logistique and the MSF headquarters in Paris, and professors Nathalie Fabbe-Costes and Marianne Jahre for their support and guidance for this case study.

# References

Beamon, B. M. (2004). Humanitarian relief chains: Issues and challenges. Proceedings of the 35th International Conference on Computers & Industrial Engineering, San Francisco, CA, USA.

Beamon, B. and Kotleba, S. (2006). Inventory management support systems for emergency humanitarian relief operations in South Sudan. *The International Journal of Logistics Management, 17*(2), 187–212.

Bucholtz, M. (2000). The policies of transcription. *Journal of Pragmatics, 32*, 1439–1465.

Cook, G. (1990). Transcribing infinity. *Journal of Pragmatics, 14*, 1–24.

Davidson, C. (2009). Transcription: Imperatives for qualitative research. *International Journal of Qualitative Methods, 8*(2), 35–52.

Dean, A. and Sharp, J. (2006). Getting the most from Nud*ist/Nvivo. *The Electronic Journal of Business Research Methods, 4*(1), 11–12.

Denzin, N. K. and Lincoln, Y. S. (2005). Introduction: The discipline and practice of qualitative research, in N. K. Denzin and Y. S. Lincoln (eds), *The Sage handbook of qualitative research*. Thousand Oaks, CA: Sage.

Ellram, L. M. (1996). The use of the case study method in logistics research. *Journal of Business Logistics, 17*(2), 93–138.

Flyvbjerg, B. (2006). "Five Misunderstandings About Case-Study Research." *Qualitative Inquiry, 12*(2), 219–245.

Gioia, D. A. and Pitre, E. (1990). Multiparadigm perspectives on theory building. *Academy of Management Review, 15*(4), 548–602.

Gralla, E., Goentzel, J. and Fine, C. (2016). Problem Formulation and Solution. *Production and Operations Management, 25*(1), 22–35.

Guba, E. G. and Lincoln, Y. S. (1989). *Fourth generation evaluation*. Thousand Oaks, CA: Sage.

Halldorsson, A. and Aastrup, J. (2003). Quality criteria for qualitative inquiries in logistics. *European Journal of Operational Research, 144*(2), 321–332.

Handfield, R. B. and Melnyk, S. A. (1998). "The scientific theory-building process: a primer using the case of TQM." *Journal of Operations Management, 16*(4), 321–339.

Jahre, M. and Jensen, L.-M. (2010). "Coordination in humanitarian logistics through clusters." *International Journal of Physical Distribution & Logistics Management, 40*(8/9), 657–674.

Kovács, G. and Spens, K. M. (2005). "Abductive reasoning in logistics research." *International Journal of Physical Distribution & Logistics Management, 35*(2), 132–144.

Kunz, N. and Reiner, G. (2012). A meta-analysis of humanitarian logistics research. *Journal of Humanitarian Logistics and Supply Chain Management, 2*(2), 116–147.

Leech, N. L. and Onwuegbuzie, A. J. (2011). Beyond constant qualitative data analysis: Using Nvivo. *School Psychology Quarterly*, 26(1), 70–84.

Manuj, I. and Mentzer, J. T. (2008). Global supply chain risk management strategies. *International Journal of Physical Distribution & Logistics Management, 38*(3), 192–223.

Mentzer, J. T. and Kahn, K. B. (1995). A framework of logistics research. *Journal of Business Logistics, 16*(1), 231–250.

Meredith, J., Raturi, A., Gyampah, K. and Kaplan, B. (1989). "Alternative research paradigms in operations." *Journal of Operations Management 8*(4), 297–326.

Miles, M. B. and Huberman, M. (1994). *Qualitative data analysis*. Thousand Oaks, CA: SAGE.

Neuman, W. L. (2007). *Social research methods: Quantitative and qualitative methods*, 2nd Edn. Boston, MA: Pearson.

Ochs, E. (1979). Transcription as theory. In E. Ochs and B. B. Schiefflin (eds), *Developmental pragmatics* (pp. 43–72). New York: Academic.

Oloruntuba, R. and Gray, R. (2006). Humanitarian aid: An agile supply chain? *Supply Chain Management: An International Journal, 11*(2), 115–120.

QSR. (2008). *Nvivo 8 fundamentals: Starting to work with your material*. QSR International.

Schulz, S. and Blecken, A. (2010). Horizontal cooperation in disaster relief logistics: Benefits and impediments. *International Journal of Physical Distribution & Logistics Management, 40*(8/9), 636–656.

Siggelkow, N. (2007). Persuasion with case studies. *Academy of Management Journal, 50*(1), 20–24.

Stock, J. R. (1997). Applying theories from other disciplines to logistics. *International Journal of Physical Distribution & Logistics Management, 27*(9–10), 515–539.

Strauss, A. and Corbin, J. (1990). *Basics of qualitative research: Grounded theory procedures and techniques*. Sage: Newbury Park, CA.

Tomasini, R. M. and Van Wassenhove, L. N. (2009). From preparedness to partnerships: Case study research on humanitarian logistics. *International Transactions in Operational Research*, 16, 549–559.

Vega, D. (2016). Exploring logistics competences and capabilities in non-for-profit environments: The case of Medecins Sans Frontières. In Kovács et al. (ed.), *Supply Chain Management for Humanitarians*, Kogan-Page.

Voss, C., Tsikriktsis, N. and Frohlich, M. (2002). Case research in operations management. *International Journal of Operations and Production Management, 22*(2), 195–219.

Walker, H. and Harland, C. (2008) E-procurement in the United Nations: Influences, issues and impact. *International Journal of Operations & Production Management*, *28*(9), 831–857.

Yin, R. K. (2009). *Case Study Research – Design and Methods*, 4th Edn. Thousand Oaks, CA: Sage.

# 7

# The Application of the Case Study Methodology: Resilience in Domestic Food Supply Chains During Disaster Relief Efforts in South Asia

Mark Wilson, Muhammad Umar and Jeff Heyl

## Introduction

This chapter will explore the execution of the field work for a research project centred on two disaster-prone regions in Pakistan. We first discuss the case study method and its suitability to humanitarian logistics researchers and then apply the method to an actual research project and discuss the data gathering phase. This work is offered as a reflective piece that would be useful for humanitarian logistics researchers and research students conducting case-based research in general and intending to work in the South Asia area in particular. The work adopts a qualitative case study approach and explores in depth the methodological justifications for the use of such a method in a context/region typically encountered by humanitarian logistics researchers. Indeed, given the difficulties of collecting data in an environment characterized by a fluid, confused, often dangerous research context with a rapid rotation of entities and personnel, traditional quantitative methods and instruments such as formal surveys are problematic to say the least. Hence, a rigorous case study framework is offered that could provide a template or an example of sorts for future researchers. This chapter takes the reader from the process of

M. Wilson (✉) · M. Umar · J. Heyl
Lincoln University, Lincoln, New Zealand
e-mail: Mark.Wilson@lincoln.ac.nz; Muhammad.umar@lincolnuni.ac.nz;
Jeff.heyl@lincoln.ac.nz

© The Author(s) 2018                                                    **203**
G. Kovács et al. (eds.), *The Palgrave Handbook of Humanitarian Logistics and Supply Chain Management*, https://doi.org/10.1057/978-1-137-59099-2_7

deriving the research problem from literature, to the detailed design of the field work and cumulates in the actual in-country data gathering phase. The focus is on the experience of the researchers and the suitability of the case method during the data gathering phase to provide some insights for humanitarian researchers.

This method of necessity can only be understood in the context of the research aims and objectives. Hence, a further offering is a conceptual framework for determining the resilience of food supply chains drawn from the supply chain resilience and disaster management disciplines. It is argued that while the literature for supply chain resilience in the disaster context is still developing, there are few consolidated frameworks that seek to explain food supply chain resilience with a focus on disaster relief. The proposed framework argues that resilient food supply chains possess the capabilities of agility, adaptability and alignment (Lee 2004) in each of the four supply chain operational areas of logistics, collaboration, sourcing and knowledge management. These capabilities are facilitated further when actor's attitudes towards supply chain orientation and risk management are enhanced (Kovács and Spens 2007). In this chapter, the readers are asked to focus on the logical progression of the *process* and *steps* taken for each section for the research formulation and then execution of the in-country data gathering as a potential exemplar for case-based research in disaster-prone regions. The concluding section offers advice and lessons learned for researchers intending to work in South Asia region in general and Pakistan in particular.

## Research Approach – Inductive/Deductive

All researchers need to decide between deductive and inductive approaches as they consider their options for empirical research. Depending upon one's philosophical position, either one of these or a combination can be used in the research. The deductive approach suits natural and physical sciences (Saunders, et al. 2011). It is mostly applied when theory leads to research. A theoretical framework is developed and the researcher tests that framework through data taken from samples. Researchers then generalize these data to the whole population (Bhattacherjee 2012). Typically the researcher, after a literature review in a particular domain, deduces certain hypothesis and then through research strategy tests these hypotheses. Basic steps involved in a deductive approach are theory, hypothesis, data collection, analysis and hypothesis testing.

When theory building is the aim of the research, this usually requires an inductive approach. Generalized inferences are extracted from observations, often on an iterative basis (Bhattacherjee 2012). Here the researcher collects data and as a result of simultaneous data analysis, a new theory is generated. This is then tested further and refined until confidence in the theory formulation can be had. Due to qualitative data usage in inductive research it is not highly structured like deductive research. As the inductive approach is dependent on words, descriptions, feelings and derived meaning from observations and narratives, it is seen as more subjective and depends on the 'perception' of the 'social actors' about how they construct 'reality'. With inductive approaches, the researcher tries to find the meaning social actors attache to the reality they perceive. Generally, induction has an open and flexible approach, which provides opportunities to deal with any unexpected issues raised during the research process (Johnsen 2011), and this flexibility is better able to cope with uncertain humanitarian research contexts.

It has been argued that humanitarian supply chain research, where inter-agency relationships are the centre of attention, is neither entirely inductive nor deductive (Dubois and Gadde 2002). Hence, this research has adopted a 'moderate constructionism perspective' where the inductive approach is primary but with elements of deductive reasoning (Dubois and Gadde 2002, Järvensivu and Törnroos 2010). The reasoning for this is that the deductive element of this research is partially driven by extant theory within the disaster management and supply chain management disciplines. Hence, research of this type will not test theory *per se*, but rather will try to build on existing theory. Thus, a conceptual framework has been developed from existing supply chain resilience and disaster response literature. This framework is presented as follows (Fig. 7.1).

Following this, an inductive approach will be followed as this research is primarily concerned with building on this theory through qualitative data collection. The intent is to build depth of insight (by no means complete) of what is happening in disaster-prone areas, such as South Asian countries, in terms of food supply chains during times of disasters. As Creswell (2013) has rightly suggested, if empirical research on the topic is limited then an inductive method of generalizing from data would be the most appropriate method.

Many research strategies have been suggested by different authors to be used in qualitative research. However, Creswell (2013) has suggested five important qualitative methods of inquiry. These are narrative, phenomenology, ethnography, grounded theory and case studies. Narrative and phenomenology are associated with study of individuals. Ethnography is concerned with broad cultural sharing of behaviour in groups, while grounded theory and case study are used when researcher wants to explore events, activities and processes where little theoretical work has been done previously. Hence,

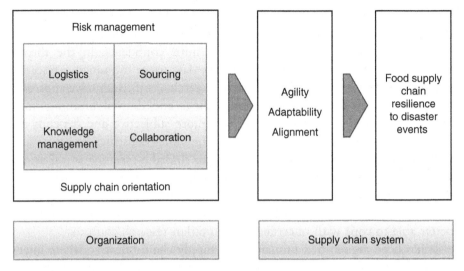

**Fig. 7.1** Conceptual framework for resilience in domestic food supply chains. Source: Authors

this work has adopted a case study inductive approach. In fact, as the focus of the study is the supply chain or multiple supply chains, it seems that the most appropriate unit of analysis is the 'supply chain' as a system. In particular, our attention is narrowed further to the retail or distribution end of the supply chain in disaster-prone regions as the most likely to be integrated into or run parallel with relief supply chains.

## Research Process

The research process used in this chapter can be categorized into three steps (Fig. 7.2). First, a review of literature and development of the conceptual framework, second the development of the survey (case study) protocols and finally the actual data gathering.

The first step was the preliminary literature review which resulted in the identification of the main extant issues. In particular, *food supply chain resilience* is a growing area of research that logically interconnects with areas such as commercial food supply chains, relief supply chains, resilience and disaster management (Fig. 7.3). The literature related to these areas was very helpful in understanding the concepts and emerging issues in the supply chain resilience discipline. The keywords that were used in search engines, databases and university library catalogues were resilience, supply chain, food

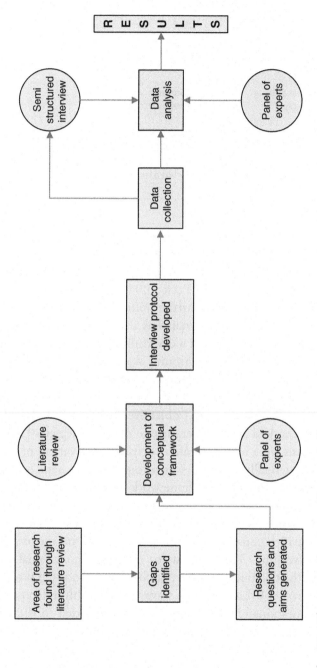

**Fig. 7.2** The research process. Source: Authors

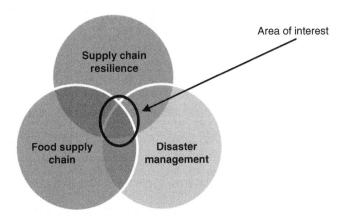

**Fig. 7.3** Main research themes. Source: Authors

supply chain, disaster management, relief supply chain, supply chain risk management and food chain resilience.

After identifying some key articles and sources (e.g. Ponomarov and Holcomb 2009; Christopher and Peck 2004) related to supply chain resilience, it became easier to identify further journals, articles and books related to this research. The quality of journals was also kept in view while searching for literature; however, this was not a determining factor when highly related papers with good theoretical background were identified. The preliminary literature review was helpful in identifying emerging issues in the supply chain resilience discipline which helped shape the overall theoretical framework. Next, research questions and objectives were refined several times in the process and checked against literature to ensure a degree of novelty. Key concepts and areas were identified after focusing on a variety of frameworks and factors. What finally emerged was a food supply chain resilience conceptual framework. Initially the framework was representation of several concepts and was piloted in front of a panel of experts and researchers from *Resilient Organizations*, a Research Centre based in Canterbury, New Zealand. The panel consisted of key personnel from the organization's supply chain discipline. The aim was to refine the conceptual framework and to increase the reliability of the research. The second step was to develop the interview protocol. Literature was again thoroughly referenced to generate relevant questions related to the concepts included in the conceptual framework. The interview protocol is major way of increasing the reliability of the research and is an essential guide for researchers in data collection phase of case research (Yin 2014). The research instrument was then pilot tested on a single food supply chain in New Zealand. Piloting case study helps to refine data collection process. Pilot tests are not a 'pretest' *per se* which is more like a dress rehearsal. For case research, pilot testing is more formative assisting the researcher to develop relevant lines of questioning and increasing the face validity of the questions and protocols (Yin 2014).

Finally in the last step, the data collection phase was conducted. The design of this research was for data to be gathered from key informants of four different food supply chains in South Asian region (more on the rationale of this design later). The data collection approach was a qualitative using the in-depth interview as the main data collection tool. A semi-structured interview technique was used in which the interview protocol played a major role. This research also used company reports and other relevant public documents as secondary data. This study also considered collecting data from a broad range of informants for comparative analysis. During the research, respondents were also asked to refine/explain their comments where meaning was not clear. This exercise is called 'respondent validation' and is used to validate the research. Subsequently, feedback questions were also asked to capture the perceptions of respondents which were used to validate the conceptual framework. Interviews were digitally recorded, field notes were also taken recoding observations and other facts. As the interview language was Urdu (the national language of Pakistan), the hand-written field notes and audio recordings were transcribed first into Urdu and then into English. A random sample of the English was then back-translated into Urdu to check for consistence of meaning over the two languages. While there were some words that had no direct translation, the meaning was compared to ensure the intent was translated. Finally, the text was then coded, condensed, displayed to allow further analysis and conclusions to be drawn.

While this outlines the research process in general, it would be helpful at this stage to step back and examine the underlying epistemological approach so as to appreciate the reasons why particular methods and techniques were used in this research.

## Case Study Methodology

A case study is 'an empirical enquiry which investigates a contemporary phenomenon in depth and within its real world context especially when boundaries between phenomenon and context may not be clearly evident' (Yin 2014, p. 13). Thus, the case study is recommended to be used in research when a researcher has to answer questions like 'how' and 'why'. Furthermore, if the researcher has no control over the behavioural events and the research is focused more on contemporary events, then case study methodology is recommended (Yin 2014). Similarly, case study methodology is appropriate for exploratory investigations of some new phenomenon which could be related to a person, group, family, situation, community or any cultural group (Meredith 1998). Hence, the case study deals with processes and puts more emphasis on a thorough analysis of a limited number of events and their interrelations. VanWynsberghe and Khan (2008) state that the case study methodology does not have a specific disciplinary orientation, thus it can be used in social science, applied science, business and humanities. Easton (1995) argues that the case study is the most suitable approach to study business relationships and supply networks. Furthermore, Gummesson (2007) and Halinen and Törnroos (2005) have also pointed out the importance of case study methodology in studying supply networks. This method gives the opportunity to the researcher to be close to the study's objects, thus enabling inductive and rich description of the phenomenon. Case study is most appropriate in a situation where little is known about the topic and where current theories seem inadequate, as is the case for our research (Easton 1995; Yin 1994).

Case studies can be used to accomplish different aims (see Table 7.1 below). Yin (2003) divides cases into exploratory, descriptive and explanatory. Eisenhardt (1989) recognizes description, but emphasizes the role of the case study in generating and testing theory. Stake (1994) highlights the value of intrinsic case study, where rich description of single case study is seen valuable as such. In the management discipline, theory generation seems the most discussed type of case research (Miles and Huberman 1994; Eisenhardt 1989; Glaser and Strauss 1967; Yin 2003).

**Table 7.1** Different types of case studies

|  | Exploratory | Descriptive | Explanatory |
|---|---|---|---|
| Purpose | This type of case study is used for those areas or situations in which the phenomenon being evaluated has no clear single set of outcomes (Yin 2014). | This type of case study is used to present complete description of the phenomenon within its real-life context (Creswell 2013). | When a case study is used to answer the question that sought to explain the presumed causal links in complex real-life context that are too complex for a survey strategy (Yin 2014). |
| Questions | Why, How | Who, What, Where | How, Why |
| Example case studies | Peck (2005), Bozkurt and Duran (2012) | Coles et al. (2012), Kneafsey et al. (2013) | Agarwal and Subramani (2013) |

*Source*: Authors

In the humanitarian logistics context, while many insights can be drawn from our commercial colleagues, much of the research can be classified as exploratory. As such exploratory studies are used to answer the 'what is happening' questions as well as seeking new insights and assessing the phenomenon in a new way (Robson 2002). This study was seeking to examine the causes (how and why questions) of resilience in food supply chains subjected to frequent disasters, the impact of resilience on these chains and also how the whole society can benefit. A significant advantage of case studies is that they are flexible and adaptable to change in the presence of new data and insights that could occur during the investigation (Saunders et al. 2011). This flexibility helped to investigate broadly the area of food supply chain resilience and as new insights unfolded, the researchers focused on areas demonstrating greater variability to the norms and hence discriminating.

Nevertheless, the case study methodology is not without its critics. This approach can be considered too situation specific and unable to generalize results (Weick and Kiesler 1979; Yin 1994). Also, it is time consuming and the extensive use of resources is also involved, such as researcher time. This later issue is of a major consideration to humanitarian logistics researchers as events often unfold/change with speed.

Regarding generalization, if the researcher has chosen a single case study with limited sample size, the results would hence not be significant in terms of statistical value (Alasuutari 2010; Ellram 1996). On the other hand, if large numbers of people are interviewed, then each would describe the complex phenomenon in a different way, which would make it difficult to interpret the situation correctly (Vissak 2010; Saunders et al. 2011). Indeed the purpose of the case study is to illuminate the detailed picture of a given phenomenon, and as suggested by Stake (1994) and Yin (2003), the expression *particularization* or *analytical generalization* should be used instead of generalization. Moreover, due to large amounts of qualitative data generated during the case study process, there may be the possibility that the researcher becomes overwhelmed and loses sight of actual issue in question or misses important larger themes altogether (Halinen and Törnroos 2005). Table 7.2 highlights the strengths and weaknesses of the case study method.

In response to some of these critiques, the case study methodology should be thoroughly designed *a priori*. 'Cases' then should be selected based on clear criteria and all the evidence of data collection should be well documented (Modell 2010). The 'unit of analysis' should be selected carefully and systematically (Gummesson 2007), and finally validity and reliability processes should be clear and give confidence as to the rigour of the research. For this study we address all these issues in the following sections.

**Table 7.2** Strengths and limitations of a case study methodology

| Strengths | Weaknesses |
| --- | --- |
| • It is commonly used in many scientific disciplines. | • Sometimes case study is considered soft, weak and unscientific. |
| • A higher response rate as compared to surveys. | • Less chances of getting published in certain journals, especially quantitative journals. |
| • Useful in generating new theory or explaining/criticizing already researched phenomenon. | • Case study is difficult and hard to conduct. |
| • Case study is very effective in explaining complex and dynamic issues in a real life context. | • Interpreting the results can be confusing. |
| • Very useful for asking 'why' and 'how' questions. It is also suitable to study organizations from multiple perspectives. | • Requires more time as compared to other methodologies. Data analysis and write up are very labour intensive and need greater word length. |
| • Theory development and empirical research can go side by side. | • Interviewee may not be telling the full story; it is also difficult to get confidential data. |
| • Flexible in the types of data that can be collected and analysed. | • Researcher bias can be high in sample selection and interviews. |
| • Flexible in reformulating and adding more questions during the data gathering process itself. | • A greater chance of ending up with a weak theory. |
| • Provides rich descriptions of phenomenon. | • It is really difficult to keep a balance between breadth and depth (single vs multiple case studies). |

Adapted from Vissak (2010), Creswell (2013) and Yin (2014)

# Case Study Design – Single and Multiple Cases

Given the nature of humanitarian logistics research outlined elsewhere in this handbook, and in light of above-mentioned specifications, it seems obvious that a case study methodology was the best approach for this research. This allows a deeper understanding of practical issues related to food supply networks in disasters in the real-life context of South Asian. What was of interest is the 'how' and 'why' of supply chain capabilities and processes that local food supply networks adopt in order to deal with natural disasters. This contemporary phenomenon was difficult to separate from its context, especially with the expected dynamics and interrelationships involved.

Further, it is essential to define what is a 'case' to understand case study design. The term 'case' in any case study is a construct, subject of interest and an empirical unit. Why it is important? Because scientific and practical interests are associated with it (Scholz and Tietje 2002). Eckstein (2000) defines a case as a phenomenon for which the researcher reports and interprets only a single measure on any pertinent variable. The case could be an account of an event or problem or activity. A case can also be an individual, organization, society or a group of organizations (Yin 2014). Hence, we argue that a 'food supply chain' is a suitable case for this research. Hence, these chains become by default an empirical unit of analysis as a whole. We provide a discussion on the 'unit of analysis' in the following sections.

A single case study is selected when the research area is unique and similar case is not available (Scholz and Tietje 2002). However, this could be quite vulnerable if the case chosen turns out not to be the case which it was thought to be. Thus, Yin (2014) suggests that a multiple case study design be adopted to provide robustness to the work. Table 7.3 provides a comparison between single and multiple case study approaches.

It is considered that humanitarian researchers would be able to enjoy the choice of single or multiple cases as the number of actors, non-governmental

**Table 7.3** Single versus multiple case studies

|  | Single case | Multiple cases |
|---|---|---|
| Typical Situation | One case<br>When a case:<br>• Is a critical case for the theory or theoretical propositions<br>• Is an extreme or unusual case, deviating from everyday circumstances<br>• Is a common case and where the objective is to capture the everyday situation<br>• Is a revelatory or longitudinal case<br>• Is used as a pilot case at the beginning of a multiple case study (Yin 2014) | Two or more cases (Yin 2014)<br>When the researcher:<br>• Is more concerned to explore differences within or across different cases<br>• The goal is to replicate findings across different cases<br>• Wants to reveal the complementary aspects of the phenomenon<br>• When the aim is to develop rich, theoretical framework (Lewis-Beck et al. 2004; Kähkönen 2011) |
| Pros | • Rich description of the phenomenon<br>• Require less time and resources | • Smaller researcher bias<br>• Provide strong base to build the theory<br>• Allow case comparisons to generate robust results<br>• Enhance external validity |
| Cons | • Generalizability<br>• The risk of exaggeration about the phenomenon<br>• Chances of misinterpreting the representativeness. | • Time consuming<br>• Less depth than single case<br>• Require extra resources |

*Source*: Authors.

organizations (NGOs), government organisation (GOs) and other agencies deployed into any relief effort is legion. If of course permissions are gained, indeed, there is an emerging trend of using the multiple case study approach and its ability to deal with a large amount of data from multiple sources (Easton 1995; Kähkönen 2011; Halinen and Törnroos 2005; Gummesson 2007). Multiple case studies have also proven to be a useful method among the researchers who study business supply networks (Batt and Purchase 2004). For this research example, a multiple case study method has been used to discover unique resilient approaches for each supply chain facing real-life disasters (floods and earthquakes). In particular, the multiple case approach facilitates cross-case comparisons and this is a very useful feature in humanitarian logistics (Coles, et al. 2012).

Yin (2014) has illustrated a useful approach to multiple case studies in Fig. 7.4 (below). The figure indicates that the first step is to generate a theoretical base from literature to guide the study. This is usually presented in form of a framework. It also reveals that case selection and protocol development are also important steps. Each individual case study should be considered as a 'whole' study. In each case, convergent evidence is sought regarding facts and conclusions. Each case conclusion is considered to be the information needing conformation/disconfirmation by the other cases. Both individual case and multiple case results should be the focus of final report. The report should also include a cross-case discussion that why certain results are found in one case study but has contrasting elements in other cases.

## Case Selection and Unit of Analysis

In case study design, an important question which a researcher always encounters concerns the number of cases that is deemed sufficient? In qualitative studies this decision is discretionary, not formulaic, similarly with quantitative research and defining the 'significant effect' in experimental science. Thus, the confidence level of accepting or rejecting a null hypothesis based on the $p$-value ($p < 0.01$, $p < 0.05$, $p < 0.1$) is a discretionary judgment call by the researcher. Yin (2014) claims that if theory is straightforward, then two or three cases can be enough. However, if theory is more latent or subtle, then four to six replications will produce reliable results. Considering this, this research relies on a four case study design. As a consequence, Eisenhardt (1989) and Miles et al. (2013) suggest that the sample chosen for qualitative research should be *purposive*, one which serves the purpose of the study. As this research is focusing on food supply chain/networks in disasters, especially in the context

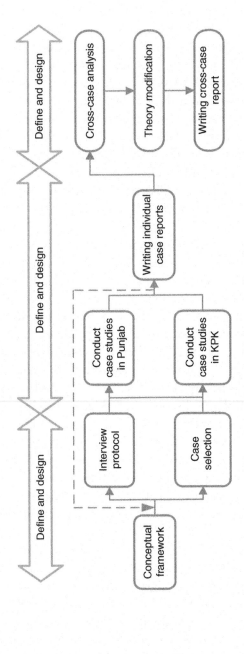

**Fig. 7.4** Multiple case study procedure. Source: Adapted from Yin (2014)

of underdeveloped South Asian country, the first step was to find the areas where disasters occur frequently in Pakistan.

To help this selection the researchers contacted the National Disaster Management Authority (NDMA) of Pakistan who deals with the whole spectrum of disaster management activities in Pakistan (www.ndma.gov. pk), and also the South Asian Disaster Knowledge Network (WWW. SAARC-SADKN.ORG) which is a knowledge sharing platform among different stakeholders of SAARC (South Asian Association of Regional Cooperation) countries. From these discussions two regions that are vulnerable to disasters (and in fact have experienced these disasters frequently/ annually) were purposively selected. The first area is the Punjab Province which is predominantly agricultural land. This area is badly affected by severe floods almost every year (Tariq and van de Giesen 2012). The second region is the Khyber Pakhtunkhwa (KPK) province which is vulnerable to earthquakes as well as floods (Khan et al, 2012) (Fig. 7.5).

Two cases from each region were selected to examine both intra- and inter-regional differences. Different relief food items were selected, which are usually provided by relief agencies (GOs and NGOs) to the community; these include rice, flour, oil, dry fruits, juice, water and food grains (Kovács and Spens 2007; Douglas 2009; Day et al. 2012; Whybark 2007). Given the research aim of seeing how local (commercial) food supply chains cope with parallel relief supply chains, we chose staple products (long shelf life) typically supplied in both channels in order to facilitate the comparisons.

However, the research was also interested in supply chains with products of a more perishable nature. Fresh fruit and vegetables supply chains are exceedingly susceptible to disasters in Pakistan. Fresh produce items are highly perishable commodities and during natural disaster, they become even more vulnerable to deterioration. Since the majority of the population in these areas is also dependent on continuous supply of fresh vegetables (Din et al. 2011; Ismail 2010), The research has also chosen a fresh produce supply chain in each region to study. Hence, the design is to study one staple and one fresh produce supply chain in each region, for a total of four case studies.

Another equally important task was to finalize the unit of analysis. Yin (2014) has suggested four basic design categories for case studies – single or multiple cases inspected from either a holistic point of view as a single unit of analysis, or they may be examined from embedded view with a multiple unit of analysis (see Fig. 7.6). Each supply network is comprised of a number of different organizations who work together to achieve the desired goals. Given that the aim is to understand resilience of a supply chain as a whole, it is

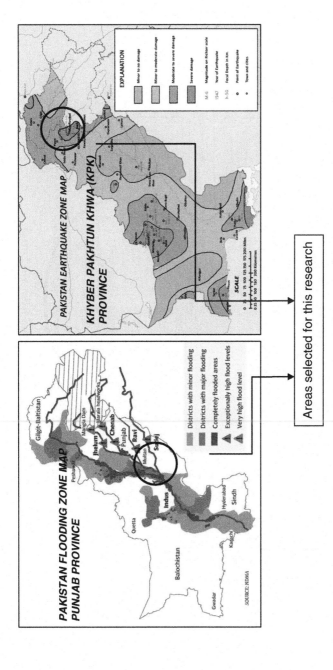

**Fig. 7.5** Sample selection decisions – Flooding and earthquake zones in Pakistan. Source: NDMA and SADKN (May 2015)

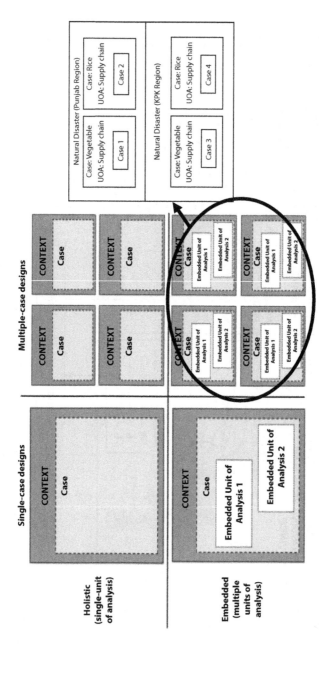

**Fig. 7.6** Case study design and unit of analysis. Source: Adapted from Yin (2014)

necessary to investigate as many organizations as possible along the entire chain. Hence, the natural unit of analysis is the 'supply chain system' or 'supply network' that produces, and distributes the sampled products of rice and fresh produce. Every researcher will have to make these 'boundary'-type decisions at some stage. The key principle is to ensure that enough data points are captured to say something your unit of analysis (i.e. firm or supply chain), but not extending the boundaries to the point where data gathering becomes wholly impractical. Hence, this study has used multiple case study approach with an embedded perspective having the supply network as unit of analysis.

## The Challenges of Network Research

Related to the unit of analysis decisions, there were three other major challenges involved in studying supply networks. As mentioned earlier, these are not mere four supply chains. Rather, each supply chain has multiple hierarchies involving hundreds of actors and suppliers, thus it can be argued that we are investigating a 'system' or complex network. It follows then that problems relating to network boundary, complexity and case comparisons were inevitable (Halinen and Törnroos 2005).

Case complexity was largely reduced by defining the number of cases and limiting the context to two main natural disasters (floods and earthquakes) as we excluded man-made and other types of disasters. Similarly, the site was limited to two main geographical regions in Pakistan that are vulnerable to these disasters. Complexity was also minimized with the help of a single interview protocol for all the respondents and by adhering to the research objectives at all times. The third important step was the selection of one staple food and one fresh produce supply chain within each region, hence resolving the issues related to case comparisons. Utilizing the same theoretical base and framework for all cases also facilitated the process of case comparison.

The major problem remaining was related to defining the boundaries of the networks, and this is similar to the issue of defining the unit of analysis. It is argued that the network boundary will clearly depend on the research problem. Halinen and Törnroos (1998) have proposed four ways of delimiting business networks (see Fig. 7.7). These four networks can be described as actor network, dyad network, micro-macro network and intranet network. As this study is concerned with food supply networks and was interested in taking a full view of the supply chain, the micro-macro network is a logical choice. At the macro level, these food networks

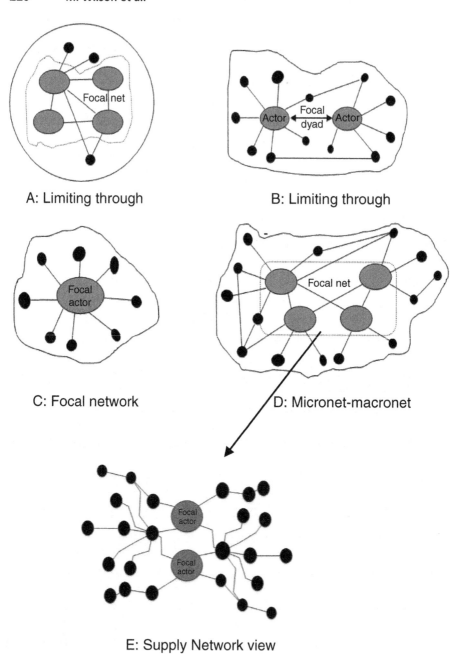

A: Limiting through

B: Limiting through

C: Focal network

D: Micronet-macronet

E: Supply Network view

**Fig. 7.7** Delimiting supply chain networks. Source: Adapted from Halinen and Törnroos (2005)

comprise thousands of actors such as different business units as well as government institutes, NGOs and humanitarian organizations. Within the micro network, the researcher approached the individual actors, thus asking them about their immediate important (dyadic) buyers and suppliers. The researcher then traversed through these referred buyers and suppliers until reaching the end of supply chain at both upstream and downstream ends. In this way the researcher was able to take a view of each buyer and supplier, as well as a horizontal view of actors at same level (tier) in the supply chain. However, there were number of challenges to reach to these actors as these networks are embedded in larger social and political networks. How the researcher reached the individual actors and the associated challenges in data collection will be discussed in the following sections.

## Systematic Combining

One of the main features of theory generation from case studies is the numerous overlaps between data collection and data analysis (Strauss and Corbin 1990). This is called the 'matching process' or the 'systematic combining' approach (Dubois and Gadde 2002). They define matching as going back and forth between the case, framework, data collection and analysis (see Fig. 7.8). The way of achieving this matching is through direction and redirection of the study. This direction and redirection holds true for theory, cases and data sources. Hence, multiple data sources is one of the techniques to achieve this. Yin (2014) and Miles et al. (2013) argue that multiple sources are required to triangulate the data which in return increase the validity of the research. However, in systematic combining not only does it increase the validity, it also leads to the discovery of new phenomenon in the given context. As a result, these new discoveries compel the researcher to search for new theories to support the results and so on.

Reading what has been written so far would seem to make it appear that designing this research was a linear set of processes and decisions made sequentially. However, the truth is it is an intertwined research processes where the researcher has gone back and forth many times between theory and real world to ensure a rigorous research process. As qualitative research has been often criticized for lack of valid processes, the researcher has used a systematic combining (Fig. 7.8) approach as suggested above. This process permits iteration, meaning that the conceptual framework, theory, fieldwork

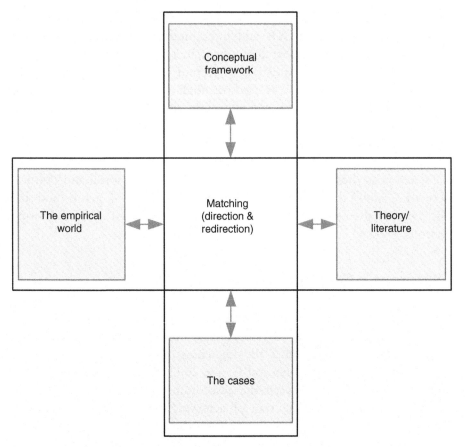

**Fig. 7.8** Systematic combining. Source: Adapted from Dubois and Gadde (2002)

and case analysis develop at the same time. As the main objective of any research is to confront theory with the real world, therefore, systematic combining makes sure that this confrontation is continuous throughout the research. This does not however preclude a deductive approach also utilizing case studies as the method.

As such, the conceptual framework is very important in this approach. A conceptual framework is a graphical representation of the main concepts and their interrelationships. This framework is developed at the start of the study and then evolves gradually as the study progresses. It works as a general guideline of the main concepts that need to be studied in the empirical world (Miles et al. 2013). Once the researcher starts the data collection and with more grip on the relevant literature, the framework gets revised continuously and becomes more precise.

Following these guidelines, systematic combining occurred many times while continuously going back and forth between different aspects of this framework during the data gathering phase of this research. Initially, the researcher was focused on disaster management, which led towards humanitarian supply chains. A partial framework was also developed at the same time to effectively manage the supply chains in disruptive events. As part of this process, a full paper based on the literature review was presented at an international academic conference, which led the researcher to explore more emergent issues within this discipline. It was found that the little had been done with commercial food supply chains and disaster management. Hence, the researcher referred back to the literature where new themes emerged that resulted in a conceptual framework more tilted towards understanding the resilience of commercial chains, but adopting critical elements from the disaster management discipline. Initially the conceptual framework was a mixture of many concepts relating to the resilience of food supply chains. However, with regular meetings with the research committee and going back and forth in the theory, a number of concepts were merged and some were discarded. The new framework along with the theory was again presented at another international academic conference. It was also discussed with members of the Resilience Organization Research Group in Canterbury, New Zealand. The following sections will explain the full data collection process.

## Sampling

This research, being qualitative in nature, used non-probability sampling to select the population for study. For this type of sampling, units are purposely selected to reflect specific features of interest in the population (Sekaran 2006). As this research was not seeking a sample that is statistically representative, we therefore *purposively* chose certain population characteristics for our selection criteria. A number of authors have recommended non-probability sampling for small-scale explorative studies (Miles, Huberman, and Saldaña 2013; Yin 2014; Sekaran 2006; Bhattacherjee 2012; Lewis-Beck et al. 2004). Purposive sampling technique identifies and selects those individuals/groups/organizations that are knowledgeable about the topic of interest or have experience in the field (Palinkas et al. 2015). Sample sizes were not fixed prior to the study as it depends on the resources, time available and theoretical saturation of the required study (Rubin and Rubin 2011). Therefore, it is more suitable for studies where analysis and data collection goes side by side such as for this research. Using purposive sampling, organizations/commission agents in the fruit and vegetable and grain markets of Punjab and KPK regions were our initial point of contact. Internet and social media platforms were also used for this purpose as well as referrals from the Disaster Management Cell of the Pakistani Government. While selecting the initial informants, three criteria were used as guidelines: knowledgeable about the situation (had experienced some disaster or its effects in recent past), willing to talk and a diversity of views (big and small markets, different business situations, different areas).

While purposively selecting the initial sample, the referral or snow balling techniques were used to follow the supply chains of the four different cases. This was an effective way of finding the immediate supply chain actors as food supply chains within these regions are usually well connected. Each informant was asked about their *main* suppliers and buyers, therefore limiting the network to those more important actors and relationships (as described earlier). In this way those in the supply chain were traversed, thus rolling the 'snow ball' to each end of the chain. For time and travel constraints, the researcher selected the study units that were easily accessible. This may not always be an option for disaster studies. This form of sampling is sometimes called convenient sampling and is highly applicable for humanitarian researchers. Qualitative samples are usually small in size as there is no hard-and-fast rules to ensure sufficient scale to statistically prove the estimates, rather looking for richness in detail. Finally, this approach yielded 38 in-depth interviews that were conducted across the four food supply chains in Punjab and KPK region.

## Data Collection

### Interview Protocol Development

The prime source of data collection in case study research is typically in-depth interviews, backed up by observations, informal conversations and a review of archival secondary sources. Research protocols are necessary to enhance the validity and reliability of qualitative research (Yin 2014). A research protocol contains the introduction, rules, procedures, questions, themes and prompts used to help guide an interview. The interview questions are the main element of this instrument, pointing to specific data that is required. Question prompts are also included to help guide the conversation and also make sure that all the topics are covered during any interview.

The protocol also helps maintains the uniformity across all the interviews, thus increasing the reliability of the research (Voss et al. 2002).

In this study, the researcher used the 'funnel format' to structure the interview protocol. This protocol starts with the broader questions concerning the introduction, supply chain partners, buyers, logistics and business history. Then by funnelling down, the core questions relating to the preparation, response and recovery from recent disasters are asked. The main research questions were refined several times as more concepts were revealed through the literature. After the development of an initial draft protocol, the researcher tested the instrument on several knowledgeable people, in particular the Head of Department, Global Value Chains and Trade, Lincoln University, New Zealand and members of research committee of Resilient Organizations, Christchurch. The initial view was that it was very lengthy as it took almost 2 hours in one of the testing interviews. The instrument was further refined based on these comments, with redundant and unnecessary questions merged or removed and where necessary any ambiguity was clarified.

## Protocol Language Translation

As the research setting was based in Pakistan where English is not common, the research instrument needed to be translated to the native language of the region (Urdu). This process was systematic involving two more researchers native to the same region and ethnic group. The instrument was independently translated word by word into the native language by these two researchers as well as the primary researcher. Google translate and other online dictionaries were used to help convert difficult words that have compatibility issues in both languages. The three translated versions were then reviewed in a combined meeting, thus leading to more changes in sentence structuring. The final drafted instrument was tested on a person of the same ethnic group and further refined. The last stage was to translate this instrument back to the English language to make the process valid. While minor inconsistencies were noted, the major themes and concepts remained intact in the back-translated English version.

## Interviews

There are three main types of interviews that can be conducted in qualitative research. These are structured, semi-structured and unstructured (Saunders et al. 2011). Structured interviews use specific questions requiring specific answers and a questionnaire (survey interview) and is a common tool. However, these interviews are most appropriate for quantitative studies (Whiting 2008). For this research semi-structured interviews were conducted. These types of interviews are more flexible, thus more suitable for the objectives of this research (exploratory). In a semi-structured interview, the researcher is able to follow lines of enquiry during the flow of the interview, but this demands more in-depth knowledge of the given topic. For this research, most of the interviews were individual one-to-one interviews; however, on several occasions group interviews were also conducted. The group interviews gave greater insights about the phenomenon capturing the collective experiences of people involved. Of interest were the notes and observations of the interpersonal interactions and reactions among the group being interviewed, thus revealing hidden meanings. Follow-up interviews were also conducted, with a number being conducted via telephone due to time and travel constraints.

In the data collection phase, the role of the interviewer was that of an investigator, who is looking for information and facts concerning the preparation, response and recovery phases of the disaster from the respondents. Leonard-Barton (1990), Yin (2003) and Creswell (2013) have all mentioned some qualities that a researcher should possess in order to conduct a good interview. These include good listening skills, unbiased, flexible and adaptable. In this particular research, some of the skills that really helped the researcher to gather quality data through the interviews are listed here:

- The researcher should be able to ask good questions and interpret the answers: these skills can be acquired by repeated rehearsals with the interview instrument.
- In order to interpret the answers, the researcher should have a full command of the local languages and culture. Some notions are culturally specific which can only be interpreted if you know the local customs. This is an important point for humanitarian researchers who typically operate in foreign environments and cultures.
- The researcher should be adaptable to the situation and be flexible. Newly developed situations should be seen as opportunities rather than threats, unless related to security and safety.
- Have full command of the subject area, but not be biased or have preconceived ideas, thus remaining sensitive to contradictory data.
- There is no need to impress the respondent with your knowledge of the subject

- Being an active and good listener is a key skill. Generally people are very sensitive to someone who is not giving them their full attention while they are talking.
- It is critical at first to develop a good rapport with the interviewee. Wear the same style of clothes and types of clothes for ethnic groups, use the same tone, maintain eye contact (if acceptable in that culture) and at all times be polite and humble.
- Always ask permission for before recording, and take any official documents with you to introduce yourself.
- Always allow the respondent the option to exit the interview at any time for any reason.

While conducting these interviews, the researcher has also noted the depth and detail, vivid and nuanced answers as well as rich content that can generate more themes (Rubin and Rubin 2011). Trust and paraphrasing questions in simpler ways were the key to achieving these characteristics. The general lack of trust and suspicion of people who ask questions was a major limiting factor within this society where the research took place. Potentially people and organizations were afraid of giving interviews for fear of some political or legal threat. Hence, good interview skills as mentioned before and social references were used to build trust. Much consideration should be given to the use of interpreters or locals where possible.

Qualitative data should be vivid and nuanced and this should emerge from one's questioning. Vividness comes through the step-by-step description of the event. The researcher enquired about the background of the respondents, their suppliers, buyers, logistic providers and any other actors involved to make the description of events fully vivid so that any reader would get a sense of not only the detail but the emotion as well. The researcher also asked for a detailed description of any meaningful moments that occurred in the recent disasters. For example, in one of the vegetable markets, the commission agent described an extreme flood which left the market completely submerged under water and silt, and then described how the market members self-organized and coordinated the clean-up and also the rationale for this behaviour. This was clearly a significant moment for the respondent and the emotion was evident. Researchers should not miss opportunities like these that allow unique moments to probe in depth.

Similarly, nuance implies that there could be several views/opinions/attitudes for the same phenomenon/event. Nuance requires a detailed description of something, not just a yes or no answer. For example, the researcher asked a question concerning trust from almost all the respondents, if someone provided a closed answer such as 'yes, we trust our supplier', the researcher then asked further questions about the meaning of trust, such as how to achieve it. Everyone seems to have a different response to this question, hence providing a quite nuanced view of trust in this context. Finally, richness comes through extended conversations. The researcher encouraged the respondents to speak openly about each situation by asking probing questions (open-ended questions). As the researcher was familiar with the local culture and every culture has its norms, often the researcher would order a cup of tea or lunch for the respondents to show the intention of spending time with them and listening to more stories.

## Secondary Data Gathering

Other than interviews, secondary data as well as data through direct observations were also collected. Observation is a more humanistic methodology and it involves the systematic recording and noting of occurrences, behaviours and processes in the social setting of the research, not just the words spoken (Marshall and Rossman 2014). In this research, observations were recorded during and before and after the interviews with different supply chain members, and also by visiting the markets where actual transactions take place. While a digital voice recorder was used to capture the words, photographs and field notes recorded the other non-verbal clues and captured actual observations of behaviours including the physical environment not described by the respondent.

Secondary data along with other methods help gain a holistic picture of the situation. Secondary data are invaluable because they helps triangulate the phenomenon under study by utilizing multiple sources of evidence. In this research, data related to the overall region's economic, social, technological and governmental situation was collected through governmental official reports and other published documents. Work process documents, handouts, receipts, transactional documents used by different actors, manuals, price lists and catalogues of items, farming brochures and reports, market manual, Punjab Disaster Management Authority (PDMA) research reports and other humanitarian company reports about the regional food supply chains were collected in the process. Triangulation is a critical component of any qualitative analysis to ensure validity and hence should be a feature of any humanitarian research project (Yin 2014).

# The Data Gathering Phase

Data collection actually started long before the formal interviews for this research. In the period of December 2013 to March 2014, the researcher conducted a number of interviews with the emergency relief providers in Pakistan, in particular the NDMA and PDMA. The researcher wrote a formal letter to the managing directors of these organizations, seeking appointment for interviews. Hence, the procurement manager in NDMA and the managing director of the PDMA were interviewed. These interviews were unstructured in order to build an initial impression of disaster management in Pakistan, and how these agencies provide relief to the affected population. Through these interviews, an idea of the most vulnerable areas and people was revealed. These organizations also shared archival data and reports, which further clarified the overall conditions in these areas concerning natural disasters and response. It was from these interviews that the idea of looking at the resilience of commercial food supply chains in the advent of natural disasters was initially conceived. Following this, a literature review was conducted that resulted in the developing research questions and conceptual framework for this study.

Data collection related to four supply chains began at the start of October 2015 and was completed by the end of February 2016. Through the interviews with the above-mentioned organizations and researcher's own knowledge of situation, it was evident that the entry points for these supply chains would need to be the large wholesale markets where commission agents conduct their business. To illustrate how these agents work, Fig. 7.9 gives an overview of how connected these agents are in the supply chain; however, a detailed analysis of these markets will be contained in a future report. Agriculture is the main driver of Pakistan's internal economy. Just over 70% of the population is directly or indirectly engaged in farming, distribution, processing and production of major food commodities (Division 2011). Rice and wheat are the major crops of Pakistan, producing 24.5 and 6.7 million tonnes, respectively (Raza 2014). Similarly, Pakistan produces almost 9 million tonnes of fresh vegetable and fruits annually (Mehmood et al. 2010).

While a percentage of these food commodities are consumed at the farm level, for home consumption or sold directly to consumers from the farm gate, the vast bulk of the products passes through the wholesale market system to the end consumers. These wholesale markets are traditionally set up by the government and they have become a central node where sellers and buyers meet to execute transactions. Commission agents are basically

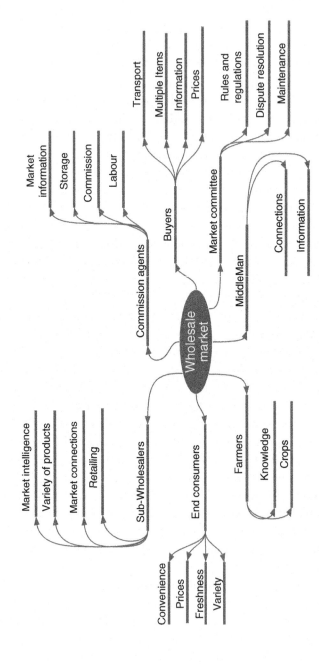

**Fig. 7.9** Wholesale market components – Food supply chains in Pakistan. Source: Author

the main custodian of these markets as they are allocated shops/premises with the main markets. Therefore, the researcher first established contact with a number of these commission agents in order to enter into these supply chains. The Agriculture Market Information System (www.amis.pk) possesses a database of commission agents operating in different markets in Punjab region. Selection of these initial contacts was made utilizing the three criteria of purposive sampling mentioned earlier. From this list the researcher contacted some of the commission agents seeking information related to the research. Most of the agents were reluctant to be part of this due to a common cultural dilemma that people tend to avoid the strangers. However, two of the commission agents agreed to give face-to-face interviews. The one major success at this point was that commission agents' business was not attached to exclusively to a single supply chain. Rather every commission agent was usually involved in supply chains for multiple products. For example, an agent dealing with vegetables would also be involved in fruits. Similarly, wheat and rice are also traded by the same person/organization. Therefore, instead of calling these vegetable and rice supply chains, the researcher has described these as fresh produce and staple food supply chains as each product group has different logistics and market characteristics. Thereafter, the researcher made sure to interview the major businesses of each of these supply chains.

Meanwhile, the researcher used his extensive network of family, friends and social acquaintances to locate other entry points. Social media mainly Facebook and Twitter were also very helpful. The researcher updated his Facebook status about the research and asked for possible contributions from someone or help in finding further respondents. A number of social activists and people involved in disaster management were also contacted through Twitter. From this approach, important new contacts were generated in the KPK region and this assured entry points; similarly more contacts were found in Punjab region. During disaster events social media is one of the emerging and main information sources. Humanitarian researchers are encouraged to make more use of these somewhat untraditional sources of contacts and data.

In November 2015, after arriving at the research site, letters of introduction were written to PDMA and other government departments (City District Government Local Body) and requests for appointments made. The reasons for this approach were that during an initial interview one respondent explained that these institutes are part of the market committees and if someone from government accompanied the researcher then respondents would be more willing to speak.

## Data Collection in Punjab Food Chains

The collection of data started by visiting one of the fruit and vegetable markets in Lahore city where the researcher made certain observations about the processes, loading and unloading of items, storage facilities and dealing with customers. A number of contacts were also made which showed interest in giving interviews. According to these observations, the interview protocol was further simplified in terms of language as the level of education of respondents was very low, making the questions around the key concepts hard to understand. Fortunately, the replies to some of the letters written to government officials were also very positive, and one of the officers (the district municipal officer in-charge of one of the largest fruit and vegetable markets in the region) agreed to assist in data collection. Being the key stakeholder, he was also interviewed. With his help, commission agents were contacted and interview times were set over the phone. The interviews were always conducted at their business sites. Initially two interviews were conducted with two separate commission agents and they also introduced their immediate suppliers and buyers. As this was the largest market in the region, farmers, middlemen and all other supply chain actors visit here regularly. Times and venues were then arranged to meet their supply chain partners.

Meanwhile, all the interviews were transcribed, and on the next visit were discussed with the actors for confirmation and accuracy. This particular supply network was spread all over Pakistan. Fresh items come not only from the immediate surrounding areas and region, but even from Sindh Province and KPK regions. The main suppliers and buyers who were in nearby areas were personally visited by the researcher to record the interviews. However, for suppliers from far away areas the researcher waited until they came to the market before being interviewed.

Being accompanied by the government officials made it easier to approach and be welcomed by these respondents. The downside was that it made it equally difficult to collect important information as these people were reluctant to provide sensitive information with officials being present. However, by sticking to best interview practices and using trust building techniques, the researcher was eventually able to gather the required information. Some of the respondents asked for an official letter from the hosting university/institution in order to assess the credentials of the researchers and the necessity of the research. Fortunately, this had been foreseen and such a letter had been obtained. It is highly recommended that researchers obtain such a letter from their host university/organization confirming, purpose and use of this research and even enrolment before the field work.

Some of the products in this market came from the KPK region, which is also part of this research design. One of the wholesalers provided the contact for a farmer in this region, which later opened up new leads for this research in that region. The Facebook page provided contacts for two main supermarkets of the region, which mainly procure the items from this market. These contacts were actually previous students of the researcher who were working in these supermarkets supply chain departments.

Besides fresh produce, respondents from food supply networks for staples were also approached. Commission agents who were sampled from the agriculture marketing information system were contacted and appointments were made over the phone. During the interviews, the respondents were also asked to supply contact details of their key buyers and suppliers. One of the respondents who was interviewed came from a social media contact. This person invited the researcher into his home and later helped in a telephone interview with one of his main suppliers. The researcher then travelled with this person to rural areas from where farmers were interviewed. This person also gave the contact of one of his major buyers, a rice mill whose general manager was interviewed later on. Gaining the active support from locals such as this is invaluable in humanitarian research.

Most of these initial interviewees urged the researcher to visit the Kamoke grain market, which is one of the largest in Pakistan. Subsequently, the researcher interviewed a trader in rice who later turned out to be from the researcher's extended family. This person was purchasing rice from the same market and had contacts within the Kamoke market. In the last week of December 2015, the researcher travelled by road to this market where commission agents were interviewed, and then one of the middlemen accompanied the researcher to off sites to different local regions where rice mills, farmers and wholesalers were interviewed.

All the interviews were recorded with the permission of the respondents, and where respondents refused to be recorded (five respondents), handwritten notes were taken instead. The main source of data were these interviews; however, observations were made by repeatedly visiting this market and other small market in the region. The observations mainly recorded actions addressing the preparation for disaster, physical conditions, the interactions of these people with their suppliers and buyers and assessing logistics infrastructure such as transportation and storage facilities. Secondary data such as information sharing sheets, rate lists, tax documents, safety rules, newspaper articles and other reports written about these chains were also collected. All the data were transcribed side by side during these interviews using '*Transcribe wreally*' (a web application). Audio files can be uploaded on this site and with the help of sophisticated tools, the transcription process becomes very easy. The transcripts were audited and checked by the researcher for accuracy.

## Data Collection in KPK Food Chains

Gathering data in the KPK region was more challenging. Firstly because of the isolated geographical location and secondly the global war on terrorism has impacted heavily on the region. The researcher travelled to Peshawar the capital of this region by local transport. Before going there, a reference was obtained from the military so that movement in the region could be facilitated. In addition, people are friendlier towards military personal. Through Twitter, one person who was associated with a humanitarian organization was contacted and with his reference, the local fruit and vegetable market was visited. Initial interviews were recorded in the largest market of the region, and then through snowballing new contacts for farmers and buyers were obtained.

A number of contacts were also referred by the commission agents in Punjab; these were also interviewed. In this region people are more friendly and hospitable; however, because of the war on terror, they are afraid of talking to strangers. It was initially found that vegetable and fruit markets more or less operate in a similar fashion like Punjab region. On the contrary, food chains of staples are quite different. As all wheat and rice are cultivated in Punjab, this region provides all the staples for the KPK region. Therefore, in KPK there are large wholesale markets in different cities. All these wholesale markets obtain their supplies from Punjab and then distribute to the local areas. One of these big wholesale markets was visited by the researcher and recorded interviews where conducted. These wholesalers supplied further contacts with their key suppliers and buyers in different regions.

In the first week of January 2016, the researcher travelled further north of the region in a military vehicle and interviewed the respondents in local markets of Mardan, Batkhela, Mingora and Takht Bhai. Some of the farmers were interviewed via telephone as the roads were damaged due to the recent earthquake making access difficult. Some of the farmers who were selling their product directly on the road side were also interviewed. During these days, interviews were transcribed immediately and the transcripts were made and validated by the respondents. However, further interviews were required which were held via telephone.

In a similar manner, observations were made regarding the damage by the earthquake and rivers, transactions between different players, market structures and conditions, body languages, dealing with customers, transportation and storage conditions. Secondary data were also collected in shape of reports, rate lists, market committee rules and regulations.

## Analysis

In qualitative studies, data analysis starts alongside the data collection. This technique helped the researcher to cycle back and forth between thinking about the existing data and coming up with new ideas to collect new data. This analysis is dependent on three contemporaneous steps: data condensation, data display and conclusion drawing (Miles et al. 2013). Data condensation is a process of focusing and simplifying the large quantities of data gathered from interviews, notes, documents and any other relevant sources. Coding, concept and theme generation are also part of this process. Data condensation in this research started with reviewing again the framework, research questions and data collection methods, thus condensing the overall information by selecting and focusing on the relevant knowledge derived from the theory framework. This process also compliments the systemic combining philosophy, where the framework, case study, collection methods and analysis evolve side by side. Concurrently, writing detailed case study descriptions and compiling matrixes to show the information is part of data display process. Data coding and themes generation are the most important steps in qualitative data analysis and these were done using NVivo software.

As recommended by Kvale and Brinkmann (2009), the written transcripts were shared with the respondents and feedback received. This process is important as it increases the internal validity. This interaction with the respondents helped generate more ideas and also strengthened the findings of the research. After the verification by the participants, all the data were then coded and concepts were grouped. Based on these codes and concepts, themes were generated and later triangulated against the observational and secondary data. Queries were then run in NVivo software to display the data, and finally these data were compared with the literature and theory to generate the conclusions.

The coding of the data is a complex process. Even from a small paragraph, a good number of codes and concepts can be emerged. The development of codes, categories and themes in the NVivo software was accomplished by a four-step process as suggested by Silver and Lewins (2014), being organizing the data, data exploration, data integration and finally interpretation. Additionally, a number of other general approaches to coding suggested by other authors were trailed (Yin 2014; Miles et al. 2013; Saldaña 2015; Hesse-Biber and Leavy 2010).

In this whole data interrogation process, the first step is to 'organize the data'. In this phase, familiarization with the data is the objective. Interview transcripts were read, re-read, grouped and notes were reviewed. Similarly, secondary data were organized, and referral to the literature base was made for more insights. Furthermore, data were sorted and an interpretative framework was also built.

The interview transcripts were imported into NVivo in the source section. Then the files were copied into the internal section and arranged into four separate folders to accommodate the four separate supply chains studied. Relevant secondary data were also copied here. In the memos section, all the observations were saved. Pictures related to the each site were also brought into the internal folder of this sources section in NVivo.

The next step was developing the interpretative framework. This should be done according to the research questions and/or the conceptual framework. In NVivo, this step is known as generating the initial 'nodes'. Nodes are basically the container in which similarly linked data/ideas are kept in order to generate themes and running queries. It also assists with displaying the data graphically (visualizations). These initial nodes were generated according to the sections in the conceptual framework of this study. For our research, these main nodes were initially vulnerabilities, capabilities, resilience and outcomes. Within these initial containers, further 'child' containers were generated according to pre-coding codes. These pre-coding codes were drawn from the literature. The reason for these child containers is that in using an inductive methodology, this research started with *a priori* theory and hence initial concepts of interest. Further codes were then generated and the initial codes were then merged or expanded based on the degree of similarity or variance.

Simultaneously, the 'classifications section' in the NVivo was used to classify the sources of data according to the different supply chain actors being interviewed. Initial coding was also done in this step. The automatic coding function of NVivo was not used here, as the researcher wanted to code the whole data manually in order to become more familiar with the contents. This process, while more time consuming, was very helpful in developing a clearer picture of how data were 'talking' and the themes started to originate even from this first round of coding.

The second step in this data interrogation is 'exploration'. Here, codes developed in first phase are transformed into concepts based on resemblances and distinctions. Also, less important or orphaned codes are subsumed into higher order codes. Codes and concepts are marked and annotated as well using the annotated tools available in NVivo. The third step is 'integration'. Here codes and categories are connected together and this then generates the patterns. These patterns were carefully observed, and based on these patterns and integration of other sources of information such as observation and literature, 'categories' are developed.

In the fourth step, 'interpretation' queries are run to see the comparison and other data display tools are used to make connections among different categories. Only then can the final report be written. We suggest that the report be written at two levels: descriptive and interpretative. The descriptive level narrates the whole supply chain and all the relevant stories told by the respondents. Often the descriptive part of the case study analysis is appended at the back of the report as an attachment or appendix. The interpretative part of the case study is by far the most important section and reveals the themes and connection of these themes to resilience of supply chain. This section will take time and effort to ensure that the analysis is unbiased and as accurate as possible. Data visualization diagrams and tables are helpful here to finally tell the story.

## Assessment Criteria

Producing reliable and rigorous research is essential for decision making but challenging in the humanitarian logistics context. As such reliability and generalizability are key assessment criteria for assessing the quality of any research. Nonetheless, these two assessment criteria are generally related to the positivist or quantitative approach (Yin 2014). As this research is more interpretive in nature, these measures need to be expressed in a different way. This study intended to study a contemporary phenomenon and other than generalizing the findings to the specific context, the interpretation and explanation of the events are the main concern (Alasuutari 2010).

Qualitative studies cannot generally be replicated as the real world is constantly changing. This is contrasted to a laboratory experiment where repeatability (reliability) is critical. Each interpretation is unique and hence replication is not as relevant in these types of studies (Strauss and Corbin 1990; Marshall and Rossman 2014; Yin 2014). On the contrary, 'authenticity' and 'internal validity' are the focal issues for qualitative research. Additionally, qualitative research is concerned about matching the findings with the reality (Patton 2005).

To summarize, Lincoln and Guba (2000) asserts that qualitative interpretations can be improved by four factors: credibility, dependability, transferability and conformability. Table 7.4 explains the steps taken to improve the quality of this study.

**Table 7.4** Measures of reliability and validity in qualitative research

| Criteria | Steps taken |
|---|---|
| **Credibility (internal validity)** Credibility establishes the extent to which the research finding is true interpretation of participant's original views. | a) Prolonged engagement in the field: research was familiar with the local culture and also contacts were established with respondents long before the data collection stage. b) Multiple case studies were used in the study, which is well established and backed by multiple recognized researchers in the field. c) Data triangulation was employed. This strategy made it easy to cross check the findings with different data sources. For example, data from interviews were triangulated with observations and secondary data. d) Respondents were given full opportunity to withdraw from the study anytime. Only genuinely interested respondents were chosen to collect the data. e) Peer debriefing: researcher has continuously taken support and feedback from the peers. Researcher attended seminars and conferences to take suggestions. Researcher was also part of Resilient Organization, New Zealand, which provided support during this whole study. |
| **Dependability (reliability)** It refers to the stability of results over time. | a) Detailed interview protocol was prepared to collect the data. This protocol includes the description of the research, concise questions about the phenomenon and has the complete list of prompt questions asked during the process. This can help future researchers to be able to follow same procedures to get similar results. |
| **Transferability (external validity)** The level to which results from one case study or real world can be applied to other case study in some different context. | a) Provide thick description: Thick and detailed description is provided for each case study as well as the setting/context with in which this case study was embedded. b) Multiple case studies are done in similar conditions which further enhance the transferability of this study. c) Purposeful sampling was used and it helped the researcher to stay focus on the key informants. It helped the researcher in in-depth findings. |

**Table 7.4** (continued)

| Criteria | Steps taken |
| --- | --- |
| **Conformability (objectivity)**<br>It refers to the degree to which results from one case study can be confirmed by other researchers. | a) Full details of the participants were collected in the process. Participants were also given chance to ready and give feedback on the transcripts. Similarly, the interpretation chapters also include the quotes from the participants' interviews. |

*Source*: Adapted from Lincoln and Guba (2000).

# Final Advice for Field Work Researchers in South Asia

We conclude this chapter with a brief summary of the lessons learnt and the limitations while the researcher was conducting the data gathering phase in South Asia. We hope that the information provided in this chapter will help all researchers deal with qualitative case study-type research in general, but for humanitarian and disaster relief researchers in particular. This type of research seems to be the most commonly published in the discipline; hence, it is critical to get it as accurate as possible.

Local knowledge of culture, area and accustoms are the key areas to be focused on before actually going into the field. Without the local language, it is difficult to communicate with the different supply chain actors. In this research, most of the respondents could only speak Punjabi and Urdu in the Punjab area, and similarly in KPK region with the addition of Pushto as a widely spoken language. It is highly desirable to have the local interpreter along with you who can translate the important insights on the spot. Secondly, it is very hard to distinguish between different food supply chains in the region as most people are trading and doing business across multiple food items. Similarly, different supply chain players are hard to distinguish based on their roles, for example, the same firm behaves as a supplier and other times as the buyer. This is especially true given the micronature of many of the businesses where the respondents have to perform multiple roles. Therefore, the researcher has to have local acumen to figure out these confusions.

A time limit was another constraint on this research. These supply chains are very fragmented and geographically spread in this region. Sometimes many kilometres have to be travelled between interviews. Therefore, researchers should allow ample time to spend in the region to collect the required data. Do not rely on the local public transport system as it is barely functional and the vehicles are not in good (safe) condition, hence one's own transport is a must.

Another interesting point that can confound the analysis is the frequency of the disasters. Some of the disasters, like floods in the Punjab region, are so frequent that the local population have become very blasé about these events and find it hard to differentiate these events from 'normal'. Thus, researchers in this field have to define what is a disaster before conducting the interviews. This should differ for humanitarian researchers in a sudden-onset disaster situation where the event is hard to miss and is certainly not normal. In this field work, researchers should differentiate those events that are 'normal' and those that are severe and have resulted in a catastrophe. Otherwise they will have to face the situation in which people will talk normally about a disaster and nothing might have changed from their business as usual (BAU) situation. Some other points worth noting are mentioned below:

- Always maintain a confidence in yourself and your research. The supply chains and business models in this research area are very disorientating and so informally connected to each other that it is very difficult to define roles and boundaries. This can be overwhelming at times. In reality, they have similar processes and problems like that of any organized business.
- Have a good knowledge of local area; first, the culture, customs, transport, road conditions and language.
- Safety first: some areas are highly vulnerable to the war on terror and other tribal conflicts, always use an escort from law enforcing authorities and/or be accompanied someone from the local area.
- People are usually very friendly, but they are afraid of or reluctant to talk to strangers because of the trust issues. Approach them through some common friend or some trustworthy government official to win their trust.
- Give yourself plenty of time because you might have to approach a targeted respondent multiple times in order to obtain accurate information.
- Start the analysis process very early in the data collection phase; this will help generating more ideas and lines of enquiry as well as validate the data concurrently.

This chapter has examined the application of the case study method to field research in a humanitarian logistics context. The main focus was to reflect on the use and application of the case method when examining food supply chains in disaster-affected regions of a developing economy. The results of the analysis will be presented at a future date. We hope that the extended discussion on the steps, process and application of the case method to our research will be of use to PhD students and humanitarian logistics researchers.

# References

Agarwal, Renu, and Preethi Subramani. 2013. 'Opportunities and pitfalls associated with coordination structures in supply chain management: An exploratory case study'. *International Journal of Supply Chain Management* 2 (4):17–31.

Alasuutari, Pertti. 2010. 'The rise and relevance of qualitative research'. *International Journal of Social Research Methodology* 13 (2):139–155.

Batt, Peter J., and Sharon Purchase. 2004. 'Managing collaboration within networks and relationships'. *Industrial Marketing Management* 33 (3):169–174.

Bhattacherjee, Anol. 2012. *Social science research: Principles, methods, and practices.* Textbooks Collection. Book 3.http://scholarcommons.usf.edu/oa_textbooks/3.

Bozkurt, Melda, and Serhan Duran. 2012. 'Effects of natural disaster trends: A case study for expanding the pre-positioning network of CARE International'. *International Journal of Environmental Research and Public Health* 9 (8):2863–2874.

Christopher, Martin, and Helen Peck. 2004. 'Building the resilient supply chain'. *International Journal of Logistics Management* 15 (2):1–14.

Coles, John B., Jun Zhuang, and Justin Yates. 2012. 'Case study in disaster relief: A descriptive analysis of agency partnerships in the aftermath of the January 12th, 2010 Haitian earthquake'. *Socio-Economic Planning Sciences* 46 (1):67–77.

Creswell, John W. 2013. *Research design: Qualitative, quantitative, and mixed methods approaches.* Thousand Oaks, California: Sage Publications.

Day, Jamison M., Steven A. Melnyk, Paul D. Larson, Edward W. Davis, and D. Clay Whybark. 2012. 'Humanitarian and disaster relief supply chains: A matter of life and death'. *Journal of Supply Chain Management* 48 (2):21–36.

Din, Ahmad, Saima Parveen, Muhammad Azher Ali, and Abdus Salam. 2011. 'Safety issues in fresh fruits and vegetables-A review'. *Pakistan Journal of Food Sciences* 21 (1–4):1–6.

Division, Statistics. 2011. *Agricultural Statistics of Pakistan.* Edited by Pakistan Bureau of Statistics, Government of Pakistan.

Douglas, Ian. 2009. 'Climate change, flooding and food security in south Asia'. *Food Security* 1 (2):127–136.

Dubois, Anna, and Lars-Erik Gadde. 2002. 'Systematic combining: An abductive approach to case research'. *Journal of Business Research* 55 (7):553–560.

Easton, Geoff. 1995. 'Case research as a methodology for industrial networks: A realist apologia. In *IMP Conference (11th): Interaction, Relationships and Networks: Past - Present - Future*, edited by Turnbull, P. W., Yorke, D., and Naudé, P. Manchester: Manchester Federal School of Business and Management. IMP; 7–9 Sep.

Eckstein, Harry. 2000. 'Case study and theory in political science'. *Case Study Method*: 119–164.

Eisenhardt, Kathleen M. 1989. 'Building theories from case study research'. *Academy of Management Review* 14 (4):532–550.

Ellram, Lisa M. 1996. 'The use of case study method in logistics reserach' *Journal of Business Logistics* 17 (2):93–138.

Glaser, B. Strauss, and Anselm Strauss. 1967. *The discovery of grounded theory*. New york.

Gummesson, Evert. 2007. 'Case study research and network theory: Birds of a feather'. *Qualitative Research in Organizations and Management: An International Journal* 2 (3):226–248. doi: doi:10.1108/17465640710835373.

Halinen, Aino, and Jan-Åke Törnroos. 1998. 'The role of embeddedness in the evolution of business networks'. *Scandinavian Journal of Management* 14 (3):187–205.

Halinen, Aino, and Jan-Åke Törnroos. 2005. 'Using case methods in the study of contemporary business networks'. *Journal of Business Research* 58 (9):1285–1297.

Hesse-Biber, Sharlene Nagy, and Patricia Leavy. 2010. *The practice of qualitative reserach*. Thousand Oaks, California: Sage Publishing.

Ismail, Ali. 2010. Pakistan floods unleash desperate economic crisis. Accessed 9 May 2015.

Järvensivu, Timo, and Jan-Åke Törnroos. 2010. 'Case study research with moderate constructionism: Conceptualization and practical illustration.' *Industrial Marketing Management* 39 (1): 100–108.

Johnsen, Thomas. 2011. 'Innovation through supply relationships, chains and networks.' Université de Grenoble.

Kähkönen, Anni-Kaisa. 2011. 'Conducting a case study in supply management.' *Operations and Supply Chain Management* 4 (1):31–41.

Khan, Shuhab D., Lize Chen, Sajjad Ahmad, Irshad Ahmad, and Fayaz Ali. 2012. 'Lateral structural variation along the Kalabagh Fault Zone, NW Himalayan foreland fold-and-thrust belt, Pakistan'. *Journal of Asian Earth Sciences* 50:79–87.

Kneafsey, Moya, Laura Venn, Ulrich Schmutz, Bálint Balázs, Liz Trenchard, Trish Eyden-Wood, Elizabeth Bos, Gemma Sutton, and Matthew Blackett. 2013. Short Food Supply Chains and Local Food Systems in the EU. A State of Play of their Socio-Economic Characteristics. Institute for Prospective and Technological Studies, Joint Research Centre.

Kovács, Gyöngyi, and Karen M. Spens. 2007. 'Humanitarian logistics in disaster relief operations'. *International Journal of Physical Distribution & Logistics Management* 37 (2):99–114.

Kvale, Steinar, and Svend Brinkmann. 2009. *Interviews: Learning the craft of qualitative research interviewing*. Los Angeles: Sage Publications.

Lee, H. L. 2004. The Triple-A supply chain, *Harvard Business Review*, *82* (10):102–112.

Leonard-Barton, Dorothy. 1990. 'A dual methodology for case studies: Synergistic use of a longitudinal single site with replicated multiple sites'. *Organization Science* 1 (3):248–266.

Lewis-Beck, Michael, Alan E. Bryman, and Tim Futing Liao. (Eds.). 2004. *The Sage encyclopedia of social science research methods*. Thousand Oaks, California: Sage Publishing.

Lincoln, Yvonna S., and Egon G. Guba. 2000. 'The only generalization is: There is no generalization'. *Case Study Method*:27–44.

Marshall, Catherine, and Gretchen B. Rossman. 2014. *Designing qualitative research*. (6th Ed.). Thousand Oaks, California: Sage Publications.

Mehmood, Waqas, Yasir Liaqat, Nauman Iftikhar, and Syed Hassan Raza. 2010. 'Managing supply chain risks in fresh food items: A case study on Makro-Habib Pakistan Limited – A wholesales chain in Pakistan'.

Meredith, Jack. 1998. 'Building operations management theory through case and field research'. *Journal of Operations Management* 16 (4):441–454.

Miles, Matthew B. and A. Michael Huberman, 1994. *Qualitative data analysis: An expanded sourcebook*, (2nd Ed.). Thousand Oakes, California: Sage Publications.

Miles, Matthew B., A. Michael Huberman, and Johnny Saldaña. 2013. *Qualitative data analysis: A methods sourcebook*, (3rd Ed.). Thousand Oaks, California: Sage Publications.

Modell, Sven. 2010. 'Bridging the paradigm divide in management accounting research: The role of mixed methods approaches'. *Management Accounting Research* 21 (2):124–129.

Palinkas, Lawrence A., Sarah M. Horwitz, Carla A. Green, Jennifer P. Wisdom, Naihua Duan, and Kimberly Hoagwood. 2015. 'Purposeful sampling for qualitative data collection and analysis in mixed method implementation research'. *Administration and Policy in Mental Health and Mental Health Services Research* 42 (5):533–544.

Patton, Michael Quinn. 2005. *Qualitative research*. Wiley Online Library, doi: 10.1002/0470013192.bsa514.

Peck, Helen. 2005. 'Drivers of supply chain vulnerability: An integrated framework.' *International Journal of Physical Distribution & Logistics Management* 35 (4):210–232.

Ponomarov, Serhiy, and Mary C. Holcomb. 2009. 'Understanding the concept of supply chain resilience'. *International Journal of Logistics Management* 20 (1):124–143.

Raza, Asmat. 2014. *Pakistan grain and feed annual report 2014*. Report prepared for the USDA Foreign Agricultural Service, Global Agricultural Information Network, Clay Hamilton (Ed.). Retrieved 3 Oct 2016 from: https://gain.fas.usda.gov/Recent%20GAIN%20Publications/Grain%20and%20Feed%20Annual_Islamabad_Pakistan_3-31-2014.pdf.

Robson, Colin. 2002. Real World Research, 2nd Edn. Malden: Blackwell Publishing.

Rubin, Herbert J., and Irene S. Rubin. 2011. *Qualitative interviewing: The art of hearing data*. Sage.

Saldaña, Johnny. 2015. *The coding manual for qualitative researchers*. Sage.

Saunders, Mark N. K., Mark Saunders, Philip Lewis, and Adrian Thornhill. 2011. *Research methods for business students, 5/e*. Pearson Education India.

Scholz, Roland W., and Olaf Tietje. 2002. 'Embedded case study methods'. *Integrating Quantitative and Qualitative*.

Sekaran, Uma. 2006. *Research methods for business: A skill building approach*. John Wiley & Sons.

Silver, Christina, and Ann Lewins. 2014. *Using software in qualitative research: A step-by-step guide*. Sage.

Stake, RE. 1994. Case studies. InN. K. Denzin & YS Lincoln (Eds.), *Handbook of qualitative research* (pp. 236–247). Thousand Oaks, CA: Sage.

Strauss, Anselm, and Juliet Corbin. 1990. *Basics of qualitative research*. Vol. 15. Newbury Park, CA: Sage.

Tariq, Muhammad Atiq Ur Rehman, and Nick van de Giesen. 2012. 'Floods and flood management in Pakistan'. *Physics and Chemistry of the Earth, Parts A/B/C* 47:11–20.

VanWynsberghe, Rob, and Samia Khan. 2008. 'Redefining case study'. *International Journal of Qualitative Methods* 6 (2):80–94.

Vissak, Tiia. 2010. 'Recommendations for using the case study method in international business research'. *The Qualitative Report* 15 (2):370–388.

Voss, Chris, Nikos Tsikriktsis, and Mark Frohlich. 2002. 'Case research in operations management'. *International Journal of Operations & Production Management* 22 (2):195–219.

Weick, Karl E., and Charles A. Kiesler. 1979. *The social psychology of organizing*, Vol. 2. New York: Random House.

Whiting, Lisa S. 2008. 'Semi-structured interviews: Guidance for novice researchers'. *Nursing Standard* 22 (23):35–40.

Whybark, D. Clay. 2007. 'Issues in managing disaster relief inventories'. *International Journal of Production Economics* 108 (1):228–235.

Yin, Robert. 1994. *Case study research: Design and methods*. Beverly Hills, California: Sage Publications.

Yin, Robert. 2003. *Case study research: Design and methods*, (3rd Ed.). Thousand Oaks, California: Sage Publications.

Yin, Robert. 2014. *Case study research: Design and methods* (5th Ed.). Thousand Oaks, California: Sage Publications.

# Part III

Collaboration - Variety of Methods

# 8

# Towards A Better Understanding of Humanitarian Supply Chain Integration

## Jihee Kim, Stephen Pettit, Irina Harris and Anthony Beresford

## Introduction

There has been an increased focus on supply chain integration (SCI) in business theory. SCI is important in defining supply chain management (SCM) and is viewed as being key to success in the commercial sector. SCI is also vital in the humanitarian sector in relation to the development of successful partnerships where collaborative responses can support effective and efficient aid delivery. Some work has been carried out on bridging the gap between regularized, commercial logistics structures and dynamic, non-standard emergency response mechanisms. However, there are very few studies that adapt SCI to fit the humanitarian context, although some research has been carried out regarding cooperation, coordination and collaboration in crisis environments.

This chapter, therefore, explores the SCI activities of major aid actors including non-governmental organizations [NGOs], United Nations [UN] and governmental organizations [GOs] from a humanitarian relief SCM perspective. The research is based on case studies in comparative design, which are useful for comparing multiple cases of situations in qualitative studies. The research, therefore, employs a qualitative approach and data

J. Kim (✉) · S. Pettit · I. Harris · A. Beresford
Cardiff Business School, Cardiff University, Cardiff, UK
e-mail: KimJ14@cardiff.ac.uk; Pettit@cardiff.ac.uk; Harris11@cardiff.ac.uk; Beresford@cardiff.ac.uk

© The Author(s) 2018                                                   **249**
G. Kovács et al. (eds.), *The Palgrave Handbook of Humanitarian Logistics and Supply Chain Management*, https://doi.org/10.1057/978-1-137-59099-2_8

are collected through semi-structured interviews and documentation. Rather than employing a standard triangulation approach, the analysis represents a synthesis of findings from the case-studies based on consensus. This qualitative approach enables researchers to gain an in-depth understanding of the topic as an explorative study and addresses the difficulties in scoping and defining topics, and generalising the findings and results due to limitations of access to key informants and elite interviewees in this field. This research adapts the concept of SCI in its commercial form to the field of humanitarian and disaster relief (HDR) logistics. While SCI has been widely covered in academic research, the concept as applied to humanitarian situations is under-researched and this study adds to the material available in this field.

## Understanding of Contexts and Characteristics

Humanitarian and Disaster Relief Supply Chain Management (HDR-SCM) has its own characters and features, which make it a group within the whole SCM. McLachlin et al. (2009) summarize the differences between business and humanitarian logistics into two dimensions: "motivation (profit vs not-for-profit [NFP]) and environment (uninterrupted vs interrupted)". Its distinct characters of HDR-SCM are related to more challenges to achieve high-level partnerships among humanitarians compared with business counterparts.

Firstly, one of the most different factors between the private and public sectors is in financial stances. Generally, humanitarian aid actors as a type of NFP organization which emphasize social objectives and social impact rather than economic objectives and profit that private companies pursue (Larson 2012). Furthermore, unlike private firms, aid organizations amass their finances primarily through donations. Consequently, they need to care about "donor desires and budget limits" (Larson 2012) and have been competing for "a shrinking base of common donors" (Van Wassenhove 2006). This has been more notable as the number of aid organizations has increased. Donors now expect higher standards of performance and impact (Thomas and Kopczak 2005). These donors often play a role in the humanitarian supply chain (SC) as the key decision makers, which "tend to inhibit high-level collaboration" (Fawcett and Fawcett 2013). Also, many NGOs sometimes have to pay attention to donors' expectations even when their expectations are not compatible with their level of effectiveness in the field (Fawcett and Fawcett 2013).

Secondly, HDR-SCM is generally situated in a more extreme and unpredictable context than its business counterparts. These dynamic environments have "a lack of stability, greater complexity, and special challenges in matching multiple sources of supply with unpredictable demand" (Larson 2012). Its complex and unique challenges lead to difficulties in controlling SCs due to a shortage of resources in terms of information, supply, technology, transportation capacity and money, short lead times and inadequate/untimely delivery. Moreover, HDR SCs do not operate on a regular basis like their for-profit counterparts.

This system is characterized as "the perfect example of temporary supply chains" due to unpredictability of disasters (Maon et al. 2009 in Fawcett and Fawcett 2013). This means that SC systems are formed and maintained for short periods which make them "not only unpredictable, but also turbulent and requiring flexibility" in the humanitarian aid context (Oloruntoba and Gray 2006 cited in Maon et al. 2009). Moreover, in HDR contexts, the SC system is hastily formed where a high level of trust cannot easily exist (Tatham and Kovács 2010 cited in Fawcett and Fawcett 2013). Hence, "how to work together" between aid actors – in other words, partnerships – has been a critical issue in disaster relief studies.

However, the implementation of effective SC partnership among multiple aid actors is not simple in HDR-SCM. Basically, there are a large number of aid actors. For example, it is estimated that there were 3,000–10,000 NGOs operating in Haiti prior to the earthquake event in 2010 (OCHA 2010 cited in Tatham and Pettit 2010). OCHA counted its humanitarian partners operating in Haiti at 512 in 2010 after the event (Human response 2016). Further, there are a variety of organization types of aid actors "from supranational aid agencies (e.g. UN agencies) and governmental organizations (GOs) to big international non-governmental organizations (BINGOs) and one-man non-governmental organizations (NGOs)" (Kovács and Spens 2009).

In addition to this, many authors include military organisations and private businesses as participants responding to disasters (Kaatrud et al. 2003; Van Wassenhove 2006; Kovács and Spens 2007). Moreover, not only do these these actors have different characteristics in terms of organizational structures and the way of operating (Larson 2012), some of them are new and inexperienced organizations in disaster relief management due to a free entry policy for volunteers (Van Wassenhove 2006). Indeed, it is very challenging to achieve effective SC partnerships among a large number and various types of aid organizations. Thus, there should be more effort applied to achieving effective partnerships among aid actors than compared to their business counterparts (Thomas and Kopczak 2005; Larson 2012).

## Scope and Definition

There were many difficulties in developing this project as many terms and concepts have not been clearly defined and demarcated between them in academics. Hence, the researcher had to put more efforts on narrowing down the research scope and defining relevant terms and ideas.

First of all, there are many synonymously used terms related to partnership in SCs because this idea has been researched under many concepts: cooperation, coordination, collaboration and integration. There are apparently differences between them, although they are often used in vague boundaries of definition. However, Spekman et al. (1998) emphasize the partnerships among SC participants as a core element for SCM and clearly describe the transition from cooperation to collaboration in different levels of partnerships as shown in Fig. 8.1.

Cooperation is regarded as a foundational level of interaction and "exchanging bits of essential information and having long-term contracts with suppliers/customers" (Spekman et al. 1998). This basic level can be refined to coordination for smooth SC linkages by "exchanging specific workflow and information" through diverse mechanisms such as just-in-time systems and electronic data interchange (Spekman et al. 1998). However, the authors argue that these activities are not sufficient for being true partners. Moving to the level of collaboration "requires high levels of trust, commitment and information sharing among SC partners" that are involved in "joint planning and process" (Spekman et al. 1998). Further, Fig. 8.1 shows SCI is considered as a prerequisite of the most intense level of partnership.

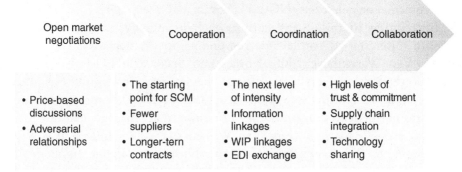

**Fig. 8.1** The key transition from open market negotiation to collaboration (Source: Adapted from Spekman et al. 1998; Mason et al. 2007)

As explained earlier, due to the presence of multiple players, collaboration is considered a very important issue in HDR-SCM (Richey 2009). Furthermore, HDR "effectiveness depends on collaboration, and the degree to which collaboration among humanitarian aid and disaster relief participants emerges is one of the factors that influence the design process" (Fawcett and Fawcett 2013). The topics related to partnerships have been widely researched in the area of HDR-SCM. In particular, Schulz and Blecken (2010) verify the benefits and impediments of horizontal cooperation in disaster relief logistics by focusing on three major tasks: storage, procurement and transportation. This research is meaningful as there is very little research regarding horizontal cooperation in HDR, and also its results show a high level of partnerships such as consolidating purchasing and sharing stocks without logos. Balcik et al. (2010) identify the attributes of SC coordination mechanism through the degree of resource sharing structure: operational, tactical, strategic levels. By using the different degrees, this research better explains coordination. Furthermore, some research uses diverse dimensions of coordination. Jahre and Jensen (2010) and Kaynak and Tuğer (2014) encompass the aforementioned three levels and two typologies of vertical and horizontal relationships when they look into coordination through the cluster system. Moshtari and Gonçalves (2012) try to categorize the types of horizontal coordination among humanitarian organizations according to the intensity and period of coordination. Tapia et al. (2012) narrow down the coordination topics and focus on the coordinative efforts on the information technology in the humanitarian area. Salmon et al. (2011) describe the impediments against coordination between aid agencies and suggest solutions. Further, Maon et al. (2009) try to find a way to improve the SC skills of humanitarians by collaborating with the private sector businesses.

However, there is very little research with respect to SCI in HDR although SCI is considered essential for excellent SCM. In particular, SCI is regarded "critical to the success of a global, responsive and agile humanitarian supply chain" (Oloruntoba and Gray 2006). However, "the nature of humanitarian personnel, their diverse backgrounds and the organizational climate in many humanitarian organizations act against process integration" (Oloruntoba and Gray 2006). Moreover, there is a shortage of appropriate human resources. Oloruntoba and Gray (2003) find that only 45 per cent of all respondent organizations have relevant staff "with a formal qualification in logistics, transport or related areas" by surveying 45 international aid organizations. Additionally, in academia, there is not much research regarding SCI. Only Afshar and Haghani (2012) propose "a comprehensive model that integrate logistics operations in response to natural disasters" which can help with "tracking of operating details of large scale disaster response operations and find the optimal allocation of scarce resources to the most critical tasks". Hence, the research concentrates on SCI in the perspectives of HDR-SCM.

The study of SCI originated from a systems perspective which takes the view that the optimization of the whole system achieves better performance than a string of optimized sub-systems (Parnaby 1979; Christopher 2011, p. 229). Christopher (2011, p. 3) asserts that "the focus of supply chain management is on co-operation and trust and the recognition that, properly managed, the 'whole can be greater than the sum of its parts'". This shows that the concepts of SCM already contain those of SCI (Pagell 2004). After this concept was adopted into the business area in the early 1980s, it has been developed and enriched and its effectiveness was proved. The idea of SCI has been regarded as a key factor of business success and "supply chain management excellence" (Childerhouse and Towill 2011). This means that "a truly integrated supply chain" functions not only to "just reduce costs" but also to "create value for the company, its SC partners and its share-holders" (Lee 2000 cited in Palomero and Chalmeta 2014). On the other hand, Zhao et al. (2015) look into the effect of SCI from a different point of view. They assert that when the degree of external integration with customer and supplier is too high, the positive effect on financial performance diminishes from some point in an inverted U-shaped relationship rather than in a linear way (Zhao et al. 2015). As described in Table 8.1, the adverse effects that SCI may bring can "offset the benefits" in the case of external SCI (Zhao et al. 2015).

Although there are several definitions suggested for SCI, the meaning of this term has not been unified by academics (Palomero and Chalmeta 2014).

Table 8.1 Major benefits and adverse effect of supply chain integration

| Benefits | Challenges |
| --- | --- |
| Promoting information exchange | Requiring considerable time (e.g. numerous meetings for a consensus decision making) |
| Facilitating mutual understanding | Leading to conflicts over goals and resources between different organizations/functions |
| Enhancing new product development performance | Conflicts may lead to poor decision making |
| Improving different types of operational performance | Opportunistic behaviours and knowledge spillover may exist |
| Increasing financial performance | Organizations lack flexibility to respond to market pressures |

Source: Adapted from Zhao et al. (2015)

Moreover, several synonyms such as cooperation, coordination and colla-boration create more confusion. In particular, SCI is often confused with collaboration and in practice intimately related to each other. Some authors cite SCI as a key component of collaboration, as shown in Fig. 8.1. Hence, there is a need to understand both collaboration and SCI. Collaboration is defined as "a fundamental agreement among SC partners to integrate their resources for mutual gains" (Näslund and Hulthen 2012). In the case of SCI, many authors "define integration as having two key components: interaction and collaboration" (Pagell 2004). When explaining SCI, the concept of collaboration is needed as Flynn et al. (2010) state:

> The degree to which a manufacturer strategically collaborates with its supply chain partners and collaboratively manages intra- and inter-organizational process in order to achieve effective and efficient flow of products, services, information, funds and decisions in order to provide maximum value to the customer at low cost and high speed.

Indeed, these two terms are intimately related and function as integral parts of each other (Mason et al. 2007; Spekman et al. 1998).

On the other hand, this research needs to consider the unique circum-stances of HDR. The above is optimized for the manufacturing and produc-tion. Also, it seems that the view taken of the relationships between manufacturers and their partners is not balanced; it inclines towards the perspectives of the manufacturing industry. Hence, this definition is not suited to other areas such as service or public sectors, and in particular, for the humanitarian contexts. There is a need to cover the unique contexts of HDR such as uncertainty and the presence of multiple actors, all of which require flexibility. Thus, as Palomero and Chalmeta (2014) suggest, this research defines SCI as below:

> SCI is a continuous process of improvement of the interactions and collabora-tions among supply chain network members to improve their ability to work together to reach mutually acceptable outcomes for their organization.

This allows the research to regard the aid actors as network members and emphasize mutual understanding and interactive relationships. Also, this definition does not limit the relationships only to internal suppliers or customers. Thus, it can include much broader concepts of relationships such as SCI with competitors or assistors.

Secondly, it was also an important issue to decide the areas where to apply this topic between logistics and SCM. Research regarding the humanitarian topic in SCs has been traditionally conducted "under the umbrella of 'humanitarian logistics'" rather than humanitarian SCM, by a margin of 3 to 1 in the number of refereed journal articles. However, the boundaries between SCM and logistics have not been clearly "demarcated" in the studies of HDR (Day et al. 2012). For instance, Thomas and Mizushima from the Fritz Institute (2005, cited in Van Wassenhove 2006) define humanitarian logistics "as the process of planning implementing and controlling the efficient, cost-effective flow of and storage of goods and materials as well as related information, from point of origin to point of consumption for the purpose of meeting the end beneficiary's requirements". This definition can be regarded as being closer to that of SCM rather than logistics (Tatham and Spens 2011). Therefore, there is a need to clearly distinguish logistics and SCM in research related to the HDR and clarify the definition of the main term used for this research because "there is a difference between logistics and SCM, insofar as these terms pertain to humanitarian and disaster relief" (Day et al. 2012).

HDR-SCM is a relatively new academic research area amongst academics (Kovács and Spens 2007) and a consensus has not been reached on its specific definition and parameters (Tomasini 2012). Nonetheless, it is clear that HDR-SCM is a broader concept generally "spanning from long term to short term", while HDR logistics deals with "short term" (Day et al. 2012). In other words, logistics is concerned more with operational and tactical issues, whereas HDR-SCM "deals with issues involving supply chain preplanning, inter-supply chain integration and supply chain terminations" (Day et al. 2012). The Council of Supply Chain Management Professionals (CSCMP 2010 cited in Sweeney 2011) also regard logistics as a part of SCM. Humanitarians generally have a complex working environment and multiple stakeholders "including large numbers of uncoordinated and disparate donors, the media, governments, the military not to mention the final beneficiaries" (Van Wassenhove 2006). In order to cover the entirety of this wide-ranging context, it seems that a broader concept needs to be adopted. This needs to view SCs along with the organic connections they share with other functions. Hence, as Day et al. (2012) proposed, this research adopts the "Unionist" perspective among the four-group taxonomy of relationships between SCM and logistics suggested by Larson and Halldorsson (2004).

As shown in Fig. 8.2, the "Unionist" perspective treats SCM as a more comprehensive term that "supply chain management completely subsumes logistics" (Larson and Halldorsson 2004) and other fields such as "marketing, operations management, purchasing, etc." (Larson and Halldórsson 2002).

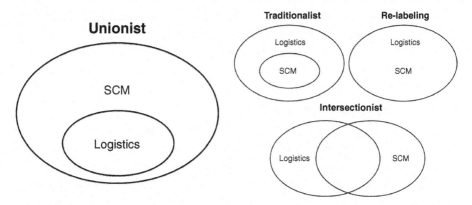

**Fig. 8.2** Perspectives on logistics versus SCM
(Source: adapted from Larson and Halldorsson 2004)

**Fig. 8.3** Relationships between HDR logistics and HDR-SCM
(Source: adapted from Day et al. 2012)

Therefore, in this research, HDR issues are dealt with under SCM as described in Fig. 8.3.

Considering this, it seems clear that disaster relief SCM contains "strong elements of supply chain management". That is to say, the concepts are relatively similar. Day et al. (2012) define HDR-SCM as follows:

The system that is responsible for designing, deploying and managing the processes necessary for dealing with not only current but also future humanitarian/disaster events and for managing the coordination and interaction of its processes with those of supply chains that may be competitive/complementary. It is also responsible for identifying, implementing and monitoring the achievement of the desired outcomes that its processes are intended to achieve. Finally, it is responsible for evaluating, integrating and coordinating the activities of the various parties that emerge to deal with these events.

This definition attempts to span the whole cyclical period of disaster relief management, from designing SC processes before the event to evaluating activities to learn lessons for future events.

## Conceptual Framework

An important underpinning of the research is a conceptual framework which is useful in order to help explain the main factors or constructs within the model; this in turn allows the researcher to investigate "the same phenomenon" in a cross-case analysis (Miles et al. 2014, p. 20). The conceptual framework is shown in Fig. 8.4.

Firstly, in order to ascertain the degree of SCI three levels of SCI are adopted: strategic, tactical and operational. This concept originate from "the needs of the business" because solutions for conflicts result from "functional attitudes and goals" and are usually concentrated at the

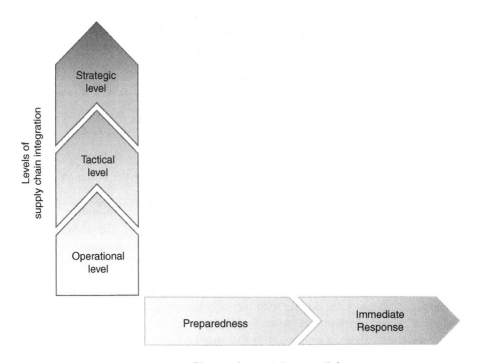

Phases of natural disaster relief management

**Fig. 8.4** Levels of supply chain integration in different phases
(Source: Authors)

operational level and are not very effective (Stevens 1989). Hence, when dealing with the issues of SCI, it is more convincing to look at all three levels. Similarly, Whipple and Russell (2007) develop a typology of collaborative relationship in three levels: "collaborative transaction management; collaborative event management; and collaborative process management". Larson (2012) adopts this concept of relationship into humanitarian logistics and specifies the activities for humanitarian contexts. At the strategic level, there is a tendency to form an integrated SC system in order to diminish the barriers between functions or units. On the tactical level, decisions or determinations are made for important issues to operate and set more detailed objectives derived from strategic goals. At the operational level, practical operations and detailed procedures are focused.

Secondly, different management skills and activities are consequently required depending on the different phases of disaster management. However, there are a variety of approaches to identifying the different phases in responding to natural disasters. Initially, these concepts stem from the National Governors Association's (1979 cited in Maon et al. 2009) suggestion regarding "a four-stage standard process model of disaster relief that includes: preparedness; response; recovery; and mitigation". Kelly (1998 cited in Maon et al. 2009) develops "the simplest disaster relief model" through "a linear sequence of prevent, disaster, and post-event". On the other hand, Safran (2003 cited in Maon et al. 2009) conceptualizes a more cyclical disaster management model viewing each phase as being intimately linked. As shown in Table 8.2, many authors divide the disaster management phases into three major timeframes: before the event, disaster and post-event, although there are a variety of approaches to identifying the different phases in responding to natural disasters. This study also adopts three clear phases of disaster management: preparedness; immediate response; and aftermath (Lee and Zbinden 2003; Kovács and Spens 2007; Perry 2007). In particular, the research focuses on the phases of preparedness and immediate response. They are relatively more important than the aftermath phase in responding to disasters effectively and also better preparedness is essential for "a better and faster response" (Van Wassenhove 2006). Thus, the conceptual framework comprises two main categories on its axes: the levels of SCI and the phases of natural disaster relief management.

Thirdly, different stances of aid actors were assumed through existing literature. For instance, Kovács and Spens (2009) depict the different perspectives of stakeholders, namely humanitarian organizations and GOs towards challenges they meet in HDR SCs. Therefore, it provides a base to assume that there might be different ideas and activities in HDR-SCI among aid actors.

**Table 8.2** Disaster relief management phases

| No | Author | Disaster relief management phases |
|---|---|---|
| 1 | Long (1997) | 1. Strategic planning to prepare for emergency project<br>2. Actual project planning when disaster strikes |
| 2 | Cottrill (2002) | 1. Planning<br>2. Mitigation<br>3. Detection<br>4. Response<br>5. Recovery phase |
| 3 | Safran (2003) | 1. Development or prevention phase<br>2. Disaster<br>3. Emergency response or transition phase<br>4. Recovery phase |
| 4 | Lee and Zbinden (2003) | 1. Preparedness<br>2. During operations<br>3. Post-operations |
| 5 | Kovács and Spens (2007) | 1. Preparation (the time before a disaster strikes)<br>2. Immediate response phase (instantly after a disaster)<br>3. Reconstruction phase (the aftermath of a natural disaster) |
| 6 | Perry (2007) | 1. Preparedness: awareness, preparatory activity and action to mitigate the full impact of a possible disaster<br>2. Response: the saving of lives and emergency relief activity<br>3. Aftermath: recovery, development and resilience activity |
| 7 | Kumar and Havey (2013) | 1. Pre-disaster (mitigation and preparedness)<br>2. Disaster (response)<br>3. Post-disaster (recovery/rebuild) |

However, in disaster events the humanitarian aid SC network includes a number of logisticians from various organizations and organizational types (Tatham and Kovács 2010). As shown in Table 8.3, many authors typically discuss five major groups of aid providers: the Non-Government Organizations (NGOs); the United Nations (UN) agencies; the Government Organizations (GOs); the military and private business (i.e. suppliers and logistics service providers. Among these five major groups of actors, three key categories were chosen for this study; NGOs, the UN agencies and GOs, while the military and private businesses were excluded. This is because, in general, the military do not consider humanitarian aid as one of their major tasks, rather they recognize it as the task of relief agencies (Byman et al. 2000 cited in Pettit and Beresford 2005). In the case of private businesses, they are more focused on economic objectives (e.g. earning profit to increase shareholder wealth (McLachlin et al. 2009), and providing support to NGOs and governments (Vega and Roussat 2015). Hence, it cannot be said that the private sector is a direct aid provider for

Table 8.3 Categories of involved actors

| Authors (Year) | Involved aid actors | NGOs | UN | GOs | Military | Private business |
|---|---|---|---|---|---|---|
| Seaman (1999) | UN, non-governmental organizations or private voluntary organizations (NGOs), governmental donors | √ | √ | √ | | |
| Kaatrud et al. (2003) | UN, the military, host governments, neighbouring country governments, other humanitarian organizations, donors and logistics service providers | √ | √ | √ | √ | √ |
| Pettit and Beresford (2005) | A number of governments, a wide range of NGOs, UN bodies, International Committee of Red Cross, military players | √ | √ | √ | √ | |
| Van Wassenhove (2006) | Humanitarian organizations, the military, governments, private business | √ | √ | √ | √ | √ |
| Kovács and Spens (2007) | Aid agencies, NGOs, governments, military, logistics providers, donors | √ | √ | √ | √ | √ |
| Larson (2012) | NGOs, UN, military, commercial service provider | √ | √ | | √ | √ |

the beneficiary, working at the same level with other aid actors. Rather, they can be regarded as a service provider for the other aid actors for the profits. In this research, this framework was applied to each aid actor, respectively.

Lastly, these entities can be regarded as the horizontal lines of SCI. SCI has been studied from various angles in terms of dimensions, directions and degrees of SCI. Academic literature has looked into SCI with "two key integration dimensions: internal and external" (Bernon et al. 2013). Internal integration is pertinent to "integration across various parts of a single organizations", while external integration "examines integration between organizations" (Pagell 2004). For external integration, there are many players involved such as suppliers, manufacturers, distributors, customers, competitors and other non-competitor organizations (Guan and Rehme 2012; Barratt 2004). Integration with customers, internally, and with suppliers, externally, can be regarded as horizontal, whilst integration with competitors, internally, and with non-competitors can be viewed as being vertical (Barratt 2004). In the research, the SCI activities of major aid actors in the horizontal line were focused on.

## Research Approach

Research in the humanitarian field has been conducted taking both quantitative and qualitative approaches. An example of quantitative research is the recent work of Van der Laan et al. (2016) who demonstrate that several factors influence forecast and planning performance, and suggest opportunities to improve for humanitarian logistics operations. The focus of their research is order forecasting as a tool for planning. Further, Acimovic and Goentzel (2016) address stock deployment issues through the use of stochastic optimization models applied to humanitarian logistics performance metrics. Roh et al. (2015) used a fuzzy analytic hierarchy approach to determine the best location for inventory prepositioning and optimum warehouse location in the context of emergency preparedness.

Here, however, a softer approach is used which takes account of measures such as experience, knowledge and tradition in an effort to gain the fullest understanding of the behavioural as well as the mechanical response mechanisms that can be observed following a disaster event. In order to gain in-depth understanding of different aid actors' stances, this study adopts a qualitative approach. The qualitative tradition started from "a recognition of the need for alternative ways to produce knowledge" in the positivism-dominant academic tradition (O'Leary 2014, p. 130). The qualitative approach generally follows the inductive logic; appreciates subjectivities, multiple perspectives and realities; and "recognizes the power of research over both participants and researchers" (O'Leary 2014). Hence, qualitative research can produce "the value of depth" which is useful in "delving into social complexity" and helps with understanding "the interactions, processes, lived experiences, and belief systems that are a part of individuals, institutions, cultural groups and even the everyday" (O'Leary 2014). This approach also allows researchers to "explore diversity rather than to quantify" and "perceptions and experiences rather than their measurement" (Kumar 2014, p. 14). Therefore, this approach is appropriate to explain the diversity of interactions between different aid actors and describe the processes of SCI in complex situations.

On the other hand, in terms of research purpose, there are four types of research studies classified by the research objective (Kumar 2014) as shown in

**Table 8.4** Taxonomy of a research study from the objectives perspective

| | |
|---|---|
| Descriptive research | Attempting to describe systematically a situation, problem, phenomenon, attitude, service or programme. |
| Correlational research | Discovering or establishing the existence of a relationship, association or interdependence between two or more aspects of a situation or phenomenon. |
| Explanatory research | Clarifying why and how there is a relationship between two aspects of a situation or phenomenon. |
| Exploratory research | Exploring an area where little is known or of investigating the possibilities of undertaking a particular research study. |

*Source*: Adapted from Kumar (2014, p. 13).

Table 8.4. The current research can be categorized as an explorative study which is useful to clarify unexplored topics and unsure problems (Saunders et al. 2012, p. 171). Because, as mentioned in the previous chapter, SCI has not been studied in the HDR-SCM area; there is a need to fundamentally understand "what is happening" and "the precise nature of the issues". A variety of ways can be used for the explorative study, primarily including "a search of the literature; interviewing experts in the subject; conducting in-depth individual interviews or conducting focus group interviews" (Saunders et al. 2012). These interviews tend to be flexible or unstructured and play a key role in leading to research progress due to the nature of explorative research (Saunders et al. 2012). Hence, in this project it is crucial to gain in-depth information and contributions from the participants.

# Research Design

The comparative design enables comparison of "two or more meaningfully contrasting cases or situations" for better understanding of social phenomena (Bryman and Bell 2011, p. 63). In this design, contrasting findings of two or more cases can be analysed and compared (Bryman and Bell 2011, p. 67). This design can be applied in both quantitative and qualitative research. "In quantitative research it is frequently an extension of a cross-sectional design", while adopted in qualitative research it is more likely to be an extended case study design (Bryman and Bell 2011). Hence, in the current study the comparative design is regarded as "an extension of a case study design" by comparing three different cases.

The extended case study research design adopted in this study also contains the underlying characteristics of the standard case study research design. Basically, the elemental case study involves "the detailed and intensive analysis of a single case" (Bryman 2012, p. 66) and is a useful method to describe rich and complex interrelationships between social actors (May 2011, p. 221). It is apparent that the case study plays an important role of "revealing the complexities in the context of phenomena and accounting for alternative interpretations", although there are critiques related to "bias, subjectivity, reliability and validity" and arguments between "generalization and particularization" (May 2011, pp. 220, 226). In addition, for qualitative case study there are specific types of research in which the case study research design suits. For instance, this research design is more appropriate to answer "why" or "how" questions and tend to be "most often used in explanatory and exploratory research" (Saunders, Lewis, and Thornhill 2012, p. 179). Thus, it is important to preliminarily know research qualifications pertinent to the case study. Drawing on Yin (2003), Baxter and Jack (2008) summarize the key conditions that the case study design is useful as follows:

(a) the focus of the study is to answer "how" and "why" questions;

(b) you cannot manipulate the behaviour of those involved in the study;

(c) you want to cover contextual conditions because you believe they are relevant to the phenomenon under study;

or (d) the boundaries are not clear between the phenomenon and context.

For these reasons, it can be clearly argued that, based on the purpose of this study and the context of the topic, the current study is highly applicable to the qualifications of the case study research design. This design has the ability to answer the "how" question of the current study and fits the exploratory nature of the research providing rich insights and considerable detail in each case.

## Unit of Analysis

Delineating and binding the case is a critical issue in the case study design. When determining the case, Baxter and Jack (2008) advise to think of the subject to be analysed, that is namely "the unit of analysis". Commonly the types of cases refer to "individuals, organizations, processes, programs, neighborhoods, institutions and even event" (Yin 2014, p. 15). Multiple aid actors are the subjects to be analysed in this project. In order to avoid questions that are too broad and to remain reasonable in scope, Baxter and Jack (2008) propose three ways of binding cases: "(a) by time and place (Cresswell 2003); (b) time and activity (Stake 1995); and (c) by definition and context (Miles and Huberman 1994)". In the current study, the cases are bounded by the last factor – "definition and context", and are analysed in the comparison design. As illustrated in the literature review earlier,

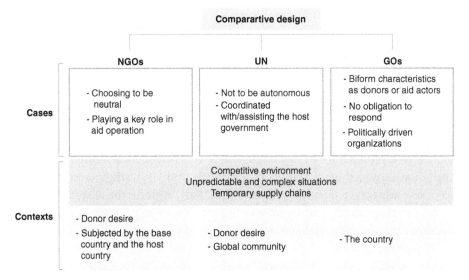

**Fig. 8.5**  Framework of comparative design
(Source: Authors, adapted from the interviews)

they were categorized by the types of organizations: the NGOs; the UN agencies; and the GOs. Although there are different aspects and diversity in each type of organizations, by and large each type of organizations is located in the specific context respectively. Fig. 8.5 shows that there are three contrasting cases to be analysed through comparison in the identical context of sudden onset natural disasters. At the same, each case is surrounded by its own context. These contexts are significant so as to capture the relevant phenomena, and cannot be separated from the cases when explaining them. From this point of view, the case study research design is useful to understand both the cases and the contextual conditions related to the cases (Yin 2014, p. 16).

## Data Collection Methods

Research in the field of humanitarian aid logistics and emergency response inevitably relies on datasets which are often fragmented, non-systematic and non-uniform. The data therefore lends itself to the case-study approach, which accepts a certain amount of non-comparability but which is often very rich in terms of opinions expressed, the nature of extreme events examined and contrasts with normal conditions. The combination of circumstances surrounding emergency or crisis events is often unique and therefore it is unlikely to be precisely repeated. Thus the value of rigorous analytical approaches, such as numerical modelling, in these cases is rather limited.

Yin (2014, p. 105) details six sources of evidence which are "the most commonly used in doing case study research": documentation, archival records, interviews, direct observations, participant-observation, and physical artefacts. The multiple sources of evidence tend to be complementarily used in case study research because each source of evidence has both advantages and disadvantages as a source of evidence and "no single source has a complete advantage over the others" (Yin 2014). Among the aforementioned forms of evidence, this study adopts the interviews as primary evidence and documentation as supplementary data.

In general, the interview is "one of the most important sources of case study evidence" and "commonly found in case study research" (Yin 2014, p. 110). The interviews and interviewing are widely understood as "the methods of maintaining and generating conversation with people on a specific topic and range of topics and the interpretations which social researchers make of the resultant data" (May 2011, p. 131). Interviews are useful to generate "rich insights into people's biographies, experiences, opinions, values, aspirations, attitudes and feelings" (May 2011). Thus, this method can provide the researcher with a "short-cut to the prior history" of relevant issues (Yin 2014, p. 113). Nonetheless, as described in Table 8.5, there are the common problems of "bias, poor recall, and poor or inaccurate articulate" in the interviewees' responses (Yin 2014). Therefore, it is a reasonable approach to "corroborate interview data with information from other sources" (Yin 2014).

Documents used for case study research take a variety of forms: personal documents including e-mails, letters and memoranda; written reports of events, agendas, announcements and meetings; internal records/administrative documents/progress reports; formal studies or evaluations; new clippings and articles in the mass media (Yin 2014, p. 105). As Table 8.5 depicts, documentary information is useful to gain "specific details to corroborate information from other sources" by verifying correct terms and titles, while it is not always accurate and sometimes does not exactly reflect on events (Yin 2014, p. 107).

May (2011, p. 132) suggests using four types of interviews: the structured interview, the semi-structured interview, the unstructured or focused interview, and the group interview or focus group. Table 8.6 depicts the key characteristics of each type of interview. In particular, this study adopts the

**Table 8.5** Two sources of evidence chosen for the research: Strengths and weaknesses

| Source of evidence | Strengths | Weakness |
|---|---|---|
| Interviews | - Targeted: focuses directly on case study topics<br>- Insightful: provides explanations as well as personal views (e.g., perceptions, attitudes and meanings) | - Bias due to poorly articulated questions<br>- Response bias<br>- Inaccuracies due to poor recall<br>- Reflexivity: Interviewee gives what interviewer wants to hear |
| Documentation | - Stable: can be reviewed repeatedly<br>- Unobtrusive: not created as a result of the case study<br>- Specific: can contain the exact names, references, and details of an event<br>- Broad: can cover a long span of time, many events, and many settings | - Retrievability: can be difficult to find<br>- Biased selectively, if collection is incomplete<br>- Reporting bias: reflects (unknown) bias of any given document's author<br>- Access: may be deliberately withheld |

*Source*: Adapted from Yin (2014, p. 106)

**Table 8.6** Four types of interviews

| Types of interview | Characteristics |
|---|---|
| **Structured interview** | - Associated with survey research, by using a questionnaire as the data collection instrument<br>- Emphasizing the neutrality of the interviewer |
| **Semi-structured interview** | - Normally preparing for specified questions and providing a greater structure for comparability over that of the focused or unstructured interview<br>- Enabling the interviewer to have more latitude to probe beyond answers and to have conversations with the interviewee |
| **Unstructured or focused interview** | - Open-ended character<br>- Enabling the interviewee to respond freely |
| **Group interview and focus group** | - Facilitating exploration of group norms and dynamics around issues and topics<br>- Providing a valuable insights into both social relations and the examinations of processes |

*Source*: Adapted from May (2011, pp. 134–139) and Bryman and Bell (2011, p. 467)

semi-structured interview as it contains advantages of both structured and unstructured interviews. This method allows the researcher to have more control over the interview than unstructured interview and to focus "more

**Table 8.7** Elite interviewing

| | |
|---|---|
| Interviewees | Elites are considered to be the influential, the prominent and the well-informed people in an organization or community |
| Advantages | - Gaining valuable information |
| | (e.g. the legal and financial structure of their organization; their organization's policies, past histories and future plans) |
| | - Providing an overall view |
| Disadvantages | - Difficulties in accessing elites |
| | - Difficulty of controlling the process of interviewing elites |

*Source*: Adapted from Marshall and Rossman (1989, p. 94)

narrowly on the planned items" to answer the research question (Rubin and Rubin 2012, p. 31). In addition to this, the interview process is likely to be flexible and the interviewer can create conversational and informal atmosphere (Bryman 2012, pp. 471–472). Hence, the semi-structured interview allows more leeway to the interviewer and interviewee and in-depth conversation through interactions between them.

The interviews used in this study tend to have characteristics as elite interviews. The interviewees selected for semi-structured interviewing are "a particular type of respondent", namely elites who have rich experience and expertise in areas relevant to HDR-SCM. Table 8.7 highlights that the biggest advantages of this method are that the elite interviewees can be great informants, providing in-depth information about organization's inside (Marshall and Rossman 1989, p. 94). Additionally, they can explain the relationships to other organizations with a big picture (Marshall and Rossman 1989, p. 94), and also know how to tactfully manage the interview process because they are usually experienced interviewees (Yin 2003, p. 57).

Hence, this "specialized treatment of interviewing" (Marshall and Rossman 1989, p. 94) is very useful for this study because these elite informants can provide in-depth knowledge and a great deal of useful information and also an accurate view with respect to complex relationships between the cases. However, there is a difficulty in controlling the interview process because elite interviewees tend to dislike the restrictions with "narrow or stereotypical questions" and prefer "provocative or open-ended questions that allow them the freedom to use their knowledge and imagination" (Marshall and Rossman 1989, p. 95). The interviewer must work hard and "establish competence" by having thorough understanding of the topic and displaying "shrewd questioning" (Marshall and Rossman 1989, p. 95).

# Data Introduction

Interviews were conducted with experts from the HDR- SCM sector. All four were carefully selected based on their width and depth of experience in the humanitarian logistics and SCM sector. This led to a high level of confidence in the validity of the opinions expressed, the judgements reached and the information given. Two interviewees were questioned by means of four face-to-face conversations and the others were by voice calls through a telecommunication application software. Initially, snowball sampling was planned to make up an appropriate sample size in the small area of humanitarian related organizations. This method is useful because it is "used most frequently to conduct qualitative research primarily through interviews" and available in a field where few respondents exist (Atkinson and Flint 2001). Nonetheless, the snowball sampling method could not proceed due to a lack of time in a month project and difficult accessibility to elite interviewees. As Marshall and Rossman (1989, p. 94) mention, elite interviewees are usually working "under demanding time constraints" and "often difficult to reach" without "sponsorship, recommendations, and introductions for assistance in making appointments". Likewise, there was a great problem of accessibility to interviewees in this project because they were very busy and physically hard to reach. Furthermore, we could not proceed with the snowballing method which would gradually increase the number of interviewees by using interviewees' recommendations or connections because some of the potential interviewees were not available due to their involvement in a recent natural disaster in Nepal.

Although this study includes a small number of interviewees, each interview provides a great deal of information because an in-depth interviewing is one of the most useful ways to gain "large amounts of data" in a short time (Marshall and Rossman 1989, p. 82). In addition, each interviewee has many years of experience in an organization working in HDR. The purpose of this study is to amass an in-depth understanding in SCI in particular that formed in the HDR contexts, rather to generalize "the rule of relationships". Hence, it is clear that the set of these interviewees in this project can fully offer rich information for the initial exploratory study.

# Data Analysis Methods

For the qualitative data analysis, there are a number of suggestions and tactics proposed. Among them, this study in the main follows the guideline of qualitative data analysis that Miles et al. (2014) propose because it logically illustrates the way of proceeding with each analysis method and application of each detailed technique.

In the current study, several analysis methods are used for deeper analysis because there is no need to stick with a single approach by using one analysis coding method. Drawing on Saldaña (2013), Miles et al. 2014. (2014, pp. 73–74) suggest two major stages of coding: "First Cycle and Second Cycle coding". In each stage, multiple coding methods can be used in a "mixed and matched" basis if they are needed. At the first cycle coding stage, codes are extracted from "the data chunks". For this, In Vivo coding and subcoding are adopted in the early stage. The In Vivo coding method is predominantly used in qualitative data analysis and usually borrows the actual words and short phrases from the interviewees' own languages for codes (Miles et al. 2014, p. 74). The advantages of using this method are that it can be applicable for all qualitative studies and reflect the interviewees' voice (Miles et al. 2014 p. 74). On the other hand, the subcoding analysis enriches the primary codes and explains them in detail (Miles et al. 2014, p. 80).

In the second stage, the in-depth analysis is conducted through the pattern codes that include: (a) categories/themes, (b) causes/explanations, (c) relationships among people and (d) theoretical constructs (Miles et al. 2014, p. 87). This method helps the researcher to draw clearly condensed results from a large amount of data and is also very useful for cross-case analysis (Miles et al. 2014,p. 86). Moreover, this is very useful in the visualization of the interconnections of components, to map the categories, or to develop the conceptual framework (Miles et al. 2014, p. 88). For this, creating codes are used in order to conduct the second cycle pattern coding analysis. This method is called "deductive coding" and starts coding based on "a provisional start list of codes prior to fieldwork" (Miles et al. 2014, p. 81). The "start list" in this research comes from the conceptual framework that was developed through the literature review.

## Discussion and Conclusions

The aim of this research was to examine horizontal SCI between different types of aid organizations (UN, NGO and GO) in the context of rapid onset natural disasters in the different phases of the disaster management. For this, the conceptual framework was applied to all the three cases and allowed the visualization of the SCI activities in the two phases. The research identified that there are more differences between SCI activities among the three cases during the preparedness phase than during the immediate response phase.

The research demonstrates that the UN leads integration activities based on the cluster system and other coordinating groups throughout all levels of SCI. In contrast, GOs tend to have very limited SCI activities and only at the tactical level by having regular meetings and sharing information for better resource allocation in the operation level. Tactical meetings and use of regular internal reviews were also observed by Roh et al. (2015) in the context of strategic pre-emergency stock placement. During the immediate post-emergency response phase, there is a trend to focus on the operational level of SCI activities among three major actors in order to respond to rapidly changing circumstances. Further, this research found that GOs have different styles of SCI activities, because unlike NGOs and UN, GOs preferred to integrate SCs with the selected partners in both phases.

The contribution of this research is to adapt the concept of SCI to the field of HDR. While SCI in standard commercial environments has been widely covered by academic research, use of the concept in humanitarian situations is under-researched. The literature thus far has focused on coordination and collaboration, but the integration of SCs requires greater scholarly focus. This study is an effort to add to the material in this important field.

Moreover, few studies, even those focused on the commercial realm, have measured the level of SCI. As Näslund and Hulthen (2012) point out, while many researchers highlight "different aspects that need to be integrated", clear guidelines are not suggested "regarding what should be integrated in the different stages of the integrative process". This means that there is a shortage of in-depth studies looking into SCI in terms of different levels or degrees of SCI. Regardless of sectors this research was a meaningful effort at measuring the level of SCI and expend the aspects of SCI.

Methodologically, this project is not in the mainstream. Quantitative methods have been predominantly used in the humanitarian studies arena. There are relatively few case studies and qualitative studies, and the qualitative studies comprise of around 15% of the research in this area (Leiras et al. 2014). This project used the extended case study research design with a qualitative approach, which is useful to gain an in-depth understandings about the topic as an explorative study. "The qualitative case study is an approach to research that facilitates exploration of a phenomenon within its context using a variety of data source" (Baxter and Jack 2008). Hence, considering a balance of quantitative and qualitative studies for further knowledge (Goffin et al. 2012), this project played a role in expanding the methodological scope of this area.

However, there are still inevitable limitations in the area of improving reliability and validity. First of all, due to time constraints and a shortage of informants in this field, this project was conducted with a small sample size of interviewees. Additionally, this study suffers from the natural weaknesses of using a single case study because it cannot confirm repeated results from a multiple case studies. Hence, this research has limitations in terms of generalising the findings of this project. Rather, this project prioritizes exploration of a new topic in the humanitarian sector and exists as a platform for an increased focus on this area of academic research.

**Acknowledgements** The authors would like to acknowledge the financial assistance provided by the Economic and Social Research Council (ESRC). Also, they would like to inform that this research is a part of the dissertation submitted to Cardiff Business School in 2015.

# References

Acimovic, J and Goentzel J. (2016). Models and metrics to assess humanitarian response capacity. *Journal of Operations Management*, 45, 11–29.

Afshar, A. and Haghani, A. (2012). Modeling integrated supply chain logistics in real-time large-scale disaster relief operations. *Socio-Economic Planning Sciences*, 46(4), 327–338.

Atkinson, R. and Flint, J. (2001). Accessing hidden and hard-to-reach populations: Snowball research strategies. *Social Research Update*, 33(1), 1–4.

Balcik, B., Beamon, B. M., Krejci, C. C., Muramatsu, K. M., and Ramirez, M. (2010). Coordination in humanitarian relief chains: Practices, challenges and opportunities. *International Journal of Production Economics*, 126(1), 22–34.

Barratt, M. (2004). Understanding the meaning of collaboration in the supply chain. *Supply Chain Management: An International Journal*, 9(1), 30–42.

Baxter, P. and Jack, S. (2008). Qualitative case study methodology: Study design and implementation for novice researchers. *The Qualitative Report*, 13(4), 544–559.

Bernon, M., Upperton, J., Bastl, M., and Cullen, J. (2013). An exploration of supply chain integration in the retail product returns process. *International Journal of Physical Distribution and Logistics Management*, 43(7), 586–608.

Bryman, A. (2012). *Social research methods* (4th edn.). Oxford: Oxford University Press

Bryman, A. and Bell, E. (2011). *Business research methods* (3rd edn.). Oxford: Oxford University Press.

Byman, D., Lesser, I., Pirnie, B., Bernard, C. and Wazman, M. (2000). *Strengthening the Partnership: Improving Military Coordination Relief Agencies and Allies in Humanitarian Operations*. DTIC Document. Washington, DC: Rand.

Childerhouse, P. and Towill, D. R. (2011). Arcs of supply chain integration. *International Journal of Production Research*, 49(24), 7441–7468.

Christopher, M. (2011). *Logistics and supply chain management* (4th edn.). New York: Pearson.

Cottrill, K. (2002). Preparing for the worst. *Traffic World*, 266(40), 15–16.

Creswell, J. (2003). *Research design: Qualitative, quantitative, and mixed methods approaches* (2nd edn.). Thousand Oaks, CA: Sage.

Day, J. M., Melnyk, S. A., Larson, P. D., Davis, E. W., and Whybark, D. C. (2012). Humanitarian and disaster relief supply chains: A matter of life and death. *Journal of Supply Chain Management*, 48(2), 21–36.

Fawcett, A. M. and Fawcett, S. E. (2013). Benchmarking the state of humanitarian aid and disaster relief: A systems design perspective and research agenda. *Benchmarking: An International Journal*, 20(5), 661–692.

Flynn, B. B., Huo, B., and Zhao, X. (2010). The impact of supply chain integration on performance: A contingency and configuration approach. *Journal of Operations Management*, 28(1), 58–71.

Goffin, K., Raja, J., Claes, B., Szwejczewski, M., and Martinez, V. (2012). Rigor in qualitative supply chain management research: Lessons from applying repertory grid technique. *International Journal of Physical Distribution and Logistics Management*, 42(8/9), 804–827.

Guan, W. and Rehme, J. (2012). Vertical integration in supply chains: Driving forces and consequences for a manufacturer's downstream integration. *Supply Chain Management: An International Journal*, 17(2), 187–201.

Humanitarian Response. (2016). *Humanitarian response* plan – January-December *2016*. May 9, 2016, from https://www.humanitarianresponse.info/en/opera tions/haiti/document/haiti-humanitarian-response-plan-2016

Jahre, M., and Jensen, L. M. (2010). Coordination in humanitarian logistics through clusters. *International Journal of Physical Distribution and Logistics Management*, 40(8/9), 657–674.

Kaatrud, D. B., Samii, R., and Van Wassenhove, L. N. (2003). UN Joint Logistics Centre: A coordinated response to common humanitarian logistics concerns. *Forced Migration Review*, 18, 11–14.

Kaynak, R., and Tuğer, A. T. (2014). Coordination and collaboration functions of disaster coordination centers for humanitarian logistics. *Procedia – Social and Behavioral Sciences*, 109, 432–437.

Kovács, G. and Spens, K. (2007). Humanitarian logistics in disaster relief operations. *International Journal of Physical Distribution and Logistics Management*, 37(2), 99–114.

Kovács, G. and Spens, K. (2009). Identifying challenges in humanitarian logistics. *International Journal of Physical Distribution and Logistics Management*, 39(6), 506–528.

Kumar, R. (2014). *Research methodology: A step-by-step guide for beginners* (4th edn). Los Angeles: Sage.

Kumar, S. & Havey, T. (2013). Before and after disaster strikes: A relief supply chain decision support framework. *International Journal of Production Economics*, 145(2), 613–629.

Larson, P. D. (2012). Strategic partners and strange bedfellows: Relationship building in the relief supply chain. In Kovács, G. and Spens, K. (Eds), *Relief supply chain management for disasters: Humanitarian aid and emergency logistics* (pp. 1–15). Hershey: Business Science Reference.

Larson, P. D. and Halldórsson, Á. (2002). What is SCM? And, where is it? *Journal of Supply Chain Management*, 38(3), 36–44.

Larson, P. D. and Halldorsson, Á. (2004). Logistics versus supply chain management: An international survey. *International Journal of Logistics: Research and Applications*, 7(1),17–31.

Lee, H. L. (2000). Creating value through supply chain integration. *Supply Chain Management Review*, 4(4), 30–36.

Lee, H. W. and Zbinden, M. (2003). Marrying logistics and technology for effective relief. *Forced Migration Review*, 18(3), 34–35.

Leiras, A., de Brito Jr, I., Queiroz Peres, E., Rejane Bertazzo, T., and Tsugunobu Yoshida Yoshizaki, H. (2014). Literature review of humanitarian logistics research: Trends and challenges. *Journal of Humanitarian Logistics and Supply Chain Management*, 4(1), 95–130.

Long, D. (1997). Logistics for disaster relief: engineering on the run. *IIE solutions*, 29(6), 26–30.

Maon, F., Lindgree, A., and Vanhamme, J. (2009). Developing supply chains in disaster relief operations through cross-sector socially oriented collaborations: A theoretical model. *Supply Chain Management: An International Journal*, 14(2), 149–164.

Marshall, C. and Rossman, G. B. (1989). *Designing qualitative research*. London: Sage.

Mason, R., Lalwani, C., and Boughton, R. (2007). Combining vertical and horizontal collaboration for transport optimisation. *Supply Chain Management: An International Journal*, 12(3), 187–199.

May, T. (2011). *Social research: Issues, methods and process* (4th edn). Maidenhead: Open University Press.

McLachlin, R., Larson, P. D., and Khan, S. (2009). Not-for-profit supply chains in interrupted environments: The case of a faith-based humanitarian relief organisation. *Management Research News*, 32(11), 1050–1064.

Miles, M. B., & Huberman, A. M. (1994). *Qualitative data analysis: An expanded source book* (2nd edn.). Thousand Oaks, CA: Sage.

Miles, M. B., Huberman, A. M., and Saldaña, J. (2014). *Qualitative data analysis: A methods sourcebook* (3rd edn). Los Angeles: Sage.

Moshtari, M., and Gonçalves, J. (2012). Understanding the drivers and barriers of coordination among humanitarian organizations. In *23rd Annual Conference of the Production and Operations Management Society*.

Näslund, D. and Hulthen, H. (2012). Supply chain management integration: A critical analysis. *Benchmarking: An International Journal*, 19(4/5), 481–501.

O'Leary, Z. (2014). *The essential guide to doing your research project* (2nd edn). Los Angeles: Sage.

Oloruntoba, R. and Gray, R. (2003). *Humanitarian Aid Organisations and Logistics*. Corby: The Institute of Logistics and Transport.

Oloruntoba, R. and Gray, R. (2006). Humanitarian aid: An agile supply chain? *Supply Chain Management: An International Journal*, 11(2), 115–120.

Pagell, M. (2004). Understanding the factors that enable and inhibit the integration of operations, purchasing and logistics. *Journal of Operations Management*, 22(5), 459–487.

Palomero, S. and Chalmeta, R. (2014). A guide for supply chain integration in SMEs. *Production Planning and Control*, 25(5), 372–400.

Parnaby, J. (1979). Concept of a manufacturing system. *International Journal of Production Research*, 17(2), 123–135.

Perry, M. (2007). Natural disaster management planning: A study of logistics managers responding to the tsunami. *International Journal of Physical Distribution and Logistics Management*, 37(5), 409–433.

Pettit, S. J. and Beresford, A. K. (2005). Emergency relief logistics: An evaluation of military, non-military and composite response models. *International Journal of Logistics: Research and Applications*, 8(4), 313–331.

Richey Jr, R. G. (2009). The supply chain crisis and disaster pyramid: A theoretical framework for understanding preparedness and recovery. *International Journal of Physical Distribution and Logistics Management*, 39(7), 619–628.

Roh, S., Pettit, S., Harris, I., and Beresford, A. (2015). The pre-positioning of warehouses at regional and local levels for a humanitarian relief organisation. *International Journal of Production Economics*, 170, 616–628.

Rubin, H. J. and Rubin, I. (2012). *Qualitative interviewing: The art of hearing data* (3rd edn). London: Sage.

Safran, P. (2003). A strategic approach for disaster and emergency assistance. Proceedings of the 5th Asian Disaster Reduction Center International Meeting and the 2nd UN-ISDR Asian Meeting, Kobe, 15–17 January.

Saldaña, J. (2013). *The coding manual for qualitative researcher* (2nd edn.). London: Sage.

Salmon, P., Stanton, N., Jenkins, D., and Walker, G. (2011). Coordination during multi-agency emergency response: Issues and solutions. *Disaster Prevention and Management: An International Journal*, 20(2), 140–158.

Saunders, M. Lewis, P., and Thornhill, A. (2012). *Research methods for business students* (6th edn). Harlow: Pearson.

Schulz, S. F. and Blecken, A. (2010). Horizontal cooperation in disaster relief logistics: Benefits and impediments. *International Journal of Physical Distribution and Logistics Management*, 40(8/9), 636–656.

Seaman, J. (1999). Malnutrition in emergencies: How can we do better and where do the responsibilities lie? *Disasters*, 23(4), 306–315.

Spekman, R. E., Kamauff Jr, J. W., and Myhr, N. (1998). An empirical investigation into supply chain management: A perspective on partnerships. *Supply Chain Management: An International Journal*, 3(2), 53–67.

Stake, R. E. (1995). *The art of case study research*. Thousand Oaks, CA: Sage.

Stevens, G. C. (1989). Integrating the supply chain. *International Journal of Physical Distribution and Materials Management*, 19(8), 3–8.

Sweeney, E. (2011). Towards a unified definition of supply chain management. *International Journal of Applied Logistics*. July-September, 2 (3), 30–48.

Tapia, A. H., Maldonado, E., Ngamassi Tchouakeu, L. M., and Maitland, C. F. (2012). Coordinating humanitarian information: The problem of organizational and technical trajectories. *Information Technology and People*, 25(3), 240–258.

Tatham, P. H. and Kovács, G. (2010). The application of "swift trust" to humanitarian logistics. *International Journal of Production Economics*, 126(1), 35–45.

Tatham, P. H. and Pettit, S. J. (2010). Transforming humanitarian logistics: The journey to supply network management. *International Journal of Physical Distribution and Logistics Management*, 40(8/9), 609–622.

Tatham, P. H. and Spens, K. (2011). Towards a humanitarian logistics knowledge management system. *Disaster Prevention and Management: An International Journal*, 20(1), 6–26.

Thomas, A. S. and Kopczak, L. R. (2005). From logistics to supply chain management: The path forward in the humanitarian sector. San Francisco: Fritz Institute. July 31, 2015 from http://www.fritzinstitute.org/PDFs/WhitePaper/FromLogisticsto.pdf

Tomasini, R. M. (2012). Humanitarian partnerships-drivers, facilitators, and components: The case of non-food item distribution in Sudan. In Kovács, G. and Spens, K. (Eds), *Relief supply chain management for disasters: Humanitarian aid and emergency logistics* (pp. 16–30). Hershey: Business Science Reference.

Van der Laan, E., Van Dalen, J., Rohrmoser, M., and Simpson, R. (2016). Demand forecasting and order planning for humanitarian logistics: An empirical assessment. *Journal of Operations Management*, 45, 114–122.

Van Wassenhove, L. N. (2006). Humanitarian aid logistics: Supply chain management in high gear. *Journal of the Operational Research Society*, 57(5),475–489.

Vega, D. and Roussat, C. (2015). Humanitarian logistics: The role of logistics service providers. *International Journal of Physical Distribution and Logistics Management*, 45(4), 352–375.

Whipple, J. M. and Russell, D. (2007). Building supply chain collaboration: A typology of collaborative approaches. *The International Journal of Logistics Management*, 18(2),174–196.

Yin, R. K. (2003). *Case study research: Design and methods* (3rd edn.). Thousand Oaks, CA: Sage.

Yin, R. K. (2014). *Case study research: Design and methods* (5th edn). Thousand Oaks: Sage.

Zhao, G., Feng, T., and Wang, D. (2015). Is more supply chain integration always beneficial to financial performance? *Industrial Marketing Management*, 45, 162–172.

# 9

# An Empirical Investigation of Swift Trust in Humanitarian Logistics Operations

Qing Lu, Mark Goh and Robert de Souza

## Introduction

Global disasters have been increasing in diversity and severity in the past decade (IFRC 2012). To mitigate the effect of such disasters, humanitarian relief organizations (HROs) across the world are busy rescuing and helping people in disaster-prone areas, where the poor infrastructure often makes humanitarian logistics challenging. In such emergency operations, there are multiple stakeholders such as commercial enterprises, donor and host governments, the military, international and local HROs, as well as local communities working together for effective response. These agencies often have varied motivations, mandates, resources, and technical expertise, and must

Q. Lu (✉)
Department of Logistics Management, Izmir University of Economics,
Izmir, Turkey
e-mail: lu.qing@ieu.edu.tr

M. Goh
The Logistics Institute Asia-Pacific (TLIAP) and NUS Business School, National
University of Singapore, Singapore
e-mail: bizgohkh@nus.edu.sg

R. de Souza
The Logistics Institute Asia-Paicifc, National University of Singapore, Singapore
e-mail: rdesouza@nus.edu.sg

© The Author(s) 2018                                                           **279**
G. Kovács et al. (eds.), *The Palgrave Handbook of Humanitarian Logistics
and Supply Chain Management*, https://doi.org/10.1057/978-1-137-59099-2_9

coordinate well to ensure the effectiveness of the emergency operations, as no single actor has sufficient resources to respond effectively to a major disaster. Therefore, coordination in emergency humanitarian logistics is receiving increased attention (Balcik et al. 2010).

Trust is a critical factor for effective coordination in supply network management (Golicic et al. 2003; Gulati and Singh 1998). It is well documented that a high level of trust between supply chain partner organizations leads to coordination effectiveness and better chain performance (Fawcett et al. 2008). However, the literature tends to focus on trust in long-term relationships. Studies on trust in the temporary networks formed by emergency logistics or quick onset disasters are scant (Tatham and Kovács 2010). In the context of humanitarian logistics, these temporary networks are often the norm in emergency relief operations, whereby a number of individual logisticians from a variety of organizations have to work together. Moreover, among the various types of temporary networks, groups in humanitarian logistics operations are better classified as hastily formed networks (HFNs) or emergent response groups (Ben-Shalom et al. 2005; Majchrzak et al. 2007). While sharing a common aim to helping the disaster victims, the logisticians in such groups may have neither worked together before, nor have gone through the same training. An emergent response group may develop, migrate, and reorganize, gaining and losing memberships in an unstructured way (Majchrzak et al. 2007). In such a context, trust building would follow a different pattern from trust in a long-term relationship, which would normally come about through positive past collaboration (Fischer 2013). Individuals within such a network are often tied together via "swift trust" or "initial trust" (Meyerson et al. 1996).

Swift trust is a form of trust occurring in temporary organizational structures, assumed by group members initially, and is later verified and adjusted (Meyerson et al. 1996). It is already recognized as an important type of trust in humanitarian operations (Stephenson 2005). Tatham and Kovács (2010) have proposed a model of swift trust in the humanitarian context with several possible facilitators. However, to date, there is no empirical work on swift trust in the study of humanitarian logistics.

To fill this research gap, we first develop a research framework with testable hypotheses to advance our knowledge in this field. We not only examine the factors affecting the forming of swift trust but also the impact of swift trust on the coordination activities as well as their effectiveness in humanitarian networks with coordination theory as the tool (Malone and Crowston 1994). By applying swift trust and coordination theory into the humanitarian logistics practice, this study would enrich our understanding in this important research field and contribute to the improvement of humanitarian relief operations on the ground. Practical implications from the study may help HROs build trust rapidly and effectively with their unfamiliar partners on-site. Such trust may lead to a smoother and hence more effective coordination and collaboration of their logistics operations, which can in turn relieve the sufferings of the beneficiaries and reduce the HRO operating cost. From the perspective of the research methodology, it is one of the few empirical investigations in the field of humanitarian logistics and may contribute to a more rigorous empirical examination in the field.

## Literature Review

Trust is a core concept in supply network management and has been studied from a range of perspectives, including economic, psychological, and sociological. It integrates "micro-level psychological processes and group dynamics with macro-level institutional arrangements" (Rousseau et al. 1998: 393). Morgan and Hunt (1994) generally define trust as "confidence in an exchange partner's reliability and integrity." In the humanitarian context with a focus on inter-personal relationships, trust is defined as "a fundamental belief that the other can be relied upon to fulfil their obligations with integrity, and will act in the best interests of the other" (Tatham and Kovács 2010: 37).

According to Stephenson (2005), interorganizational trust in the humanitarian context can be classified into four aspects:

- Trust based on the judgment of goodwill and how much one considers the other to be a friend (companion)
- Trust based on the perceived ability of others to carry out the needed tasks or to get the job done (competence)
- Trust based on whether the behavior is consistent with contractual agreements (commitment)
- Trust based on expediency because of the need to accomplish the goals quickly (swiftness)

As HFNs are commonly seen in emergency humanitarian logistics operations, swift trust is crucial to HFNs by the achievement of trusting inter-personal relationship in a very short time. Thus, we focus on swift trust in this study.

The concept of swift trust is first proposed by Meyerson et al. (1996). This concept is developed as an explanation of trust development in temporary, nonconventional teams within or between organizations. It is "a unique form of collective perception and relating that is capable of managing issues of vulnerability, uncertainty, risk, and expectations." Instead of the typical trust built through the passage of time as an evidence-driven information process, swift trust is created by category-driven processes under very tight time constraints. A temporary team would interact as if trust were present, but then must verify that the team can manage the expectations of all stakeholders. It is conditional and is in need of reinforcement and calibration by action. Hung et al. (2004) have developed a framework for the initial formation and further growth of the attribute of swift trust. Three routes to trust, the peripheral, central, and habitual, are proposed in Hung et al.'s framework. The peripheral route refers to the early establishment of trust, and the central one is its further development in relationships with a long-term perspective, while the habitual one is at a higher level where trust is based on patterns developed within the relationship.

In the context of emergency humanitarian logistics operations, networks are often formed with little or no prior warning, and the peripheral route of trust building would be more relevant and important. According to Hung et al. (2004), there are five antecedent conditions influencing the formation of swift trust, namely, third-party information, dispositional trust, rule, category, and role. Tatham and Kovács (2010) further proposed a model for the route to swift trust. Besides the five conditions, the model includes a feedback loop with the communication environment and perceived risk as moderators. In a related discussion, Tatham and Kovács (2010) also explored the importance of third-party information and the development of common rules in humanitarian logistics operations when forming swift trust.

Building trust is not the end in itself. The purpose of forming trust is to facilitate more effective interorganizational coordination and collaboration. The most commonly accepted definition of coordination is "the act of managing dependencies between entities and the joint effort of entities working together towards mutually defined goals" (Malone and Crowston 1994). Based on coordination theory, proposed by Malone and Crowston (1994), we may see that the coordination in humanitarian logistics arises from the task interdependency, where a single entity is unable to meet the needs of the beneficiaries in one location. One coordination mechanism is to assign a single lead agency (often called the umbrella organization) as the coordinator to facilitate horizontal coordination (Akhtar et al. 2012). It is often called the cluster approach and is widely used in humanitarian relief operations (Jahre and Jensen 2010). However, mechanism alone is insufficient for effective coordination as most HROs are independent from one another with different motives; interorganizational trust is essential for effective coordination. In the situation of complex and dynamic environments, a context similar to emergency humanitarian operations, Hossain and Uddin (2012) have developed a framework to model coordination within social networks. Similarly, Saab et al. (2013) have explored the connection between trust and coordination among the field-level Information and Communications Technology (ICT) workers in HROs and shown that trust building through collaborative activities is essential for successful interorganization coordination.

While there is a growing recognition of the importance of trust in humanitarian logistics operations, and specifically swift trust, there is no known empirical study on the forming of swift trust in emergency relief operations as the existing works are largely based on theoretical applications such as Tatham and Kovács (2010) or case studies such as Saab et al. (2013). This study is thus initiated to fill the research gap.

## Hypotheses and Framework

To develop a framework with empirically testable hypotheses, we first examine the model presented in Tatham and Kovács (2010: 38). The five antecedent conditions in the model are then further developed into testable hypotheses in the context of emergency relief operations.

Third-party information is the first factor in the original model. It is mainly in the form of reputation or certification from our field study with humanitarian logisticians on the ground. Third-party information can also manifest in the form of reference, particularly for the small local HROs. When a partner is introduced by a trusted person or organization, two HROs without any prior work experience would be easier to trust each other. We thus posit the following hypothesis.

**H1**: *It is easier to generate swift trust toward a partner if the partner is introduced by a trusted person or organization.*

The second factor, disposition trust, is not specific to the humanitarian context (Tatham and Kovács 2010), and as such, we do not explore it further. Rule is the third factor, which is important in relief operations. It has been called to develop common rules and procedures among HROs in the same cluster to facilitate interorganizational coordination, though in practice, there is still a long way to go (Balcik et al. 2010). Two HROs with similar operating rules and procedures may generate trust in each other much easier, resulting in the following hypothesis.

**H2:** *Two HROs are more likely to generate swift trust toward each other if they follow similar rules and procedures in their humanitarian operations.*

Category is an important though often divisive factor in the forming of swift trust. Here, we specifically explore the impact of organizational belief and value, one important type of category. Sharing the same organizational value or belief would be particularly important for swift trust forming among the small, local HROs. In addition to organizational values, religious belief and conviction could also play an important role in relief operations as many nongovernmental organizations (NGOs) are faith based. Anecdotal information from the field suggests that it is relatively easier for two Christian HROs to work together as compared to a Muslim organization working with a Christian one. We thus have the next two hypotheses.

**H3a:** *Two HROs are more likely to generate swift trust toward each other if they are similar or share the same organizational beliefs.*

**H3b:** *Two HROs are more likely to generate swift trust toward each other if they are similar or share the same religious belief or values.*

Role is another important factor, which is affected by the competency of a person or an organization. It is reported that experience in prior disaster relief operations is important for trust building (Saab et al. 2013). A person or organization experienced in humanitarian operations may be viewed as being more competent and as such is easier to be trusted, resulting in the following hypothesis.

**H4:** *It is easier to generate swift trust toward a partner if the partner is perceived as being competent by his/her background or experience.*

In addition to the five antecedent factors, perceived risk can act as a moderator on swift trust building. In the humanitarian context, the competition for media attention and the subsequent funding would be an important risk as most HROs do not have stable revenues but rely on donations from the goodwill of various individuals and organizations (Tomasini and Van Wassenhove 2009). A sense of the potential competition may affect swift trust building between two HROs and can thus lead to them withholding critical information and deterring coordination effectiveness. Another possible risk is the potential clash due to value differences, which is a common factor in interorganizational conflicts and happens also in humanitarian relief operations (Akhtar et al. 2012). We thus propose the next two hypotheses.

**H5a:** *It is more difficult to generate swift trust toward a partner if the partner is perceived to be a potential competitor for funds.*

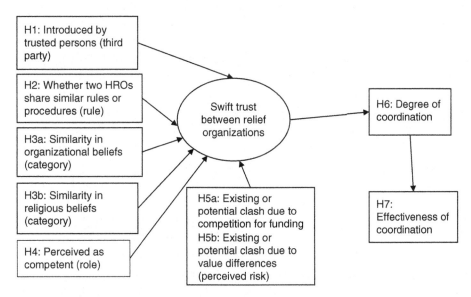

**Fig. 9.1** Research framework

**H5b:** *It is more difficult to generate swift trust toward a partner if the partner is perceived to be significantly different in organizational values.*

In addition to the antecedents of swift trust, we also investigate the impact of swift trust on the coordination activities as well as coordination effectiveness in the humanitarian context. These relationships are well known in the coordination literature (e.g., Gulati and Singh 1998; Rampersad et al. 2010). We now posit the following two hypotheses.

**H6:** *The higher the level of swift trust among the coordinating partners, the higher the degree of their coordination activities.*

**H7:** *The higher the degree of coordination activities among the partners, the better the coordination effectiveness.*

Figure 9.1 summarizes the six hypotheses into a framework.

# Research Sample, Measures, and Results

## Research Sample

We choose HROs in Southeast Asia as the research sample. Several countries in the region such as the Philippines, Indonesia, and Myanmar are particularly disaster prone, given the various recent disasters in the region such as tsunamis (2004 Indian Ocean tsunami in Aceh), earthquakes (2009 Sumatra earthquake in Padang), cyclones and typhoons (2008 Cyclone Nargis in Myanmar, 2013 Typhoon Haiyan in Philippines), floods (2011 Bangkok flood), and volcanic eruptions (2010 Merapi eruption in Java). In addition, there are man-made disasters such as ethnic conflicts in Myanmar and Southern Philippines. Many large international HROs have manned active operations in the region to support their extensive relief and development programs. It is, indeed, an appropriate location for our study.

Moreover, most countries in the region are democratic countries with a vibrant private sector and strong networks of local albeit much smaller HROs. For instance, Indonesia, the largest country in the region, is estimated to host tens of thousands of local NGOs, of which at least 9,000 are officially registered with the Ministry of Home Affairs (Figge and Pasandaran 2011). Many NGOs are heavily involved in humanitarian operations and are HROs as well. There are both religious and secular NGOs, those focusing on emergency relief and those having both relief and development activities. On religious NGOs alone, there are Protestant, Catholic, Muslim, and Buddhist organizations operating in the region. Thus, it would be interesting to explore the forming of swift trust in such a complex and dynamic environment.

We decide to perform a survey rather than a case study, the common approach in most humanitarian logistics studies for a number of reasons and challenges. A case study involving multiple languages and levels of interpretation is often difficult to undertake. At the same time, a standardized questionnaire with well-designed constructs and larger sample size would make the study results more objective and empirical verification easier in the future.

The questionnaire for this survey was developed through a rigorous process of screening the survey questions for ease of response from the field. In addition to the English version, it was translated into the local language, that is, Bahasa Indonesia, for a survey conducted in Indonesia. It would enable us to reach more local or regional NGOs there who are poor in foreign languages, as suggested by Harkness and Schoua-Glusberg (1998). A large-scale survey was initiated in early 2014. Giving the explorative nature of the study and the scant knowledge about the actual work of the humanitarian organizations in the region, we used the humanitarian logistics education centers in Southeast Asian countries to conduct the surveys among the NGOs participating in the training sessions conducted by these centers. A researcher visited these centers with the trainers, distributed the

**Table 9.1** Organizational affiliation of respondents (*n* = 80)

|  | Number | Percentage (%) |
|---|---|---|
| Government agencies | 11 | 13.8 |
| Government-affiliated associations | 11 | 13.8 |
| Local NGOs | 4 | 5.1 |
| Regional NGOs | 6 | 7.6 |
| International NGOs | 15 | 18.8 |
| UN agencies and other multinational organizations (e.g., Red Cross) | 15 | 18.8 |
| Private sector | 7 | 8.8 |
| Academia | 11 | 13.8 |

questionnaires, and collected them back on the spot. As most humanitarian organizations are not accustomed to answering public inquiries and surveys, handling questionnaire personally would be more convenient and effective for them. The researcher could also explain and clarify their questions during the process. We managed to collect 90 questionnaires from three training sessions in Singapore (33 responses), Indonesia (24 responses), and the Philippines (33 responses), respectively.

On examining the responses, we find one questionnaire unusable due to the missing of all critical information. Thus, the actual sample size for most analyses is 89. A few questionnaires only answered part of our questions and missed some information, making the sample size for hypothesis testing not exactly equal. So where necessary, we will report the actual sample size used for the results found in each of the tables presented in this chapter. Table 9.1 presents the respondent profiles.

Among the respondents, nine of them omitted their profile information such as organization type and size. Among the rest (80), the largest group is the NGO sector (including local, regional, international NGOs, as well as multinational organizations like the UN agencies) (50%), followed by the public sector (28% from government agencies and related associations), academia (14%), and finally the private sector (both corporations and private foundations, 9%). It largely fits with the overall humanitarian landscape in the region where the NGOs and governments are major players.

## Measures

The measures for the constructs such as swift trust and coordination are drawn from the extant literature with some adjustments according to the context of emergency relief operations. On swift trust, we adopt three items from Robert et al. (2009):

- My colleagues who might interact with them would probably consider them trustworthy.
- Given their track record, I see no reason to doubt their competence and preparation for the task.
- If I were working with them on a specific task, I believe I can rely on them not to cause me trouble by careless work.

The degree of coordination is measured by the frequency and openness of information sharing, readiness to maintain a positive relationship, proactive in information sharing, and accessibility according to Hossain and Uddin (2012), and Rampersad et al. (2010). The last construct, coordination effectiveness, is developed based on Hossain and Uddin (2012) and Rampersad et al. (2010) with some adjustments to the humanitarian context with the following five items:

- The relief activities of our organization are well coordinated with the new partner.
- The relief activities of our organization with the new partner are well coordinated within the humanitarian network we belong to.
- There exists an effective centralized coordination body in our humanitarian network.
- The centralized coordination body can process all the information from the network.
- The centralized coordination body can coordinate well with the new partner.

## Results

Based on the survey results, we first test hypotheses H1–H4, with answers from the first survey question, "based on your experience, when you work with organizations or persons you did not know previously, to what extent do the following factors induce your trust in your unknown partners?" Factor analysis through principal components analysis managed to derive factors from the seven items used in the survey. The result is presented in Table 9.2 with four loaded factors. As these factors account for 81% of the observed variance in the data and the Kaiser-Meyer-Olkin (KMO) measure is 0.64, the exploratory factor analysis is deemed valid.

**Table 9.2** Factor analysis on factors that induces trust ($n = 88$)

| Items | Factor 1 Third-party information | Factor 2 Value or competency | Factor 3 Similar rules | Factor 4 Same beliefs |
|---|---|---|---|---|
| Person from organization I know | **0.768** | 0.190 | −0.062 | 0.100 |
| Person introduced by a person I know | **0.878** | 0.068 | 0.097 | −0.086 |
| Having friends in the organization | **0.770** | −0.168 | 0.337 | 0.226 |
| The organization follow similar rules or procedures | 0.122 | 0.22 | **0.897** | 0.087 |
| The person is competent based on background and experience | 0.035 | **0.912** | 0.046 | 0.138 |
| Have same value with the organization | 0.111 | **0.725** | 0.454 | 0.009 |
| Have same religious belief with the organization or person | 0.092 | 0.127 | 0.084 | **0.974** |

The three items in the first factor, "the person is from an organization I know," "the person is introduced by someone I know," and "I have some good friends in the organization," are used to measure the variable for H1, "introduced by trusted person." Reliability analysis also supports the grouping with the Cronbach's alpha at 0.76. The two items in the second factor are conceptually inconsistent as the first "competency by background or experience" is quite different from the second "sharing same values" and reliability analysis does not support the grouping either with Cronbach's alpha at 0.68, below the threshold for item consistency. Moreover, both factors three and four contain single items, and we thus treat the rest four items individually.

For the testing of H2, H3a, H3b, and H4, the single items in the questionnaire are therefore used. The items "the organization follows similar rules or procedures in humanitarian operations as mine," "we share the same values with the organization," "we share the same religious beliefs with the organization or the person," and "given his/her background and experience, the person is competent in humanitarian operations" are employed for H2, H3a, H3b, and H4, respectively.

We then conduct $t$-tests to test the first four hypotheses as we have single variable for each hypothesis. The result is presented in Table 9.3, which shows that H1, H2, H3a, and H4 are supported while H3b is not. H1, H2, H3a, H4 are all strongly supported when compared with the null hypothesis (mean = 3). On the other hand, H3b is strongly rejected and religious belief has been viewed as having no impact on swift trust generation.

**Table 9.3** t-Test results for H1–H4 for null hypothesis (mean = 3) (n = 89)

| Variables | Mean | t-Value | p-Value |
|---|---|---|---|
| Introduced by trusted person (H1) | 3.38 | 4.92 | <0.001 |
| Sharing similar rules and procedures (H2) | 3.49 | 5.38 | <0.001 |
| Sharing similar organizational values (H3a) | 3.91 | 10.1 | <0.001 |
| Sharing similar religious belief (H3b) | 2.17 | −7.47 | <0.001 |
| Perceived competent (H4) | 3.84 | 10.2 | <0.001 |

**Table 9.4** t-Test results for H5 for null hypothesis (mean = 3) (n = 88)

| Variables | Mean | t-Value | p-Value |
|---|---|---|---|
| Potential competition for funding (H5a) | 2.88 | −1.21 | 0.229 |
| Potential clash due to differences in value (H5b) | 3.31 | 3.03 | 0.003 |

To test H5, we use the question "based on your experience, when you work with organizations or persons you did not know previously, to what extent do the following factors lower your trust in your unknown partners?" Two items "potential competition for funding" and "potential clash due to differences in value" are used to measure the variables for H5a and H5b, respectively. t-Tests are similarly employed, and the results in Table 9.4 show that H5a is rejected but H5b is supported.

For the testing of H6 and H7 on coordination activities, a factor analysis is conducted by principal components analysis to derive the coordination variables from the multiple items reported in the survey. The result is presented in Table 9.5 with three loaded factors. As these factors account for 77% of the observed variance in the data and the KMO measure is 0.75, the explanatory factor analysis is deemed valid.

The five items in the first factor, coordination with the new partner, coordination in the network, effective centralized coordinator, centralized coordinator with information, and good coordination with the new partner by the central body, are measures for coordination effectiveness. The second factor includes the openness, regularity, and proactivity of information sharing, which measures the different aspects of information sharing, an aspect of coordination. The third factor includes approachable and active assistance for the new partners, measuring the active assistance in coordination. Reliability analysis supports the grouping of variables with Cronbach's alpha at 0.92 for coordination effectiveness, 0.85 for information sharing, and 0.70 for active assistance, respectively, which supports their internal consistencies.

**Table 9.5** Factor analysis on coordination activities ($n = 84$)

| Items | Loaded factor 1 Coordination effectiveness | Loaded factor 2 Information sharing | Loaded factor 3 Active assistance |
|---|---|---|---|
| Open to share information with new partners | 0.128 | **0.852** | 0.070 |
| Regularly share information with new partners | 0.176 | **0.880** | 0.126 |
| Proactively share information with new partners | 0.084 | **0.832** | 0.239 |
| New partner can approach us for help needed | 0.136 | 0.255 | **0.816** |
| We try our best for a positive coordination experience with the new partner | 0.187 | 0.094 | **0.839** |
| Our activity well coordinated with the new partner | **0.662** | 0.149 | 0.365 |
| Our activity with the new partner well coordinated within the network | **0.762** | 0.164 | 0.284 |
| There is an effective central body in our network | **0.909** | 0.048 | 0.0911 |
| The central body can process all information from the network | **0.931** | 0.116 | 0.001 |
| The central body can coordinate well with the new partner | **0.917** | 0.156 | 0.101 |

After the factor analysis, we average the item scores for the three factors and derive the value of all coordination variables, coordination effectiveness, information sharing, and active assistance, respectively. H6 is thus further divided into two sub-hypotheses:

**H6a:** *The higher the swift trust among the coordinating partners, the higher the degree of their coordination activities in information sharing.*

**H6b:** *The higher the swift trust among the coordinating partners, the higher the degree of their coordination activities in active assistance.*
Similarly, hypothesis H7 is divided into two sub-hypotheses:

**H7a:** *The higher the degree of the coordination activities in information sharing, the better the coordination effectiveness.*

**H7b:** *The higher the degree of the coordination activities in active assistance, the better the coordination effectiveness.*

**Table 9.6** Linear regression on H6 ($n = 86$)

| Dependent variable | Coordination on information sharing (H6a) | | Coordination on active assistance (H6b) | |
|---|---|---|---|---|
| Independent variables | b | Std. error | b | Std. error |
| Swift trust | 0.247[*] | 0.100 | 0.099 | 0.090 |
| Organizational type | −0.068 | 0.081 | 0.046 | 0.073 |
| $R^2$ | 0.079 | | 0.018 | |

[*]$p < 0.05$

**Table 9.7** Linear regression on H7 ($n = 86$)

| Dependent variable | Coordination effectiveness | | | |
|---|---|---|---|---|
| Independent variables | b | Std. error | b | Std. error |
| Information sharing (H7a) | 0.342[**] | 0.106 | | |
| Active assistance (H7b) | | | 0.432 | 0.119 |
| Organization type | 0.081 | 0.081 | 0.036 | 0.080 |
| $R^2$ | 0.115 | | 0.141 | |

[**]$p < 0.01$

Four linear regressions are conducted to test the four hypotheses with organizational type (public, private, NGOs, and others) as the control variable. The results are reported in Tables 9.6 and 9.7.

Tables 9.6 and 9.7 show that H6a, H7a, and H7b are supported by regression analysis but not H6b, and control variable organization type has no impact on our dependent variables.

# Discussion

With a reasonable sample size, we are able to conduct more rigorous empirical analysis on the forming and impact of swift trust in the field of humanitarian operations. In general, most of our hypotheses are well supported by the empirical data. Introduced by a trusted person or organization can lead to higher trust (H1), similarity in rules and procedures can generate trust (H2), sharing similar organizational value can generate trust (H3a), and a competent partner is more likely to be trusted (H4). However, there are also surprises. Contrast to our expectation (H3b), religious belief or values have no impact on the forming of swift trust. Actually, most respondents strongly agree that religion should not have any impact on their professional behavior. In another similar question on the barrier to the forming of swift trust, most respondents also strongly disagree that religious differences should be a source of organizational conflict. It shows that humanitarian workers are largely professional in their views on religion. In Southeast Asia, a region with many religions and occasional religious conflicts, the humanitarian workers in general are able to put religion into their private domain and maintain a professionally neutral position when dealing with organizations and folks from different religious backgrounds.

Our test on H5a and H5b also shows the differences between principles and monetary benefits. While organizational value differences is an important barrier to the forming of swift trust (H5b), potential conflict in fund raising (H5a) is not. Humanitarian workers are not so concerned about the competition for funding among the humanitarian organizations, but focus more on the ground operations which demand high trust among the different organizations. Here again, we note the professionalism of the humanitarian staff.

Moving from the forming of swift trust to its impact, H6 and H7 present a mixed picture. While swift trust is found to be inductive to coordination in information sharing (H6a), its linkage to active assistance in coordination is not supported by the data (H6b). It shows the limitation of swift trust in the field. While humanitarian organizations are willing to trust unfamiliar partners quickly for the groundwork, their coordination is still limited in scope. Some swift trust is good enough for low cost coordination like information sharing, but is insufficient for the more costly forms of coordination such as active assistance. Especially due to the chaotic nature on the ground for emergency relief operations, it is difficult for an organization to spend additional time and effort on unfamiliar partners when there are tons of tasks already in the activity pipeline. Permanent and long-term trust and close relationships from past interactions may be necessary for more active assistance in the coordination. Moreover, both H7a and H7b are supported, showing that coordination in either information sharing or active assistance can enhance the effectiveness of coordination.

## Conclusion

The humanitarian aid supply network in disaster relief operations is a typical HFN where members come from organizations with different backgrounds and organizational culture. Nurturing swift trust in such a group is critical for the coordination in the network and thus its effectiveness in the relief operation, particularly so when it concerns rapid response situations. This study investigates the antecedents of swift trust and develops an empirically testable framework linking trust, coordination activity, and performance. We conducted a survey among the humanitarian organizations in Southeast Asia, yielding 89 usable responses. The results show that most hypotheses on swift trust generation are supported, with some interesting exceptions as well. However, being the first empirical investigation without a large sample size, the usual caveat applies and thus limits our conclusion and generalizations.

Our findings highlight the importance of swift trust in humanitarian operations and identifies several means to enhancing the trust. NGOs and governments should use their means effectively to improve swift trust among the humanitarian players. For example, third-party certification and personal competency are inductive to swift trust. Organizing more external training activities would be beneficial for humanitarian workers in both network building, communication, coordination understanding, and competency enhancement.

Clearly, as with all empirical studies, the richness of the sample and the size of the sample do help in providing more accurate and deeper insights into the phenomenon of study. In this chapter, our small sample size naturally calls for a guarded conclusion of our results.

Future studies could increase the sample pool and examine the empirical results more rigorously, and test the five antecedent conditions for swift trust with better proxies, drawn from other domains of study such as Fischer (2013) who has dealt with the issues of trust, communication, and past collaboration. The connection between swift trust and coordination effectiveness can be explored in depth, following the footsteps of Gulati and Singh (1998) and other management scholars. It is also interesting to note that religious belief has no statistical impact on swift trust generation. It would be interesting to explore this anomaly more carefully at the country level and explore the means to achieving such a harmony which is one hallmark of the professionalism of the NGOs. We defer this to another study.

# References

Akhtar, P., Marr, N.E., Garnevska, E. (2012). Coordination in humanitarian relief chains: Chain coordinators. *Journal of Humanitarian Logistics & Supply Chain Management*, 2(1), 85–103.

Balcik, B., Beamon, B.M., Krejci, C.C., Muramatsu, K.M., Ramirez, M. (2010). Coordination in humanitarian relief chains: Practices, challenges and opportunities. *International Journal of Production Economics*, 126(1), 22–34.

Ben-Shalom, U., Lehrer, Z., Ben-Ari, E. (2005). Cohesion during military operations. *Armed Forces and Society*, 32(1), 63–79.

Fawcett, S.E., Magnan, G.M., McCarter, M.W. (2008). Benefits, barriers, and bridges to effective supply chain management. *Supply Chain Management*, 13(1), 35–48.

Figge, K., Pasandaran, C. (2011). Indonesian NGOs must set transparency example: Study, *Jakarta Globe*, Sept 3, http://jakartaglobe.beritasatu.com/archive/indonesian-ngos-must-set-transparency-example-study/

Fischer, C. (2013). Trust and communication in European agri-food chains. *Supply Chain Management: An International Journal*, 18(2), 208–218.

Golicic, S.L., Foggin, J.H., Mentzer, J.T. (2003). Relationship magnitude and its role in interorganizational relationship structure. *Journal of Business Logistics*, 24(1), 57–76.

Gulati, R., Singh, H. (1998). The architecture of cooperation: Managing coordination costs and appropriation concerns in strategic alliances. *Administrative Science Quarterly*, 43(4), 781–794.

Harkness, J.A. and Schoua-Glusberg, A. (1998). Questionnaires in translation. *ZUMA-nachrichten spezial*, 3(1), 87–127.

Hossain, L., Uddin, S. (2012). Design patterns: Coordination in complex and dynamic environments. *Disaster Prevention and Management*, 21(3), 336–350.

Hung, Y.-T.C., Dennis, A.R., Robert, L. (2004). Trust in virtual teams: Towards an integrative model of trust formation, *Proceedings of the 37th Hawaii International Conference on Systems Science*, 1–11. Hawaii.

IFRC. (2012). *World Disasters Report 2011*. Geneva, Switzerland: International Federation of Red Cross and Red Crescent Societies.

Jahre, M., Jensen, L.-M. (2010). Coordination in humanitarian logistics through clusters. *International Journal of Physical Distribution & Logistics Management*, 40(8/9), 657–674.

Majchrzak, A., Jarvenpaa, S.L., Hollingshead, A.B. (2007). Coordinating expertise among emergent groups responding to disasters. *Organization Science*, 18(1), 147–161.

Malone, T.W., Crowston, K. (1994). The interdisciplinary study of coordination. *Computing Surveys*, 26(1), 87–119.

Meyerson, D., Weick, K.E., Kramer, R.M. (1996). Swift trust and temporary groups. In R.M. Kramer, & T.R. Tyler (Eds.), *Trust in Organizations: Frontiers of Theory and Research*, 166–195. Thousand Oaks, CA: Sage.

Morgan, R.M., Hunt, S.D. (1994). The commitment trust theory of relationship marketing. *Journal of Marketing*, 58(3), 20–38.

Rampersad, G., Quester, P., Troshani, I. (2010). Examining network factors: Commitment, trust, coordination and harmony. *Journal of Business and Industrial Marketing*, 25(7), 487–500.

Robert, L., Dennis, A.R., Hung, Y.-T.C. (2009). Individual swift trust and knowledge-based trust in face-to-face and virtual team members. *Journal of Management Information Systems*, 26(2), 241–279.

Rousseau, D.M., Sitkin, S.B., Burt, R.S., Camerer, C. (1998). Not so different after all: A cross discipline view of trust. *Academy of Management Review*, 23(3), 393–404.

Saab, D., Tapia, A., Maitland, C., Maldonado, E., Tchouakeu, L.-M. (2013). Inter-organizational coordination in the wild: Trust building and collaboration among field-level ICT workers in humanitarian relief organizations. *VOLUNTAS: International Journal of Voluntary and Nonprofit Organizations*, 24(1), 194–213.

Stephenson, M. (2005). Making humanitarian relief networks more effective: Operational coordination, trust and sense making. *Disasters*, 29(4), 337–350.

Tatham, P., Kovács, G. (2010). The application of "swift trust" to humanitarian logistics. *International Journal of Production Economics*, 126(1), 35–45.

Tomasini, R., Van Wassenhove, L.N. (2009). *Humanitarian Logistics*. New York: Palgrave Macmillan.

# 10

# Drivers of Coordination in Humanitarian Relief Supply Chains

Rameshwar Dubey and Nezih Altay

## Introduction

Natural disasters destroy infrastructure and property, displace families, and disrupt our daily lives. The objective of disaster relief operations is to provide humanitarian assistance in the forms of water, food, shelter, and supplies to areas affected by large-scale emergencies (Beamon and Balcik 2008). Responding to such large-scale events is a complex task (Tomasini and Van Wassenhove 2009). One reason for this complexity is the sheer number and diversity of organizations taking part in a disaster relief operation. Therefore, a quick, organized response requires a coordinated effort. The United Nations Office of Coordination for Humanitarian Assistance (OCHA) recognized the need for coordination in the wake of the inadequate initial international response to the Indian Ocean Tsunami in late 2004. The 2005 Humanitarian Response Review process and the subsequent establishment of the cluster approach as a coordination mechanism are the results of this recognition (OCHA 2005).

Coordination has also been recognized by academic scholars as one of the drivers of success in disaster relief operations (van Wassenhove 2006;

R. Dubey (✉)
Symbiosis International University, Pune, India
e-mail: rameshwardubey@gmail.com

N. Altay
Driehaus College of Business, DePaul University, Chicago, IL, USA
e-mail: NALTAY@depaul.edu

© The Author(s) 2018     **297**
G. Kovács et al. (eds.), *The Palgrave Handbook of Humanitarian Logistics and Supply Chain Management*, https://doi.org/10.1057/978-1-137-59099-2_10

Balcik et al. 2010). Coordination should help organizations to manage complex relationships to respond to disasters effectively and efficiently (Akhtar et al. 2012). Kabra and Ramesh (2015) note that poor coordination among actors often results in further suffering. To alleviate suffering relief supply chains must avoid duplication of resources and services, whether by filling gaps or preventing overlaps, and ensure that various organizations are synchronized to work together to achieve a common objective, thereby enabling a more coherent, effective, and efficient response (Gillmann 2009). Akhtar et al. (2012) note that tangible (e.g., finance, technology, and people) and intangible resources (e.g., leadership, extra efforts, relevant experiences and education, relationship management skills, research abilities, and performance measurement skills) are very important to ensure coordination among actors involved in disaster relief operations. Relying on organizational structure theory, Akhtar et al. (2012) also argue that in horizontal structures such as NGOs, an umbrella organization should play a coordinator role in the supply chain. This idea is similar to UN's cluster approach where an umbrella organization is expected to take the lead role in formulating an action plan.

Existing studies on coordination in relief supply chains have either focused on factors of coordination (Akhtar et al. 2012; Kabra and Ramesh 2015) or attempted to model the decision making behaviors of humanitarian actors using discrete-event simulation (Krejci 2015). Few studies utilize a theory-focused approach to understand the role of key factors in improving coordination among actors in a humanitarian relief supply chain (HRSC). Furthermore, humanitarian logistics and supply chain management scholars have expressed the need towards theory generation to advance the field (Jahre et al. 2009; Overstreet et al. 2011; Tabaklar et al. 2015). Tabaklar et al. (2015) note that the field has been borrowing theories from other established disciplines. Here, we argue that borrowing theories from other established fields can indeed help us advance the HRSC literature up to a point, but there is still a pressing need for theories suited to address the unique complexities of HRSCs. To generate theories on an emerging field one has to address the complexities of the field first (Eisenhardt 1989; Pagell and Wu 2009; Markman and Krause 2014; Dubey et al. 2015a). Along these lines, some theories have helped to offer a better explanation to HRSC-related problems such as swift trust (Tatham and Kovács 2010), temporary supply chain networks (Jahre et al. 2009), and information diffusion in clusters (Altay and Pal 2014). Our aim with this chapter is to enhance our understanding of coordination among humanitarian actors by developing a theoretical model of coordination using total interpretive structural modeling

(TISM). To address our research objective, we refer to Whetten (1989) and outline the following research questions:

*RQ1: What are the drivers of coordination in HRSCs?*

To address RQ1, we use an extensive literature review followed by an expert opinion survey to arrive to the key drivers of coordination in HRSCs.

*RQ2: How identified drivers are integrated into a theoretical framework?*

To address RQ2 there are several alternative methods that could be utilized such as case studies (Eisenhardt 1989), grounded theory (Egan 2002; Chermack 2007), action research (Coughlan and Coghlan 2002; Taylor and Taylor 2009), and graph theory approach (Sushil 2012; Dubey et al. 2015a). In this study we advocate in favor of the graph theory approach, specifically TISM to generate our theoretical framework. TISM in recent years has been used extensively (see Yadav 2014; Khatwani et al. 2015; Jain and Raj 2015; Dubey et al. 2015a; Yadav and Barve 2016), however the use of TISM in generating theory has been limited (Dubey et al. 2015a). Thus, we propose in our study a TISM-based approach to develop a framework to explain coordination in HRSCs.

In the subsequent sections we first discuss drivers of coordination in HRSCs, followed by the TISM method, resulting theoretical framework and research propositions, discussion of findings, and we close the chapter with conclusions.

## Drivers of Coordination

Balcik et al. (2010) define coordination in HRSCs as the relationship and interactions among different actors operating within the relief environment. They further argue that coordination in humanitarian relief chains may appear horizontal or vertical. Horizontal coordination refers to the extent to which an umbrella organization coordinates with their partners at the same level within the chain. NGO's prefer horizontal coordination (Balcik et al. 2010; Akhtar et al. 2012). Vertical coordination refers to the traditional command-control structure of linking with partners in the chain. Government organizations and armed forces follow vertical coordination. To answer RQ1, which is exploratory in nature, we first have used keywords to identify drivers from the literature. Following Ketchen and Hult (2007), we utilized existing organizational theories as our bases of identifying the drivers. First, based on the resource-based view (RBV) we note the resources (tangible or intangible) and capabilities that may play a significant role in explaining coordination in disaster relief chains. Second,

**Table 10.1** Drivers of the coordination

| Theory | Driver | References |
|---|---|---|
| Resource-based view | Information and communication technologies (ICTs) | Pettit ad Beresford (2009); Kabra and Ramesh (2015) |
| | Information sharing | Balcik et al. (2010); Altay and Pal (2014); Kabra and Ramesh (2015) |
| | Visibility | Kabra and Ramesh (2015) |
| | Training | Kabra and Ramesh (2015) |
| | Mutual learning | Kabra and Ramesh (2015) |
| | Contingency leadership | Akhtar et al. (2012) |
| | Performance management systems (PMS) | Akhtar et al. (2012) |
| Relationship theory | Swift-trust | Tatham and Kovács (2010) |
| | Commitment | Pettit and Beresford (2009); Kabra and Ramesh (2015) |
| | Cultural cohesion | Balcik et al. (2010); Kabra and Ramesh (2015) |
| | Regular meetings | Balcik et al. (2010); Kabra and Ramesh (2015) |

on the basis of relationship theory we identify key drivers of coordination. Using these two theories we gathered 11 drivers and classified them as shown in Table 10.1. All of these drivers are organizational-level drivers.

## Use of Information and Communications Technology

An organization's Information and Communications Technology (ICT) infrastructure is considered an important business resource (Zhu and Kraemer 2002). ICTs make up a critical part of the resources humanitarian organizations need to assist local populations and host governments. Thus, based on the resource based view of the organization we argue that use of such strategic resources as ICTs may lead to competitive advantage (Barney 1991). ICTs are key elements of the global response to disasters and armed-conflict scenarios (Wentz 2006). Asplund et al. (2008) argue that emerging information infrastructures play a critical role in improving cooperation among actors in disaster relief operations. Therefore, we consider ICTs a driver of coordination in HRSCs.

## Information Sharing

Information sharing is a critical but not so straightforward component of information flows (Premkumar and King 1994). The utility of information sharing depends on the quality of information being shared (Zhou and

Benton 2007). Information shared among humanitarian actors must possess quality, accuracy, accessibility, and relevancy (Cao and Zhang 2011). Kabra and Ramesh (2015) suggest that not only the quality of information but also the quality of information sharing is critical for coordination among humanitarian actors. Altay and Pal (2014) investigate the impact of information exchange for effective response, and find it to be a driver for coordination. Hence, we argue that information sharing is one of the drivers of coordination in HRSCs.

## Visibility

Visibility is an important capability in managing supply chains (Barratt and Oke 2007; Brandon-Jones et al. 2014). Visibility is related to the flow of information (Brandon-Jones et al. 2014) and allows supply chain partners to coordinate as they can see each other's inventory levels and replenishment quantities. This transparency in information flows can improve confidence and reduce interventions, which in turn improves decision making (Christopher and Lee 2004). We suggest that visibility, similar to commercial supply chains, is also a driver for coordination in humanitarian relief chains.

## Training

Lai et al. (2009) point out that lack of local capacity impacts disaster relief operations in most of the underdeveloped regions. Therefore, in under-developed regions capacity building is crucial. Kovács and Spens (2007) argue in favor of training to reduce the impact of disaster. Training can be then viewed as a way of capacity building. Another effect of training is the reduction of stress of humanitarian workers. Stress among relief workers may negatively influence the effectiveness of disaster relief operations (Paton 1996). Therefore, to minimize the negative effects of stress training can be viewed as a driver of coordination.

## Mutual Learning

We have seen in the previous section how cohesion of professional culture can improve coordination and therefore effectiveness of response. One way of building this cultural cohesion involves mutual learning. If humanitarian organizations can build a culture of learning from previous lessons and adopting best practices, which most humanitarian organizations already do, and carry this culture outside of their boundaries sharing their knowledge with others, that can improve coordination in future operations (Kabra and Ramesh 2015). We propose then that mutual learning is a driver for coordination among actors in HRSCs.

## Contingency Leadership

Stoner et al. (1995) define leadership as the process of directing and influencing the task-related activities of group members. There are several theories of leadership which includes trait leadership theory, contingency leadership theory, behavioral leadership theory, and full range theory of leadership. Here in this study, we argue that disaster relief chains are hastily formed. Hence, in such situations contingency leadership theory may offer better insight to explaining coordination among humanitarian organizations. In other words, contingency theory proposes that effective leadership is contingent on factors independent of an individual leader. As such, the theory predicts that effective leaders are those whose personal traits match the needs of the situation in which they find themselves. Adapting Stoner et al.'s work to HRSCs a leader first must be able to involve all the actors in the disaster relief chain. Second, the leader must be able to use power (reward power, coercive power, legitimate power, referent power, or expert power) to improve coordination among the humanitarian actors. Third, the leader must possess the ability to influence the actors towards a common action. And finally, the leader should emphasize shared values. Leadership has already been considered as one of the critical drivers of coordination in disaster relief chains (Waugh and Streib 2006; Kabra and Ramesh 2015; Dubey et al. 2015b). Thus, we too propose contingency leadership as a driver for coordination in HRSCs.

## Performance Measurement System

Performance measurement system (PMS) refers to the process of collecting, analyzing, and presenting data regarding the performance of each actor engaged in disaster relief operations (Beamon and Balcik 2008). Poister (2003) suggests that PMS is vital for the non-profit sector and can help organizations make better decisions, allocate resources more effectively, evaluate the efficacy of alternative solutions, and improve performance. Additionally, Kabra and Ramesh (2015) point out that PMS is an important driver for improving coordination among actors in disaster relief chains. Consequently, in this study we include PMS as one of the drivers for coordination.

## Swift-Trust

Following the seminal work of Morgan and Hunt (1994), management scholars examined complex relationships among partners using relationship theory. However, HRSC scholars argue that this new field of research has its own unique characteristics (Kovács and Spens 2011; Holguin-Veras et al. 2012). Hence to explain the complexity of building relationships in humanitarian networks, which are usually hastily formed (Jahre et al. 2009), the use of trust may not provide an adequate explanation. Therefore, Tatham and Kovács (2010) argued that most of the time in emergency situations there is a need for swift-trust building. Consequently, we propose that swift-trust is a critical driver for coordination among actors in HRSCs.

## Commitment

Morgan and Hunt (1994) argue that commitment is one of the antecedents of relationship building. Additionally, Min et al. (2005) argue that "... Commitment implies the parties are tolerant of each other's deficiencies (within reason) and that each will cooperate and not act opportunistically. This is important because most collaborative partners are not equal in terms of clout or bargaining power...". Hence, it is important for all participating actors to have a personal stake in the coordination effort and its operational outcomes. Thus, we propose that commitment among humanitarian actors as one of the drivers of coordination in HRSCs.

## Cultural Cohesion

Coordination suggests multiple organizations with different resources and governance structures acting together to accomplish a common task. Balcik et al. (2010) argue that relief actors operate in an environment which does not encourage coordination. Mainly because the situation is stressful, there is time pressure, and organizations from various nations and plethora of cultures converge at the same location. We believe however, that despite coming from various national cultures, humanitarian workers still share certain norms and values that may help with a feeling of stability (Schein 1985) and allow them to perform better (Wilkins and Ouchi 1983). Van Wassenhove (2006) reminds us that each of the actors involved in a disaster relief operation has the same general goal, to help people and alleviate suffering. These shared values among humanitarians create a cultural cohesion in the sense of a professional culture which can encourage members of different organizations to act in concert for the good of the people they are helping (Borys and Jemison 1989; Kabra and Ramesh 2015). Hence we argue that cultural cohesion is a driver for coordination among actors in HRSCs.

## Regular Meetings

Hicks and Pappas (2006) say that meeting regularly helps improve coordination of disaster relief operations. Regular meetings facilitate information sharing among humanitarian actors operating on the field and reduce information asymmetry, which acts as one of the barriers of the trust building process (Tatham and Kovács 2010). Therefore, in case of hastily formed networks holding regular meetings would help reduce uncertainty and restore confidence among humanitarian actors, which leads to building trust, and therefore is a driver for coordination in HRSCs.

# Total Interpretive Structural Modeling

TISM is a qualitative research method with roots in graph theory, and lends itself well to theory building by identifying linkages between constructs (Dubey et al. 2015a). Because there is no theory testing, TISM can be used with a small set of respondents who are either interviewed or surveyed. Sushil (2012) argues that TISM is an extended version of interpretive structural modeling (ISM). For a detailed description of ISM we refer the reader to consult Warfield (1973) and Mandal and Deshmukh (1994). Similar to ISM, the TISM method also uses interpretive logic to build connections between any two nodes, but unlike ISM, TISM provides an explanation for the nature of each connection and transitive link (Sushil 2012; Dubey et al. 2015a; Khatwani et al. 2015; Yadav and Barve 2016). In the following subsections we describe the method in detail and discuss the steps followed to develop a TISM model to explain coordination in disaster relief supply chains.

## The Interpretive Logic Knowledge Base

To derive a conceptual model using TISM, first the nodes (drivers of coordination) were identified through a review of literature. In this chapter we identified and explained 11 drivers of coordination in disaster relief supply chains (see Table 10.1). The 11 drivers were then validated by consulting ten experts, a group that consisted of academics who have published related research in reputable journals and disaster relief workers with more than ten years' experience on the field. Our expert pool did not suggest adding any new drivers or dropping any of the 11 drivers identified. Other than minor wording adjustments no other changes were made in the list of 11 drivers of coordination. Since ISM is an interactive process to explain the relationship among a set of variables, a questionnaire was developed to receive expert opinion on the relationships between the 11 nodes.

## Sampling Design and Data Collection

The drivers we identified in section "Drivers of Coordination" of this chapter may be interacting with each other and/or they may not necessarily share the same level of criticality/importance in practice. This means we need to understand the directional relationships between them. To accomplish this, a survey instrument was developed in which, for each possible connection between two drivers two questions were asked: for example "*Training leads to mutual learning*" and next "*Mutual learning leads to training.*" Each relationship between two drivers were measured on a five-point Likert scale with anchors ranging from strongly disagree (1) to strongly agree (5), to ensure high statistical variability among survey responses.

Prior to data collection, the survey instrument was pre-tested for content validity in two stages. In the first stage, three experienced researchers were asked to critique the questionnaire for ambiguity, clarity, and appropriateness of the drivers used. Based on the feedback received from these researchers minor modifications in language were made to enhance clarity of the questions. Following Dillman's (2007) total design test method the survey then was e-mailed with a cover letter to senior members from The Chartered Institute of Logistics and Transport (CILT) India, and the National Disaster Management Authority (NDMA) of India. From the membership bodies of CILT-India and NDMA, 62 respondents with more than ten years of experience in disaster relief operations were identified. Some of the respondents were also associated with Sphere India and other humanitarian agencies involved in preparing guidelines related to humanitarian operations. We do understand that the fact that all of our expert pool is based in India is a limitation of this study as this could bring a cultural bias to the findings. Our intention in this chapter however, is to demonstrate the use of TSIM methodology in theory building and hope that the reader will keep this limitation in mind while considering the results of the study.

We received 46 usable responses representing 74.19% response rate. We believe that we owe such a high response rate to the use of email for the survey and follow-up telephone calls to each respondent. Furthermore, it is important to mention that personal relationships with the bodies like CILT-INDIA and NDMA played a significant role in the data collection process.

# Analysis and Results

## The Interpretive Logic Matrix

Based on the 46 survey responses, we calculated a mean score for each direct relationship between two drivers. In our case, we have assumed that a driver does not impact the other if the mean score is less than three. A sample of the response we received from the 46 respondents is displayed in Appendix A. The bidirectional relationship ($i{\rightarrow}j$, $j{\rightarrow}i$) is represented with mean scores as ($\bar{w}_{ij}, \bar{w}_{ji}$). We captured the bidirectional relationship between two drivers using the letters $V$, $A$, $X$, and $O$.

The letter $V$ denotes a relationship in which node $i$ leads to node $j$ ($\bar{w}_{ij} > 3$) but the connection is not reciprocal (i.e., $j$ does not lead to $i$ or $\bar{w}_{ji} \leq 3$). Letter $A$ denotes a relationship in which driver node $j$ helps to achieve node $i$ ($\bar{w}_{ji} > 3$) but the reverse is not true (i.e., $i$ does not lead to $j$ or $\bar{w}_{ij} \leq 3$). Hence, $A$ is the opposite of $V$. The letter $X$ denotes a relationship in which both nodes impact each other (i.e., $i$ impacts $j$, but also $j$ impacts $i$ ($\bar{w}_{ij} > 3$ and $\bar{w}_{ji} > 3$)). Similarly, the letter $O$ represents a relationship in which neither node is associated with each other (i.e., there is no connection between $i$ and $j$ ($\bar{w}_{ij} \leq 3$ and $\bar{w}_{ji} \leq 3$)).

The SSIM matrix in Table 10.2 is further converted into a binary matrix, called the initial reachability matrix (see Table 10.3) by substituting $V$, $A$, $X$, and $O$ by binary values 1 or 0 such that $V$ generates 1 for ($i \rightarrow j$) and 0 for ($j \rightarrow i$); $A$ generates 0 for ($i \rightarrow j$) and 1 for ($j \rightarrow i$); $X$ generates 1 for ($i \rightarrow j$) and for ($j \rightarrow i$); and finally, $O$ generates 0 for ($i \rightarrow j$) and for ($j \rightarrow i$). From the initial reachability matrix in Table 10.3 the final reachability matrix in Table 10.4 is generated using the transitivity principle. For example, if node $i$ leads to node $j$, and node $j$ leads to node $k$, then the transitivity principle implies that node $i$ relates to node $k$. The final reachability matrix is constructed by pair-wise

**Table 10.2** Structural self-interaction matrix (SSIM)

|                             | 11 | 10 | 9 | 8 | 7 | 6 | 5 | 4 | 3 | 2 | 1 |
|-----------------------------|----|----|---|---|---|---|---|---|---|---|---|
| 1. Training                 | A  | A  | X | O | V | O | A | V | O | V |   |
| 2. Use of ICTs              | O  | X  | A | X | V | O | A | O | O |   |   |
| 3. Swift-Trust              | A  | O  | A | A | V | A | A | X |   |   |   |
| 4. Visibility               | O  | A  | A | A | V | O | A |   |   |   |   |
| 5. Contingency leadership   | X  | V  | V | V | O | V |   |   |   |   |   |
| 6. Information sharing       | A  | A  | O | A | V |   |   |   |   |   |   |
| 7. Commitment               | A  | A  | A | A |   |   |   |   |   |   |   |
| 8. PMS                      | A  | A  | A |   |   |   |   |   |   |   |   |
| 9. Regular meetings         | O  | A  |   |   |   |   |   |   |   |   |   |
| 10. Cultural cohesion       | A  |    |   |   |   |   |   |   |   |   |   |
| 11. Mutual learning         |    |    |   |   |   |   |   |   |   |   |   |

**Table 10.3** Initial reachability matrix

|                             | 1 | 2 | 3 | 4 | 5 | 6 | 7 | 8 | 9 | 10 | 11 |
|-----------------------------|---|---|---|---|---|---|---|---|---|----|----|
| 1. Training                 | 1 | 1 | 0 | 1 | 0 | 0 | 1 | 0 | 1 | 0  | 0  |
| 2. Use of ICTs              | 0 | 1 | 0 | 0 | 0 | 0 | 1 | 1 | 0 | 1  | 0  |
| 3. Swift-Trust              | 0 | 0 | 1 | 1 | 0 | 0 | 1 | 0 | 0 | 0  | 0  |
| 4. Visibility               | 0 | 0 | 1 | 1 | 0 | 0 | 1 | 0 | 0 | 0  | 0  |
| 5. Contingency leadership   | 1 | 1 | 1 | 1 | 1 | 1 | 0 | 1 | 1 | 1  | 1  |
| 6. Information sharing       | 0 | 0 | 1 | 0 | 0 | 1 | 1 | 0 | 0 | 0  | 0  |
| 7. Commitment               | 0 | 0 | 0 | 0 | 0 | 0 | 1 | 0 | 0 | 0  | 0  |
| 8. PMS                      | 0 | 1 | 1 | 1 | 0 | 1 | 1 | 1 | 0 | 0  | 0  |
| 9. Regular meetings         | 1 | 1 | 1 | 1 | 0 | 0 | 1 | 1 | 1 | 0  | 0  |
| 10. Cultural cohesion       | 1 | 1 | 0 | 1 | 0 | 1 | 1 | 1 | 1 | 1  | 0  |
| 11. Mutual learning         | 1 | 0 | 1 | 0 | 1 | 1 | 1 | 1 | 0 | 1  | 1  |

comparisons and by inference and presented in Table 10.4, where the numbers with an asterisk denote transitivity.

From the final reachability matrix in Table 10.4 we derive the reachability and antecedent sets (Warfield 1973). The reachability set consists of the node itself and the other nodes that it leads to. The antecedent set on the other hand, consists of the node itself and the other nodes that lead into it. For each node, we then find the intersection of these two sets. The nodes for which the reachability and the interaction sets are identical occupy the top level in the hierarchy. The top-level node in the hierarchy would not lead into any other node. Once the top-level nodes have been identified, they are removed from both sets and the process continues iteratively (see Appendix B). Levels for the 11 drivers are provided in Table 10.5. These levels help in building the directional graph in Fig. 10.1 and the final model.

**Table 10.4** Final reachability matrix

| | 1 | 2 | 3 | 4 | 5 | 6 | 7 | 8 | 9 | 10 | 11 | Driving power |
|---|---|---|---|---|---|---|---|---|---|---|---|---|
| 1. Training | 1 | 1 | 1* | 1 | 0 | 1* | 1 | 1* | 1 | 1* | 0 | 9 |
| 2. Use of ICTs | 1* | 1 | 1* | 1* | 0 | 1* | 1 | 1 | 1* | 1 | 0 | 9 |
| 3. Swift-Trust | 0 | 0 | 1 | 1 | 0 | 0 | 1 | 0 | 0 | 0 | 0 | 3 |
| 4. Visibility | 0 | 0 | 1 | 1 | 0 | 0 | 1 | 0 | 0 | 0 | 0 | 3 |
| 5. Contingency leadership | 1 | 1 | 1 | 1 | 1 | 1 | 1* | 1 | 1 | 1 | 1 | 11 |
| 6. Information sharing | 0 | 0 | 1 | 1* | 0 | 1 | 1 | 0 | 0 | 0 | 0 | 4 |
| 7. Commitment | 0 | 0 | 0 | 0 | 0 | 0 | 1 | 0 | 0 | 0 | 0 | 1 |
| 8. PMS | 1* | 1 | 1 | 1 | 0 | 1 | 1 | 1 | 1* | 1* | 0 | 9 |
| 9. Regular meetings | 1 | 1 | 1 | 1 | 0 | 1* | 1 | 1 | 1 | 1* | 0 | 9 |
| 10. Cultural cohesion | 1 | 1 | 1* | 1 | 0 | 1 | 1 | 1 | 1 | 1 | 0 | 9 |
| 11. Mutual learning | 1 | 1* | 1 | 1* | 1 | 1 | 1 | 1 | 1* | 1 | 1 | 11 |
| Dependence power | 7 | 7 | 10 | 10 | 2 | 8 | 11 | 7 | 7 | 7 | 2 | |

*Indicates transitivity

**Table 10.5** Level partition of reachability matrix

| Drivers of commitment | Level |
|---|---|
| Commitment | One |
| Swift-Trust | Two |
| Visibility | Two |
| Information sharing | Three |
| Use of ICTs | Three |
| Training | Three |
| PMS | Four |
| Regular meetings | Four |
| Cultural cohesion | Four |
| Contingency leadership | Five |
| Mutual learning | Five |

## Structural Model

The hierarchical levels of the drivers for coordination are used to create the structural model presented in Fig. 10.1. The structural model displays the drivers in seven levels (hierarchical model). The level 1 driver (commitment) is dependent on other drivers. The lowest level (seventh-level) drivers, contingency leadership and mutual learning represent those drivers

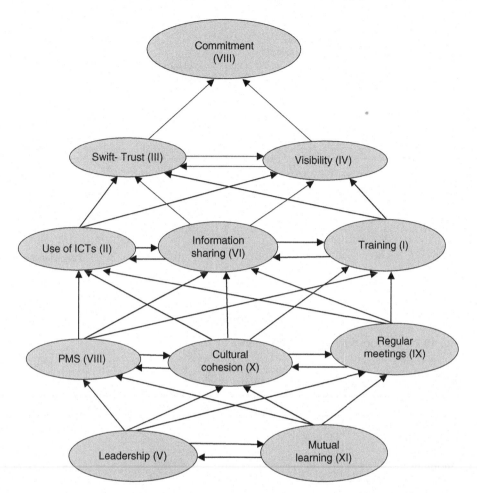

**Fig. 10.1**   Structural model

which lead to commitment through mediating drivers. The links on the model capture experts' opinions and reflect the binary interactions presented in Table 10.4.

Next, we further classify the drivers into four groups as shown in Fig. 10.2 based on their driving power and dependence (which were calculated in Table 10.4) using MICMAC (Cross Impact Multiplication Matrix) analysis. To accomplish this, first position coordinate's matrix is utilized as shown in Table 10.6, and then the position coordinates are displayed in the form of scatter plot as shown in Fig. 10.2. The scatter plot obtained is then divided into four quadrants. Drivers in the first quadrant are *autonomous drivers* because they are in a way independent of other drivers. Autonomous drivers are weak

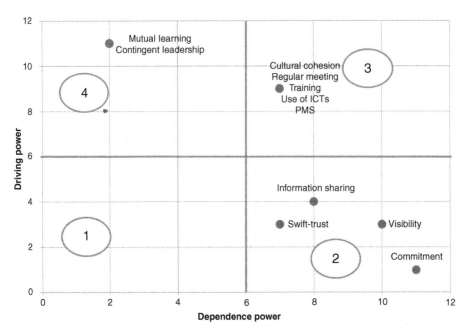

**Fig. 10.2** Driving power and dependence

**Table 10.6** Position coordinates of enablers

| Drivers | Dependence power (X) | Driving power (Y) |
|---|---|---|
| Training | 7 | 9 |
| Use of ICTs | 7 | 9 |
| Swift-trust | 7 | 3 |
| Visibility | 10 | 3 |
| Contingent leadership | 2 | 11 |
| Information sharing | 8 | 4 |
| Commitment | 11 | 1 |
| PMS | 7 | 9 |
| Regular meetings | 7 | 9 |
| Cultural cohesion | 7 | 9 |
| Mutual learning | 2 | 11 |

drivers and weak dependents. They do not have much influence on the system. The absence of autonomous drivers in the undertaken study indicates that all the considered drivers play a significant role in the coordination of HRSC.

Second quadrant drivers are known as *dependent drivers* because they have high dependence power but poor driving power. In our case, we observe four drivers in this cluster: swift trust, information sharing, visibility, and commitment. The drivers in the third quadrant are *linkage drivers*. In our case we have found five drivers which are linkage drivers. These drivers are training, use of ICTs, PMS, regular meetings, and cultural cohesion. These drivers tend to act as mediators or may be termed as interacting variables. Finally, the fourth quadrant contains *driving drivers*. The drivers in this cluster have high driving power and weak dependence power. We have found two drivers in this cluster. These drivers are contingent leadership and mutual learning. Hence we can conclude that contingent leadership and mutual learning leads to swift trust, information sharing, visibility, and commitment via training, use of ICTs, PMS, regular meetings, and cultural cohesion.

The ISM model in Fig. 10.1 is an attempt to extend the literature on coordination in HRSC management. However, there are some shortcomings of ISM models that should be mentioned (Sushil 2012). First, ISM models fail to reflect on the nature of the links. Moreover, these models lack complete transparency (Sushil 2012; Dubey et al. 2015a). These limitations are remedied by developing a TISM model (see Fig. 10.3) following the steps suggested by Sushil (2012):

Step 1: Identify drivers using extensive literature review and further validate those drivers consulting experts;

Step 2: Ask a separate group of experts to define the contextual relationships among drivers;

Step 3: Interpret pairwise comparisons. There will be in all [n(n-1)/2] paired comparisons. To further upgrade to TISM, the researcher needs to explain the interpretive logic for the dominance of drivers (Dubey et al. 2015a);

Step 4: Develop an interpretive logic knowledge base;

Step 5: Derive final reachability matrix from the interpretive logic knowledge base;

Step 6: Draw a directed graph from conical matrix;

Step 7: The TISM model is developed in which links are interpreted;

Step 8: We have developed interpretive matrix on the basis of links in TISM Model (see Table 10.7)

In Table 10.7 we developed an interpretive matrix which is the source for the commentary on each of the links in Figure 10.3. For this we consulted two of our experts. Therefore, this interpretation is purely based on the opinion of the experts and requires further validation using a survey with a large sample size. We note that this is a limitation of the interpretive logic. However, as we have argued in the initial section of this chapter the TISM method is useful in developing hypotheses in the absence of sufficient literature. Next we discuss our results and the limitations of this methodology.

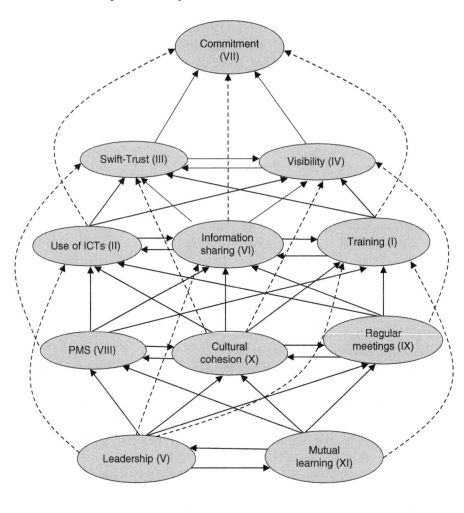

– – – – – – – ▶  Represents transitive link

**Fig. 10.3**  TSIM-based model

## Discussion

This study demonstrates the implementation of a little known qualitative method which lends itself well to theory building. Specifically, using TISM we attempted to generate a theoretical model which explains how drivers of coordination in humanitarian relief supply chains interact with each other. The resulting model indicates that the most important driver for coordination is commitment by the humanitarian actors. The other ten drivers

**Table 10.7** Interpretive matrix

| | TG | ICT | Swift trust | Visibility | Leadership | Information sharing | Commitment | PMS | RM | CC | ML |
|---|---|---|---|---|---|---|---|---|---|---|---|
| Training(TG) | | Reduces behavioral uncertainty | Reduces uncertainty | Improves exchange of information among actors. | | Reduces behavioral uncertainty and increases mutual understanding. | | | | | |
| Use of ICTs | | | Improves quick exchange of quality information among actors. | With the help of ICTs all information related to physical stock of relief items and disaster relief efforts are clear. | | With the help of ICTs, the right information related to right goods and right place improves the disaster relief efforts. | | | | | |
| Swift-Trust | | | | Swift-trust helps to improve quality information exchange which further improves visibility in disaster relief chain. | | Swift-trust helps to improve engagement of all the humanitarian actors which increases the commitment among all the actors. The commitment is an important ingredient for building coordination among players in disaster relief chain. | | | | | |
| Visibility | | | Visibility reduces behavioral uncertainty which further improves swift-trust among actors in the network. | | | Visibility is key for building commitment. Availability of right information related to relief items inventory and KPIs of each actor in the disaster relief network increases dependence on each other. | | | | | |
| Contingency Leadership | | | | | | Belief and participation of senior members in performance evaluation is important for PMS culture. | | | Facilitate regular interaction. | Leadership participative styles helps in building humanitarian culture. | |
| Information sharing | Knowledge | Supporting tool | Reduces uncertainty | Right information related to inventory, current action, future strategies | | | | | | | |
| Commitment | | | | | | This is the outcome of all remaining ten drivers. This is the most important antecedent of coordination among actors in disaster relief chain. | | | | | |
| PMS | It helps to control the deviation. | The feedback is further utilized to upgrade existing ICTs. | | | | The PMS encourages actors to exchange right information in right time to reduce deviation. | Promote performance measures. | | | It builds right attitude. | |
| Regular meetings(RM) | Needs identification | Resource selection strategies which include ICTS | | | | Promote information exchange through brainstorming. | Promote equality and respect for each other. | | | Brainstorming culture. | |
| Cultural cohesion (CC) | Helps in learning. | Belief in usage of ICTs | | | | Belief in right information exchange | | | | | |
| Mutual learning (ML) | Helps to adapt to the situation | | | | | Fixes the KPI and measures | | | It encourages participation | Build attitude | |

identified in our literature review are all antecedents to commitment. Commitment of an organization to coordination is affected by their trust (specifically swift-trust) to others and the humanitarian system as well as visibility. Trust and visibility both are greatly influenced by the use of ICTs, quality information sharing and training. Information to be shared is organization-specific since situational data usually is distributed to all humanitarian actors involved in a relief operation by cluster leads, host governments, and humanitarian data repositories such as ReliefWeb. Organization-specific data comes from the organization's performance management system (assuming the organization has a PMS). For sharing to happen humanitarian organizations need to invest in information and communications technologies. Systems (whether ICTs or PMS) need to be tested routinely during training exercises and regular meetings. Organizations should be taking part in these exercises and meetings because they all share common values of humanitarianism. Finally, our model indicates that organizational leadership and mutual learning are two factors that influence professional culture, training, and attendance to meetings. Mutual learning through lessons learned reports and shared best practices should augment the professional culture among humanitarian actors.

## Theoretical Contributions

Coordination among humanitarian actors has been of interest to academic scholars and practitioners even before the 2005 Humanitarian Response Review identified the lack of coordination in humanitarian response as a major barrier to effectiveness. What is less understood is what makes coordination go and how the key drivers of coordination interact with each other. These two key aspects, that is, identification of key drivers and their relationships in a conceptual model, signify our contribution to the humanitarian relief supply chain management literature. Our work in this chapter is built on the findings of prior studies, and our model extends this literature.

Another contribution of this chapter is the use of an alternative method in the context of humanitarian operations. TISM is a method that combines qualitative and quantitative approaches to aid with theory development. The constructs in the resulting conceptual model are found in the literature but TISM builds the links between the constructs through expert opinion. Therefore, the conceptual model presented in this chapter reflects the opinions and experiences of humanitarian practitioners, thus enhancing its applicability and relevance.

## Managerial Implications

The conceptual model of coordination proposed in this chapter should provide some guidance to disaster relief agencies and other humanitarian actors. First of all, the model suggests that commitment is the critical element for coordination and lays the foundation for organizations interested in coordinating with their relief chain partners. In addition, the model presented in this chapter identifies the mediating factors that would have an influence on organizational commitment at different levels. It gives clues on how cultural cohesion, training, having regular meetings, as well as resources such as ICTs and PMS create a platform for information sharing, and shows that information sharing helps build swift-trust among actors and creates visibility in the disaster relief supply chain. And finally, it shows that leadership and mutual learning form the basis of establishing coordination. The hierarchical structure with linkages should help disaster relief agencies understand the inner-workings of coordination.

## Further Research Directions

Clearly, the conceptual model presented in this chapter needs to be tested and validated using large data set. There is no doubt that some of the linkages or even drivers we presented in this chapter may not have a significant role (at least statistically) in coordination among humanitarian actors. In future studies the present model can be tested using confirmatory factor analysis (CFA) and the research hypotheses can further be examined using covariance based structural equation modeling (SEM).

In our current study we have identified our drivers on the basis of resource based view of the organization and relationship theories. However, if we use institutional, information diffusion, actors network or any other organizational theories then our list of drivers may increase significantly. This further provides an opportunity to extend the current study using other existing organizational theories. Future studies may identify additional drivers or can reduce the number of drivers using exploratory factor analysis (EFA). Hence the current framework can utilize the combination of TISM-EFA and TISM-CFA techniques to strengthen the argument presented in this chapter.

There are studies that have investigated the impact of one or more of the drivers we listed here on coordination but the mediating role of some these drivers are yet to be tested. For example, Altay and Pal (2014) postulate that information sharing improves coordination, but they did not consider the mediating effect of visibility and commitment in their study. Therefore, the model presented in this chapter not only fills a gap in the coordination literature, but also provides a spring board for future research.

## Conclusions

Our interest in developing a framework for explaining coordination among humanitarian actors was triggered by two facts: first, coordination in HRSCs is highly complex due to the sheer number and diversity of organizations involved in hastily formed supply chains. Despite growing academic interest in coordination in humanitarian operations, there is still a need for a theoretical framework that can lay the foundation for future research on coordination. Secondly, existing literature on coordination has failed to embrace diverse research methods which can help to fill gaps and lead to new research questions.

There is a clear need for theory focused research in the field of humanitarian relief supply chain management. Tabaklar et al. (2015) argue that to advance existing humanitarian operations management literature theories from other disciplines need to be borrowed. In this chapter we argue that although borrowing theories from other disciplines may help to advance the field such development would be incremental and is bound to get stuck at a point since humanitarian operations have fundamental differences than commercial operations.

Eisenhardt (1989) argues that in an emerging field alternative methods may help generate theories which can then be tested using cross-sectional or longitudinal data. In this chapter, using a graph-theory-based qualitative technique we developed a conceptual model for coordination among humanitarian organizations. Our findings indicate that commitment is the key driver that leads to coordination. The theoretical framework also shows that trust and visibility in the supply chain can be built through information sharing, which is enabled by information and communications technologies and PMSs. We also present that leadership and mutual learning together provide the basis for building commitment among humanitarian actors.

The HRSC field would benefit tremendously from more theory building. Our study is exploratory in its nature since the relationships between the drivers are identified by a small group of field experts. Thus, the next step should be to develop measurement scales for these relationships and conduct a large scale study to check their strength and validity.

**Acknowledgments** The authors are extremely grateful to the editors and two anonymous reviewers for their excellent inputs during review stage and in final production phase.

# Appendix A

| Respondents | 1→11 | 1→10 | 1→9 | 1→8 | 1→7 | 1→6 | 1→5 | 1→4 | 1→3 | 1→2 |
|---|---|---|---|---|---|---|---|---|---|---|
| 1 | 1 | 4 | 2 | 1 | 4 | 3 | 1 | 3 | 2 | 3 |
| 2 | 2 | 4 | 1 | 1 | 5 | 2 | 2 | 2 | 3 | 2 |
| 3 | 2 | 2 | 5 | 1 | 5 | 1 | 2 | 3 | 2 | 3 |
| 4 | 2 | 2 | 5 | 1 | 5 | 3 | 2 | 3 | 3 | 3 |
| 5 | 1 | 3 | 1 | 1 | 3 | 3 | 1 | 1 | 1 | 1 |
| 6 | 3 | 3 | 4 | 3 | 4 | 3 | 3 | 4 | 1 | 4 |
| 7 | 1 | 1 | 3 | 1 | 4 | 1 | 1 | 4 | 1 | 4 |
| 8 | 2 | 2 | 4 | 2 | 4 | 2 | 2 | 5 | 2 | 5 |
| 9 | 4 | 4 | 5 | 3 | 5 | 3 | 4 | 4 | 1 | 4 |
| 10 | 1 | 1 | 5 | 1 | 5 | 1 | 1 | 5 | 1 | 5 |
| 11 | 2 | 2 | 5 | 2 | 4 | 2 | 2 | 5 | 2 | 5 |
| 12 | 1 | 1 | 5 | 1 | 4 | 1 | 1 | 4 | 1 | 4 |
| 13 | 2 | 1 | 5 | 2 | 4 | 1 | 2 | 4 | 2 | 4 |
| 14 | 1 | 1 | 1 | 1 | 5 | 1 | 1 | 5 | 1 | 5 |
| 15 | 2 | 1 | 4 | 1 | 5 | 1 | 2 | 5 | 2 | 5 |
| 16 | 1 | 1 | 4 | 1 | 4 | 1 | 1 | 4 | 1 | 4 |
| 17 | 2 | 2 | 4 | 2 | 4 | 1 | 2 | 4 | 2 | 4 |
| 18 | 1 | 1 | 5 | 1 | 5 | 1 | 1 | 5 | 1 | 5 |
| 19 | 1 | 1 | 5 | 1 | 5 | 1 | 1 | 5 | 1 | 5 |
| 20 | 2 | 2 | 5 | 2 | 5 | 2 | 2 | 5 | 2 | 5 |
| 21 | 1 | 1 | 5 | 1 | 5 | 1 | 1 | 5 | 1 | 5 |
| 22 | 1 | 1 | 5 | 1 | 4 | 1 | 1 | 5 | 1 | 5 |
| 23 | 1 | 1 | 4 | 1 | 4 | 1 | 1 | 4 | 1 | 4 |
| 24 | 2 | 2 | 4 | 2 | 5 | 2 | 2 | 4 | 2 | 4 |
| 25 | 2 | 2 | 5 | 2 | 5 | 2 | 2 | 5 | 2 | 5 |
| 26 | 2 | 2 | 5 | 2 | 5 | 2 | 2 | 5 | 2 | 5 |
| 27 | 1 | 1 | 5 | 1 | 5 | 1 | 1 | 5 | 1 | 5 |
| 28 | 3 | 3 | 5 | 3 | 5 | 3 | 3 | 5 | 3 | 5 |
| 29 | 3 | 3 | 5 | 3 | 5 | 3 | 3 | 5 | 3 | 5 |
| 30 | 1 | 1 | 5 | 1 | 5 | 1 | 1 | 5 | 1 | 5 |
| 31 | 2 | 2 | 3 | 2 | 4 | 2 | 2 | 3 | 2 | 3 |
| 32 | 1 | 1 | 4 | 1 | 4 | 1 | 1 | 4 | 1 | 4 |
| 33 | 2 | 2 | 5 | 2 | 5 | 2 | 2 | 5 | 2 | 5 |
| 34 | 2 | 2 | 5 | 2 | 5 | 2 | 2 | 5 | 2 | 5 |
| 35 | 2 | 3 | 5 | 2 | 5 | 3 | 2 | 5 | 2 | 5 |
| 36 | 1 | 2 | 4 | 1 | 4 | 2 | 1 | 4 | 1 | 4 |
| 37 | 1 | 4 | 5 | 1 | 5 | 3 | 1 | 5 | 1 | 5 |
| 38 | 1 | 1 | 5 | 1 | 5 | 1 | 1 | 5 | 1 | 5 |

(continued)

(continued)

| Respondents | 1→11 | 1→10 | 1→9 | 1→8 | 1→7 | 1→6 | 1→5 | 1→4 | 1→3 | 1→2 |
|---|---|---|---|---|---|---|---|---|---|---|
| 39 | 2 | 3 | 5 | 2 | 4 | 3 | 2 | 5 | 1 | 5 |
| 40 | 2 | 2 | 5 | 2 | 3 | 1 | 2 | 5 | 2 | 5 |
| 41 | 3 | 1 | 5 | 3 | 3 | 1 | 3 | 5 | 4 | 5 |
| 42 | 3 | 1 | 5 | 3 | 4 | 1 | 3 | 5 | 1 | 5 |
| 43 | 2 | 1 | 3 | 1 | 5 | 1 | 2 | 4 | 2 | 4 |
| 44 | 2 | 1 | 3 | 1 | 5 | 3 | 2 | 4 | 2 | 4 |
| 45 | 1 | 1 | 5 | 1 | 2 | 1 | 1 | 5 | 1 | 5 |
| 46 | 2 | 3 | 5 | 3 | 4 | 2 | 2 | 3 | 1 | 3 |
|  | 1.74 | 1.87 | 4.30 | 1.61 | 4.43 | 1.74 | 1.74 | 4.35 | 1.63 | 4.35 |
| **Respondents** | 11→1 | 10→1 | 9→1 | 8→1 | 7→1 | 6→1 | 5→1 | 4→1 | 3→1 | 2→1 |
| 1 | 5 | 3 | 4 | 3 | 1 | 4 | 5 | 3 | 2 | 1 |
| 2 | 5 | 2 | 4 | 1 | 3 | 4 | 5 | 1 | 2 | 1 |
| 3 | 4 | 3 | 4 | 1 | 1 | 2 | 3 | 2 | 2 | 1 |
| 4 | 3 | 3 | 4 | 4 | 3 | 2 | 4 | 1 | 2 | 1 |
| 5 | 2 | 1 | 3 | 1 | 2 | 3 | 4 | 3 | 3 | 2 |
| 6 | 4 | 4 | 4 | 1 | 2 | 3 | 4 | 3 | 3 | 3 |
| 7 | 5 | 4 | 4 | 1 | 1 | 1 | 4 | 1 | 1 | 1 |
| 8 | 5 | 5 | 4 | 2 | 1 | 2 | 4 | 2 | 2 | 2 |
| 9 | 5 | 4 | 4 | 3 | 3 | 4 | 4 | 4 | 4 | 4 |
| 10 | 5 | 5 | 5 | 1 | 1 | 1 | 5 | 1 | 1 | 1 |
| 11 | 5 | 5 | 4 | 2 | 2 | 2 | 5 | 2 | 2 | 2 |
| 12 | 4 | 4 | 4 | 1 | 1 | 1 | 4 | 1 | 1 | 1 |
| 13 | 4 | 4 | 4 | 2 | 1 | 1 | 4 | 2 | 2 | 2 |
| 14 | 5 | 5 | 5 | 1 | 1 | 1 | 5 | 1 | 1 | 1 |
| 15 | 5 | 5 | 5 | 2 | 1 | 1 | 5 | 2 | 2 | 2 |
| 16 | 4 | 4 | 4 | 1 | 1 | 1 | 4 | 1 | 1 | 1 |
| 17 | 4 | 4 | 4 | 2 | 2 | 2 | 4 | 2 | 2 | 2 |
| 18 | 5 | 5 | 5 | 1 | 1 | 1 | 5 | 1 | 1 | 1 |
| 19 | 5 | 5 | 5 | 1 | 1 | 1 | 5 | 1 | 1 | 1 |
| 20 | 5 | 5 | 5 | 2 | 2 | 2 | 5 | 2 | 2 | 2 |
| 21 | 5 | 5 | 5 | 1 | 1 | 1 | 5 | 1 | 1 | 1 |
| 22 | 4 | 5 | 4 | 1 | 1 | 1 | 4 | 1 | 1 | 1 |
| 23 | 4 | 4 | 4 | 1 | 1 | 1 | 4 | 1 | 1 | 1 |
| 24 | 5 | 4 | 5 | 2 | 2 | 2 | 5 | 2 | 2 | 2 |
| 25 | 5 | 5 | 5 | 2 | 2 | 2 | 5 | 2 | 2 | 2 |
| 26 | 5 | 5 | 5 | 2 | 2 | 2 | 5 | 2 | 2 | 2 |
| 27 | 5 | 5 | 5 | 1 | 1 | 1 | 5 | 1 | 1 | 1 |
| 28 | 5 | 5 | 5 | 3 | 3 | 3 | 5 | 3 | 3 | 3 |
| 29 | 5 | 5 | 5 | 3 | 3 | 3 | 5 | 3 | 3 | 3 |
| 30 | 5 | 5 | 5 | 1 | 1 | 1 | 5 | 1 | 1 | 1 |
| 31 | 4 | 3 | 4 | 2 | 2 | 2 | 4 | 2 | 2 | 2 |
| 32 | 4 | 4 | 4 | 1 | 1 | 1 | 4 | 1 | 1 | 1 |
| 33 | 5 | 5 | 5 | 2 | 2 | 2 | 5 | 2 | 2 | 2 |
| 34 | 5 | 5 | 5 | 2 | 2 | 2 | 5 | 2 | 2 | 2 |
| 35 | 5 | 5 | 5 | 2 | 3 | 3 | 5 | 2 | 2 | 2 |

(continued)

(continued)

| Respondents | 1→11 | 1→10 | 1→9 | 1→8 | 1→7 | 1→6 | 1→5 | 1→4 | 1→3 | 1→2 |
|---|---|---|---|---|---|---|---|---|---|---|
| 36 | 4 | 4 | 4 | 1 | 2 | 2 | 4 | 1 | 1 | 1 |
| 37 | 5 | 5 | 5 | 1 | 4 | 4 | 5 | 1 | 1 | 1 |
| 38 | 5 | 5 | 5 | 1 | 1 | 1 | 5 | 1 | 1 | 1 |
| 39 | 4 | 5 | 4 | 2 | 3 | 3 | 4 | 2 | 2 | 2 |
| 40 | 5 | 5 | 3 | 2 | 2 | 2 | 3 | 2 | 2 | 2 |
| 41 | 5 | 5 | 3 | 1 | 1 | 1 | 5 | 2 | 2 | 4 |
| 42 | 4 | 5 | 4 | 1 | 1 | 1 | 5 | 2 | 3 | 3 |
| 43 | 5 | 4 | 5 | 2 | 3 | 1 | 5 | 1 | 2 | 2 |
| 44 | 5 | 4 | 5 | 2 | 1 | 1 | 3 | 2 | 3 | 2 |
| 45 | 5 | 5 | 2 | 1 | 2 | 1 | 4 | 3 | 1 | 1 |
| 46 | 4 | 3 | 4 | 3 | 2 | 3 | 1 | 1 | 3 | 1 |
|  | 4.59 | 4.35 | 4.35 | 1.65 | 1.74 | 1.87 | 4.41 | 1.74 | 1.83 | 1.70 |

# Appendix B

Iteration Table 10.1

| Drivers | Reachability set (RS) | Antecedent set (AS) | RS∩AS | Level (RS∩AS=RS) |
|---|---|---|---|---|
| Training | 1,2,3,4,6,7,8,9,10 | 1,2,5,8,9,10,11 | 1,2,8,9,10 | |
| Use of ICTs | 1,2,3,4,6,7,8,9,10 | 1,2,5,8,9,10,11 | 1,2,8,9,10 | |
| Swift-Trust | 3,4,7 | 1,2,3,4,5,6,8,9,10,11 | 3,4 | |
| Visibility | 3,4,7 | 1,2,3,4,5,6,8,9,10,11 | 3,4 | |
| Leadership | 1,2,3,4,5,6,7,8,9,10,11 | 5,11 | 5,11 | |
| Information sharing | 3,4,6,7 | 1,2,5,6,8,9,10,11 | 6 | |
| Commitment | 7 | 1,2,3,4,5,6,7,89,10,11 | 7 | I |
| PMS | 1,2,3,4,6,7,8,9,10 | 1,2,5,8,9,10,11 | 1,2,8,9,10 | |
| Regular meetings | 1,2,3,4,6,7,8,9,10 | 1,2,5,8,9,10,11 | 1,2,8,9,10 | |
| Cultural cohesion | 1,2,3,4,6,7,8,9,10 | 1,2,5,8,9,10,11 | 1,2,8,9,10 | |
| Mutual learning | 1,2,3,4,5,6,7,8,9,10,11 | 5,11 | 5,11 | |

Iteration Table 10.2

| Drivers | Reachability set (RS) | Antecedent set (AS) | RS∩AS | Level (RS∩AS=RS) |
|---|---|---|---|---|
| Training | 1,2,3,4,6,8,9,10 | 1,2,5,8,9,10,11 | 1,2,8,9,10 | |
| Use of ICTs | 1,2,3,4,6,8,9,10 | 1,2,5,8,9,10,11 | 1,2,8,9,10 | |
| Swift-Trust | 3,4 | 1,2,3,4,5,6,8,9,10,11 | 3,4 | II |

(continued)

(continued)

| Drivers | Reachability set (RS) | Antecedent set (AS) | RS∩AS | Level (RS∩AS=RS) |
|---|---|---|---|---|
| Visibility | 3,4 | 1,2,3,4,5,6,8,9,10,11 | 3,4 | II |
| Leadership | 1,2,3,4,5,6,8,9,10,11 | 5,11 | 5,11 | |
| Information sharing | 3,4,6 | 1,2,5,6,8,9,10,11 | 6 | |
| PMS | 1,2,3,4,6,8,9,10 | 1,2,5,8,9,10,11 | 1,2,8,9,10 | |
| Regular meetings | 1,2,3,4,6,8,9,10 | 1,2,5,8,9,10,11 | 1,2,8,9,10 | |
| Cultural cohesion | 1,2,3,4,6,8,9,10 | 1,2,5,8,9,10,11 | 1,2,8,9,10 | |
| Mutual learning | 1,2,3,4,5,6,8,9,10,11 | 5,11 | 5,11 | |

Iteration Table 10.3

| Drivers | Reachability set (RS) | Antecedent set (AS) | RS∩AS | Level (RS∩AS=RS) |
|---|---|---|---|---|
| Training | 1,2,6,8,9,10 | 1,2,5,8,9,10,11 | 1,2,8,9,10 | III |
| Use of ICTs | 1,2,6,8,9,10 | 1,2,5,8,9,10,11 | 1,2,8,9,10 | III |
| Leadership | 1,2,5,6,8,9,10,11 | 5,11 | 5,11 | |
| Information sharing | 6 | 1,2,5,6,8,9,10,11 | 6 | III |
| PMS | 1,2,6,8,9,10 | 1,2,5,8,9,10,11 | 1,2,8,9,10 | |
| Regular meetings | 1,2,6,8,9,10 | 1,2,5,8,9,10,11 | 1,2,8,9,10 | |
| Cultural cohesion | 1,2,6,8,9,10 | 1,2,5,8,9,10,11 | 1,2,8,9,10 | |
| Mutual learning | 1,2,5,6,8,9,10,11 | 5,11 | 5,11 | |

Iteration Table 10.4

| Drivers | Reachability set (RS) | Antecedent set (AS) | RS∩AS | Level (RS∩AS=RS) |
|---|---|---|---|---|
| Leadership | 5,8,9,10,11 | 5,11 | 5,11 | |
| PMS | 8,9,10 | 5,8,9,10,11 | 8,9,10 | IV |
| Regular meetings | 8,9,10 | 5,8,9,10,11 | 8,9,10 | IV |
| Cultural cohesion | 8,9,10 | 5,8,9,10,11 | 8,9,10 | IV |
| Mutual learning | 5,8,9,10,11 | 5,11 | 5,11 | |

Iteration Table 10.5

| Drivers | Reachability set (RS) | Antecedent set (AS) | RS∩AS | Level (RS∩AS=RS) |
|---|---|---|---|---|
| Leadership | 5,11 | 5,11 | 5,11 | V |
| Mutual learning | 5,11 | 5,11 | 5,11 | V |

# References

Akhtar, P., Marr, N. E., & Garnevska, E. V. (2012). Coordination in humanitarian relief chains: Chain coordinators. *Journal of Humanitarian Logistics and Supply Chain Management, 2*(1), 85–103.

Altay, N., & Pal, R. (2014). Information diffusion among agents: Implications for humanitarian operations. *Production and Operations Management, 23*(6), 1015–1027.

Asplund, M., Nadjm-Tehrani, S., & Sigholm, J. (2008). Emerging information infrastructures: Cooperation in disasters. In *Critical information infrastructure security* (pp. 258–270). Berlin, Heidelberg: Springer.

Balcik, B., Beamon, B. M., Krejci, C. C., Muramatsu, K. M., & Ramirez, M. (2010). Coordination in humanitarian relief chains: Practices, challenges and opportunities. *International Journal of Production Economics, 126*(1), 22–34.

Barney, J. (1991). Firm resources and sustained competitive advantage. *Journal of Management, 17*(1), 99–120.

Barratt, M., & Oke, A. (2007). Antecedents of supply chain visibility in retail supply chains: A resource-based theory perspective. *Journal of Operations Management, 25*(6), 1217–1233.

Beamon, B. M., & Balcik, B. (2008). Performance measurement in humanitarian relief chains. *International Journal of Public Sector Management, 21* (1), 4–25.

Borys, B., & Jemison, D.B. (1989). Hybrid arrangements as strategic alliances: Theoretical issues in organizational combinations. *Academy of Management Review, 14*(2), 234–249.

Brandon-Jones, E., Squire, B., Autry, C. W., & Petersen, K. J. (2014). A contingent resource-based perspective of supply chain resilience and robustness. *Journal of Supply Chain Management, 50*(3), 55–73.

Cao, M., & Zhang, Q. (2011). Supply chain collaboration: Impact on collaborative advantage and firm performance. *Journal of Operations Management, 29*(3), 163–180.

Chermack, T. J. (2007). Disciplined imagination: Building scenarios and building theories. *Futures, 39*(1), 1–15.

Christopher, M., & Lee, H. (2004). Mitigating supply chain risk through improved confidence. *International Journal of Physical Distribution & Logistics Management, 34*(5), 388–396.

Coughlan, P., & Coghlan, D. (2002). Action research for operations management. *International Journal of Operations & Production Management, 22*(2), 220–240.

Dillman, D. A. (2007). *Mail and internet surveys: The tailored design — 2007 update.* Hoboken: John Wiley.

Dubey, R., Gunasekaran, A., Sushil, & Singh, T. (2015a). Building theory of sustainable manufacturing using total interpretive structural modelling. *International Journal of Systems Science: Operations & Logistics, 2*(4), 231–247.

Dubey, R., Singh, T., & Gupta, O. K. (2015b). Impact of agility, adaptability and alignment on humanitarian logistics performance: Mediating effect of leadership. *Global Business Review, 16*(5), 812–831.

Egan, T. M. (2002). Grounded theory research and theory building. *Advances in Developing Human Resources, 4*(3), 277–295.

Eisenhardt, K. M. (1989). Building theories from case study research. *Academy of Management Review, 14*(4), 532–550.

Gillmann, N. (2009). Interagency coordination during disaster strategic choices for the UN. NGOs, and other Humanitarian Actors in the Field. Baden-Baden: Nomos.

Hicks, E. K., & Pappas, G. (2006). Coordinating disaster relief after the South Asia earthquake. *Society, 43*(5), 42–50.

Holguín-Veras, J., Jaller, M., Van Wassenhove, L. N., Pérez, N., & Wachtendorf, T. (2012). On the unique features of post-disaster humanitarian logistics. *Journal of Operations Management, 30*(7), 494–506.

Jahre, M., Jensen, L. M., & Listou, T. (2009). Theory development in humanitarian logistics: A framework and three cases. *Management Research News, 32*(11), 1008–1023.

Jain, V., & Raj, T. (2015). Modeling and analysis of FMS flexibility factors by TISM and fuzzy MICMAC. *International Journal of System Assurance Engineering and Management, 6*(3), 350–371.

Kabra, G., & Ramesh, A. (2015). Analyzing drivers and barriers of coordination in humanitarian supply chain management under fuzzy environment. *Benchmarking: An International Journal, 22*(4), 559–587.

Ketchen, D. J., & Hult, G. T. M. (2007). Bridging organization theory and supply chain management: The case of best value supply chains. *Journal of Operations Management, 25*(2), 573–580.

Khatwani, G., Singh, S. P., Trivedi, A., & Chauhan, A. (2015). Fuzzy-TISM: A fuzzy extension of TISM for group decision making. *Global Journal of Flexible Systems Management, 16*(1), 97–112.

Krejci, C. C. (2015). Hybrid simulation modeling for humanitarian relief chain coordination. *Journal of Humanitarian Logistics and Supply Chain Management, 5*(3), 325–347.

Kovács, G., & Spens, K. M. (2007). Humanitarian logistics in disaster relief operations. *International Journal of Physical Distribution & Logistics Management, 37*(2), 99–114.

Kovács, G., & Spens, K. M. (2011). Humanitarian logistics and supply chain management: The start of a new journal. *Journal of Humanitarian Logistics and Supply Chain Management, 1*(1), 5–14.

Lai, A. Y., He, J. A., Tan, T. B., & Phua, K. H. (2009). A proposed ASEAN disaster response, training and logistic centre enhancing regional governance in disaster management. *Transition Studies Review, 16*(2), 299–315.

Mandal, A., & Deshmukh, S. G. (1994). Vendor selection using interpretive structural modelling (ISM). *International Journal of Operations & Production Management, 14*(6), 52–59.

Markman, G., & Krause, D. (2014). Special topic forum on theory building surrounding sustainable supply chain management. *Journal of Supply Chain Management, 50*(2), 106.

Min, S., Roath, A. S., Daugherty, P. J., Genchev, S. E., Chen, H., Arndt, A. D., & Glenn Richey, R. (2005). Supply chain collaboration: What's happening? *The International Journal of Logistics Management, 16*(2), 237–256.

Morgan, R. M., & Hunt, S. D. (1994). The commitment-trust theory of relationship marketing. *The Journal of Marketing, 58*(3),20–38.

OCHA. (2005). *Humanitarian Response Review.* An Independent Report Commissioned by the UN Emergency Relief Coordinator & Under-Secretary-General for Humanitarian Affairs. United Nations Office for the Coordination of Humanitarian Affairs. New York and Geneva: United Nations.

Overstreet, R. E., Hall, D., Hanna, J. B., & Kelly Rainer Jr., R. (2011). Research in humanitarian logistics. *Journal of Humanitarian Logistics and Supply Chain Management, 1*(2), 114–131.

Pagell, M., & Wu, Z. (2009). Building a more complete theory of sustainable supply chain management using case studies of 10 exemplars. *Journal of Supply Chain Management, 45*(2), 37–56.

Paton, D. (1996). Training disaster workers: Promoting wellbeing and operational effectiveness. *Disaster Prevention and Management: An International Journal, 5*(5), 11–18.

Pettit, S., & Beresford, A. (2009). Critical success factors in the context of humanitarian aid supply chains. *International Journal of Physical Distribution & Logistics Management, 39*(6), 450–468.

Poister, T.H. (2003), *Measuring performance in public and nonprofit organizations.* San Francisco, CA: Jossey-Bass.

Premkumar, G., & King, W. R. (1994). Organizational characteristics and information systems planning: An empirical study. *Information Systems Research*, *5*(2), 75–109.

Schein, E. (1985). *Organizational culture and leadership*. San Francisco, CA: Jossey-Bass.

Stoner, J., Freeman, E., & Gilbert, D. (1995). *Management*. Englewood Cliffs, NJ: Prentice Hall, 267, 268.

Sushil, (2012). Interpreting the interpretive structural model. *Global Journal of Flexible Systems Management*, *13*(2), 87–106.

Tabaklar, T., Halldórsson, Á., Kovács, G., & Spens, K. (2015). Borrowing theories in humanitarian supply chain management. *Journal of Humanitarian Logistics and Supply Chain Management*, *5*(3), 281–299.

Tatham, P., & Kovács, G. (2010). The application of "swift trust" to humanitarian logistics. *International Journal of Production Economics*, *126*(1), 35–45.

Taylor, A., & Taylor, M. (2009). Operations management research: Contemporary themes, trends and potential future directions. *International Journal of Operations & Production Management*, *29*(12), 1316–1340.

Tomasini, R. M., & Van Wassenhove, L. N. (2009). From preparedness to partnerships: Case study research on humanitarian logistics. *International Transactions in Operational Research*, *16*(5), 549–559.

Yadav, N. (2014). Total interpretive structural modelling (TISM) of strategic performance management for Indian telecom service providers. *International Journal of Productivity and Performance Management*, *63*(4), 421–445.

Yadav, D. K. and Barve, A. (2016). Modeling post-disaster challenges of humanitarian supply chains: A TISM approach. *Global Journal of Flexible Systems Management*, *17*(3), 321–340.

Van Wassenhove, L. N. (2006). Humanitarian aid logistics: Supply chain management in high gear. *Journal of the Operational Research Society*, *57*(5), 475–489.

Warfield, J. N. (1973). Binary matrices in system modeling. *Systems, Man and Cybernetics, IEEE Transactions*, *3*(5), 441–449.

Waugh, W. L., & Streib, G. (2006). Collaboration and leadership for effective emergency management. *Public Administration Review*, *66*(s1), 131–140.

Wentz, L. (2006). *An ICT primer: Information and communication technologies for civil-military coordination in disaster relief and stabilization and reconstruction*. National defense University, Center for technology and national security policy. Washington, DC.

Whetten, D. A. (1989). What constitutes a theoretical contribution? *Academy of Management Review*, *14*(4), 490–495.

Wilkins, A.L, & Ouchi, W.G. (1983). Efficient cultures: Exploring the relationship between culture and organizational performance. *Administrative Science Quarterly*, *28*, 468–481.

Zhou, H., & Benton, W. C. (2007). Supply chain practice and information sharing. *Journal of Operations Management, 25*(6), 1348–1365.

Zhu, K., & Kraemer, K. L. (2002). E-commerce metrics for net-enhanced organizations: Assessing the value of e-commerce to firm performance in the manufacturing sector. *Information Systems Research, 13*(3), 275–295.

# 11

# Agility Learning Opportunities in Cross-Sector Collaboration. An Exploratory Study

Alessandra Cozzolino, Ewa Wankowicz and Enrico Massaroni

## Introduction

Since the end of the 1990s, we have witnessed a shift towards profit and non-profit engagement, especially in humanitarian logistics; before that time, "collaboration between the two sectors seemed unfeasible" (Stapleton et al. 2012, p. 220). Traditionally, business has considered the social sector "a dumping ground for spare cash, obsolete equipment, and tired executives" (Kanter 1999, p. 123). Conversely, from the viewpoint of the humanitarian sector, profit-driven companies have been perceived "to be the cause of, rather than solution to, problems affecting the developing world" (Stapleton et al. 2012, p. 220), e.g., child exploitation, environmental disasters, pollution and intensive monocultures.

In the past, the humanitarian sector has had an interest in dealing with businesses only when they are needed, on the basis of purely commercial exchanges, such as the purchase of the goods or services that are relevant to the fulfilment of specific humanitarian needs. In some cases, individual companies have carried out philanthropic donations so that the humanitarian organizations considered, for a certain

A. Cozzolino (✉) · E. Wankowicz · E. Massaroni
Department of Management, Sapienza University of Rome, Rome, Italy
e-mail: Alessandra.Cozzolino@uniroma1.it; ewa.wankowicz@uniroma1.it; enrico.massaroni@uniroma1.it

© The Author(s) 2018

**327**

G. Kovács et al. (eds.), *The Palgrave Handbook of Humanitarian Logistics and Supply Chain Management*, https://doi.org/10.1057/978-1-137-59099-2_11

time period, monetary contributions as the only appropriate forms of corporate giving (Stapleton et al. 2012).

Recently, however, humanitarian organizations have shown greater interest in the resources, skills, processes and technologies that can be found in the business sector (Van Wassenhove et al. 2008). The humanitarian sector has, in fact, begun to consider investing in its own growth by not only obtaining more goods, more services and more funds but also by placing importance on the professional and managerial skills of its employees, stimulating them, improving them and, above all, by acquiring and learning from the for-profit sector (Blansjaar and Van Der Merwe 2011).

Companies have also increased their interest in the humanitarian sector. In addition to pure philanthropic contributions, companies may also be interested in welcoming humanitarian organizations as their new clients. Companies in the pharmaceutical, packaging, food and logistics services industries have begun to develop tailored solutions for humanitarian purposes (Kovács 2011). In addition, companies may be interested in reaching certain geographical areas, for example, after a disaster, to build new relationships with local governments to identify new markets and new business opportunities in those countries where they do not yet have a presence.

Between these two extremes lies an area of Corporate Social Responsibility (CSR), "where commercial and philanthropic intentions can easily overlap", even in humanitarian logistics (Tomasini and Van Wassenhove 2009b, p. 140). Under the common umbrella of CSR, companies may seek opportunities to improve their impact on society through responsible actions, including obtaining economic benefits. This development is based on the assumption, which is now widely accepted, that companies can increase their competitiveness through initiatives in which social value and economic value overlap because "there is no inherent contradiction between improving competitive context and making a sincere commitment to bettering society" (Porter and Kramer 2002, p. 66).

Business–humanitarian collaboration seeks "to build on synergies between the business and humanitarian communities to advance humanitarian objectives and at the same time support CSR" (Andonova and Carbonnier 2014, p. 350). Companies often provide a mix of "cash donation, in-kind donation of goods or services, the provision of technical or managerial expertise, cause-related marketing, employee giving schemes and sponsoring, or logistical support and collaboration specific to field activities"; in such cases, the humanitarian organization that is involved generally "grants its corporate partner the possibility of using its name or logo in public communication, thus creating a public association of image or brand between the two parties" (Andonova and Carbonnier 2014, p. 350).

Companies may also be interested in establishing the continuity of their business after a disaster and in playing an active role in relief operations where their plants, offices, employees, suppliers and/or customers are located. In this way, they can personally maintain company's activities that have been affected by a disaster (Cozzolino 2012, 2014).

These are more traditional motivations for companies to engage with the humanitarian sector. A new trend was indicated by Kanter (1999, p. 123), according to whom "smart companies are approaching the social sector as a learning laboratory"– especially in terms of the potential to learn "complementary skills" (Oglesby and Burke 2012).

One potential area of learning that is a specific competency of the humanitarian sector for the benefit of firms has only recently been identified by some authors (Tomasini and Van Wassenhove 2009a/2000b; Charles et al. 2010; Cozzolino 2012, 2014) in the agility of the supply chain.

We refer to agility, in this chapter, as the capability to respond to unpredictable events in a simultaneously fast, effective and flexible way and at a reasonable cost. This insight comes from the observation of specific experience that the humanitarian sector – and especially the world's largest humanitarian organizations – has developed in managing logistics and supply chains in the extreme conditions of emergency response operations, which are based on the principle of agility.

When agility is discussed in the humanitarian logistics and supply chain management context, it is mostly associated with its importance and usefulness during emergency relief operations, as noted by many authors such as Van Wassenhove (2006), Tomasini and Van Wassenhove (2009a/2009b), Maon et al. (2009), Christopher and Tatham (2011), Cozzolino (2012) and Cozzolino et al. (2012). Further, in the final report of its Policy and Research Conference held in 2011, the United Nations Office for the Coordination of Humanitarian Affairs identified agility as a priority research theme (L'Hermitte et al. 2015). However, although agility is repeatedly mentioned, the academic literature on humanitarian logistics and supply chain management on the possibility for companies to learn agility from the humanitarian sector is limited (Van Wassenhove 2006; Tomasini and Van Wassenhove (2009a/2009b); Maon et al. 2009; Cozzolino 2012), and the extent to which they grasp such an opportunity is not empirically investigated.

In summary, there is still no settled understanding of the concrete possibility that companies have to learn agility during a cross-sector collaboration with the humanitarians during disaster relief operations. Thus, this chapter is designed to fill this gap through a preliminary empirical analysis of a case study, which represents a best practice in cross-sector partnerships in humanitarian logistics, and aims to investigate the following research questions:

*RQ1: Can companies concretely learn agility from the humanitarian sector in emergency relief operations?*
*RQ2: What do they concretely learn in terms of agility?*

To address these points, we organize the remainder of this chapter as follows. The next section outlines the theoretical background of this study in a synthetic manner. We present the main insights from the literature on the chances that businesses can learn supply-chain agility from the field of humanitarian emergency management (section "Agility in Humanitarian Supply Chains"), the importance of the mutual benefits of a collaboration (section "Mutual Benefits That Are Derived from Collaboration"), the cross-sector learning opportunities (section "Cross-Sector Learning Opportunities"), and partnership models for cross-sector collaboration in humanitarian logistics (section "Partnership Models for Cross-Sector Collaboration in Humanitarian Logistics"). We then focus more on the empirical investigation that adds the most value. The case study is presented in section "Case Study Analysis". We choose a best practice case study (section "Methodology") and describe it in section "The LET Initiative". The results obtained from the case study analysis and discussion are provided in sections "Key Findings" and "Discussion". In the conclusion, limitations and suggestions are indicated for future research.

# Theoretical Background

## Agility in Humanitarian Supply Chains

In the literature, although many authors define agility in different ways, it is generally described as the ability to respond quickly and effectively to unexpected changes, both on the demand side and on the supply side (Charles et al. 2010; Scholten et al. 2010; Kovács and Spens 2009; Pettit and Beresford 2009; Taylor and Pettit 2009; Oloruntoba and Grey 2006; Narasimhan et al. 2006; Christopher 1992, 2000, 2005; Sheffi 2005; Aitken et al. 2002; Van Hoek et al. 2001; Christopher and Towill 2000; Towill and Christopher 2002;

Childerhouse and Towill 2000; Mason-Jones et al. 2000; Naylor et al. 1999). "In essence it is about being demand-driven rather than forecast-driven" (Christopher et al. 2006, p. 6). To do this "sometimes means putting spare or redundant capacity aside to cope with unpredictable surges in the pipeline, but that is part of the price you pay" (Gattorna 2006, p. 161); moreover it could require "a massive and periodic source of employment" (Peck 2005). Because agility is not achievable at a "low cost" (Lapide 2006; Gattorna 2006), the availability of goods and services is therefore more properly connected to "reasonable costs" (Hofman and Cecere 2005).

The concept of agility goes beyond the level of an individual firm and refers, rather, to an entire supply chain (Van Hoek et al. 2001). In fact, despite the fact that a single firm may have established internal processes to guarantee agility, it would still be limited if it were to, for example, face long lead times from suppliers. In reality, therefore, an important aspect of agility is the presence of agile partners upstream and downstream of a focal firm (Christopher 2005), which may provide an agile supply chain.

We can also identify some guidelines as a starting point in the creation of an agile supply chain (Christopher 2005; Lee 2004; Harrison et al. 1999):

- Synchronization of activities by sharing information with other actors in the supply chain to align logistics processes. Synchronization requires all partners to share scheduling and use the same reference codes, with the ability to observe and communicate with other partners in the refurbishing and replenishment processes to monitor and maintain inventory levels.
- Creating collaborative relationships with suppliers, especially with those with the capacity to respond to unforeseen or unforeseeable changes. Suppliers should not be chosen based on cost.
- Construction of a reliable logistics system, creating stable relationships with logistics providers who can provide expertise and logistical resources.
- Reduction of the complexity of products at the design stage process: the sources of complexity vary along the supply chain and increase with variety. Complex products do not always allow simplification; however, simplification can be achieved in the design of common parts for more products or groups of products. Complex processes can be re-engineered to delete activities that correspond to waste and do not create value. It is also possible to increase concurrent actions, or, in parallel, to decrease lead time.
- Implementation of the postponement: such postponement refers to the process by which the assembly of a product (good and/or service) in its final form or the physical availability is delayed as long as possible pending an actual customer request. If the market is characterized by strong

heterogeneity, products that are assembled according to customer requests, after the time of the actual request, can reduce the likelihood that the product no longer fulfils the needs of the market;

• Design of contingency plans and building of crisis management teams: a successful response to a crisis event is challenging; the more that is invested in preparation, the more effective the response phase.

The principle of agility has been combined with the concepts of emergency and humanitarian logistics in several academic contributions (Charles et al. 2010; Scholten et al. 2010; Kovács and Spens 2009; Pettit and Beresford 2009; Taylor and Pettit 2009; Oloruntoba and Gray 2006; Towill and Christopher 2002), and it has also been closely linked with theories of unexpected shocks that affect supply chains (Van Wassenhove 2006; Lee 2004). More specifically, the agile approach is applied during a disaster relief operation in the response phase; this phase covers all of the operations that must be carried out directly after the occurrence of a sudden disastrous event (Cozzolino 2012, 2014; Cozzolino et al. 2012; Conforti et al. 2008). It is, therefore, during the response operations after a disaster that the agile principle – according to the objective of urgent effectiveness – finds its highest expression, and it is actually in this context that companies can learn agility from the humanitarian sector. The only way for companies to be present at such dire moments is through strategic collaboration with humanitarian actors in response to disasters.

## Mutual Benefits That Are Derived from Collaboration

The essence of collaborative relationships is in the mutual benefits (Maon et al. 2009). There are several factors that motivate the private sector to engage in humanitarian initiatives, even if there is misalignment between the two sectors in terms of goals. The former focuses on making a profit, while the latter focuses on saving lives and assuring the wellbeing of affected people. Nevertheless, the advantages that can be derived from business-humanitarian collaborations can benefit both sectors.

Companies can identify new market opportunities that are otherwise difficult to obtain (Van Wassenhove et al. 2008; Van Wassenhove 2006), and they can demonstrate the efforts that they have made to meet their social responsibility (Thomas and Fritz 2006). They can also improve employee job satisfaction and retention (Binder and Witte 2007). The benefits for the humanitarian sector relate to the expertise that can help them to operate more efficiently and effectively, incorporating the best supply chain practices to balance the flexibility and efficiency that can be of great benefit in life-and-death situations (McLachlin et al. 2009). Furthermore, as Murphy et al. (2012) state, the new knowledge that can be derived from cross-sector experiences is more likely to "accrue to society rather than for the firm" (p. 1704). From this point of view, going beyond profit, the principles of corporate social responsibility can be realized, and companies can demonstrate good corporate citizenship (Maon et al. 2009; McDonald and Young 2012; Labib Eid and Sabella 2014). The private sector's engagement in humanitarian logistics can be projected to serve a variety of conditions and crisis contexts (Zyck and Kent 2014). As Christopher and Tatham (2011) state, the involvement of companies in the humanitarian aid market will continue, as they can obtain benefits that can be derived from the realization of corporate social responsibility.

On the other hand, the humanitarian sector recognizes that the potential benefits that can be obtainable from the collaboration go well beyond cash donation, which is the most common form of contribution of the private sector. In fact, cross-sector collaboration brings several benefits in terms of velocity of support during disasters, back office support for disaster preparedness, capacity building between disasters and best practices exchanges among partners (Van Wassenhove et al. 2008; Tomasini and Van Wassenhoe 2009a/2009b; Stapleton et al. 2012). Businesses can offer immaterial resources, such as expertise, knowledge and best practices that are as essential as technology and infrastructure, but the private sector's technical expertise can be a key factor in meeting humanitarian challenges (Zyck and Kent 2014). The process of systematic learning to create shared value (Porter and Kramer 2011) is a highly relevant result of these partnerships as "every joint project either between or during a disaster is an opportunity to learn" (Tomasini and Van Wassenhove 2009b, p. 135).

## Cross-Sector Learning Opportunities

The engagement of business in partnership with the humanitarian sector is guided by goals such as the potential for learning and business development (Tomasini and Van Wassenhove 2009b). The concept of cross-sector collaboration as a vehicle for new knowledge creation requires going beyond the mere transfer of existing knowledge (Arya and Salk 2006; Anand and Khanna 2000; Larsson et al. 1998; Kale et al. 2000), and it constitutes a breeding ground for the parties that are involved in cross-sector collaboration to benefit from cross-learning opportunities (London et al. 2005).

In particular, in these cross-learning opportunities, knowledge management implies the continuous involvement and sharing of the lessons that have been learned among the partnership members. These processes could allow the company to convert knowledge from tacit to explicit and from individual to organizational, resulting in a "spiral of knowledge", by which the assets of the enterprise' knowledge are extended and deepened, according to the perspective offered by the "knowledge-based view of the firm" by Nonaka (1994).

Knowledge management, which is one of five key elements of effective disaster management, can be translated in the context of humanitarian logistics in "learning from previous disaster by capturing, codifying and transferring knowledge about logistics operations" (Tomasini and Van Wassenhove 2009a, p. 182). Moreover, in the context of high uncertainty, mutual learning in cross-sector collaboration requires that the sharing of learned experience be done so rapidly (L'Hermitte et al. 2016; Redding and Catalanello 1994) to improve practices and prevent them from becoming obsolete. As Tomasini and Van Wassenhove (2009b) explain, sharing lessons learned facilitates the making of faster and better decisions.

Relief operations require fast and timely responses from the numerous members who are involved in a humanitarian supply chain. The continuous improvement in the performance of humanitarian operations entails mutual understanding and alignment of their objectives, sharing of information and undertaking joint planning (L'Hermitte et al. 2016). The effective exploitation of the core competences of both sectors can contribute to the improvement of disaster preparedness (Van Wassenhove et al. 2008). The combined knowledge of partners can affect the achievement of mutual goals (Murphy et al. 2012).

## Partnership Models for Cross-Sector Collaboration in Humanitarian Logistics

In the humanitarian logistics context, Thomas and Fritz (2006) identify four types of "private corporation disaster-relief agency partnership": "single-company philanthropic partnership"; "multi-company philanthropic partnership"; "single-company integrative partnership"; and, "multi-company integrative partnership".

Taking the number of partners into account, this classification is based on the taxonomy that was proposed by Austin (2000a/2000b), which more generally identifies different approaches to collaboration between businesses and non-profits, encompassing a wide range of industries and social sectors (Austin 2000a/2000b; Wymer and Samu 2003). In particular, Austin (2000a/2000b) conceptualizes a "cross-sector collaboration continuum", along which there are three types and stages of relationships: "*philanthropic*", "*transactional*" and "*integrative*".

"*Integrative*" refers to a smaller but growing number of collaborations that evolve into strategic alliances, which involve deep mission mesh, strategy synchronization and value compatibility. Core competencies are not only simply deployed in such cases, but they are also combined to create unique and high value combinations.

An integrative partnership in particular may be of interest because it has features that specifically support cross-learning in the context of humanitarian logistics. In cooperation, the two sectors can learn from each other and together can build a cross-transfer process of their best practices, which is precisely one of the most successful drivers for this type of cross-sector collaboration (Tomasini and Van Wassenhove 2009a/2009b).

Collaboration between the two sectors is not easy because there is a high degree of heterogeneity in terms of culture, purpose, interests, mandates, capacity and expertise (Balcik et al. 2010) – but the diversity can become an asset if they can build on their comparative advantages and complement each other's contributions (Global Humanitarian Platform 2007).

# Case Study Analysis

## Methodology

We conducted an empirical investigation based on the study of a case. The methodology of the case study is well recognized as a valid approach through which to deepen understanding of a phenomenon that is still in development, and/or the dimensions of which have not yet fully explained (Yin 1994).

As the company contributions with the highest impact on the social sector use "the core competencies of the business" (Kanter 1999), for disaster relief operations, the supply chain and logistics functions are crucial for an operation's success (Van Wassenhove 2006); by virtue of their logistics and supply chain management competencies, logistics companies are among the best private organizations to partner with humanitarian organizations "not only from a charitable concern but also as an opportunity for learning and business development" (Tomasini and Van Wassenhove 2009a, p. 557).

For the purpose of this study, it is of interest to verify the research questions, beginning with an overview of logistics service providers.

To choose the case, we mapped integrative collaborations at the international level (in the literature on humanitarian logistics) between humanitarian and logistics providers in emergency response operations. Integrative types of partnership, as defined in Austin (2000a/2000b), are recognized as the most favourable for inter-organizational learning.

The partnerships that have emerged among global logistics providers have included Agility, DHL, FedEx, Geodis, Kuehne+Nagel, Maersk, Toll, TNT, and UPS (Thomas and Fritz 2006; Spring 2006; Binder and Witte 2007; Maon et al. 2009; Tomasini and Van Wassenhove 2009b; Samii 2008; Van Wassenhove 2006; Samii and Van Wassenhove 2004; Quinn 2010; Stadler and Van Wassenhove 2012; Oglesby and Burke 2012; Cozzolino 2012 and 2014; Vega and Roussat 2015; Abidi et al. 2015). These types of partnership are limited and involve well-known global organizations, so it was quite simple to identify them in the literature. They are also communicated on the institutional web sites, but to go in-depth, it is necessary to contact the person responsible for each specific initiative.

From this analysis emerges the first (historically) and still the only international experience of multi-company integrative partnership that has focused on logistics services and been composed of companies in the logistics sector with humanitarians that work in emergency responsiveness: Logistics Emergency Teams (LETs) in collaboration with the World Food Programme, as a Global Logistics Cluster for the entire system of the United Nations and other organizations that belong to the international humanitarian community (www.logcluster.org).

This type of relationship represents "a platform for private sector–humanitarian collaboration" at global level (Oglesby and Burke 2012), and it is a way to "pioneer a new partnership model" as part of the emergency response (Stadler and Van Wassenhove 2012), as it is the first case of its kind in the world (http://www.logcluster.org/logistics-emergency-teams).

It is not a coincidence that the first initiative of this type was born out of a collaboration with the WFP, which is the largest humanitarian logistics expert at the international level and which implements the principles of agility in its supply chains in its relief operations (Cozzolino et al. 2012; Conforti et al. 2008).

We decided to take an in-depth view of this important case. Therefore, we proceed to analyse different sources, to consolidate and enrich the inquiry findings and to ensure proper data triangulation, which would ensure the different perspectives of observation (the LETs' views on individual logistics providers belonging to the initiative, on the one hand, and the WFP's views on logistics clusters and the World Economic Forum, on the other): institutional websites; official videos, internal reports and public files that describe the initiative of the LET; publications of academic research that specifically analyse the LETs (in the Media section of the website www. logisticsemergency.org); interviews that have been published in other academic research and institutional video that describe the initiative of the LETs, in terms of individual missions, success factors and critical issues of cooperation and the results that have been obtained; and, at the end, data collected through a specific questionnaire that was composed for this research project.

After investigating on desk the elements from the perspective of business-humanitarian collaboration through transcribed and analysed interviews from secondary sources, the study was completed with a field analysis suitable for the specific purpose in our research. This was necessary because no other studies have specifically addressed this aspect of the learning the agility.

The empirical investigation was based on a questionnaire (with both open and closed questions) completed by the three top managers for each of the three companies of the LET Steering Committee. We consider this number of interviews to be sufficient because the managers are the highest proponents of the business sector in the LET/LC partnership and have years of collaboration and involvement in the initiative, and their point of view represents their own companies. They all appreciated being part of our research. Because of the geographical distance, there was no opportunity to meet with them personally, so the interviews were conducted through email or Skype; hopefully, face-to-face interviews can be conducted in the next step of the research.

The secondary data and the data from the questionnaires were analysed through qualitative content analysis (Krippendorff 2004). To assure the trustworthiness of this research, the model that was proposed by Guba was selected. Following Guba's framework (1981), a trustworthy study should follow the four criteria of credibility, transferability, dependability and confirmability. Furthermore, to ensure the reliability of the study, a formal protocol (see Table 11.1) was developed, taking into account as a primary driver the objectives of the current research, combined with the insights that were gathered from the literature review.

A pilot test was performed before the interviews with one practitioner, experts in the logistics field, and one academic professor in supply chain management. As a result, the wordings of some of the questions were

**Table 11.1** The structure of the questionnaire

| Section | Title | | Aim |
|---|---|---|---|
| Section I | Business-humanitarian collaboration as a cross-learning opportunity | | Description of the cross-learning opportunities in the collaboration between business and humanitarian sectors |
| | Section I (a) | Logistics service providers-humanitarians collaboration as a cross-learning opportunity | |
| | Section I (b) | WFP-LET collaboration as a cross-learning opportunity | |
| Section II | Learning agility from the humanitarian supply chain | | Analysis of the possibilities of learning the agility of the supply chain of humanitarian emergency management |
| | Section II. (a) | Definition of "agility" | |
| | Section II. (b) | Learning agility from the humanitarian supply chains (LSPs-humanitarians) | |
| | Section II. (c) | Learning agility from the humanitarian supply chain in WFP-LET collaboration | |
| Section III | Cases and experiences in WFP-LET collaboration (documents, blogs and business case studies) | | Collection of cases and experiences |

*Source*: Our elaboration.

changed to make them both easier to understand and more focused on the areas of interest. This step aimed to provide a solid structure for the interviews and facilitate a comparison of the cases at the analysis stage.

If it took the form of an oral conversation, the questionnaire was shared with the interviewed manager after its transcription. The information that was collected was treated confidentially.

## The LET Initiative

"The annual meeting of world economic leaders in Davos has become one of several platforms for brokerage of public–private partnerships in the humanitarian field" (Andonova and Carbonnier 2014, p. 349): at the 2008 World Economic Forum (WEF) summit, United Nations agencies and WEF member companies announced a new initiative that considered substantial contributions by multinational logistics companies to Logistics Emergency Teams (LETs) that intervene in disasters.

As Sean Doherty, Head of Logistics and Transport Industry of the WEF, stated: "Logistics Emergency Teams provide surge capacity – warehouse space, offices, airlifts, shipping, trucking – but most importantly, they have experts with on-the-ground experience, knowledge, and relationships" ("Logistics Emergency Teams" video, see at https://www.youtube.com/watch?v=lLwWfjQ7vPU&feature=player_embedded).

LETs unite the capacity and resources of the logistics industry with the expertise and experience of the humanitarian community to provide more effective and efficient disaster relief. A key reason for cooperating through LETs is to provide a demand-driven, efficient response. LETs are the first partnership of this type, formalizing a multi-stakeholder cooperation between the private and public sector. It remains one of the best WEF-initiated and operationalized public-private partnerships (http://www.logclus ter.org/logistics-emergency-teams).

Josette Sheeran, Executive Director del World Food Programme, said: "When disaster strikes, our job is to mobilize massive assistance and to make sure it reaches those in need – fast! Private sector expertise and corporate partnerships are critical to helping us save lives" (www.wfp.org).

The WEF facilitated the partnership in 2005. The concept behind LET was the result of important dialogues that took place at the international level after the Asian tsunami of 2004. On that occasion, in fact, many companies that belong to the WEF sought to determine lessons learned as a result of aid operations in response to huge natural disasters and the possibility and/or need to supplement the available resources of the various companies within the humanitarian relief system. With the increasingly clear awareness of the extreme criticality of logistics in humanitarian relief operations, in 2005 Agility, TNT and UPS officially announced their willingness to work through a multi-company and cross-sector partnership. After some years the composition of LETs changed. In the first phase, Maersk joined the team, and in the second phase, TNT left the initiative, but the aim of the initiative remained the same. The LET is currently composed of Agility, UPS and Maersk.

The formal collaboration, however, began only in 2008, given the complex organization that was required by a partnership of this magnitude, which was unprecedented. The first field operation was in Myanmar and, later, in other locations, such as Mozambique, Haiti, the Philippines, Indonesia, Pakistan, Chile and Japan.

As Olivia Bessat, Senior Manager del Global Agenda Council Team del World Economic Forum, declared: "The strength of LETs lies in engaging, in advance, all of the private and humanitarian members in the design of the entire mechanism behind their partnership. The result is a set of pre-arrangements and an effective contingency plan ready to be triggered to support the relief effort for large-scale natural disasters" (www.weforum.org).

LETs are designed to provide effective and rapid logistical support for survivors after a disaster, and, to achieve such a performance, all of the business partners that support the WFP must faithfully follow the agreement that was set forth in the Memorandum of Understanding and in the operative procedures that govern the partnership (www.logcluster.org) through which they have agreed to contribute with their "core competences (1) on a pro-bono basis, and (2) only upon request of the LC to support humanitarian response operations in the event of (3) a natural disaster affecting more than 500.000 people" (Stadler and Van Wassenhove 2012 p. 6).

Support is provided through pre-agreed operating procedures and training, and it includes: logistics specialists (e.g., airport coordinators, airport managers, and warehouse managers); logistics assets (e.g., warehouses, trucks, and forklifts); and, logistics services (e.g., airlifts, trucking and customs management).

The LET business partners are all top companies in the logistics and transportation industry. They have robust corporate social responsibility programmes and previous experience in disaster-relief operations. The dedication to help in disaster response is explicitly included in the priorities of social responsibility initiatives.

The teams are made up of the LET staff with logistics experience, and they are prepared to mobilize within 48 hours of an emergency at the request of the WFP. As stated by one of the volunteers of the LET on the field as part of the interview that was released during one of the post-disaster relief operations: "We are in a very closed cooperation with WFP. We know each other, and we know each other's needs very well. So, in the case of a disaster like this, we come together very quickly, and we generate concrete plans".

Staff recruitment takes place among the employees of partner companies, in voluntary mode for a total availability of two years. Every year there is a training to prepare volunteers for their missions in the field, so that, as Matteo Perrone of WFP (Stadler and Van Wassenhove 2012, p. 6) stated: "In the field, the deployed employees are no more Agility, Maersk, UPS or TNT. They are part of our team; they are living with us".

Even in the perception of the participants, this is an important aspect, as two LET volunteers declared during the annual training meeting (LET training session video by Maersk): "I am sitting in a room with a lot of dedicated professionals, and [...] it is very evident that there is a sense of community even if we are competitors" (Marketing Executive – TNT Netherlands) and "This is a very special partnership: we are all in the logistics and transportation industry, and […] we come together as one team" (CSR Associate – Agility Kuwait).

The LET values and combines the capabilities and resources of the logistics industry with the skills and experience of the humanitarian community: "A spirit of cooperation, good faith, and willingness to learn from each other are key to success" ("Relationship guidelines for LET Members/ Global Logistics Cluster Collaboration" see at www.logcluster.org).

# Key Findings

Based on the conceptual framework, this first exploratory study analyses the empirical evidence on the concrete opportunities for companies to learn agility in collaboration with the humanitarian sector during disaster relief management.

The following considerations emerged from secondary data and from the questionnaire completed by the three top managers for each of the three companies of the LET Steering Committee. For confidentiality reasons, in the following empirical analysis, the letters attached to the quotations reflect the codes that we assigned to each interviewee/organization. The other quoted sentences from secondary sources have explicit references.

## Results from Secondary Data

Secondary data analysed in this section are derived in particular from two previous manuscripts: Stadler and Van Wassenhove (2012), and Cozzolino (2014).

Stadler and Van Wassenhove (2012) is mainly useful for the present research because it specifically treats in depth the case of the LET in partnership with WFP/LC. From the above-mentioned study, some interesting considerations on partnership, joint benefits and learning possibilities emerged. In particular, it was possible to understand the point of view of LET's representatives on four elements of agility (effectiveness, flexibility, quicker response, reasonable costs). The companies' perspective primarily considers the first three elements, as shown in Table 11.2. Referring to the costs, there are no specific quotes from the companies, but this come only from the WFP.

**Table 11.2** Elements of agility

| | |
|---|---|
| Chairman and Managing Director (Agility) | Effectiveness<br>"Engaging in a cross-industry collaborative approach not only required jointly shaping the partnership design and operations, but also adapting the members' own organizational procedures and systems to ensure smooth and coordinated implementation" |
| Director of Corporate Social Responsibility (Agility) | Flexibility<br>"Humanitarian logistics if they want X, Y, and Z and you're busy preparing it, the next day they may rather need A, B, and C. That is sometimes frustrating but it might be that they initially wanted to deliver food but then cholera has become the main problem in the camp, so the priority has moved from food to medical and hygiene equipment. You have to learn flexibility" |
| Director of Corporate Social Responsibility (Agility) | Quicker response<br>"Working in a disaster areas is incredibly challenging. The total communication infrastructure can break down and the humanitarians succeed in setting up an operation within two hours. The humanitarian system has to work with very few resources and they are very creative with new solutions. We can learn a lot with regard to efficiency" |
| Logistics Officer (WFP) | Reasonable costs<br>"They [the LET companies] don't want it to be too costly for them" |

*Source*: Cozzolino (2014) from Stadler and Van Wassenhove (2012).

Cozzolino (2014) is mainly useful for the present research because it has explicitly investigated with an empirical study which opportunities the companies may have to learn agility of the supply chain from humanitarian emergency management, in the perspective of the humanitarian sector. From this work, it was possible then to extrapolate if LET companies may learn agility in the perspective of the WFP/LC, which is the opposite perspective that we have chosen instead in the present work. The quotes extracted from Cozzolino (2014) and reported below refer to an interview of the author of the Deputy Global Logistics Cluster Coordinator in 2013. The LC manager noted that "all volunteers and managers absorb a great deal from humanitarian operations in conjunction with WFP at both the operational and strategic levels" and that this specific ability to adapt and respond as quickly as possible to events can be learned in the field. He stated that such an ability "cannot be learned in a short time (the time of a single volunteer of the LET in the field) but can only come from years of experience". In particular, compared with employees who work in, for example, Dallas or Liege, employees who work in countries that are subject to natural disasters or critical climate issues obtain more immediate and valuables benefits from their volunteer experience with the LET initiative. In fact, the next time a natural disaster occurs in an area where a former volunteer with the WFP initiative of the LET works, he will know what action to take, potentially personally intervening and handling the emergency for his headquarter and his colleagues.

## Results from the Questionnaire

The data from the questionnaires administered to the LET Steering Committee are aligned with the primary objective of our research, that is, to capture variations in theory and concepts and not generalizability (McCracken 1998; Strauss 1987), aiming to explore unusualness and not only typicality (Hartley 2004). Difference and similarities among the three companies' perspectives emerged, as outlined in the following paragraphs.

Solving the most complex humanitarian and global health challenges requires enhanced collaboration and partnerships (Z). In the specific collaboration between LET and WFP/LC, each organization wants to support humanitarians on a long-term basis and to contribute its expertise to sustain the community as part of a CSR programme. The engagement in the LET/LC partnership expresses each company's corporate citizenship through both community and employee commitment (X and Y). The LET has helped bring life sustaining supply chain solutions to disaster-impacted communities over the past decade: this is a tremendous example of how the transportation sector has worked together to share its expertise to help beneficiaries (Z).

As shown in Table 11.3, these are the reasons why logistics companies should collaborate with the humanitarian sector and, in particular, serve as the rationale for a collaboration between LET initiative and the WFP/LC.

By virtue of their worldwide presence the LET' global LSPs are present in almost every markets in the world, and many of the markets where they are present, with a business activity, they are countries that are disaster risk prone and rely a lot on international humanitarian support, so partnering in LET/LC they can demonstrate that in these markets they are there not only to make money, but also with a long-term partnership with the community where they operate to support them in case of crisis (X). Moreover a lot of their own employees ask what they do as big company for the society, so that

**Table 11.3** Reasons to collaborate

|  | In general | | | In LET/WFP | | |
|---|---|---|---|---|---|---|
|  | X | Y | Z | X | Y | Z |
| Possibility for the companies to enhance their reputation (and demonstrate their good intentions) | Yes | Yes | Yes | Yes | Yes | Yes |
| Possibility to improve the risk management (companies can improve the management of events with low probability and high risk) | Yes* | Yes | Yes | Yes | Yes | Yes |
| Companies can achieve higher customer loyalty | No | No | Yes | No | No | No |
| Retention and job satisfaction of employees | Yes | Yes | Yes | Yes | Yes | No |
| Possibility for the companies to reach new clients and/or new markets | Yes | No | Yes | No | No | No |
| Possibility of mutual learning of best practices and innovation | Yes | Yes | Yes | No | No | Yes |
| Humanitarian sector's need for specialized logistics expertise/knowledge | Yes | Yes | Yes | Yes | Yes | Yes |

*Only some of them.
*Source*: Our elaboration.

partnering with WFP/LC it "is the right thing to do": "our employees want us to do it and we have the fully resources to help in this way" (Y).

In the companies perspective, the primary motivation in collaborating in LET/LC initiative is to contribute to the humanitarian cause by providing their resources and logistics expertise, as is clear declared in the official communications of the LET initiative, in the institutional LET web site, and in the CSR section of the single companies member of the initiative. The intent of the business is to express and communicate its humanitarian conscience – in terms of CSR programmes – to its customers and employees, offering itself as a stable partner in emergency operations.

"The two sectors can learn each other", as all three companies (X, Y and Z) confirmed, and they embrace the opportunity to learn other best practices from their partners and apply those to their supply chains (Z). In emergency management "every moment is a learning moment" as well as every disaster provides an opportunity to learn how casualties could have been prevented; those learnings can be shared with communities to build resilience prior to the next disaster (Z). However learning is not necessarily the main reason for engaging in such a partnership, as shown in Table 11.4.

Referring to the definition of agility used in this work, we asked the respondents to confirm or, if they disagree, give their own definition, as shown in

Table 11.4 Importance of mutual learning

| | In general | | | In LET/WFP | | |
|---|---|---|---|---|---|---|
| | X | Y | Z | X | Y | Z |
| The importance of learning opportunity among the reasons that lead to collaboration* | Very important (4) | Not very important (2) | Extremely important (5) | Very important (4) | Not very important (2) | Extremely important (5) |
| The importance of mutual learning of logistic best practices in particular among the reasons that lead to collaboration* | Somewhat important (3) | Not very important (2) | Extremely important (5) | Somewhat important (3) | Not very important (2) | Somewhat important (3) |

*Please express your opinion on this statement using a five-point scale: where 1 = completely disagree and 5 = completely agree.
Source: Our elaboration.

**Table 11.5** Definition of "agility"

|  | X | Y | Z |
|---|---|---|---|
| Agility refers to the capability to respond to unpredictable events in a way that is simultaneously fast, effective, flexible and at reasonable costs*. | 5 | 4 | 5 |
| As an agile supply-chain needs a massive source of employment, and it cannot be reached at a low cost, "reasonableness" in cost configuration is defined as the perspective to keep a response to uncertainty *. | 4 | 2 | 5 |

*Please express your opinion on this statement using a five-point scale: where 1 = completely disagree and 5 = completely agree.

*Source*: Our elaboration.

**Table 11.6** Learning agility

|  | In general | | | In LET/WFP | | |
|---|---|---|---|---|---|---|
|  | X | Y | Z | X | Y | Z |
| Can logistics service providers learn from humanitarians how to manage unexpected shocks that affect supply chains, in order to adopt and transfer the learned competencies into their business supply chains? | Yes | Yes | Yes | No | Yes | Yes |
| Can logistics service providers learn agility from humanitarians during disaster relief operations? | Yes | Yes | Yes | No | Yes | Yes |

*Source*: Our elaboration.

Table 11.5. Each of them provided confirmation, but what is interesting is that one of the interviewed managers noted that "agile supply chains do not necessarily require massive amounts of employees or high costs" (Y).

As shown in Table 11.6, logistics service providers can learn agility from humanitarians during disaster relief operations. Only from the point of view of X there was a contrasting view expressed: "the specific LET/LC collaboration is not for the purpose of learning agility, it is not really based on something to learn".

From a business perspective, LSPs may learn from the humanitarian sector about responsiveness, change management, working with limited resources and, particularly in the LET/LC partnership, responsiveness and change management (Y). In the business perspective, the humanitarian sector may learn from business LSPs about planning, process management, business applications and, particularly in the LET/LC partnership, planning and process management (Y). According to Z, the humanitarian sector may learn from leading LSPs, especially those in LET, "what they do best": efficiency, problem solving, innovation, and safety. While LSPs may approach the humanitarian sector as a laboratory of innovation and collaboration into a very complex supply chain. According to X, the humanitarian sector may learn from business LSPs, particularly from those in LET, about access to information about countries and infrastructures (how to access a certain place, how it works in different countries), transport optimization, and going to new countries (where companies have their own structures and employees and WFP/LC do not). In contrast, large LSPs, especially those in LET, already have all of their expertise in house, so there is much more room for the humanitarian sector to learn from main LSPs in logistics (X). According to X, the humanitarian sector relies on large international LSPs such as those in LET to respond to disasters.

However, because humanitarians must work in dynamic work environments and still deliver, private sector companies should be able to learn from this to improve service quality because change management is a critical part of any supply chain, particularly in the humanitarian context (Y). By virtue of good teamwork and dialogue between the LET/LC partnership, LSPs could have the chance to learn some of the rules of agility from WFP/LC in disaster relief operations (Y), as reported in Table 11.7.

Negative answers (of the X company) indicate that learning agility is not the reason for this partnership.

## Discussion

From these preliminary results, learning agility seems to be almost an unintentional consequence and not a primary motivation to cooperate. However, at the same time, it is considered an important point in the cross-sector collaboration.

However it seems that the learning theme is just little or not communicated. Some hypotheses are described in the following sentences.

This, above all, because agility is already a capability that those global LSPs – as leaders in their business sector – have learned before others during their competition in an instable context. Thus, more than learning it, the opportunity could be to continue training in the field and increasingly implement their agile capabilities in new challenging contexts.

If they do not already have this capability, some other options emerge. It may be that there is still no full awareness of the learning opportunity, or also

**Table 11.7** Rules of agility that companies can learn

| Rules of agility | In general | | | In LET/WFP | | |
|---|---|---|---|---|---|---|
| | X | Y | Z | X | Y | Z |
| Reacting to events rather than relying on the forecasts (on the demand side) | Yes | Yes | Yes | No | Yes | Yes |
| Handling short lead time of supply (on the supply side) | Yes | Yes | Yes | No | Yes | Yes |
| Synchronizing tasks sharing information among actors of the humanitarian supply chain (shared scheduling) | Yes | No | Yes | No | Yes | Yes |
| Re-organizing processes by eliminating activities that do not add value | Yes | No | No | No | Yes | No |
| Creating collaborative relationships with suppliers and, in particular, working with suppliers to reduce the time of in-bound and usefulness of delivery | Yes | No | Yes | No | Yes | No |
| Reducing complexity (too many product variations, too many suppliers, mode of transportation, etc.) | Yes | Yes | No | No | Yes | No |
| Planning for postponement | Yes | Yes | Yes | No | Yes | Yes |
| Setting up buffer of low-cost stocks of key-components | Yes | Yes | Yes | No | No | Yes |
| Building a reliable logistics system, creating stable relationships with 3PLs | Yes | Yes | Yes | No | Yes | Yes |
| Drawing contingency plans and setting up crisis management | Yes | Yes | Yes | No | Yes | Yes |
| Innovating to respond quickly and effectively to an emergency | Yes | Yes | Yes | No | Yes | Yes |

*Source*: Our elaboration.

because concrete results of the learning process are not yet visible. Another option is that the learning opportunity has not a proper space in the institutional communication of the companies because the communication is directed to the target of customers and stakeholders not directly interested in this topic, but in the CSR area.

An alternative reason it could be the desire not to communicate this opportunity because valuable element of differentiation from the competition. In this sense, the companies involved could develop important innovations or even new business models. Companies are focused on understanding the needs that humanitarian agencies have in terms of logistics; and, they are also interested in knowing the type of materials most frequently handled during rescue operations – that, compared to those that normally manage, are much more simple and standard – in order to speed up their supply chains in response to the needs of humanitarian actors. Consider, for example, the interest that the LET companies manifest in understanding the types of materials handled by the WFP and their distribution methods: learn how to handle these products appropriately has an advantage on the success of pro-bono partnership (in the present and for the future) and an advantage if they wish to eventually propose themselves at a later time for money to other humanitarian organizations; but also there is the possibility for the company to invest in new lines of services, opening also the way to new business models for logistics for-profit clients. This could be in line with the idea that one of the primary motivations for companies to engage in partnership with humanitarians is, in the humanitarian perspective, to open new markets, no longer served pro-bono but for-profit; but that could be coherent with CSR approach, where economic and philanthropic intentions in same ways simultaneously occur.

## Conclusion

With this contribution, we aim to investigate the opportunity for companies to learn about the agility of supply chains in the context of humanitarian emergency operations.

The literature and the analysed operational conditions reveal that companies and humanitarians can learn from each other during disaster relief, not only the humanitarian sector from the business sector but also the other way around, in terms of agility.

The results of this research may be of particular interest to academics and practitioners in both the profit and non-profit sectors because such learning opportunities are reflected in the best outcome for the logistics of humanitarian aid to benefit people in need. It can also support the creation of an agenda for their engagement in the realization of corporate social responsibility goals.

This first exploratory study, despite having provided unprecedented findings on the topic, needs to be deepened especially in its empirical investigation. The selected methodology permits a thorough exploration of a phenomenon that is still at an early stage, but requires further analysis. It is important to be in constant communication with the parties that participate in the initiative explored in this research to obtain their points of view. First, it might be useful to go in-depth with more questions through a semi-structured interview to the LET Steering Committee. Second, further investigation might consider collecting opinions from other profiles in the companies belonging to different functions, such as volunteers and logisticians. We should also complete the research from the WFP/LC perspective on the topic by giving a questionnaire/interview to the major exponents of the partnership on the humanitarian side. Moreover, it would also be interesting to investigate sectors other than logistics.

Through such additional studies (with the direct involvement of managers/professionals from both business and humanitarian sector), it will be possible to create a deeper understanding of the agility learning opportunities for companies.

**Acknowledgements** The authors would like to thank the organizations that were involved in this research for their support. The data were treated confidentially. The authors take exclusive responsibility for everything that is written in this chapter. Any opinions, findings, conclusions or recommendations that are expressed in this material are those of the authors and do not necessarily reflect the views of the organizations that are analysed.

# References

Abidi, Hella, Sander De Leeuw, and Matthias Klumpp. "The value of fourth-party logistics services in the humanitarian supply chain." *Journal of Humanitarian Logistics & Supply Chain Management* 5 (2015): 35–60.

Aitken, James, Martin Christopher, and Towill Denis Royston. "Understanding, implementing and exploiting agility and leanness." *International Journal of Logistics: Research & Applications* 5 (2002): 59–74.

Anand, Bharat N., and Tarun Khanna. "Do firms learn to create value? The case of alliances." *Strategic Management Journal* 21.3 (2000): 295–315.

Andonova, Liliana B., and Gilles Carbonnier. "Business–humanitarian partnerships: Processes of normative legitimation." *Globalizations* 11.3 (2014): 349–367.

Arya, Bindu, and Jane E. Salk. "Cross-sector alliance learning and effectiveness of voluntary codes of corporate social responsibility." *Business Ethics Quarterly* 16.02 (2006): 211–234.

Austin, James E. "Strategic collaboration between nonprofits and business". *Nonprofit and Voluntary Sector Quarterly* 29. Suppl 1 (2000a): 69–97.

Austin, James E. *The collaboration challenge: How nonprofits and businesses succeed through strategic alliances.* San Francisco: Jossey-Bass, 2000b.

Balcik, Burcu, Benita M. Beamon, Caroline C. Krejci, Kyle M. Muramatsu, and Magaly Ramirez. "Coordination in humanitarian relief chains: Practices, challenges and opportunities." *International Journal of Production Economics* 126.1 (2010): 22–34.

Binder, Andrea, and Jan Martin Witte. *Business engagement in humanitarian relief: Key trends and policy implications*. London: Global Public Policy Institute (GPPi), 2007.

Blansjaar, Martijn, and Charl van Der Merwe. "The importance of information technology in humanitarian supply chains: Opportunities and challenges in the Helios project." In *Humanitarian logistics. Meeting the challenge of preparing for and responding to disasters*, edited by Martin Christopher and Peter Tatham, 46–63. London: Kogan Page, 2011.

Charles, Aurelie, Matthieu Lauras, and Luk N. Van Wassenhove. "A model to define and assess the agility of supply chains: Building on humanitarian experience." *International Journal of Physical Distribution & Logistics Management* 40.8/9 (2010): 722–741.

Childerhouse, Paul, and Denis Towill. "Engineering supply chains to match customer requirements." *Logistics Information Management* 13.6 (2000): 337–346.

Christopher, Martin. *Logistics and supply chain management*. London: Pitman Publishing, 1992.

Christopher, Martin. "The agile supply chain: Competing in volatile markets." *Industrial Marketing Management* 29.1 (2000): 37–44.

Christopher, Martin. *Logistics and supply chain management: Creating value-added networks*. New Jersey: Pearson Education, 2005.

Christopher, Martin, and Peter Tatham. "Introduction". In *Humanitarian logistics. Meeting the challenge of preparing for and responding to disasters*, edited by Martin Christopher and Peter Tatham. London: Kogan Page, 2011.

Christopher, Martin, and Denis R. Towill. "Supply chain migration from lean and functional to agile and customised." *Supply Chain Management: An International Journal* 5.4 (2000): 206–213.

Christopher, Martin, Helen Peck, and Denis Towill. "A taxonomy for selecting global supply chain strategies." *The International Journal of Logistics Management* 17.2 (2006): 277–287.

Conforti, Alessio, Alessandra Cozzolino, and Silvia Rossi. "Il supply chain management delle emergenze umanitarie. Il caso del World Food Programme." *Finanza Marketing e Produzione* 2.2 (2008): 25–48.

Cozzolino, Alessandra. *Humanitarian logistics: Cross-sector cooperation in disaster relief management*. SpringerBriefs in Business Series, 2012.

Cozzolino, Alessandra. "Agilità nella logistica delle emergenze. Le imprese apprendono dalle organizzazioni umanitarie." *Sinergie Italian Journal of Management* (2014): 75–98.

Cozzolino, Alessandra, Silvia Rossi, and Alessio Conforti. "Agile and lean principles in the humanitarian supply chain: The case of the United Nations world food programme." *Journal of Humanitarian Logistics and Supply Chain Management* 2.1 (2012): 16–33.

Gattorna, John. *Living supply chains: How to mobilize the enterprise around delivering what your customers want*. London: Pearson Education, 2006.

Global humanitarian platform. Global Humanitarian Principles of Partnership. A Statement of Commitment Endorsed by the Global Humanitarian Platform. Geneva, 2007.

Guba, Egon G. "Criteria for assessing the trustworthiness of naturalistic inquiries." *Educational Communication and Technology Journal* 29.2 (1981): 75–91.

Harrison, Alan, Martin Christopher, and Remko I. van Hoek. *Creating the agile supply chain*. London: Institute of Logistics and Transport, 1999.

Hartley, Jean. "Case study research". In *Essential guide to qualitative methods in organizational research*, edited by Cassell, Catherine, and Gillian Symon. London: Sage, 2004.

Hofman, Debra, and Lora Cecere. "The agile supply chain." *Supply Chain Management Review* 9.8 (2005): 18–19.

Kale, Prashant, Harbir Singh, and Howard Perlmutter. "Learning and protection of proprietary assets in strategic alliances: Building relational capital." *Strategic Management Journal* 21.3 (2000): 217–237.

Kanter, Rosabeth Moss. "From spare change to real change. The social sector as beta site for business innovation." *Harvard Business Review* 77.3 (1999): 122–132.

Kovács, Gyöngyi. "So where next? Developments in humanitarian logistics". In Christopher, Martin and Peter Tatham (Eds.) *Humanitarian logistics. Meeting the challenge of preparing for and responding to disasters* (2011): 249–263. London: Kogan Page.

Kovács, Gyöngyi, and Karen Spens. "Identifying challenges in humanitarian logistics." *International Journal of Physical Distribution & Logistics Management* 39.6 (2009): 506–528.

Krippendorff, Klaus. *Content Analysis An Introduction to Its Methodology*. Thousand Oaks, California: Sage Publications, 2004.

Labib Eid, Niveen, and Anton Robert Sabella. "A fresh approach to corporate social responsibility (CSR): Partnerships between businesses and non-profit sectors." *Corporate Governance* 14.3 (2014): 352–362.

Lapide, Larry. "The essence of excellence." *Supply Chain Management Review* 10.3 (2006): 18–25.

Larsson, Rikard, Lars Bengtsson, Kristina Henriksson, and Judith Sparks. "The interorganizational learning dilemma: Collective knowledge development in strategic alliances." *Organization Science* 9.3 (1998): 285–305.

Lee, Hau L. "The triple-A supply chain." *Harvard Business Review* 82.10 (2004): 102–113.

L'Hermitte, Cécile, Peter Tatham, Marcus Bowles, and Ben Brooks. "Developing organisational capabilities to support agility in humanitarian logistics: An exploratory study." *Journal of Humanitarian Logistics and Supply Chain Management* 6.1 (2016): 72–99.

L'Hermitte, Cécile, Marus Bowles, Peter Tatham, and Ben Brooks. "An integrated approach to agility in humanitarian logistics." *Journal of Humanitarian Logistics and Supply Chain Management* 5.2 (2015): 209–233.

London, Ted, Dennis A. Rondinelli, and Hugh O'Neill. "Strange bedfellows: Alliances between corporations and nonprofits." In *Handbook of strategic alliances*, edited by Shenkar, Odded and Jeffrey J. Reuer, 353–366. California: Sage Publications, 2005.

Maon, François, Adam Lindgreen, and Joëlle Vanhamme. "Developing supply chains in disaster relief operations through cross-sector socially oriented collaborations: A theoretical model." *Supply Chain Management: An International Journal* 14.2 (2009): 149–164.

Mason-Jones, Rachel, Ben Naylor, and Denis R. Towill. "Lean, agile or leagile? Matching your supply chain to the marketplace." *International Journal of Production Research* 38.17 (2000): 4061–4070.

McCracken, Grant. *The long interview (Qualitative Research Methods)*. Beverly Hills: Sage, 1998.

McDonald, Sharyn, and Suzanne Young. "Cross-sector collaboration shaping corporate social responsibility best practice within the mining industry." *Journal of Cleaner Production* 37 (2012): 54–67.

McLachlin, Ron, Paul D. Larson, and Soaleh Khan. "Not-for-profit supply chains in interrupted environments: The case of a faith-based humanitarian relief organisation." *Management Research News* 32.11 (2009): 1050–1064.

Murphy, Matthew, Francois Perrot, and Miguel Rivera-Santos. "New perspectives on learning and innovation in cross-sector collaborations." *Journal of Business Research* 65.12 (2012): 1700–1709.

Narasimhan, Ram, Morgan Swink, and Soo Wook Kim. "Disentangling leanness and agility: An empirical investigation." *Journal of Operations Management* 24.5 (2006): 440–457.

Naylor, J. Ben, Mohamed M. Naim, and Danny Berry. "Leagility: Integrating the lean and agile manufacturing paradigms in the total supply chain." *International Journal of Production Economics* 62.1 (1999): 107–118.

Nonaka, Ikujiro. "A dynamic theory of organizational knowledge creation." *Organization Science* 5.1 (1994): 14–37.

Oglesby, Rosie, and Joanne Burke. "Platforms for private sector: Humanitarian collaboration." *Platforms for private sector: Humanitarian collaboration*. London: King's College, 2012.

Oloruntoba, Richard, and Richard Gray. "Humanitarian aid: An agile supply chain?" *Supply Chain Management: An International Journal* 11.2 (2006): 115–120.

Peck, Helen. "Finding better way to deal with disasters." *Logistics and Transport Focus* 7.10 (2005): 19–21.

Pettit, Stephen, and Anthony Beresford. "Critical success factors in the context of humanitarian aid supply chains." *International Journal of Physical Distribution & Logistics Management* 39.6 (2009): 450–468.

Porter, Michael E., and Mark R. Kramer. "The competitive advantage of corporate philanthropy." *Harvard Business Review* 80.12 (2002): 56–68.

Porter, Michael E., and Mark R. Kramer. "Creating Shared Value". *Harvard Business Review*, 89 (2011): 1–2.

Quinn, Emma. "Logistics for food assistance: Delivering innovations in complex environments". In *Revolution: From food aid to food assistance. Innovations in overcoming hunger*, edited by World Food Programme Omamo Steven Were, Ugo Gentilini, Susanna Sandström, 307–328 http://documents.wfp.org/stellent/groups/public/documents/newsroom/wfp225973.pdf, 2010.

Redding, John C., and Ralph F. Catalanello. *Strategic readiness, The making of the learning organization*. San Francisco: Jossey-Bass, 1994.

Samii, Ramina, and Luk N. Van Wassenhove. *Moving the world: TNT-WFP partnership-learning to dance*, INSEAD, (2004) Case study n. 2004–5194.

Samii, Ramina. "Leveraging logistics partnerships. Lessons from humanitarian organizations", PhD dissertation, Erasmus University Rotterdam, Rotterdam, 2008.

Scholten, Kirstin, Pamela Sharkey Scott, and Brian Fynes. "(Le) agility in humanitarian aid (NGO) supply chains." *International Journal of Physical Distribution & Logistics Management* 40.8/9 (2010): 623–635.

Sheffi, Yossi. *The resilient enterprise: Overcoming vulnerability for competitive advantage*. Cambridge, MA: MIT Press Books, 2005.

Spring, Silvia. "Relief when you need it. Can FedEx, DHL and TNT bring the delivery of emergency aid into the 21st century?" *Newsweek-International Edition* 11 (2006). (http://www.fritzinstitute.org/PDFs/InTheNews/2006/newsweek-I-091106.pdf).

Stadtler, Lea, and Luk N. Van Wassenhove. "The logistics emergency teams: Pioneering a new partnership model." *INSEAD Case Study* 10 (2012): 2012–5895.

Stapleton, Orla, Lea Stadtler, and Luk N. Van Wassenhove. "Private-humanitarian supply chain partnerships on the silk road" In *Managing supply chains on the silk road. Strategy, performance, and risk*, edited by Haksöz, Çağrı, Sridhar Seshadri, and Ananth V. Iyer, 217–238, Florida: CRC Press, 2012.

Strauss, Anselm L. *Qualitative analysis for social scientists*. New York: Cambridge University Press. 1987.

Taylor, David, and Stephen Pettit. "A consideration of the relevance of lean supply chain concepts for humanitarian aid provision." *International Journal of Services Technology and Management* 12.4 (2009): 430–444.

Thomas, Anisya, and Lynn Fritz. "Disaster relief, inc." *Harvard Business Review* 84.11 (2006): 114–126.

Tomasini, Rolando M., and Luk N. Van Wassenhove, "From preparedness to partnerships: Case study research on humanitarian logistics." *International Transactions in Operational Research* 16.5 (2009a): 549–559.

Tomasini, Rolando M., and Luk N. Van Wassenhove. *Humanitarian logistics*. New York: Palgrave Macmillan, 2009b.

Towill, Denis, and Martin Christopher. "The supply chain strategy conundrum: To be lean or agile or to be lean and agile?" *International Journal of Logistics* 5.3 (2002): 299–309.

Van Hoek R.I., Remko, Alan Harrison, and Martin Christopher. "Measuring agile capabilities in the supply chain." *International Journal of Operations & Production Management* 21.1/2 (2001): 126–148.

Van Wassenhove, Luk N. "Humanitarian aid logistics: Supply chain management in high gear." *Journal of the Operational Research Society* 57.5 (2006): 475–489.

Van Wassenhove, Luk N., Rolando M. Tomasini, and Orla Stapleton. "Corporate responses to humanitarian disasters: The mutual benefits of private-humanitarian cooperation." Conference Board, 2008.

Vega, Diego, and Christine Roussat. "Humanitarian logistics: The role of logistics service providers." *International Journal of Physical Distribution & Logistics Management* 45.4 (2015): 352–375.

Wymer, Walter W., Sridhar Samu, "Dimensions of business and non-profit colla-borative relationships", In *Nonprofit and business sector collaboration. Social enter-prises, cause-related marketing, sponsorships, and other corporate-nonprofit dealings*, edited by Wymer, W.W. and Samu, S (2003) 3–22, Best Business Books, The Haworth Press, Binghamton, NY.

Yin, Robert. *Case study research: Design and methods*. California: Sage Publications, (1994).

Zyck, Steven, and Randolph Kent. "Humanitarian crises, emergency preparedness, and response: The role of business and the private sector." Final report, HPG Paper. London: Humanitarian Policy Group, Overseas Development Institute (2014), http://www.odi.org/publications/8534-private-sector-business-compa nies-humanitarian-emergencies-disasters-csr.

# Part IV

## Variety of Topics

# 12

# How Flexibility Accommodates Demand Variability in a Service Chain: Insights from Exploratory Interviews in the Refugee Supply Chain

Kirstin Scholten, Carolien de Blok
and Robbin-Jan Haar

## Introduction

The exodus of hundreds of thousands of refugees from the Middle East, Northern Africa and Eastern Europe has caused major challenges for the European Union. In 2015 alone, more than 800,000 refugees entered the European Union, the majority from Syria, Afghanistan, Iraq, Eritrea or Somalia (Human Rights Watch 2015). The backgrounds of these refugees vary to a large extend in terms of gender, nationality, age, taken route, religious beliefs et cetera, which ultimately implies different medical, social and legal needs when they arrive in Europe (Arnold et al. 2015; Burnett and Peel 2001). This variability in needs that the consumer, in this case the refugee (unintentionally) introduces, is also known as demand variability. Demand variability is not only a challenge in refugee services, but has a negative effect on the aims of for-profit (service) organizations as well (Frei 2006; Germain et al. 2008; Yao et al. 2008). Given the often limited resources available to organizations that deal with refugees, it is important to find effective ways of dealing with variability in demand to be able to continuously adapt and quickly respond to the diversity in needs.

K. Scholten (✉) · C. de Blok · R.-J. Haar
University of Groningen, Groningen, The Netherlands
e-mail: k.scholten@rug.nl; c.de.blok@rug.nl; Robbin-Jan.haar@live.nl

© The Author(s) 2018                                                              **359**
G. Kovács et al. (eds.), *The Palgrave Handbook of Humanitarian Logistics
and Supply Chain Management*, https://doi.org/10.1057/978-1-137-59099-2_12

Even though the practical use of supply chain management (SCM) in the refugee chain has been recognized, little effort has been put into developing a sound basis on how SCM could operate within this chain. Aid and service provision to refugees is treated as a series of discrete activities on various levels of the system, with little connections between the various stages and levels of service delivery (Human Rights Watch 2015). In order to improve the current refugee situation various key factors such as coordination, relocation mechanisms, capacity management, prevention of backlogs and delays, streamlining of procedures and processes, and access to service networks have been highlighted (Human Rights Watch 2015), which are all topics and concepts well-known to the supply chain and operations fields. Fulfilling customer needs through information management, processes, resources and service performances, from the earliest supplier to the end-user is what Baltacioglu et al. (2007) referred to as service SCM. Service SCM has an academic basis in more general supply chain literature (Sampson 2000) and both product- and service-oriented supply chains have employed efforts to reduce and accommodate demand variability. These two approaches of reducing versus accommodating have been in constant tension with each other (Frei 2006; Lambert and Cooper 2000). Nonetheless, Frei (2006) mentioned that for service organizations it is unwise and even impossible to eliminate variability due to (1) the fact that value is perceived by the amount of variability accommodated and (2) customers (in our case refugees) themselves being inputs for the delivery of services. Hence, accommodating variability appears to be the most feasible approach. One way of accommodating demand variability is through flexibility, which enables organizations to deal with high levels of uncertainty (Manuj and Mentzer 2008) and to continuously adapt to the ever-changing diversity in needs of refugees.

As activities of refugee service organizations consist of different interlinked steps and stages linking flexibility to accommodating demand variability would help service organizations to serve their customers better and ultimately improve the situation for many refugees. To the best knowledge of the authors, however, there exists no literature that explicitly relates service supply chain flexibility to the accommodation of demand variability. In fact, flexibility in a service setting is subject to multiple ambiguities, making it difficult to express a relationship between flexibility and demand variability from literature alone. As both service organizations and governments have expressed a need for flexibility to manage the variability of refugee needs (Jamal 2000; Karakas 2015; Mesco and Pop 2016; OM International 2015) an exploration of both concepts, how they manifest in the refugee chain and how they relate to and influence each other is required. In order to discover how service organizations can respond to the diversity in needs through flexibility, using the European refugee crisis (particularly within the Netherlands) as a research context, this research aims to explore *how flexibility can enable service supply chains to accommodate refugee-introduced demand variability.*

This chapter is set up as follows. First, we review relevant literature on flexibility and demand variability in the service supply chain context. Following, we give further background on the research context of the study (the refugee application procedure in the Netherlands) and we outline the methodological approach employed to answer the research question in depth. As insight into service supply chains in general, and how variability and flexibility are dealt with in these chains in particular are still in their infancy, we set up a qualitative study based on exploratory interviews. The underlying principles, best practice and challenges of employing this method will be outlined in detail. Next, the findings are presented and discussed in light of literature. We conclude with implications for theory and methods used.

# Theoretical Background

## Demand Variability

Research on demand variability to date is limited to commerce; however, the parallel to the refugee setting can be drawn, bearing in mind two main differences: firstly, different to regular customers refugees are not in a position of power or leverage as they are (sometimes even with their lives) dependent on the services offered similar to the humanitarian aid setting (Oloruntoba and Gray 2009). Hence, it is argued that non-voluntary consumers like refugees are inclined to simply accept the services that are offered (Jung et al. 2015). Secondly, demand variability is not always the result of a direct request from the refugee or customer, but can also be the result of an assessment or diagnosis of needs by the service provider; for instance the identification of different health-care needs (e.g., Burnett and Peel 2001; Busch-Armendariz et al. 2011). Therefore, demand variability in services can be defined as the variety in requests and needs introduced by the customer or as perceived by the service provider (Frei 2006).

Demand variability comes in different forms: arrival variability, request variability, capability variability, effort variability and subjective preference variability (see Table 12.1 for further definition and explanation) (Frei 2006).

**Table 12.1** Five types of demand variability (based on Frei 2006)

| Type of variability | Explanation |
| --- | --- |
| Arrival variability | Customers do not request for service at the same time, or at times specified by the organization. |
| Request variability | Customers ask for a wide range of services, or have unique needs that are difficult to accommodate. |
| Capability variability | Customers have different capabilities in terms of knowledge, skills, etcetera, while participating in the service process. |
| Effort variability | Customers apply various amounts of effort and energy in participating in the service process. |
| Subjective preference variability | Customers have different opinions and perceptions on how they are treated and serviced. |

These five types of demand variability are strongly interrelated and may occur in sequential order from a customer arriving, requesting a service, being part of a delivery process (capability and effort) to assessing the delivered service (Frei 2006; Yang 2011). Additionally, customers are not merely recipients of the service but often part of the service delivery process (Maull et al. 2012). Therefore, a customer that introduces one type of variability may simultaneously introduce other types of variability as a result of a discrepancy in perceptions between customer and service provider (Yang 2011). This suggests that a customer introducing for example arrival variability by neglecting a reservation policy may also introduce capability variability in vaguely describing the service request, implying the customer's perception on how the request is treated, is subject to variability as well.

In a service setting, demand variability has two faces; on the one hand, a lot of value is perceived from how the variability the customer introduces is accommodated rather than turned down (Frei 2006; Yang 2006). This implies that demand variability can function as an opportunity for service organizations to add additional value, if their service model supports it. On the other hand, demand variability has shown to decrease the productivity of service operations and service levels, as the high variety of tasks make it more difficult to measure and manage employee performance and specialize in certain tasks (Devroye and Eichfeld 2009). Cross-trained employees, for example, are able to cover a wider range of tasks but can cause lower levels of quality as they are less experienced in specific areas when compared to more specialized employees (Sayin and Karabati 2007). Other effects of demand variability are related to increased costs (Boutsioli 2010; Frei 2006), decreased efficiency (Frei 2006) and excess capacity of personnel and equipment (Almeida and Cima 2015; Boutsioli 2010). Research on overcoming demand variability has resulted in an overview of various management tactics (for an outline of the most effective tactics, see Appendix A). However, as most of the management tactics require the service organization to respond quickly to changing customer needs and changing conditions, flexibility is required. This implies that flexibility could also enable service organizations to accommodate the different demand variabilities introduced by refugees as outlined above.

## Flexibility in Service Supply Chains

Although there is no clear and uniform definition of supply chain flexibility, it has been defined by means of different dimensions or components (e.g., Duclos et al. 2003; Stevenson and Spring 2007; Vickery et al. 1999). While these dimensions and components often differ in relation to the supply chain perspectives they take (e.g., supplier perspective versus customer perspective), they all point towards the goal of accommodating the different needs of the customer. Above all, it is mentioned that flexibility enables organizations to deal with high levels of uncertainty (Manuj and Mentzer 2008), which in this research relates to the uncertainty that is introduced by demand variability. Particular to the service supply chain setting, Arias-Aranda (2003) identified nine dimensions of supply chain flexibility. Table 12.2 provides an overview and explanation of the nine types of flexibility. The third column of Table 12.2 gives an example of the relevance for refugee service organizations specifying the types of service flexibility applicable to the research context.

While literature on flexibility in services does not explicitly state how or when to achieve the different types of flexibility it has been stated that flexibility should have a strategic, rather than operational focus before it can enable the management of demand variability (Duclos et al. 2003). Furthermore, Merschmann and Thonemann (2011) emphasize that flexibility needs to fit the changing environment as implementing and sustaining flexibility is costly. Literature on more specific means to operationalize the types of flexibility, however, is lacking. Yet, flexibility could for example be achieved by altering capacity levels (expansion flexibility), a platform for connectivity (information distribution flexibility), cross-trained employees (labor and equipment flexibility), being able to step aside from bureaucracy (services and servuction flexibility), or creating a citizenship culture (volume flexibility). Note that process flexibility and programming flexibility might not be applicable to the refugee setting, due to their systems focus.

**Table 12.2** Nine types of service flexibility

| Type of service flexibility | Explanation | Example of relevance for refugee service organizations |
|---|---|---|
| Expansion flexibility | The ability to which capacity can be added when needed. | The management of a refugee facility hiring extra personnel or drawing on the volunteer-database when forecasting a spike in refugee influx. |
| Information distribution flexibility | The ability to distribute and share information through the service delivery system. | A psychologist making the lawyer aware that the refugee under issue is suffering from a severe trauma, which could delay his appointment, so the lawyer can build slack in the schedule. |
| Routing flexibility | The ability to use alternative processing routes to deliver a service. | A refugee lawyer unable to drive to the various locations due to time constraints, who decides to set up a consult for refugees through a video call. |
| Labor and equipment flexibility | The ability of personnel and machines to perform different operations. | The cook or restaurant at a refugee facility being able to deliver both Halal food and regular food to serve both Islamic and non-Islamic refugees. |
| Market flexibility | The ability of the service delivery system to adapt to market changes. | A refugee facility adapting from an influx of mostly exploring Syrian men to an influx of mostly families, due to new political actions. |
| Services and servuction* flexibility | The ability of the system to add or substitute services without major efforts.<br>*Note that servuction refers to the production of services (Arias-Aranda, Bustinza and Barrales-Molina 2011). | Offering a refugee psychological assistance when a refugee appears to be in need of that, even though the refugee initially needed medical needs only. |
| Process flexibility | The ability of a system to operate unattended for longer periods. | *Not applicable.* |
| Programming flexibility | The ability to produce different part types without major effort. | *Not applicable.* |
| Volume flexibility | The ability to operate at different levels of output. | Administrative clerks skipping lunch breaks when seeing a large line of refugees before the office to increase capacity. |

Adapted from Creswell (2003) and Lincoln and Guba (1985)

## Relationship Between Service Supply Chain Flexibility and Demand Variability

While literature suggests accommodation tactics for organizations to deal with variability (see Appendix A), to the best of the authors' knowledge, no clear link has been established with flexibility to date. Connections between flexibility and demand variability are difficult to make for several reasons. Firstly, one can argue that different types of flexibility may be used to accommodate one type of demand variability, while at the same time one type of flexibility may be used to accommodate multiple types of demand variability: request handling, for example, may be an approach to accommodate effort as well as capability variability; both volume flexibility and expansion flexibility increase the amount of service delivered; only the means and prerequisites through which that increase is achieved are different (Sawhney 2006). Additionally, in terms of capacity, one may say that different types of flexibility can be both collectively exhaustive and mutually exclusive. When deciding, for instance, to implement routing flexibility by ensuring capacity at multiple locations, service organizations can gain total capacity (incorporating expansion flexibility at the same time), which is then spread over multiple locations or departments. Hence, one may still need to implement additional expansion flexibility to ensure capacity at one (for instance, the busiest) service location. The extra capacity, however, does not automatically lead to additional flexibilities as these extra employees might not have been trained to also add service content (service and servuction flexibility) or handle variety in requests (labor and equipment flexibility). This results in a lot of ambiguity and tension between the types of flexibility and how these can be used in practice. In line with the aim of this chapter we explore *how* flexibility (as represented by the flexibility types in Table 12.2) can be used to accommodate demand variability (as represented by the demand variability types in Table 12.1) in service supply chains.

## Research Context (The Netherlands)

Europe has seen a large influx in refugees from around the summer of 2014, which increased drastically in spring 2015 (Brunsden and Wagstyl 2015). To strive for continuity, Human Rights Watch (2015) identified the different stages that refugees go through: acute service provision at Europe's border, the asylum procedure in a particular country and, when granted asylum, integration in that country. This allows us to derive three types of service chains: acute services chain (shelter, food, safety), short-term (ST) services chain (asylum process, health-care, temporary housing, financial assistance) and long-term (LT) services chain (education, labor integration, housing). In this study, we will particularly focus on the ST and LT service supply chain in the Netherlands.

Once arrived in the Netherlands, the refugee application processes, hence ST service chain in the Dutch context consists of mainly four phases (not considering the possibilities for appeal in case of a negative decision on the asylum appeal) (Vluchtelingenwerk 2015a; UNHCR 2015): phase one – application and registration; phase two – preparation for procedure (rest period); phase three – start asylum procedures; phase four – request accepted/rejected. During these four phases, different organizations interact in a chain to provide services to the refugees. Refugees request asylum from the government in phase one. During the four phases temporary shelter is provided by a governmental organization (GO). Additionally, interpreters and lawyers are contracted by the government; health-care providers help to cover essential needs of the refugees and to ensure that applicants are "fit for interviews." A nongovernmental organization (NGO) helps refugees by providing additional information about procedures. In case of minors applying for asylum a specific GO is activated. Sometimes another NGO is also involved to help find family members that might be in disperse locations all over Europe. The procedure during the four phases is quite standardized in terms of the overall procedure and process steps. This changes once asylum has been granted and refugees become part of the LT service supply chain.

Only after asylum has been granted, refugees are transferred to an asylum center. Here, they receive some standard services such as basic insurances and continued free public transport as well as services that are reflecting individual needs and capabilities. These services concern physical and mental care, financial support and education. Once accepted, refugees receive a residence permit for five years. They must attend to integration and language courses and obtain the same rights as Dutch citizens. The emphasis is now on integration of the different refugees into the existing structures and setups of municipalities and Dutch society. This requires additional organizations to get involved, that is, health-care insurances and providers, schools, local governments and so on. A graphical representation of the ST and LT chains and involved parties is given in Fig. 12.1a, b.

**(a)**

| | Short-term service chain | | | |
|---|---|---|---|---|
| **What**<br>**Whom** | Application and registration | Rest period | Asylum procedures | Request accepted/rejected |
| Shelter org. | X | X | X | X |
| Health care | X | X | | |
| Lawyer | X | | X | X |
| Translator | X | X | X | X |
| Psychologist | X | | | |
| Volunteers | X | X | X | |
| National govt. | X | | | X |

**(b)**

| | Long-term service chain | | | |
|---|---|---|---|---|
| **What**<br>**Whom** | Receive permit | Placement in center | Basic living arrangements | Ongoing integration activities |
| National govt. | X | | | |
| Local govt. | | X | X | X |
| Health care | | | X | |
| Insurers | | | X | |
| Housing org. | | X | X | |
| Education orgs. | | | | X |
| Financial support | | | X | X |
| Public transport | | | X | |

**Fig. 12.1** (a) Activities and parties involved in short-term refugee supply chain. (b) Activities and parties involved in long-term refugee supply chain

Over the past 12 months (second half of 2015 and first half of 2016), 42766 refugees applied for asylum in the Netherlands of which about 80 percent received asylum and hence, permission to stay in the Netherlands for the longer term (Vluchtelingenwerk 2015b). Figure 12.2 depicts the arrival of refugees in the Netherlands in terms of volume, age and gender. Additionally, Fig. 12.3 shows that the refugees applying for asylum in the

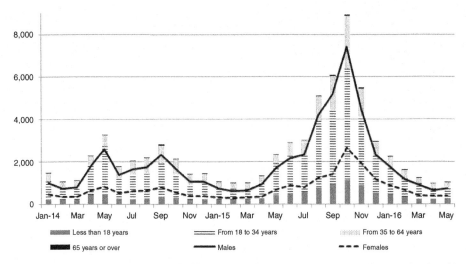

**Fig. 12.2** Age and gender of first time asylum applicants in the Netherlands (based on Eurostat 2016)

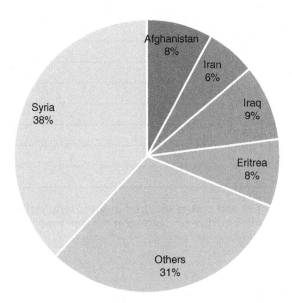

**Fig. 12.3** Country of origin of first asylum applicants in the Netherlands from September 2015 to August 2016 (based on IND 2016)

Netherlands differ in their nationality and background. At the same time, these figures show how arrival, request and capability variability are introduced to the asylum procedure system that service providing organizations try to accommodate.

# Methodology

Exploratory research is often used in early research stages, when the purpose is to gain familiarity with a phenomenon or acquire new insight, for example in new contexts or to formulate more precise relations. There is little knowledge available on the refugee chain in Europe and how flexibility can enable service supply chain organizations to accommodate refugee-introduced demand variability, hence, exploratory research will allow us to gain insights and explore the relationship between demand variability and flexibility in this specific setting. The unit of analysis was set as an organization in the refugee service supply chain.

Particularly qualitative research is often perceived to accommodate exploratory research because it aims to find meaning, description, concepts, definitions, metaphors, symbols or characteristics in textual data and the spoken word, rather than numerical data through the use of statistical methods (Berg and Lune 2012). As such, qualitative research enables a deep understanding of the issue under investigation by providing thick and detailed descriptions of concrete actions in real-life contexts that preserve the actual meanings that participants ascribe to these actions and settings (Gephart 2004). Qualitative research enables a researcher to get first-hand knowledge of the subject under investigation (Näslund 2002) and develop active skills which include identifying the key issues, working out how they might be resolved and understanding the intellectual, practical, moral and political implications of different ways of resolving them (Mason 2002). While the close relationship between the researcher and the subject matter is important, particular attention has to be paid to staying as objective as possible. In the study at hand, various guidelines in the composition, data collection and analysis were followed to avoid pitfalls in relation to objectivity so that trustworthiness could be ensured (see Table 12.3).

## Data Collection

To gather data on how flexibility enables service supply chains to accommodate demand variability, exploratory semi-structured interviews were conducted. Interviews are one of the most frequently used forms of qualitative research methods (Mason 2002). It is a form of conversation that enables the gathering of valuable in-depth understanding on how concepts relate and helps to build theory (Ellram 1996). Semi-structured interviewing was deemed to be the most appropriate data collection method for this study as it facilitated the needed flexibility during the interviews allowing for in-depth

**Table 12.3** Trustworthiness assessment

| Trustworthiness criteria | Phase of research | Measures taken in this study |
|---|---|---|
| **Credibility** (Ensures that findings are congruent from the perspective of the participants) | Data collection | • Early familiarization with the culture of the participants' organizations through studying and analyzing website, press releases and annual reports before the first data collection dialogue took place.<br>• Interviewee triangulation: Using multiple sources of evidence. |
| | Composition | • Key informants reviewed and provided feedback on draft interview reports. |
| **Dependability** (Assesses the consistency of data collection, data analysis and theory generation over time) | Data collection | • Used case study protocol and interview guide.<br>• Continuous reflection of multiple researchers. |
| | Data analysis | • Developed interview database.<br>• Continuous reflection of multiple researchers. |
| | Composition | • Provided detailed description of methodology employed.<br>• Continuous reflection of multiple researchers. |
| **Transferability** (Degree to which findings can apply or transfer in a different project) | Data analysis | • Established a chain of evidence of coding. |
| | Composition | • Provided thick descriptions of contextual background wherever possible without compromising anonymity of participants. |
| **Confirmability** (Measure of how well the inquiry's findings are supported by the data collected) | Composition | • External audits through discussion of findings with academic experts, review process of book chapter.<br>• While every effort was taken to minimize shortcomings, those limitations which could not be overcome are recognized in the limitations of this study. |

Adapted from Arias-Aranda (2003)

exploration of the variables under study while at the same time enabling to use a core set of questions for easy data comparison. Flexibility in the interviews was believed to be particularly important as we aimed to interview a large variety of organizations and people involved in different stages of the refugee application procedure ranging from GOs to NGOs and commercial businesses. We were aware of the risk that this might introduce a broad variety of motives and practices of organizations, yet given the exploratory nature of the subject, we wanted to ensure that we investigate the topic from every possible angle. While this created challenges, for example when engaging with an organization involved in public governance in terms of ensuring that we do not get involved in the political nature of the topic, it allowed us to get an in-depth understanding of the different stakeholders, their practices and forces at play in the refugee service supply chain. To stay focused and on track, the interviews were guided by selection criteria for interviewees, an interview protocol and procedures during the interview process.

Interviewees were selected based on (i) the organization the interviewee works for having to be a partner in the refugee service chain and (ii) the interviewee being either on a management level or in an operational position with authority to make decisions related to the accommodation of variability. We had several discussions on whether to interview refugees or not. On the one hand, the perspective of the refugee on the subject of our research would provide additional insights, on the other hand, there were ethical concerns in engaging with people that might be traumatized, psychologically unstable or simply exhausted from a long journey. Ultimately, the decision taken was to exclude the refugees' perspective from our study, which meant at the same time, that we had to exclude one of the variables (i.e. subjective preference variability) from the data collection.

An interview protocol was developed compromising the set of questions to be used in interviews (Voss et al. 2002) (see Appendix B), an information sheet (see Appendix C) and an informed consent form (see Appendix D) to enhance the trustworthiness of this study – see also Table 12.3. Accordingly, all interviews started with general questions about the background and position of the interviewee. The second part of the interview concentrated on the setup of the organization, the role of the organization in the refugee chain and in fulfilling the needs of refugees. The main part of the interviews followed a standard core (to facilitate data comparison) with open-ended questions and probes. We aimed to gain insights into the extent to which demand variability exists in a refugee setting, is perceived, and is managed by the organizations involved as well as in the chain as a whole. Additionally, we asked questions building on how demand variability is managed, seeking for aspects of flexibility. We purposefully designed the main part of the interview protocol to contain broad exploratory questions given the nature of the study and to be able to capture the possible broad array of answers from the different interviewees. At the same time, we asked interviewees to recall specific situations to have rich examples that would help to find answers to the research questions. At the end of the interview participants were asked for their feedback and additional comments to create a feeling of closure of the interview process.

Interviews with 13 people from different levels (operational staff, functional managers and higher strategic positions) within their respective organizations were conducted for the researchers to be able to get a deep and informed understanding about specific situations and reactions in relation to flexibility and variability. An overview of the interviews conducted is depicted in Table 12.4. Because of the exploratory character of the study, getting access to a diverse pool of interviewees was deemed more important than a balanced or equal representation of organizations active in the chain. Moreover, since the aim of this study is to get a first and broad insight into practices conducted in the refugee chain and not to compare organizations or cases (based on literal or theoretical replication) we freely approached organizations and interviewees. As such, we used personal contacts as well as social media (e.g., LinkedIn) to

**Table 12.4** Overview of data collection

| Organization - interviewee # | Type of service | Interviewee position | Part of chain | Duration of interview |
|---|---|---|---|---|
| A – 1 & 2 | Refugee assistance (NGO) | Team leaders | ST | 65 minutes (two interviewees) |
| B – 3 | Reception services (GO) | Case manager | ST | 45 minutes |
| C – 4 | Legal services (service organization) | Refugee lawyer | ST | 58 minutes (via phone) |
| D – 5 | Health-care insurance (NGO) | Division manager | ST | 60 minutes |
| E – 6 | Public governance (GO) | Program manager chain information | ST | 58 minutes |
| F – 7 | Refugee assistance (NGO) | Advisor public affairs | ST | 38 minutes |
| G – 8 | Refugee decision services (GO) | Deputy director | ST | 40 minutes |
| H – 9 | Health care and welfare (NGO) | Policy advisor | ST & LT | 46 minutes |
| I – 10 | Public governance (GO) | Municipality council member | LT | 28 minutes |
| J – 11 | Public governance (GO) | Municipality council member | LT | 38 minutes |
| K – 12 & 13 | Public governance operations (GO) | Project manager and trainee | LT | 50 minutes (two interviewees) |
| A – 14 | Refugee assistance (NGO) | Team leader | LT | 64 minutes |
| L – 15 | Refugee education (NGO) | Educational manager | LT | 52 minutes |

approach 34 potential interviewees and check their fit with and interest in our study. Moreover, snowballing, based on the contacts of people that were interviewed in early stages of the study, was used to approach potential interviewees to be included at later stages. Although there is no common benchmark on what amount of interviews is enough to saturate the data, Guest, Buhnse and Johnson (2006) propose 12 interviews. In line with that, we were able to reach saturation by conducting 13 interviews.

In terms of the interview process, interviews were whenever possible conducted by two researchers to limit researcher bias, were recorded and transcribed verbatim to provide for a comprehensive data analysis. All transcripts were sent back to the interviewees for verification within 48 hours, in order to prevent interpretative issues and hence, impinge on validity. Where necessary, data collection was followed up with emails and calls to fill in missing details. After the transcript had been approved by the interviewee, the audio file was deleted. All interviews followed best practice of interviewing.

## Data Analysis

In accordance with Miles and Huberman (1994) data collection, coding and analysis in this study took place simultaneously allowing for flexibility in the research process. In a first analysis step, we reduced all data to quotes, phrases or paragraphs that were truly applicable to answer the research question. Following, we deduced first order codes based on the two sets of variables coding each quote once for a type of variability (see Table 12.1) and a second time for a type of flexibility (see Table 12.2). This then allowed us to juxtapose the two first order codes with the aim of searching for tactics that show how flexibility can accommodate variability. In doing so, we were able to identify eight accommodation tactics (second order categories) that could be categorized into the three third-order themes of capacity related, communication related and service delivery related tactics. An excerpt of coding can be found in Table 12.5. In a final step we distinguished the data between ST and LT to further compare and contrast differences in accommodation tactics and categories. Furthermore, it is notable that some second order categories could not be juxtaposed, that is, they related to a flexibility type or a variability type, but not to both. To overcome this challenge, several discussion between the researchers took place which lead to the conclusion that this was mostly due to the fact that these quotes related to facilitators of flexibility or variability. A decision was taken to exclude these quotes from

Table 12.5 Excerpt of coding

| Quotes | First-order code: variability | First-order code: flexibility | Second-order categories | Third-order themes |
|---|---|---|---|---|
| "Well, in light of the high influx we've developed an asylum dashboard what at a certain point in time really showed some issues from the logistics center on a daily basis" (Org. E) | Arrival | Information distribution | Coordination meetings | Communication related |
| "And that [the capacity meeting] has been evoked due to the increased influx (…) it has been a wish from the participating institutions. And it works very well" (Org. D) | | | | |
| "It depends on whether there are few people [refugees] coming in, and a lot of people [refugees] going out…so one week you have a job and two weeks later you don't have a job, that's how it works" (Org. A, Int. 1) | | Expansion | Adapt capacity or output | Capacity related |
| "Yes, put more hours into it, and just follow and give full measure" (Org. C) | | Volume | | |
| "But these kind of things [the increase of demand], well, they hit you and you simply have to deal with it" (Org. I) | | Volume | Facilitate ad hoc response | Service delivery related |
| "Someone with the skills of an ambulance nurse, which is between 10 PM and 8 AM on location is first going to check with the client if something needs to be done" (Org. D) | | Labor and equipment | | |

further analysis as considerations of facilitators of the two leading concepts under scrutiny were deemed to be outside the scope of this study.

# Results

In exploring how flexibility can help organizations to accommodate variability introduced by consumers (refugees), the analysis of data resulted in the identification of eight "accommodation tactics" (adapt capacity or output, coordination meetings, establishing a supply chain database, facilitating an ad hoc response, segmenting the market, modifying service to reduce required capability, developing capability through training, and stressing the importance of consumer effort) over three categories (capacity, communication and service delivery related). Furthermore, a distinction between the ST and the LT refugee chain shows, that not all accommodation tactics are relevant for either of the two. Following, we present the detailed findings in relation to each variability type.

## Accommodating Arrival Variability

We found that arrival variability can be accommodated with capacity, communication and service delivery related tactics. In particular, the analysis shows that adapting capacity or output, coordination meetings and facilitating an ad hoc response via expansion, volume, information distribution and labor and equipment flexibility can help to deal with customers that request services at different times or at times not specified by the service provider. Table 12.6 gives an overview of the different tactics in the ST and LT supply chains.

**Table 12.6** Accommodation tactics for arrival variability

| Accommodation category | Accommodation tactic | | Flexibility type |
| --- | --- | --- | --- |
| | Short term | Long term | |
| Capacity related | Adapt capacity or output | Adapt capacity or output | - Expansion flexibility<br>- Volume flexibility |
| Communication related | Coordination meetings | Coordination meetings | Information distribution flexibility |
| Service delivery related | Facilitate ad hoc response | Facilitate ad hoc response | - Labor and equipment flexibility<br>- Volume flexibility |

The analysis of data shows, that capacity related tactics (i.e. scaling up or down) are frequently used to manage the influx of refugees over the past 18 months: "*How does one creatively manage such an issue? How does an organization do that? Well, scaling up and scaling down, which has to do with governance and thinking across borders*" (Org. D). We found that most organizations make use of volume flexibility, that is, adding additional working hours or working more efficient ("*we have to change gears to realize certain things now*" (Org. A, Int. 1)) rather than expansion flexibility, that is, hiring additional staff "*because the demand, the influx, it goes up and it goes down*" (Org. C). Hence, expanding might lead to redundancies when having to down-scale in response to a decreasing influx in the future. While we found volume and expansion flexibility to be applicable in both the ST and the LT the analysis of data reflects that organizations involved in the ST chain put greater emphasis on volume flexibility than organizations in the LT chain. As the influx of refugees in the ST chain is much more uncertain than in the LT, applying expansion flexibility becomes more difficult: "*it depends, on whether there are few people [refugees] coming in, and a lot of people [refugees] going out... so one week you have a job and two weeks later you don't have a job, that's how it works*" (Org. A, Int. 1). Therefore, volume flexibility is used to compensate for the high level of uncertainty. This is somewhat different in the LT where incoming numbers of refugees can be derived from developments in the ST chain and allow for more LT planning in terms of expansion flexibility.

Additionally, we found the communication related tactic of coordination meetings with chain partners to be relevant in both the ST and LT chain for accommodating arrival variability. Coordination meetings enable flexibility in relation to information distribution as they allow to set and divide tasks and roles within the chain: "*It's denoted as the 'field table', and there are all the key players at one table with a whole lot of organizations [at which the most important thing to discuss is] of course that you do this and I do that, don't sit on each other's chair, and I take over when you're finished so I can return this*" (Org. J). As the aim of such coordination meetings is to enable organizations to better deal with arrival fluctuations and hence differing demand levels, status updates help chain organizations to coordinate their own efforts. For example, Organization E referred to RAG (Red, Amber, Green) status criteria for updates and Organization J highlighted that "*what works particularly well with [chain summit] is making it insightful by means of eh, diagrams and such. Very simply: 'do you deliver what you had to deliver?', 'yes I did, my diagram is green, but yours is red', and then these parties can address these things at the table (...).*" Findings suggest that such coordination meetings happen in relation to different topics, for example, capacity either physical or online ("*Well, in light of the high influx we've developed an asylum dashboard what at a certain point in time really showed some issues from the logistics center on a daily basis*" (Org. E)) and with different chain members involved.

Furthermore, we also found that the service delivery related tactic of facilitating an ad hoc response accommodates arrival variability via labor and equipment as well as volume flexibility in both the ST and LT chain. "*These kind of things [the increase of demand], well, they hit you and you simply have to deal with it*" (Org. I). Examples in the data that we found related to sharp increases in day care needs in the ST or housing in the LT. Furthermore, night time needs required additional considerations as organizations "*saw people just calling 911 when something was the matter, sometimes as much as three times in a single night.*" As a solution for this issue, a flexible way of assessing needs in the middle of the night was introduced where "*someone with the skills of an ambulance nurse, which is between 10 PM and 8 AM on location is first going to check with the client if something needs to be done*" (Org. D). While the ad hoc response suggests some overlap with the capacity related tactic of adapting capacity or output, it is different in terms of operationalization as it involves labor and equipment flexibility.

## Accommodating Request Variability

In relation to request variability we found that the communication related tactics of establishing a data base with chain partners and the service delivery related tactics of market segmentation, and facilitating an ad hoc response accommodated customers asking for a wide range of or unique services via market, information distribution, labor and equipment, volume, routing, and services and servuction flexibility. Table 12.7 gives an overview of the findings in relation to request variability for the ST and LT chain.

We found that request variability requires information sharing and hence flexibility in terms of distributing information. The analysis of data shows that the communication related tactic of establishing a database with chain members enables individual organization to be aware and know about the different needs and requests of a refugee in the ST and LT chain. This is reflected upon by Organization A (Int. 1): "*Sometimes, for example: a wife comes in and the husband is trying to find here, but she doesn't really want to be found. It is quite useful if [chain partner] wrote a memo [in the system] like 'miss X is here, and she does not want to be found by her husband.*" While this quote demonstrates the need for a shared system across the supply chain to

**Table 12.7** Accommodation tactics for request variability

| Accommodation category | Accommodation tactic | | Flexibility type |
|---|---|---|---|
| | Short term | Long term | |
| Communication related | Establish database with chain partners | Establish database with chain partners | Information distribution flexibility |
| Service delivery related | Market segmentation | | Market flexibility |
| | Facilitate ad hoc response | | - Routing flexibility |
| | | | - Services and servuction flexibility |

accommodate request variability, at the time of conducting this research, no single database was in place in the ST chain: "*Of course not! Well we have the [intranet name], that's for the disclosures, information on countries and so on but of course I don't have any access, [laughter] on databases from other eh, partners. And sometimes it's very difficult to receive information...*" (Org. C) or in the LT chain: "*(...) we receive no information about the refugee, except from himself*" (Org. L). At the same time, however, we found evidence for the intention and importance of developing a joint database as indicated by Organization E: "*(...) so that all loose information systems will be provided with a single search engine, so that, if you find someone from safety and migration you can check 'I know him from asylum, I know him from visa, I know him from criminal records, I know him from Schengen, I know him from stolen/lost travelling documents', and that all with secure privacy.*" Similarly, Organization G confirms that a joint data base is on their agenda "*we are working on a central planning system, but it is still a long way to go.*"

Additionally, we found that the service delivery related tactics market segmentation, and facilitating an ad hoc response can help to accommodate request variability in the ST chain via market, labor and equipment, services and servuction, volume and routing flexibility. Here, the analysis of data highlights tension between responding to request on an individual or group level. While organizations intend to focus on individual requests ("*no I consider them all as individual, (...) but of course cases, a lot of these cases are similar (...) well, hmmm, you know the cases are similar so perhaps I approach them the same way, that's possible, yes*" (Org. C)), this is due to the large influx of refugees not always possible and hence, segmentation of needs in groups is required. One way of segmentation on a group level is the Dutch five-track system: "*The state secretary has tried to make a division for each asylum seeker in five tracks, so someone comes here and can in five different tracks... so can be assigned to five different groups [based on their country of origin]*" (Org A., Int. 1). Organization E adds the supply chain benefits that follow the 5-track system: "*Shelter capacity is scarce, and with this approach we are differentiating with what's called the track policy to at least make sure that people from safe countries or known from another country, so Dublin claimers, that a very quick decision can be made – by plucking them out of the line and not treat them according to the time they entered, which was the old logistical model.*" Therefore, market segmentation relates to market flexibility, as it concerns different groups of refugees and helps to deal with request variability. Lastly, we found that organizations facilitate an ad hoc response for ST requests via routing as well as services and servuction flexibility. Examples that we found relate to exceptions or irregular needs of refugees that required an ad hoc service response in the moment that they arose: "*(...) and in [reception location] we have, when the influx was really booming, facilitated an obligatory washing ritual as all people that came here through human traffickers had scabies*" (Org. D.) or an ad hoc response in relation to routing: "*few weeks ago one of my clients was in the hospital and then I travelled to the hospital [instead of the refugee travelling to me]*" (Org. C).

## Accommodating Capability Variability

We found that to accommodate capability variability, organizations employ service delivery related tactics that modify their services to reduce the required capabilities (ST chain) or develop new capabilities via training (ST and LT chain) – see Table 12.8. Hence, labor and equipment, services and servuction, expansion and volume flexibility help to deal with, for example, a customer's (limited) knowledge or skills of the service delivery process.

Our data shows that capability variety requires organizations to adjust (aspects of) their services to meet the existing capabilities of the refugee. Examples that we found particularly relate to capabilities in language: "*(...) and with [supportive organization] I have a lot of contact, but that's more about translating letters people get that they don't understand; then they can go to [supportive organization]. (...)*" (Org. B) or "*And on the locations a lot of awareness sessions are held in their own language, information folders are handed out about accessing health care, there are posters hanging... Well people of security often know what to say (...)*" (Org. D). Changing the language of the letter or translating information sessions into different languages helps to adjust an

**Table 12.8** Accommodation tactics for capability variability

| Accommodation category | Accommodation tactic | | Flexibility type |
|---|---|---|---|
| | Short term | Long term | |
| Service delivery related | Adjust service to reduce required capability | | - Labor and equipment flexibility<br>- Services and servuction flexibility |
| | Develop capability through training | Develop capability through training | - Expansion flexibility<br>- Services and servuction flexibility<br>- Volume flexibility |

aspect of the service which in turn reduces the need for the refugee to understand Dutch or English. Therefore, labor and equipment flexibility as well as services and servuction flexibility is required. At the same time, however, we found that the tactic of adjusting services to meet capability variability does not always work in practice. In relation to refugees not showing up for certain appointments one interviewee reflects: "*Well, that is what we are trying to figure out. We first thought that it maybe was the invitation because it was in Dutch…but now we translated the letters and we made it different than it was before; we tried to push a bit more, like please attend to the course, but it didn't really work out…*" (Org. A, Int. 1). As one of the aims within the overall refugee chain is to make refugees more self-sufficient to function in their "new society", adjusting services to meet refugee capability variability is considered a ST chain tactic rather than a LT chain tactic. This links closely to the second tactic that we found to accommodate capability variability: facilitating training to transfer additionally required capabilities to the refugees, which is used in the ST and LT chain. "*We're starting [project name], a nice project to teach people to learn how it works financially in Holland. We do that in the first year they are here, and they are fond to have the project*" (Org. A, Int. 14). Facilitating training, hence, relates to services and servuction flexibility (additional service) as well as expansion and volume flexibility, due to the high influx and different levels of capabilities of refugees requiring organizations to have enough training capacity available.

## Accommodating Effort Variability

Effort variability relates to customers applying different amounts of effort and energy in participating in the service delivery process. We found that stressing the importance of consumer effort, a communication related tactic,

**Table 12.9** Accommodation tactics for effort variability

| Accommodation category | Accommodation tactic | | Flexibility type |
|---|---|---|---|
| | Short term | Long term | |
| Communication related | Stress importance of consumer effort | | Services and servuction flexibility |

via services and servuction flexibility can help accommodate such variability in the ST chain (see Table 12.9).

Overall, there was little data in our analysis that related to effort variability. However, some effort variability between different refugees is evident, as clearly illustrated by organization C: "*Sometimes you have an individual who speaks broadly, and sometimes it has to do with nationality as well. If you have an Armenian refugee, well, sure the interview is longer. From Iran: long interview – it has to with the refugee as well.*" We found that this is not just apparent in the length of procedural interviews, but also in relation to attendance of appointments as organizations highlight that "*one nationality is much more loyal in making appointments than others (…), so you try to find solutions for that through better awareness sessions (…)*" (Org. D). Hence, the interviewee from Organization D suggests to stress the importance of consumer (refugee) effort using additional services (awareness sessions) and hence, service and servuction flexibility, to try and overcome effort variability.

# Discussion and Conclusion

With the refugee crisis ongoing but the future uncertain, it is crucial for organizations to know how to continue accommodating the variety of needs of refugees. Accordingly, this research set out to explore how flexibility can enable service supply chains to accommodate refugee-introduced demand variability. The analysis of qualitative data from semi-structured interviews allowed us to identify eight flexibility based accommodation tactics that were either communication, service delivery or capacity related. These accommodation tactics all relate to different forms of demand variability and ask organizations to be flexible in different areas. An overview of our findings is depicted in Fig. 12.4. It is noticeable from our findings, that there are more accommodation tactics for the ST chain than for the LT chain. As a matter of fact, there seemed to be no accommodation tactics specifically applicable to the LT chain. While this could be due to interview selection or the strong focus of organizations on the ST chain due to its urgency, another

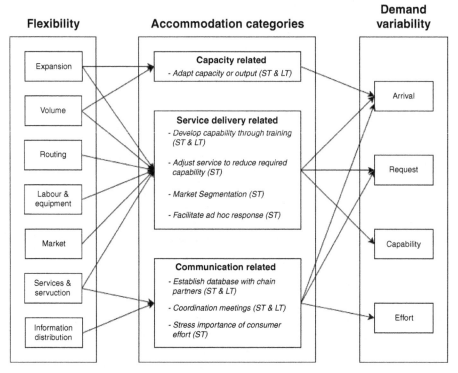

**Fig. 12.4**  Relationships between variability and flexibility

explanation could be the inherent characteristics and underlying goals of the two chains. While in the ST chain the focus is on assessment of eligibility of asylum based on specific personal characteristics, in the LT chain the aim is to integrate refugees into society. Hence, by the nature of the task, the needs of people should become more homogenous in the LT chain focusing on, for example, learning the language of the country of asylum, understanding the society, attending school or finding work et cetera.

The identified mechanisms suggest some overlap with earlier variability accommodation tactics described by Frei (2006) and Yang (2011). Yet, the novelty of this research lies in the extension of these tactics to the service supply chain setting via the concept of flexibility. While earlier research focused on the concept of variability itself and how it could be accommodated, our results provide additional tactics enabled by flexibility that are relevant for organizations collaborating in the service delivery process. Demand management can be considered the primary function of SCM (Baltacioglu et al. 2007) and relates to the ability of an organization to understand customer demand requirements and balance these against the capabilities of the network (Croxton et al. 2002; Lambert and Cooper 2000) either by managing demand or by managing supply (Sasser 1976). Hence, we were not surprised to find that organizations in the refugee chain adapted their capacity or output (manage supply) to deal with arrival variability.

At the same time, however, due to the immediate nature of services, the production and consumption of services is inseparable (e.g., Parasuraman et al. 1985). Hence, for capacity alterations to be effective they have to be planned for in advance, which was hardly possible in the refugee service chain: the large influx of refugees took many organizations by surprise and additionally little information was available on the diversity of refugees needs in advance. This required organizations to find alternative ways of dealing with variability in the *service delivery process*. We found that organizations strategically managed demand via training refugees to increase their capabilities or via segmentation. Segmentation is a strategic demand management approach that allows the grouping of different needs of key (groups of) consumers with the aim of establishing more standardized ways of dealing with the variety in terms of requests (Childerhouse et al. 2002; Lambert and Cooper 2000). At the same time, however, we also found tactics that dealt with the sudden nature of the influx and resulting variability in the ST chain. Services were adjusted to be able to deal with capability variability and with arrival and request variability had to be accommodated ad hoc rather than planned.

Service supply chain theory postulates that the service delivery process is bi-directional and initiated by the input of the consumer (Sampson 2000). Hence, we expected to find *communication-related tactics* that would help organizations to accommodate variability. However, the communication related tactics that we found, do not focus on information exchange between the refugee and the service providing organizations, but more on collaboration between the different organizations involved in the service delivery process. There are two possible explanations for this. Firstly, there is a time component to accommodating needs. Once a refugee arrives at a reception center services have to be delivered promptly. Hence, rather than having a refugee going around different organizations highlighting his or her needs, information needs to be shared and services coordinated amongst organizations to enable the fast identification of need requirements and actions to be taken accordingly. Secondly, refugees can be considered non-voluntary consumers (passive in nature) rather than customers (who pay for their needs fulfillment and expect their needs to be fully satisfied) (Jung et al. 2015). In line with that, there is little input from refugees about their needs and requirements that could guide service providers in managing arrival or request variability. Hence, there is an emphasis on sharing information between service organizations to be able to delivery services in an effective and efficient manner. At the same time, it is important to stress the importance of consumer effort to be able to gather as much information and input as possible.

## Managerial Implications

As the development of the refugee crises in Europe remains uncertain, the contribution of this research is more than merely the added theoretical knowledge. Interestingly, this research also allows to draw parallels between the refugee setting and the broader (public) health-care setting; in both supply chains consumers have limited input in the service delivery process. Hence, some of the accommodation tactics might also be relevant there. By knowing how demand variability can be accommodated by flexibility, refugee service and public health-care organizations can make specific investments in practices relevant for the types of variability they encounter. The suggested procedure to accommodate demand variability via flexibility would be to firstly, carefully assess what forms of demand variability are present in the service supply chain, and which organization(s) can or should accommodate it. This assessment also prevents "redundant" flexibility which might increase costs. And then, secondly, decide by what means the organization aims to accommodate the variability, hence choose the relevant accommodation tactics. Furthermore, thirdly, to prevent redundant investments and inefficiencies, focus on specific investments and continuously monitor performance of the accommodation tactics that enable flexibility for the different types of variability encountered. Overall, this will allow organizations to be efficient while remaining effective (flexible).

## Limitations and Suggestions for Future Research

As with all studies, this one has certain challenges and limitations, some of which are common critiques of qualitative research, whereas others stem from the particular research design of this study. Much attention and consideration has been given to possible ways of accounting for these limitations and how to minimize their impact. Firstly, the sheer quantity of sources and growing volume of rich information from qualitative data (Eisenhardt 1989) can present a huge challenge. For many issues that concern SCM, service operations and especially information around refugees it is difficult to read all available and relevant primary documents, journal articles, books and websites, or to interview all possible participants and/or different stakeholders of the refugee chain. Therefore, the researchers had to select only a small number of sources from the overall population to be studied in depth in this research. This situation can create opportunities for bias in relation to sampling (overlooking important sources or dismissing others) and analysis of data. To avoid biases the researchers made sure to use external informants and documentation to support the sampling process. Snowballing of interviewees and involvement in established projects helped to keep focus and to identify the most relevant sources of data. Nevertheless, there was limited control over the selection of candidates for interviews. While the selection of organizations to approach was determined by the researcher, the interviewees were largely decided by a possible contact person as well as interviewee availability given the busy and pressing times that the organizations were experiencing to deal with the influx of refugees. The researcher could only ask for participants in the position level and/or area of staff that would be ideal. Gaining access to organizations and interviewees within governmental organizations was at times difficult because of protective nature of some organizations due to high political sensitivity of our research context.

Secondly, during the interviews, the central focus was on the establishment of a deep and informed understanding about specific situations and reactions in relation to flexibility and variability. While the focus on specific actions is an advantage in that it reduces retrospective bias, interview questions were formulated in a way that allowed respondents to choose which examples to talk about during the interviews. Therefore, it is possible that interviewees choose more successful examples of dealing with variability to highlight achievements rather than pitfalls and difficulties. Although such a risk could not be fully eliminated, in the introduction to this study it was highlighted to the respondents that its central aim was to understand the underlying mechanisms, avoiding any references to outcomes.

Thirdly, this study investigates a specific situation, which has only been experienced by organizations in the refugee chain in the past year. As such, organizations are working hard to adapt to their new reality, implying that they are in the process of establishing a LT focus and improvement. To develop the concepts of interest, it would be useful to collect data that allows even richer insights through, for example, longitudinal research drawing on participant observations, action research and ethnographic inquiries to further understand the nature of these actions and interactions in shaping service supply chain flexibility in the refugee application procedure. As the refugee crises in Europe is constantly evolving, future research can gain more insights to ensure the accommodation of refugees in the coming years.

**Acknowledgment**  The authors would like to thank Szymon Idzikowski for his help in the data collection stage of this study.

# Appendix

## Appendix A: Most Effective Demand Variability Management Tactics

| Type of variability | Approaches to accommodate |
|---|---|
| Arrival variability | 1. Ensure capacity at peak times<br>2. Require reservation<br>3. Outsource non-strategic functions |
| Request variability | 1. Employee training to handle different requests<br>2. Ensure specialized employees to be available<br>3. Segment customers based on their requests |
| Capability variability | 1. Ensure availability of employees that can adapt to different skills levels<br>2. Do work for customers<br>3. Create low-skilled self-service options |
| Effort variability | 1. Ensure availability of employees who compensate for lack of effort<br>2. Do work for customers<br>3. Use rewards and penalties as incentives |
| Subjective preference variability | 1. Enhance communication and explanations to customers<br>2. Enhance understanding of service content and standard<br>3. Ensure availability of employees who can diagnose and adapt to different expectations |

Most effective demand variability management tactics (based on Yang, 2011)

## Appendix B: Interview Protocol (Probes in Italic)

1. Can you please describe the organization and how it fits into the refugee application procedure?
2. What services does the organization offer?
3. What's your role in the organization and can you describe your work activities?

4. What are the needs of the refugees for your organization?

- *How do needs differ? In what exactly?*
- *What are the reasons for this diversity/variability (other needs)?*

5. How do you address the different needs of refugees?

- *Is there a common denominator in the needs?*
- *Do you use standardized working procedures? Or use a group-wise approach?*
- *What is difficult in addressing needs, and why?*
- *What goes well in addressing needs, and why?*

6. How do you deal with the unexpected increase of refugees and their needs?

- *Did you foresee the large increase in demand over the past few years? How?*
- *How do you try to manage the increase in needs?*

7. Did the increase introduce more other needs and how did you manage this? *Do you feel like you have a degree of control over the needs increase? How?*

8. Given the current situation, how do you think this increase in needs will develop over the coming years?

- *How will it affect the need for your organization's services?*
- *How will it change the current way of working?*
- *How will it affect diversity in needs?*
- *What are you putting in place now to prepare?*
- *Are you able to already influence needs of refugees?*
- *-What information would you need to manage future developments?*

9. How are you involved with other related organizations that are concerned with refugees and their needs? *Could you give specific examples?*

10. What information is shared between other related organizations? *In what way is information shared, and with what purpose?*

11. Can you tell me something about the way you work with other organizations?

- *Governmental organizations?*
- *Private organizations?*
- *What are the chances for improvement in further collaboration with other organizations?*

12. Do you have any way of evaluating working in relation to

a. internal aspects (demand managing)
b. collaboration (information sharing and collaborating in a network)
c. external sources (doing something better than others or something you can learn from others)?

# Appendix C: Information Sheet

## Introduction and Goals of the Research

The largest exodus of refugees since the Second World War has brought major challenges for refugee service organizations across Europe. One of the main challenges faced concerns managing the wide range of needs of the refugees. At the same time it is difficult to establish what exactly the needs of these asylum seekers are, as their backgrounds vary in terms of nationality, age, gender, etcetera, which in the end implies different (service) needs.

We believe that challenges concerning management of asylum seeker needs can be overcome through (i) *flexibility*, by enabling organizations to deal with high levels of uncertainty, and (ii) *interorganizational information sharing*, which has shown to enhance supply chain performance. Through our research, we intend to explore how these challenges can be dealt with. The goal of this interview is to gather a wide range of knowledge for our research project on what we call "the refugee chain"; the European refugee crisis as seen from a service supply chain management perspective. With the insights gathered, we hope to contribute to managing the crisis, and serving the best interest of the refugee.

## Procedure of the Interview

Before the interview starts a form of confidentiality will be filled in, in order to maintain common interests and values. The interview will try to restrict itself to approximately 60 minutes. Questions about the focal firm, the internal business, and finally concerning external business will be asked. After the interview, there is room for feedback and further questions on the procedure. The information gathered will be transcribed and used to be coded into condensed information for the research. The transcriptions of the interview will be sent to the interviewee within one week after the interview to have a look at it and check if the interviewer interpreted everything correctly. If the interviewee wishes not to answer a question, or its subsequent questions, of course that is all right. The interviewee may withdraw at any time. If there are any questions before, during or after the interview, please ask.

## Further Notes

If you permit us to make audio files to ensure accuracy and ease analysis, please be aware that they are treated confidentially. This means that audio files are available for the researchers only and will not be redistributed. Audio files will be deleted when the transcriptions are approved by the interviewee and supervising researchers. The things agreed upon in the consent form have to be signed by both the interviewer and interviewee before proceeding with the actual interview in order to maintain common interest. We explicitly emphasize that this interview is treated anonymously, and that by no means any answers will be traced back to you nor the organization you work for. If you have any questions regarding the interview or protocol, feel free to contact us. *[contact information deleted]*

# Appendix D: Consent Form

To maintain common interests and values, the following consent form has been developed.

---

**Researcher's Name:**

**Faculty/School/Department**: Faculty of Economics and Business, University of Groningen

**Field of Study**: Research project on the refugee chain

**Location of interview:**

**Function/organization of interviewee:**

**Time at start:**

**To be completed by the interviewee:**

1.1 Have you been fully informed/read the information sheet about this study? YES/NO

1.2 Have you had an opportunity to ask questions and discuss this study?

1.3 Have you received satisfactory answers to all your questions? YES/NO

1.4 Do you understand that you are free to withdraw from this study? YES/NO
   • at any time YES/NO
   • without giving a reason for withdrawing
   • without affecting your future relationship with the institute

1.5 Have you been informed that this consent form shall be kept in the confidence of the researcher? YES/NO

1.6 Do you agree that the interview will be recorded?

1.7 Do you agree to be quoted in the main text anonymously? YES/NO

1.8 Do you agree to take part in this study, of which the results are likely to YES/NO
   be published? YES/NO

---

(continued)

(Please note: no information will be traced back to you).                    YES/NO

1.9 If there any other preferences or restrictions you would like to mutually
agree upon, please write them down below. In case there are no other
preferences or restrictions, please leave this open:

_____

_____

_____

Signed_____ Date _____

Name in Block Letters _____

Signature of Researcher _____ Date _____

# References

Almeida, A. S. and Cima, J. F. "Demand uncertainty and hospital costs: An application to Portuguese public hospitals." *The European Journal of Health Economics: HEPAC: Health Economics in Prevention and Care* 16 2015: 35–45.

Arias-Aranda, D. "Service operations strategy, flexibility and performance in engineering consulting firms." *International Journal of Operations & Production Management* 23 2003: 1401–1421.

Arias-Aranda, D., Bustinza, O. F. and Barrales-Molina, V. "Operations flexibility and outsourcing benefits: An empirical study in service firms." *The Service Industries Journal* 31 2011 1849–1870.

Arnold, F., Katona, C., Cohen, J., Jones, L. and McCoy, D. "Responding to the needs of refugees." *British Medical Journal* 351 2015: 1–2.

Baltacioglu, T., Ada, E., Kaplan, M. D., Yurt, A. O. and Kaplan, Y. C. "A new framework for service supply chains." *The Service Industries Journal* 27 2007: 105–124.

Berg, B. L. and Lune, H. *Qualitative research methods for the social science.* Upper Saddle River, NJ: Pearson Education, 2012.

Boutsioli, Z. "Demand variability, demand uncertainty and hospital costs: A selective survey of the empirical literature." *Global Journal of Health Science* 2 2010: 138–149.

Brunsden, J. and Wagstyl, S. "EU forecasts growth dividends from projected 3m migrant influx." *Financial Times*, November 6, 2015. Accessed 12 February 2016. https://www.ft.com/content/d4a39baa-83bd-11e5-8095-ed1a37d1e096

Burnett, A. and Peel, M. "Asylum seekers and refugees in Britain: Health needs of asylum seekers and refugees." *British Medical Journal* 322 2001: 544–547.

Busch-Armendariz, N. B., Nsonwu, M. B. and Heffron, L. C. "Human trafficking victims and their children: Assessing needs, vulnerabilities, strengths, and survivorship." *Journal of Applied Research on Children* 2 2011: 13–34.

Childerhouse, P., Aitken, J. and Towill, D. R. "Analysis and design of focused demand chains." *Journal of Operations Management* 20 2002: 675–689.

Creswell, J. W. *Research design: Qualitative, quantitative, and mixed method approaches.* London: Sage Publications, 2003.

Croxton, K. L., Lambert, D. M., Garcia-Dastugue, S. J. and Rogers, D. S. "The demand management process." *International Journal of Logistics Management* 13 2002: 51–66.

Devroye, D. and Eichfeld, A. "Taming demand variability in back-office services." *McKinsey* Company, September 2009. Accessed 27 September 2016. http://www.mckinsey.com/business-functions/operations/our-insights/taming-demand-variability-in-back-office-services

Duclos, L. K., Vokurka, R. J. and Lummus, R. R. "A conceptual model of supply chain flexibility." *Industrial Management & Data Systems* 103 2003: 446–456.

Eisenhardt, K. M. "Building theories from case study research." *Academy of Management Journal* 14 1989: 532–550.

Ellram, L. M. "The use of the case study method in logistics research." *Journal of Business Logistics* 17 1996: 93–138.

Eurostat. "Asylum and first time asylum applicants – monthly data (rounded)." Accessed 2 September 2016. http://ec.europa.eu/eurostat/tgm/table.do?tab=table&init=1&language=en&pcode=tps00189&plugin=1

Frei, F. X. "Breaking the trade-off between efficiency and service." *Harvard Business Review* 84 2006: 92–105.

Gephart, R. P. "Qualitative research and the academy of management journal." *Academy of Management Journal* 47 2004: 454–462.

Germain, R., Claycomb, C. Dröge, and C. "Supply chain variability, organizational structure, and performance: The moderating effect of demand unpredictability." *Journal of Operations Management* 26 2008: 557–570.

Guest, G., Bunce, A., and Johnson, L. "How many interviews are enough? An experiment with data saturation and variability." *Family Health International* 18 2006: 59–82.

Human Rights Watch. *"Europe's Refugee Crisis: An Agenda for Action."* 16 November 2015. Accessed 27 September 2016. https://www.hrw.org/report/2015/11/16/europes-refugee-crisis/agenda-action

IND Available at: https://ind.nl/Documents/AT%20August%202016.pdf

Jamal, A. "Minimum standards and essential needs in a protracted refugee situation." *Evaluation and Policy Analysis Unit United Nations High Commissioner for Refugees* November 2000. Accessed 27 September 2016. http://www.unhcr.org/research/evalreports/3ae6bd4c0/minimum-standards-essential-needs-protracted-refugee-situation-review-unhcr.html

Jung, H., Lee, C. and White, C. C. "Socially responsible service operations management: An overview." *Annals of Operations Research* 230 2015: 1–16.

Karakas, C. "Economic challenges and prospects of the refugee influx." *European Parliamentary Research Service* 3 December 2015. Accessed 27 September 2016. http://www.europarl.europa.eu/thinktank/en/document.html?reference=EPRS_BRI%282015%29572809

Lambert, D. M. and Cooper, M. C. "Issues in supply chain management." *Industrial Marketing Management* 29 2000: 65–83.

Lincoln, Y. S. and Guba, E. G. *Naturalistic inquiry.* London: Sage Publications, 1985.

Manuj, I. and Mentzer, J. T. "Global supply chain risk management strategies." *International Journal of Physical Distribution & Logistics Management* 38 2008: 192–223.

Maull, R., Geraldi, J. and Johnston, R. "Service supply chains: A customer perspective." *Journal of Supply Chain Management* 48 2012: 72–86.

Mason, J. *Qualitative researching.* London: Sage Publications, 2002.

Merschmann, U. and Thonemann, U. W. "Supply chain flexibility, uncertainty and firm performance: An empirical analysis of German manufacturing firms." *International Journal of Production Economics* 130 2011: 43–53.

Mesco, M. and Pop, V. "Italy seeks flexibility on EU deficit rules to meet refugee costs." *The Wall Street Journal,* 4 February, 2016. Accessed 18 March 2016. http://www.wsj.com/articles/italy-seeks-flexibility-on-eu-deficit-rules-to-meet-refugee-costs-1454592327

Miles, M. B. and Huberman, M. A. *Qualitative data analysis.* London: Saga Publications, 1994.

Näslund, D. "Logistics needs qualitative research – Especially action research." *International Journal of Physical Distribution and Logistics Management* 32 2002: 321–338.

Oloruntoba, R. and Gray, R. "Customer service in emergency relief chains." *International Journal of Physical Distribution & Logistics Management* 39 2009: 486–505.

OM International. "Flexibility is key in supporting refugees – International." *OM News* 21 December, 2015.Accessed 18 March, 2016. http://news.om.org/feature-article/r48229

Parasuraman, A., Zeithaml, V. A., and Berry, L. L. "A conceptual model of service quality and its implications for future research." *The Journal of Marketing,* 1985 Oct 1: 41–50.

Sampson, S. E. "Customer-supplier duality and bidirectional supply chains in service organizations." *International Journal of Service Industry Management* 11 2000: 348–364.

Sasser, W. E. "Match supply and demand in service industries." *Harvard Business Review* 54 1976: 44–51.

Sawhney, R. "Interplay between uncertainty and flexibility across the value-chain: Towards a transformation model of manufacturing flexibility." *Journal of Operations Management* 24 2006: 476–493.

Sayin, S. and Karabati, S. "Assigning cross-trained workers to departments: A two-stage optimization model to maximize utility and skill improvement." *European Journal of Operational Research* 176 2007 1643–1658.

Stevenson, M. and Spring, M. "Flexibility from a supply chain perspective: Definition and review." *International Journal of Operations and Production Management* 27 2007: 685–713.

UNHCR. "Aantal Syrische vluchtelingen bereikt een record van 4 miljoen," 2015. Accessed 27 September 2016. http://www.unhcr.nl/home/artikel/24dd0a6fdd63 d87160ebdde85a059d9d/unhcr-aantal-syrische-vluchtelingen.html

Vickery, S., Calantone, R. and Dröge, C. "Dimensions of supply chain flexibility." *The Journal of Supply Chain Management* 35 1999: 16–24.

Vluchtelingenwerk. "Naar een visie voor VluchtelingenWerk 2015a. Accessed 27 September 2016. https://www.vluchtelingenwerk.nl/sites/public/ Vluchtelingenwerk/migrate/pdf-bibliotheek/Rapporten_Vlw/2010-06-Visie2015 compleetdef.pdf?phpMyAdmin=7w5ZyEx7eG8GI5V6d7lLiau64 Ca&phpMyAdmin=d103b040daaa28b558cce86d2a2af0e5

Vluchtelingenwerk. "Feiten & cijfers." 2015b. Accessed 27 September 2016. http:// www.vluchtelingenwerk.nl/feiten-cijfers

Voss, C., Tsikriktsis, N. and Frohlich, M. "Supply chain risks: A review and typology." *International Journal of Operations & Production Management* 22 2002: 195–219.

Yang, C. C. "Establishment of a quality-management system for service industries." *Total Quality Management & Business Excellence* 17 2006: 1129–1154.

Yang, C. C. "Implementation and effectiveness of strategic actions used to reduce customer variability." *The Service Industries Journal* 31 2011: 527–544.

Yao, Z., Leung, S. C. H. and Lai, K. K. "Analysis of the impact of price-sensitivity factors on the returns policy in coordinating supply chain." *European Journal of Operational Research* 187 2008: 275–282.

# 13

# Developing Individual Competencies for Humanitarian Logistics

Graham Heaslip, Peter Tatham
and Alain Vaillancourt

## Introduction

One organisational tactic designed to enhance individual skills and align them with organisational needs is to develop a competency framework (Autry et al. 2005) but, to date, no technical competency framework had been developed to describe the skills required for humanitarian logistics preparedness, response and recovery. This is important, not least because logistics represents a sector within the humanitarian system that is experiencing serious gaps in capacity including a notable lack of skilled staff, and this situation has existed for many years (Allen et al. 2013; Bölsche et al. 2013).

As an example, the lack of professional logistical capacity resulted in poor decisions being made among humanitarian aid (HA) organisations in the aftermath of the 2004 tsunami, where 42% of HA organisations conducted

G. Heaslip (✉)
Galway Mayo Institute of Technology, Galway, Ireland
e-mail: graham.heaslip@gmit.ie

P. Tatham
Department of International Business and Asian Studies,
Griffith University, Nathan, Australia
e-mail: p.tatham@griffith.edu.au

A. Vaillancourt
Jönköping International Business School, Jönköping, Sweden

© The Author(s) 2018                                                            **395**
G. Kovács et al. (eds.), *The Palgrave Handbook of Humanitarian Logistics
and Supply Chain Management*, https://doi.org/10.1057/978-1-137-59099-2_13

assessments without expert logistics input. This resulted in both a failure to anticipate bottlenecks in the supply chain and a poor evaluation of beneficiaries' needs (Tatham and Pettit 2010). Importantly, the cost of logistics including procurement, the transportation of materials, warehousing, and distribution has been estimated to be as high as 60–80% of the income of aid agencies (Van Wassenhove 2006; Tatham and Pettit 2010), and up to 30% of aid delivered has been identified as wasted in some post-crisis situations (Pettit and Beresford 2009). These percentages should be set against the high cost of humanitarian activities worldwide which, for 2011, was estimated to be some $12 billion in humanitarian aid and a further $156 billion in development assistance (Global Humanitarian Assistance 2015). Furthermore, it should be recognised that these numbers do not meet the entirety of the needs; indeed in 2013 consolidated funding appeals raised at best 77% of their funding target, and at worst 21% (Smith and Swithern 2013). It is argued that improvements in the skills of logistic staff will help to mitigate these inefficiencies and, thereby, allow the overall humanitarian activities to better meet the needs of the intended beneficiaries.

Unsurprisingly, therefore, a key element of the humanitarian reform process has focused on developing the capacity of, in particular, suitably skilled personnel (Overstreet et al. 2011; Kovács et al. 2012; Allen et al. 2013). This clearly requires a range of cognitive and operational skills which will need to be identified, created and supported (Eisenhardt et al. 2010). The ability of logistics and supply chain managers to adapt and operate an agile supply chain in international, unstable and complex conditions requires professional skills, competence and knowledge (Kovács and Spens 2009; Tatham and Christopher 2014). To date, however, there is limited understanding of the ways in which the recruitment, training, retaining and deployment of humanitarian logisticians might be advanced (Overstreet et al. 2011; Kovács et al. 2012; Allen et al. 2013).

It has been argued (Tatham and Pettit 2010; Kovács et al. 2012) that a recognised set of standards for humanitarian staff would improve performance and promote quality and accountability, and also both promote the development of a professional career path as well as inter-agency staff mobility. There is already research on performance (Schultz and Heigh 2009; Gralla et al. 2014) and some research on skills (Kovács et al. 2012) in relation to the humanitarian context. However, in order to develop a proper understanding of employee-level competencies for humanitarian logistics there is a need to further explore the required knowledge and behaviour of logisticians and supply chain managers. Once established, the specific skills, knowledge and behaviours from the humanitarian sector, in combination with those from a normal ("for-profit") supply chain context, will offer a better understanding of the relevant competencies. This will then underpin further research on employee-level competencies and performance for humanitarian logisticians.

The aim of this chapter is, therefore, to develop a Humanitarian Logistics Competency Framework (HLCF) that can be used by those within the sector to understand the gaps in their portfolio of skills. The framework that will be presented within the chapter will also provide the basis for organisations to test and adjust their existing approaches to skills and competencies and, as such, is designed to be an initial exemplar that has the potential to form the basis of a sector-wide common approach. This will not only help to design and develop a career path for humanitarian logisticians, but will also aid inter-organisational mobility of staff by offering a "neutral" baseline against which individual organisations' models (to the extent that they exist) can be mapped.

## Definitions

To avoid confusion, we adopt the definitions used by the Chartered Institute of Personnel and Development (CIPD 2014, p. 2).

> *Competency Framework:* is a structure that sets out and defines each individual competency (such as problem-solving or people management) required by individuals working in an organization or part of an organization.
>
> *Competency Domain:* are the high-level groups, or clusters, of competency areas within a given competency framework.
>
> *Competencies:* are defined as the behaviours and technical attributes that individuals must have, or acquire, to perform effectively in a particular role.

What can be seen from the literature is that the use of a competency framework is designed to support the identification and subsequent development of a range of skills, including those required to be flexible. Flexibility – which is a key requirement for HL practice (Gattorna 2015; L'Hermitte et al. 2016) – can, in theory, be supported through the development of skills such as innovating, problem solving, creativity, resilience and adaptability (Weinert 2001; Rodriguez et al. 2002), and is often operationalised through the adoption of a competency framework (see for example TCSW 2013). However, the competencies themselves are not always so clearly set out in the literature. For example, competencies for top management could be defined as leadership skills, general management skills, interpersonal skills, communication skills, creativity and personality traits such as dependability and adaptability (Thornton III and Byham 2013), whereas competencies for middle management might be seen as intellectual, interpersonal, adaptability and results orientation (Dulewicz 1989).

In order to be able to determine the requisite competencies to become a humanitarian logistician we first need to define the concept of humanitarian logistics (HL), the accepted definition of which is provided by Thomas and Kopczak who define it as:

> ...the process of planning, implementing and controlling the efficient, cost-effective flow and storage of goods and materials, as well as related information, from the point of origin to the point of consumption for the purpose of alleviating the suffering of vulnerable people. The function encompasses a range of activities, including preparedness, planning, procurement, transport, warehousing, tracking and tracing, and customs clearance. (2005, p. 2)

As humanitarian supply chains are both enormously complex and also staffed by a multiplicity of workers at different levels, with varying types and levels of education and training backgrounds, there is no single cadre of worker that can be educated and trained to undertake all the functions and tasks that are required to manage them efficiently and effectively. For this reason, our core approach has been to develop a compendium of all competencies needed within a humanitarian supply chain. Depending on the local context and configuration of the humanitarian supply chain, these competencies will be distributed across a range of different workers.

Most competency frameworks consist of two core elements: (i) the occupation specific knowledge and skills and (ii) the competencies required to work effectively with others in the organisation in order to achieve effective outcomes (Mangan and Christopher 2005; Kovács et al. 2012; Uhlenbrook and de Jong 2012). In some ways, this can be seen as mirroring the T-shaped profiles adopted in engineering, logistics or IT related industries where the vertical part of the T is the in depth occupational knowledge, and the horizontal part on the top is the set of skills required to work across boundaries with other knowledge or skill sets (see, for example, Mangan and Christopher 2005; Karjalainen et al. 2009; Uhlenbrook and de Jong 2012). Using this approach as our guide, we have developed HLCF as described in the next section.

# The Need for HLCF

In developing the HLCF it is important to note that competency models differ from traditional job analysis in that the latter focuses on job attributes and this, in turn, allows applied measurement. By contrast, competency management aims to orient employee activities in order that they better link into the organisation's strategy (PtD 2015).

It is argued that, in a similar way, there is a clear need for efficient and effective logistic managers especially in organisations with complex supply chains such as those found in a humanitarian context (Overstreet et al. 2011; Kovács et al. 2012; Allen et al. 2013). This has led to calls for the further development of humanitarian logistics training and the elaboration of standards for skills as a means of improving the effectiveness of logisticians (Thomas and Mizushima 2005; Kovács and Spens 2011). This call was followed by research papers on skills and training in humanitarian logistics (Kovács and Tatham 2010; Kovács et al. 2012; Allen et al. 2013), as well as general competencies in this sector (Bölsche et al. 2013) but, to date, the question of the required competencies for humanitarian logisticians remains to be fully addressed.

The proposed HLCF is a foundation for the full range of humanitarian logistics workforce management and development activities: role design and description; recruitment; performance management; learning and development and strategic workforce planning. The HLCF provides a systematic and integrated approach to these activities and offers the humanitarian logistics sector a shared language with which to describe the knowledge, skills and abilities needed to perform their role across all clusters and agencies.

# Humanitarian Logistics Competencies

Murphy and Poist (1991, 2007) suggest that the senior-level logistics manager needs to be proficient in three skills categories namely: business skills, logistics skills and management skills. The key finding from their body of research is the importance of management skills in the supply chain context. In a similar way, Gammelgaard and Larson (2001) posited a three-factor model of SCM skill areas for executive development and other programmes aimed at logistics managers: interpersonal/managerial basic skills, quantitative/technological skills and SCM core skills.

Logistics research has also linked skills to various competencies, for example, Ramsay (2001) and Hunt and Davis (2008) single out purchasing as a competency, while Autry et al., (2005), Lai et al. (2008) and Daugherty et al. (2009) all stress the importance of information technology and logistics information systems. Logistics itself has been assessed as a dynamic competency (André 1995; Zhao et al. 2001; Autry et al. 2005; Esper et al. 2007), whilst Grant (2009) points at "supply chain management" as an example of a relational capability. Importantly, however, there is general agreement on the concept of distinct skill sets, and also that while technical logistics knowledge is important, it needs to be complemented by other "softer" (Vereecke et al. 2008) or "emotional" (Van Hoek et al. 2002) skills.

This has led to Mangan and Christopher (2005) adapting Leonard-Barton's (1995) T-shaped skills profile to supply chain managers. This model emphasises the difference in breadth versus depth of knowledge, skills and competencies in the different areas. In other words, logisticians need to have a combination of a depth of logistics skills together with broader competence in a number of other areas. The consensus view across the above studies of logistics managers would appear to be that respondents regarded themselves as "managers first and logisticians second" (Mangan and Christopher 2005, p.180) with requisite skills and competencies sets that comprise both general management skills and competencies and specific logistics/supply chain skills and competencies (Mangan et al. 2001).

Drawing on the existing business-related supply chain skills and competencies literature, a number of authors have considered its application in a humanitarian logistics context. Thus, Kovács and Tatham (2010); Kovács et al. (2012); Bölsche et al. (2013); Allen et al. (2013) all draw on the T-shaped model which identifies the requirement for knowledge areas and competencies/skills required by logistics and supply chain managers to create a profile where "managers have an in-depth expertise in one discipline combined with enough breadth to see the connection with others" (Mangan and Christopher 2005, p 181).

Kovács and Tatham (2010) compared the skills needs of business, military and humanitarian logisticians. Their results highlight that marketing was not among the otherwise typical management skills needed by humanitarian logisticians. This is not entirely surprising as, arguably, this outward-facing role is conducted by the "Programmes" staff within a humanitarian agency. However, their research also suggested that there is a stronger emphasis in the humanitarian logistics group on technical, "core" logistics skills such as warehousing, and transportation management, but also that leadership and supplier relationship management skills stood out as highly important in this sector. This is in contrast to the studies by Walker and Russ (2010) on the professionalisation of the overall humanitarian sector that emphasises the need for skills in the areas of needs assessment, security and safety, monitoring and evaluation, and particular relief item and mandate-based areas such as, water and sanitation. Allen et al. (2013) carried out a survey amongst members of the Humanitarian Logistics Association (HLA) in which they found that a career path in humanitarian logistics requires extra skills and training, particularly in human resource management (HRM) and general management. These authors argue that their research shows evidence of a "hierarchy of skills that is important to humanitarian logistics and the needs for these skills depend on the levels of responsibility" (Allen et al. 2013, p.143). Kovács et al. (2012), who analysed over 200 advertisements for humanitarian logisticians, went on to develop skills hierarchies from another perspective, looking at skill sets that come as bundles on different levels. They further suggest the addition of a set of "contextual" skills to the T-shaped model – which, in the case of humanitarian logistics, would encompass skills from emergency preparedness to fleet management, from security management to the training of other logisticians.

Apart from contextual skills, logistics skills models typically contrast general management skills that are needed in breadth to technical (sometimes called "functional") logistics skills that are needed in depth. The above studies shed some light on the importance of various skills and skill sets for humanitarian logisticians. However, the contextual knowledge of humanitarian logisticians is generally not recognised as a separate entity in the competency framework of humanitarian logisticians. Thus, we stress its relevance and the unstated, perhaps taken-for-granted, presumption that local and global contextual awareness and knowledge is implicit in general management skills, is, in fact, a gap in previous considerations of competency frameworks for humanitarian logisticians. Indeed, it is argued that local and global knowledge are, in reality, crucial competencies for humanitarian logisticians, without which many humanitarian missions would undoubtedly fail. Whilst it may seem obvious that general core humanitarian competencies are an important part of any role in this field, this research has found that many are sorely neglected when it comes to training with the resultant diminution in individual and collective effectiveness.

The setting of a developing country or an area affected by a disaster or complex emergency, creates a complicated set of challenges such as difficulties in predicting demand (in terms of timing, location, type and size) coupled with sudden occurrences of large demands with short lead times for different supplies, the importance of timeliness in deliveries and a general lack of resources (material, human, technological and financial) (Balcik and Beamon 2008; Bölsche et al. 2013; Allen et al. 2013). Issues that typically

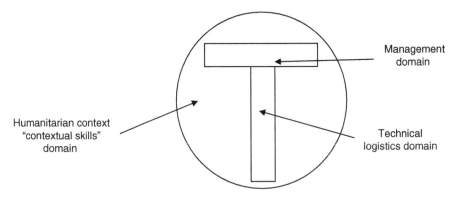

**Fig. 13.1** Relationship of management, technical logistics and humanitarian domains

arise include the "4 W" (who wants what where?) needs assessment process, difficulties in accessing the affected populations due to a lack of or a compromised infrastructure and/or a degraded security situation (Heaslip et al. 2012). Other contextual issues that humanitarian logisticians must take into account are disaster types (the type, speed of onset and probability of disasters in the region) (Van Wassenhove 2006; Tatham et al. 2013), the focus and location of their own organisation (their mandate, regional presence and declaration of a state of emergency) (Kovács and Tatham 2010), the general stakeholder environment (Kovács and Spens 2009), and the logistic performance of the country of operations.

To summarise this discussion, Fig. 13.1 demonstrates our understanding of the relationship between the humanitarian context, the technical logistics requirement and management skills required for a humanitarian logistician.

## Research Approaches for Humanitarian Competencies

Research methods that investigate the competencies of humanitarian logisticians can take many forms; their underlying aim is to understand the role and contribution of an individual inside a humanitarian organisation. This type of research can use both quantitative and qualitative methods and can be achieved through indirect and direct enquiry and sometimes a mix of both. Indirect enquiry can use data sources such as literature reviews, training materials from humanitarian organisations, job adverts and requirements from donors. Since humanitarian logisticians are often pressed for time in their work, indirect enquiry offers the possibility to identify the required competencies without hindering ongoing operations. However, the required competencies are not necessarily related to what the logisticians are actually doing in the field and, as such, there is a need for direct enquiry. Direct enquiry targets humanitarian logisticians and can include surveys and case studies with interviews and helps develop an understanding of the conditions in the field but can be subject to bias.

Kovács et al. (2012) is a great example of indirect research inquiry into job skills where job advertisement for humanitarian logisticians were analysed. Job advertisement help identify gaps, industry trends, and skills and competencies that employers search for and that job applicants should demonstrate. These job advertisements were then considered using content analysis which ensures a systematic review of the material at hand. This type of research data is easily accessible through online job websites that specialise in the humanitarian sector, whilst content analysis is a well-recognised method for textual analysis.

Allen et al. (2013) is an example of a direct research enquiry into the training needs of humanitarian logisticians. This research uses a survey to assess what priorities logisticians identify for further training based on their self-reported job profiles. To underpin the validity of the survey, 11 telephone interviews were undertaken with HLA members who matched the target population. The low survey response rate of 17% indicates the difficulty of accessing data directly from the field in the humanitarian context. Furthermore, there was an additional risk of bias from the sample group since the survey participants were on a mailing list of logistician members of the HLA. Nevertheless, a direct survey of humanitarian logisticians, where a variety of job profile are present, is helpful in gaining an understanding of the responsibility and priorities for professional development in the field. This, in turn, could be linked to different types of competencies to be acquired by training. Kovács and Tatham (2010) use a similar survey approach to help test logistics skills in the light of logistics performance. To ensure the validity of this research a pilot survey was conducted with the help of 75 participants. The survey was then sent out through different mailing lists and the link forwarded from colleague to colleague (snowball sampling). Ultimately, however, there was also a relatively low response rate by people in the humanitarian sector (17%), although it has previously been noted by Larson (2005) that responses of the order of 10% are typical in such electronic surveys.

## Developing an HCLF

To achieve our research goal of developing an HLCF, we undertook a systematic literature review (see Fig. 13.2) and supplemented this with data from a pilot qualitative study where eight semi-structured interviews with senior logisticians in humanitarian agencies and United Nations (UN) organisations were conducted.

We conducted a number of interviews with humanitarian logisticians in order to (a) confirm the groupings and their labels and to further consolidate the categories where possible, and (b) to understand the differences in the significance of various competency domains in light of their career progression. For the interviews, we turned to senior humanitarian logisticians as "field experts" and the final sample consisted of eight

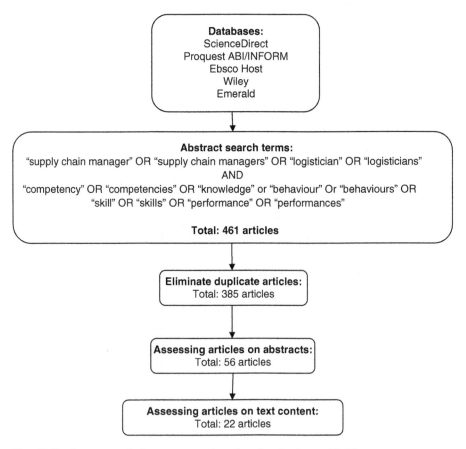

**Fig. 13.2** A systematic literature review for developing a HLCF

respondents, two from UN agencies, one employee from an international humanitarian organisation and five employees from international non-governmental organisations (NGOs) (see Table 13.1). Respondents were selected by the means of stratified sampling, that is, in such a way as to cover organisations across different types of operational mandates including: multi-country, food, water, shelter, education and health. A further criterion for inclusion was that respondents had to have a minimum of 10 years of experience in HL (rather than in logistics/supply chain management in general). Being senior humanitarian logisticians with such a length of experience, they all had worked in field and country offices as well as in headquarters, and were thus able to bring both these perspectives into the discussions.

During the interview process, respondents were first asked to provide a full and descriptive account of their experiences as humanitarian logisticians. This facilitated a sensitisation to the context, language and operations of the interviewees and permitted the development of appropriate interview protocols.

We followed the suggestion in Kovács et al. (2012) that collecting qualitative data from humanitarian logisticians would shed light on the actual use of skills and thereby overcome the lack of understanding for this sector. This recognised the reality that their data was on skill requirements in job advertisements, which they themselves criticised as potentially being a human resource manager's, rather than a supply chain manager's, view of the job requirements, reflecting a lack of understanding the actual priorities and the use of skills on the job from this data. Other previous studies (CILT UK 2008; Kovács and Tatham 2010; Walker and Russ 2010; Allen et al. 2013) have collected data through surveys that were based on given lists of skills, and whilst these offered interesting results relating to the significance of various skills, such an approach does not allow skills that did not make the lists in the questionnaires in the first place – for example those in the "contextual skills" category.

The different potential competencies present in the literature numbered a total of 53 unique categories. However, some of these categories of potential competencies were similar and when these are grouped together, they lead to a shorter list of nine competency domains (see Table 13.2).

The next step was to expand each of the competency domains and identify the specific competencies within each, and resultant expanded competency domains are shown in Fig. 13.3. In doing so, it is important to appreciate that there is not necessarily an even coverage across each of these domains. For example, in terms of gaps in skills, the main theme that

**Table 13.1** List of respondents

| Organisation | Position held | Years involved in humanitarian logistics | Previous logistics experience: Commercial logistics (C)/military logistics (M) | Logistics experience in field office (F)/headquarter office (HQ) | Type of relief involvement | Personnel employed in organisation | Expenditure US $ 2015 |
|---|---|---|---|---|---|---|---|
| United Nations Organisation A | Supply chain manager | 16 years | 9 years (C) | 7 years (F) 9 years (HQ) | Over 75 countries, Emergencies, livelihoods, food, education | 11,500 employees | 2.97 billion |
| United Nations Organisation B | Procurement and logistics coordinator | 20 years | 12 years (M) | 8 years (F) 12 years (HQ) | Over 125 countries Emergencies, livelihoods, legal, protection, education. | 7,600 employees | 1.8 billion |
| International humanitarian organisation | Supply chain manager | 11 years | 8 years (C) | 7 years (F) 4 years (HQ) | Over 189 countries Emergencies, shelter, livelihoods, legal, health. | 100,000,000 employees/volunteers | 394.2 million |
| International NGO A | Logistics manager | 12 years | 15 years (M) | 7 years (F) 5 years (HQ) | Over 20 countries Emergencies, livelihoods, legal, protection, education. | 2,500 employees | 150.3 million |
| | | 10 years | 8 years (C) | 4 years (F) | | 2,500 employees | 60.8 million |

| | | | | | | | |
|---|---|---|---|---|---|---|---|
| International NGO B | Logistics manager | | | 6 years (HQ) | Over 15 countries Emergencies, health, livelihoods, education | | |
| International NGO C | International logistics officer | 10 years | 5 years (C) | 7 years (F) 3 years (HQ) | Over 50 countries Emergencies, livelihoods, legal, protection, education. | 5,000 employees | 350.3 million |
| International NGO D | Logistics manager | 12 years | 20 years (M) | 10 years (F) 2 years (HQ) | Over 25 countries Emergencies, health, livelihoods, education | 3,000 employees | 80.3 million |
| International NGO E | Logistics manager | 13 years | N/A | 6 years (F) 7 years (HQ) | Over 15 countries Emergencies, health, livelihoods, education | 2,000 employees | 50.8 million |

**Table 13.2** Competency domains

| Competency domain | Explanation |
| --- | --- |
| General management | The competencies a humanitarian logistician must have to lead and manage a team. |
| Resource management | The competencies a humanitarian logistician must have to manage money, people and information to ensure systems work effectively. |
| Supply planning | The competencies a humanitarian logistician must have to be able to develop the operational plan for the timely provision of the correct supplies in a humanitarian environment. |
| Personal and interpersonal | The competencies a humanitarian logistician must have to manage her/his responsibilities and create a future career path. |
| Supply management | The competencies a humanitarian logistician must have to procure the relevant supplies needed for the humanitarian environment. |
| Transport/distribution | The competencies a humanitarian logistician must have to transport and distribute supplies within the humanitarian environment. |
| Warehousing | The competencies a humanitarian logistician must have to store and manage supplies within the humanitarian environment. |
| Information systems and technology | The competencies a humanitarian logistician must have to manage information systems within the humanitarian environment. |
| Humanitarian setting | The competencies a humanitarian logistician must have to operate within the humanitarian context. |

emerged from the interviews was related to management and leadership, which was mentioned by the majority of respondents. One interviewee stated:

> Management and leadership skills are not taught…yet when you become a senior manager you are expected to possess these skills.

Other limiting competencies mentioned include: understanding and adhering to guidelines, analysing data, report writing, training others, working well with different teams, strategy, coordination, adapting programmes to suit the specific context, communicating with media, funding applications, and knowing where to find resources.

The resultant HLCF contains nine competency domains with 32 specific competencies and it provides senior humanitarian logisticians with a tool to define the expected competencies for specific roles within their organisation, and individuals with an overview of where they may need to develop

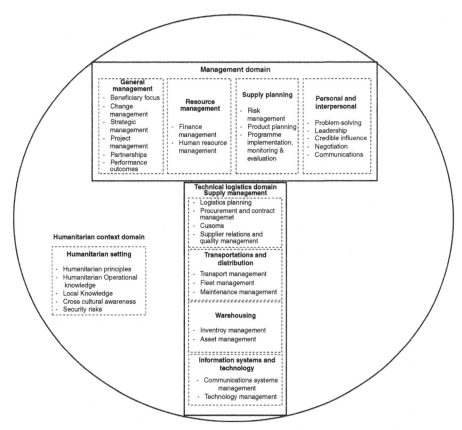

**Fig. 13.3** T-shaped model populated with the domains and competency areas (high level)

particular aspects of a competency to more effectively and efficiently perform their role, or one to which they aspire.

## Conclusion

In this chapter we propose the structure and contents for a competency framework for practitioners in humanitarian logistics and describe how it could be used to improve staff recruitment, assessment and professional development. The benefits of a competency-based approach have been understood, and these include the introduction of transparent standards and increased public accountability. The standardisation of training and provision of a clear framework also encourage learning and professional development (Voorhees 2001).

The proposed HLCF was constructed from previous literature relating to logistics skills in a business logistics context, but was amended to reflect insights from humanitarian logistics literature and from senior humanitarian logisticians across a range of humanitarian aid organisations. We have also extracted and synthesised the resulting competencies. The resulting model also demonstrates both the overall importance of functional logistics skills and the need to incorporate additional skills related to the international humanitarian context.

In developing the proposed HLCF, this chapter highlights a lack of research on competency management. When it comes to humanitarian logistics, the research also highlights the paucity of research that investigates the links (if any) between the context and knowledge in this field. We, thus, offer further research directions for competencies in humanitarian logistics as well as in business logistics and supply chain management.

Given that competency models have been the object of attention in supply chain management and logistics literature, further investigation in both the business and HA contexts is likely to lead to additional insights in the design or improvement of proper competency-based management activities in organisations which aim to link employee-level competencies to their performance or strategic goals. Fisher et al. (2010) observe that, as businesses do not own anybody, they are only entitled to the services of employees so long as they can assure the highest possible pay-off on the investment in employees' skills. This suggests the need for a balance between the HR agenda and professional autonomy to humanitarian logistics. This also implies the need for research into how individuals' perceptions of their "worth" and the perceived scope to appropriate the benefits from their expertise impact on the effort-reward bargain. Similarly, a greater understanding of the contextual factors that impact on differences in HR requirements, for example through an examination from a contingency factor perspective, could be illuminating for those in the sector.

Further research is required to increase the understanding of skills on different levels of the job. Current research (Kovács et al. 2012; Allen et al. 2013) does not differentiate between staff working at country levels or in headquarters and those in field-based appointments, and this is a clear gap in the literature. Although every effort has been made to identify all essential competencies, it is fully accepted that the list may not be exhaustive due to the various limitations of the present research. It is also noted that the competencies highlighted through expert interviews are likely to have been biased towards each individual's area of expertise and reflect international rather than national perspectives. Ideally a larger sample of field experts and national staff would have been canvassed, with experts included from government departments, training institutions, donor organisations and other NGOs (national and international). Further research may also accentuate a more thorough understanding of the current and future context of humanitarian logistics and, in turn, require further investigation into the proposed key performance areas, as well as the core competencies and resultant skills, knowledge and behaviours going forward – the development of Cash Transfer Programmes (CTP) being an obvious example.

The move to a competency-based approach is a logical step to strengthen the humanitarian logistics sector and to build human resource capacity. However, the competency framework proposed here requires further review involving a wider range of stakeholders that includes beneficiary populations, in order to encourage sector-wide adoption and use. Further research is required in testing our proposed framework in practice.

# References

Allen, A. M., Kovács, G., Masini, A., Vaillancourt, A. and Van Wassenhove, L. (2013),"Exploring the link between the humanitarian logistician and training needs", *Journal of Humanitarian Logistics and Supply Chain Management*, Vol. 3 Iss. 2, pp. 129–148.

André, R. (1995), "Leading diverse management teams in Logistics", *Journal of Business Logistics*, Vol. 16 Iss. 2, pp. 65–84.

Autry, C. W., Griffis, S. E., Goldsby, T. J. and Bobbitt, L. M. (2005), "Warehouse management systems: Resource commitment, capabilities, and organizational performance", *Journal of Business Logistics*, Vol. 26 Iss. 2, pp. 165–183.

Balcik, B. and Beamon, B. M. (2008), "Performance measurement in humanitarian relief chains", *International Journal of Public Sector Management*, Vol. 21 Iss. 1, pp. 4–25.

Bölsche, D., Klumpp, M. and Abidi, H. (2013), "Specific competencies in humanitarian logistics education", *Journal of Humanitarian Logistics and Supply Chain Management*, Vol. 3 Iss. 2, pp. 99–128.

CILT [Chartered Institute of Logistics and Transport UK] (2008), "Humanitarian and emergency logistics personnel: logisticians job description assessment", Available at: www.ciltuk.org.uk/download/helpanalysis.pdf.

CIPD [Chartered Institute of Personnel and Development] (2014), "Competence and competency frameworks", *Chartered Institute of Personnel and Development*, Available at: http://www.cipd.co.uk/hr-resources/factsheets/competence-competency-frameworks.aspx

Daugherty, P. J., Chen, H., Mattioda, D. D. and Grawe, S. J. (2009), "Marketing/logistics relationships: Influence on capabilities and performance", *Journal of Business Logistics*, Vol. 30 Iss. 1, pp. 1–18.

Dulewicz, V. (1989), "Performance appraisal and counselling", in Herriot, P., *Assessment and selection in organizations: methods and practices for recruitment and appraisal*, New York: John Wiley & Sons, pp. 645–649.

Eisenhardt, K. M., Furr, N. R. and Bingham, C. B. (2010), "CROSSROADS-Microfoundations of performance: Balancing efficiency and flexibility in dynamic environments", *Organization Science*, Vol. 21 Iss. 6, pp. 1263–1273.

Esper, T. L., Fugate, B. S. and Davis-Stramek, B. (2007), "Logistics learning capability: Sustaining the competitive advantage gained through logistics leverage", *Journal of Business Logistics*, Vol. 28 Iss. 2, pp. 57–81.

Fisher, S. L., Graham, M. E., Vachon, S. and Vereecke, A. (2010), "Don't miss the boat: Research on HRM and supply chains", *Human Resource Management*, Vol. 49, pp. 813–828.

Gammelgaard, B. and Larson, P. D. (2001), "Logistics skills and competencies for supply chain management", *Journal of Business Logistics*, Vol. 22 Iss. 2, pp. 27–50.

Gattorna, J. (2015), *Dynamic Supply Chains* (3rd Edn). Harlow, UK: Pearson Education Ltd., pp. 339–374.

Global Humanitarian Assistance. (2015), Global Humanitarian Assistance Report http://www.globalhumanitarianassistance.org

Gralla, E., Goentzel, J. and Fine, C. (2014), "Assessing trade-offs among multiple objectives of humanitarian aid delivery using expert preferences", *Production and Operations Management*, Vol. 23 Iss. 6, pp. 978–989.

Grant, R. M. (2009), *Contemporary strategy analysis* (7th edn), Hoboken, NJ: John Wiley & Sons, Inc.

Heaslip, G., Sharif, A. M. and Althonayan, A. (2012), "Employing a systems-based perspective to the identification of interrelationships within Humanitarian Logistics", *International Journal of Production Economics*, Vol. 139 Iss. 2, pp. 377–392.

Hunt, S. D. and Davis, D. F. (2008), "Grounding supply chain management in resource-advantage theory", *Journal of Supply Chain Management*, Vol. 44 Iss. 1, pp. 10–21.

Karjalainen, T-M., Koria, M. and Salimäki, M. (2009), "Educating T-shaped design, business and engineering professionals", *Proceedings of the 19th CIRP Design Conference – Competitive design*, Cranfield University, 30–31 March https://dspace.lib.cranfield.ac.uk/bitstream/1826/3645/3/Educating_T-shaped_Design_Business_and_Engineering_Professionals-2009.pdf?origin=publication_detail

Kovács, G. and Spens, K. M. (2009), "Identifying challenges in humanitarian logistics." *International Journal of Physical Distribution & Logistics Management*, Vol. 39 Iss. 6, pp. 506–528.

Kovács, G. and Spens, K. M. (2011), "Humanitarian logistics and supply chain management: The start of a new journal", *Journal of Humanitarian Logistics and Supply Chain Management*, Vol. 1 Iss: 1, pp. 5–14.

Kovács, G., Tatham, P. H. and Larson, P. D. (2012), "What skills are needed to be a humanitarian logistician?", *Journal of Business Logistics*, Vol. 33 Iss. 3, pp. 245–258.

Kovács, G. and Tatham, P. H. (2010), "What is special about a humanitarian logistician? A survey of logistic skills and performance", *Supply Chain Forum: An International Journal*, Vol. 11 Iss. 2, pp. 32–41.

Lai, F., Li, D., Wang, Q. and Zhao, X. (2008), "The information technology capability of third-party logistics providers: A resource-based view and empirical evidence from China", *Journal of Supply Chain Management*, Vol. 44 Iss. 3, pp. 22–38.

Larson, P. D. (2005), "A note on mail surveys and response rates in logistics research", *Journal of Business Logistics*, Vol. 26 Iss. 2, pp. 211–222.

Leonard-Barton, D. (1995), *Wellsprings of knowledge: Building and sustaining the sources of knowledge*, Harvard Business School Press: Boston, MA.

L'Hermitte, C., Tatham, P. H., Brooks, B. and Bowles, M. (2016), 'Supply chain agility in protracted operations'. *Journal of Humanitarian Logistics and Supply Chain Management*, Vol. 6 Iss. 1, pp. 72–99.

Mangan, J. and Christopher, M. C. (2005), "Management development and the supply chain manager of the future", *International Journal of Logistics Management*, Vol. 16, Iss. 2, pp. 178–191.

Mangan, J., Gregory, O. and Lalwani, C. (2001), "Education, training and the role of logistics managers in Ireland", *International Journal Logistics: Research and Applications*, Vol. 4 Iss. 3, pp. 313–327.

Murphy, P. R. and Poist, R. F. (1991), "Skill requirements of senior-level logistics executives: An empirical assessment", *Journal of Business Logistics*, Vol. 12 Iss. 2, pp. 73–94.

Murphy, P. R. and Poist, R. F. (2007), "Skill requirements of senior-level logisticians: A longitudinal research assessment", *Supply Chain Management: An International Journal*, Vol. 12 Iss. 6, pp. 423–431.

Overstreet, R. E., Hall, D., Hanna, J. and Rainer, R. K. (2011), "Research in humanitarian logistics". *Journal of Humanitarian Logistics and Supply Chain Management*, Vol. 1 Iss. 2, pp. 114–131.

Pettit, S. J. and Beresford, A. K. C. (2009), "Critical success factors in the context of humanitarian aid supply chains", *International Journal of Physical Distribution & Logistics Management*, Vol. 39 Iss. 6, pp. 450–468.

PtD [People that Deliver] (2015), "Health supply chain competency framework for managers & leaders", *People that Deliver*, Available at http://www.peoplethatdeliver.org/sites/peoplethatdeliver.org/files/FINAL%20Validated%20SCM%20leadership%20%20management%20framework%2013th%20April%202015.pdf

Ramsay, J. (2001), "The resource based perspective, rents, and purchasing's contribution to sustainable competitive advantage", *Journal of Supply Chain Management*, Vol. 37 Iss. 3, pp. 38–47.

Rodriguez, D., Patel, R., Bright, A., Gregory, A. and Gowing, M. K. (2002), "Developing competency models to promote integrated human resources practices", *Human Resource Management*, Vol. 41 Iss. 3, pp. 309–324.

Schultz, S. F. and Heigh, I. (2009), "Logistics performance management in action within a humanitarian organization", *Management Research News*, Vol. 32 Iss. 1, pp. 1038–1049.

Smith, K. and Swithern, S. (2013), *The 2014 UN appeal: Different process, greater needs*. Global Humanitarian Assistance. http://www.globalhumanitar ianassistance.org/wp-content/uploads/2013/12/UN-response-crisis-2014-final2.pdf

Tatham, P. H. and Christopher, M. G. (2014), "An introduction to humanitarian logistics", in Tatham, P. H. and Christopher, M. G. (eds) *Humanitarian logistics: Meeting the challenge of preparing for and responding to disasters* (2nd Edn), London: Kogan Page.

Tatham, P. H. and Pettit, S. J. (2010), "Transforming humanitarian logistics: The journey to supply network management", *International Journal of Physical Distribution & Logistics Management*, Vol. 40 Iss. 8/9, pp. 609–622.

Tatham, P. H., L'Hermitte, C., Spens, K. M. and Kovács, G. (2013), "Humanitarian Logistics: Development of an Improved Disaster Classification Framework". Proceedings of ANZAM OM/SC Conference, Brisbane, 20-21 Jun 2013. ISBN: 978-0-646-90576-1

The College of Social Work (TCSW). (2012), "Professional Capabilities Framework," The College of Social Work. http://www.tcsw.org.uk/profes sional-capabilities-framework/, (accessed 14 Nov 2014).

Thomas, A. S. and Kopczak, L. R. (2005), "From logistics to supply chain management" *Fritz Institute*, Available at: www.fritzinstitute.org/PDFs/WhitePaper/FromLogisticsto.pdf

Thomas, A. and Mizushima, M. (2005) Logistics training: Necessity or luxury? *Forced Migration Review*, Vol.22, pp. 60–61.

Thornton, G. C. and Byham, W. C. (2013), *Assessment centers and managerial performance*, New York: Academic Press, Harcourt Brace Jovanovich Publishers.

Uhlenbrook, S. and de Jong, E. (2012), "T-shaped competency profile for water professionals of the future", *Hydrology and Earth System Sciences Discussions*, Vol. 9, pp. 2935–2957.

Van Hoek, R., Chatham, R. and Wilding, R. (2002), "Managers in supply chain management, the critical dimension", *Supply Chain Management*, Vol. 7 Iss 3/4, pp. 119–125.

Van Wassenhove, L. N. (2006), "Humanitarian aid logistics: Supply chain management in a high gear", *Journal of the Operational Research Society*, Vol. 57, May, pp. 475–489.

Vereecke, A., Boute, R., Dierdonck, R. and Seernels, S. (2008), "Supply chain managers – Who needs them? Insights from a European Survey on the Profile and the Role of the Supply Chain Manager", Vlerick Leuven Gent Management School, pp. 1–34.

Voorhees R. A. (2001), "Competency-based learning models: A necessary future", *New Direct Institut Res*, pp. 5–13.

Walker, P. and Russ, C. (2010), "Professionalising the Humanitarian Sector", *ELRHA*, Available at: http://www.elrha.org/uploads/Professionalising_the_humanitarian_sector.pdf

Weinert, F. E. (2001), "Concept of competence: A conceptual clarification", in Rychen, D. S. and Salganik, L. H. (Eds.) *Defining and selecting key competencies*, Ashland, OH, USA: Hogrefe & Huber Publishers, pp. 45–65.

Zhao, M., Dröge, C. and Stank, T. P. (2001), "The effects of logistics capabilities on firm performance: Customer-focused vs. information-focused capabilities", *Journal of Business Logistics*, Vol. 22 Iss. 2, pp. 91–107.

# 14

# Governance of Service Triads in Humanitarian Logistics

## Graham Heaslip and Gyöngyi Kovács

## Introduction

In the continuous search for new ways of creating and capturing value, many organizations are looking for diversification opportunities in service markets related to their products (Visnjic Kastalli et al. 2013). Although companies constantly offer services to the market, they have only in recent years seen the integration of products and services as a possibility for growth and competitiveness (Jacob and Ulaga 2008). The provision of services has now turned into a conscious and explicit strategy with services becoming a main differentiating factor in a totally integrated products and service offering (Baines et al. 2009).

How to manage services in an organization-to-organization (O2O) setting is becoming important as increasing competition forces organizations to work more closely with external partners in the supply chain (Williams et al. 2006; Tate et al. 2010; Van Iwaarden and Van der Valk 2013). An example of such collaboration is the service triad, in which purchased services are directly delivered by service providers to customers (Van Iwaarden and

G. Heaslip (✉)
Galway Mayo Institute of Technology, Galway, Ireland
e-mail: graham.heaslip@gmit.ie

G. Kovács
Humanitarian Logistics at Hanken School of Economics, Helsinki, Finland
e-mail: gyongyi.kovacs@hanken.fi

© The Author(s) 2018                                                                 **417**
G. Kovács et al. (eds.), *The Palgrave Handbook of Humanitarian Logistics and Supply Chain Management*, https://doi.org/10.1057/978-1-137-59099-2_14

Van der Valk 2013). This raises the issue of governance within the service triad which to date has received little attention (Selviaridis and Spring 2010; Van der Valk, and Van Iwaarden 2011). As observed by Selviaridis and Spring (2010), "very little is known about how exchanged services take shape and how/why they are reshaped during the pre- and post-contract phases" (p. 172). The paucity of research relating to governance in the service triad raises questions with regard to alignment of contracts and which contract prevails in case of, for example, service delivery failure (Li and Choi 2009; Van der Valk and Van Iwaarden 2011).

Within humanitarian logistics (HL) the focus has shifted from core products towards the services because offering a mixture of goods and services allows UN agencies and IHOs to differentiate (Kovács 2014). However, applying the customer concept in the humanitarian setting is a bit more problematic. A traditional concept of a customer is the party that pays for goods or services, and is thus involved in a commercial transaction. Financial flows are, however, differently organized in the humanitarian setting. Yet, the notion of beneficiaries (end users) as well as implementing partners (organizational counterparts) having differing and varying requirements applies all the same also here.

Many humanitarian organizations do exactly the same things (provide food, water, sanitation, shelter, health care, education), they seek funding and resources from the same donors (governments, institutional and private), they use the same mass media to raise awareness and funds; their marketing strategies are very similar; and they use the same transport carriers and logistics service providers (Heaslip 2013; Oloruntoba and Gray 2009). Consequently, whatever marketing strategies they employ are quickly copied by other IHOs, who in essence are in competition (Oloruntoba and Gray 2009). Organizations trying to create or maintain differentiation in the humanitarian sector often find that whatever changes they make are greeted by counter moves from competing relief organizations (Oloruntoba and Gray 2009). For many humanitarian organizations the way to sustainable competitive advantage may not lie in changes in the product, promotion, or pricing strategies of the organization, but rather in improving customer service within HL, ancillary services, such as logistics and distribution (Oloruntoba and Gray 2009) and service offerings (Heaslip 2013).

Overall, there is a myriad of actors in the humanitarian supply chain (for an overview, see Heaslip et al. 2012), all with differing functions and roles. Table 14.1 provides an overview of those that are relevant to the service triad at hand, adding on the role of beneficiaries, who, though not directly included in an O2O service triad, are the final recipients of products and services, and the very reason for the existence of humanitarian service triads in the first place.

**Table 14.1** Different actors and their roles related to the humanitarian service triad

| Actor | Function | Commercial transaction | Authors |
|---|---|---|---|
| Beneficiaries | The end-user of the product or service whose needs or requirements must be accommodated | None | Oloruntoba and Gray (2009), Kovács and Spens (2007) and Altay and Green (2006) |
| Implementing partner (IP) | These are specific organizations, with specific functions (such as water, shelter etc.) operating between the international humanitarian organizations (IHOs) and the aid beneficiaries/end-users of the relief effort. | Yes between IP and IHO. | Matopoulos et al. (2014), Kovács and Spens (2011) and Thomas and Mizushima (2005) |
| Donor (governmental, institutional, private) | Provides funding for IHOs to procure staff, relief goods and transport them to disaster sites for relief distribution. The donor not only provides funding but may also provide supplies such as clothing, food or cooking oil, here the donor acts like a supplier, except that the donor does not get paid. | Yes between donor and IHO. None when donor acts as a supplier (in-kind donations). | Heaslip (2013) Holguín-Veras et al. (2013), Oloruntoba and Gray (2009) and Van Wassenhove (2006) Kovács and Spens (2009) and Van Wassenhove (2006) |
| IHO | Can act as donor, implementing partner, or delivery partner in particular programmes or through Clusters. | Yes between IHOs. | Kovács (2014) and Jahre and Jensen (2010) |
| UN Agency | Specific organization, with specific functions (such as water, shelter etc). Can act as delivery partners in particular programmes or through Clusters. | Yes between donor, IHO and IP. | Heaslip (2013), Kovács and Spens (2011) and Jahre and Jensen (2010) |

In this chapter we adopt an agency theory (AT) perspective to gain a better understanding of how contractual agreements influence the service triad in humanitarian supply chains. This is in essence an O2O triad between the donor, a UN agency or IHO, and the UN's or IHO's implementing partner (IP, another, usually local organization) in the field. AT explicitly addresses under which contractual arrangements the relationship between a buyer (the principal) and a service provider (the agent) operates most efficiently (Eisenhardt 1989; Tate et al. 2010). As observed by Van der Walk and Van Iwaarden (2011), when service production is outsourced there is a third actor involved: the "end customer" (another agent). In this research the buyer (the principal) is therefore confronted with two agents (the service provider, which is either an UN agency or an IHO, and "end customer", which in the humanitarian service triad would be the IP) who may each have their own specific and possibly conflicting objectives (Tate et al. 2010; Van der Walk and Van Iwaarden 2011). In AT the contractual question becomes should the agent be measured by relational (such as salaries, hierarchical governance) or contractual outcomes (commissions, market governance) (Logan 2000). As Eisenhardt (1989, p. 58) points out, "[…] the focus of agency theory [centres] on determining the most efficient contract governing the principal-agent relationship […]".

This leads to the following research question: how can AT be applied in a service triad in HL in order to gain a better understanding of how contractual arrangements influence the buyer-service provider alignment in an O2O service triads? To assist in answering this question we use descriptive exploratory research to obtain primary data directly from humanitarian in-country programmes.

## Service Triads

There are two unique features to service triads overall. Firstly, there is direct contact between service provider and end customer (Li and Choi 2009; Van der Valk et al. 2009; Van der Valk and Van Iwaarden 2011). Hence, the service provider's performance is determinative for end customer satisfaction, and the buyer cannot directly control this performance other than through contracts and monitoring activities (for example through contracts and/or Service Level Agreements). Secondly, while there is a contract between end customer and buyer and between buyer and service provider, there is however no contract between the service provider and end customer. So far, service triads and their governance have been largely neglected in scholarly research (Li and Choi 2009; Van der Valk et al. 2009; Selviaridis and Spring 2010; Van der Valk, and Van Iwaarden 2011). Table 14.2 provides an overview

**Table 14.2** Triad literature in supply chain management

| Authors | Service triad composition | Research theory | Setting manufacturing / service | Results |
|---|---|---|---|---|
| Wu and Choi (2005) | 1 buyer and 2 suppliers | Social network theory | Manufacturing | Relational dynamics of the supplier-supplier relationship as a link indirectly connected to the buyer |
| Dubois and Frediksson (2008) | 1 buyer and 2 suppliers | Network theory | Manufacturing | Triadic sourcing occurs |
| Choi and Kim (2008) | 1 supplier and 2 buyers | Social network theory | Manufacturing | Structural embeddedness exist in these triads |
| Rossetti and Choi (2008) | Supplier, service provider, and an end user (customer) | Agency theory | Manufacturing | Supply chain disintermediation occurs between the customer and the supplier |
| Choi and Wu (2009) | 1 buyer and 2 suppliers | Balance theory and Social network theory | Manufacturing | Triadic relational dynamics in the collective go beyond individual actors |
| Li and Choi (2009) | Buyer, service provider and end user (customer) | Social network theory | Services | • Bridging role of the service provider is potentially critical<br>• Nature of the relationship between buying firm and service provider before service provision begins affects the relationship between service provider and customer after it begins<br>• Ongoing interaction between the service provider and the customer, once service delivery begins, may undermine the relationship between the buying organization and the customer |

(continued)

**Table 14.2** (continued)

| Authors | Service triad composition | Research theory | Setting manufacturing / service | Results |
|---|---|---|---|---|
| Wu et al. (2010) | 1 buyer and 2 suppliers | Co-opetition theory | Manufacturing | • A significant relationship between supplier–supplier co-opetition and supplier performance<br>• Buyer plays a role in building supplier-supplier relationships |
| Van der Walk and Van Iwaarden (2011) | Buyer, service provider and end user (customer) | Agency theory | Services | Outsourced service production can be properly governed by the right combination of contracts and monitoring activities |
| Hartmann and Herb (2014) | Buyer, service provider and end user (customer) | Social capital theory | Services | Social capital in one relationship does not only improve dyadic supply performance but also impacts other relationships in the network. |

of the antecedent literature of service triads in supply chain management. In line with previous research in service triads (Li and Choi 2009; Van der Valk and Van Iwaarden 2011), this research focuses on business-to-business, or rather, O2O services.

The service triad proposed for this research follows the service triad composition initially proposed by Li and Choi (2009) – buyer organization, service provider and end customer. Translating this composition into HL, we propose a buyer organization would be similar to a donor, a service provider is similar to a UN agency or IHO, and the end customer equates to an implementing partner (IP), see Fig. 14.1. The nature of the relationships between these actors and the level of integration and trust are major determinants of the capability of the supply chain to deliver services.

When acting as "service providers", UN agencies or IHOs can provide services such as information consultancy, procurement, customs clearance, warehousing, distribution, inventory management, fleet services and management, postponement, and training. Prominent examples are UNICEF's procurement services to their "partners" (governmental agencies, or NGOs that act as implementing partners), or the International Federation of the Red Cross and Red Crescent Societies (IFRC) provides fleet services to national chapters of the Red Cross/Red Crescent movement. In the latter case, IFRC manages a global fleet that they can lease to national chapters (their IPs) on demand (Pedraza Martinez et al. 2011). However, it is donors providing the funding for this to happen. Donors are intrinsically interested in the results of humanitarian programmes, and set the constraints of these programmes (Jahre and Heigh 2008; Majewski et al. 2010).

As in third-party logistics, there are various possibilities for these relationships. Material flows can originate from donors if they are suppliers at the same time,

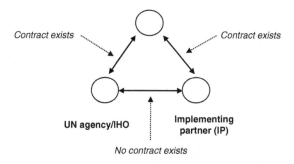

**Fig. 14.1**   A humanitarian service triad

and go through IHOs to IPs, or just be administered by IHOs to reach IPs. Financial flows from donors can target IHOs, IPs, or both – though the most typical situation would foresee a financial transaction from donor to IHO to IP, which is why the situation is sometimes described as consisting of sequential principal-agent relationships (Lundin 2011) and not triads. Interestingly, there is no one common set-up for how formal contracts exist between the three entities in this service triad. Donors may have a contract with the UN agency/IHO or the IP, or both. UN agencies /IHOs may have a contract with the IP directly, or the arrangement may be set through the donors. Then again, also in third-party logistics (Bask 2001), it is the sum of the flows (material, information, finance, and title flows) that determines the triad.

Meeting the demands of beneficiaries has become more complex (and more global), the providers of HL and distribution services have responded in a number of ways. Some have diversified into complete one-stop shops, others have remained more narrowly focused on providing a limited range of functions. Some examples illustrate the trend. The traditional view of UN (e.g. WFP and UNICEF) and IHOs (e.g. Oxfam and World Vision International) is in providing tangible relief (such as water, food, and shelter), see Fig. 14.2. Post the 2004 Asian tsunami the asset-based UN agency (e.g. WFP) and IHO (e.g. IFRC) developed. This was primarily from the diversification of some traditional IHOs into more complex offerings. Several of the world's leading UN agencies and IHOs moved in this direction (e.g. United Nations Humanitarian Response Deport – UNHRD). With

| | Asset based | Skills based |
|---|---|---|
| **Physical service** | *Major functions*<br>Warehousing<br>Inventory management<br>Postponement<br>Transportation<br>Distribution | *Major functions*<br>Information consultancy<br>Supply        chain<br>management<br>Financial services<br>Training |
| | **Traditional** | **Network based** |
| | *Major functions*<br>Food<br>Water<br>Sanitation<br>Shelter<br>Health care<br>Education | *Major functions*<br>Track and trace<br>Procurement<br>Custom clearance<br>Service standardization |

Management services ⟶

**Fig. 14.2** Types of UN agencies and IHOs (Source: Authors)

this move towards asset-based services, it is as if the goods an IHO provides had become a "qualifier", whereas the service offered has become the "order winner". The focus has shifted from core products towards the services because offering a mixture of goods and services allows the IHO to differentiate and create a more satisfied and loyal customer – though with a focus on donors as customers, not beneficiaries.

In the early 2000s, a number of network-based UN and IHOs appeared, most notably United Nations Children's Fund (UNICEF), IFRC and WFP. This move to offering value-added services includes procurement services being offered by agencies such as the UNICEF, the UNHRD network and the United Nations Office for Project Services (UNOPS) to other UN agencies as well as to governments (Kovács 2014). Procurement works like a pivot in the internal supply chain process turning around requests into actual products/commodities or services to fulfil the needs. Beyond the UN family, IFRC have developed a procurement centre and procurement portal that has been accredited by the European Commission's Humanitarian Aid & Civil Protection agency (ECHO), and through which third parties (for example, Caritas) outside Red Cross/Red Crescent national chapters can ask for their services. Other value-added services are also available, for example the IFRC is offering its services in areas such as "procurement and transportation", "warehousing and handling", "contingency stock", "fleet service" and "insurance" (IFRC 2012; Kovács 2014). These service offerings are offered both in disasters settings and long-term development (IFRC 2012). In addition to these, Heaslip (2013) has demonstrated the existence of further applications of service operations in humanitarian supply chains, for example the WFP acting as a consignee in major disasters (and consolidating transportation), as well as service standardization. The nature of these services necessitates creating geographically extensive and tightly integrated networks of operations. The development of "common services" has even become one of four key points on the agenda of the Global Logistics Cluster meeting in Copenhagen in November 2014. The global strategy of the Logistics Cluster for 2013–2015 (GLC 2013) includes the point of developing a "service catalogue" that would be available for addressing and filling gaps in logistics services in risk areas but also to build national preparedness – albeit it remains disputed which role the cluster should play in the latter.

The fourth type of IHO – the skill based – has been a recent phenomenon. These are UN and IHOs that provide a range of primarily information based services. These encompass consultancy services (including supply chain configuration) and training. Examples of this type of IHO include UNWFP, which has developed the Logistics Response Team Training (LRT training) that it has offered to other organizations in the Logistics Cluster since 2007. Interestingly, an integral part of this is a "service mindset training" for logisticians.

As discussed earlier, UN agencies and IHOs are moving to offering value-added services (see Fig. 14.2). The provision of services by UN agencies and IHOs has now turned into a conscious and explicit strategy with services becoming a main differentiating factor in a totally integrated products and service offering (Heaslip 2013; Kovács 2014). As this research is focused on O2O services, it rules out the possibility of beneficiaries being part of the service triad, instead the implementing partner is considered the end customer. As noted by Kovács (2014, p. 280),

> ...the role of implementing partners also deserves more attention. Largely neglected in research, it is often not the big international NGOs (BINGOs) or aid agencies which conduct the last mile distribution but their implementing partners on the ground.

## Agency Theory

AT is concerned with the study of problems that arise when one party, the principal, delegates work to another party, the agent (Zsidisin and Ellram 2003). The focus of AT is on deciding on the type of contract between a principal and an agent (Eisenhardt 1989; Van der Valk and Van Iwaarden 2011). AT advances two types of contract – contractual and relational. The formal contractual approach (or structural approach) identifies complex contracts that mitigate the perceived risk of opportunistic behaviour (Cao and Lumineau 2015; Poppo and Zenger 2002). In contrast, the relational perspective promotes a more relational governance strategy in which partners rely on trust to address issues of safeguarding and coordination (Cao and Lumineau 2015; Malhotra and Lumineau 2011). These two perspectives have their specific assumptions, theoretical bases and governance structures. Contractual governance relies more on monetary sanctions and legal enforceability for curtailing abnormal behaviours. Relational governance on the other hand utilizes trust-based principles such as self-enforceability and social sanctions for restraining self-interest-driven, opportunistic behaviours (Mahapatra et al. 2010). Table 14.3 summarizes the two types of contracts.

**Table 14.3** Types of contract between principal and agent

| Contract type | Focus of contract | Main assumptions | Proposed governance structures | Authors |
|---|---|---|---|---|
| Contractual | Emphasizes measurable results or contractual effectiveness and are more likely to lead the agent to behave in the interests of the principal. | 1. Single transaction <br> 2. Parties tend to act opportunistically. <br> 3. Performance is driven by quality of the initial structural design. | • Formal governance <br> • Complex contracts | Eisenhardt (1989), Zsidisin and Ellram (2003), Tate et al. (2010) and Van der Valk and Van Iwaarden (2011) |
| Relational | Focus on processes, tasks and activities that will accomplish the desired results and are most appropriate when the agent's behaviour can be readily monitored and measured at a reasonable cost. | 1. Inter-firm relationship <br> 2. Parties tend to act in a trustworthy fashion. <br> 3. Performance is driven by the quality of the ongoing relational processes. | • Informal governance <br> • Trust | Eisenhardt (1989), Zsidisin and Ellram (2003), Tate et al. (2010), Van der Valk and Van Iwaarden (2011) |

Underlying AT are specific assumptions about human nature (self-interest, bounded rationality, risk aversion), information (seen as a commodity that can be purchased), and organizations (goal conflict among members) (Eisenhardt 1989; Tate et al. 2010; Van der Valk and Van Iwaarden 2011). AT builds on specific assumptions regarding whether suppliers can be expected to act in the best interest of their (customers') customers, or are likely to display opportunistic behaviour (Tate et al. 2010; Van der Valk and Van Iwaarden 2011). Firstly, regarding human nature, the assumptions of self-interest, and bounded rationality and differing risk preferences (Tate et al. 2010) explain why in many cases agents are unlikely to act in the best interest of their principals. Secondly, information is viewed as a commodity that can be exchanged (Eisenhardt 1989). If interests are misaligned and there is goal incongruence, then information may be hidden, thereby creating information asymmetry (Tate et al. 2010). Thirdly, organization relates to the fact goal congruence between principal and agent reduces the risk of opportunistic subcontractor behaviour (Van der Valk and Van Iwaarden 2011). Essentially the principal wants the provider to meet or exceed agreed upon service levels and the agent wants to be fairly rewarded for his efforts as noted by Fayezi et al. (2012) "typically, the principal seeks to minimise the agency costs, such as, specifying, rewarding and monitoring, and policing the agent's behaviour, while the agent works towards maximising rewards and reducing principal control" (p. 557). Efficient management of agency problems such as information acquisition (or communication) (Eisenhardt 1989), preference mismatch (or conflict of interest) (Tate et al. 2010), effort (or moral hazard) and capability (or adverse selection) (Van der Valk and Van Iwaarden 2011), mainly associated with the agent (Fayezi et al. 2012) is also imperative to any principal-agent relationship. The greater the goal congruence between the agent and the contract, the more likely the agent will meet the terms of the contract (Rossetti and Choi 2008).

In situations where an agent's action is difficult to observe, such as in HL (largely due to the complex nature of the task), the principal is exposed to a heightened risk of opportunism by its agent. Similarly, where agents know more than the principals the potential for opportunism increases. This according to Hartmann and Herb (2014) provides an opportunity for the agent to both evade control and misrepresent its capabilities. To avoid opportunism governance emerges from the values and agreed-upon processes found in social relationships which may minimize transaction costs (Tangpong 2011; Malhotra and Lumineau 2011).

As humanitarian operations are being pressured to become more transparent (Van Wassenhove 2006), UN agencies and international humanitarian organizations (IHOs) have focused on "getting the job done" and have put little effort into performance measurement other than reporting to donors on the amount of relief and usage of funds for a given operation. When performance is difficult to measure, parties have incentives to limit their efforts toward fulfilling the agreement. Poppo and Zenger (2002) found that when mangers could not easily measure the performance of an outsourced activity, it strongly damaged the user's evaluation of the provider's cost performance. According to Poppo and Zenger (2002, p. 709), "managers have two choices in such a situation, either realize lower performance, or expend resources and create more complex contracts to improve performance measurement, and service levels". The AT assumptions are applied to the service triad agency relationships in Table 14.4.

Recently scholars have used AT to develop propositions on the design of contractual arrangements between two principals and an agent (Tate et al. 2010) and triads (Van der Valk and Van Iwaarden (2011). We draw on the work of Li and Choi (2009); Tate et al. (2010); and Valk and Van Iwaarden (2011) to build propositions. In the humanitarian service triad, as in third-party logistics, the actual material, financial, information and title flows determine the triad, regardless of the contractual set-up. In any case, financial flows originate from donors, hence they are the principal in the humanitarian service triad, whereas the UN agency or IHO as service provider, and the IP will conduct agent-like behaviour. The IP is mainly interested in the desired outcome of the service encounter and possibly in the process that brings about that outcome.

Eisenhardt (1989) proposes that a contractual contract is more likely to lead any agent to behave in the interests of the principal. Based on this, we propose the following:

*Proposition 1: Within the service triad, the contract applying to the donor-IP dyad is contractual based.*

Zsidisin and Ellram (2003) point out that the buyer (here donor) will primarily be interested in pricing, compliance and performance information as a means to reduce risk and monitor supplier behaviour. Van der Valk and Van Iwaarden (2011) posit that cost reduction may be an important buyer objective, while quality is likely an end customer objective. Building on Tate et al. (2010) we propose the following:

*Proposition 2: Within the service triad, the contract applying to the donor-UN agency /IHO dyad is contractual based.*

**Table 14.4** Agency assumptions applied to service triads in humanitarian logistics

| Assumption | | Buyer/donor (Principal) | Service provider/UN agency or IHO (Agent) | End customer/implementing partner (Agent) |
|---|---|---|---|---|
| **People** | Self interest | Focus on cost control and efficacy of contracts. | The Agent may or may not behave as agreed. | The Agent may or may not behave as agreed. |
| | Bounded rationality | Limitations are due to an over-emphasis on tangible issues at the potential expense of critical, but less tangible performance issues. | Limitation comes from lack of information about Principal's future needs and commitment. | Limitation comes from lack of information about Principal's future needs and commitment. |
| | Risk aversion | Risk neutral when the opportunity exists to multisource. | Risk averse when the relationship is important, prefer multisource. | Risk averse when security and income are often tied to a single donor. |
| **Information** | Information | Information requirements are high with regard to conformance to outcome oriented metrics. | Information requirements are high with regard to conformance to outcome oriented metrics. | Want communication flows limited to relational issues but will exchange information to achieve security and income. |
| | | Use information to control supplier opportunism. | Use information to improve the relationship. | |
| | Utility of information | View information as contributor to and outcome of good relationships. | View information as a commodity. | Use information as a commodity. |
| **Organization** | Goal conflict | Wants relationship more formalized and the service more commoditized. Reduced cost, timely delivery, and measurable quality. Overarching goal is to control agency costs and achieve contractual results. | Wants to provide a highly individualized service with limited interference on process. Overarching goal is to maximize profit, which includes maintaining the relationship. | Wants a strong alliance with the supplier and highly creative output. Overarching goal is to create a positive image for the organization and increase sales. |

Source: Adapted from Eisenhardt (1989) and Tate et al. (2010)

In summary, AT can be used to help design the most effective types of contracts and relationships to provide fair outcomes to all parties. The contractual question concerns the management of the agent using contractual or relational contracts while balancing the service triad. The next section describes the research design and data collection used for this research.

## Research Design and Data Collection

The research followed a systematic combining approach, as described by Dubois and Gadde (2002). The aim was to link theory to the empirical world, where the case itself as well as theoretical constructs served as intermediating links between theory and empirics. One approach designed to tackle real problems and to develop a capacity to learn is a case study (Yin 2003). Due to lack of suitable frameworks that offer explanation for effective service triad contracts in HL, we adopted exploratory case study as the methodological approach for this research (Eisenhardt 1989). Case studies allow exploration of areas with little pre-existing theory (Voss et al. 2002), and help develop frameworks by using data collected through direct interaction with subjects of interest (Eisenhardt and Graebner 2007).

Since humanitarian service triads are a contemporary phenomenon that show their potential in real-life contexts and can hardly be replicated in experiments, the case study design is deemed as an appropriate research methodology. Our empirical study used one case study examining the response to the Typhoon Yolanda. The case in focus was the service triad between the Irish Aid, WFP and Concern Worldwide (CWW). Primary data were collected through semi-structured interviews. Informants were chosen to cover persons who had [...] lived experiences related to the focus of the study, who were willing to talk about their experiences, and who were diverse enough from one another to enhance rich and unique stories of the particular experience.

This study is based on field research, utilizing participant observation and in-context interview techniques for rich data collection. It was felt that field research would be the only way to obtain data that would be rich in detail and which could be related to the context in which it was occurring. Observation provided a means of studying the whole system with its many interrelationships in great detail. Participant observation has been described as when the "ethnographer participates in the daily routines of this setting, develops ingoing relations with the people in it, and observes all the while what is going on". The complexity of the humanitarian context meant that case study research offered the methodological fit (Edmonson and McManus 2007; Fisher 2007) to advance relevant theory on service triads.

The selected organizations capture the heterogeneity in the humanitarian sector and facilitate comparisons (Eisenhardt and Graebner 2007). The size and profile of the organizations interviewed fit with the time, budget and accessibility constraints of the research project. The selected organizations (see Table 14.5) facilitated access to their sites and personnel for interviews.

We operationalized research quality as credibility, transferability, dependability, and confirmability (see e.g. (Golafshani 2003). By triangulating sources of information, the researcher's perceptions were corrected from different angles. Transferability is explained by Halldorsson and Aastrup (2003) as to what extent "the study is able to make general claims about the world". Transferability between the context of defence logistics and the context of HL will be discussed later in the chapter. As for dependability, that is stability of data over time, Halldorsson and Aastrup (2003) suggest to document the whole research process. Ideally, all research material should be made available. Some texts are not publicly available. Confirmability was ensured by transcribing and redistributing audio-taped recordings to each respondent. The rationale of so doing was to ascertain that the respondents agreed with the researcher's interpretation of what was said, and allow additional comments from the respondents. Finally, we combined information from the interviews with secondary data.

Data collection took place during a period of 4 weeks in 2014 and was mainly performed by means of semi-structured, in-depth interviews (Table 14.5), and through document studies and participant observation. The interviews focused on the contracts/SLAs in place, incentives used, and the monitoring activities employed. At IA, interviews of about 1.5–2 hours were conducted with the three managers that are most strongly involved in the dealings with each of the agents. These interviews resulted in an understanding of how IA works and how IA views the relationships with WFP and CWW. At the service provider, two interviews of approximately 1.5–2 hours were conducted with strategic and tactical representatives. The interviews focused on what agreements were made between WFP and IA and WFP and CWW. At CWW interviews tool place strategic, tactical and operational managers, each interview lasting approximately 1.5–2 hours. The interviews focused on what agreements were made between CWW and IA and CWW and WFP.

**Table 14.5** Interviewees

| Triad participant | Organization | Job title | Function level | Services |
|---|---|---|---|---|
| Donor | Irish Aid (IA) | Head of Development Cooperation Division | Strategic | *Buying:* Information consultancy; |
| | | Humanitarian Development Specialist | Tactical | Procurement; Customs clearance; |
| | | Humanitarian Development Specialist | Operational | Warehousing; Distribution; Inventory Management; Fleet service; Postponement; Training |
| Service provider (UN agency/IHO) | WFP | Network Coordinator | Strategic | *Providing:* Information consultancy; |
| | | Procurement and logistics coordinator | Operational | Procurement; Customs clearance; Warehousing; Distribution; Inventory Management; Fleet service; Postponement; Training |
| IP | Concern World Wide (CWW) | Supplies and Logistics Manager | Strategic | *Receiving:* Procurement; |
| | | Logistics manager | Tactical | Customs clearance; Warehousing; Distribution; |
| | | Logistics manager | Operational | Inventory Management; Fleet service; Postponement; Training |

Critical to the usefulness of the analysis is the clarity of the case boundary (Perren and Ram 2004); in this research the case boundary was around the senior logistical personnel of Irish Aid, WFP and Concern Worldwide rather than the individual organizations *per se*. Because we relied on key informants, we needed influential decision makers who led service initiatives for their organization, so we only invited senior managers to participate.

In terms of data management, digital folders were created for archiving system for each case study. A chain of evidence was established by documenting data sources in the case study reports and analysis. There are no predetermined criteria for sample size in qualitative research but according to Edmonson and McManus 2007) the sample size can be fixed at what the researcher considers reliable within the constraints of time and resources. Data analysis involved a process of data reduction and reconstruction. In the data reduction phase, collected data were subjected to a coding process that allowed them to be disaggregated so that key themes in the data became apparent. Data were analysed in a two-stage process that was heavily inductive (Lofland and Lofland 1995). During the first stage, field notes and transcribed interviews were examined for instances during which issues pertaining to the collaborative nature of the project (working together) were noted. Initial labels were then attached to these data elements that in some way pertained to collaboration, either between the military and the agencies or the agencies themselves. The second stage of coding was an analysis of the initial codes. During this focused coding (Lofland and Lofland 1995), the initial codes were sorted into similar groups, to which labels were then attached. This enabled systematic organization of our data and reducing complexity. Examples of labels used are contract type, service specification and so on. Subsequently the analysis and synthesis of results was carried out through feedback and discussion with associated humanitarian service triad participants.

The next section presents the findings from the case study, which is used to provide validation of the two propositions.

# Results

In this section, we first provide a case history. The discussion is based on data that we obtained through data triangulations (i.e., data collected at different times at multiple locations from multiple participants). The case studied involved the service triad of Irish Aid (donor) – WFP (UN agency) – Concern Worldwide (IP).

## The Donor

Irish Aid (IA) has been in the top 20 of government contributions to humanitarian aid of the past decade (GHA 2011). In 2013, the Irish Government spent €637 million on Ireland's aid programme. This is called Official Development Assistance (ODA) and represented 0.46% of Gross National Product (GNP) or 46 cents in every €100 that the country produces (Irish Government 2014). €497 million or approximately 78% of this funding was managed by IA. Table 14.5 provides an overview of the services IA purchase from WFP. IA does not deliver aid on the ground; in emergencies it uses its various implementing partners to deliver aid on its behalf.

## The UN Agency as Service Provider

WFP procures, manages, stores and transports emergency supplies on behalf of the humanitarian community, Table 14.5 provides a more detailed list of services. WFP through its affiliate the United Nations Humanitarian Response Depot (UNHRD) pre-positions inventory in six locations worldwide – Panama, Ghana, Dubai, Subang, Las Palmas and Brindisi. The case of WFP was selected, because of WFP being the lead agency of the Logistics Cluster, and has therefore developed numerous "common services" for other agencies and organizations in the cluster.

## The Implementing Partner

Concern Worldwide are dedicated to tackling poverty and suffering in the world's poorest countries. They work in partnership with the very poorest people in these countries, directly enabling them to improve their lives. Concern Worldwide operate as an IP for Irish Aid delivering aid on their behalf.

## Findings

This section delves deeper into the case study findings, interpreting the data in the light of the contractual considerations of AT. The data available from the case studies provide new insights into the relationships in O2O service triads, beyond those available from quantitative data analysis (Eisenhardt and Graebner 2007).

## Proposition 1

For proposition 1, similar to Eisenhardt (1989) who suggested: "When the principal has information to verify agent behaviour, the agent is more likely to behave in the interest of the principal" (p. 60), our research finds that IPs will opt for contractual-based contracts. Our findings are comparable to Neely (1999) who found that people focus on the issues that are measured and rewarded within an organization, and it " is likely that the agent will behave in its own interest by complying with the objectives that are more easily measured and thus are used to evaluate its performance" (p. 220). In the contract between Irish Aid (IA) and Concern Worldwide the contract is based on measureable outcomes, such as cost, timeliness and issue resolution. IA observed, "As we got more experience in the area [humanitarian sector] we required more information regarding what outcomes needed to be included in our contracts. Part of this was to adhere to transparency and accounting procedures". It should be noted, however, that certain aspects of the contract such as beneficiary satisfaction was not considered.

These findings show that if contracts are not designed carefully, opportunistic behaviour may occur in the unmeasured areas, so that the spirit of the contract may be lost. For example, IA had to continuously modify its measures, or its IP would act in their own self-interest and try to "game" the system. IA remarked, "there have been situations in the past where agencies have tried to take advantage and act in their self-interest and not in Irish Aids interest, even though we would be purchasing the goods." This finding is similar to those reported by Tate et al. (2010) when investigating the purchasing of marketing services in a triadic relationship.

In this contractual contract, criteria had to be modified to take all possible deviations from the intent of the contract into account. The IP focused on what was measured, rather than performing to the behaviour that they clearly knew that IA was interested in. These findings show that if contracts are not designed carefully, opportunistic behaviour may occur in the unmeasured areas, so that the spirit of the contract may be lost. It is thus highly important that appropriate measures are identified. Similar to Mishra et al. (1998) and Tate et al. (2010) this research found that even if the IP possess the "right" skills, they may still fail to use them if information asymmetry allows such actions and if there are cost savings involved. Similarly buyers (donors) seek information to help make better choices. IA commented: "It is important for our IPs to tell us what services they would like...We have frank conversations with our IPs so that we can understand their position".

New insights were obtained regarding the presence of relational contracts in the donor – IP relationship. The research suggests that a hybrid (mixed) contract exits. The hybrid approach had the benefit of providing detailed performance data regarding relational elements such as processes for accessing funding as well as contractual criteria such as cost, timeliness and issue resolution. While the relational monitoring may be perceived by the IP to be obtrusive, the presence of a relational contract looks like an aid in preventing the IP from displaying reactant behaviour. IA commented, "We have very good relationships with Concern Worldwide and in some cases personal friendships which facilitates more of the soft skills when negotiating contracts; we try to co-create with our implementing partners." The presence of relational contracts reduces the possibility of misalignment of contracts. This finding suggests that in the cases studied, relational governance outweighs contractual governance.

To avoid opportunistic behaviour, incentive capability (Hurwicz 1972) was adopted in the contract design. Contracts were subsequently designed so that the actions with the highest pay-off to the IP are also the actions that are most appropriate from the donor's point of view.

## Proposition 2

Proposition 2 stated that the contract applying to the donor-service provider (UN agency /IHO) dyad is contractual-based. In line with Grönroos (2011) and Tate et al. (2010), we observe that the way in which the service is perceived governs much of the contractual behaviour related to services. The IP's preference for contractual contracts with the donor is not necessarily reflected in the service provider – donor contract. IA has a three-year contract with WFP which is a hybrid contract consisting of contractual-based measurable outcomes, such as cost, timeliness and issue resolution and relational outcomes. Underlying the contract is a service-level agreement, which includes arrangements for the service delivery process. It seems that the donor prefers to focus on aspects like measurability of performance in determining their contracts, and to specify a relational-based contract rather than to transfer their IP's requirements to WFP. While the relational monitoring may be perceived by the service provider to be meddlesome, the presence of a relational contract looks like an aid in preventing the service provider from displaying opportunism behaviour. Contrary to earlier research by Van der Valk and Van Iwaarden (2011), this research determines that the preferred contract between the buyer (donor) – service provider is a hybrid-based contract.

Eisenhardt (1989) observed that in AT the right type of contract varies with the length of relationship. While this may be true, we did not find support for this in the practices among the case studies. For example, prior to WFP involvement, IA used relational-based contracts with its service providers within long-term relationships. Later, when WFP became involved, IA modified its contracting approach to improve measureable performance, and developed a mix of relational-based and contractual-based contracts. IA remarked: "We learnt so much from our previous involvement in humanitarian aid. With WFP we think we have struck the right balance of accountable measurements." A major characteristic of humanitarian contexts is the lack of information available to humanitarian logisticians. The major difficulty is that the quality of service provision is difficult to assess; whereas the service provider may know product quality, the buyer often does not (Kastalli et al. 2013). This asymmetry of information between service providers and buyers creates problems for their market provision. WFP remarked: "We try to build relationships with our customers, build trust maintain a connection and jointly overcome any unexpected problems."

A hybrid approach reduces the conflict between IA and WFP by allowing both to incorporate their goals. From a logistics perspective, the hybrid approach also has the benefit of providing detailed performance data regarding the relational-based elements, while retaining WFP's preferred contractual focus. For IA, the hybrid approach allows the positive relationship with the service provider while still achieving the desired results. Since the hybrid contractual arrangement includes both relational- and contractual-oriented elements, the agent will be more likely to behave in the interests of the principal. This is similar to Eisenhardt's (1989) observation that, "When the contract between the principal and agent is outcome-based, the agent is more likely to behave in the interests of the principal" (p. 60). By standardizing coordination with WFP, IA is able to obtain a good overview of the service provider's activities, learn from them and make appropriate investments in their capabilities.

## Conclusion

This chapter has drawn on AT to conceptualize the service triadic relationship between a donor, service provider and IP of HL services. We wanted to gain an understanding of how contractual agreements influence the alignment of goals and behaviours between the buying organization and the service provider and between the buying organization and an implementing partner. For this purpose, we examined data from a case study.

A key characteristic of commercial service triads is that services are directly delivered by the service provider to the end customer. Hence, the service provider's performance is determinative for end customer satisfaction, and the buyer cannot directly control this performance other than through contracts and monitoring activities. AT provides valuable suggestions regarding contracts, yet, has only limitedly been applied to triadic settings.

Considering the novelty of research regarding the supply of services in general and regarding HL services in particular, the next few sentences present the theoretical contributions of this research. This research contributes to the governance of service triad relationships in the context of HL services. Our research allows for theoretical elaboration of AT, and a greater understanding of the service triad context. The introduction of the agency triad creates an opportunity for improved contractual relationships. This research helps elaborate upon existing theory to develop an understanding of the service triad relationship. It highlights the value of alignment, and suggests the appropriate type of contractual arrangements between a donor – service provider and a donor – IP. This research suggests that a hybrid of elements of contractual-based and relational-based contracts in HL services results in improved performance.

For practitioners, our findings suggest that it is highly important that relational outcomes are established between donor–service provider and donor–IP, as it appears to guide the service provider and IP towards desired behaviour. Aligning all three parties in the triad by means of the right type of contract is beneficial not only for the donor, but certainly also for the IP and the service provider. This research suggests that cooperation between the principal and two agents can improve performance through sharing of information, knowledge, and improved coordination. However, this alignment seems to be more easily achieved through relational contracts rather than legal arrangements.

This research argues that governance structures that integrate the complementary elements of relational- and contractual-based contracts are likely to be advantageous. Mahapatra et al. (2010) notes that in these mechanisms, complementary elements such as potential for future business, contractual adaptability and penalties for unjustifiable breaches limit dysfunctional outcomes that are inherent to contractual or relational governance. Developing an arrangement that appropriately balances relational- and contractual-based elements however involves a great deal of experiment in a mutually supportive atmosphere.

In examining an HL service triad AT helps to answer two questions: what can the donor do to encourage quality service and fair treatment by the service provider and what can the service provider do to keep the donor and IP satisfied and at the same time reach its goals.

The service triad clearly is a special situation, since contracts and service production do not occur on one and the same link, but across multiple links in the triad. This has implications for what kind of contract and what kind of governance structures is appropriate. Further research is required to examine different contractual governance mechanisms such as transactional cost economics or social exchange theory to determine which the appropriate governance structure for contracts in service triads. Future research could add insight to the phenomena briefly explored here by studying triads in these more enduring service contexts. Follow-up research could be aimed at further validating and developing the propositions presented in this research. Overall, we believe our research provides a good starting point for additional research on governance in service triads in various other service contexts.

# References

Altay, N. and Green, W.G. (2006). "OR/MS research in disaster operations management", *European Journal of Operational Research*, 175(1), 475–493.

Baines, T. S., Lightfoot, H. W., Benedettini O. and Kay, J. M. (2009), "The servitization of manufacturing", *Journal of Manufacturing Technology Management*, 20(5), 547–567.

Bask, A. (2001). "Relationships among TPL providers and members of supply chains – A strategic perspective", *Journal of Business & Industrial Marketing*, 16(6), 470–486.

Cao, A. and Lumuneau, F. (2015) "Revisiting the interplay between contractual and relational goverance: A qualitative and meta-analytic investigaation", *Journal of Operations Management*, 33, 15–42.

Choi, T.Y. and Kim, Y. (2008). "Structural embeddedness and supplier management: A network perspective", *Journal of Supply Chain Management*, 44, 5–13.

Choi, T.Y. and Wu, Z. (2009). "Triads in supply networks: Theorizing buyer-supplier-supplier relationships", *Journal of Supply Chain Management*, 45(1), 8–25.

Dubois, A. and Fredriksson, P. (2008). "Cooperating and competing in supply networks: Making sense of a triadic sourcing strategy". *Journal of Purchasing and Supply Management*, 14, 170–179.

Edmonson, A.C. and McManus, S.E. (2007). "Methodological fit in management field research". *Academy of Management Review*, 32(4), 1155–1179.

Eisenhardt, K.M. (1989). "Agency Theory: An assessment and review. Academy of management". *Academy of Management Review*, 14(1), 57–74.

Eisenhardt, K. and Graebner, M.E. (2007). "Theory building from cases: Opportunities and challenges". *Academy of Management Journal*, 50(1), 25–32.

Fayesi, S., O'Loughlin, A. and Zutshi, A. (2012). "Agency theory and supply chain management a structured literature review", *Supply Chain Management: An International Journal* 17(5), 556–570.

Fisher, M. (2007). "Strengthening the empirical base of operations management". *Manufacturing & Service Operations Management* 9(4), 368–382.

Global Humanitarian Assistance Report (2013). *Who's who in humanitarian financing*, http://www.globalhumanitarianassistance.org/reports/

Global Logisitcs Cluster (2013), Global Strategy 2013–2015, http://www.logcluster.org/sites/default/files/logistics_cluster_glcsc_strategic_plan_2012-2015_0.pdf

Golafshani, N. (2003). "Understanding reliability and validity in qualitative research", *The Qualitative Report*, 8(4), 597–606.

Grönroos, C. (2011). "A service perspective on business relationships: The value creation, interaction and marketing interface". *Industrial Marketing Management*, 40(2), 240–247.

Halldórsson, Á. and Aastrup, J. (2003). "Quality criteria for qualitative inquiries in logistics" *European Journal of Operational Research*, 144(2), 321–332.

Hartmann, E. and Herb, S. (2014). "Opportunism risk in service triads – A social capital perspective", *International Journal of Physical Distribution & Logistics Management*, 44(3), 242–256.

Heaslip, G. (2013). "Services operations management and humanitarian logistics", *Journal of Humanitarian Logistics and Supply Chain Management*, 3(1), 37–51.

Heaslip, G, Sharif, A.M. and Althonayan A. (2012). "Employing a systems-based perspective to the identification of inter-relationships within humanitarian logistics", *International Journal of Production Economics*, 139(2), 377–392.

Holguín-Veras, J., Pérez, N., Jaller, M., Van Wassenhove, L. N. and Aros-Vera, F. (2013). "On the appropriate objective function for post-disaster humanitarian logistics models", *Journal of Operations Management*, 31, 262–280.

Hurwicz, L. (1972). "On informationally decentralized systems". In R. Radner & C.B. MacGuire (Eds.), *Decision and organization: A volume in honour of Jacob Marschak* (pp. 297–336). North Holland Publishing Company: Amsterdam.

International Federation of Red Cross and Red Crescent Societies (IFRC). (2012). Logistics Preparedness, Available at: http://www.ifrc.org/en/what-we-do/disaster-management/preparing-for-disaster/disaster-preparedness-tools/logistics-preparedness Accessed 14/04/14.

Irish Government (2014) *Irish Aid Annual, Department of Foreign Affairs and Trade*, Government Publications, Dublin.

Jacob, F. and Ulaga, W. (2008). "The transition from product to service in business markets: An agenda for academic inquiry". *Industrial Marketing Management*, 37(3), 247–253.

Jahre, M. and Heigh, I. (2008). "Does the current constraints in funding promote failure in humanitarian supply chains?" *Supply Chain Forum: An International Journal*, 9(2), 44–54.

Jahre, M. and Jensen, L. M. (2010). "Coordination in humanitarian logistics through clusters", *International Journal of Physical Distribution and Logistics Management*, 40(8/9), 657–674.

Kastalli, V., Van Looy, I. B. and Neely, A. (2013). "Steering Manufacturing Firms Towards Service Business Model Innovation". *California Management Review* 56(1), 100–123.

Kovács, G. (2014). "Where next? The future of humanitarian logistics". In: Martin Christopher and Peter Tatham (eds.) *Humanitarian logistics: Meeting the challenge of preparing for and responding to disasters*, (pp. 275–285, 2nd edn.). Kogan Page: London, UK.

Kovács, G. and Spens, K. (2007). "Humanitarian logistics in disaster relief operations", *International Journal of Physical Distribution & Logistics Management*, 37(2), 99–114.

Kovács, G. and Spens, K.M. (2011). "Trends and developments in humanitarian logistics – A gap analysis", *International Journal of Physical Distribution and Logistics Management*, 41(1), 32–45.

Kovács, G. and Spens, K. M. (2009). "Identifying challenges in humanitarian logistics", *International Journal of Physical Distribution and Logistics Management*, 39(6), 506–528.

Li, M. and Choi, T.Y. (2009). "Triads in services outsourcing: Bridge, bridge decay and bridge transfer", *Journal of Supply Chain Management*, 45, 27–39.

Lofland, J. and Lofland, L. (1995). *Analyzing social settings*. Wadsworth: Belmont, CA.

Logan, M. (2000). "Using agency theory to design successful outsourcing relationships", *The International Journal of Logistics Management*, 11(2), 21–32.

Lundin, S. (2011). Den icke-statliga organisationens agerande inom utvecklingsbiståndskedjan ur ett samarbets- och maktperspektiv, Masters thesis, at http://hdl.handle.net/10138/27941, Accessed Mar 27, 2015.

Mahapatra, S.K., Narasimhan, R. and Barbieri, P. (2010). "Strategic interdependence, governance effectiveness and supplier performance: A dyadic case study investigation and theory development". *Journal of Operations Management* 28 (6), 537–552.

Majewski, B., Navangul, K.A. and Heigh, I. (2010). "A peek into the future of humanitarian logistics: Forewarned is forearmed". *Supply Chain Forum: An International Journal*, 11(3), 4–18.

Malhotra, D., Lumineay, F., (2011). "Trust and collaboration in the aftermath of conflict: The effects if contract", *Academy of Management Journal*, 54(5), 981–998.

Matopoulos, A., Kovács, G. and Hayes, O. (2014). "Local resources and procurement practices in humanitarian supply chains: An empirical examination of large scale house reconstruction projects". *Decision Sciences*, 45, (4), 621–646.

Mishra, D. P., Heide, J. B., & Cort, S. G. (1998). Information asymmetry and levels of agency relationships.Journal of marketing Research, 277–295.

Neely, A. (1999). The performance measurement revolution: Why now and what next? *International Journal of Operations & Production Management*, 19(2), 205–228.

Oloruntoba, R. and Gray, R. (2009). Customer service in emergency relief chains, *International Journal of Physical Distribution & Logistics Management*, 39(6), 486–505.

Pedraza Martinez, A.J., Stapleton, O. and van Wassenhove, L.N. (2011). "Field vehicle fleet management in humanitarian operations: A case-based approach", *Journal of Operations Management*, 29(5), 404–421.

Perren, L., & Ram, M. (2004). Case-study method in small business and entrepreneurial research mapping boundaries and perspectives. International small business journal, 22(1), 83–101.

Poppo, L. and Zenger, T. (2002). "Do formal contracts and relational governance function as substitutes or complements?" *Strategic Management Journal* 23, 707–725.

Rossetti, C. and Choi, T. (2008). "Supply management under high goal incongruence: An empirical examination of disintermediation in the aerospace industry", *Decision Sciences*, 39 (3), 507–540.

Selviaridis, K. and Spring, M. (2010). "The dynamics of business service exchanges: Insights from logistics outsourcing", *Journal of Purchasing & Supply Management*, 16, 171–184.

Tangpong, C. (2011). "Content analytic approach to measuring constructs in operations and supply chain management". *Journal of Operations Management* 29, 627–638.

Tate, W., Ellram, L., Bals, L., Hartmann, E. and van der Valk, W. (2010). "An agency theory perspective on the purchase of marketing services". *Industrial Marketing Management* 39 (5), 806–819.

Thomas, A. and Mizushima, M. (2005). "Logistics training: Necessity or luxury?" *Forced Migration Review*, 22, 60–61.

Van der Valk, W., Wynstra, F. and Axelsson, B. (2009). "Effective buyer–supplier interaction patterns in ongoing service exchange". *International Journal of Operations and Production Management*, 29 (8), 807–833.

Van der Valk, W. and Van Iwaarden, J. (2011). "Monitoring in service triads consisting of buyers, subcontractors and end customers", *Journal of Purchasing & Supply Management*, 17, 198–206.

Van Iwaarden, J. and Van der Valk, W. (2013). "Controlling outsourced service delivery: managing service quality in business service triads", *Total Quality Management and Business Excellence*, 24, 9–10.

Van Wassenhove, L.N. (2006). "Humanitarian aid logistics: supply chain management in high gear", *Journal of the Operations Research Society*, 57, 475–489.

Voss, C., Tsikriktsis, N. and Frohlich, M. (2002). "Case research in operations management", *International Journal of Operations & Production Management*, 22(2), 195–219.

Williams, R., Van der Wiele, T., Van Iwaarden, J., Bertsch, B. and Dale, B. (2006). "Quality Management: The new challenges". *Total Quality Management & Business Excellence*, 17(10), 1273–1280.

Wu, Z. and Choi, T.Y. (2005). "Supplier-supplier relationships in the buyer-supplier triad: Building theories from eight case studies". *Journal of Operations Management*, 24(1), 27–52.

Wu, Z., Choi, T. Y., & Rungtusanatham, M. J. (2010). Supplier–supplier relationships in buyer–supplier–supplier triads: Implications for supplier performance. Journal of Operations Management, 28(2), 115–123.

Yin, R.K. (2003). *Case study research: Design and methods*, 3rd edn. SAGE Publications, London.

Zsidisin, G.A. and Ellram, L.M. (2003). "An agency theory investigation of supply risk management". *Journal of Supply Chain Management* 39(3), 15–27.

# 15

# Multimodal Logistics in Disaster Relief

Syed Tariq, Muhammad Naiman Jalil
and Muhammad Adeel Zaffar

## Introduction

A disaster is defined as a major ecological breakdown between man and the environment (Gunn 2003). Disasters can be natural like earthquakes, floods, hurricanes, or man-made like chemical leakages or terrorist attacks. The number of natural disasters has increased in an exponential manner in the past few decades (see Fig. 15.1). Damages caused by disasters amounted to USD 155.8 billion from 2005 to 2014 (Guha-Sapir et al. 2014). Logistics is an important element of disaster operations, accounting for close to 80 percent of relief efforts (Trunick 2005). For example, in the 2010 Earthquake in Haiti, both sea and airports were damaged. Portable air traffic control equipment was brought in to make the airport functional. However,

S. Tariq (✉)
Suleman Dawood School of Business, Lahore University of Management Sciences, Lahore, Pakistan
e-mail: 14080009@lums.edu.pk

M.N. Jalil
Rotterdam School of Management, Erasmus University, Rotterdam, The Netherlands
e-mail: muhammad.jalil@lums.edu.pk

M.A. Zaffar
Information Technology, University of North Carolina, Chapel Hill, NC, USA
e-mail: adeel.zaffar@lums.edu.pk

© The Author(s) 2018                                                         **445**
G. Kovács et al. (eds.), *The Palgrave Handbook of Humanitarian Logistics and Supply Chain Management,* https://doi.org/10.1057/978-1-137-59099-2_15

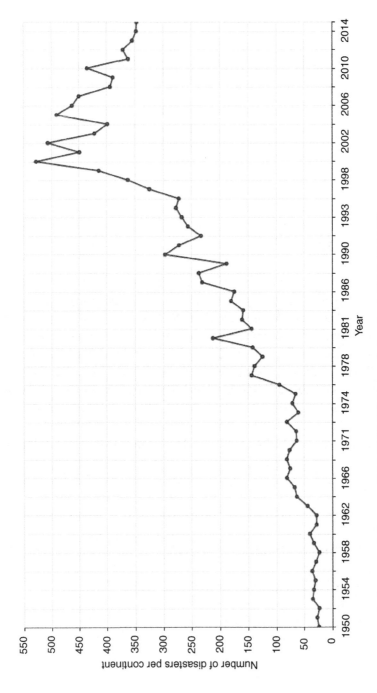

**Fig. 15.1** Trend of reported disasters 1950–2015 (With permission from EM-DAT 2016)

the seaport could not resume function for weeks as the piers and two cranes had been destroyed. Alternate logistics arrangements and emergency equipment were deployed to resume the flow of relief goods and medical teams (Holguín-Veras et al. 2012a). Such disruption of logistics infrastructure is one of the reasons for the utilization of alternative modes of transportation in disaster operations. This chapter is concerned with multimodal transportation during disasters and the elements of logistics that enable its use in disaster response.

Multimodal transportation of freight is defined as the utilization of more than one transportation mode in delivering a shipment of goods (UNECE 2009). The objective of this chapter is to review and understand problem settings in disaster scenarios concerned with multimodal logistics in order to provide areas of future research. This review includes a comparison of literature with cases from practice to glean interesting future areas of research. Literature relevant to multimodal planning in disaster operations is discussed in section "Literature Review". Section "Case Methodology" discusses the research methodology of two case studies—the 2005 Kashmir Earthquake and the 2010 Pakistan Floods. The cases are presented in sections "Kashmir Earthquake 2005" and "Pakistan Floods 2010", respectively, from a relief logistics viewpoint. Finally, in section "Analysis and Conclusions", we analyze the logistics problems faced in the two cases to obtain insights for future research in the field.

# Literature Review

## Disaster Operations Management

Humanitarian operations are geared toward alleviating suffering in general and helping people survive. These can be divided into two streams of activities: relief activities and development activities (Beamon and Balcik 2008). Relief activities alleviate suffering in large-scale emergencies. Disaster response is a relief activity targeted toward affectees of natural or man-made disasters. The purpose of relief activities is to provide immediate response to minimize human suffering and loss of life. Development activities—sometimes called continuous aid work—are long-term commitments toward the development of infrastructure, self-sufficiency, and sustainability in a community. These activities are sometimes conducted after disasters. However, their core purpose is to provide long-term stability and introduce self-sufficiency in an affected area.

The process of disaster operations management consists of four distinct phases: mitigation, preparedness, response, and recovery (McLoughlin 1985). Mitigation is concerned with reduction in disaster risk through steps in advance that reduce impact on populations. Preparedness phase facilitates disaster response through training personnel, deploying disaster response facilities, evacuating vulnerable population, and pre-stocking goods in preparation for the disaster. Disaster response phase occurs after a disaster has struck. The response phase is focused on minimizing human suffering through delivery of relief goods and medical assistance to the affectees. The recovery phase is a long-term effort to provide economic stability and resume daily activities in the affected area.

Disaster logistics problems occur in the last three stages, that is preparedness, response, and recovery stages (Özdamar and Ertem 2015). Certain characteristics of disaster logistics planning as highlighted by Sheu (2007) are:

1. Challenges in coordination and communication during disaster response arising from damaged communication infrastructure and increased complexity of communication due to multiple stakeholders.
2. Difficulties in achieving efficiency and timeliness in logistics.
3. Scarce resource availability given the magnitude of the impact.
4. Increased sources of uncertainty including high demand uncertainty as well as uncertainty due to impact of disaster on infrastructure capabilities of the region.

Caunhye et al. (2012) mention that recovery takes place after the chaotic environment of disaster response subsides. Hence, we focus on logistics planning during preparedness and response stages of disaster operations management which are more focused on the chaotic nature of disaster operations.

## Multimodality of Logistics in Disaster Operations

Multimodal transportation of freight is broadly defined as the utilization of more than one transportation modality to ship goods (UNECE 2009). Other terminologies have also been introduced in the literature that refer to shipment of goods through multiple modes of transportation. They represent concepts that qualify multimodal transportation planning according to techniques employed for improving efficiency or flexibility in the system. We will discuss three terms here: intermodal transportation, co-modal transportation, and synchromodal transportation. Intermodal transportation refers to the transportation of goods through at least two transportation modes over the travel itinerary (Crainic and Kim 2006). Co-modal transportation refers to the consolidation of shipments from a consortium of shippers utilizing smart methods to maximize benefit for the entire group (Verweij 2011). Synchromodal transportation is less clearly defined in literature. However, there is agreement that it introduces the element of real-time flexibility in multimodal transportation planning (Behdani et al. 2014; Verweij 2011). SteadieSeifie et al. (2014) discuss multimodal transportation planning in detail in their literature review and conclude that the terms multimodal and intermodal are often used interchangeably in academic literature.

This chapter differentiates between multimodality and intermodality in light of the definitions presented earlier. The intermodal problem here involves more than one vehicle selection decision for the travel itinerary between supply and demand points. Facilities are required in this scenario to connect the different vehicle routes and shift the goods from one transportation mode to the other if required. The multimodal problem is considered as the choice of transportation mode between origindestination pairs. The last mile distribution problem, for example, can be described as a multimodal problem where vehicles of multiple transportation modalities deliver goods from a supply location to a demand point without shifting their load to another vehicle.

The logistics aspect is introduced when we define an intermodal logistics network. Intermodal logistics networks are characterized by transportation through two or more modes on a network that contains facilities that enable modal switch during transportation from an origin to a destination (Woxenius 2007). Hence, consolidation of shipments and modal shift introduce facility and inventory-related problems.

We divide the work on multimodal logistics in disaster operations into three key areas based on the nature of multimodality in the problem: (1) multimodal transportation, (2) intermodal transportation, and (3) intermodal logistics problem. Transportation and logistics problems in disaster operations undertaking co-modal or synchromodal work are scarce. The key reason for this is the dearth of sophisticated coordination models in literature which is discussed in detail in section "Analysis and Conclusions". Table 15.1 provides an overview of key papers based on the types of logistics problems and multimodality. In the following section, literature is discussed with relevance to the phase and type of the problem. Section "Preparation Phase" provides problem aspects relevant to the preparation phase, while section "Response Phase" presents problem aspects relevant to the response phase of disaster operations. We summarize the concepts presented in these sections in section "Literature Summary".

**Table 15.1** Literature map based on problem type and type of multimodality

| Paper | Problem type | Type of multimodality | Preparation | Response |
|---|---|---|---|---|
| Nolz et al. (2010) | Location-routing | Intermodal logistics | √ | √ |
| Rennemo et al. (2014) | Location-routing | Intermodal logistics | √ | √ |
| Bozorgi-Amiri and Khorsi (2015) | Location-routing | Intermodal logistics | √ | √ |
| Zhu et al. (2008) | Resource allocation | Intermodal logistics | √ | √ |
| Adivar and Mert (2010) | Vehicle requirement-routing | Intermodal logistics | | √ |
| Yi and Özdamar (2007) | Location-Routing | Intermodal transportation | | √ |
| Afshar and Haghani (2012) | Location-routing | Intermodal logistics | | √ |
| Ruan et al. (2014) | Location-routing | Intermodal logistics | | √ |
| Haghani and Oh (1996) | Routing | Intermodal transportation | | √ |
| Barbarosoglu and Arda (2004) | Routing | Intermodal transportation | | √ |
| Özdamar et al. (2004) | Routing | Intermodal transportation | | √ |
| Ye and Liu (2011) | Routing | Intermodal transportation | | √ |
| Özdamar and Demir (2012) | Routing | Intermodal transportation | | √ |
| Najafi et al. (2013) | Routing | Intermodal transportation | | √ |
| Battini et al. (2014) | Routing | Intermodal transportation | | √ |
| Zhao and Qian (2014) | Routing | Intermodal transportation | | √ |
| Ozkapici et al. (2016) | Routing | Intermodal transportation | | √ |
| Wang et al. (2015) | Routing and scheduling | Multimodal transportation | | √ |
| Zheng and Ling (2013) | Routing and scheduling | Multimodal transportation | | √ |
| Hu (2011) | Routing and scheduling | Intermodal transportation | | √ |

## Preparation Phase

The disaster logistics problem in the preparation phase of disaster operations management includes locating response facilities and pre-stocking relief goods. The preparation phase problems relevant to multimodal logistics often include response phase vehicle routing in addition to facility location and/or stock pre-positioning.

### Location-Routing Problems

Facilities for disaster relief include permanent distribution centers, warehouses, and temporary response facilities (Afshar and Haghani 2012). All of these facilities receive and dispatch relief goods. The intermodal logistics of disaster relief goods requires facilities that can handle multiple modes of transportation to assist in shipment consolidation and transshipment between nodes and transportation modalities. Temporary response facilities are often deployed in the response phase to assist in relief goods distribution.

The facility location problem is related to the vehicle routing problem. The integration of the two problems provides significant gains in productivity (Min et al. 1998). The location routing problem is faced with a number of uncertainties including uncertain supply, uncertain demand, and uncertain facility capacities after a disaster strikes (Rennemo et al. 2014). Hospitals and clinics in disaster-struck areas have uncertain capacities and processing capabilities as a result of the disaster (Najafi et al. 2013).

### Stock Pre-positioning

Pre-positioned relief goods provide a hedge against possible shortages. The disaster preparation planning must also be sensitive to possible vulnerabilities to transportation infrastructure after a disaster. Zhu et al. (2008) consider stock pre-positioning in preparation for disasters. The transportation network connecting warehouses to affected areas is vulnerable to disaster-related damage. The response phase multimodal logistics is accounted for in the problem through scenario analysis. Location-routing problems also consider pre-positioning of stock in the facilities (Nolz et al. 2010; Rennemo et al. 2014; Bozorgi-Amiri and Khorsi 2015).

*Vehicle Requirement Problem*

Vehicle requirement planning calls for assessing each link in the transportation network for its transportation mode requirement and the amount of commodity that would traverse the link. Adivar and Mert (2010) present a problem that plans for international response to a disaster scenario with vehicle requirement decision. Response phase damage to the network makes the vehicle requirement and routing decisions more difficult.

## Response Phase

*Temporary Facility Location*

Temporary facilities are located closer to affected areas to assist in the distribution of goods and the provision of shelter and medical attention for affectees. Ruan et al. (2014) discovered that greater numbers of temporary facilities often increase the efficiency and utility of medical supplies due to decreased distance between affected areas and temporary facilities. They also discovered that more vehicles are required to serve the increased number of temporary facilities.

One way of locating temporary facilities is seabasing. It originates from the military where a container ship forms a floating warehouse to deliver supplies where required. The application of seabasing provides flexibility in facility location to enable better response time. The floating warehouse can be anchored at a single point or move to other locations as required. Seabasing expands the horizon of multimodal logistics from transportation multimodality toward multimodality of warehouse facilities. Ozkapici et al. (2016) applied the seabasing concept for intermodal transportation in a disaster response scenario.

*Routing*

Disasters may cause massive damage to transportation networks. This impacts the amount of goods that can be transported through a transportation mode in time for the response efforts (Barbarosoglu and Arda 2004). The damage to transportation infrastructure can also cut off some affected areas from access through some transportation modes. This results in the need for alternative modes of transportation.

Disasters like earthquakes are difficult to predict and plan for. This leads to scenarios where both demand and consequently supply of relief goods is not easy to plan (Barbarosoglu and Arda 2004). The affected areas have to be surveyed after the disaster in order to assess the damage. The survey process takes time to calculate actual demand figures. This leads to the possibility of a mismatch between supply and demand in disaster-affected areas. Some demand points may be overstocked initially while other demand points may be realized later. The supply-demand mismatch results in ineffective response due to increased response time (Ye and Liu 2011). As a clearer demand picture is received, transportation between demand nodes may occur in order to resolve the initial mismatches (Özdamar et al. 2004). Another approach to tackle the demand-supply mismatch is to calculate demand in the form of a cluster. Since the areas affected by a disaster can generate several demand points, the problem becomes easier to solve when the demand is clustered (Özdamar and Demir 2012).

Vehicles involved in disaster response activities may or may not start travelling from supply points. The supply of vehicles may originate from points other than those for relief goods. This is especially true for disasters like earthquakes which are difficult to predict (Özdamar et al. 2004).

Human lives are at stake in disaster response efforts. This makes delivery speed an important aspect of the problem for medical supplies in particular. Damage to the transportation network aggravates the problem for some transportation modes. Helicopters are utilized for their capability to take off and land vertically in relatively small places. They are also able to avoid some disruptions in the transportation network and take a more direct route via air. However, helicopters are often in short supply and must be utilized efficiently. Ruan et al. (2014) found that as the difference between travel times of road vehicles and helicopters increased, intermodal transportation of medical supplies became more advantageous. Having said that, once the difference in speeds exceeded a threshold, intermodal transportation became less effective because of superior helicopter speeds and comparatively inferior road transportation speed. This implies that when roads are severely damaged, the use of helicopters is a better choice.

A number of different commodities are required to provide an effective response in disaster-affected areas. These include food, clothing, medicine, medical supplies, and machinery. Different commodities may require different modes of transportation (Haghani and Oh 1996). Fragile and temperature-sensitive medicine and medical supplies may require a transportation mode that can ensure better handling and speed of delivery than, for example, transportation for clothing.

Multimodal logistics involve the transfer of shipments from one mode of transportation to the other. The transshipment time and cost and accidents during transshipment are important considerations in multimodal logistics planning. All transportation modes are vulnerable to accidents. This problem is further aggravated in disaster scenarios when networks are damaged. Accidents can happen during transportation or during transshipment of goods. Zhao and Qian (2014) present an analytical approach to plan for minimum accidents, cost, and time.

Casualty transportation during non-disaster times is usually done through specialized vehicles like ambulances. Some transportation modes can be adapted in disaster scenarios to transport both goods and casualties in some sequence leading to a pickup and delivery-type scenario (Yi and Özdamar 2007). The injured people are spread in the affected areas in a similar fashion as the demand for relief goods. The extent of injuries also varies among affectees (Najafi et al. 2013).

*Scheduling*

The uncertainties encountered in disaster response make disaster transportation planning a complex problem. The problem is aggravated when multimodal transportation is considered. Hence, the scheduling of multimodal vehicles in disaster response planning is tackled through heuristics, fuzzy optimization, and an immune-based model (Zheng and Ling 2013; Wang et al. 2015; Hu 2011).

**Literature Summary**

The multimodal logistics literature in disaster management has improved from routing decisions to decisions spanning multiple phases of disaster operations management. The key area where the literature lacks is in accommodating the complex interactions of humanitarian actors in the multimodal logistics planning problem. Applications of co-modal and synchromodal transportation require attention due to their potential for greater efficiency and flexibility in dealing with the problem. Battini et al. (2014) tested their model for a possible co-transportation scenario and inferred that such a possibility would improve cost performance. They also mentioned the lack of such arrangements in the humanitarian community. Rodriguez et al. (2007) mentioned a number of tangible and intangible factors that can inhibit the utilization of co-transportation. They recommended the use of techniques like the analytic hierarchy process to resolve conflicts between potential partners. The efficiency and effectiveness of co-modal and synchromodal transportation networks in disaster scenarios require further exploration.

There are some general limitations of optimization models. The amount of data required may not be available in large-scale emergencies or may be difficult to communicate. Optimal solutions might take very long even when sufficient data are available. Disaster scenarios require urgent directives rendering improvement in solution algorithms important. Better solution algorithms are critical to making large, realistic models practical.

After discussing select papers from literature, we now focus our attention on the cases.

# Case Methodology

## Sample

Kashmir earthquake 2005 and Pakistan floods 2010 were selected for study on the basis of their impact. Table 15.2 highlights their impact among similar incidents in the history of the country by mortality count. The two disasters are among the top ten disasters by fatality counts and the number of people affected. The earthquake tops the list in mortality count and the floods top the list in the number of people affected. As recent events that caused large-scale destruction, both serve as instructive cases for our study.

Our distinct advantage in studying these cases lies in first-hand access to experts and individuals who were involved during disaster logistics operations. Both disasters occurred in terrains that, to a great extent, involved

**Table 15.2** Top 10 natural disasters in Pakistan by mortality count for the period 1900–2011

| Disaster | Date | Casualties | No. total affected | Damage (000 USD) |
|---|---|---|---|---|
| Earthquake | 8-Oct-05 | 73,338 | 5,128,000 | 5,200,000 |
| Earthquake | 31-May-35 | 60,000 | | |
| Storm | 15-Dec-65 | 10,000 | | |
| Earthquake | 28-Dec-74 | 4,700 | | |
| Earthquake | 27-Nov-45 | 4,000 | | |
| Flood | 1950 | 2,900 | | |
| Flood | 28-Jul-10 | 1,985 | 20,202,327 | 9,500,000 |
| Flood | 8-Sep-92 | 1,334 | 6,655,450 | 1,000,000 |
| Flood | 2-Mar-98 | 1,000 | | |
| Flood | Sep-12 | 571 | 4,849,841 | |

Source: SAARC (2016)

extreme conditions and damaged infrastructure. Such conditions are commonly observed in large-scale disasters (Ferris 2010). All these aspects combined presented significant challenges during the disaster logistics operations management of the cases.

## Methodology

The case study method was employed in assessing the state of practice in planning, coordinating, and managing the logistics of disaster operations. The research framework was primarily exploratory and explanatory in nature.

We decided to base our research on primary and secondary data by utilizing a mixed method research design. We collected primary data by interviewing key officials to understand on-ground realities of disasters operations. These expert interviews facilitated our understanding of intra- and interorganizational dynamics and structural dependencies during disaster operations that transpired in a rather chaotic and time-pressured environments. We shall discuss these aspects in greater detail later.

In addition to this, archives, organizational documents, and academic literature were used to understand and present a deeper understanding of disaster logistics operations of the chosen cases. The archival and literature research was also used to triangulate the findings of expert interviews. We used these sources to create a chronological depiction of the events and their logistics. The chosen sample and its analysis are discussed later in the chapter. The focus of the cases was toward understanding the logistics and coordination problems in the two disasters. The coordination problem was included due to the interesting co-modal possibilities that can be utilized to improve productivity.

## Data Collection

The data for case studies were collected through two methods—key respondent interviews and archival research. For detailed interviews, two respondents were selected. Lt. Col. (R) Raza Iqbal was interviewed. He is working in the UN-OCHA as Humanitarian Affairs Officer. He has also worked with the National Disaster Management Authority (NDMA), Pakistan, as Director Response. The second interview was with Lt. Col. (R) Ali Haider Kazi who worked as Director Coordination for the Earthquake Reconstruction and Rehabilitation Authority (ERRA) and was Logistics Head at the NDMA during the 2010 floods. The interviews were semi-structured and explored the coordination of multiple vehicle modes during the two disasters and relevant logistics elements. Interview data were utilized to understand: (1) the background of the disaster; (2) the intra- and inter-organizational contexts of logistic function during disaster preparedness and response phases; and (3) the nature of decisions taken during disaster relief efforts.

Both academic and practitioner literature were utilized for data collection. Academic literature included published work from journals like *Natural Hazards, Disasters*, and the *International Journal of Emergency Management*. Unpublished papers and theses were also utilized to triangulate interview data. Practitioner literature includes reports by the Asian Development Bank, the World Bank, the United Nations, the NDMA, the ERRA, and other government agencies as well as news items. Literature was searched using "2005 Kashmir Earthquake response," "2005 Kashmir Earthquake logistics," and similar keywords for the 2010 floods. The data obtained in literature were utilized for: (1) accurate descriptions of the disasters; (2) coordination setup during the disasters; (3) preparation and response phase logistics; and (4) supporting evidence for the interviews. Methodological primacy was given to literature which ensured that the biases of the interviewees or the researchers did not impact the study.

## Overview of the Cases

There are some similarities between the two cases. Both cases pertain to the same country and are among the worst disasters faced by it. Disaster operations were in a developing state throughout the two cases. A sophisticated and systematic approach to disaster operations planning was not fully functional. Coordination aspect of the logistics problem did not accommodate all stakeholders at a similar level throughout the two disasters.

Disaster logistics planning demonstrated improvement from the 2005 case to the 2010 case. The 2005 earthquake presented a challenge for which the country was not prepared. Logistics plans were developed and certain elements of coordination were established during the disaster. This was partly because earthquakes are difficult to forecast. The terrain was mountainous and made road transportation less viable. The NDMA had established better coordination mechanisms before the 2010 floods hit the country. Floods can be forecasted with reasonable accuracy, but the forecast in this case arrived late. Hence, the advantage that could have been attained due to a timely forecast of the flood was lost. The terrain was more diverse in this scenario as the floods originated from mountains and the waters travelled downstream to plains and desert areas.

The cases present scenarios which are somewhat similar to responses to other disasters. The disaster response efforts were on a massive scale in both scenarios. Hence, problems faced by logistics planners were vivid. The two cases may provide little help in disaster relief planning for man-made disasters like terrorist attacks or chemical spills.

# Kashmir Earthquake 2005

## Background of the Disaster

Northern Pakistan was struck by a 7.6 Mw earthquake on October 8, 2005. This earthquake caused a surface rupture 70 km long and up to 7 m wide that ran from Bagh in Kashmir to Balakot in the Khyber Pakhtunkhwa (KPK) province, then called the North-West Frontier Province (Kaneda et al. 2008). The main affected region was in the Lesser Himalaya which had main valley floor altitudes at a height of approximately 500 m to more than 2,000 m above sea level and peaks rising up to more than 3,000 m above sea level. The Jhelum River and its tributaries, the Neelum and the Kaghan Rivers, flow in these areas. The lower slopes of the valley reach 10–25° and toward the peaks the slopes rise to more than 50° (Owen et al. 2008).

Snowfall in this region occurs at altitudes greater than 1,500 m above sea level December through March. At the peaks the snow drifts exceed several meters in thickness. The earthquake occurred in the post-monsoon period when the weather was mild. A timeline of the 2005 Kashmir Earthquake response is given in Table 15.3.

## Coordination

"Logistics is a very precise activity…one cannot have too much coordination in disaster logistics"—Lt. Col. (R) Ali Haider Kazi

The interviewees emphasized that coordination is a key element in logistics in general and disaster logistics in particular. The resource shortages faced in disasters can be avoided or reduced through effective coordination of relief logistics. Hence, we also discuss coordination aspect in our case studies.

**Table 15.3** Timeline of 2005 Kashmir Earthquake response

| 8:50 October 8, 2005 | October 9, 2005 | October 10, 2005 | October 24, 2005 | March 31, 2006 |
|---|---|---|---|---|
| Earthquake occurs | United Nations Disaster Assessment and Coordination team arrives | Federal Relief Commission is formed | Earthquake Reconstruction and Rehabilitation Authority formed | Government of Pakistan announces end of relief, Federal Relief Commission subsumed into Earthquake Reconstruction and Rehabilitation Authority |

## Pre-disaster

### Government Structure

The roles of government departments when the 2005 earthquake struck are summarized in Table 15.4. The Pakistan Meteorological Department (PMD) was responsible for predicting weather and geophysical phenomena. In coordination with the Geological Survey of Pakistan, the PMD had formulated a seismological map.

The key stakeholders under the National Calamity (Prevention and Relief) Act 1958 for relief provision are the Provincial relief departments. The Directorate General Civil Defense has to work under the supervision of the provincial governments. The Emergency relief cell of the Cabinet Division works directly under the Prime Minister. This cell was responsible for coordinating between donors and provincial relief departments.

**Table 15.4** Roles of government departments

| Prediction/ confirmation | Pakistan Meteorological department (PMD) | |
|---|---|---|
| **Response lead institution** | Provincial Relief Department-**Provincial** | Emergency Relief Cell-**National** |
| **Support institutions** | SUPARCO-**Geographic Information System/Mapping** | Civil Defense-**Response** |
| **Provider of last resort** | Pakistan Army | |

Another key stakeholder is the Space and Upper Atmosphere Research Commission (SUPARCO) that utilizes satellite imaging techniques to assist in disaster management. The Pakistan Army's role in disaster operations includes inspection, assessment, and the last line of resort for relief work. All corps headquarters are equipped for emergency relief in times of disaster (GoP 2005).

## Structure of the United Nations

United Nations was working on the pilot for the cluster approach to operating in disaster scenarios. The cluster approach was formulated as a response to the Darfur crisis 2004–2005. The UN Emergency Relief Coordinator Jan Egeland commissioned a report evaluating the global humanitarian system prevalent up to 2004–2005. The report concluded that the prevalent coordination mechanisms operated independently of each other (Adinolfi et al. 2005). It identified a need for closer coordination and proposed specialization in certain areas/clusters for disaster response. The proposed cluster approach was bolstered by the lead agency approach prevalent within the UNHCR in the mid-1990s. Nine clusters were implemented for the pilot project. The Kashmir Earthquake was identified as the pilot project for the cluster approach. The cluster lead agencies (CLAs) for each cluster in the earthquake are listed in Table 15.5.

The coordination mechanism for the cluster approach was such that the CLAs would coordinate between various international non-governmental organizations (NGOs) operating in the clusters. The UN Emergency Relief Coordinator was to coordinate between the clusters. Given its responsibility to coordinate between various organizations, the cluster lead was to be the provider of last resort in its cluster.

**Table 15.5** Cluster lead agencies for earthquake 2005

| Cluster | Cluster Lead Agency |
|---|---|
| Logistics | WFP |
| Emergency shelter | IOM |
| Camp management | UNHCR |
| Food and nutrition | WFP |
| Water Sanitation and Hygiene (WASH) | UNICEF |
| Protection | UNICEF |
| Health | WHO |
| IT and telecommunication | OCHA |

Adapted from Stoddard et al. (2007).

## After Disaster Occurrence

The president and the prime minister set up the Federal Relief Commission (FRC) on 10 October 2005, 2 days after the disaster, to further streamline the operations. The FRC proceeded to communicate with two primary stakeholders: the military and the civilian stakeholders. The military relief work was coordinated through a dedicated wing responsible for the execution of rescue and relief operations. Similarly, there was a dedicated wing for civilian stakeholders which managed inter-agency coordination between the various civilian departments and the NGOs.

Qureshi (2006) found that civilian institutions were not emphasized in the disaster response. Local government representatives and the civilian structure of the government worked with little support from the army and the international NGOs. The army representatives were of the opinion that the civilian institutions had failed to provide relief during the disaster response phase. The Federal Relief Commission was headed by Major General Farooq Ahmed Khan which led Qureshi (2006) to believe that FRC legitimized the military's role in disaster response. Thompson (2008) is of the view that the Emergency Response Cell was untested in large-scale disaster scenarios. This inexperience might be the reason why the Pakistan Army General Headquarters took charge of response efforts.

An NGO staff member reported for the Kashmir earthquake 2005: "If we had good maps, we would be on top of things" (Currion 2005, p. 17). Thompson (2008) noted that the implications of this observation are the lack of situational awareness and inability to provide a common operational picture to all stakeholders. The United Nation's Humanitarian Information Centre (HIC) introduced their "Who is doing what where?" maps and related products through relief improve coordination.

*Logistics Structure*

The logistics coordination structure that emerged during the disaster relief was such that an Army Logistics Cell coordinated the collection and receipt of all incoming relief materials and dispatched them to the humanitarian hubs as indicated by their demands. Another cell was formed to coordinate all the air traffic flowing within the country as well as from abroad. This Air Operations Center worked under the General Officer Commanding Military Aviation and comprised the Pakistan Army Air Wing, the UN Helicopter Air Service, and the United States Navy (Cahill 2007).

The principle by which the Army and the local authorities coordinated with the humanitarian agencies was that of "non-interfering coordination". This meant that the information and the assessment of the damage would be disbursed to all humanitarian stakeholders as transparently as possible and would allow them to make their choices in relief participation. The only action required of them was to report their decisions to the Pakistani authorities. This led to better relief provision as the humanitarian actors chose the areas they were most competent in while the Army and the government agencies filled up remaining gaps (MacLeod 2007).

## Preparedness

### Facility Location

According to a report by the Government of Pakistan (2005), the emergency relief cell operated a warehouse in Islamabad when the earthquake occurred. Islamabad, being the federal capital, was to be the last resort for relief goods. However, Islamabad was also affected by the earthquake and the respondents report some damage at the relief cell warehouse as well.

### Stock Pre-positioning

The details of stocks pre-positioned in the emergency relief cell warehouse at Islamabad could not be acquired. However, according to the interviewees, the stocks were insufficient for disaster response. The key reason why preparedness was so low was because the last earthquake that caused similar destruction in this region had occurred about four centuries ago (Thakur 2006).

### Vehicle Requirement Planning

An Aviation Squadron comprising four helicopters was at the emergency relief cell's disposal to assist in rescue operations and to provide logistics to disaster struck areas. This was an insufficient amount of transportation as discovered after the disaster. A number of deficiencies in planning were also discovered by Alexander (2006, p. 1) including the "lack of preparedness", as well as the untrained and unequipped state of local first responders.

## Response

According to a joint report by the Asian Development Bank and the World Bank (2005), the disaster event resulted in direct damages of USD 2.3 billion. The top three sectors that bore the damage were private housing, transportation (roads and bridges), and education. The damage to private housing amounted to USD 1.03 billion which was the major portion of damage sustained in the earthquake. The second largest component of the damage was sustained by roads and bridges which amounted to USD 340 million. The education sector was the third highest component of the damage amounting to USD 335 million. The damages to the education sector primarily comprised school buildings. Schools were in session on the day the disaster struck, leading to a high casualty count of school-going children.

### Temporary Facility Location

The president requested the UNDAC (UN Disaster Assessment and Coordination) to assist in damage assessment and coordination of international relief organizations. A UNDAC team was on ground within 24 hours of the disaster and set up an On-Site Operations Coordination Centre (OSOCC) at Muzaffarabad. Further humanitarian hubs were set up in the disaster region as shown in Fig. 15.2 with Civil Military Liaison officers in each (Cahill 2007). The interview respondents were of the opinion that the temporary facilities were located keeping in view alternative road routes and helicopter landing areas. The redundancy of road and helicopter access was necessary because of excessive road damage that was causing major problems in relief delivery. Helicopter access was not a major problem for hub facilities, but in smaller clusters of population the heavily forested mountainous terrain caused some difficulty.

### Routing

The coordination and cooperation aspects were not evident in routing relief goods. The Edhi Foundation, the largest NGO in Pakistan, responded by directing all of its ambulances in the Punjab and KPK toward the disaster region. They filled their ambulances with wheat flour and burial shrouds. They later introduced lentils, oil, and drinking water in their relief items.

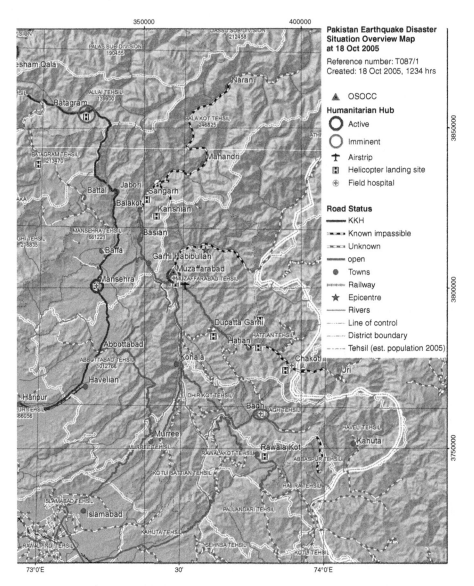

**Fig. 15.2** UN OSOCC and Humanitarian Hubs as placed on the map (With permission from MapAction 2005)

Their transportation mode included inflatable boats for evacuation of affectees and transportation of relief goods across rivers (Syed 2015). Although they set up their relief network at a quick pace, there is not much evidence of their coordination with other stakeholders. This was not a stand-alone case as indicated by the interview respondents. Most of the local NGOs and independent volunteers adapted their own strategies to route their relief vehicles. This led to a lot of stress on the road network in particular.

ADB-WB (2005) reported strong response from the civil society including local and international NGOs such as the Edhi Foundation, Islamic Relief, the Red Crescent Society, the Agha Khan Foundation, Oxfam, and the Rural Support Program Network. They also reported a large number of self-help groups supported by several thousand people collecting relief goods for the earthquake affectees. The donations amounted to USD 100 million excluding in-kind items and services. Interview respondents noted that the in-kind donations were excessive and included material that did not meet any requirements. This led to the problem of material convergence where unusable items were sorted out. However, some material went through the relief chain to the affectees causing nuisance for them.

A total of approximately 6,440 km of roads were damaged in the disaster region. This included a total of 175 km of national highways, cutting off road access to the Kashmir region from Pakistan (ERRA 2006). This led to a greater need for other modalities of transportation, especially helicopters and other air assets. The interview respondents noted that volunteer road vehicles aggravated the problem. The mountainous terrain of the affected region was already limited in its capacity to handle road vehicles. Evacuating traffic and excessive independent volunteer vehicles chocked what remained of the road network. This led to early efforts in restoring road infrastructure to ease the traffic.

As winters were about to begin and the vulnerability to extreme colds in the mountains was termed as the second impending disaster, the relief operation was dubbed Operation Winter Race. The operation started as a race against time. Extensive use of aircraft led to around 500 sorties by the Pakistan Air Force, about 30,000 helicopter sorties by the Pakistan Army Aviation, and around 11,000 sorties by the United Nations for rescue, relief, and evacuation. According to the United Nations Joint Logistics Committee (UNJLC) data, 75 percent of the cargo coordinated through the Cargo Movement Coordination Cell (CMCC) was moved through the UN Humanitarian Air Service (UNHAS) and the rest was moved through road transportation (Benini et al. 2009). The UNJLC prioritized food and shelter and utilized air transportation for the same. Construction material was delivered through road transportation as road network became usable. Trucks were owned by independent transporters. The truck drivers were familiar with the mountainous terrain and the interview respondents regard their driving skills highly.

### Helicopters-Fleet Management

Helicopters are a terrain-independent mode of transportation and a key-transportation resource in many disasters. The Pakistan Army Air Operations Centre (AOC) coordinated and approved all helicopter missions in the disaster area. The AOC determined appropriateness of a mission through urgency and accessibility of the region through other modes of transportation. Urgency meant the immediacy of the requirement and accessibility meant whether the area could be covered through ground vehicles or not. Most of the aviation units operated primarily at the Chaklala airbase with the AOC (Thomspon 2008).

Efficient usage of air assets involves minimizing ground time to improve work achieved per blade hour. Thompson (2008) notes that in the first week after the disaster, several aircrews sat idle due to lack of situational awareness by the planners. The information asymmetry continued later into the disaster when relief was dispatched to locations which were already well-supplied. The inefficient usage of helicopters coupled with the high costs of operating them led to a cash crisis threatening further usage of this transportation mode (BBC 2005). The employment of helicopters for scouting ground routes and assessing relief provision situation proved useful. The AOC maintained a map of this information.

### Mules

In the disaster area, road boundaries were classified by the ease with which various ground vehicles could move on them. These comprise road head and jeep head. A road head is the limit up to which normal road transportation can travel. A jeep head is a path beyond the road head up to which a jeep can travel. The area beyond a jeep head cannot be accessed through most vehicles. In the earthquake, mountainous terrain presented areas where jeep heads ended. Such areas were accessed through the army Animal Transportation Units (ATUs). These units comprised trained mules deployed by the Pakistan Army. These mules could carry up to 72 kg load and travel up to 26 km without rest (BBC 2005). About 250 mules were deployed by the Army while the extent of

**Table 15.6** 2005 Earthquake case summary on developed framework

| Preparedness | Response |
|---|---|
| *Facility location* Emergency Relief Cell operated a central facility in Islamabad for disaster relief. | *Temporary facility location* Four facilities located in disaster area by the government and UN. |
| *Stock pre-positioning* Centralized stocks at Islamabad warehouse of Emergency Relief Cell. | *Routing* Routes were surveyed by Pakistan Army and decided based on their recommendation for military and international NGO response. However, independent volunteers and local NGOs decided routes by themselves. |

the civilian usage of mules is unknown. The usage of mules in the Ganul/Ghanoul valley near Mansehra in KPK was reported by *The Telegraph UK* (Wilkinson 2005).

## Case Summary

The 2005 earthquake case employed an intermodal logistics approach in the response phase with collection and distribution of relief goods performed in an intermodal fashion. Response phase logistics included temporary facility location and routing. Key transportation modalities included trucks and helicopters in distribution. A summary of the earthquake case is presented in Table 15.6.

# Pakistan Floods 2010

## Background of the Disaster

The monsoon rains began around 18 July and lasted till 10 September 2010. The intensity of rainfall reached a peak on 28–29 July 2010. A secondary peak in rainfall was observed on 5–9 August 2010. The flooding began from River Swat in the northern region of Khyber Pakhtunkhwa in the last week of July. Fatality reports from heavy rains and flooding were first reported on 22 July 2010, from Khyber Pakhtunkhwa, the Punjab, and Balochistan provinces. The overall impact of the flood was such that 6 million ha of land were inundated out of which 3.3 million ha were cultivated land (Iqbal et al. 2015).

# Coordination

## Pre-disaster

### Government Structure

The provincial governments were responsible for dealing with floods through the National Calamity Act 1958. The provincial government requested federal level planning and mitigation of floods after the heavy floods in 1973 and 1976 (Rahman 2010). This led to the establishment of the Federal Flood Commission (FFC) in 1977. The FFC is responsible for planning flood protection at the national level. It reviews damage assessment and plans for reconstruction when flooding occurs (GoP 2011).

The National Disaster Management Ordinance was promulgated in 2006 in an effort to avoid the stress faced in the 2005 earthquake. The National Disaster Management Authority (NDMA) led the preparation for the floods of 2010. The guidelines on disaster management were detailed in the National Disaster Response Plan 2010 and the National Monsoon Contingency Plan 2010. The Emergency Relief Cell was operative in parallel with the NDMA. The cell's role was important in obtaining funds and procuring relief goods. However, the cell was undermined in the planning process leading to difficulties in implementation. A timeline of the 2010 floods and their response is given in Table 15.7.

The Federal Flood Commission prepares National Flood Protection Plans on ten-year horizons. The practice began in 1978 and the 2010 floods happened during the 4th planning horizon. The 3rd plan 1998–2008 included the development of the first computer-based flood early warning system. The 4th plan had been submitted to the Ministry of Water and Power in November 2006 for approval, but awaited approval by the Planning Commission until after the 2010 floods (GoP 2011).

The National Disaster Response Plan 2010 prepared by the NDMA outlined major institutions and their broad responsibilities in a disaster scenario (see Table 15.8). The Hyogo Framework for Action inspired the organizational structure for disaster coordination in Pakistan. The structure in which these institutions were to coordinate is captured in Fig. 15.3.

The NDMA captured most of these planning elements in 2007 through the National Disaster Risk Management Framework (NDMA 2007). The National Disaster Response Plan 2010 provided standard operating procedures

**Table 15.7** Timeline of 2010 Pakistan floods

| **July 18–24, 2010** | | | |
|---|---|---|---|
| July 21: First Monsoon rainfall | Swat, Kabul and Indus Rivers started rising | Flooding in Mianwali and Layyah districts | |
| **July 28–30, 2010** | | | |
| July 29: Torrential rainfall | Rivers started spilling over embankments | In the northern region Swat valley and Charsadda/Nowshera districts affected through rivers Kabul and Swat, respectively | Mianwali, Layyah, D.G. Khan, and Rajanpur districts affected through River Indus |
| **August 2–9, 2010** | | | |
| Incessant rains for 8 days: August 2–9 in the catchment areas of the rivers | Breaches in Indus River on August 2 at Mulanwala and Dibwala, Southern Punjab causing 3–4 m high waves flooding Muzaffargarh district | Peak flood in Indus River extending beyond Sukkur Barrage, Sindh | |
| **August 10–20, 2010** | | | |
| Floods peaked in Punjab | Breaches of Indus River in Tori and Ghuaspur exposing further areas in Balochistan and Sindh to flooding | Two discharge peaks observed at Sukkur Barrage one on August 12 and the other on August 17 | |
| **August 21–September 18, 2010** | | | |
| KPK and Punjab provinces cleared of flood water, except low-lying pockets | Flood water receded toward Dadu district, Sindh | Deltaic region in Thatta district inundated | |
| **September 19–30, 2010** | | | |
| Large areas in Sindh and some in Balochistan under deep flood water | Sowing of Rabi crop season not possible in the affected region | | |

**Table 15.8** Institutions and their functions in a disaster scenario

| Institution | Responsibilities |
|---|---|
| NDMA | National planning, coordination, monitoring and technical assistance |
| PDMA | Provincial planning, coordination, monitoring, evaluation, technical assistance, and direction to provincial departments |
| DDMA | District planning, coordination, monitoring, implementation, monitoring, community training, early warning system implementation and maintenance, establish relief centers and relief stock |
| Local authorities | Training employees for disaster management, resource maintenance, construction monitoring, carrying out relief, rehabilitation and reconstruction |
| Armed forces | Support civil administration in relief, rescue and evacuation; search and rescue; provision of helicopters, airplanes, ships, etc. for evacuation; assist in flood contingency planning; security provision |
| Provincial Relief Departments | Relief Commissioner is responsible for coping with disaster situation; disbursal of funds and relief goods |
| Civil Defense | Assist in rescue, evacuation and relief; formation and training of search and rescue teams in all districts; first aid training; maintenance of volunteers database at district level; community awareness |
| Pakistan Red Crescent Society (PRCS) | Disaster preparedness and response |
| Punjab Emergency Services (Rescue 1122) | Handling all types of emergencies |
| Local Charity Organizations (Edhi, etc) | Ambulance services, evacuation, food and nonfood items |
| NGOs | Provision of relief services and promotion of recovery |
| Community Based Organizations | Local-level disaster risk management and relief activities |
| UN Agencies | Capacity building, technical support, and coordination of International NGOs (INGOs) through Inter Agency Standing Committee (IASC) |
| Media | Disseminating information about early warnings, relief, recovery and gaps |

Adapted from NDMA (2010).

and job descriptions for emergency operation centers at district, provincial, and national levels. The emergency operation centers (EOCs) were hubs for coordination and management of relief operations at respective levels. The provincial and national-level EOCs were to be activated as the district and province authorities became overwhelmed by the disaster needs, respectively.

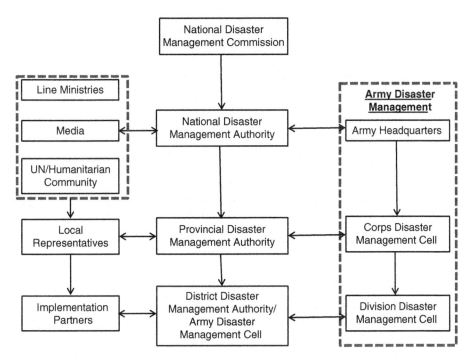

**Fig. 15.3** Disaster management organizational structure (Adapted from NDMA 2010)

## UN Structure

The UN cluster approach had evolved since its deployment as a pilot during the 2005 Kashmir earthquake. The number of clusters had increased from the pilot number of 9 to 11. The list of clusters and their lead agencies is given in Table 15.9.

## After Disaster Occurrence

SUPARCO had become the regional support office for the UN Space-based Information for Disaster Response program on 12 February 2010. The UN and the Pakistan government worked together to create maps for the disaster region. These included damage assessment maps, daily updates, thematic mapping, and time series analyses through maps of the disaster region. The information contained in the maps was utilized by the NDMA, the UN, the INGOs, and some local NGOs to plan their response for the disaster scenario (Iqbal et al. 2015).

**Table 15.9** UN clusters and cluster lead agencies

| Type | Cluster | Cluster lead agency |
|---|---|---|
| Response | Agriculture | Food and Agriculture Organization (FAO) |
| | Camp Coordination, Camp Management (CCCM) | International Organization for Migration (IOM) |
| | Early Recovery | United Nations Development Programme (UNDP) |
| | Nutrition | United Nations Children's Emergency Fund (UNICEF) |
| | Emergency Shelter | International Federation of Red Cross and Red Crescent Societies (IFRC) |
| | Health | World Health Organization (WHO) |
| | Education | UNICEF/Save the Children |
| | Protection | United Nations High Commissioner for Refugees (UNHCR) |
| | Water, Sanitation and Hygiene (WASH) | UNICEF |
| Service | Logistics | World Food Programme (WFP) |
| | Emergency Telecommunications | Office for Coordination of Humanitarian Affairs (OCHA)/WFP/UNICEF |

Adapted from Steets et al. (2010)

## *Logistics Coordination*

The NDMA (2011) reported a total of 316 foreign relief flights, 6 relief trains, and 5 shipments through the sea. Almost half of the flights were received at the Main Operating Base at Chaklala, Rawalpindi. The remaining relief flights were received in the five Forward Operating Bases.

A Joint Aviation Coordination Cell (JACC) was formed between the Pakistan Army, the Pakistan Air Force, the UN Helicopter Air Service (UNHAS), the US Air Force, the US Marines, the USAID, the WFP, and the NDMA. This cell was chaired by the General Officer Commanding of the Pakistan Army Aviation. The cell places special emphasis on managing fixed wing and rotary wing flying crafts for relief operations. According to the NDMA (2011), helicopter support included 48 helicopters from Pakistan, 24 from the US, 5 from China, 4 from Japan, 4 from Afghanistan, 3 from the UAE, and 8 from UNHAS/WFP. In addition to rotary wing resources, 16 fixed wing flying aircraft were dispatched to Pakistan for relief operations. The US provided 2 C17s and 3 C-130s while Turkey and Egypt provided a C-130 each for relief operations. The US fixed wing aircraft were the first to arrive in Pakistan on 4 August 2010.

The Pakistan Navy established Emergency Response and Coordination Centers at Head Quarters of commander north in Islamabad and naval headquarters Karachi for water-based transportation. Teams were deployed in KPK and Sindh. The navy employed 3 hovercraft and more than 200 boats in the relief effort over flood waters. Almost 1,000 boats were deployed by other institutions of the Pakistan government (UN-OCHA 2010).

## Preparedness

### Facility Location

Before the 2010 floods, the NDMA had formed ad hoc warehouses at the federal and provincial capitals with the help of other government agencies. In the federal capital, Islamabad, four warehouses were present. Two of these warehouses were operated by the Pakistan Army which allowed some space to the NDMA to store relief goods. One was operated by the Emergency Relief Cell and another warehouse was owned and operated by the NDMA. Two warehouses were present in Karachi, the provincial capital of the Sindh province. One was an army warehouse with space allocation for relief goods, and the other was operated by the Relief Goods Dispatch Organization which came under the Emergency Relief Cell. The Army Ordinance Depot in Quetta and the Army Engineer Store Depot in Lahore were also engaged with an allocated area for disaster relief goods. The WFP was running a warehouse in Pir Piai, KPK province.

### Stock Pre-positioning.

The PMD forecasted normal monsoon rains in 2010. This forecast was revised on June 21st, 2010, when the PMD issued a warning for flash floods in the northern region of the country. The warning announced an additional 10 percent rain with "few very heavy rainfall events" (GoP 2011, p. 30). Rahman and Khan (2011) explain this as a defect in the early warning system as the catchment area of Kabul and Swat rivers was outside its coverage. This led to a higher number of mortalities and damages in the Kabul and Swat river basins. Out of 1,961 deaths, 1,156 were reported in the Khyber Pakhtunkhwa province where the Kabul and Swat river basins are situated (Rahman and Khan 2011). Another cause of the flood was snowmelt (Rasul and Ahmad 2012) generated by high snowfall during 2004–2009 (NDMA 2009) and aggravated by record high summers in 2010 (Vidal and Walsh 2010). Once the record high rainfalls had occurred in the northern areas, the

PMD provided a reasonably accurate picture of flooding for the rest of the country with 2–3 days warning (NDMA 2011). This resulted in a short window for relief agencies to pre-position an adequate amount of relief stocks.

Relief good stocks were acquired and placed in accordance with the flood forecast. There was severe shortage of relief items especially at the beginning of the disaster response. Polastro et al. (2011) attributed this to the shipment of locally produced relief items to Haiti for earthquake relief since Pakistan produces 85 percent of the world's emergency tents. However, international NGOs were able to cope with the situation through national and regional contingency stocks.

## Response

### Temporary Facility Location

The map of the disaster region with the NDMA operating bases and the UN provincial/area hubs as of 6 September 2010 is given in Fig. 15.4. The UN humanitarian coordinator and Country Team were located with the NDMA Main Operating base (MOB). The UN was focused toward creating humanitarian hubs closer to disaster struck communities. In Sindh, the UN formed the first hub in Sukkur to cater for northern Sindh and later established another one in Hyderabad. The Provincial Disaster Management Authority (PDMA) Sindh is based in Karachi, but the NDMA created Forward Operating Bases (FOBs) in Sukkur and Hyderabad. The PDMA structure favored MOB in provincial capital and forward bases closer to disaster-affected regions. The UN presence in Karachi increased over time due to better cargo handling capabilities of this port city. This also improved coordination between the UN and the PDMA Sindh. The Pakistan government and the UN worked in tandem on the cluster-based coordination pattern. The clusters were assigned governmental counterparts to interact with, as shown in Table 15.10.

### Routing and Resource Allocation

The 2010 flood response provides a better case for multimodal logistics in both the receipt and the disbursal of relief goods. The improvements happened as the result of a better coordination structure. The NDMA

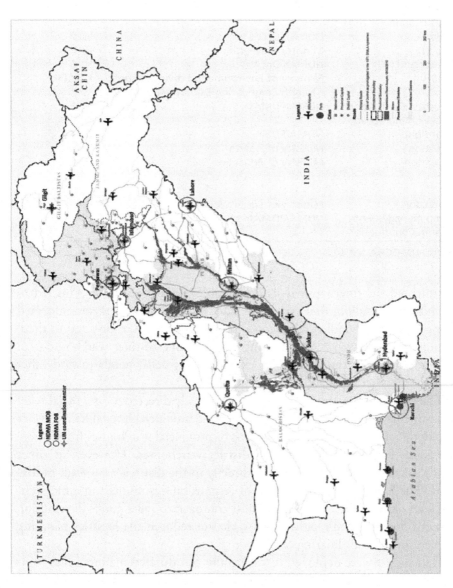

**Fig. 15.4** Location of NDMA MOB/FOBs and UN hubs as of September 6th, 2010 (Adapted from MapAction 2010; NDMA 2011 and UN-OCHA 2010)

**Table 15.10** Clusters, cluster lead agencies and governmental counterparts

| Cluster | Primary Governmental Counterpart | Cluster Lead Agency |
|---|---|---|
| Agriculture | Ministry of Agriculture | FAO |
| Community Restoration | NDMA/PDMAs | UNDP |
| Food | NDMA/PDMAs | WFP |
| Health | Ministry of Health | WHO |
| Shelter and NFIs | NDMA/PDMAs | IOM |
| WASH | Ministry of Environment, Provincial Public Health Engineering Departments | UNICEF |
| Logistics, Emergency Telecommunications | NDMA/PDMAs | WFP |
| Coordination | NDMA/PDMAs | OCHA |
| Nutrition | Ministry of Health | UNICEF |
| Education | Ministry of Education | UNICEF/Save the Children |
| Protection | Ministry of Social Welfare | UNHCR |
| Camp management/ Camp Coordination | NDMA/PDMAs | UNHCR |

Source: UN-OCHA (2010)

coordinated the international- and federal-level relief response. This led to the NDMA handling relief goods in bulk. Interview respondents informed that the NDMA handled relief goods procured by them or donated to them through multiple ways: (1) receiving goods at one of their warehouses; (2) receiving goods at the airport; or (3) redirecting relief goods toward other warehouses where demand was urgent.

The goods shipped by the NDMA were mostly directed to provincial relief departments in bulk to enable response at the provincial level. The NDMA's role in this situation was to route goods to provincial warehouses from where the goods could be dispatched to district warehouses. However, at times goods were shipped by the NDMA directly to the districts as a result of dire need. The hierarchical distribution of responsibilities resulted in a hierarchical level of networks. This hierarchical approach to relief goods distribution reduced the size of the logistics network and reduced the logistics planning burden on the coordinating bodies.

Helicopters were deployed in a centrally coordinated manner. The Joint Aviation Coordination Cell cleared the helicopters for their pickup and drop off points as well as the routes to travel. This special treatment was due to the strategically important terrain-independent characteristic of helicopters and to avoid any air traffic-related accidents. Road and water-based transportation were less systemically routed. Transporters were identified for shipment through trucks. Independent volunteers and NGOs provided relief supplies based on their own knowledge of the transportation networks.

## Case Summary

The case of the 2010 floods employed an intermodal logistics approach in the preparation and response phases with collection and distribution of relief goods performed in an intermodal fashion. The logistic problems of the preparation phase included locating disaster response facilities and stock pre-positioning. Response phase logistics included temporary facility location and routing. Key transportation modalities included airplanes and ships in collection and trucks, boats, and helicopters in distribution. A summary of the 2010 floods case is presented in Table 15.11.

# Analysis and Conclusions

The 2005 Kashmir earthquake was a wake-up call for disaster management institutions in Pakistan in a number of ways. There was no planning or preparation for this disaster or any disaster of a similar nature. There was a complete lack of logistics planning in the preparedness phase. The planning elements in disaster management emerged slowly during the response phase. The terrain was already difficult to navigate and became more difficult to work with as a result of the disaster. This required extensive use of helicopters which the country did not possess in sufficient numbers. The number of aircraft serving the area by November 2, 2005, rose to 125 through assistance

**Table 15.11** 2010 Floods case summary on developed framework

| Preparedness | Response |
|---|---|
| *Facility location* One warehouse each was being operated by World Food Programme, National Disaster Management Authority and Emergency Relief Cell | *Temporary facility location* Ad hoc facilities were arranged with Pakistan Army |
| *Stock pre-positioning* Stocks were available in the warehouse facilities, but were not sufficient for a disaster of such a scale | *Routing* Helicopter routes were decided by Joint Aviation Coordination Cell. Road and water-based transportation problem was not decided centrally. |

from other nations (ADB-WB 2005). Lack of funds and accessibility issues led to the utilization of mules as an alternative mode of transportation. However, the abruptness of the disaster, the lack of preparedness and mostly ad hoc response led to a situation where the different modes of transportation were not efficiently utilized.

The response to floods in 2010 improved through lessons learned from the earthquake. The most important development was the establishment of an institution for coordinating and monitoring disaster operations management, that is the NDMA. This institution led the efforts for the establishment of functioning warehouses with pre-positioned relief goods stock. The last mile distribution problem was decentralized through the framework of this institution. As small autonomous bodies became responsible for their areas, improvements in relief goods distribution were realized. The logistics problem was split into several hierarchies. At the national level, the distribution problem was to deliver to the provinces only. The provinces were in turn responsible for supplying district demands. The districts were then responsible for delivering supplies to affectees in their areas. A centralized coordination mechanism for last mile distribution would have heavily taxed the resources of the central coordinating body leading to inefficiencies. As a result the logistics problem was broken down into smaller problems at different hierarchical levels; however, the utilization of some logistics modes—helicopters, for instance—remained centralized. The assignment of governmental counterparts to the UN clusters was another mechanism that synchronized coordination between international NGOs and the distribution of the workload. A major weakness of the system was the delay in the deployment of a sophisticated warning system. Table 15.12 summarizes research ideas gleaned from the two cases.

In light of the literature and analysis of the two disasters, it is obvious that there is a gap between research and practice. The response teams are overwhelmed with operational tasks and have little time for systematic planning during the response phase. This increases the importance of planning tools that can provide solutions in a quick and efficient manner. However, we find that multimodal logistics models are computationally difficult to solve and Özdamar and Ertem (2015) conclude that these models are not integrated into decision support systems. Furthermore, these multimodal logistics solutions are difficult to implement in the chaotic environment of disaster response due to inherent issues in coordination and information asymmetry.

**Table 15.12** Comparison of literature and implementation in the two disasters

| Preparedness | Response |
| --- | --- |
| *Facility location*: (1) Facilities as alternative to costly transportation modalities, (2) inclusion of forecasting to improve short-term location problem, (3) coordinated facility location by multiple humanitarian actors | *Temporary facility location*: (1) Inclusion of multimodal accessibility score, (2) consideration beyond distribution point |
| *Stock pre-positioning*: (1) Lot-size planning, (2) multimodal sourcing transportation for short-notice stocking | *Routing*: (1) Planning for congestion/returning traffic, (2) hierarchical transportation planning in practice, (3) modeling the transportation coordination incentives/contracts to enable co-modal and synchromodal transportation, (4) introduction of volunteer vehicles, (5) consideration of material convergence |

# Preparation

### Facility Location Problem

The interview respondents viewed warehouse facilities as an alternative to the acquisition of costly vehicles. Locating permanent facilities closer to disaster-prone areas and pre-stocking them with relief goods can be costly exercises. However, the trade-off between facility acquisition and vehicle procurement needs to be explored for an efficient and effective disaster response.

The inclusion of forecasting and risk assessment elements in stock pre-positioning makes it easier to plan for future requirements. Garrido et al. (2015) included a flood forecasting model in their study on emergency preparation and response during flood disasters. The model improved the pre-stocked inventory and vehicle allocation for disaster response. The integration of forecasting/risk assessment and multimodal access to facility location decisions requires further research. Models considering risk assessment with pre-planned accessibility of facilities through multiple modes of transportation can improve response time logistics.

The warehouse sharing arrangements observed in the response to the 2010 floods provide hope for possible co-modal planning of logistics. The trust and credibility established while sharing permanent facilities can be utilized in sharing transportation vehicles of various modes to deliver goods owned by different humanitarian actors.

The problem of facility location could also be planned in a coordinated manner to minimize costs and human suffering while maximizing coverage and cooperation between humanitarian actors. Formation of contracts that offset expensive capital investment through rent agreements with multiple parties is an observable phenomenon in the field.

## Stock Pre-positioning

The pre-positioning of stocks provides a hedge against sourcing costs during the disasters. There is a tradeoff between sourcing and transportation costs during the disaster and costs of obsolescence, material management, and maintenance of pre-positioned stocks. Problems of lot-sizing for procurement are relevant to the problem of pre-positioning.

The multimodal logistics problem in stock pre-positioning is not usually pressed for delivery time performance. However, delivery time performance becomes relevant in late warnings when the stock pre-positioned in warehouses needs to be augmented before the disaster. Pre-positioning stock during these late warnings might face delays due to evacuating traffic congestion. Development of models for routing and scheduling vehicles of multiple modes to pre-position stocks in a timely fashion is another area for future research.

## Response

### Temporary Facility Location

Temporary facilities include distribution centers, evacuation shelters, and medical camps closest to the affectees. Location planning for the temporary facilities is possible after the disaster has struck and the affected locations have been identified. However, since these temporary facilities are last mile distributions points, better accessibility needs to be ensured for them.

There can be situations where the temporary facility is not the actual consumption point for relief goods. In the case of the Kashmir earthquake, certain affected areas were so remote that distribution points were also further from their location. Another reason for the distance between distribution centers and affected areas was a lack of accessibility to a feasible location in that area. The last mile problem begins at such temporary facilities. Transportation through mules was one such example in the case of the Kashmir earthquake.

## Multimodal Routing

The routing problem is linked to vehicle allocation, scheduling, and coordination problems. The damaged links in the network are not identified immediately after the disaster has occurred. The condition of some routes might be updated much later. The condition of the routes is also dynamic as some repair begins during the disaster to facilitate routing.

Relief distribution can be hampered by transportation bottlenecks on some routes due to evacuating traffic. The Kashmir earthquake is an illustration of this with mountainous terrain and scarce road capacity. Few attempts have been made to model congestion in relief distribution with Wang et al. (2015) modeling it as arc capacity constraint.

The logistics decision-making setup that emerged in the 2010 floods—and is prevalent in Pakistan today—was hierarchical and distributed in most cases. This despite the fact that the majority of multimodal routing literature for disaster scenarios assumes a central planner who decides for all the goods movement and location decisions. The hierarchical logistics model observed in the 2010 case separates bulk movement from last mile distribution. The planners for routing are different and in some cases they are independent agents. The centralized coordination of helicopters presents a further complexity in modeling this system. However, for almost all other transportation modalities the routing decision is decentralized. A hierarchical model of the disaster routing problem with multiple transportation modes may be an area of future research. Applications of agent-based models for multimodal routing in a decentralized network can also be promising areas of research.

The key challenge is to improve multimodal routing in the disaster context to co-modality and eventually to synchromodality. The application of a co-modal system in a disaster context is often difficult due to severe coordination problems inherent in humanitarian relief chains. Balcik et al. (2010) discovered that transportation is an area where coordination mechanisms in relief chains need to be improved. They suggest that incentives and contracts for transportation-based collaboration are a future area of research in disaster logistics.

The role of volunteer vehicles is often overlooked in disaster operations management. A number of independent volunteers come forward to assist in disaster settings. These volunteers may be able to own and operate vehicles of different modalities. This exogenous supply of vehicles can be directed by humanitarian actors to assist in disaster response. Technologies like crowd-mapping can provide valuable data and improve utilization of volunteer vehicles, but sophisticated mechanisms are required for establishing the credibility and believability of the data (Poblet et al. 2012).

Material convergence is a phenomenon in disaster relief where a lot of unsolicited goods are accumulated at the relief distributor's facility. These materials contain a large proportion of goods not suitable for use. Material convergence was observed in the 2005 earthquake where large amounts of in-kind donations required processing. The planners had not foreseen this issue which resulted in less-effective utilization of transportation (Wilder 2008). Although a major problem, the literature is scarce in this area (Holguín-Veras et al. 2012b).

## Scheduling

The two case studies present similar problems in scheduling. The centrally coordinated helicopters were scheduled in a more systematic manner compared to road and water-based transportation. Articles addressing the scheduling aspect of multimodal vehicles in disaster response are scarce. We came across only three such articles as shown in Table 15.1. This dearth of articles can be attributed to the need for more effective and efficient solution algorithms to solve this complex problem (Wang et al. 2015).

Multimodal scheduling problems need to schedule heterogeneous products with different vehicle requirements. Fragile and temperature-sensitive medical products cannot be transported alongside tents and other nonperishables. Similarly, other products have different transportation requirements. Scheduling problems must consider the product-vehicle match.

The scheduling problem also needs to take into consideration the prevalent status of the network. Bad weather might ground helicopters just like land-sliding might stop ground vehicles. A dynamic program which updates these conditions during disaster response might improve scheduling.

# References

Adinolfi, C., Bassiouni, D. S., Lauritzsen, H., and Williams, H. R. (2005). Humanitarian response review. Retrieved from *ALNAP*, April 1, 2016, from http://www.alnap.org/pool/files/adinolfi-et-al-(2005)-humanitarian-response-review.pdf

Adivar, B., & Mert, A. (2010). International disaster relief planning with fuzzy credibility. *Fuzzy Optimization and Decision Making, 9*(4), 413–433.

Afshar, A., and Haghani, A. (2012). Modeling integrated supply chain logistics in real-time large-scale disaster relief operations. *Socio-Economic Planning Sciences*, *46*(4), 327–338.

Alexander, D. (2006). *Earthquake in Kashmir: A Question of Responsibilities*. An unpublished paper. Retrieved April 1, 2016, from http://www.radixonline.org/resources/kashmiralexander.doc

Asian Development Bank and World Bank (ADB-WB). (2005). Preliminary Damage and Needs Assessment—Pakistan 2005 Earthquake.

Balcik, B., Beamon, B. M., Krejci, C. C., Muramatsu, K. M., and Ramirez, M. (2010). Coordination in humanitarian relief chains: Practices, challenges and opportunities. *International Journal of Production Economics*, *126*(1), 22–34.

Barbarosoglu, G. and Arda, Y. (2004). A two-stage stochastic programming framework for transportation planning in disaster response. *Journal of the Operational Research Society*, *55*(1), 43–53.

Battini, D., Peretti, U., Persona, A., and Sgarbossa, F. (2014). Application of humanitarian last mile distribution model. *Journal of Humanitarian Logistics and Supply Chain Management*, *4*(1), 131–148.

BBC. (2005, October 28). Cash crisis for quake helicopters. Retrieved April 1, 2016, from *BBC News*: http://news.bbc.co.uk/2/hi/south_asia/4384204.stm

Beamon, B. M., and Balcik, B. (2008). Performance measurement in humanitarian relief chains. *International Journal of Public Sector Management*, *21*(1), 4–25.

Behdani, B., Fan, Y., Wiegmans, B., and Zuidwijk, R. (2014). Multimodal schedule design for synchromodal freight transport systems. Available at SSRN *2438851*.

Benini, A., Conley, C., Dittemore, B., and Waksman, Z. (2009). Survivor needs or logistical convenience? Factors shaping decisions to deliver relief to earthquake affected communities, Pakistan 2005–06. *Disasters*, *33*(1), 110–131.

Bozorgi-Amiri, A., and Khorsi, M. (2015). A dynamic multi-objective location–routing model for relief logistic planning under uncertainty on demand, travel time, and cost parameters. *The International Journal of Advanced Manufacturing Technology*, *85*(5-8), 1633–1648.

Cahill, K. M. (2007). *The Pulse of Humanitarian Assistance*. Oxford, UK: Oxford University Press.

Caunhye, A. M., Nie, X., and Pokharel, S. (2012). Optimization models in emergency logistics: A literature review. *Socio-Economic Planning Sciences*, *46*(1), 4–13.

Crainic, T. G., and Kim, K. H. (2006). Intermodal transportation. *Transportation*, *14*, 467–537.

Currion, P. (2005). Assessment report: Pakistan Earthquake Response. Inter-agency Working Group on Emergency Capacity, Retrieved April 1, 2016, from ALNAP: http://old.alnap.org/resource/3381.aspx.

EM-DAT. (2016). Number of disasters reported: 1950–2015. EM-DAT: The OFDA/CRED International Disaster Database – www.emdat.be – Université

Catholique de Louvain – Brussels – Belgium. Retrieved April 1, 2016, from http://www.emdat.be/disaster_trends/index.html

ERRA. (2006). *Annual Review 2005–2006*. Islamabad: Government of Pakistan.

Ferris, E. (2010). *Earthquakes and floods: Comparing Haiti and Pakistan*. Brookings Institution, 26.

Garrido, R. A., Lamas, P., and Pino, F. J. (2015). A stochastic programming approach for floods emergency logistics. *Transportation Research Part E: Logistics and Transportation Review, 75*(C) 18–31.

Government of Pakistan (GoP). (2005). A review of disaster management policies and systems in Pakistan. UN-World Conference on Disaster Reduction. Retrieved April 1, 2016, from http://presidentofpakistan.gov.pk/gop/index.php?q= aHR0cDovLzE5Mi4xNjguNzAuMTM2L2dvcC8uL3BkZnMvZGlzYXN0ZXIgb WFuYWdlbWVudCBwb2xpY3kucGRm

Government of Pakistan (GoP). (2011) *Annual Flood Report 2010*. Government of Pakistan, Ministry of Water and Power, Federal Flood Commission, Islamabad

Guha-Sapir, D., Hoyois, P., and Below, R. (2014). *Annual Disaster Statistical Review 2013: The Numbers and Trends*. Brussels: CRED.

Gunn, S. W. A. (2003). The language of disasters: A brief terminology of disaster management and humanitarian action. *In Basics of International Humanitarian Missions*, 37–40. New York City, New York, USA: Fordham University Press.

Haghani, A., and Oh, S. C. (1996). Formulation and solution of a multi-commodity, multi-modal network flow model for disaster relief operations. *Transportation Research Part A: Policy and Practice, 30*(3), 231–250.

Holguín-Veras, J., Jaller, M., Van Wassenhove, L. N., Pérez, N., and Wachtendorf, T. (2012a). On the unique features of post-disaster humanitarian logistics. *Journal of Operations Management, 30*(7), 494–506.

Holguín-Veras, J., Jaller, M., Van Wassenhove, L. N., Pérez, N., and Wachtendorf, T. (2012b). Material convergence: Important and understudied disaster phenomenon. *Natural Hazards Review, 15*(1), 1–12.

Hu, Z. H. (2011). A container multimodal transportation scheduling approach based on immune affinity model for emergency relief. *Expert Systems with Applications, 38*(3), 2632–2639.

Iqbal, I., Iqbal Z., and Ravan, S. (2015). Effective use of Space-based information to monitor disasters and its impacts: Lessons Learnt from Floods in Pakistan. Retrieved April 9, 2016, from *UN-SPIDER.org*: http://www.un-spider.org/ sites/default/files/150112_SUPARCOBooklet_online.pdf

Kaneda, H., Nakata, T., Tsutsumi, H., Kondo, H., Sugito, N., Awata, Y., Akhtar, S. S., Majid, A., Khattak, W., Awan, A.A. and Yeats, R.S. (2008). Surface rupture of the 2005 Kashmir, Pakistan, earthquake and its active tectonic implications. *Bulletin of the Seismological Society of America, 98*(2), 521–557.

MacLeod, A. (2007). *ERRA Annual Review 2006–2007*, 119–132. Islamabad: Government of Pakistan.

MapAction. (2005). Pakistan Earthquake Disaster Situation Overview Map, T087/
1, 18 October 2005. Retrieved from MapAction.org, April 1, 2016, from http://
maps.mapaction.org/dataset/7-1293.

MapAction. (2010, September 9). Pakistan-Overview-Transport, PAK215,
v2_A0, 19 August 2010. Retrieved from MapAction.org, April 1, 2016,
from http://maps.mapaction.org/dataset/196-2111/resource/97b59d32-d56d-
4323-8675-df54e9406ee7

McLoughlin, D. (1985). A framework for integrated emergency management.
*Public Administration Review, 45*, 165–172.

Min, H., Jayaraman, V., and Srivastava, R. (1998). Combined location-routing
problems: A synthesis and future research directions. *European Journal of
Operational Research, 108*(1), 1–15.

Najafi, M., Eshghi, K., and Dullaert, W. (2013). A multi-objective robust optimization
model for logistics planning in the earthquake response phase. *Transportation
Research Part E: Logistics and Transportation Review, 49*(1), 217–249.

NDMA. (2007). *National Disaster Risk Management Framework.* Islamabad:
Government of Pakistan.

NDMA. (2009). *Annual Report 2009.* Islamabad: Government of Pakistan.

NDMA. (2010). *National Disaster Response Plan 2010.* Islamabad: Government of
Pakistan.

NDMA. (2011). *Pakistan Floods 2010: Learning from Experience.* Islamabad:
Government of Pakistan.

Nolz, P. C., Doerner, K. F., & Hartl, R. F. (2010). Water distribution in
disaster relief. *International Journal of Physical Distribution & Logistics
Management, 40*(8/9), 693–708.

Owen, L. A., Kamp, U., Khattak, G. A., Harp, E. L., Keefer, D. K., and Bauer, M. A.
(2008). Landslides triggered by the 8 October 2005 Kashmir earthquake.
*Geomorphology, 94*(1), 1–9.

Özdamar, L., and Demir, O. (2012). A hierarchical clustering and routing procedure for large scale disaster relief logistics planning. *Transportation Research Part
E: Logistics and Transportation Review, 48*(3), 591–602.

Özdamar, L., and Ertem, M. A. (2015). Models, solutions and enabling technologies
in humanitarian logistics. *European Journal of Operational Research, 244*(1), 55–65.

Özdamar, L., Ekinci, E., and Küçükyazici, B. (2004). Emergency logistics planning
in natural disasters. *Annals of Operations Research, 129*(1–4), 217–245.

Ozkapici, D. B., Ertem, M. A., and Aygüneş, H. (2016). Intermodal humanitarian
logistics model based on maritime transportation in Istanbul. *Natural Hazards,
83*(1), 1–20.

Poblet, M., Leshinsky, R., and Zeleznikow, J. (2012). Digital neighbours: Even Good
Samaritan crisis mappers need strategies for legal liability. *Planning News, 38*(11), 20.

Polastro, R., Nagrah, A., Steen, N., and Zafar, F. (2011). *Inter-Agency Real Time
Evaluation of the Humanitarian Response to Pakistan's 2010 Flood Crisis.* Madrid:
DARA.

Qureshi, J. H. (2006). Policy briefing Pakistan: Political impact of the earthquake. Crisis Group Asia Briefing No. 46. Retrieved April 10, 2016, from crisisgroup. org: http://www.crisisgroup.org/~/media/Files/asia/south-asia/pakistan/b046_ pakistan_political_impact_of_the_earthquake.pdf

Rahman, A. (2010) *Disaster Risk Management: Flood Perspective.* VDM Verlag Publishing: Saarbrücken, 192 pp. *ISBN 978-3-639-29891-8*

Rahman, A., and Khan, A. N. (2011) Analysis of flood causes and associated socio-economic damages in the Hindu Kush region. *Natural Hazards 59*(3): 1239–1260.

Rasul, G., and Ahmad, B. (2012). *Climate change in Pakistan.* Focused on Sindh Province, Pakistan Meteorological Department Report.

Rennemo, S. J., Rø, K. F., Hvattum, L. M., and Tirado, G. (2014). A three-stage stochastic facility routing model for disaster response planning. *Transportation Research Part E: Logistics and Transportation Review, 62*, 116–135.

Rodriguez, R. R., Saiz, J. J. A., and Bas, Á. O. (2007). Tangible and intangible factors for supply chain co-transportation practices. In *XI Congreso de Ingeniería de Organización: Madrid, 5-7 de Septiembre de 2007*, 923–927. Madrid, Spain: Asociación para el Desarrollo de la Ingeniería de Organización (ADIGNOR).

Ruan, J., Wang, X., and Shi, Y. (2014). A two-stage approach for medical supplies intermodal transportation in large-scale disaster responses. *International Journal of Environmental Research and Public Health, 11*(11), 11081–11109.

SAARC. (2016). Disaster profile of Pakistan. Retrieved April 1, 2016, from http:// www.saarc-sadkn.org/countries/pakistan/disaster_profile.aspx

Sheu, J. B. (2007). Challenges of emergency logistics management. *Transportation Research Part E: Logistics and Transportation Review, 43*(6), 655–659.

SteadieSeifi, M., Dellaert, N. P., Nuijten, W., Van Woensel, T., & Raoufi, R. (2014). Multimodal freight transportation planning: A literature review. *European Journal of Operational Research, 233*(1), 1–15.

Steets, J., Grünewald, F., Binder, A., De Geoffroy, V., Kauffmann, D., Krüger, S., Meier, C. and Sokpoh, B. (2010). Cluster approach evaluation 2 synthesis report. IASC Cluster Approach Evaluation 2nd Phase, Groupe URD and the Global Public Policy Institute.

Stoddard, A., Harmer, A., Haver, K., Salomons, D., and Wheeler, V. (2007). Cluster approach evaluation—Final. *Development*, 10121, 10150.

Syed, S. (2015, October 4). 10 years on, we have learnt no lessons from the earthquake. Retrieved April 1, 2016, from Dawn: http://www.dawn.com/news/1210665

Thakur, V. C. (2006). Lessons learnt from the 8 October 2005 Muzaffarabad earthquake and need for some initiatives. *Current Science-Bangalore, 91*(5), 566.

Thompson, W. C. (2008). *Practitioner's Hands and Academic Eyes: A Practical Approach to Improving Disaster Preparedness and Response* (Doctoral dissertation). Corvallis, Oregon, USA: Oregon State University.

Trunick, P.A. (2005). "Special report: Delivering relief to tsunami victims", *Logistics Today, 46*(2), 1–3.

UNECE. (2009). Illustrated glossary for transport statistics. ISBN: 978-92-79-17082-9.

United Nations Office for the Coordination of Humanitarian Affairs (UN-OCHA). (2010) Pakistan floods emergency response plan, September revision. UN-OCHA

Verweij, K. (2011). Synchronic modalities – Critical success factors. In P. J. van der Sterre (Ed.), *Logistics Yearbook Edition 2011*. Rotterdam (pp. 75–88). ISBN: 978-90-79470-00-6.

Vidal, J. and Walsh D. (1 June 2010). "Temperatures reach record high in Pakistan". *The Guardian*, London.

Wang, L., Song, J., and Shi, L. (2015). Dynamic emergency logistics planning: Models and heuristic algorithm. *Optimization Letters*, *9*(8), 1533–1552.

Wilder, A. (2008). Perceptions of the Pakistan earthquake response: Humanitarian agenda 2015—Pakistan country study. Medford, MA: Feinstein International Center, Tufts University.

Wilkinson, I. (2005, November 7). Mules provide constant hope for villages cut off by quake. Retrieved April 1, 2016, from *The Telegraph*: http://www.telegraph.co.uk/news/worldnews/asia/pakistan/1502434/Mules-provide-constant-hope-for-villages-cut-off-by-quake.html

Woxenius, J. (2007). Generic framework for transport network designs: Applications and treatment in intermodal freight transport literature. *Transport Reviews*, *27*(6), 733–749.

Ye, Y., and Liu, N. (2011, June). A sequential approach for emergency logistics planning in natural disasters. In *International Conference on* Service Systems and Service Management (ICSSSM), 2011 8th (pp. 1–6). Tianjin, China: IEEE.

Yi, W., and Özdamar, L. (2007). A dynamic logistics coordination model for evacuation and support in disaster response activities. *European Journal of Operational Research*, *179*(3), 1177–1193.

Zhao, Y., and Qian, Y. (2014). The construction of emergency logistics and integrated transport system based on "Scenario-Response" mode. *International Journal of Control and Automation*, *7*(3), 359–370.

Zheng, Y. J., and Ling, H. F. (2013). Emergency transportation planning in disaster relief supply chain management: a cooperative fuzzy optimization approach. *Soft Computing*, *17*(7), 1301–1314.

Zhu, J., Huang, J., Liu, D., and Han, J. (2008). Resources allocation problem for local reserve depots in disaster management based on scenario analysis. In *The 7th International Symposium on Operations Research and its Applications*, 395–407. Beijing, China: World Publishing Corporation.

# Part V

## Applications - Most Typical

# 16

# Structuring Humanitarian Supply Chain Knowledge Through a Meta-Modeling Approach

Laura Laguna Salvadó, Matthieu Lauras, Tina Comes
and Frederick Bénaben

## Introduction

Humanitarian organizations purpose is to alleviate human suffering. For a long time, it has been understood that getting the right resources to the right place and at the right time is crucial for a successful relief response. Thus, humanitarian organizations have concentrated their efforts on logistics performance improvements, with effectiveness and responsiveness as key objectives.

Moreover, the competition for funding, which is insufficient to cover all humanitarian needs, is a reality today (UN OCHA 2014). With restricted funding and an overall increase of humanitarian needs, efficiency[1] has become a new objective for humanitarian logistics.

---

[1] Efficiency is a measure of how economically the firm's resources are utilized when providing a given level of customer satisfaction (Neely, Gregory, and Platts 1995). In the HSC context, it is the ability to avoid wasting resources (materials, energy, efforts, money, and time) in responding to the beneficiaries' needs.

L.L. Salvadó (✉) · M. Lauras · F. Bénaben
University of Toulouse—Mines Albi, Toulouse, France
e-mail: laura.lagunasalvado@mines-albi.fr; matthieu.lauras@mines-albi.fr;
Frederick.benaben@mines-albi.fr

T. Comes
University of Agder, Grimstad, Norway
e-mail: tina.comes@uia.no

© The Author(s) 2018                                                    **491**
G. Kovács et al. (eds.), *The Palgrave Handbook of Humanitarian Logistics
and Supply Chain Management*, https://doi.org/10.1057/978-1-137-59099-2_16

Looking at humanitarian operations, we identify many opportunities to improve the balance between effectiveness (order qualifier) and efficiency (order winner) to boost the long-term sustainability of humanitarian organizations (Laguna Salvadó et al. 2015). An example of these challenges is the contingency stock management of humanitarian organizations, which shows a significant misalignment with actual needs, producing excessive stock coverage, and important bullwhip effects all along the supply chain.

Decision support systems (DSS) can improve the decision support performance (Liu et al. 2010). A DSS is a computerized information system to support decision-making activities such as warehouse location (Balcik and Beamon 2008), transport planning (Balcik et al. 2008), or inventory management (Beamon and Kotleba 2006). DSS generally consists of a computer knowledge base linked to a quantitative model that recommends optimal solutions to a concrete decision-making question (Laguna Salvadó et al. 2016). The knowledge base contains information of the "real world" to fill in the optimization model. An important step toward DSS is hence the development and design of humanitarian supply chain (HSC) knowledge management (KM) systems. Gathering, formalizing and exploiting the knowledge and information about HSC is thus a critical requirement to develop adequate DSS.

However, the adoption of "humanitarian technology," even if promising, is a difficult task as outlined in the Red Cross World Disaster Report (2013). The causes of limited adoption range from political or cultural barriers, to the low accessibility of existing tools that require specialized expert knowledge not available in the field. It is therefore imperative to develop a context-aware approach that can cope with the complexity of a disaster environment, and take into account the practices of responders.

Consequently, the HSC challenge has attracted a lot of research interest, and the number of publications on HSC has increased considerably during the past twenty years. The academics insist on the potential of improving decision-making processes (Overstreet et al. 2011). Some of them argues that to bridge the technological gap while developing humanitarian technology, research should consider real-world problems and data on past and present disaster response, as well as forecasted strategies (Holguín-Veras et al. 2012; Galindo and Batta 2013b; Laguna Salvadó et al. 2016). Several reviews of disaster management literature identifies strengths and weaknesses of this research area (Altay and Green 2006; Simpson and Hancock 2009; Lettieri et al. 2009; Galindo and Batta 2013). The authors propose clear directions to increase the relevance and impact of research on practitioners. In particular, they suggest: (i) building realistic assumptions and scenarios, (ii) improving the efficiency capabilities of humanitarian networks, and (iii) considering the effect of data uncertainty on the results. It is commonly accepted that practitioners will apply research in the humanitarian sector only if they trust the findings. As a consequence, more research should be done in collaboration with practitioners.

## Field Research Challenges

More and more HSC researchers have developed field-oriented approaches to formulate models that use realistic assumptions and produce more applicable research. Academics argue the need of multidisciplinary field research to meet this challenge (Chan and Comes 2014).

While conducting field research in HSC, the objective for researchers is (i) to get as much relevant data as possible with a limited time window and (ii) to organize this knowledge to inform rigorous research models or theory-building. On the practitioner's side, the objective is (i) to learn from previous disasters by capturing, codifying, and transferring knowledge and (ii) co-develop a reliable trusted solution that can be deployed in practice.

There is consequently a need for specific methods and tools able to support the data collection step (semi-structured interviews) and the data structuring and analysis step (i.e., knowledge base) of such an approach. Particularly, this requires the definition of a framework, or common universe of discourse dedicated to HSC, which is essential to solving the various semantic conflicts (concepts definition and name) that are bound to occur between academics and practitioners.

To contribute on breaking the technological barrier, we have conducted two field research missions in two different contexts. One during the Ebola Outbreak in West Africa on December 2014 (Comes et al. 2015a), and the second one, at the America's IFRC Regional Logistic Unit (RLU) on October 2015, during a "noncrisis" period (Laguna Salvadó et al. 2016). The objective in both missions was identifying humanitarian practitioner's needs related to HSC decision-making.

The methods used to capture the knowledge where mainly semi-structured interviews and observations. Prior to these interviews, a deep investigation of "open data" (data accessible on the web, e.g., rieliefweb.org) on the crisis was conducted to gather a maximum of raw data regarding the management and monitoring of HSCs flows of goods. From the concrete aims of the field research, qualitative structured interview protocol for the practitioner's interviews are defined.

Even if both missions were relevant and we could identify some challenges of the HSC in different contexts, the difficulty was to structure all the gathered knowledge as a whole. We did use modeling languages from the art like Business Process Modeling Notation (BPMN) to formalize process, or Value Stream Mapping (VSM) to formalize material flows. However, the information gathered was never structured on a standard database or shared it with any stakeholder.

The ideal would be to have a "standard" model of the HSC to be used as reference. This would support field research design and fulfillment (verify the integrity of the data gathered, compare between different campaigns, etc.) and also would facilitate the shared understanding of the HSC between academics, practitioners, and any stakeholder.

## Increasing the Relevance of Field Research

This chapter aims at going a step forward a standard HSC reference knowledge by developing a meta-modeling approach. Meta-models facilitate integration among stakeholders, information systems, intelligent processing, and shared reuse of knowledge among systems (Pinto and Martins 2004). It is particularly promising in a humanitarian context that requires making the knowledge of the relations among the relief stakeholders explicit (Humphries 2013).

The meta-model brings a shared and common understanding of the HSC, to facilitate the design and fulfillment of academic field research. In the following, firstly, we present the background on meta-modeling approaches, particularly in crisis and disaster management. Secondly, we discuss the field-research methods used to build the HSC meta-model (Ebola outbreak and America's International Federation of Red Cross), and thirdly, we present a meta-model for managing the knowledge of HSC build with the field-research works and the HSC related literature. Finally, section "Potential Uses of the HSC Meta-Model and Conclusion" discusses the applicability and limits of the HSC meta-model.

# Meta-Modeling Background and Methodology

## Meta-Modeling and Ontology

Over the past decades, there has been a tremendous growth in meta-modeling and ontology development (see Henderson-Sellers and Bulthuis 2012). Following Guizzardi (2005). We understand a model as an abstraction of reality according to a certain conceptualization. A meta-model is then a "model of models" that (i) describes a domain that is representative of more than one instance in a less abstract domain and (ii) is the core of a modeling language used to describe those instances (Bataille and Castellani 2001; Henderson-Sellers 2011).

An ontology is a formal explicit specification of a shared conceptualization for a domain of interest (Gruber and others 1993). It describes knowledge that can be used and reused to facilitate the comprehension of *concepts* and *relations* in a given domain as well as the communication between different domain actors. There are two kinds of ontology that are useful for engineering:

- Domain ontologies, which are used to create common vocabulary for a specific application domain.
- Meta-ontologies, which are equivalent in nature to the meta-model of a modeling language and thus encapsulate the concepts needed for creating domain ontologies.

The logistics activities of HSC domain can be structured and formalized as meta-ontologies. Therefore, the center of our contribution lies in developing a structure of HSC concepts and relations between them.

Given our research question, we provide here an overview of models in (i) HSC management and (ii) disaster/crisis management.

### Humanitarian Supply Chain Management Meta-Models

In commercial supply chain management (SCM), many process reference models have been developed; they mainly focus on the behavioral aspects of an organization through the analysis of business processes. The most famous is probably the supply chain operations reference (SCOR) model (Zhou et al. 2011). Beyond this, Grubic and Fan (2010) reviewed meta-models dedicated to SCM. They identify a set of gaps that have to be considered in future developments. The most important ones regarding HSC meta-models are the following:

- Level of granularity: There is no related work at tactical and operational levels, despite their importance.
- Lack of models grounded in empirical or field research—similar to the situation for HSC. Therefore, there is a lack of deeper order and structure of reality.
- Lack of knowledge of dyadic relationships or external supply chains. This point is critical for the humanitarian stakeholders.
- Very few meta-models have formally represented and acknowledged the importance of time. This point is critical for HSC, due to the different time frames of HSC (slow-onsets vs. low onsets, see section "Humanitarian Operations Life Cycle").

In addition, Daniele and Ferreira Pires (2013) identify five concepts that have to be integrated in a supply chain meta-model:

- Activity represents the relevant actions to achieve logistics and provides value for customers.
- Actor denotes individuals or companies that could be a provider or demander of activities and operate those activities on related resources.
- Physical resource denotes the objects that are used in the activities.
- Location denotes the geographical area used to define the place relevant for the activities.
- Time denotes the start/end time or the time interval associated to activities.

In the specific HSC literature, we identify different reference models that have been developed. Blecken (2010) proposes a specific reference model framework based on supply chain reference models. It is organized in two dimensions. The hierarchical decomposition organizes SCM tasks at strategic, tactical, and operational levels. The structural decomposition organizes SCM tasks related to assessment, procurement, warehousing, and transport. Franke et al. (2011) combine the Blecken's reference process model with a tool for ensuring a shared understanding on coordination aspects. These contributions are relevant for our problematic as they can support on the identification and the definition of concepts to be included in the HSC meta-model. However, both do not formalize their meta-model, which limits their re-usability. In addition, these two reference models are focused on the behavior aspects of the logistics operations, whereas the aim of this research work is to consider a large vision of HSC system.

Overstreet et al. (2011) provides a literature review on future research with a framework for conducting research in humanitarian logistics. None of the models discussed addressed the challenge of data gathering and structuring through a meta-model.

A different contribution to the HSC KM is the Humanitarian eXchange Language (HXL) Situation and Response Standard (Clark et al. 2015). HXL is a project by the United Nations Office for the Coordination of Humanitarian Affairs that aims at defining data management and exchange for disaster response. This is a joint project between academics and practitioners with a KM approach, developed with the specific humanitarian field constraints that may be considered. Thus, this standard is oriented to the interoperability of humanitarian knowledge and could be considered on the development of specific DSS.

## Crisis/Disaster Meta-Model

On the larger domain of crisis and disaster management, along with the open data movement and semantic web, a lot of interest has been dedicated to developing crisis and disaster management ontologies (Aaltonen 2009; Asadi et al. 2011; Bénaben et al. 2008; Comes et al. 2015b; Imran et al. 2013). Only few, however, attempts to represent crisis and disaster management knowledge structures in a meta-model in reusable form. The following non exhaustive list highlights some examples: Othman and Beydoun (2010), Blecken (2010), Lauras et al. (2015) and Bénaben et al. (2016). These meta-models have begun to unify the terminology, sharpening the definition of terms and their semantic relationships. Each of the models is focused on a specific case, and such not suitable for a generic analysis. Moreover the main domain is civil protection, critical infrastructure, and/or homeland security and we focus in the following on the very few that are interesting from an HSC perspective.

Othman and Beydoun (2010) propose a meta-model based on ten earlier crisis meta-models composed of four packages corresponding to the phases of the crisis management cycle: mitigation, preparedness, response, and recovery. While this meta-model unifies and facilitates access to crisis management expertise, it has several limitations:

* The majority meta-models used are not formalized.
* The meta-model does not provide detail of each crisis management phase.
* The extraction of general concepts relates to specific types of crisis, such as a cyclone, is not generalizable.
* The meta-model is not instantiated to create a concrete ontology.

Based on this, Bénaben et al. (2016) have developed a more detailed crisis meta-model and associated ontology to facilitate knowledge sharing and develop advanced crisis management systems. They propose a methodology to define a meta-model and develop its characteristics: (i) the studied system, corresponding to the sub-part of the world impacted by the crisis; (ii) the crisis system, corresponding to the properties of a specific crisis; (iii) the treatment system, corresponding to a description of the abilities of actors, which can be deployed in a crisis response; and (iv) the collaborative process, corresponding to a description of the crisis response. The meta-model proposed is based on a core meta-model that describes the knowledge associated with any kind of collaborative situation and develops application-domain layers (crisis management in that case). Based on this principle, it could be possible to design a specific layer for HSC that would be linked with existing layer dedicated to generic crisis management situation.

# Research Methods

## Meta-Model Engineering

Several authors have tried to structure the creation, use, and management of meta-models. According to Pinto and Martins (2004), a meta-model can be built from scratch or by re-using previous knowledge. We decided to build the HSC meta-model from both existing meta-models and field-research works. With this porpoise we use the ENTERPRISE methodology. This methodology is composed of four steps (Uschold and King 1995):

* *Identify purpose and scope*: intended uses, and range of intended users.
* *Build the meta-model*
* *Evaluate*
* *Document*

The ENTERPRISE methodology, even if clear and simple, it presents some inconveniences that have to be considered. First, it does not have a cyclic approach, so after the evaluation phase, a loop may be added to the first two steps to improve the meta-model. Second, the meta-model is build from the users perception of the system (HSC in our case). Other approaches consider "use cases" to identify the concepts. We think that linking both approaches may result on a more relevant meta-model. And third, the methodology do not considers the meta-model life cycle, and this is an inconvenience as long as the meta-model has to adapt to the changes on the HSC configuration.

We present on this chapter the detail of the two first steps of the meta-model development, while evaluation and documentation are left for further discussions.

To formalize the meta-model, we have used Unified Modeling Language (UML) class model as some authors, among whom Colomb and Ahmad (2010) have suggested. It is a type of static structure diagram that describes the structure of a system by showing the system's classes and the relationship between them (association, inheritance, dependency, etc.) (Fowler 2004).

To define the concepts, we have used field-research analysis and targeted literature (as discussed in previous section). In the following section, we implement the two first steps of the ENTERPRISE methodology to build a relevant meta-model for HSC.

## Field Research and Data Collection

To build the meta-model, we followed a field-oriented gathering and validation step. Practically, we used the information gathered previously during the Ebola Outbreak in West Africa on December 2014 (Comes et al. 2015a), and the second one, at the America's IFRC Regional Logistic Unit (RLU) on October 2015 (Laguna Salvadó et al. 2016). The benefit of these missions is the difference on the context characteristics (see Table 16.1). Concerning the Ebola mission, it was a field research on the downstream part of the HSC (see Fig. 16.1), with a lot of actors working in a health emergency crisis. From a supply chain perspective, it was an interesting crisis as long as there where few item references to supply, and the items became difficult to provide (rupture). The second mission was to an IFRC RLU. This is a permanent hub located at Panamá, and dedicated to manage the contingency stock for the Americas region. The observed par of the supply chain was the upstream during a preparation phase (no crisis), with only one humanitarian actor

**Table 16.1** Field missions framework

| | HSC observed part | Crisis phase | Scope | Setup |
|---|---|---|---|---|
| Ebola Outbreak (several objectives, within logistic operations) | HSC downstream | Response phase | Several humanitarian actors, horizontal coordination | A multi-disciplinary field team (Africa) + back office team (Europe) |
| Americas IFRC RLU (logistic operations focus) | HSC upstream | Preparation | One humanitarian actor, vertical coordination | Single researcher to the field (Panamá) + remote supervision (Europe) |

(IFRC). In both missions there was the objective of identifying the business processes and material flows of logistic operations to detect weakness and opportunities to improve the performance.

# HSC Meta-Model Building

## Identify the Purpose and Scope

We come back here to the key factors that justify the purpose and the scope of the HSC meta-model.

In any disaster, there is a diversity of decision-makers: within each organization, there is a typical dichotomy between fields-based operations and

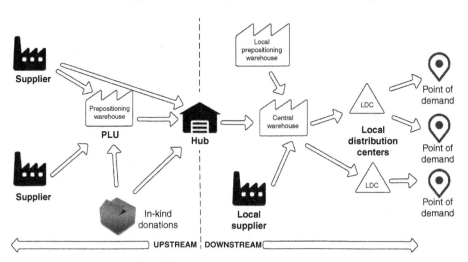

**Fig. 16.1** Humanitarian supply chain

coordination at headquarters (Comes et al. 2015b). In addition, digital volunteers largely organized remotely have become increasingly influential since the Haiti earthquake (Altay and Labonte 2014). Their role as decision-makers, shaping the perception of a disaster as well as their contribution for operational decisions is, however, not yet clearly understood or analyzed (Comes 2016). This confusion of mandates, aims, and differences in communication is insufficient to provide each member with a global view of the situation.

The usual perception of humanitarian world, together with the division of knowledge, implies building a shared knowledge system, based on the representation and the characterization of an HSC. As discussed in the introduction, the purpose of the meta-model is to allow dealing with the problem of structuring and sharing the implicit and explicit HSC knowledge.

To sum up, both HSC academics and practitioners needs a knowledge structuration to better understand the HSC behaviors to improve them.

## Build the Meta-Model

To build the meta-model there are two main stages (Uschold and King 1995):

a) Capture knowledge:

- Identify key concepts and relationships (empirical-research and/or existing meta-models or ontologies).
- Produce text definitions for such concepts and relationships.
- Define terms to refer to the developed concepts and relationships.

b) Code knowledge:

- Organize concepts in a hierarchical way
- Transform the conceptual description into a formal model

### Capture Knowledge

In today's standard configuration, an HSC can be modeled in two main parts. Permanent Logistics Units (PLU), organized as linear supply chains, constitute the upstream part of the HSC (Fig. 16.1, upstream on the left side). They are permanent units and have a role throughout the disaster cycle, that is, preparedness; immediate response; support; and dismantling. PLUs include the operational activities from the sourcing of material resources, warehouse management, to the distribution of items to a relief hub. The downstream part (right side in Fig. 16.1) refers to the dynamic supply structure created in the immediate aftermath of a disaster.

Although the humanitarian sector has become aware of logistics importance to be performing, the approach of humanitarian organizations is very different from the private sector, who realized longtime ago the importance of using efficient supply chains. Several authors (Van Wassenhove 2006; Jahre, Jensen, and Listou 2009; Tomasini and Van Wassenhove 2009; Charles et al. 2010; Gralla et al. 2016) have tried to identify the characteristics of the former's particular context.

Based on field research and a literature review, we have identified five main categories that have to be considered in our meta-model:

- The Stakeholders
- The Categories of Flows Managed
- The Funding Process
- The Dynamics and the Complexity of the Environment
- The Humanitarian Operation Life Cycle

*The Stakeholders*

The humanitarian distribution channel goes through different many stakeholders—that we call Strategic Humanitarian Units (SHU)—starting from suppliers and going to beneficiaries. These SHUs are of a different nature: They are international agencies such as the World Food Program (WFP), international nongovernmental organizations (INGOs) such as Care International, nongovernmental organizations (NGOs), implementing partners, the military, donors, private companies, and governmental agencies. All these SHUs have, to some extent, the following proprieties:

- They are under-resourced, with limited skills availability and high employee turnover that limits institutional memory and efficiency
- Ineffective leverage of technology (i.e., nonrobust equipment) and in particular, information systems that are relatively basic. Many relief logistics departments rely on manual systems without any Information Technology
- Command/control systems are lacking
- Several operations need to be done at the same time

In addition, not all of these stakeholders have the same incentives.

*The Categories of Flows Managed*

The humanitarian distribution channels manage the traditional categories of flows, but these present some specificity:

- Physical flows are material (food, relief items, etc.) and human (organizational skills).
- Informational flows (order transmission, tracking, and coordination of physical flows) that are poorly structured and managed.
- Financial flows, which are unilateral (from donors).

Moreover, because the media places such high pressure on agencies to compete for visibility, organizations have to consider the media flow (even if they are not able to manage it effectively). For instance, Van Wassenhove (2006) explains that ineffective use of the media by humanitarian organizations can lead to waves of unsolicited donations (with resulting bottlenecks) instead of the much-needed resources.

*The Funding Process*

HSC is funded by donors (governments, companies, and the private sector). The funding process is a channel for donations from individual people or donor organizations to the beneficiaries (through several SHUs). Thus, contrary to commercial supply chains, the financial flows are not parallel with the material flows.

*The Dynamics and the Complexity of the Environment*

The dynamics of HSC are very specific because they endeavor to respond to certain vital needs due to sudden or long-term crises. An HSC does not start with a customer's expression of needs and does not want to make a profit. Under these conditions, it is quite difficult to apply best practices in terms of planning and scheduling. There is evidence of a frequent lack of planning in relief supply chains, resulting in inefficiencies. For example, the overuse of expensive and unsafe air charters, failure to pre-plan stocks, congestion at ports caused by unplanned deliveries, delivery of useless or unwanted items to disaster victims and a lack of inter-organizational collaboration for information systems (Oloruntoba and Gray 2009). Generally, an HSU has to:

- Assess needs
- Consider unforeseeable conditions and very short-time frames
- Work under emergency conditions and to be agile
- Deal with a lack of transparency

The environment of HSCs includes several specific characteristics that intensify its complexity:

- A politically volatile climate in which humanitarian organizations have to operate.
- The humanitarian principles: humanity, neutrality, impartiality, and independence.
- A high level of uncertainty in terms of demand, supply, and environment.

Other constraints on managing an HSC come from unforeseeable, complex, particular, and unstable external actors such as local governments (where the crisis takes place), donor governments, the military (third-party service providers), or private-sector logistics providers (i.e., transportation, warehousing).

## The Humanitarian Operation Life Cycle

If we consider a project to be a temporary endeavor undertaken to achieve a particular aim, then HSC operations can be defined as a project. In fact, humanitarian organizations are responsible for producing relevant outputs and hence they must be constantly aware of the project goal (minimizing the impact of a disaster), project purpose, and of course, the internal measurements of project management efficiency. Concretely, there are two kinds of project environments for implementing humanitarian logistics operations:

- Slow-onset disasters: Droughts, epidemics, famine/food insecurity, population movements, and man-made disasters. In this case, the focus is on capacity building, using national staff, cost savings, low budgets, planning, and scheduling, and long time frames.
- Sudden-onset disasters: Hurricanes, cyclones and typhoons, earthquakes, floods, volcanic eruptions, technological and man-made disasters. In this

case, the focus is on providing medical assistance, providing food and nonfood items, launching appeals, globally assessing needs, using international staff, high budgets and very short time frames.

The four different phases in the life cycle of a humanitarian operations have been described as: Preparedness, Immediate Response (Ramp Up), Support (Maturity), and Dismantling (Ramp Down) (Charles et al. 2009). However, this life cycle description has different phases if we consider only the relief mission time as described by Balcik et al. (2008): Assessment, Deployment, Sustainment, and Reconfiguration. In both descriptions, the duration of the operations vary according to the function of the project's characteristics (sudden or slow onset). Nevertheless, the duration is much less important than it would be for any comparable industrial project. In this project, we consider a view of the HSC at a given time (like a picture).

## Code Knowledge

The purpose of this chapter is to structure the knowledge about HSC into a dedicated meta-model, based on the knowledge identified on the previous sections.

### Overview of the Meta-Model

According to Bénaben et al. (2016), we propose a layered meta-model structure (Fig. 16.2). The main layer is a core meta-model relating to the general concepts of collaboration. It is common to all collaborative situations whatever the application domain is.

Then, a set of layers that allows defining the concepts associated to a particular domain of application. In our case, we develop two complementary layers. The first one is about generic knowledge on crisis management and it is inspired from Lauras et al. (2015) and Bénaben et al. (2016). The second one is about HSC knowledge, based on previous sections discussions.

### The Core

As described in Bénaben et al. (2016) the core meta-model (Fig. 16.3) is composed by four packages (Context, Partners, Objectives, and Behavior) that contain concepts dedicated to crisis situation:

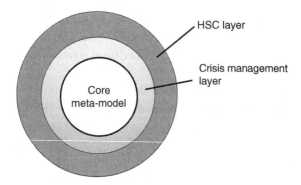

**Fig. 16.2** HSC-layered meta-model structure (inspired from Lauras et al. 2014)

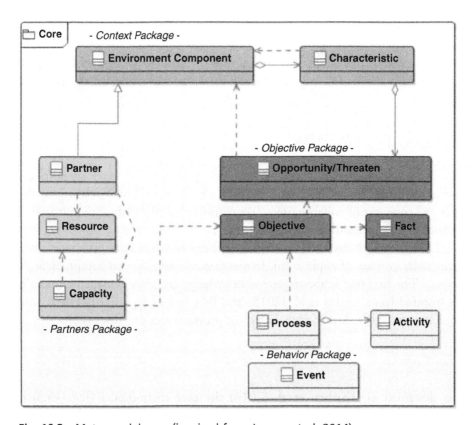

**Fig. 16.3** Meta-model core (inspired from Lauras et al. 2014)

- Context package: components and characteristics of the environment considered, along with related opportunities, threats, and risks.
- Objective package: common objectives, which have to be managed by the network.
- Partner package: resources and know-how of partners, including capabilities, patterns, instructions, resources (people, material, information, etc.), flows (links among capabilities), and mediators, which orchestrate the processes.
- Behavior package: characteristics of the collaboration. This package includes the business activities or processes, and associated events.

The different packages are shown in Fig. 16.3.

### The Crisis Management Layer

The crisis management layer is connected to the core one, with three packages: Context, Partners, and Objectives packages. The fourth package (crisis management behavior) it contains concepts dedicated to deduce collaborative behavior described as process model. As long as our first approach is not to deduce processes, but to structure knowledge related to the current processes, this behavior layer is not considered in the HSC meta-model.

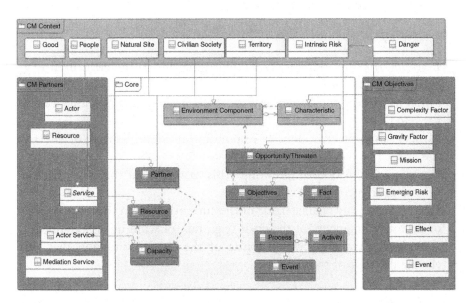

**Fig. 16.4**   Core + crisis management layer

In Fig. 16.4 the idea of layers is illustrated with all the described concepts (Bénaben et al. 2016).

Context package:

- *Good*: any human-made elements (e.g., building, road, etc.).
- *People*: any group of person (e.g., students of a school, employees of a plant, etc.).
- *Natural site*: any natural element of the environment (e.g., lake, forest, etc.).
- *Civilian society*: any social actors (e.g., media, intellectual society, etc.).
- *Territory*: any administrative area (e.g., county, island, etc.).
- *Danger*: any specific dangerous characteristic of the environment (e.g., seismic area, social instability, etc.).
- *Intrinsic risk*: any permanent risk due to identified danger (e.g., earthquake, riot, etc.).

Partners package:

- *Actor*: any stakeholder involved in crisis management (e.g., firemen, EMS, etc.).
- *Resource*: any resource used by actors (e.g., truck, decontamination tent).
- *Service*: any capability of actors (e.g., evacuate victims, treat injured people, etc.).
- *Actor service*: any service specifically provided by actors.

Objectives package.

- *Emerging risk*: any risk specifically emerging due to the crisis itself (e.g., collapse of a building, panic, etc.).
- *Effect*: any direct consequence of the crisis itself (e.g., 10 injured people, fire, etc.).
- *Mission*: any objective directly responding to identified risk or effect of the crisis.
- *Event*: any event occurring during crisis management that must be considered as triggering and effect.
- *Gravity factor*: any characteristic of the current situation that may increase or decrease the gravity of the crisis (e.g., rain or wind on a large fire).
- *Complexity factor*: any characteristic of the current situation that may change the type of the crisis.

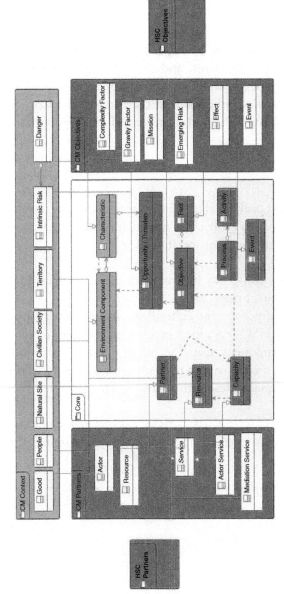

**Fig. 16.5**  HSC meta-model schema

## The HSC Layer

In Fig. 16.5 a big picture of the meta-model is showed. We can identify the three layers: core, crisis management, and HSC.

To build the HSC layer, the concepts specifics from the HSC domain have been added with the same package structure as in the crisis management KM generic layer. The HSC packages are called: (i) HSC Context, (ii) HSC Partners, (iii) HSC Objectives, and (iv) HSC Behavior. The components inside the new packages inherit from components appearing in the crisis management layer that inherits from the meta-model Core. Regarding the fourth package (HSC Behavior), it inherits directly from the core concepts.

### i. HSC Context

The HSC Context package (Fig. 16.6) permits to define the ecosystem where the HSC system has to evolve. We have defined the concepts listed below to characterize the environment specificities.

- *Logistics Infrastructure*: any human-made elements related to logistic activities (e.g., airport, bridge, etc.).
- *Cultural Considerations*: the cultural specificities of any group of humans that can affect HSC (e.g., food exceptions, hygiene standards, etc.).
- *Media*: any component related to media that can influence HSC.
- *Administrative procedure*: any procedure related to an administrative area (customs, pharmaceutical authorizations, etc.).

Moreover, the HSC system has intrinsic risks related to the context; we have identified three main permanent risks due to the existence of the HSC.

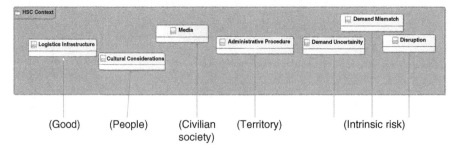

**Fig. 16.6**  HSC Context

- *Demand uncertainty:* As consequence of the crisis uncertainty.
- *Demand mismatch:* There can be misalignment as consequence of the context (i.e., bullwhip effect caused by logistic infrastructures disruption, as observed for the Haiti crisis, 2010; or the Nepal Earthquake, 2015).
- *Disruption:* Suppliers may be not able to supply some item references, as observed during the Ebola Outbreak for the Personal Protection Equipment (PPE).

## ii. HSC Objectives

The goal of the HSC is to supply products to the populations affected by a humanitarian crisis. The *material resources need* is considered an *effect* that inherits from a *fact* so concerned by the *objective* of the core meta-model. The *vulnerability elements* are emerging a risk that threats the HSC objectives. So the HSC objective (Fig. 16.7) is defined as covering the material needs and to ensuring that even if part of the HSC is destroyed the main objective is achieved.

## iii. HSC Partners

The HSC Partner's package (Fig. 16.8) includes all the elements that enable to describe the HSC system (actors, resources, and skills) and the links between.

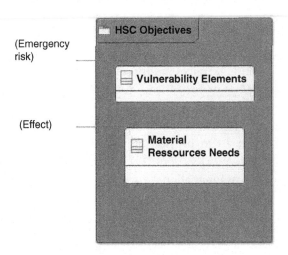

**Fig. 16.7** HSC Objectives layer

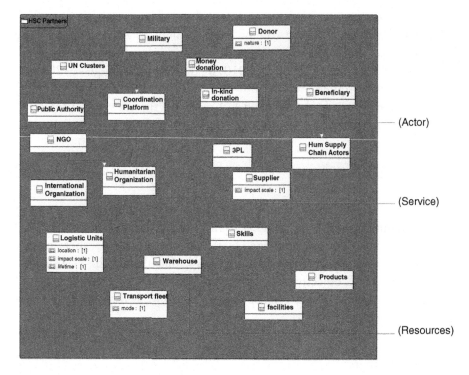

**Fig. 16.8**  HSC Partners

*Humanitarian Supply Chain Actors: I*nherits from *Actor* and Regroups:

- *Donor:* can be a private or a public actor. They provide cash, or "in-kind donation" like resources (products, materials, facilities, transportation) or skills (services) support. Donations are either for a concrete crisis response or for general humanitarian responses.
- *Beneficiary:* the community receiving the humanitarian aid.
- *Humanitarian Organization:* the parent concept of *NGO* or *International Organization.* They can provide HSC services for other humanitarian organizations, as the IFRC does (Laguna Salvadó et al. 2016).
- *Military:* national or international forces collaborating on HSC operations.
- *3PL:* or Third-Party Logistics are private companies specialized on logistic services. There are experiences of collaboration between them and humanitarian organizations (Laguna Salvadó et al. 2016).

- *Supplier:* can be local or international. Suppliers can provide warehouse services or deliver items as consignment inventory. Thus, humanitarian organizations do not pay for the prepositioned items before consumption.
- *Public authority:* local, regional, or national authority that can play a role on the HSC decisions related to location or access authorizations.
- *Coordination platform:* the concept related to all the actors' interoperability initiatives, like the *UN Clusters*.
- *Logistic units:* part of the Humanitarian Organizations, with a location, an impact scale (local, regional, international), and a lifetime (permanent or temporary). They can be composed of:
  - *Skills:* all the human capabilities (management and operational)
  - *Transport fleet:* the transportation modes owned by the humanitarian organizations or other actors (car, plane, lorry...)
  - *Warehouses:* composed by the *Facilities* and the *Products*. Facilities concern all the buildings and materials necessaries for the warehouse operation. Products are the emergency items that can be medical, food or nonfood items (shelters, hygiene kits, etc.)

iv. HSC Behavior

This package (Fig. 16.9) defines the operational processes that the HSC partners does to achieve the objectives in a given context. This package includes two views of the behavior: a process oriented view, with the business activities or processes, and a flow oriented view, with material flows.

On the BPMN standard language, a *Logistic process* can be related to a pool, or group of actors, Key Performance Indicators (KPI), and the start and end *Events*. To define the business processed, the *Pool* contains:

- *Partner Tasks:* defined by their attributes (type, duration, resources, start and end events)
- Gateways: to define the tasks sequence

And to define the flow perspective, we relate the pool to the *material flow* inputs and outputs.

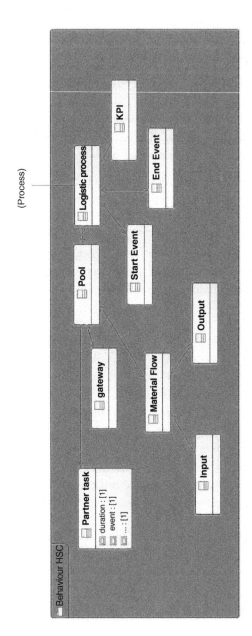

**Fig. 16.9** HSC Behavior

# Potential Uses of the HSC Meta-Model and Conclusion

As discussed on the introduction, the conceptualization of the HSC knowledge is required for both academics and practitioners to make the relations among the stakeholders explicit. The HSC meta-model proposed aims to provide a shared and common understanding of the HSC concepts and relationships, to be able to (i) support the field research design and to (ii) design and monitor future decision-making support tools and/or dedicated DSS. It defines a framework to keep, compare, and reuse information. In the following, we describe uses of such a contribution.

## To Support Field Research Works

The strategy to collect the data in the field is often based on observation and interviews of practitioners. The HSC meta-model can support field research design and execution in the future by supporting the interview design, ensuring that the concepts that are asked/gathered have a place in the model, and vice versa.

## To Support Decision Support System Design

The model can be the base of future DSS design. It can be expected to create "knowledge bases" that supports on the HSC meta-model to support design, development, and evaluation of DSS. On DSS application, the meta-model plays the role of reference for a shared database (instance model), that can be used then as input for optimization based DSS or deductive business-processes DSS. The use of "standard" database has a huge potential to improve the collaboration between humanitarian stockholders. Coordination is a difficult exercise in a crisis situation, and sharing information is a recurrent problem of humanitarian crises. To carry out this objective, the actors need to coordinate their activities and share data. Lauras et al. (2015) illustrates the potential of meta-model during a response crisis (train crash for their use case). Thanks to a common model, each actor can first describe his abilities in a way understandable to everyone and all actors of the crisis response can share the same picture of the situation. This has a potential to improve the agility and collaboration of HSC by proposing detection and adaptation systems based on real-time knowledge update. Second, it is possible to use this structured knowledge to develop and use some advanced crisis management tools, like Mediation Information Systems (MIS) that supports the orchestration of business-processes between stockholders.

A significant limitation of this study is that validity and reliability in qualitative research is controversial. For the instance, the validation step of the methodology proposed has not been conducted. This step requires joining a large spectrum of humanitarian actors including academics and practitioners. The different perspectives of the actors may produce some misunderstanding on the concepts included in the model, or the identification of missing concepts ignored by the authors.

The current HSC meta-model is a first attempt to describe all the concepts related to the HSC as a layered meta-ontology, developed by a limited group of experts. More works have to be done to obtain a generic HSC meta-model that can be accepted by the humanitarian community as standard. The results of current and future research works should be helpful considering that each organization—each actor—possesses its own knowledge, with its own semantic, usually limited to its core activity. However, even if all actors own all the knowledge of the domain collectively, none of them will master the whole knowledge or its boundaries individually.

Moreover, the meta-model gives a static view of the HSC. By implementing it, we can obtain a "picture" of the HSC as observed in a given moment. Due to the dynamic nature of the HSC, we consider the need of introducing a time dimension concept to the meta-model.

**Acknowledgments** The authors would like to thank the Disaster Resilience Laboratory for managing the exciting adventure of the Ebola Outbreak field research, and also to share their results and methodologies related to previous field research.

We also thank the Americas IFRC logistic department for their warm welcome to the Panama Regional Logistic Unit facilities, and specially to Mathieu Grenade (former Americas IFRC Logistic Development Coordinator) for sharing his knowledge of the HSC.

# References

Aaltonen, Mika. 2009. "Multi-Ontology, Sense-Making and the Emergence of the Future". *Futures* 41 (5): 279–283.

Altay, Nezih, and Walter G. Green. 2006. "OR/MS Research in Disaster Operations Management". *European Journal of Operational Research* 175 (1): 475–493. doi:10.1016/j.ejor.2005.05.016.

Altay, Nezih, and Melissa Labonte. 2014. "Challenges in Humanitarian Information Management and Exchange: Evidence from Haiti". *Disasters*. doi:10.1111/disa.12052.

Asadi, Sahar, Costin Badica, Tina Comes, Claudine Conrado, Vanessa Evers, Frans Groen, Sorin Illie, Jan Steen Jensen, Achim J. Lilienthal, and Bianca Milan. 2011. "ICT Solutions Supporting Collaborative Information Acquisition, Situation Assessment and Decision Making in Contemporary Environmental Management Problems: The DIADEM Approach". In *Conference on Innovations in Sharing Environmental Observation and Information* (EnviroInfo 2011), October 5–7, 2011, Ispra, Italy, 920–931.

Balcik, B., and B. M. Beamon. 2008. "Facility Location in Humanitarian Relief". *International Journal of Logistics Research and Applications* 11 (2): 101–121. doi:10.1080/13675560701561789.

Balcik, Burcu, Benita M. Beamon, and Karen Smilowitz. 2008. "Last Mile Distribution in Humanitarian Relief". *Journal of Intelligent Transportation Systems* 12 (2): 51–63. doi:10.1080/15472450802023329.

Bataille, V., and X. Castellani. 2001. "Métamodélisation et Ingénierie Des Systèmes D'information". *Ingénierie Des Systèmes d'Information:* 149–174.

Beamon, Benita M., and Stephen A. Kotleba. 2006. "Inventory Modelling for Complex Emergencies in Humanitarian Relief Operations". *International Journal of Logistics Research and Applications* 9 (1): 1–18. doi:10.1080/13675560500453667.

Bénaben, F., M. Lauras, S. Truptil, and N. Salatgé. 2016. "A Metamodel for Knowledge Management in Crisis Management". In *2016 49th Hawaii International Conference on System Sciences (HICSS)*, 126–135. doi:10.1109/HICSS.2016.24.

Bénaben, Frédérick, Chihab Hanachi, Matthieu Lauras, Pierre Couget, and Vincent Chapurlat. 2008. "A Metamodel and Its Ontology to Guide Crisis Characterization and Its Collaborative Management". In *Proceedings of the 5th International Conference on Information Systems for Crisis Response and Management (ISCRAM)*, Washington, DC, USA, May, 4–7.

Blecken, Alexander. 2010. "Supply Chain Process Modelling for Humanitarian Organizations". Edited by Peter Tatham. *International Journal of Physical Distribution & Logistics Management* 40 (8/9): 675–692. doi:10.1108/09600031011079328.

Chan, Jennifer, and Tina Comes. 2014. "Innovative Research Design—A Journey into the Information Typhoon". In *Procedia Engineering, Humanitarian Technology: Science, Systems and Global Impact 2014, HumTech2014*, 78: 52–58. doi:10.1016/j.proeng.2014.07.038.

Charles, Aurélie, Matthieu Lauras, and Rolando Tomasini. 2009. "Learning from Previous Humanitarian Operations, a Business Process Reengineering Approach". In *Proceedings of the 6th International ISCRAM Conference*, Gothenburg, Sweden.

Charles, Aurélie, Matthieu Lauras, and Luck N. Van Wassenhove. 2010. "A Model to Define and Assess the Agility of Supply Chains: Building on Humanitarian Experience". *International Journal of Physical Distribution & Logistics Management* 40 (8/9), doi:10.1108/09600031011079355.

Clark, Tim, Carsten Keßler, and Hemant Purohit. 2015. "Feasibility of Information Interoperability in the Humanitarian Domain". In 2015 AAAI Spring Symposium Series. http://carsten.io/ClarkKesslerPurohit.pdf.

Colomb, Robert M., and Mohammad Nazir Ahmad. 2010. "A Perdurant Ontology for Interoperating Information Systems Based on Interlocking Institutional Worlds." *Applied Ontology* 5 (1): 47–77.

Comes, Tina. 2016. "Cognitive and Motivational Biases in Humanitarian Sensemaking and Decision-Making". In *IEEE International Multi-Disciplinary Conference on Cognitive Methods in Situation Awareness and Decision Support (CogSIMA)*, 56–62. San Diego: IEEE.

Comes, Tina, Bartel Van de Walle, Laura Laguna Salvadó, and Matthieu Lauras. 2015a. "Understanding the Health Disaster: Research Design for the Response to the 2014 West African Ebola Outbreak". *Procedia Engineering* 107 (2015): 81–89.

Comes, Tina, Olga Vybornova, and Bartel Van de Walle. 2015b. "Bringing Structure to the Disaster Data Typhoon: an Analysis of Decision-Makers' Information Needs in the Response to Haiyan." Proceedings of the AAAI Spring Symposium Series (SSS-15) on Structured Data for Humanitarian Technologies: Perfect Fit or Overkill.

Daniele, Laura, and Luis Ferreira Pires. 2013. "An Ontological Approach to Logistics'. In Enterprise Interoperability, Research and Applications in the Service-oriented Ecosystem, IWEI 2013, 26 March 2013, Enschede, the Netherlands (pp. 199–213).

Emanuele Lettieri, Cristina Masella, and Giovanni Radaelli. 2009. 'Disaster Management: Findings from a Systematic Review'. *Disaster Prevention and Management: An International Journal* 18 (2): 117–136. doi:10.1108/09653560910953207.

Fowler, Martin. 2004. *UML Distilled: A Brief Guide to the Standard Object Modeling Language.* Boston: Addison-Wesley Professional.

Franke, Jörn, Adam Widera, François Charoy, Bernd Hellingrath, and Cédric Ulmer. 2011. 'Reference Process Models and Systems for Inter-Organizational Ad-Hoc Coordination-Supply Chain Management in Humanitarian Operations'. *In 8th International Conference on Information Systems for Crisis Response and Management (ISCRAM'2011), Lisbon, Portugal.* https://hal.inria.fr/inria-00593290/.

Galindo, Gina, and Rajan Batta. 2013. 'Review of Recent Developments in OR/MS Research in Disaster Operations Management'. *European Journal of Operational Research* 230 (2): 201–211. doi:10.1016/j.ejor.2013.01.039.

Gralla, Erica, Jarrod Goentzel, and Charles Fine. 2016. 'Problem Formulation and Solution Mechanisms: A Behavioral Study of Humanitarian Transportation Planning'. *Production and Operations Management* 25 (1): 22–35. doi:10.1111/poms.12496.

Gruber, Thomas R., and others. 1993. 'A Translation Approach to Portable Ontology Specifications'. *Knowledge Acquisition* 5 (2): 199–220.

Grubic, Tonci, and Ip-Shing Fan. 2010. 'Supply Chain Ontology: Review, Analysis and Synthesis'. *Computers in Industry*, Semantic Web Computing in Industry, 61 (8): 776–786. doi:10.1016/j.compind.2010.05.006.

Guizzardi, Giancarlo. 2005. '*Ontological Foundations for Structural Conceptual Models*'. Enschede: Universiteit Twente. http://doc.utwente.nl/50826/1/thesis_Guizzardi.pdf.

Henderson-Sellers, B. 2011. 'Bridging Metamodels and Ontologies in Software Engineering'. *Journal of Systems and Software* 84 (2): 301–313. doi:10.1016/j.jss.2010.10.025.

Henderson-Sellers, B., and A. Bulthuis. 2012. *Object-Oriented Metamethods*. New York: Springer Science & Business Media.

Holguín-Veras, José, Miguel Jaller, Luk N. Van Wassenhove, Noel Pérez, and Tricia Wachtendorf. 2012. 'On the Unique Features of Post-Disaster Humanitarian Logistics'. *Journal of Operations Management* 30 (7–8): 494–506. doi:10.1016/j.jom.2012.08.003.

Humphries, Vanessa. 2013. 'Improving Humanitarian Coordination: Common Challenges and Lessons Learned from the Cluster Approach. |The Journal of Humanitarian Assistance'. *The Journal of Humanitarian Assistance*. http://sites.tufts.edu/jha/archives/1976.

Imran, Muhammad, Shady Elbassuoni, Carlos Castillo, Fernando Diaz, and Patrick Meier. 2013. 'Extracting Information Nuggets from Disaster-Related Messages in Social Media'. In ISCRAM, 791–800. Baden-Baden.

Jahre, Marianne, Leif-Magnus Jensen, and Tore Listou. 2009. 'Theory Development in Humanitarian Logistics: A Framework and Three Cases', Edited by Peter H. Tatham. *Management Research News* 32 (11): 1008–1023. doi:10.1108/01409170910998255.

Laguna Salvadó, Laura, Matthieu Lauras, Tina Comes, and Mathieu Grenade. 2016. 'A Study on the Sub-Regionalization of Humanitarian Supply Chain: The IFRC Case'. In Proceedings of the ISCRAM 2016 Conference – Rio de Janeiro, Brazil, May 2016.

Laguna Salvadó, Laura, Matthieu Lauras, Tina Comes, and Bartel Van de Walle. 2015. 'Towards More Relevant Research on Humanitarian Disaster Management Coordination'. In. Kristiansand.

Lauras, Matthieu, Frédérick Bénaben, Sébastien Truptil, Jacques Lamothe, Guillaume Macé-Ramète, and Aurélie Montarnal. 2014. 'A Meta-Ontology for

Knowledge Acquisition and Exploitation of Collaborative Social Systems'. In *Behavior, Economic and Social Computing (BESC), 2014 International Conference on*, 1–7. IEEE.

Lauras, Matthieu, Sébastien Truptil, and Frédérick Bénaben. 2015. 'Towards a Better Management of Complex Emergencies through Crisis Management Meta-Modelling'. *Disasters* 39 (4): 687–714. doi:10.1111/disa.12122.

Liu, Shaofeng, Alex H. B. Duffy, Robert Ian Whitfield, and Iain M. Boyle. 2010. 'Integration of Decision Support Systems to Improve Decision Support Performance'. *Knowledge and Information Systems* 22 (3): 261–286. doi:10.1007/s10115-009-0192-4.

Neely, Andy, Mike Gregory, and Ken Platts. 1995. 'Performance Measurement System Design: A Literature Review and Research Agenda'. *International Journal of Operations & Production Management* 15 (4): 80–116. doi:10.1108/01443579510083622.

Oloruntoba, Richard, and Richard Gray. 2009. 'Customer Service in Emergency Relief Chains'. Edited by R. Glenn Richey. *International Journal of Physical Distribution & Logistics Management* 39 (6): 486–505. doi:10.1108/09600030910985839.

Othman, Siti Hajar, and Ghassan Beydoun. 2010. 'A Disaster Management Metamodel (DMM) Validated'. In *Knowledge Management and Acquisition for Smart Systems and Services*, Edited by Byeong-Ho Kang and Debbie Richards, 111–125. Lecture Notes in Computer Science 6232. Springer: Berlin Heidelberg. http://link.springer.com/chapter/10.1007/978-3-642-15037-1_11.

Overstreet, Robert E., Dianne Hall, Joe B. Hanna, and R. Kelly Rainer. 2011. 'Research in Humanitarian Logistics'. *Journal of Humanitarian Logistics and Supply Chain Management* 1 (2): 114–131. doi:10.1108/20426741111158421.

Pinto, Helena Sofia, and João P. Martins. 2004. 'Ontologies: How Can They Be Built?' *Knowledge and Information Systems* 6 (4): 441–464. doi:10.1007/s10115-003-0138-1.

Simpson, N. C., and P. G. Hancock. 2009. 'Fifty Years of Operational Research and Emergency Response'. *Journal of the Operational Research Society* 60 (1): S126–S139. doi:10.1057/jors.2009.3.

Tomasini, Rolando M., and Luk N. Van Wassenhove. 2009. 'From Preparedness to Partnerships: Case Study Research on Humanitarian Logistics'. *International Transactions in Operational Research* 16 (5): 549–559. doi:10.1111/j.1475-3995.2009.00697.x.

UN OCHA. 2014. 'Global Humanitarian Overview'. Status Report. http://fts.unocha.orghttp://www.unocha.org/cap.

Uschold, Michael, and Martin King. 1995. *Towards a Methodology for Building Ontologies*. Citeseer. http://citeseerx.ist.psu.edu/viewdoc/download?doi=10.1.1.480.1214&rep=rep1&type=pdf.

Van Wassenhove, L N. 2006. 'Humanitarian Aid Logistics: Supply Chain Management in High Gear†'. *Journal of the Operational Research Society* 57 (5): 475–489. doi:10.1057/palgrave.jors.2602125.

Zhou, Honggeng, W. C. Benton, David A. Schilling, and Glenn W. Milligan. 2011. 'Supply Chain Integration and the SCOR Model'. *Journal of Business Logistics* 32 (4): 332–344. doi:10.1111/j.0000-0000.2011.01029.x.

# 17

# Decision Support Systems for Urban Evacuation Logistics in Practice

Marc Goerigk, Horst W. Hamacher
and Sebastian Schmitt

## Introduction

The application of operations research to the field of humanitarian logistics has been a major topic of research since about one decade ago (Altay and Green 2006; Beamon and Kotleba 2006) and has attracted an ever increasing number of researchers since (Apte 2010; Van Wassenhove and Martinez 2012).

But while numerous approaches have been successfully applied to individual scenarios (Martinez et al. 2011; Özdamar and Ertem 2015), recent surveys conclude that only few of them have been incorporated into general-purpose decision support systems (DSS) that are used in practice nowadays (Ortuño et al. 2013).

The vast majority (more than 93 percent) of the models proposed so far have been designed based on individual snapshots of the underlying data

M. Goerigk (✉)
Department of Management Science, Lancaster University, Lancaster, UK
e-mail: m.goerigk@lancaster.ac.uk

H.W. Hamacher · S. Schmitt
University of Kaiserslautern, Kaiserslautern, Germany
e-mail: hamacher@mathematik.uni-kl.de; schmitt@mathematik.uni-kl.de

© The Author(s) 2018 **523**
G. Kovács et al. (eds.), *The Palgrave Handbook of Humanitarian Logistics
and Supply Chain Management*, https://doi.org/10.1057/978-1-137-59099-2_17

instead of taking into account automated or even real-time data sources (Sokat et al. 2014).

This has been recognized as a gap between academic work and practical requirements. The main reason behind this gap is the highly fragmented landscape of stakeholders and institutions that cope with disaster management in practice. This fragmentation results in heterogeneous, isolated and incompatible IT infrastructures that make an automated gathering of all the relevant data nearly impossible.

While the European Commission raises attention to this problem and proposes specific measures to tackle it (Annoni et al. 2005), several interviews that we conducted with members of popular institutions that are participating in disaster management – namely the German Federal Agency For Technical Relief, the German Red Cross and representatives of the German fire departments – have shown that the actual implementation of these measures in practice is still far out of sight.

About this chapter: We propose the establishment of a standardized software layer whose design is kept simpler than the design proposed by the European Commission, is solely based on open standards, and targets a cost- and time-effective setup process from the beginning. Besides these differences, the target stays the same: By equipping the actors involved in the management of disasters with full-featured data warehouses that are easy and inexpensive to set up and extend while allowing for an automated exchange of information without further adjustments, this software layer is meant to minimize organizational and technological barriers not only between different institutions but also between academics and practitioners.

To detail our proposal as well as to encourage its adoption, this chapter describes an actual implementation of such a layer and its usage during a current research project that investigates the application of mathematical optimization methods to evacuation planning within an urban setting in Germany.

In section "Design and Techniques", we outline the basic design of the software layer and describe the techniques we used to implement different aspects of it. Section "Urban Evacuation in Germany" introduces the reader to the context of the aforementioned research project and its evacuation settings. The extensions we applied to the server side as well as the implementation of a graphical user interface (GUI) are described in section "Deploying the System Within the Evacuation Context". Section "Results" elaborates on the observations we made after having deployed the entire software system in practice. A conclusion is drawn in section "Conclusion and Outlook".

# Design and Techniques

Since the main target of the software layer is the minimization of organizational and technological barriers to implement relevant functionalities in form of technical modules and to exchange information between different actors in an automated way, its implementation should build on open and standardized technologies while following a simple and generic design.

## Architecture

Regarding the overall technical architecture, we chose a simple client-server topology whose actors are linked together using the Internet Protocol Suite. The communication between clients and the server is completely based on RESTful (Fielding and Taylor 2002) services which eases the development of new modules (i.e. the clients) that connect to the central software layer (i.e. the server) even further.

## Data Format

We chose the open-standard data format JSON to represent individual records as well as to compose messages that are exchanged in the form of HTTP payloads between the different actors of the overall system.

Each record is a value of the JSON type *Object* and consists of the following four key/value-pairs:

- **id** → *String*: It has assigned a unique identifier of type *String* that is immutable and serves as a reference throughout the record's life cycle. Records can be retrieved, updated or deleted using their respective *id* values as references.
- **tags** → *Object*: The *tags* value represents the actual data that is stored by the record. Its structure is not predefined but rather has to be agreed on by the subsequent clients and server-extensions. A set of records can be specified by a query. Each query either states a specific constraint on one of the key/value-pairs residing inside the *tags* value, or represents a Boolean combination of multiple other queries.
- **geometry** → *Object*: This key is optional. If it is present, the value it maps to is meant to encode a geometry in compliance with the GeoJSON

standard (GeoJSON 2016). The *geometry* key can be used to express queries in the form of spatial constraints.

- **name → *String*:** This key is optional. The value it maps to is indexed in a special way to allow for fuzzy searches and auto-complete functionalities.

Examples of actual records can be seen in Fig. 17.2.

## Storage Engine

We chose Elasticsearch (Elasticsearch 2016) as the underlying storage engine. Elasticsearch fits in perfectly with our key/value-structure and provides us with rich search capabilities and a mature query language – including an appropriate parser for user input – out of the box. We use the geo_shape type to index the *geometry* values, configured with QuadTree as the PrefixTree at a precision of 100 m. All the other values residing inside the *tags* object are indexed using the default type-mapping that is computed by the Elasticsearch engine while applying updates to the dataset.

## Webserver and Server-Side Modules

While user interfaces as well as some of the computational modules will be implemented as independent clients to our software layer, some other modules may have to work side-by-side to the server. Examples are extensions to the storage engine that provide specific aggregations of the data, or modules that allow for proprietary communications apart from the RESTful interface between separate clients. Since we chose the Node.js platform (Tilkov and Vinoski 2010) to implement all of the server-side functionalities, authors of those modules are bound to the JavaScript programming language running inside the Node.js Virtual Machine and the modularization structure that is imposed by this platform.

Our Webserver is solely implemented using the standard libraries provided by Node.js and does not depend on third party extensions. We therefore use a simple stack of HTTP-Handlers combined with a map that routes specific HTTP targets to their respective endpoints.

Figure 17.1 shows the basic interface of our implementation that exposes all the functionalities of the individual components listed above.

```
1   public interface BasicLayer {
2       Record create(JsonObject tags, Geometry geometry);
3       Record read(String recordId);
4       Record update(String recordId, String[] keyPath, Object value);
5       Record delete(String recordId);
6       RecordIterator search(String query, long offset, int maxHits);
7   }
```

**Fig. 17.1** The API of the software layer as it is exposed without applying any further extensions at the server side

# Urban Evacuation in Germany

To demonstrate the practicability of our implementation, we deployed it within the context of one of our current research projects that investigates the application of mathematical optimization methods to evacuation planning within an urban setting in Germany. This section is meant to describe this context in more detail.

We define an urban evacuation scenario as an organized relocation of humans, animals and material goods over a longer period – i.e. several days – from an endangered to a safe region. This includes the determination of respective regions, the notification of affected people as well as their transport, accommodation and lodging.

## Organizational Structure

To illustrate the process of such an evacuation in more detail, we discuss the corresponding organizational structure in Germany. The political leader who is responsible for the affected region is entrusted with mandating an evacuation as a measure to fend of danger from people. In the case of a city, this is the mayor of this city; in case of several affected cities, it is the respective chief administrative officer of the federal state. The law equips this politician with the authority to delegate his power of decision to another person of his choice. Usually the chief of the respective fire department is chosen to take over leadership in case of an evacuation. This led to the German fire departments having established special task forces that are entrusted with evacuation management and other tasks related to catastrophes and their appropriate responses in general.

Thus, the leaders of local authorities and organizations that are entrusted with security and emergency tasks are the end users of any decision support system in the field of urban evacuation logistics. These authorities and organizations are called "Authorities and Organizations that are Entrusted With Safety Tasks" ("Behörden und Organisationen mit Sicherheitsaufgaben", BOS).

## Official Guidelines for Evacuation Scenarios in Germany

Similar to other federal states, the state Rhineland-Palatinate has published official guidelines that should be followed in case of an urban evacuation (Ministerium des Innern und für Sport Rheinland-Pfalz 2002). These guidelines provide a basic evacuation plan that has to be adapted by the individual communities by providing total numbers about their demography and task forces. The guidelines summarize empirical numbers and thoughts that have been gathered throughout exercises and real world scenarios that took place all over the country throughout the last decades.

Since an evacuation is seen as a public duty, the responsible politicians have to prove their appropriate preparedness. Thus, the guidelines published by the state are widely adopted and followed by the responsible authorities.

Each instance of a process that follows these official guidelines to evacuate an urban region must reach the decisions listed below at some point in time. All those decisions are derivatives of the general question about the "who" and "where". In practice, they have to be combined with an overall schedule that answers the question about "when" to do "what". Note that these questions can be answered with the help of optimization tools (Bish 2011; Goerigk et al. 2014).

### Which Region Has to Be Evacuated?

We start our investigation by looking at the simplest scenario a decision-maker can be confronted with when he has to decide upon the region that has to be evacuated: An insecure explosive body in practice always leads to a radial region that is centred at the explosive body itself and whose radius is calculated by a simple rule of thumb that only considers the weight of the explosive body and neglects the details of the surrounding urban infrastructure.

There are other scenarios – as well as other models to determine the affected region in case of explosive bodies – that are more complex. An example is the spread of toxic gas which not only leads to regions that are hard to compute but also depend on and vary over time.

Therefore, the location of the inhabited buildings has to be included in the set of information that an evacuation process relies on. When it comes to more complex scenarios than ours, one may also require information about the topography of the affected area.

## Where to Establish Evacuation-Related Places?

**Shelters.** Those people who have no other place to go, must be provided with appropriate shelters by the public authorities. Thus, information about the demography of the affected region is crucial to retrieve any estimations on the required capacities of these shelters. Additionally, the set of possible shelters as well as information about their maximum capacities, preparation and maintenance costs have to be managed.

**Gathering Points.** People are meant to gather at the so-called gathering points to get picked up in groups. To keep both the evacuation plan itself as well as its communication simple, those places should be popular places like bus stops, pharmacies, popular buildings, big street crossings, etc. Thus, the set of such places needs to be available when coordinating an evacuation.

**Force Accumulation Places.** Large-scale evacuations sometimes require the operation controllers to mobilize external task forces. Those are usually gathered first at the so-called force accumulation places and from there on deployed in groups, instead of letting them reach the danger zone individually. Since a large gathering of emergency forces impose special demands on the technical infrastructure as well as on the traffic connections of the respective place, appropriate spots are usually chosen and listed upfront as possible force accumulation places by the local representatives of the BOS. This list is part of the required information.

**Sources of Support.** Since the evacuation of people also includes their accommodation and lodging, those people who gather at the established shelters have to be served with food, information and basic health care. All the possible sources of support like canteens, drugstores or supermarkets have to be known to the decision-makers.

## Which Routes Should Be Used by the Public Transportation?

When selecting the routes that should be used to transport the people from the gathering points to the shelters, the decision-makers not only have to know about the static structure of the street network but they also need to know about its behaviour under load. Thus, information about both the network and empirically gathered numbers concerning the traffic have to be accessible when planning an evacuation. Models that deliver estimations on traffic as it would result from the majority of people leaving the affected region by car additionally require demographic information about this region.

## Which Forces have to be Mobilized?

To decide on which forces to mobilize, the operation controllers first of all have to know about the available forces and about the time it would take to mobilize them respectively. Which and how many task forces actually are required to allow the evacuation to happen as planned, depend on both the demographic characteristics of the affected region as well as on previously made decisions like which gathering points, shelters and other places have to be established and maintained or which routes to prepare for transportation. Thus, not only information about the available task forces has to be managed but also do the information about gathering points, shelters, routes and the like has to be combined with information about the expected resulting personnel costs.

## How to Inform the Affected People?

Since many of the sirens in Germany nowadays have been shut down and replaced by personal mobile alarms, there are ongoing efforts to establish alternative systems to reach the population in case of emergency again (Bundesamt für Bevölkerungsschutz und Katastrophenhilfe 2008; Wikipedia: eCall 2016). As long as there is no such a system established, the current approach is simply to drive by car through the streets and shout out the warning texts to the people. The main problem here is the determination of the vehicle routes as well as the scheduling of the single shouts. The target is to minimize the amount of time it takes to reach all the people, and to avoid a single household to be shouted at by two different speakers at the same time.

## The End Users and Their Actual Scenario

Since the 107 fire departments in Germany synchronize each other on a regular basis considering methods, techniques and systems they deploy in practice, we may consider the "Working Group on Danger Defense" ("Arbeitskreis Gefahrenabwehr", AKGA) as being representative for the general German end-user-group that we are targeting at. They are the local representatives of the BOS at Kaiserslautern, a city within the federal state of Rhineland-Palatinate with approximately 100,000 inhabitants.

The basic scenario that is used as the starting point of our research is a radial evacuation area that spans over 2,000 m and affects more than 40,000 inhabitants of the city of Kaiserslautern. Such a scenario may result from a bomb disposal and is similar to large-scale evacuation scenarios that have taken place in the recent past, for example, in Koblenz 2011 (Wikipedia: Evakuierung in Koblenz 2016). It has been discussed and set up in cooperation with the AKGA and the German authority entrusted with bomb disposals.

## The Current "State of the Art"

The current decision-making process not only relies heavily on non-technical tools like paper maps and rulers but also lacks a unified protocol considering the access to the information that the operation managers depend on to find the right decisions in the course of an evacuation. This information is stored – if at all – in different formats and is communicated via network attached storage, email services and in some cases even via sheets of paper that are exchanged between the different actors using fax or the (non-electronic) mail service.

This leads to severe delays of several hours or even days. Therefore, the overall evacuation process can already be considerably improved by gathering all the required information in a single place and providing the decision-makers with appropriate technical tools to access it fast and in a unified way.

Furthermore, practitioners often base their decisions solely on experiences derived from previous evacuation scenarios or exercises. Usually, they do not have any scientific models at hand that provide them with forecasts based on the current scenario, or allow them to adapt their experiences gathered so far to the current scenario in a rational – or even automated – way. If such a model is to be established in practice and if it requires computers to perform its calculations, the entire input of the model has to be available and accessible in a digital form. This makes the establishment of technical tools to manage evacuation related information a necessary first step.

On the other hand, there already exist evacuation-related DSS that have been – and still are – used to conduct large-scale exercises and planning-games to generate a priori knowledge and expertise (CAE Elektronik 2013; REPKA 2016; Ministerium des Innern und für Sport Rheinland-Pfalz 2010). But except from this person-bound experience, the outcome of such systems is neither fed back into practice nor is there any synchronization mechanism to keep their input up-to-date. Thus, a large effort is needed to prepare exercises of this type on a regular basis, and the outcome of these exercises are questionable as acceptable patterns for real-world scenarios.

# Deploying the System Within the Evacuation Context

To further detail our proposal as well as to encourage its adoption, the following section describes the actual deployment of our system as it has been described in section "Design and Techniques" during a current research project that investigates the application of mathematical optimization methods to an evacuation planning process like the one described above.

## User Requirements

In the following subsection, we list typical end user requirements according to their priority, highest priority first.

### Management of Different Scenarios

The system should provide the user with the possibility to manage several, independent evacuation scenarios.

After choosing (or creating) such a scenario, the user should be able to define all the different aspects of the scenario like affected regions, gathering points, shelters and the like. These changes should be persisted for later use.

### Marking of a Radial Area

The user should be able to specify a radial area by providing the location of the centre of the circle and its radius in meter. The resulting region should be aligned to the street network, that is, whenever a building intersects the given circle and is thus marked for evacuation, each other building that belongs to the same block must also be marked as to be affected by the evacuation. A block of a building B is the set of buildings that can be "reached" starting from B without crossing any street.

### Retrieving Information About the Affected Population

The user should be provided with aggregated numbers of habitants that are affected by the current evacuation scenario. Besides categorizing people according to their medical requirements during the transportation, the BOS usually distinguishes between children, teenagers, adults and seniors because those groups result in different numbers of required task forces to support them during the transportation and the number of seats and standings in busses. Therefore, any additional information about the population regarding their medical condition and their distribution over the aforementioned classes would be of great value.

### Marking of Blocks

Marking a block means to mark all of its buildings for evacuation. Unmarking it is meant as the reverse operation. The user interface should provide the user with the ability to mark or unmark single blocks by clicking somewhere inside them. Blocks that have been marked before should be unmarked, and vice versa.

### "Intelligent" Search

If the name of a record is not known exactly, or if the searched record is known under different names, the search should propose all those candidates that have "similar" names to the one provided by the user. Furthermore, the search should work case insensitive. When typing a query, the user should be provided with suggestions for completion of the currently advancing query.

### Gathering Point Information

Having marked buildings for evacuation as well as having defined a set of gathering points, the user needs to be provided with some estimate of the expected number of people that are going to gather at the individual points to get picked up by the BOS.

## Street Network Manipulation

The user interface should provide the user with possibilities to modify the street network in the following ways:

* Block roads and/or single lanes of a road.
* Add and/or remove lanes from a road.
* Force a direction on a lane.

These modifications are seen as the complete set of operations on the street network to reproduce both real world modifications as they are applied by the BOS on purpose, as well as situations as they are imposed unintentionally by, for example, traffic, damages to streets or zones of imminent danger.

The system should also provide the user with a list of all the modifications that have been conducted so far.

## Points of Interest Warnings

The user should be provided with a list of special places that lie within the region that has to be evacuated. A place is meant to be special, if it belongs to at least one of the following types:

* School
* Kindergarten
* Senior Residence
* Hospital
* Others (explicitly marked by the BOS)

If possible, the system should provide additional information like the number of pupils of a specific school or the capacity of a hospital.

We found all of those features being well accepted by all of the different parties of end users that we were in dialog with and which spread over a wide range of different positions at the organizations that take part in emergency response. We chose an iterative and incremental development process to adapt the basic version of our software layer to meet these requirements. Each iteration started by presenting the current status of the user interface to the AKGA and afterwards agreeing on the current set of feature requests ranked by their importance to the users. Our average iteration length was three weeks. After each iteration, a software system has been developed that implemented a subset of the current feature requests completely. Thus, during the initial requirements analysis meeting at the start of each new iteration, the end users were presented with a software system that was ready to be used in practice.

## Data Import

To support user interfaces that implement features to meet the requirements listed above, as well as to support further computations on the so derived evacuation scenarios, the dataset managed by our system has to contain at least the following information:

- Where are the possible shelters, gathering points and other evacuation-related places as stated in section "Where to Establish Evacuation-Related Places?"
- Where are the homes of the people and how many inhabitants do actually live there?
- How does the street network of the city look like?

To provide this information, we imported data from different sources to our storage engine upfront. While our final vision is a broad range of customized user interfaces and computational modules that act as individual clients to our software layer and allow the daily management of all this data in place, we relied on a periodical, automated import of this data from external systems for now.

### Buildings, Streets and Points of Interest

Upfront to the initial data import, we compared the cartographic data that we have been provided with by the public authorities of the city of Kaiserslautern to a snapshot of the OpenStreetMap database by overlaying respectively rendered maps and highlighting all those features that intersected each other. This way we found that the OpenStreetMap dataset not only conforms to the officially measured one geometrically but also enriches it by providing additional semantics like street capacities, speed limits and detailed information about the so-called Points of Interest (i.e. special places like gymnasiums, stores, monuments and the like) all over the city.

Therefore, we decided to use the OpenStreetMap database as our exclusive cartographic data source. Depending on the individual context of a DSS, one may come to a different decision when looking at another city.

## Demographic Data

The public authorities of the city of Kaiserslautern also provided us with anonymized demographic data per building that we attached to the respective records in form of a specific key-to-object pair. Analogously, we attached the capacities of the local gymnasiums as they have been chosen as the set of possible shelters by the AKGA and were provided to us in form of excel sheets.

Figure 17.2 shows three examples of records after importing the different data sources mentioned above.

# Extending the Server Side

The following extensions have been implemented on top of the Node.js platform at the server side to provide the user interface – as well as other clients – with the evacuation related functionalities as they have been derived from the set of requirements listed above.

## Serving Pre-rendered Maps

The affected region is served to the clients as a pre-rendered map layer using the Web Map Tile Service (WMTS) standard (Open Geospatial Consortium 2010). The individual tiles are transferred in the form of images encoded as Portable Network Graphics (PNG) files. These tiles visualize all those buildings, that are marked for evacuation by drawing them as filled polygons on a translucent canvas. This way the client can show them as an additional tile layer to the user and is thus relieved from heavy rendering when it comes to large regions that have to be evacuated. Furthermore, simple and generic caching algorithms that result from the use of the WMTS standard can be applied to both sides, the server and the client.

# Serving Images of Buildings, Streets and Places

The same algorithm that is used to render the above-mentioned WMTS layer is used to compute images of individual records that have a value attached to the *geometry* key. Thereby, the desired dimensions of the resulting image are given by the client and the server computes the appropriate zoom level.

```
{
    "id": "AVWgbapPPWDciF3r1AUV",
    "tags": {
        "building": "home",
        "people": {
            "children": 3, "teenager": 2,
            "adults": 10, "seniors": 1
        }
    },
    "geometry": {
        "type": "Point",
        "coordinates": [7.7546343, 49.438729]
    },
    "name": "Königstraße 92"
}
```

```
{
    "id": "AVRM4HjWavectaKnDPHp",
    "tags": {
        "building": "shelter",
        "capacity": 300
    },
    "geometry": {
        "type": "Point",
        "coordinates": [7.7557577, 49.4288567]
    },
    "name": ["Barbarossahalle", "TSG Sporthalle"]
}
```

```
{
    "id": "AVY1rDtecmknSDUTqcav",
    "tags": {
        "osm_reference": "way/45073854",
        "highway": "tertiary",
        "maxspeed": 50,
        "capacity": 300
    },
    "geometry": {
        "type": "LineString",
        "coordinates": [...]
    },
    "name": "Logenstraße"
}
```

**Fig. 17.2** Basic examples of the three basic primitives

```
1    public interface EvacuationLayer extends BasicLayer {
2        void markCircle(String scenarioId, Point center, int radiusInMeter);
3        void toggleMark(String scenarioId, String recordId, EvacuationMark mark);
4        void toggleMarks(String scenarioId, String[] recordIds, EvacuationMark mark);
5        Record[] getBuildingsOfBlock(Point location);
6        void clearAllMarks(String scenarioId);
7        Image getTile(Box mapBox, int width, int height);
8        Image getMergedTile(int x, int y, int z);
9        Image getDetailImage(String recordId, int width, int height);
10   }
```

**Fig. 17.3** The interface of the server after three iterations

## Computing Blocks of Buildings

To compute block of buildings, first, the street next to the given point is chosen using the spatial index. From there on, the algorithm iterates from street to street – always using the one that results in the tightest slope around the given point – until the first chosen street is reached again. Thereby dead ends are neglected and the algorithm aborts after a fixed maximum number of streets visited.

## Estimate the Number of People Per Gathering Point

To estimate the number of evacuees that are supposed to gather at a given gathering point, we use Voronoi regions, the spatial index and appropriate intersection tests. In practice, only a fraction of the resulting number is used as the final estimation.

Figure 17.3 shows the resulting application programming interface (API) that is provided by the server. We iterated three times to reach this version. The GUI as it is described by the following subsection is based on this snapshot.

## The GUI

The final GUI provides the user with an interactive map that can be zoomed in and out, moved around and clicked or tapped to get a geographic overview as well as to search for records in a graphical way. Additionally, the user can type in a query and send it to the database. Queries are supposed to conform to the query language defined by Elasticsearch. The result of such a query is visualized afterwards by highlighting its hits (i.e. the set of records that match the given query) on top of the map in form of pins which can then be clicked or tapped upon to get a detailed view of the corresponding records. Additionally, all the tools that are implemented so far can be accessed via a menu that is designed according to the "Sliding Menu UI-Pattern" as it is seen as a current standard for app development on the Android platform (Navigation drawer 2016).

## Reaching for Platform Independence

To avoid two separate codebases for desktop and mobile operating systems, we set up an intermediate layer on top of both, the Android OS and the desktop platform. This layer consists of basic components such as buttons, images, text and containers, as well as a layout engine and a few tools to allow for platform-independent access to basic features of the underlying operating systems.

## Rendering the Map as a Stack of Map Layers

To show a rendered map to the user, we also use the WMTS standard and access a public server that deploys Mapnik (2016) as its rendering engine. These Mapnik tiles are used to show a basic layer of the map to the user. Thin clients as Android phones can thus be served with pre-rendered content that is presented to the user as a separate map layer without imposing high requirements on the underlying hardware.

The set of buildings that are marked as to be evacuated is rendered as a tile-based image that can also be delivered according to the above-mentioned WMTS standard and is drawn right above the basic map layer. All those records that are marked as either gathering points, shelters or force accumulation points are highlighted by showing pins in different colours. Numbers about affected habitants are presented by a separate dialog, whereas the approximations concerning the number of people that are supposed to gather at a single gathering point are drawn right above the pin of this gathering point.

## Viewing and Marking Records

Whenever the user clicks or taps onto the map, the area that lies below the user's pointer or fingertip is computed by the underlying platform and is sent to the server in form of a getrecordsWithin-request. If the resulting set

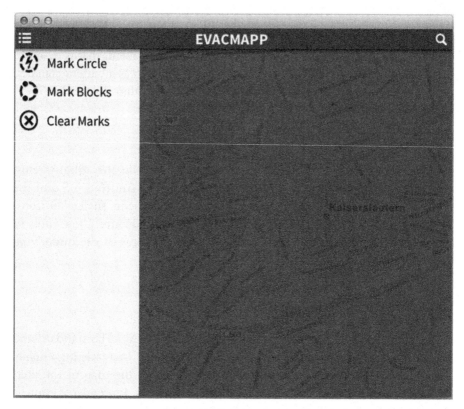

**Fig. 17.4** The basic GUI. Search is triggered via the menu bar, while other tools can be selected from the menu (© OpenStreetMap contributors)

counts more than one record, those are presented to the user in form of a scrollable list. Else, the detail view of the clicked or tapped record is shown immediately. The latter view – as well as each row of the list-view in case of several records – uses the getDetailImage-API-endpoint to retrieve an excerpt of the rendered map showing the respective record in detail (i.e. at a high zoom level). Furthermore, the user is provided with four buttons to attach single EvacuationMarks to the primitive. To apply several updates to different records at once, the user is meant to double-click or double-tap onto the individual pins consecutively. This action triggers a special menu to appear at the bottom of the map and equips the user with buttons to send different bulk-updates to the server or to discard his selection.

Figures 17.4–17.6 show screenshots of the user interface that demonstrate the basic process of setting up an evacuation scenario.

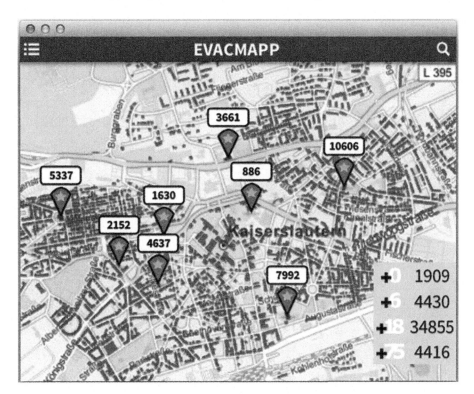

**Fig. 17.5** After specifying a set of buildings that have to be evacuated, the affected habitants are shown at the lower right. The selected gathering points have their expected number of people attached above their pins (© OpenStreetMap contributors)

## Results

All of the implemented services take advantage of the underlying Elasticsearch database managing a current excerpt from the OpenStreetMap dataset. Using these technologies, we can not only provide the end users with access to more information than they had at hand before but we are also able to manage millions of database entries simultaneously with response times constantly below 500 ms on moderate hardware (2.5 GHz intel core 2 duo with 4 GB of RAM and a hard disc drive). Furthermore, the end users are provided with rich search capabilities that were not available before. Using the Elasticsearch query language, they are now able to state queries like "all bus stops that intersect the affected region", or "all shelters that do not intersect the affected region and that provide sufficient capacity to accommodate more than 500 people".

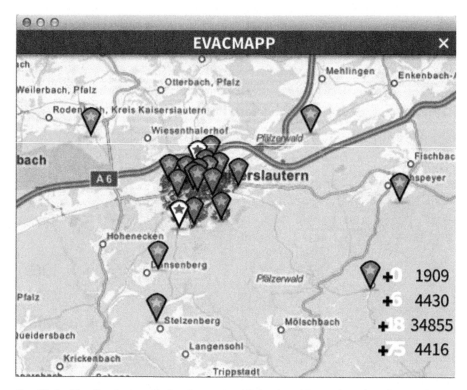

**Fig. 17.6** The final scenario has been established and is ready to be given as input to scientific modules (© OpenStreetMap contributors)

We evaluated the platform-independence and scalability of our system by importing Open Street Map (OSM) records of an entire federal state and accessing the database not only from stationary PCs running the most popular Operating Systems (MS Windows, Mac OS X, Linux) but also from different smartphones running the Android OS. Without exception, the resulting user experience has been free from delays, the GUI adapted well to the different screen sizes and complete evacuation scenarios of arbitrary scale could be set up without reaching any hardware limits on all platforms.

After a short introduction (<5 minutes) to the Elasticsearch query language, the practitioners were able to use the system without any further assistance right after the presentations that we gave during our requirements analysis meetings at the start of each iteration. The GUI was adopted well and has been in heavy use since then. If this trend continues, there are good chances for further modules to base on near-real-time data.

Several meetings of the AKGA have taken place that were attended by people who are working at emergency-unrelated departments of the municipality. They expressed interest in our system and stated that they were willing to follow future developments – trusting that they could connect their departments too. Such a development would lead to even higher potentials regarding scope, quality and actuality of the entire dataset.

In the course of a current research project that investigates the application of mathematical optimization methods to evacuation planning within an urban setting in Germany used our software system as the basic source of data. The connection to our services has been set up within hours using standard libraries of the Java programming language. Since we could not only provide an up-to-date snapshot of all the relevant information but also specific evacuation scenarios that have been defined by actual practitioners, the project could save a severe amount of effort and base its research on high-quality, real-world data.

## Conclusion and Outlook

DSS have the potential to play a vital role in the success of emergency management and planning. This chapter exemplifies the process of developing a DSS from collecting end user requirements, to suitable software solutions.

Looking at evacuation logistics as they are applied in Germany nowadays, we found the practitioners not only in need of scientific models to support them with finding decisions but we also realized the lack of technical tools to allow for the deployment of respective software systems. Therefore, we propose the establishment of a generic software layer that provides digital and uniform access to all the information that underlies urban evacuation logistics. We developed such a layer and deployed it in cooperation with local authorities that are entrusted with emergency tasks and thus are the actual end users of any evacuation-related software system in Germany.

We avoided the use of expensive and overloaded systems and developed each component of our system with typical constraints of public authorities and low budgets in mind. This way, we kept our software free of any licensing issues as well as extremely lightweight.

Following an iterative and incremental development approach that maintained a minimalistic graphical interface, the users have been able to use the individual increments to get inspired and encouraged to participate actively in the development process. We thus not only received constantly feedback but we also achieved a high acceptance of our system in practice.

We integrated all the different data sources that we were provided with by the end users as well as the OpenStreetMap database. We chose a storage engine that is known to scale horizontally and can handle several millions of data entries. All of the queries we implemented so far complete in a few milliseconds and thus can be integrated to set up an interactive toolchain.

All the different sources of information that are accessed by the AKGA nowadays have been imported to our software layer and are accessible faster and more conveniently than before. Combined with the tools that are implemented so far, like marking circles and blocks, our system replaces not only the heterogeneous and old-fashioned data sources that decision-makers have to cope with nowadays but also paper maps and rulers when it comes to the determination of the affected region.

Hence, we developed a technical platform that not only is capable of speeding up the preparation of an evacuation process from days to minutes but also provides programmatic access to all the evacuation-related information. Thus, we paved the road to the use of scientific modules within DSS in practice.

Plenty of additional DSS features are possible, such as functionalities that enable task forces to provide additional data or updates via mobile devices. Equipping them with fast access to the cameras, microphones and keyboards of their mobile phones and attaching the current time as well as their current positions to the so created records, the head of operations could be provided with an additional map layer that presents an overview of all those "messages". Besides this live-feedback, these features could also be used to track an evacuation and deliver a log file at the end, which is hard to get access to in practice nowadays, and, at the same time, is a highly desired part of the result of an evacuation.

**Acknowledgements** The authors would like to thank all the members of the BOS for supporting us with great ideas and a deep insight into their daily work, which has been the fundamental source of both our inspiration as well as our knowledge on evacuation logistics in practice. The work was partially supported by the German Ministry of Research and Technology (BMBF), Grant Numbers 13N13198 and 13N12826.

# References

Altay, Nezih, and Walter G Green. "OR/MS research in disaster operations management." *European Journal of Operational Research* 175, no. 1 (2006): 475–493.
Annoni, Alessandro, Lars Bernard, John Douglas, Joseph Greenwood, Irene Laiz, Michael Lloyd, Zoheir Sabeur, Anne-Marie Sassen, Jean-Jacques Serrano, and Thomas Usländer. "Orchestra: Developing a unified open architecture for risk management applications." Peter van Oosterom, Siyka Zlatanova, Elfriede M. Fendel (Ed.), In *Geo-information for disaster management*, 1–17. Berlin, Heidelberg: Springer, 2005.

Aruna Apte. "Humanitarian Logistics: A New Field of Research and Action", *Foundations and Trends in Technology, Information and Operations Management* 3, no. 1 (2010): 1–100.

Beamon, Benita M, and Stephen A Kotleba. "Inventory modelling for complex emergencies in humanitarian relief operations." *International Journal of Logistics: Research and Applications* 9, no. 1 (2006): 1–18.

Bish, Douglas R. "Planning for a bus-based evacuation." *OR spectrum* 33, no. 3 (2011): 629–654.

Bundesamt für Bevölkerungsschutz und Katastrophenhilfe. *Warnung der Bevölkerung mit dem Satellitengestützten Warnsystem (SatWaS)*. Bundesamt für Bevölkerungsschutz und Katastrophenhilfe, Bonn, 2008.

CAE Elektronik GmbH. *SIRA – Simulationssystem für Rahmenübungen*. CAE Elektronik GmbH, Stolberg, 2013.

*Elasticsearch*. Website. https://www.elastic.co/. Accessed April 2016. 2016.

Fielding, Roy T, and Richard N Taylor. "Principled design of the modern Web architecture." *ACM Transactions on Internet Technology (TOIT)* 2, no. 2 (2002): 115–150.

*GeoJSON*. Website. http://geojson.org/. Accessed April 2016. 2016.

Goerigk, Marc, Kaouthar Deghdak, and Philipp Heßler. "A comprehensive evacuation planning model and genetic solution algorithm." *Transportation Research Part E: Logistics and Transportation Review* 71 (2014): 82–97.

Mapnik. Website. http://www.mapnik.org. Accessed April 2016. 2016.

Martinez, Alfonso J Pedraza, Orla Stapleton, and Luk N Van Wassenhove. "Field vehicle fleet management in humanitarian operations: A case-based approach." *Journal of Operations Management* 29, no. 5 (2011): 404–421.

Ministerium des Innern und für Sport Rheinland-Pfalz. *Empfehlungen für die Planung von Evakuierungen im Rahmen von vorbeugenden Manahmen des Katastrophenschutzes*. Ministerium des Innern und für Sport Rheinland-Pfalz, Mainz, 2002.

Ministerium des Innern und für Sport Rheinland-Pfalz. *SAFER – Simulation in der Ausbildung für Einsatzkräfte in Rheinland-Pfalz*. Ministerium des Innern und für Sport Rheinland-Pfalz, Mainz, 2010.

*Navigation drawer*. Website. https://www.google.com/design/spec/patterns/naviga tion-drawer.html. Accessed April 2016. 2016.

Open Geospatial Consortium Inc. *OpenGIS Web Map Tile Service Implementation Standard*. OGC 07-057r7. 06.04.2010. Open Geospatial Consortium Inc., 2010.

Ortuño, MT, P Cristóbal, JM Ferrer, FJ Martín-Campo, S Muñoz, G Tirado, and B Vitoriano. "Decision aid models and systems for humanitarian logistics. A survey." In *Decision aid models for disaster management and emergencies*, 17–44. Amsterdam, Paris, Beijing: Atlantis Press, 2013.

Özdamar, Linet, and Mustafa Alp Ertem. "Models, solutions and enabling technologies in humanitarian logistics." *European Journal of Operational Research* 244, no. 1 (2015): 55–65.

*REPKA*. Website. http://www.repka-evakuierung.de/. Accessed April 2016. 2016.

Sokat, Kezban Yagci, Rui Zhou, Irina S Dolinskaya, Karen Smilowitz, and Jennifer Chan. *Capturing real-time data in disaster response logistics*. Technical report. Citeseer, 2014.

Tilkov, Stefan, and Steve Vinoski. "Node. js: Using JavaScript to build high-performance network programs." *IEEE Internet Computing* 14, no. 6 (2010): 80.

Van Wassenhove, Luk N, and Alfonso J Pedraza Martinez. "Using OR to adapt supply chain management best practices to humanitarian logistics." *International Transactions in Operational Research* 19, nos. 1–2 (2012): 307–322.

*Wikipedia, The Free Encyclopedia: eCall*. Website. http://de.wikipedia.org/wiki/ECall. 2016.

*Wikipedia, The Free Encyclopedia: Evakuierung in Koblenz*. Website. http://de.wiki pedia.org/wiki/Evakuierung_in_Koblenz_am_4._Dezember_2011.     Accessed April 2016. 2016.

# 18

# Advances in Network Accessibility and Reconstruction after Major Earthquakes

Andréa Cynthia Santos

## Introduction

Natural and man-made disasters have a serious impact on populations, environment and urban infrastructures, which is a consequence, among others, of the population density in urban areas. Nowadays, 54% of the world population lives in such areas UN Prospects (2016), increasing the complexity of operations in case of major disasters. Each year different kinds of disasters (floods, fire, earthquakes, hurricanes etc.) leave millions of people dead, injured or homeless and represent billions of dollars in humanitarian aid and reconstruction EMDAT (2016). This explains part of the political, scientific and community interest in improving operations post disasters. This study is a result of co-operation (collaborative project "Optimizing logistics for large scale disasters" (OLIC (2015))) between representative organizations in crisis management, in particular partners from the International Charter on Space and Major Disasters (ICSMD (2015)), and researchers trying to connect theoretical Operations Research (OR)/ Management Science (MS) models and methods with the real problems faced on the ground. The integration of ideas from both members of the International Charter and scientists was mandatory to legitimate the proposed models and approaches. Moreover, it is important to highlight that the members of ICSMD

A. Cynthia Santos (✉)
Institut Charles Delaunay, Université de Technologie de Troyes,
Troyes Cedex, France
e-mail: andrea.duhamel@utt.fr

© The Author(s) 2018                                                              **547**
G. Kovács et al. (eds.), *The Palgrave Handbook of Humanitarian Logistics and Supply Chain Management*, https://doi.org/10.1057/978-1-137-59099-2_18

involved in the project have provided a support to obtain and to treat real data from major disasters. This has allowed us to define standard inputs to the algorithms, as well as to produce outputs for rescue teams. As a consequence, the problems surveyed here have been tested using real data.

The problems were investigated for major earthquakes, which represent the third most frequent disaster type in the world, and the sixth in terms of damage caused EMDAT (2016). OR/MS foundations have been applied, together with information obtained by satellite images from ICSMD. The results were compiled to add value and produce maps with decision support information. Real data from Port-au-Prince, Haiti, in 2010 and from Kathmandu, Nepal, in 2015 was used to fix the context, define realistic scenarios and treat key points for humanitarian operators. Road accessibility to the population was a relevant issue pointed out in OLIC project. This topic should be considered in its own right and also together with other post-disaster problems, such as relief distribution, reconstruction, etc. (not necessarily in an integrated optimization model). In fact, road networks and buildings can be seriously affected after a major earthquake. The former greatly disrupts accessibility to the population which is very significant to the rescue teams and for routing supplies. The latter is relevant to the rehabilitation of the affected cities, and in some cases becomes an opportunity to improve their urban infrastructures. The earthquake in Port-au-Prince, Haiti, 2010 damaged several buildings and blocked routes, in which the blocked routes appear with different levels of disruption such as light blockage (vehicles can still access routes) and major disruption (a building fell over the route). Port-au-Prince is still suffering the consequences of this disaster in terms of urban infrastructure rehabilitation and private and public building reconstruction. Recently, in 2015, a number of earthquakes hit Nepal and damaged several historic monuments and buildings in Kathmandu. These require particular attention to achieve their restoration, starting with the careful removal of precious debris.

In this chapter, basic and complex problems concerning the accessibility to the population, the road rehabilitation problem, and methods for solving them Sakuraba et al. (2016a, b) are surveyed. For the sake of clarity, "Accessibility to the population" is a generic term used here to indicate if a path exists from starting points (referred also as origins) to destinations and how long they are. A number of trends and opportunities related to this topic are also discussed. In particular the lack of studies dedicated to long-term reconstruction phase, raising new challenges. In addition, it is important to highlight that accessibility issues can also be considered together with other problems (e.g. relief distribution) in a more pragmatic way than in previous studies. Few works considered such an aspect. For instance, authors in Yan and Shih (2009); Liberatore et al. (2014) designed optimization models combining infrastructure recovery decisions with distribution to minimize the time required for the reparation and distribution operations. Work of Liberatore et al. (2014) focuses on this problem, using multi-criteria decisions and optimizes time, cost, reliability, security and demand satisfaction. It is worth mentioning that integrated optimization models are interesting and challenging from a scientific point. However, in the context of crisis management, they do not seem to be an initial good approach to apply in the response phase and in practice, since different decision-makers such as governments, civil safety, nongovernmental organizations (NGO) and Red cross are involved in post-disaster relief operations. Each one has its own tasks, organization, coordination and way of operating. Moreover, some organizations can be even in competition. Huachi et al. (2015a, b) present an acceptable way to handle the network disruption by considering the network changes dynamically and providing vehicle routing solutions for the last mile of distribution.

Several excellent surveys can be entry points to OR/MS applied to disaster operations. For instance, relief distribution, routing and transportation, as well as models and metrics are reviewed in Anaya-Arenas et al. (2014); Caunhye et al. (2012); Huang et al. (2012). Facility location is additionally focused on by Caunhye et al. (2012). The study Diaz et al. (2013) classifies the literature into two categories of problems. The ones dedicated to "emergency management" which includes transportation, routing, supply chain and "emergency procurement logistics, and humanitarian logistics" covering aid, facility locations and resource distribution and allocation. Leiras et al. (2014) propose a systematic way to review the literature on humanitarian logistics both in terms of qualitative and quantitative models and strategies. Work by Altay and Green III (2006) presents a classification and reviews problems based on the well-known phases of disaster operations management: mitigation, preparedness, response and recovery. A number of basic concepts are presented in Ortuño et al. (2013), followed by a literature review also based on disaster phases. Among other issues, it covers problems in mitigation and preparedness phases (assessment, facility location, evacuation, inventory planning, among others), response (e.g. last mile and large-scale distribution) and disaster recovery (e.g. civil infrastructure systems, power system restoration, economic recovery, health care and mental health recovery). Moreover, work by Duhamel et al. (2016) clarifies how OR/MS strategies can improve resilience, and presents models and strategies for solving a location-allocation problem, considering the population dynamics and the type of disaster.

A number of works in the literature do not distinguish between emergency accessibility and medium and long-term accessibility. Nevertheless, accessibility covers different problems according to the time scale of a disaster. Two problems are detailed in this chapter, accessibility in the initial emergency and in the medium term, respectively, the Road Network Accessibility Problem (RNAP) and the Work-troops Scheduling Problem (WSP). RNAP can be solved by polynomial time algorithms, while the WSP appears at the interface between emergency and the beginning of the reconstruction phase, and belongs to the NP-hard class of combinatorial optimization problems. The RNAP consists of providing both an estimation in terms of time periods to make the population accessible, and defining paths to travel to target zones. Some paths can be immediately used, while others are inaccessible depending on the time period. The WSP aims at assigning Work-Troops (WT) to remove debris and improve the overall accessibility. For the sake of clarity, let a WT be composed of bulldozers, excavators, dump trucks and the human resources to pilot these equipments. Several constraints and parameters close to practice are considered by Sakuraba et al. (2016b) such as a limited number of WT, physical road limits (e.g. primary, secondary and tertiary), road blockage level (e.g. partially or complete blocked), time periods and the use of more than one WT to clean a route. The network rehabilitation dynamic is considered to update the accessibility situation per time period.

The remainder of this chapter is organized as follows. Initially, in section "Network Accessibility After Earthquakes", an overview of accessibility problems found in the literature is provided, together with a description of RNAP and WSP. Then, trends and opportunities are given in section "Trends and Opportunities". The essential data treatment, which is a key point for applying OR/MS methods in real contexts is discussed in section "Systematic Data Treatment for Network Accessibility" for RNAP and WSP, followed by examples of standard input and output maps. Finally, concluding remarks are done in section "Concluding Remarks".

# Network Accessibility After Earthquakes

In the literature, there are several studies on improving accessibility during mitigation and preparedness phases by defining recommendations to prevent major disruptions, Hu et al. (2012); Faturechi and Miller-Hooks (2015); Fiondella (2013). Furthermore, some authors investigate the emergency accessibility, while others look at scheduling WT to restore the network transportation. An overview on accessibility contributions in the response phase and applying quantitative models and strategies is given below. Then, RNAP and WSP are presented.

## Literature Review on Network Accessibility Problems

Network accessibility in the first three days of response is handled by Aksu and Ozdamar (2014). The proposed model assumes a limited number of WT, each WT can restore one route at a time and aims at maximizing the total weighted earliness of all path restoration completion times. The time period in which a road becomes available is defined by the proposed model. Instances based on the road networks of two districts in Istanbul, Turkey are used in the experiments, considering up to 49 blocked roads out of 212, and 4 to 18 WT. Study by Duque and Sorensen (2011) is dedicated to the inter-city accessibility problem and develops a hybrid heuristic (i.e. Greedy Randomized Adaptive Search Procedure with a Variable Neighborhood Descent) to define which roads should be repaired to minimize the weighted sum of the shortest paths for all destinations, with manpower and financial budget constraints. Results and analysis of the budget constraints impact are provided for a realistic instance of three regional centers in Haiti (i.e. Port-au-Prince, Les Cayes, and Cap Haitian) after the quake in 2010.

Highway restoration considered by Yan and Shih (2007) is modeled using a network indexed over time, referred to as time-space network. The authors assume a WT repairs a single road at a time and present a flow-based model which optimizes the repair time. Experiments are addressed using an instance of Nantou County, Taiwan with 24 damaged points and 24 WT. Highways emergency rehabilitation, that is, up to 72 hours is addressed in Feng and Wang (2003). Thus, the authors assume that it is possible to do repairs in the critical and chaotic period of emergency. A multi-objective model is optimized in a given priority order for the following three objectives: maximizing the length of usable roads, maximizing the number of nodes with injured people that can be accessed by roads, referred to by the authors as maximizing the number of lives saved, and minimizing the risk of working in sensitive areas. Experiments have also been carried out in an instance of Nantou County, Taiwan, considering 10 damaged nodes and 3 WT. The restoration of roadways in the main arteries of Taiwan rural areas is modeled using an integer multiple-commodity network flow in Yan et al. (2014). The order of repairs is implicitly handled by the model as the possibility of routing vehicles flow on a specific road. The goal is to minimize the maximum time required to repair all highway segments and the model is tested over the instances from Yan and Shih (2007).

Scheduling problems to improve accessibility in the medium and long term have been investigated by Chen and Tzeng (1999). The authors Chen and Tzeng (1999) propose a bilevel model, where the first level considers the

WT scheduling and the second level addresses the asymmetrical assignment traffic model. The fuzzy multi-objective bi-level model is solved by means of a genetic algorithm, using an instance with 4 WT and 10 blocked routes.

## Road Network Accessibility Problem

The main decisions about and answers to RNAP rely on the time required to arrive at points (destinations) on an urban network and the order to repair routes, restoring or improving (i.e. access destinations faster) the network connectivity. However, some characteristics impose specific operations to treat accessibility problems properly. For example, removing debris is very different from doing majors repairs, as illustrated in Fig. 18.1. Here, both RNAP and WSP focus on accessibility and removing debris. The problem of repairs requiring long civil engineering, is discussed in section "Trends and Opportunities".

The RNAP is defined in a graph $G = (V,E)$, where $V$ and $E$ stand respectively for the set of vertices and edges, defining the urban transportation network. The vertex set $V = O \cup D \cup T$, where $O$, $D$ and $T$ are respectively the origins (network nodes to be defined, e.g. humanitarian aid points, WT origins and others), destinations (nodes to be accessed) and the transshipment nodes. In addition, $t_{ij} \in N$ is the estimated time required to repair an edge $[i,j] \in E$, and $p_j$ is the population at every destination $j \in D$. It should be noted that the volume of debris can be computed using data treatment of satellite images based on the debris volume. Moreover, the population can migrate after an earthquake. Thus, an estimation of population per area based on satellite images, using the habitable surface still available and the spontaneous points of inhabitant grouping can also be computed. Traveling costs (time) are assumed to be irrelevant to available edges, while the number of

**Fig. 18.1**   Examples of severe route damage, Nepal 2015 (Source: Quanjing, 2016)

time periods required to restore/clean a blocked edge is considered as its costs. Thus, if $[i, j] \in E$ is blocked, $c_{ij}$ is equal to the number of time periods to remove debris in $[i,j]$ using a single WT, otherwise $c_{ij} = 0$. RNAP has been mathematically modeled as a flow-based model by Sakuraba et al. (2016b), where a unit of flow is sent to each destination. Whenever several origins are available, an artificial node is used to connect all origins. The objective is to provide an overview estimation of the number of periods required to arrive at each destination, defined by variables $y_i \geq 0$ associated with every node $i \in D$. Implicitly, the solutions indicate the edges in the path to arrive at large population areas, blocked or not. One may note that, the objective function can be weighted by the number of inhabitants to define a priority on populated regions. It allows us to analyse the impact on repairing/ cleaning the blocked routed (modeled by edges) in such paths. Another factor is that if an area is difficult to access in the emergency phase, alternative transportation vehicles can be deployed like helicopters or drones.

Figure 18.2-(a) depicts a simple example of an instance for RNAP, where the gray nodes correspond to destination (D = {5, 6, 8}). There is a single starting point (O = {0}), dashed lines indicate impassable routes, and the number of periods required to repair them are also presented. Available edges cost are set to zero since the traveling times are assumed to be less than a unique repair on the given blocked routes (edges). Fig. 18.2-(b) and (c) show two solutions, where $p_i$ is the number of inhabitants at $i$ and $y_i$ is equal to the number of time periods required to arrive at each destination. The first solution in Fig. 18.2-(b) has a blocked edge, that is [0, 3], while the second one has two disrupted edges [2,3] and [4,8]. However, the second

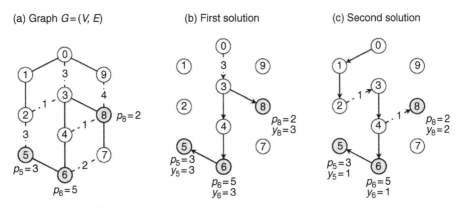

**Fig. 18.2**  Examples of an instance and solutions to RNAP

**Fig. 18.3** Graph for Port-au-Prince, Haiti

solution requires less effort and allows the destinations to be reached in fewer time periods than the first solution, even if two blocked routes are considered in the paths. It is worth mentioning that the destination 8 can be reached faster than in the second solution (see Fig. 18.2-(c)) by using the path $\{0,1,2,3,8\}$, that is, $y_8 = 1$.

This problem can be easily solved by a shortest path algorithm, such as Dijkstra or Bellman-Ford, where costs are the number of periods to arrive at each destination. The algorithm complexity is relevant since the urban graphs can be very large. For instance, the Port-au-Prince graph representing its urban transportation network has 16 660 vertices (origins, destinations and transshipment nodes) and 19 866 edges (road segments), as depicted in Fig. 18.3. Djikstra's algorithm can be implemented using a binary heap in $O(m \log n)$ Cormen et al. (2009), where $m$ and $n$ correspond, respectively, to the number of arcs and vertices of a given graph. Note that undirected graphs can be transformed in directed ones. Thus, edges can be represented by arcs.

In spite of the simplicity of this problem, it quickly provides important insights to a decision-maker. A basic example concerns the available resources, whenever they do not allow the proposed routes to be repaired/cleaned, accessibility can be ensured by other kinds of vehicles as mentioned earlier.

## Work-Troops Scheduling Problem

Studies Sakuraba et al. (2016a, b) present a cutting edge model for the WSP. In particular, this model allows ground dynamics to be integrated, the mathematical model is indexed per time period with constraints not still handled in the literature, and the heuristic methods are fast which allow new parameters to be updated and solutions to be reoptimized, whenever necessary. Moreover, significant aspects not still treated by previous works have been considered. For example, the road network connectivity constraints together with the WT scheduling are done using a flow model. In addition, more than one WT can work to repair a route according to its physical limitations and relevance to the network connectivity. Furthermore, it considers an overall urban area relying on large-scale graphs. Last but not least, the model and methods have been designed with experts in situation on the ground, and data treatment received as much attention as the model and methods (section "Systematic Data Treatment for Network Accessibility").

The following input parameters are used. The road network is represented by a graph $G = (V, E)$ as previously defined, where the origins and destinations belong to the set of vertices. The origins contain the information about the number of available WT, while destinations have an estimation of population. The edges also have parameters stating their distance and the amount of time periods necessary to repair them, if they are blocked. Without loss of generality, "an edge repair" means the route represented by the corresponding edge will be repaired. A limitation on the number of WT that can work simultaneously on a route is given for each edge according to the type of route (primary, secondary and tertiary), as well as the number of WT is assumed to be known in advance. It is important to mention that the estimation of population and the volume of debris are computed from satellite images. A pro of this data treatment is that it gives the state of the situation, that is, population migration, volume of debris, etc. in real-time and a con is that weather conditions can disturb getting satellite images.

The mathematical model uses two levels of flow: one level to follow the evolution of the shortest paths from origins to destinations and network connectivity, and the second level to ensure WT arrive at the destination if and only if there is a path to route them. Moreover, the objective function is weighted by the number of inhabitants. According to this objective function, priority is given to populated regions. The model selects edges, requiring repairs such that resource constraints are satisfied. It decides the assignation of WT to edges' extremities, how many WT to be sent for blocked edges, and in which time period the repairs will be performed. The goal is to reduce the shortest paths, considering populated areas as priority. The mathematical model gives a formal definition of the problem, which is very relevant in the scientific context. However, it is time consuming for large-scale graphs. Thus, Sakuraba et al. (2016a, b) propose simple and efficient heuristics described below, able to address the problem in real cases.

A relevant result observed in the experiments with the mathematical model is that the allocation of WT in the first time period is determinant to obtain good quality solutions in terms of accessibility to the population. Using this information, the authors in Sakuraba et al. (2016a) propose ranking heuristics which work as follows. Initially, blocked edges are classified to repair in a priority order. The first ranking heuristic (H1) basically classifies edges according to the gain on the objective function used in the mathematical model. The second ranking heuristic (H2) classifies blocked edges according to the number of times they appear in shortest paths to destinations. Once the ranking is done, both heuristics allocate available WT on-the-fly to repair edges (routes) in the order they appear on the classification. This is done without violation of the constraints (e.g. number of WT, route limitations, etc.). In Sakuraba et al. (2016b), more sophisticated heuristics have been proposed, named Lexicographic Classification Heuristic (LCH). LCH uses several criteria to choose edges to be repaired such as time required to repair, the reduction on the shortest paths to destinations and the size of population at destinations. The allocation of WT is done by time period, ensuring constraints are satisfied. LCH performs better than H1 and H2. Moreover, LCH results are close enough to the optimal solutions achieved by CPLEX (i.e. up to 2.7% from optimal solution values) using simulated instances.

The choice of doing simple, but efficient heuristics in Sakuraba et al. (2016a, b) and not metaheuristics is justified by the connection with practice. In fact, operators are constantly receiving radio messages informing them about unexpected events, for example, an apparently intact building finally collapses, earthquake aftershocks frequently occur (especially in the first days), equipment like bulldozers fails, the trucks to evacuate the ruins can be late, a dumping site may become saturated, etc. Thus, several simulations need to be done to answer the many "what if?". In conclusion, metaheuristics and other methods can also be developed, providing that they will not consume much time, which is crucial in this context.

In summary, several points have been overcome in studies Sakuraba et al. (2016a, b) such as a model closer to the ground situation, efficient heuristics able to run in a real context, systematic production of inputs and outputs maps (see section "Systematic Data Treatment for Network Accessibility"), and validation by disaster operators for this kind of problem. Moreover, several interesting problems for further research have emerged during this collaboration.

## Trends and Opportunities

Several interesting decision problems that can be solved by means of OR/MS strategies, appear on road accessibility and city reconstruction. Figure 18.4 illustrates a simple classification covering some of these problems, and in particular some problems with lack of methods, mathematical models, etc. The problems are separated according to time scale since this has a major impact on the choice of models and methods to solve them, on the objectives to be targeted, among other aspects. For instance, in an emergency, relevant information for a decision-maker is how quickly one can access population areas and identifying which paths can actually be used according to the situation on the ground (population migration,

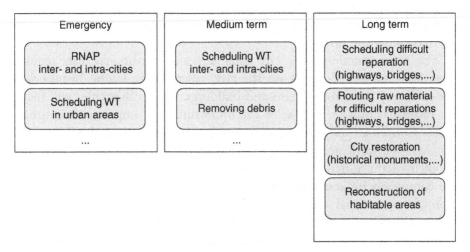

**Fig. 18.4** A classification of problems to clean and reconstruct cities after a major earthquake

congestion, blocked roads, etc). For this purpose, RNAP can produce an answer efficiently, providing the data is available. Scheduling emergency WT can also be done for critical tasks like security. A building which is threatening to collapse may have to be secured, and in some cases early demolition may have to be anticipated. In the emergency phase, the important thing to keep in mind is that there is no time for long resolution methods, and that the operators on the ground are essential and, in some cases, more appropriate to get good decisions. In spite of that, maps with decision information such as the ones shown in section "Systematic Data Treatment for Network Accessibility", see Figs. 18.5 and 18.6, can be a very useful support.

In the medium term (covering the frontier between the emergency and the weeks after an earthquake), several combinatorial optimization problems can be properly treated with a global gain on the overall operations. One example is the intra-city WSP presented in this survey. For other problems, such as removing debris, there is clearly a lack of studies. In an emergency, debris is sometimes just pushed to one side of a street. On the contrary, in the medium term, they are removed to specific areas. Debris comes from the road network but also from buildings. Dealing with this situation relies on a vehicle routing problem (VRP) with some interesting characteristics such as multi-trips. This problem can be integrated into WSP in some cases, whenever the responsible for such operations are handled by a co-ordinate team. Otherwise, gains from integrating WSP into the corresponding VRP model in a unique optimization model can be lost in practice due to the lack of coordination between the involved teams. Removing debris of monuments and historical zones is a different problem since each piece needs to be classified and numbered. This allows the puzzle to be put back together in the reconstruction phase.

The reconstruction of a city after a major earthquake can require months/years, and depends on the city: towns with a long history will try to restore their monuments and buildings, while other cities will focus on reconstruction or may seize the opportunity to improve their urban areas. Combinatorial optimization problems are found in this phase for the road network accessibility and reconstruction. For the former, the problems require major and difficult civil engineering work as the routes are completely broken (e.g. Fig. 18.1). The scheduling and the transportation of raw material are examples of problems. In terms of highways and infrastructure reconstruction, there are works in the scientific literature as mentioned in section "Network Accessibility After Earthquakes". For the latter, it can be an opportunity to reorganize urban areas better and also to construct resilient buildings able to resist earthquakes.

# Paths map

*Shortest paths from origins to warehouses and population gathering points*

**Nodes**

◉  Origins

▲  Destination - population gathering points

□  Warehouses

**Network**

———  Shortest path from the origin to a warehouse or population gathering point

------  Road

N

0        2.5        5
▬▬▬▬▬▬▬▬▬▭ Km

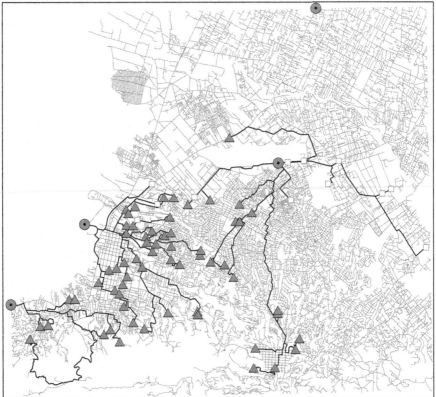

**Fig. 18.5**  Example of maps with a RNAP solution for Port-au-Prince, Haiti

# Gradient map

*Distances from the origins*

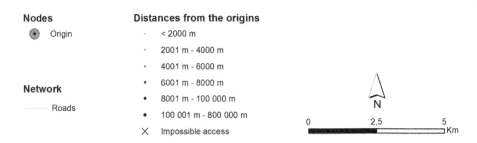

**Nodes**

⊙ Origin

**Network**

——— Roads

**Distances from the origins**

·    < 2000 m

·    2001 m - 4000 m

·    4001 m - 6000 m

•    6001 m - 8000 m

•    8001 m - 100 000 m

●    100 001 m - 800 000 m

✕    Impossible access

N

0       2,5       5
━━━━━━━━━━━━━━━━ Km

**Fig. 18.6** Example of map with a gradient determining the accessibility of the overall urban network for Port-au-Prince, Haiti

# Systematic Data Treatment for Network Accessibility

Many studies in the literature have tested methods using realistic instances, that is, only a part of the data is real. The data and parameters required to solve just-in-time decision problems is still a challenge that was partially overcome in OLIC project. In fact, full-scale test was done in 2015 with the quakes that struck Nepal. Data from several sources was combined: satellites images, real time information from social networks, Geographical Information Systems (GIS), etc. An interesting and prospective study by Bono and Gutiérrez (2011) applies similar ideas to data treatment to handle road network accessibility.

The road network, including the type of routes (primary, secondary and tertiary) was recovered from GIS and database as Google earth and Openstreetmap for RNAP and WSP. Then additional information was added to edges and nodes of the final graph. The blockage levels were computed by the volume of debris and added as a parameters of edges, while the population estimation are attached to the nodes. Relevant information such as hubs, depots, points where spontaneous population gatherings happened, was distinguished from other nodes in the graph. Dimensioning the human and material resources has been done for Port-au-Prince based on past information. The evolution of the network accessibility is then updated according to the dynamics on the ground based on satellites images treated in the ICSMD.

Figs. 18.5 and 18.6 are examples of maps with added decision information produced in OLIC project. Fig. 18.5 illustrates a RNAP solution for Port-au-Prince some hours after the quake in 2010, where the gray circles, the gray triangles and the squares represent respectively the origins (Port, Airport and relevant road entry points), points where spontaneous population gatherings happened, and the depots of supplies. The RNAP solution is given and shows the best paths to arrive at the target gathering points of population. Fig. 18.6 provides an estimation in meters on the accessibility to regions in the city by means of a gradient. The smaller the black circles are, the faster the access (paths from origins to destinations) to the corresponding region is.

Several experts working on disaster operations from different organizations have analysed the maps produce in OLIC project. The feedback from them is that they expect OR/MS methods to remain decision-support information, rather than a tool to replace human decisions. Moreover, it is important to make clear the criteria used to set up solutions. Thus they can choose from the various possible solutions, the ones which seem the most relevant to the context and the so many subjective appreciations.

## Concluding Remarks

Post-disaster operations are a very rich topic, both in terms of theoretical and practical issues. In this context, there are many opportunities to apply OR/MS strategies to improve operations on the ground in case of major catastrophes: providing data is available and the decision-making operators trust the solutions generated by the OR/MS methods. Some initiatives have contributed to overcoming these obstacles such as OLIC project, and consortia like the ICSMD.

Road accessibility and reconstruction problems after major earthquakes are crucial for a return to normal life. In this context, an overview of the available literature for road accessibility problems has been done in this chapter. Moreover, two problems, the RNAP and WSP, have been described, together with methods and main results. RNAP and WSP are the initial problems faced on road accessibility and provide a base for studies on this subject.

Data remains a critical factor for producing solutions in the initial response phase of a disaster. Although difficult, it is not an impossible task due to technological advances and available computational tools (GIS, collaborative platform as Openstreetmap, etc). Considerable efforts based on relevant information from satellite images have been made in the past 15 years, which it is now possible to exploit. Other technologies such as sensor networks, drones, etc. can also support information gathered in the field. In any case, parameters required to run methods for decision problems can already be used in the time scale of a disaster.

Finally, a picture of trends and opportunities involving road network accessibility and reconstruction in the emergency, medium term and long term has also been developed. It is easy to see that there is still room for further research on the development of mathematical models and methods for such problems. In particular, it is relevant to investigate how to connect existing OR/MS methods for solving real-life problems. In this context, sometimes less is more and the goal is to provide good, just-in-time solutions using scalable and efficient methods.

# References

Aksu, D. T., & Ozdamar, L. (2014). A mathematical model for post-disaster road restoration: Enabling accessibility and evacuation. *Transportation Research Part E: Logistics and Transportation Review, 61*, 56–67.

Altay, N., & Green III, W. G. (2006). OR/MS research in disaster operations management. *European Journal of Operational Research, 175*, 475–493.

Anaya-Arenas, A. M., Renaud, J., & Ruiz, A. (2014). Relief distribution networks: A systematic review. *Annals of Operations Research, 223*, 53–79.

Bono, F., & Gutiérrez, E. (2011). A network-based analysis of the impact of structural damage on urban accessibility following a disaster: The case of the seismically damaged Port au Prince and Carrefour urban road networks. *Journal of Transport Geography, Special section on Alternative Travel futures, 19*, 1443–1455.

Caunhye, A. M., Nie, X., & Pokharel, S. (2012). Optimization models in emergency logistics: A literature review. *Socio-Economic Planning Sciences*, Special Issue: Disaster Planning and Logistics: Part 1, *46*, 4–13.

Chen, Y.-W., & Tzeng, G.-H. (1999). A fuzzy multi-objective model for reconstructing the post-quake road-network by genetic algorithm. *International Journal of Fuzzy Systems, 1*, 85–95.

Cormen, T. H., Stein, C., Rivest, R. L., & Leiserson, C. E. (2009). *Introduction to Algorithms* (3rd ed.). MIP Press, London, UK.

Diaz, R., Behr, J., Toba, A.-L., Giles, B., Ng, M., Longo, F., & Nicoletti, L. (2013). Humanitarian/emergency logistics models: A state of the art overview. In *Proceedings of the 2013 Summer Computer Simulation Conference* (pp. 24:1–24:8), Toronto, Canada.

Duhamel, C., Santos, A. C., Brasil, D., Châtelet, E., & Birregah, B. (2016). Connecting a population dynamic model with a multi-period location-allocation problem for post-disaster relief operations. *Annals of Operations Research*, Special issue OR Confronting Crisis, *247*(2), 693–713.

Duque, P. M., & Sorensen, K. (2011). A GRASP metaheuristic to improve accessibility after a disaster. *OR Spectrum, 33*, 525–542.

EMDAT (Access 2016). EM-DAT - The international disaster database. http://www.emdat.be/publications.

Faturechi, R., & Miller-Hooks, E. (2015). Measuring the performance of transportation infrastructure systems in disasters: A comprehensive review. *Journal of Infrastructure Systems, 21*, 04014025:(1–11).

Feng, C., & Wang, T. (2003). Highway emergency rehabilitation scheduling in post-earthquake 72 hours. *Journal of the Eastern Asia Society for Transportation Studies, 5*, 3276–3285.

Fiondella, L. (2013). An algorithm to prioritize road network restoration after a regional event. *In Proceedings of the IEEE International Conference on Technologies for Homeland Security* (pp. 19–25), Waltham, USA.

Hu, Y., Liu, X., & Jiang, Y. (2012). Overviews of failure mode and reconstruction of road traffic facilities in Wenchuan earthquake-stricken areas. *Procedia Environmental Sciences, 12*, 615–627.

Huachi, P., Santos, A. C., & Prins, C. (2015a). Last-mile distribution in post disaster relief. In 6th International triennial workshop on Freight Transportation and Logistics (Odysseus) (p. 4p), Ajaccio, France.

Huachi, P., Santos, A. C., & Prins, C. (2015b). Uma heurística para o problema de roteamento de veículos com frota heterogênea e múltiplos depósitos aplicadas à distribuição pós-catastrofes. In *XLVII Simpósio Brasileiro de Pesquisa Operacional (SBPO), Porto de Galinhas*, (pp. 4118–4129), Brazil.

Huang, M., Smilowitz, K., & Balcik, B. (2012). Models for relief routing: Equity, efficiency and efficacy. *Transportation Research Part E: Logistics and Transportation Review, 48*, 2–18.

ICSMD (2015). International Charter on "Space and Major disasters". https://www.disasterscharter.org.

Leiras, A., de Brito Jr, I., Peres, E. Q., Bertazzo, T. R., & Yoshizaki, H. T. Y. (2014). Literature review of humanitarian logistics research: Trends and challenges. *Journal of Humanitarian Logistics and Supply Chain Management, 4*, 95–130.

Liberatore, F., Ortuño, M. T., Tirado, G., Vitoriano, B., & Scaparra, M. P. (2014). A hierarchical compromise model for the joint optimization of recovery operations and distribution of emergency goods in humanitarian logistics. *Computers & Operations Research, 42*, 3–13.

OLIC (2015). OLIC project - Optimizing logistics for large scale disasters. https://www.csfrs.fr/recherche/projets-en-cours/OLIC.

Ortuño, M. T., Cristóbal, P., Ferrer, J. M., Martín-Campo, F. J., Muñoz, S., Tirado, G., & Vitoriano, B. (2013). Decision aid models and systems for humanitarian logistics. A survey. In B. Vitoriano, J. Montero, & D. Ruan (Eds.), *Decision aid models for disaster management and emergencies, 7*, 17–44.

Quanjing (Access 2016) - Beijing Quanjing Visualization Network Co. Ltd. Quanjing.com.

Sakuraba, C. S., Santos, A. C., & Prins, C. (2016a). Work-troop scheduling for road network accessibility after a major earthquake. *Electronic Notes in Discrete Mathematics, 52*, 317–324.

Sakuraba, C. S., Santos, A. C., Prins, C., Durand, A., Bouillot, L., & Allenbach, B. (2016b). Road network emergency accessibility planning after a major earthquake. *EURO Journal on Computational Optimization, Special Issue on Disaster Risk management, 4*, 381–402.

UN Prospects (Access 2016). United nations, population division, world population prospects. http://esa.un.org/unpd/wpp/.

Yan, S., & Shih, Y.-L. (2007). A time-space network model for work team scheduling after a major disaster. *Journal of the Chinese Institute of Engineers, 30*, 63–75.

Yan, S., & Shih, Y.-L. (2009). Optimal scheduling of emergency roadway repair and subsequent relief distribution. *Computers & Operations Research, 36,* 2049–2065.

Yan, S., Chu, J. C., & Shih, Y.-L. (2014). Optimal scheduling for highway emergency repairs under large-scale supply. *IEEE Transactions on Intelligent Transportation Systems, 16,* 2378–2393.

# 19

# Information Technology in Humanitarian Logistics and Supply Chain Management

Dorit Schumann-Bölsche

## Introduction

Information technologies change rapidly in a complex and dynamic environment with opportunities and challenges for humanitarian logistics and supply chain management (SCM). Some of the technologies are innovations from the past few years whereas others have been established since decades. One example for an established technology is the mobile phone in combination with Short Message Service (SMS) for replenishment of humanitarian aid in sub-Saharan Africa. Examples for newer technologies are drones and big data with several applications after acute disasters such as earthquakes in Haiti and Nepal, floods on the Philippines and epidemics in Western Africa (see, e.g., Meier 2015). It can be stated that the access to information technologies differentiates between countries, regions, and their development status; with impacts on their access and values for humanitarian logistics and the people in need (ITU 2015). Which is the value of information technology (IT) solutions for humanitarian logistics and SCM? There is no general answer. It differs in dependence of the region, the kind and scale of a disaster and the special application of the technology in humanitarian logistics and SCM. Before going into detail to answer the question the definition, aims and goals of humanitarian logistics are needed.

D. Schumann-Bölsche (✉)
German Jordanian University, Amman, Jordan
e-mail: Dorit.Schumann@gju.edu.jo

© The Author(s) 2018
G. Kovács et al. (eds.), *The Palgrave Handbook of Humanitarian Logistics and Supply Chain Management*, https://doi.org/10.1057/978-1-137-59099-2_19

Humanitarian logistics is defined as "the process of planning, implementing and controlling the efficient, (cost-) effective flow and storage of goods and materials, as well as related information, from the point of origin to the point of consumption for the purpose of alleviating the suffering of vulnerable people (Thomas and Kopczak 2005)". The aims and goals are part of the definition: efficient, effective and for the purpose of alleviating the suffering of vulnerable people. It is that part of humanitarian aid which should bring the right products of humanitarian aid, to the right people, at the right time, in the right quality, in the right amount and to the right costs, especially in the aftermaths of acute or permanent disasters and crisis. With a good or even optimal logistics service the supply is quick, save and reliable. If the right goods (e.g. food and medicines) are received by the right people (the most affected people and people in need), at the right place, at the right time (as fast as necessary) and with the right quality (e.g. high quality of food items or medicine even in situations of extreme weather), then humanitarian logistics can contribute to alleviate the suffering of vulnerable people. Often it even can save lives. The right logistics costs (e.g. for IT, human re-sources, food, and non-food items) are part of the aims, as well. If humanitarian organizations lower the logistics costs, they can use the budget for the core tasks of humanitarian aid. The application of information technologies in humanitarian logistics and SCM must be geared to these aims of logistics service and logistics costs, which are often conflicting ones (Blansjaar and Stephens 2014; Bölsche and Herbinger 2014). "Humanitarian technology refers to the use and new applications of technology to support efforts at improving access to and quality of prevention, mitigation, preparedness, response, recovery and rebuilding efforts" (Vinck 2013; Sandvik et al. 2014).

This chapter focuses on information technologies which are able to meet the aims and goals of humanitarian logistics and SCM. It addresses researchers, students, practitioners and politicians, who are interested in integrating information technologies into concepts and applications for humanitarian logistics and SCM. An introduction to the relevance of the topic is presented in section "Relevance and Empirical Data", where empirical data with regard to IT, logistics, disasters, development and health is presented from international reports and statistics. From a broad variety of information technologies, which are assigned to the disaster management cycle in section "Information Technology in the Disaster Management Cycle" some adequate technologies for humanitarian logistics and SCM are presented with their chances, challenges and open research questions in more detail in section "Examples for Information Technologies in Humanitarian Logistics – Status Quo and Open Questions". These are: mobile phones, single-board computers, drones and big data. Concepts and applications from logistics and SCM are presented, for example, replenishment with mobile phones in sub-Saharan Africa as well as temperature and humidity control with single-board computers, cash and voucher solutions to supply refugees inside and outside camps. In addition some new information technologies and their application for humanitarian logistics and SCM are presented: drones and big data. Open research questions in section "Examples for Information Technologies in Humanitarian Logistics – Status Quo and Open Questions" address in particular lacks in the current conceptual research in integrating the technologies into humanitarian logistics and SCM. In the last section an evaluation approach is presented.

## Relevance and Empirical Data

Why does humanitarian aid need innovative logistics concepts? And why does humanitarian logistics need information technologies? Which humanitarian technologies are available and which suit best to meet the above mentioned aims and goals? The answers could be based on worldwide statistics, literature analysis and existing applications. The Human Development Report, the World Health Statistics, reports from the UN Refugee Agency UN HCR, the Annual Disaster Statistical Review, the Logistics Performance Index (LPI) from the Worldbank and the Information Society Report are suitable to give some fundamental background. The mentioned statistics about human development, health, refugees and disasters document the need of humanitarian aid in general (UN DP 2015; WHO 2016; UN HCR 2016; Guha-Sapir et al. 2015). In addition, reports about logistics performance and technologies give further insights for the chapter regarding strengths and weaknesses in logistics and relevant information technologies (Arvis et al. 2016; ITU 2015). In addition to the empirical chapter the state of the art will be completed by literature and experiences from own experiences and research activities, especially in the three countries Germany, Jordan and Cameroon.

In Table 19.1 some selected values from reports about human development, health and refugees are given. Three different human development groups are selected, and for each group one country as an example: Germany, Jordan and Cameroon. These three countries are typical for their corresponding development group and will be addressed in this publication (Abushaikha and Schumann-Bölsche 2016; Schumann-Bölsche and Schön 2015).

The data in Table 19.1 document that there are tendencies for a higher rate of poverty, lower rate of population living in urban areas and higher mortality rates in countries with a lower human development index. For sub-Saharan Africa can

Table 19.1 Statistics and indicators about human development, health and refugees (UN DP 2015; WHO 2016; UN HCR 2016)

| Example for human development index group | Human development Index, from 0 (lowest) – 1 (highest) 2015 UN DP 2015 | Population living on less than US$1.25 per day, % average 10 years UN DP 2015 | Living in urban areas % 2014 UN DP 2015 | Life expectancy at birth years 2015 WHO 2016 | Malaria incidence, per 1000 population at risk 2013 WHO 2016 | Total refugees and total population of concern total amount, 2015 UN HCR 2016 |
|---|---|---|---|---|---|---|
| Germany (very high human development) | 0.916 (Rank 6) | – | 74.3 | 81.0 | – | 749,309 |
| Jordan (high human development group) | 0.748 (Rank 80) | 0.1 | 83.4 | 74.1 | – | 689,053 |
| Cameroon (low human development group) | 0.512 (Rank 153) | 27.6 | 53.8 | 57.3 | 271,8 | 459,650 |
| ... | ... | ... | ... | ... | ... | ... |
| World | 0.711 | – | 53.5 | 71.4 | 98.6 | 63,912,738 |

be stated that droughts and hunger occur regularly and that life expectancy is comparatively low. Droughts are the most frequent kind of disasters in sub-Saharan Africa. Experiences from the past show that the negative impacts on the population are particularly high in countries with situations of political instability, crisis or war. For the year 2015, 528 disasters are reported; 90 million people were affected and 30,000 died. In comparison to more industrialized regions the impacts in Africa are significant higher numbers of deaths and victims and significant lower economic damages (Guha-Sapir et al. 2015). These are just some values from the broad spectrum of data in reports on development, health and disasters, which also incorporate data about a broad range of health, education, nutrition, gender equality, infrastructure for energy and sanitation, etc. (Guha-Sapir et al. 2015; UN DP 2015; WHO 2016). The UN Millennium Development Goal Report summarizes: "The region continues to lag behind. More than 40 percent of the population in sub-Saharan Africa still lives in extreme poverty in 2015" (UN MDGs 2015, p. 15). Lower life expectancy, higher mortality and malnutrition rates, lower educational level, less people living in urban areas – all these are situations for African countries which become even more apparent for the regions of sub-Saharan Africa. Many challenges have to be addressed to overcome the existing situation, for example, the supply with food and medicines must be enhanced and there are necessities to improve the infrastructural situation as well as education and political conditions. In the following some IT applications for humanitarian logistics are presented, some of them are especially suitable for humanitarian logistics in sub-Saharan African countries. When addressing these challenges special circumstances such as heat, humidity, power outages and others have to be taken into account.

Logistics performance in less-developed countries is comparatively low (see Table 19.2) and the distribution of mobile phones is worldwide – and even in low income countries – high (see Table 19.3). In 2016 the World Bank published the fifth edition of the LPI which compares the logistics performance of 160 countries in the world regarding six components: The efficiency of customs, the quality of trade and transport infrastructure, the ease of arranging competitively priced shipments, the competence and quality of logistics services, the ability to track and trace consignments, and the frequency of scheduled delivery times (Arvis et al. 2016). For each of the six components the value is determined between 5 (highest value) and 1 (lowest value). The summarized LPI is documented in Table 19.2 for three countries, with Germany on rank 1 with the highest LPI (4.23), Jordan ranked 67th and Cameroon ranked 148nd (LPI: 2.15) from 160 counties. Whereas Germany and Jordan could rise the overall LPI in comparison to the former report from the year 2014 (Germany from 4.12 to 4.23 and

**Table 19.2** Statistics and indicators about logistics performance (Arvis et al. 2016 and 2014)

| Country: | Logistics performance, 2016 rank | LPI: Logistics performance index 2016, between 1 (lowest) and 5 (highest) | Lead time, import 2016 days for port and land | Transport costs import, in US$ for 40 foot dry container (from 2014) |
|---|---|---|---|---|
| Germany | 1 | LPI: 4.23 | 7 | 2,218 |
| Jordan | 67 | LPI: 2.96 | No data available | 2,125 |
| Cameroon | 148 | LPI: 2.15 | 21 | 5,281 |

Jordan from 2.87 to 2.96); the LPI for Cameroon is lower than 2 years before (from 2.30 to 2.15) and also the ranking is lower from 142 to 148. Two important details for effectiveness and efficiency are given in the table: The average import lead time for containers, which is in Cameroon three times higher than in Germany, and the corresponding costs, which are in Cameroon more than double as high as in Germany and Jordan (from the 2014 survey; they are not published in the 2016 LPI report).

Reasons for lower efficiency and effectiveness are analysed and documented in publications, which focus on logistics and logistics processes in (sub-Saharan) Africa. Some of the reasons are administrative processes for customs clearance in combination with a high bureaucracy; conditions of infrastructure at the seaports, the airports, streets and bridges; conditions of the means of transport; several check and control points and corruption. On a wider macro-level reasons can be found in the financial and political situation of many African countries. Unstable, extreme weather conditions and daily power failures due to a fragile electricity network aggravate the situation. Furthermore well-educated personnel and IT infrastructure are missing. One of the problems most countries in sub-Saharan Africa do have is the lack of connectivity within supply chains and global networks. In many cases the IT systems used in African supply chains are incompatible with each other, thus, many organizations and logistics providers use paper-based documentation instead of IT systems. Visibility, transparency and controllability of supply chains are not possible within this situation. This leads to congestions of sensitive hubs (like ports and central distribution hubs), long leading times and high costs of operation (Abushaikha and Schumann-Bölsche 2016; Buatsi and Mbohwa 2014; Kessler 2013; Maathai 2010; Schöpperle 2013). In the following especially IT and the corresponding IT infrastructure are addressed.

Regarding ITs this publication refers in Table 19.3 to the report "Measuring the Information Society" from the International Telecommunication Union

**Table 19.3** Statistics and indicators about information society

| Region/country | ICT rank | Mobile/cellular phone subscribers, per 100 population in 2014 | Costs for mobile-cellular sub-basket US$ per month in 2014 | Internet users (%) % of population in 2014 | Costs for fixed-broadband basket US$ per month in 2014 |
|---|---|---|---|---|---|
| Example for 1: Germany | 14 | 120.4 | 18.02 | 89.5 | 46.37 |
| Example for 2: Jordan | 92 | 147.8 | 4.96 | 60.0 | 30.28 |
| Example for 3: Cameroon | 147 | 75.7 | 16.22 | 6.5 | 40.45 |
| World | | 92 | | 43.4 | 30.40 |

Data from ITU (2015)

(ITU; 2015). The overall index about IT is a mixture of the three components access (40 percent), use (40 percent) and skills (20 percent), which themselves consist of a huge amount of IT data from each country. Details are documented in the ITU (2015) report. One main commonality to the LPI ranking from above can be stated: Whereas developed countries are usually ranked on top levels (Germany on rank 14) most of the developing countries – and especially those from sub-Saharan Africa – constitute the end of the ranking (Cameroon on rank 147 from 167 listed countries).

Regional differences in the access and use of the technologies can be observed and measured. Mobile phones are highly distributed worldwide with 92 mobile phone subscribers per 100 population in 2014 (and 97 in 2015), and even in developing countries the distribution rate is high (e.g. Cameroon with 76 subscribers per 100 population). Worldwide the urban population is covered widely by mobile-cellular signals, but even the covering rate of the rural population is high with 98 percent in Europe, 87 percent worldwide and 79 percent in Africa with a rising trend. The access and use of Internet in 2014 is considerably lower: only 43 percent of the worldwide population is Internet user, and there is a huge difference between developed countries 82 percent (Germany 89 percent) and developing countries 35 percent (Cameroon 6 percent). One aim is to make the Internet accessible for 55 percent of the worldwide population until 2020. The growth of the Internet of Things – a combination of the Internet with physical objects – is stated as 70 percent per year since 2002. For humanitarian logistics those information technologies which require an Internet access cannot be applied in regions where the Internet is not accessible. Transferring big data or even small data via the Internet is possible in those regions where an Internet access is available, stable and fast enough for the application. Many applications for humanitarian logistics need an access or transmission of data via the Internet, such as 3D printing in humanitarian logistics, for example, for humanitarian aid in sanitation (McNamara and Marsillac 2013; Tatham et al. 2015); drones, enterprise resource planning systems, tracking and tracing are other examples – most of them require a transfer of data. Furthermore, huge cost differences can be observed, some of them are documented in Table 19.3. Costs for fixed broadband as shown in Fig. 19.1, but also for mobile pre- and post-paid broadband are high, especially for African countries. In relation to the average income per person in the countries the differences between the countries and technologies become even more substantial (ITU 2015).

In addition to quantitative data the ITU report also refers qualitatively to the 2015 UN Millennium Development Goals and the new UN Sustainable Development Goals (SDGs) from 2015 with its 2030 agenda (UN MDGs 2015; UN SDGs 2015). The new set of goals aims to end poverty and hunger

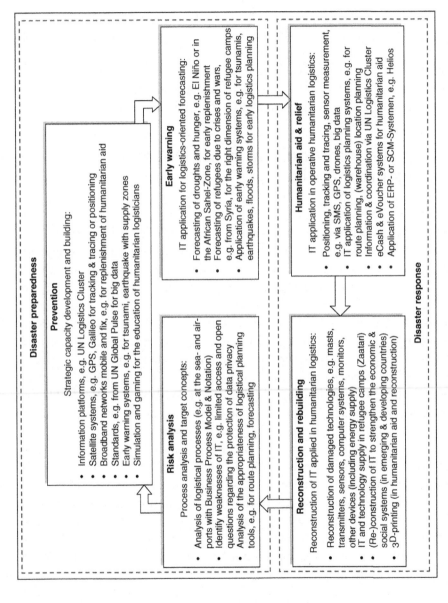

**Fig. 19.1** Information technologies in the disaster management cycle

**Disaster preparedness**

**Prevention**

Strategic capacity development and building:

- Information platforms, e.g. UN Logistics Cluster
- Satellite systems, e.g. GPS, Galileo for tracking & tracing or positioning
- Broadband networks mobile and fix, e.g. for replenishment of humanitarian aid
- Standards, e.g. from UN Global Pulse for big data
- Early warning systems, e.g. for tsunami, earthquake with supply zones
- Simulation and gaming for the education of humanitarian logisticians

**Early warning**

IT application for logistics-oriented forecasting:

- Forecasting of droughts and hunger, e.g. El Niño or in the African Sahel-Zone, for early replenishment
- Forecasting of refugees due to crises and wars, e.g. from Syria, for the right dimension of refugee camps
- Application of early warning systems, e.g. for tsunamis, earthquakes, floods, storms for early logistics planning

**Humanitarian aid & relief**

IT application in operative humanitarian logistics:

- Positioning, tracking and tracing, sensor measurement, e.g. via SMS, GPS, drones, big data
- IT application of logistics planning systems, e.g. for route planning, (warehouse) location planning
- Information & coordination via UN Logistics Cluster
- eCash & eVoucher systems for humanitarian aid
- Application of ERP- or SCM-Systemen, e.g. Helios

**Disaster response**

**Reconstruction and rebuilding**

Reconstruction of IT applied in humanitarian logistics:

- Reconstruction of damaged technologies, e.g. masts, transmitters, sensors, computer systems, monitors, other devices (including energy supply)
- IT and technology supply in refugee camps (Zaatari)
- (Re-)construction of IT to strengthen the economic & social systems (in emerging & developing countries)
- 3D-printing (in humanitarian aid and reconstruction)

**Risk analysis**

Process analysis and target concepts:

- Analysis of logistical processes (e.g. at the sea- and airports with Business Process Model & Notation)
- Identify weaknesses of IT, e.g. limited access and open questions regarding the protection of data privacy
- Analysis of the appropriateness of logistical planning tools, e.g. for route planning, forecasting

by 2030; future should be one where living on less than $1.25 a day is a thing of the past. The ITU report explains how technologies are able to contribute to the Development Goals with an ICT 2020 agenda and related goals: Growth, inclusiveness, sustainability, innovation and partnership (ITU 2015).

Open questions and weaknesses must also be mentioned with regard to the empirical studies presented above. A compilation of the data from different sources is challenging. Regions, continents and developing groups are merged differently from each other in the reports. For future research activities regarding the empirical data some new standards for the grouping of data is needed and could be one topic for future research activities.

# Information Technology in the Disaster Management Cycle

Information technologies in humanitarian logistics are changing rapidly. The technologies are related to a typical disaster management cycle from preparedness to response and back again, in which a continuous improvement of IT, humanitarian logistics and humanitarian aid is aimed. Actual surrounding conditions, technological innovations and experiences from the present and past must be considered when IT for humanitarian logistics should be identified, applied and evaluated. The following Fig. 19.1 documents for each phase of the cycle suitable technologies for humanitarian logistics and SCM. Some of them are more strategic-oriented, others are suitable for ad hoc operative humanitarian logistics processes during the humanitarian aid response phase. More detailed descriptions about the mentioned technologies in Fig. 19.1 are available (e.g. Abushaikha and Schumann-Bölsche 2016; Altay and Labonte 2014; Harke and Leeuw 2015; Huth and Romeike 2016; Meier 2015; Schmitz 2013).

Some technologies and activities can be allocated to all stages of the disaster management cycle, for example, the UN Global Logistics Cluster. On the strategic level of disaster preparedness the Cluster creates standards with regard to coordination, logistics and technologies. In addition maps with regional basic logistics information are built up and available on the Logistics Cluster webpage. On the more operative level of disaster response actual logistic-oriented information is available, for example, about closed bridges and streets, the situation at the airports and seaports, capacities in the warehouses and for transport and a tracking and tracing system. Risks are analysed on the basis of evaluation and feedback from the users. Important adjustments from the past few years are the renewing of the webpage, the development of the tracking and tracing system RITA (Relief Item Tracking Application) and new activities in social networks. In the year 2014 the UN Global Logistics Cluster was active in 13 operations, with 160 involved organizations, 670 new webpages with 330 thousand views and in addition numerous blogs, tweets and posts in social media. The biggest and most expensive operation in the year 2014 was Ebola in Western Africa with 20 thousand affected people. The activities of the Cluster have a broad range from typical logistical activities – such as the establishment of a logistics hub, tracking and tracing, and the coordination of transport and storage – to the development of a telecommunication cluster for the affected countries Liberia, Guinea and Sierra Leone (Altay and Labonte 2014; Birge 2013; UN Logistics Cluster 2014 and 2016).

# Examples for Information Technologies in Humanitarian Logistics – Status Quo and Open Questions

From the broad range of information technologies, which are available for humanitarian logistics and SCM (shown in Fig. 19.1) some are described more deeply in this publication: mobile phones with SMS, single board computers, drones and big data. The four technologies address the variety and diversity of humanitarian technologies. From established to innovative IT; from low-cost IT solutions to high investments; with different rates of access and usage and which need different IT skills from education and training. Each application must consider the different conditions in the countries and in dependence of the kind of disaster. Despite all technological innovation we should bear in mind that "man remains irreplaceable" (Jorio 2016; Merckens and Schneider 2013).

## Mobile Phones

In most countries of the world mobile phones are still established. In comparison to other technologies mobile phones provide some important advantages, which suit well to the aims and goals of humanitarian logistics regarding effectiveness and efficiency: In their application they are capable to save at once time and money, the technology is reliable, and in addition their rate of accessibility and usage is currently the highest regarding existing technologies for international humanitarian logistics (see Table 19.3). Whereas landline wires and web servers often fail during disaster and crises, cell phone towers typically withstand extreme weather events and other harsh conditions (Korenblum 2012). In the disaster management cycle the mobile phone technology belong especially to the stage of humanitarian aid and relief, but further applications are feasible.

Some first mobile phone applications in humanitarian logistics from 2008 to 2010 can be identified as the first documented ones. In 2008 mobile phones were used for cash transfers to vulnerable people in Kenya during the post-election violence. Beneficiaries lived in insecure and remote rural areas where adequate supplies of food were locally available. The Haiti earthquake in 2010 can be identified as one of the most documented adaption of the mobile phone technology in humanitarian aid and logistics, where text messages sent by trapped survivors became crucial catalysts for humanitarian logistics (ALNAP 2016; Korenblum 2012; Parker 2016; Sandvik 2014). Two further applications are described more deeply: "SMS for Life" and "mobile cash and vouchers".

"SMS for Life", a pilot project from sub-Saharan African documents, that efficiency and effectiveness of physical replenishment can be enhanced by the application of mobile phones in humanitarian logistics and SCM in the collaboration between private enterprises and public health organizations. The enterprise Novartis uses text messages via mobile phones in combination with SMS and electronic mapping technology to track stock levels for malaria medicine at public health facilities in Tanzania (and later for other diseases in further sub-Saharan countries). The replenishment of medicines in rural areas is supported by the SMS-generated stock-level information with an improved access to essential malaria medicines and in consequence a reduced number of deaths from malaria via eliminating stock-outs. The core of the solution is the use of SMS messaging between the health facilities that dispense antimalarial medicines and their district medical officers who are responsible for treatment availability in the districts. The first pilot pro-gramme was conducted in 2009/2010 over a period of 7 months in three districts in Tanzania, covering 229 villages, 5,000 health facilities and a population of 1.2 million people. Stock-outs for malaria medicine have been reduced from 79 percent to less than 26 percent in the districts. Stock-outs can thus be avoided or restocked within one or two days whereas in the past this would have taken 1 or 2 months. The costs are less than US$80 per health facility per year. SMS for Life is a flexible logistical solution, which is expandable to other countries and products. In Tanzania it has been applied to tuberculosis and leprosy medicines, and the project has been rolled out to other countries (Kenya, Ghana, Democratic Republic of Congo and Cameroon). Adaptions of the project can lead to further innovations, for example, the ideas can be transferred to cooled logistical processes for medical products, to food and non-food items in humanitarian aid, and the results can be integrated into a broader process analysis for logistical processes in sub-Saharan African countries (e.g. Buatsi and Mbohwa 2014; Kessler 2013; Mc Guire 2015; Novartis 2016; Schöpperle 2013; UN Foundation 2016).

Other applications of mobile phones in humanitarian logistics focus on refugees and the delivery of humanitarian aid to refugees (see data in Table 19.1). Mobile cash and vouchers are good solutions to enhance effectiveness and efficiency of humanitarian logistics for refugees. By the end of 2015 displacement has surpassed 63 million people. The main contributing factor has been the war in the Syrian Arab Republic with effects on neighbouring countries such as Jordan, but also on Europe. The Syrian Arab Republic remained the largest source country of refugees, with a refugee population of more than 4.8 million by end 2015. A broad distribution of mobile phones amongst Syrian refugees has been noticed and documented, especially to use the phone as a compass and map, to keep contact with family and friends and to gain information about the countries and regions. The development of mobile phone applications for humanitarian logistics must consider the different conditions in the source and host countries of refugees and on their route. Instead of shipping bags, relief organizations use mobile phone networks to distribute electronic cash vouchers where viable. Mobile cash and vouchers are sent directly to mobile phones through SMS and recipients can withdraw cash or goods at identified merchants. This reduces shipping and other overhead costs, speeds up delivery and requires fewer staff for humanitarian aid and logistics. Mobile cash can be used in supermarkets inside or outside refugee camps, where refugees can buy their food and other goods what is less degrading for refugees as standing in line for aid. Mobile cash systems would save considerable amount of travel time, queuing time and offer quicker response to their needs (Abushaikha and Schumann-Bölsche 2016; Habekuß and Schmitt 2015; IFRC 2013; UN HCR 2016; Zeug 2015).

But also gaps are documented regarding usage, acceptance rates and logistical processes. One citation from Oxfam's mVoucher project in Somalia for non-food water and sanitation items characterizes these gaps: The logistics supply chain was very long and costly and regional retailers had been integrated too late into the logistics chain. Furthermore education and training for retailers and logisticians was missing with special regard to the voucher system. Other problems arose from the beneficiaries who requested vouchers electronically but did not pick the goods for sanitation up physically. As a consequence the pilot project was reduced in a first correction from an aimed amount of 50 thousand goods to 5 thousand and finally the project was realized with 3 thousand deliveries via the voucher system. There are needs to combine the technical aspects of IT with the planning, design and application of the physical HSCs. With regard to the "SMS for Life" project research question arise, as: Which are the impacts of Vendor Managed Inventory (VMI) on the involved actors and beneficiaries? In this concept the responsibility for inventory management is transferred from traditional orders by the health facilities and medical officers to the supplier, in this case Novartis (Abushaikha and Schumann-Bölsche 2016; Chopra and Meindl 2016; O'Donnell 2015).

## Single Board Computer

A single board computer can be a fast and low-cost temperature and humidity control system for humanitarian logistics in sub-Saharan Africa. One option for a small, low-cost computer with sufficient processing power is the Raspberry Pi. This single-board computer of the size of a credit card was developed by the British Raspberry Pi Foundation and costs in dependence of the model between US$25 and 35. It is easy to implement, to use and to maintain and works effectively (fast and reliable). A light bulb is one possible solution for an alarm system which is in the off-status if the temperature is within the required temperature zone and is switched on by the Raspberry Pi, if the temperature leaves this zone. A sound system could be integrated alternatively or additionally. Furthermore the alarm system could be connected to a mobile phone network sending SMS in case that a defined temperature zone is left. The visibility and transparency within the supply of medicines, vaccines and food have positive impacts on the quality of the products and therewith a positive impact on the health of the inhabitants, for example, in sub-Saharan Africa (Bell 2013; Raspberry Pi Foundation 2016; Schön et al. 2014; Schumann-Bölsche and Schön 2015). In the disaster management cycle from Fig. 19.1. such a temperature and humidity control system can be assigned to the early warning systems, but the technical development of solutions for humanitarian logistics is part of the prevention phase and applications of single board computers are additionally conceivable in further parts of the disaster management cycle. To verify, if such systems meet the aims and goals of humanitarian logistics, different factors have to be considered, for example, personnel requirements, power requirements and overall costs, all of them with open research questions.

   With regard to the operative usage by personnel the monitoring system is easy to understand – even for people with little educational background, as the alarm system provides immediate and understandable information about temperature and humidity. Nevertheless, it is beneficial to have a person with IT affinity on-site as well as Internet connectivity close-by (with access to online manuals) because Raspberry Pi and other single-board computers come without any installed programmes. Other open questions concern the education of personnel and IT experts, for example, open access learning environments for African students and other locals could be build up (Harke and Leeuw 2015; Kessler 2013). Concerning the power requirements possible energy failures must be considered, especially in developing countries. Power packs can be connected to the Raspberry Pi and the sensor network. As the energy failure usually happens without warning, the power pack needs to be connected to the system continuously to avoid system failures. Such power packs have a limited operating life and need to be changed regularly. Alternatives could be, for example, self-sufficient systems with renewable energy. The Raspberry Pi costs are given above, but to make it fully usable, further components are necessary, for example, monitor, radio receiver, sensor, power-pack, cable, keyboard, mouse, adapter, connectors, batteries, etc. All needed parts added up create costs of approx. US$300–400 (market prices in the EU). For each application a detailed calculation is needed, which considers the special application and requirements. If African countries succeed in negotiating special prices from vendors and retailers, quantity discounts in case of higher amounts or second hand products, the overall costs could possibly be reduced. In addition, shipping costs and customs have to be taken into account if some of the products are not available in African countries and personnel costs could arise if further education and training is necessary. The single-board computer can be substituted, for example, by another type such as Banana Pi, and the components of the sensor network could be replaced, as well. Alternative systems to a single-board computer are notebooks, tablet PCs and mobile phones. Further investigations are necessary to decide if the investment is advisable or not, for example, considering the effects of visibility including reduced waste and higher potencies of medicines, vaccines and food (Schön et al. 2014; Schumann-Bölsche and Schön 2015).

## Drones

The application of drones in humanitarian logistics and SCM is in the discussion and practical implementation since few years. In the military the technology of drones is still established and applied as IT but also in a wider sense as a technology for physical processes, for example, as a transport mode. In terms of an demarcation from the military drones are applied in the humanitarian context under headlines such as "drones for good" (UAE

2016). In the disaster management cycle drones are especially assigned to disaster response, because of their application in the direct aftermaths of a disaster within the first hours and days of humanitarian aid and relief. But in the prevention phase of disaster preparedness it is necessary to build up original and primary maps for vulnerable regions, so that a comparison is possible before and after the occurrence of a disaster; the technology of drones must be developed and the application must be trained. Successful implementations of drones in the logistical processes of disaster preparedness and disaster response are documented, for example, after the typhoon Haiyan on the Philippines and in the aftermaths of two devastating earthquakes in Nepal in the year 2015. Compared to the application of satellites, maps could be generated faster and with a higher resolution by drones. The maps show in 2D or 3D images the location and scale of destruction and can be compared with the primary situation. For humanitarian logisticians this is useful and valuable information about the condition of infrastructure and impression of destruction, location of affected population and needs for humanitarian aid. Maps and images from drones are important sources for further planning, design and execution of humanitarian logistics. In addition to the generation of maps drones can be applied for sensory measurements, for example, to measure the contamination after explosions on chemical plants or nuclear power plants and in cases of biological contamination. Drones reach regions where logisticians do not have any access or restricted access. The implementation as an IT can be exceeded to a transport mode in humanitarian logistics as drones are able to load few kilograms (in dependence of their configuration) so that small amounts of humanitarian relief goods can be transported even into regions, where epidemics or contaminations appear (HumTech 2015; Meier 2015; UAE 2016).

But there is a huge amount of critical and unsolved problems in the implementation of drones in humanitarian logistics, beneath them: Missing international standards and code of conduct, open questions of security and data privacy protection, high costs, small carry loads and short operation times; and in a wider context the impact on people, society and environment. With a focus on security the question arises how the air space above an affected region can be protected in a way, that mutual hazards between drones and other flying objects (airplane, helicopter or others) can be avoided. Additional hazards from drones for the affected population or other humans caused by accidents or other hazards must be avoided. Beside security aspects the influence of applied drones on the population must be considered with a broad spectrum from negative to positive side-effects. Negative effects can be fear of the unknown flying object or just a feeling of disturbance, as reported from Nepal with hundreds of drones in the sky. In contrast people and humanitarians relate to positive effects from drones in Western Africa during the Ebola epidemic. Pictures from drones about prohibited zones paled by huge fences could enhance the comprehension of the people outside the restricted areas. With the images from the drones they were able to understand what happened inside the fences (Jorio 2016; Meier 2015). Future research is necessary to solve open questions and unsolved problems. For humanitarian logisticians interesting fields for research activities should consider interdisciplinary research at the interfaces of the technology "drone", management and logistics, humanitarian aid, legal systems, politics and ethics. In all these fields a need of empirical, methodological and application-oriented demand of interdisciplinary research can be stated.

## Big Data

Big data is another innovation from the past few years with opportunities and challenges for humanitarian aid and humanitarian logistics. A first "Guidance for Incorporating Big Data into Humanitarian Operations" was published in cooperation with several UN organizations and universities in 2015 (Whipkey and Verity 2015). Big data refers to large and/or complex datasets that go beyond the capabilities of people and traditional software to capture, store, manage and analyse them in their entirety. They can be characterized by the four Vs, which represent "Volume – great volume", "Variety – various modalities", "Velocity – rapid generation" and "Value – huge value and low density". For the purpose of humanitarian logistics, big data can be applied in situations with a large amount of data coming from different sources with an automated data collection and data analysis for information, communication and the decision-making process. In this process they can be used to answer where the affected populations are, where they come from and where are they going to, what they need and which gaps need to be addressed. Typically they are not alternatives to the above-mentioned information technologies rather they build up complementary IT solutions and networks on a high level of development. Big data come, for example, from email, SMS, websites (e.g. UN Logistics Cluster), messaging and mobile apps, photo and video sharing, social media, blogs and tweeds, satellites, drones, security cameras, mobile phone tracking, tracking and tracing, passport tracking, radio and television transmissions, sensors, facial recognition, etc. In the disaster management cycle (Fig. 19.1) big data are denominated several times; they can be applied in all phases of the cycle and in various realizations in humanitarian logistics (Gray et al. 2016; UN Logistics Cluster 2016; Whipkey and Verity 2015).

Since the 2010 Haiti earthquake, several examples for big data application in humanitarian aid and logistics are documented. Within few days an SMS life line for Haiti was established including translation from Creole into English, and a battle with the huge amount of big data was described. Up to 1 year after the earthquake movements of Haitian inhabitants were tracked with mobile data from a mobile provider with 85 percent accurateness in predicting locations. In the aftermaths of the earthquake a cholera epidemic occurred in Haiti with further implementations of big data use. Informal sources from Twitter and HealthMap were able to make the epidemic trend in volume available 2 weeks earlier. The informal "big" data was available in real-time as opposed to official data which was released after a delay. Using informal big data provides earlier insight into the evolution of an epidemic, which had positive implications for disease control measures, humanitarian logistics planning and ultimately saved lives. Some of the experiences from Haiti could be transferred and expanded in Nepal 2015 where big data from mobile phones and SMS were integrated with data from drones, images and tweets as a basis for humanitarian logistics planning and execution (Meier 2015; Whipkey and Verity 2015).

In 2015 the UN World Food Programme (WFP) started a new mobile phone flagship Global Pulse which aims to analyse how real time data from mobile phone usage could support networks in fighting hunger and in supporting humanitarian logistics. The analysis of Call Detail Records (CDRs) collected by mobile phone operators provides real-time insights about human behaviour, their communication and movement during critical events. Privacy and anonymity play a central role in the UN Global Pulse projects. While the content of the voice call or SMS will not normally be recorded, the basic facts (metadata, e.g. the calling and called connections, time and duration of calls, use of services as SMS, the location IDs of the cells in use) are routinely captured under CDR. First ideas are documented to integrate information and data about the Syrian conflict, refugees and refugee camps into the UN Global Pulse project. Applications for the support of refugees on route are still in their initial phase (Abushaika and Schumann-Bölsche 2016; ACAPS 2016; Rutherford 2015; UN Global Pulse 2016).

The existing challenges in the use of big data in humanitarian logistics are enormous and as a consequence demands for research activities still exist and will arise in the future. The challenges concern technical solutions; in addition non-technical factors have to be considered including political, legal, cultural (including language) and commercial dimensions. The limited access to technologies and vulnerable infrastructure, for example, in developing countries and vulnerable regions, would limit the amount of big data that can be reported and collected. In addition there is a need for qualified professionals. IT experts, logisticians and interdisciplinary educated people are missing in most parts of the world, and especially in developing countries. Focusing on humanitarian logisticians they must be able to ensure the validity of the data, and to integrate them with planning systems for logistics and SCM. Furthermore there are needs to develop standard list of protocols and nomenclatures adhering to established humanitarian ethics and principles with privacy and beneficiary confidentiality in datasets. The use of IT for collecting and processing data in humanitarian settings engenders dilemmas concerning data responsibility. There is a trade-off between increasing the efficiency of humanitarian action and protecting the privacy of beneficiaries in crises (ACAPS 2016; Kumar and Vidolov 2016; Meier 2015; Montjoye et al. 2014; Sandvik et al. 2014; Whipkey and Verity 2015; UN Global Pulse 2016; Vinck 2013).

Open research questions are mentioned above for each presented IT. Therewith the last chapter does not deal with research questions but with introducing ideas for an evaluation approach for the choice of information technologies in humanitarian logistics and SCM.

## Concluding: An Evaluation Approach

For humanitarian organization it is not important to choose the most innovative technology, rather the choice should be oriented at the contribution of the technologies to the aims and goals of humanitarian aid and humanitarian logistics. In the introducing chapter a definition as well as the aims and goals for humanitarian logistics are given; they refer to "the purpose of alleviating the suffering of vulnerable people" and to logistics service and logistics cost, so that the evaluation approach is geared to these basic principles.

- Logistics service in dependence of the IT in humanitarian logistics: With a high or maximal logistics service the suffering of vulnerable people can be alleviated or eliminated. IT influences logistics effectiveness (e.g. speed, reliability, flexibility).
- Logistics costs in dependence of the IT in humanitarian logistics: With low or minimal logistics costs there is more money available for the core tasks of humanitarian aid. IT influences logistics efficiency. Calculations must consider cost effects in both directions: Costs for IT in humanitarian logistics have an increasing effect, but they possibly lower other cost

components in humanitarian logistics and a waste of the available budget for humanitarian aid.

These both aims and goals are in many cases conflicting ones. For example the costs for single-board computers are in comparison to other technologies comparatively low; in the same time the positive effects on the logistics service by the use of sensor measures and warning systems are quite low, as well. In contrast the costs and investments for big data solutions – with high potentials for humanitarian logistics – are for some countries, regions and organizations too high, so that an implementation is not possible for them (especially in developing countries and rural areas). Consequently decisions about IT in humanitarian logistics neither should be geared one-sided to the logistics service nor one-sided to the logistics costs. High effectiveness of technologies has its (high) price. Each decision about the choice and application of information technologies in humanitarian logistics should be oriented on the organizations strategy and objective. Criterions of exclusion should be defined and used for the purpose of monitoring if the application of the technology is excluded because of technical, ethical, legal, political, other constraints or risks. Unreasonably high risks and technological dependencies should be excluded (Chopra and Meindl 2016; Blansjaar and Stephens 2014; Huth and Romeike 2016).

A further evaluation and decision support for the choice of information technologies can be based on a scoring model because of multiple objectives, aims, goals and decision criteria for humanitarian logistics. This model is able to integrate logistics costs and logistics services with their different specifications and other decision criteria such as risks, integration and coordination and others, which are relevant for information technologies humanitarian logistics and SCM. Such constraints which are not part of the exclusion criteria can be part of the scoring model, for example, the required energy supply and educational level for the implementation and application of the technology, the possibilities to use the technology in rural areas and the influence of the technology on the further economical and societal development of the region. In its evaluation the scoring model assigns scores for each IT and decision criteria and weights them in relation to the proportionate significance of the decision criteria. Finally all weighted scores are summed up for each technology to its total score. The scoring model is one model which enables organizations to evaluate information technologies in humanitarian logistics and SCM. Some weaknesses can be mentioned, for example, the subjective assignment of scores and weights as well as weaknesses caused by the summation of weighted scores. The model can be replaced or complemented by other evaluation methods, for example, by a SCOR model, a SWOT analysis, a balanced scorecard, key performance indicators, etc. (see, e.g., Chopra and Meindl 2016; Durán et al. 2016; Mc Guire 2015). This is another field of future research activities, namely the further selection, modification and application of adequate methods for the purpose of evaluating information technologies in humanitarian logistics.

# References

Abushaikha, I., and Schumann-Bölsche, D. "Mobile Phones: Established Technologies for Innovative Humanitarian Logistics concepts." *Elsevier Procedia Engineering*, Vol. 159 (2016): 191–198.

ACAPS Assessment Capacities Projects. "Call Detail Records – The Use of Mobile Phone Data to Track and Predict Population Displacement in Disasters." Accessed August 20th, 2016. http://www.gsdrc.org/document-library/call-detail-records-the-use-of-mobile-phone-data-to-track-and-predict-population-displacement-in-disasters/.

ALNAP Active Learning Network for Accountability and Performance in Humanitarian Action. "Cash Transfers through Mobile Phones: An Innovative Emergency Response in Kenya." Accessed August 20th, 2016. http://www.alnap.org/resource/5763.

Altay, N., and Labonte, M. "Humanitarian Logistics and the Cluster Approach." In *Humanitarian Logistics*, edited by P. Tatham, and M. Christopher, 97–114, 2nd Ed. London: Kogan Page, 2014.

Arvis, J.-F. et. al. *Connecting to Compete, Trade Logistics in the Global Economy – The Logistics Performance Index and Its Indicators.* Washington D.C.: World Bank, 2014 and 2016.

Bell, C. *Beginning Sensor Networks with Arduino and Raspberry Pi* (Technology in Action). New York: Springer, 2013.

Birge, C. "Relief Item Tracking and Reporting for the Logistics Cluster." In *Managing Humanitarian Supply Chains*, edited by B. Hellingrath, D. Link, and A. Widera, 87–94. Hamburg: DVV Media Group, 2013.

Blansjaar, M., and Stephens, F. "Information Technology in Humanitarian Supply Chains." In *Humanitarian Logistics*, edited by P. Tatham, and M. Christopher, 57–76, 2nd Ed. London: Kogan Page, 2014.

Bölsche, D., and Herbinger, W. "Ernährungssicherheit durch humanitäre Logistik". *Welttrends – Special Edition Ernährung garantiert? Ernährungssicherheit im 21. Jahrhundert*, (2014): 89–106.

Buatsi, P., and Mbohwa, C. "The Journey to Humanitarian Supply Network Management – An African Perspective." In *Humanitarian Logistics*, edited by P. Tatham, and M. Christopher, 151–173, 2nd Ed. London: Kogan Page, 2014.

Chopra, S., and Meindl, P. *Supply Chain Management – Strategy, Planning, and Operation*, 6th Ed. London: Pearson Education, 2016.

Durán, O., Ruiz, E., and Esquivel, C. "Towards a Monitoring and Follow Up System for the Costa Rican Risk Management System." In *Proceedings of the 13th International Conference on Information Systems for Crisis Response and Management*, edited by A. H. Tapia et al. Rio de Janeiro, 2016.

Gray, B., Weal, M., and Martin, W. "Social Media and Disasters: A New Conceptual Framework." In *Proceedings of the 13th International Conference on Information Systems for Crisis Response and Management*, edited by A. H. Tapia et al. Rio de Janeiro, 2016.

Guha-Sapir, D., Hoyois, P., and Below, R. *Annual Disaster Statistical Review 2014 – The Numbers and Trends*. Brussels: Centre for Research on the Epidemiology of Disasters (CRED), 2015.

Habekuß, F., and Schmitt, S. "Refugees: Why Do You Need a Mobile Phone?" *Zeit online*, October 1st 2015. Accessed August 20th, 2016. http://www.zeit.de/ gesellschaft/zeitgeschehen/2015-09/smartphones-mobil-phones-refugees-help.

Harke, J., and Leeuw, S. d. "Enhancing Sustainability in Managing Inventory Prepositioning Networks for Disaster Relief through a Simulation Game." In *Humanitarian Logistics and Sustainability*, edited by M. Klumpp et al., 215–233. Cham: Springer International, 2015.

HumTech – Humanitarian Technology. Science, Systems and Global Impact. Cambridge-Boston: *Elsevier Procedia Engineering*, 2015 and 2016.

Huth, M., and Romeike, F. *Risikomanagement in der Logistik – Konzepte, Instrumente, Anwendungsbeispiele*. Wiesbaden: Springer Gabler, 2016.

IFRC. The Digital Humanitarian. *The Magazine of the International Red Cross and Red Crescent Movement* (IFRC), No. 3 (2013).

ITU International Telecommunication Union. *Measuring the Information Society Report*. Genf: Telecommunication Development Bureau, 2015.

Jorio, L. "Drohnen – von der Kriegswaffe zum humanitären Helfer". *Swiss Info*. Accessed August 20th, 2016. http://www.swissinfo.ch/ger/ein-jahr-nach-dem-erdbeben-in-nepal_drohnen—von-der-kriegswaffe-zum-humanitaeren-helfer/ 42098960.

Kessler, M. *Logistics Network Design in Africa.*, Vol. 20. Berne: Haupt, 2013.

Korenblum, J. "Mobile Phones and Crisis Zones – How Text Messaging Can Help Streamline Humanitarian Aid Delivery." *Humanitarian Exchange*, No. 52 (2012): 38–39.

Kumar, A., and Vidolov, S. "Reconsidering the Ethics of Community Engagement and the Role of Technology." In *Proceedings of the 13th International Conference on Information Systems for Crisis Response and Management*, edited by A. H. Tapia et al. Rio de Janeiro, 2016.

Maathai, W. *The Challenge for Africa*. New York: Anchor, 2010.

Mc Guire, G. *"Handbook of Humanitarian Health Care Logistics. "* 3rd Ed., 2015. Accessed August 20th, 2016. www.humanitarianhealthcarelogistics.com.

McNamara, T., and Marsillac, E. "Make to Demand with 3-D Printing: The Next Big Thing in Inventory Management?" In *The Supply Chain Management Casebook*, edited by C. Munson, 180–183. Upper Saddle River: FT Press, 2013.

Meier. P. *Digital Humanitarians – How Big Data is Changing the Face of Humanitarian Response*. Boca Raton: CRC Press, 2015.

Merckens, K., and Schneider, B. "Practical Logistics in the End of the World – Man Remains Irreplaceable." In *Managing Humanitarian Supply Chains*, edited by B. Hellingrath, D. Link, and A. Widera, 130–136. Hamburg: DVV Media Group, 2013.

Montjoye de, Y.-A., Kendall, J., and Kerry, C. F. "Enabling Humanitarian Use of Mobile Phone Data." *Issues in Technology Innovation* (2014): 1–12.

Novartis. "SMS for Life." Accessed August 20th, 2016. http://malaria.novartis.com/ innovation/sms-for-life/index.shtml.

O'Donnell, A. *Using Mobile Phones for Polio Prevention in Somalia*. Oxford: United Kingdom, Oxfam GB, 2015.

Parker, E. "Providing SMS Solutions for Humanitarian and Disaster Relief." Accessed August 20th, 2016. http://www.onereach.com.

Raspberry Pi Foundation. Accessed August 20th, 2016. http://www.raspberrypi.org/.

Rutherford, A. "Exploring the Role of Data Science in Assisting UN Relief Efforts in Syria." March 2015. Accessed August 20th, 2016. http://www.unglobalpulse. org/exploring-role-data-science-assisting-un-relief-efforts-syria.

Sandvik, K. B. et al. "Humanitarian Technology: A Critical Research Agenda." *International Review of the Red Cross*, Vol. 96, Iss: 893 (2014): 219–242.

Schmitz, P. "Katastrophen Management". In *Handbuch Humanitäre Hilfe*, edited by J. Lieser, and D. Dijkzeul. Berlin/Heidelberg: Springer, 2013.

Schön, A., Streit-Juotsa, L., and Schumann-Bölsche, D. "Raspberry Pi and Sensor Networking for African Health Supply Chains." *6th International Conference on Operations and Supply Chain Management*. Bali, 2014.

Schöpperle, A. *Analysis of Challenges of Medical Supply Chains in Sub-Saharan Africa Regarding Inventory Management and Transport and Distribution*. London: University of Westminster, 2013.

Schumann-Bölsche, D., and Schön, A.-M. "A Raspberry in Sub-Saharan Africa? Chances and Challenges of Raspberry Pi and Sensor Networking in Humanitarian Logistics." *Procedia Engineering*, Vol. 107 (2015): 263–272.

Tatham, P., Loy, J., and Peretti, U. "Three Dimensional Printing – A Key Tool for the Humanitarian Logistician?" *Journal of Humanitarian Logistics and Supply Chain Management*, Vol. 5, Iss: 2 (2015): 188–208.

Thomas, A., and Kopczak, L. *From Logistics to Supply Chain Management – The Path Forward to the Humanitarian Sector*. U.S: Fritz Institute, 2005.

UAE United Arab Emirates. "Drones for Good." Accessed August 20th, 2016. http://www.dronesforgood.ae.

UN DP United Nations Development Programme. *Human Development Report 2015 – Work for Human Development.* New York: United Nations, 2015.

UN Foundation. "What We do: Mobile Health for Development." Accessed August 20th, 2016. http://www.unfoundation.org/what-we-do/issues/global-health/mobile-health-for-development.html.

UN Global Pulse. Accessed August 20th, 2016. www.unglobalpulse.org.

UN HCR United Nations High Commissioner for Refugees. *UN HCR Global Trends Forced Displacement in 2015.* Geneva: United Nations, 2016.

UN Logistics Cluster. *Logistics Cluster Annual Report.* Rome: United Nations, 2014.

UN Logistics Cluster. Accessed August 20th, 2016. www.logcluster.org.

UN MDGs United Nations Development Programme. *The Millennium Development Goals (MDG) Report 2015.* New York: United Nations, 2015.

UN SDGs United Nations Development Programme. *The Sustainable Development Goals Booklet.* New York: United Nations, 2015.

Vinck, P. *World Disasters Report - Focus on Technology and the Future of Humanitarian Action.* IFRC, Geneva, 2013.

Whipkey, K., and Verity, A. *Guidance for Incorporating Big Data into Humanitarian Operations.* Mountain View, CA: Creative Commons, 2015.

WHO World Health Organization. *World Health Statistics 2016 – Monitoring Health for the SDGs.* Geneva: United Nations, 2016.

Zeug, K. "Arroganz des Helfens." *enorm magazin*, No. 5. (2015).

# 20

# Bridging Research and Practice in Humanitarian Logistics: A Diagnostic Tool to Assess Organizational Agility

Cécile L'Hermitte, Marcus Bowles, Peter H. Tatham and Benjamin Brooks

## Introduction

The cultural differences and disconnect between academic research and the practice of business management have long been debated in the literature (e.g. Friedman 2001; Van de Ven and Johnson 2006; Thomas and Tymon 1982; Brannick and Coghlan 2006; Schön 1983; Argyris and Schön 1974) and more practice-oriented research has been repeatedly called for (Shapiro et al. 2007). Due to its focus on oversimplified models (Chopra et al. 2004), its inability to capture the intricacies and dynamics inherent in real-world

C. L'Hermitte (✉)
Waikato Management School, University of Waikato, Hamilton,
New Zealand
e-mail: cecile.lhermitte@waikato.ac.nz

M. Bowles
Centre for Regional & Rural Futures, Deakin University, Geelong, Australia
e-mail: m.bowles@deakin.edu.au

P.H. Tatham
Department of International Business and Asian Studies, Gold Coast, Australia
e-mail: p.tatham@griffith.edu.au

B. Brooks
Australian Maritime College, University of Tasmania, Launceston, Australia
e-mail: Benjamin.Brooks@utas.edu.au

© The Author(s) 2018                                                        **591**
G. Kovács et al. (eds.), *The Palgrave Handbook of Humanitarian Logistics and Supply Chain Management*, https://doi.org/10.1057/978-1-137-59099-2_20

problems (Besiou and Van Wassenhove 2015), its complexity (e.g. highly sophisticated mathematical models), its lack of immediate relevance and/or its limited usefulness, academic research is often ignored by practitioners (Panda and Gupta 2014; Brannick and Coghlan 2006; Sodhi and Tang 2008). In part, this is because significant differences exist in the way researchers and business practitioners approach the creation/utilization of knowledge. Whilst scholarly excellence requires a thorough, analytical and methodologically sound approach to expand theoretical knowledge, practitioners tend to prefer practical knowledge that bears relevance to the problems faced by their organizations and that provides useful as well as quickly and easily applicable solutions to improve performance (Van de Ven and Johnson 2006; Panda and Gupta 2014).

According to Chopra et al. (2004), this gap could be bridged if research would not only develop an academically valid argument that builds the theory underlying the practice, but would also extend its reach to practitioners by clearly articulating its significance and practical applicability. Going one step further, Chopra et al. (2004) argue that academics need to understand the evolving industrial reality and respond to the real problems faced by practitioners in order to make their work practically valuable. Similarly, Sodhi and Tang (2008) recommend that academics and practitioners support each other and note that reinforcing the links and interactions between universities, journal editors and the professional community will help researchers produce practice-driven studies that better meet the needs of end users (i.e. middle/senior management and industry leaders) without compromising on methodological rigour. For example, rather than producing mathematical models with limited practical applicability, researchers could focus on modelling real phenomena and on empirically validating these models (Sodhi and Tang 2008).

This so-called rigour vs. relevance (Schön 1983, 1987) or knowing vs. doing gap (Brannick and Coghlan 2006) relates not only to business-oriented research, but can also be observed in the humanitarian logistics discipline. For example, Kovács and Spens (2011) note that humanitarian logistics research is not sufficiently focused on implementation and practice, whilst Pedraza-Martinez et al. (2013) argue that humanitarians tend to misunderstand and mistrust academics because both communities exhibit fundamental differences in the way they think, talk and work. The two communities also have different approaches to humanitarian logistics problems. Whilst aid workers are action-oriented and pragmatic, that is, they give priority to their day-to-day operations and to the improvement of these operations (Pedraza-Martinez et al. 2013), academics typically conduct long and thorough studies that have been criticized for their limited practicality and applicability to field operations (Ferguson 2005; Kovács and Spens 2011). Taking a similar view, Besiou and Van Wassenhove (2015) note that research in humanitarian operations tends not only to focus on issues that are seen by practitioners as rather trivial and/or inaccurate representations of the reality, but also to make assumptions that are impractical in real humanitarian circumstances.

Humanitarian research has also been blamed for its lack of accessibility. In particular, practitioners are not familiar with academic discourse and conventions, and even less with academic jargon. They have no time and/or willingness to read long, detailed and theoretical analyses even if the topics relate directly to their daily concerns. Rather, practitioners prefer easily accessible reports, that is, studies that are not only to the point but which also provide details as to how to get the job done (Ferguson 2005).

These differences between research and practice are, in part, the result of humanitarians and academics working towards the achievement of different goals: on one hand, saving lives and alleviating human suffering for humanitarian organizations and, on the other hand, publishing scholarly valid studies in order to gain academic credit for researchers. Thus, academic recognition comes from publishing in well-established journals rather than ensuring that research is accessible by, and well communicated to, practitioners (Pedraza-Martinez et al. 2013; Ferguson 2005). And yet, working together and leveraging the strengths of research and practice can be beneficial to both academics and practitioners (Van de Ven and Johnson 2006). In this regard, Dijkzeul et al. (2013) observe that humanitarian organizations can benefit from academic research that provides analytical distance and rigour, whereas researchers can benefit from working with humanitarian organizations in order to achieve a better understanding of the reality of the humanitarian work. Similarly, Pedraza-Martinez et al. (2013) note that research disseminated in a format that is accessible to, and applicable by, practitioners can result in a win-win situation, that is, the creation of academic knowledge and, at the same time, the development of relevant solutions for humanitarian logisticians.

Following from the above discussion, we argue that there is a need for research in humanitarian logistics to be more easily understandable and applicable by practitioners. Therefore, this chapter provides an example of how the gap between research and practice can be bridged and demonstrates that academics can, relatively easily, make their research more practice-oriented and more attractive to humanitarian organizations. It builds on our 3-year academic project that investigated the concept of organizational capacity building and its contribution to agility, that is, the ability to swiftly identify and respond to sudden and short-term risks and uncertainties encountered along the humanitarian supply chains. In particular, our research demonstrates that agility originates not only from operational and functional (i.e. logistics) skills and expertise, but also from the systems, structure and culture of an organization. More precisely, agility relates to the way the organization operates, that is, how it shares information, makes decisions, builds skills, formulates processes and procedures, allocates responsibility and authority, learns from past experiences, etc. (L'Hermitte et al. 2015, 2016; 2017). However, to date, no clear line of action has been provided for the leaders and managers of humanitarian organizations. In other words, it remains unclear how, practically speaking, they can implement our research in order to evaluate the level of agility of their organizations and, subsequently, develop it by changing their organizational practices.

In order to address this limitation, a quick and simple diagnostic tool in the form of a maturity test has been developed. This tool is expected to enable the leaders of humanitarian organizations to easily assess the current level of agility of their organizations and to identify potential avenues to improve it. In doing so, we aim to illustrate, more generally, how the gap between academic rigour and practical relevance can be filled and how academic research can be more focused on implementation and practice.

The remainder of this chapter is structured as follows. Section "Research Background" provides details on the background of our research. An overview of the maturity model approach is presented in section "Maturity Models" and a maturity test to assess agility at the organizational level is proposed in section "The Proposed Maturity Test". Subsequently, section "Contributions" focuses on the contributions of the study before section "Limitations and Further Research" addresses its limitations and further research avenues. Section "Concluding Comments" provides concluding comments.

# Research Background

Change, uncertainty and disruptions are part of the routine of humanitarian organizations. Not only do they need to set up emergency supply chains in response to what are, sometimes, totally unpredictable disasters (Beamon and Balcik 2008), but they also deal with multiple disruptive events and turbulence in the environment of relief operations. This includes, for example, extreme weather and challenging topographic conditions that restrict the access to the affected areas, cumbersome bureaucratic regulations and corruption that impede the flow of humanitarian goods, as well as the lack of reliable transport and/or storage services available locally (Kunz and Reiner 2012; L'Hermitte et al. 2014). As a consequence, humanitarian organizations need to build and maintain a high level of agility, that is, they need to be able to respond swiftly to sudden and short-term field-level changes, uncertainties and disruptions, and to rapidly adapt their logistics and supply chain operations to meet the specific field requirements (L'Hermitte et al. 2015).

The existing humanitarian logistics literature (e.g. Charles et al. 2010; Oloruntoba and Gray 2006; Jahre and Fabbe-Costes 2015) mainly studies agility at the technical and functional level (i.e. as the ability of the logistics function to respond to disruptions and to adapt operations) and does not consider agility as a result of the organization's systems, structure and culture (L'Hermitte et al. 2015). Similarly, humanitarian practitioners associate agility with fundamentally operational considerations such as the skills, expertise and creativity of their logistics staff (L'Hermitte et al. 2015, 2016). This approach is consistent with the current perception that humanitarian logistics is an operational function rather than one with a strategic dimension (Whiting and Ayala-Öström 2009) and with the fact that overstretched field workers focus predominantly on solving visible problems at the field level rather than being involved in strategic reflections on what could be done better within their department and/or organization (Pedraza-Martinez et al. 2013).

A different approach has been taken in the business management literature which has established that operational agility requires a long-term perspective and stems from organizational capacity building (e.g. Yusuf et al. 1999; Appelo 2011; Sharifi and Zhang 2001). In other words, being agile goes beyond technical skills and expertise, and requires strategic inputs and leadership commitment. We have transferred this organizational perspective of agility to the humanitarian logistics discipline and, by drawing on Teece's Dynamic Capabilities Model (Teece and Pisano 1994; Teece et al. 1997), identified a set of four strategic-level capabilities that contribute to operational agility, that is, to enhancing responsiveness and flexibility in the field. In our research, responsiveness is defined as the ability to rapidly sense and identify turbulence along the supply chain, as well as to swiftly draw up a suitable response. Flexibility is defined as the ability to act in a timely manner and to swiftly adjust logistics operations (L'Hermitte et al. 2015). The four identified strategic-level capabilities are:

- Being purposeful (the capacity to maintain a clear direction for humanitarian action),

- Being action-focused (the capacity to build readiness and marshal the organization to respond to the risks and uncertainties encountered along the humanitarian supply chains),
- Being collaborative (the capacity to build and sustain relationships within and outside the humanitarian organization in order to solve problems collaboratively),
- Being learning-oriented (the capacity to identify and capture past field experiences, to share them across operations, and to turn them into improved practices).

The first capability, *being purposeful*, enhances agility because a clear and strong organizational purpose serves as a reference point in turbulent and constantly changing environments and, thereby, enables humanitarian logisticians to move proactively in a known and agreed direction rather than simply reacting to unfolding events (L'Hermitte et al. 2015). Humanitarian organizations, which are typically driven by a clear and meaningful mandate (i.e. saving lives and alleviating human suffering), are frequently seen in the literature as highly purposeful organizations (Maon et al. 2009; Tomasini and Van Wassenhove 2009).

The second capability, *being action-focused*, is developed by leaders who understand the challenges that field workers face and equip them with the tools needed to overcome these challenges and make the necessary operational changes in a timely manner. These tools include, for example, standardized processes and procedures that enable field workers to manage common operational situations, short and rapid decision making lines to deal swiftly with exceptional circumstances, and the use of information technology to make timely and accurate information available (L'Hermitte et al. 2015). Since swift responses to unpredictable events and to highly volatile environments are a fundamental requirement in the aid sector, humanitarian organizations are generally considered as action-focused and, in this regard, as liable to offer learning opportunities to their private sector counterparts (Van Wassenhove 2006; Charles et al. 2010).

The third capability, *being collaborative*, supports agility because field logisticians know on whom they can call and who, within and outside the organization, can assist them in overcoming the disruptions encountered in rapidly changing humanitarian environments (L'Hermitte et al. 2015). Although collaboration is an essential requirement in humanitarian operations and coordination mechanisms such as the Logistics Cluster have been developed, aid organizations have been frequently criticized for working in silos (Overstreet et al. 2011; Howden 2009), for the lack of cross-organizational collaboration in their field operations and for the resultant duplication of efforts (Kovács and Spens 2009; McLachlin and Larson 2011).

The fourth and final capability, *being learning-oriented*, contributes to the development of agility through continuous learning and ongoing improvement. Specifically, learning-oriented humanitarian organizations rapidly identify past experiences, reflect on them to improve operating practices, and swiftly transfer the lessons learned throughout the organization and across operations in order to support faster and more informed decisions and action (L'Hermitte et al. 2015). Whilst the benefits of organizational learning and continuous improvement have been repeatedly highlighted in the humanitarian literature, significant improvements remain to be achieved in this regard. In particular, humanitarian organizations still need to better integrate continuous improvement into the design and implementation of their projects, to develop formal mechanisms in order to capture and disseminate the lessons from evaluations in a more timely and effective manner, and to translate this information into improved practices and processes (WFP 2009; Ramalingam et al. 2009).

The leaders of humanitarian organizations have a critical role to play in the development of the four above-mentioned capabilities. In particular, this development needs to be supported by a number of key drivers that underpin the capabilities, including expertise (i.e. trained and experienced people who are creative, proactive, adaptable and collaborative), appropriate organizational structures and processes (in order, for example, to support swift decision making and information sharing), as well as adequate technology that supports not only the availability of timely and accurate logistics information, but also collaborative practices within and outside an organization (L'Hermitte et al. 2015).

From a methodological perspective, our research followed a three-step process. Firstly, we drew on the Dynamic Capabilities Model (Teece and Pisano 1994; Teece et al. 1997) and on the business literature on agility in order to identify the four above-mentioned strategic-level capabilities (L'Hermitte et al. 2015). Secondly, qualitative exploratory data were gathered within a best practice organization. More specifically, a total of 29 interviews of logistics experts were performed in June 2014 at the Rome headquarters of the United Nations (UN) World Food Programme (WFP). A content analysis of these interviews was undertaken to corroborate the empirical relevance of the four capabilities to the humanitarian context, as well as to provide insight into the role played by each of them in the ability of humanitarian organizations to conduct agile field operations. In doing so, we were able to identify an emergent relationship between organizational practices and agile logistics operations (L'Hermitte et al. 2016).

WFP has been selected because the organization sees logistics as an important part of its relief operations (WFP Logistics 2015) and has been recognized for its logistics expertise (Logistics Manager 2014). Our research was, therefore, grounded in this particular case study and may, as a consequence, have produced knowledge that Flyvbjerg (2006) defines as context-dependent. It is fully accepted that the exact mechanisms underlying agility may differ from one organization to another and that those identified in relation to WFP, namely a large UN agency that, in 2015, attracted US$4.8 billion funding and delivered 3.2 million metric tons of food to 76.7 million people in 81 countries (WFP 2016), may not be fully applicable to smaller and medium-sized organizations. That said, WFP constitutes a critical case and the overall considerations highlighted in our research are, therefore, expected to transcend its empirical context and to bear relevance to other organizations.

Thirdly, a shift to quantitative data collection and analysis was necessary to measure the strength of the identified relationship between organizational practices and agile logistics operations. To this end, both prior research and the interviews conducted in Rome were used to inform the development of a questionnaire and to gather quantitative data through an online survey. The survey questionnaire included a total of 46 items to be measured on a five-point Likert scale. Forty of these items measured the four strategic-level capabilities (collectively referred to as organizational capacity building) and six items measured two operational outcomes, namely responsiveness and flexibility (collectively referred to as operational agility) (L'Hermitte et al. 2017). Figure 20.1 illustrates our research's approach to agility.

The survey was conducted with 11 international aid and development organizations (Acted, Concern Worldwide, IFRC, International Medical Corps, MSF, Save the Children, UNDP, UNHCR, UNICEF, WFP, and World Vision International) between November 2014 and February 2015 and a total of 59 usable responses were received. A structural equation analysis was subsequently undertaken in order to quantify the causal relationship between organizational capacity building and operational agility. This analysis demonstrated that, collectively, the four strategic-level capabilities account for 52 percent of the variance in operational agility. In less academic words, this means that the four capabilities support over half of the ability of humanitarian organizations to deal with field-level change and uncertainty. In addition, the quantitative analysis provided strong evidence of shared

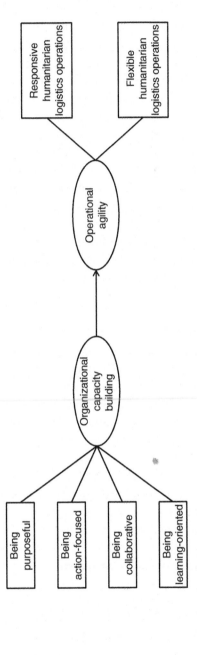

**Fig. 20.1**  Research's approach to agility

variance among the four capabilities. Simply stated, this means that the four capabilities form an integrated whole, that is, they play a collective role in the development of agility in humanitarian logistics operations and require, therefore, to be considered as a whole (L'Hermitte et al. 2017). Ultimately, the 3-year research project confirmed the multi-dimensional and multi-level nature of agility in humanitarian logistics, that is, that an agile organization not only exhibits various characteristics (it is purposeful, action-focused, collaborative, and learning-oriented), but it also builds agility at all levels of the organization, that is, beyond the operational level.

Whilst our research provides a framework for expanding the scope of agility to organizational considerations and identifies the higher-level dimensions and determinants of agility in humanitarian logistics, it has not been translated into a practical tool that can be used by humanitarian organizations. It may, as a consequence, be difficult for the leaders of humanitarian organizations who desire to assess and improve their agility to know where and, indeed, how to start. This chapter, therefore, proposes a maturity test which is expected to support a structured approach to the evaluation and the development of the four above-mentioned capabilities. Before presenting this tool, the next section provides an overview of the maturity model approach.

## Maturity Models

Initially rooted in developmental psychology (e.g. Piaget 1971) and later translated into organizational approaches such as quality management, information technology, knowledge management, innovation, product design, research and development, collaboration, and leadership (Fraser et al. 2002; Netland et al. 2007), maturity tests are diagnostic tools providing an improvement path in the form of a series of development stages called maturity levels. They are typically used by organizations to evaluate the achievement of a range of elements (e.g. processes, projects, capabilities, etc.) and to identify what needs to be done to improve performance. As such, maturity models are not only assessment tools, but also provide a framework for identifying suitable actions, prioritizing these actions and measuring progress over time as part of an improvement process (Fraser et al. 2002; Humphrey 1997).

Maturity models come in all shapes and forms, ranging from quick audit schemes (e.g. Netland and Alfnes 2011) to very sophisticated assessment and improvement models, the implementation guidelines of which are detailed in reports that can exceed 500 pages (e.g. Carnegie Mellon University 2010).

Within this significant body of literature, a number of maturity tests have been developed and used in order to measure and enhance agility. For example, Dove (2001) builds a comprehensive "change proficiency maturity model" that can be used at different levels of an organization (i.e. from the level of the entire organization to the level of key processes) in order to gauge the degree of agility achieved at each level. Perkins (2012) develops an organizational change maturity model based on three key organizational dimensions (strategic change leadership, business change readiness and project change management) which, according to the author, organizations need to develop to become truly agile and able to manage change successfully. Going into the details of what should be done to achieve agility (i.e. the development of agile values, agile technology, agile people and agile structures), Wendler (2014) proposes a maturity model to assess the level of organizational agility achieved by organizations in the software and IT service industries. Schweigert et al. (2014) describe a number of other agility maturity models developed in systems engineering, software engineering and software process improvement.

In the area of business supply chain management, maturity models focus on specific aspects of the discipline and, in particular, on inter-organizational collaboration or on supply chain processes but they rarely involve a higher-level approach to the management of an organization's supply chains (Netland et al. 2007). More specifically, supply chain maturity models are primarily used to control, measure and improve demand management and forecasting, production planning and scheduling, procurement, distribution, as well as integrated supplier and/or customer management (de Oliveira et al. 2011; Lockamy and McCormack 2004). Going one step further, Netland et al. (2007) propose a model that focuses on the inter-functional management of an organization's supply chains and includes core organizational dimensions such as its relation to the overall business strategy, the information and material flows, control, and the extent to which a supply chain-oriented organizational culture exists.

In a similar way to the function- and process-oriented perspective to supply chain maturity models primarily found in the business literature, a functional approach is dominant in the field of humanitarian logistics. In particular, Charles et al. (2010) develop a maturity model to assess the agility of humanitarian supply chains based on a number of capabilities (flexibility, reactivity, velocity, effectiveness and visibility). Importantly, however, the primary focus of Charles et al. (2010) is on logistics operations and their study does not address the organizational determinants of agility in humanitarian logistics, a perspective which is consistent with the above-mentioned operational approach to agility adopted within the humanitarian logistics literature.

A more comprehensive approach is taken by the United States Agency for International Development (USAID) which has developed the "Supply Chain Compass", a diagnostic and planning tool that supports the integration of the supply chains for essential health products made available to developing countries (for example to prevent HIV/AIDS and malaria, or to support family planning). This tool includes a maturity model covering a number of key managerial and functional areas in relation to supply chain management, that is, strategic planning and performance management, information systems, human resources, forecasting and supply planning, product selection and procurement, warehousing and inventory control, as well as transportation (USAID 2016, 2015a). Whilst this maturity model has the advantage of taking a broader and multi-functional perspective, it remains focused on integrating health supply chains, that is, on integrating the work of the various actors involved in the management and deliveries of health supplies. As a consequence, the core focus of this maturity model is not agility.

In summary, it can be seen from the above discussions that no maturity model taking a higher-level, organizational approach to the concept of agility in humanitarian logistics has been developed to date. The next section contributes to addressing this gap by proposing a maturity model that, similarly to that developed by Netland et al. (2007), focuses on core organizational dimensions rather than operational processes.

# The Proposed Maturity Test

## Key Features

The maturity test presented in this section reflects Netland and Alfnes' (2011) approach, that is, it has been designed as a quick and simple audit tool that aims to provide insights into the current state of organizational practices. As recommended by Netland and Alfnes (2011), it is both sufficiently simple to be easily understood and adopted by organizations, and sufficiently comprehensive to cover a range of areas (4 capabilities and 40 practices) related to the development of organizational agility. As such, the tool has been developed to meet the rapidity, simplicity and applicability requirements discussed earlier.

It should be noted that our maturity test is not only designed to be an assessment tool, but also an improvement tool. Thus, the results are not only intended to describe how well an organization has achieved each of the capabilities described previously, but also to point out potential action directions in order to enhance these capabilities and to move to a higher maturity level. From this perspective, our maturity test is expected to provide practical guidance and inform decision making.

That said, we recognize that humanitarian organizations are diverse in their purpose, size and operating methods (Long and Wood 1995; Kovács and Spens 2007), and that their approach to organizational design and development will most certainly differ from one organization to another (Clarke and Ramalingam 2008). Therefore, section "The Proposed Maturity Test" does not aim to present a one-size-fits-all solution to increase organizational agility. Rather, and as will be further explained in section "Test Process", the test process can be adapted to and by each organization. More than proposing a prescriptive and rigid method for evaluating and enhancing the agility capabilities, the test is designed to inform the thinking of the leaders and managers of humanitarian organizations and to provide potential avenues to support and improve the agility of their logistics operations by considering a number of organizational mechanisms.

## Test Content

The initial structure of the proposed model has been developed by drawing on the literature on maturity models (e.g. Fraser et al. 2002; Netland and Alfnes 2011; Humphrey 1997; Netland et al. 2007). In light of these studies, our maturity test includes the following key elements:

- Broad categories of interest in the form of four capabilities, along with a set of practices supporting the development of these capabilities,
- Five maturity levels with a descriptor for each level and a generic description of the characteristics of an organization at each developmental stage,
- An assessment questionnaire designed to measure the level of achievement of the key practices and capabilities.

### Capabilities and Key Practices

The proposed maturity model includes four broad dimensions in the form of the four previously described organizational capabilities, namely being purposeful, action-focused, collaborative and learning-oriented. The model also includes a set of key practices that are the elements that impact on the achievement of the capabilities, that is, the practical factors that leaders can address and leverage in order to make their organizations purposeful, action-focused, collaborative and learning-oriented. We use the 40 above-mentioned scale items developed in L'Hermitte et al. (2017) to delineate and measure the four capabilities. In order to maintain the deliberate simplicity of the model, the key practices are equally weighted, that is, they are all treated with the same degree of importance.

As indicated in Table 20.1, these key practices have been identified at four different levels (i.e. individual, team, organization and supply chain network) in order to ensure a substantial coverage of the multiple dimensions associated with a particular capability (L'Hermitte et al. 2017).

## Maturity Levels

Maturity levels are evolutionary stages that describe the typical behaviour exhibited by an organization along a number of pre-defined stages and in relation to the categories of interest (Fraser et al. 2002). In other words, maturity levels determine how well a humanitarian organization is achieving the four capabilities. Our model includes a five-level path developed by considering the sample of maturity models compiled by Fraser et al. (2002) as well as a number of practice-oriented tools (USAID 2015a, b; Bowles 2011, 2000). These five developmental stages reflect an increasing level of activity and performance achieved by the organization towards the development of the capabilities, that is, a growing level of maturity. The allocated descriptors include:

- Level 0: Unrecognized
- Level 1: Fragmented
- Level 2: Developing
- Level 3: Established
- Level 4: Optimized

A generic description of each of these five maturity levels is provided in Table 20.1.

## Questionnaire

Diagnostics questions are needed in order to evaluate the organization's current practices and, ultimately, to implement the model. A Likert-scale questionnaire can be used for this purpose. As explained by Fraser et al. (2002), Likert scales present strong similarities with maturity grids, and only differ in the level of description provided. Thus, whilst maturity levels describe the organization's typical deployment of the capability at each

**Table 20.1** Capabilities and associated practices

| Capabilities | Practices | | Level |
|---|---|---|---|
| **Being purposeful** | P1 | The organization has a clear purpose | Organization |
| | P2 | The organization enhances its consistency of purpose by aligning goals and objectives across all levels | Organization |
| | P3 | The organization's processes and procedures are set up to achieve the overall purpose | Organization |
| | P4 | Individuals fully identify with the organization's purpose | Individual |
| | P5 | Individuals' actions are guided by the organization's purpose | Individual |
| | P6 | Teams/groups clearly understand what has to be done to fulfil the organization's purpose | Team |
| | P7 | Partners across the supply chain share a sense of common purpose | Supply chain network |
| **Being action-focused** | A1 | Individuals have the skills needed to meet the requirements of their positions | Individual |
| | A2 | Individuals feel confident in their ability to take the initiative as necessary | Individual |
| | A3 | Teams/groups have the necessary resources | Team |
| | A4 | Teams/groups are provided with suitable processes and procedures for dealing with common situations | Team |
| | A5 | Teams/groups are authorized to adapt processes and procedures when necessary | Team |
| | A6 | The organization has an extensive field presence (including offices in remote areas) | Organization |
| | A7 | The organization has short and rapid decision-making lines and approval protocols | Organization |
| | A8 | The organization delegates authority and responsibilities to support action | Organization |
| | A9 | The organization has effective leaders in place who drive action | Organization |
| | A10 | The organization makes accurate logistics information available (e.g. track-and-trace information, availability of resources, etc.) | Organization |

(continued)

**Table 20.1** (continued)

| Capabilities | Practices | | Level |
|---|---|---|---|
| | A11 | The organization disseminates risk-related information to assist decision-making in uncertain situations (e.g. political or weather risks) | Organization |
| | A12 | The organization disseminates demand-related information (e.g. what is needed, in which quantities, when, where) in a timely manner | Organization |
| | A13 | The organization provides the right information to the right people at the right time | Organization |
| | A14 | Partners across the supply chain actively engage in information sharing (e.g. logistics data, predictive analysis, etc.) | Supply chain network |
| | A15 | Partners across the supply chain develop consistent policies and procedures to support their action | Supply chain network |
| Being collaborative | C1 | Individuals maintain positive and active relationships with others within the organization | Individual |
| | C2 | Individuals maintain positive and active relationships with people outside the organization | Individual |
| | C3 | Teams/groups are fully aware of the expertise of other units/divisions within the organization | Team |
| | C4 | Teams/groups actively collaborate with other units/divisions within the organization to solve problems | Team |
| | C5 | Teams/groups actively collaborate with others outside the organization to solve problems | Team |
| | C6 | The organization has mechanisms in place to support trust and coordination between the different units/divisions | Organization |
| | C7 | The organization eliminates functional silos by supporting the integration of the different parts of the organization | Organization |

**Table 20.1** (continued)

| Capabilities | Practices | | Level |
|---|---|---|---|
| | C8 | Partners across the supply chain have a clear understanding of the role and competencies of the different parties with which they are working | Supply chain network |
| | C9 | Partners across the supply chain work together to solve problems | Supply chain network |
| **Being learning-oriented** | L1 | Individuals are committed to active learning and self-development | Individual |
| | L2 | Individuals generate new insights and share information with others in the team/group | Individual |
| | L3 | Teams/groups continuously learn from communicating with other units/divisions | Team |
| | L4 | Teams/groups reflect on past experiences and generate their own procedures based on best practices | Team |
| | L5 | The organization has mechanisms in place for identifying lessons from past operational successes and failures | Organization |
| | L6 | The organization translates the lessons from past experiences into improved and more relevant processes and practices | Organization |
| | L7 | The organization shares best practices throughout the organization and across operations | Organization |
| | L8 | Partners across the supply chain learn from each other | Supply chain network |
| | L9 | Partners jointly evaluate their performance in order to improve their future work | Supply chain network |

developmental stage, a Likert scale provides a unique statement of good practice together with a rating scale which enables the respondents to assess their level of agreement with the statement (e.g. a scale ranging from strongly agree to strongly disagree).

Fraser et al. (2002) qualifies as "hybrid" such models combining a Likert-based questionnaire and overall descriptions of a number of maturity levels. An advantage of using hybrid models is that Likert scales simplify the respondents' rating process. With an eye to the deliberate simplicity of our maturity model,

**Table 20.2** Maturity levels

| Level | Descriptor | Description |
|---|---|---|
| 0 | Unrecognized | The capability has not been identified as an essential driver of agility in humanitarian logistics operations by any level of the organization. As a consequence, the organization is in a state of no awareness, no effort, and no action in regard to the capability. |
| 1 | Fragmented | The capability is recognized by a small number of people and/or teams as an essential driver of agility in humanitarian logistics operations. As a result, the capability is ill-defined and the action taken to develop the capability is limited and fragmented across departments, regional/country offices and/or operations. The corporate level of the organization is not committed to the development of the capability and no formal action is taken to develop it at the organizational level. |
| 2 | Developing | The capability is being recognized by the highest level of the organization as an essential driver of agility in humanitarian logistics operations and the initial commitment of senior leaders to its development is becoming visible. In particular, formal plans are emerging to raise awareness and communicate about the capability at all levels of the organization, systems are being designed and implemented, and resources are being mobilized to develop the capability. The development process remains, however, at an early stage. |
| 3 | Established | The highest level of the organization is committed to developing the capability and formal processes and systems are in place to this end. However, these plans do not cover all aspects of the capability and/or are not applied in a systematic and consistent way by all levels of the organization. |
| 4 | Optimized | All levels of the organization (people, teams, functions, departments, geographical entities, etc.) are aware of the need to develop the capability. The formal systems and processes in place to enhance this capability are routinely applied, well functioning and continuously improved. The capability is embedded in the organizational culture. |

we adopt Fraser et al. (2002) hybrid approach. Thus, the 40 above-mentioned practices are measured on a five-point scale by the questionnaire respondents who answer the following question: "To what extent are the following practices applied within your organization?". Specifically, respondents are invited to score the extent to which the practices listed in Table 20.1 are in place using the following five-point rating scale: (4) routinely applied (3) mostly applied (2) partly applied (1) rarely applied, and (0) never applied. This five-point rating scale, that has been developed by drawing on the work of Netland et al. (2007), reflects the five maturity levels described in Table 20.2.

According to Netland and Alfnes (2011), the qualitative nature of the test, which is based on subjective measures (i.e. the perceptions of the participants), has the advantages of being simple, rapidly carried out and inclusive (all levels of the organization can be involved). On the other hand, since the answers are not based on objective measures (i.e. facts and numbers), the statements scored by the participants may be subject to interpretation. For this reason, the survey participants should be carefully selected based on their expected insights, and the quality of language should be given particular attention. These points will be further developed in the next section related to the test process.

## Test Process

The seven-step test process described below has been developed by using the work of Netland and Alfnes (2011) as well as the previously mentioned practice-oriented tools (USAID 2015a, b; Bowles 2011, 2000).

*Step 1: Determine the relevance and importance of each of the 40 practices*

As a first step, it is important that the leaders of humanitarian organizations consider the 40 practices listed in Table 20.1. As previously mentioned, humanitarian organizations are very different in terms of their mandate, size, scope of intervention, level of resources available, modes of operation (Long and Wood 1995; Kovács and Spens 2007) and, as a result, in the way they build agility. For this reason, some of the 40 practices associated with the four capabilities may not be fully relevant to all humanitarian organizations. This includes, for example, the elements requiring structural investments such as an extensive field presence with offices in remote areas, or the availability of a sophisticated, IT-based logistics management information system.

As a consequence, the leaders of humanitarian organizations need to consider, discuss and determine the applicability of each of the 40 practices to their particular organization, and discard any irrelevant practices from the questionnaire. Ideally, these discussions should include field logisticians in order to gain a solid understanding of which tools/practices best support the ability of field workers to overcome disruptions and ensure the continuity of the logistics operations. On the other hand, some organizations may have implemented a number of agility-enhancing practices that are not listed in Table 20.1. This should also be considered and discussed, and any omitted practices supporting the development of agility in humanitarian logistics should be added to the questionnaire.

In addition to considering the relevance of the practices, the accuracy and consistency of the language of the best practice statements should be assessed in order to ensure that the test is valid and reliable. Given that each organization has, over time, developed its own terminology and jargon, the wording of the questionnaire should be adjusted if it does not reflect the organization's actual practices.

*Step 2: Select respondents*

As previously mentioned, the test is a qualitative diagnostic tool designed to provide experience-based answers to each of the 40 statements. The staff members invited to participate in the test should, therefore, be selected carefully on the basis of their experience in humanitarian logistics and their understanding of the topics covered. In addition, the selected respondents should include staff at all levels of the organization (from the operational level to the senior management level), staff involved in various operations (in various geographic locations and in various types of operations such as emergencies, recovery operations and development programs), and staff working at centralized and decentralized locations (e.g. headquarters and country/regional offices). Doing so will ensure that all perspectives are taken into consideration, and that the test is perceived by those taking part as a broad and inclusive consultation and engagement process.

Ideally, a minimum number of test participants is required in order to ensure that the results accurately reflect the target population (i.e. the surveyed staff). The minimum size of the sample depends on the three following elements (Lind et al. 2015):

– The number of people making up the target population,
– The margin of error, that is, the plus-minus percentage points that estimate how the sample is likely to deviate from the population (commonly ±5 percent),
– The confidence level, that is, the probability that the sample accurately reflects the population within the margin of error (commonly 95 percent).

Several sample size calculators are available online (see, for example, Survey Monkey 2016) and can be used to easily and quickly determine the minimum number of test participants.

*Step 3: Administrate the test*

Once participants have been selected, the test can be administered via email. An online questionnaire reflecting the best practices listed in Table 20.1 can be easily created by using a survey software tool and by inserting a survey link into the text of the email. The benefits of conducting the test online are, among other things, the rapidity of distribution, the ability for participants to respond immediately, the automatic collection of data, and cost effectiveness (Sue and Ritter 2007). All these factors contribute to the deliberate simplicity and rapidity of the overall test process.

In addition to including the best practice statements in the questionnaire, humanitarian organizations may want to include demographic questions, that is, questions about the profile and experience of the respondents (e.g. where they currently work, what their grade level is, how long they have been working for the organization, and any other significant elements). Doing so will facilitate the interpretation of the results, as further explained below. Beyond these general demographic questions, the questionnaire should, preferably, be designed as an anonymous data collection tool in order to obtain more honest responses from the participating staff members.

*Step 4: Aggregate the results*

The overall score achieved by an organization for each of the four capabilities is computed as follows. Initially, an average score is calculated for each of the 40 key practices by aggregating the individual scores obtained for each of these items and by dividing the total by the number of participants. Next, an average score is calculated for each of the four capabilities by aggregating the average scores obtained for each of the items associated with a particular capability and by dividing the total by the number of items associated with the capability. The overall score obtained for each of the four capabilities ranges from 0 to 4 and should be interpreted in the light of the maturity levels described in Table 20.2. The aggregated results are important parts of the scorecards presented in the next section.

*Step 5: Present the results*

The test results can be displayed in two different formats, namely scorecards and diagrams. Scorecards are a simple and organized way of presenting the results obtained for each of the key practices associated with a particular capability. According to Chiesa et al. (1996), scorecards provide an overview of the organization's strengths and weaknesses and can, therefore, be usefully employed to rapidly evaluate the results of a maturity test. Table 20.3 shows how these scorecards can be presented.

**Table 20.3** Scorecards

| | Being purposeful | | | Being action-focused | | | | Being collaborative | | | Being learning-oriented | | |
|---|---|---|---|---|---|---|---|---|---|---|---|---|---|
| | P1 | P2 | … P7 | A1 | A2 | … | A15 | C1 | C2 | … C9 | L1 | L2 | … L9 |
| Total number of 4 scores | | | | | | | | | | | | | |
| Total number of 3 scores | | | | | | | | | | | | | |
| Total number of 2 scores | | | | | | | | | | | | | |
| Total number of 1 scores | | | | | | | | | | | | | |
| Total number of 0 scores | | | | | | | | | | | | | |
| Overall practice score | | | | | | | | | | | | | |
| Average practice score | | | | | | | | | | | | | |
| **Overall capability score** | | | | | | | | | | | | | |

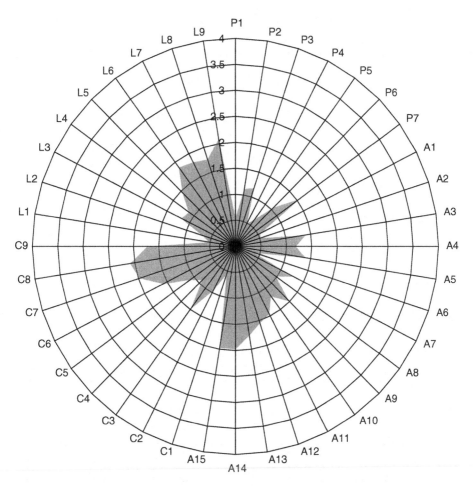

**Fig. 20.2**   Two-dimensional spider diagram (key practices)

The test results can also be displayed in a two-dimensional spider diagram that visually represents the average maturity scores obtained for each of the key practices. Figure 20.2, which provides an example based on our survey results, was developed using the Microsoft Excel charts function. Alternatively, four separate spider diagrams can be created to represent only the key practices associated with each capability and/or a single diagram can be used to represent the broader dimensions, that is, the capabilities (although, as illustrated in Fig. 20.3, such a diagram offers less differentiation). The benefit of using spider diagrams is that the results can be more easily visualized and, in turn, more easily interpreted. For example, the key practices that could be further developed are detectable at a glance in Fig. 20.2.

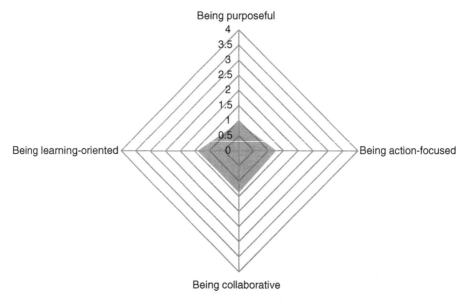

**Fig. 20.3** Two-dimensional spider diagram (capabilities)

In addition, a spider diagram enables the test results to be presented in a more accessible and communicable format.

Figures 20.2 and 20.3 are provided as an example only and serve no other purpose than to illustrate how the test results can be displayed in spider diagrams. They should not be seen as representative of any humanitarian organization or group of organizations and constitute no empirical validation of the model developed and presented in this chapter.

*Step 6: Analyse the test results*

Based on the results displayed on the spider diagram representing the broader capabilities, the leaders of humanitarian organizations can easily differentiate between the capabilities with a higher level of maturity (i.e. what the organization is doing well) and the capabilities with a lower level of maturity (i.e. what needs to be improved within the organization). For example, Fig. 20.3 shows that scope for improvement exists in respect of all four capabilities. The spider diagram representing the key practices (Fig. 20.2 in our illustration) can also be used to identify, in a greater level of detail, what the organization is doing well and where the focus should be in order to further develop the capabilities and achieve a higher level of maturity.

Since a spider diagram is based on average scores, it may be useful to consider the detail of the results presented in the scorecards and, in particular, to study the variability in the scores obtained for each practice. For example, do the results congregate around a specific value (e.g. around 2), do they congregate around a lower and around a higher value (e.g. around 1 and around 4), or are they spread out evenly from 0 to 4? In the first case, the results are likely to reflect a consensus view of the staff members throughout the organization. In the second case, the results show some fragmentation and it may be helpful to investigate the source of variation further. For example, do staff members working in the headquarters have a different opinion from those working in the field? The third case may be more difficult to interpret and the leaders of humanitarian organizations may need to assess if patterns of variation exist between specific operations, between organizational levels (e.g. operations, front-line management, middle management, senior management), or between staff members recently recruited and those employed by the organization for a longer time.

In any event, the analysis of the results will highlight a number of gaps that should be considered, discussed and, if necessary, addressed in order to develop the four capabilities (i.e. achieve a higher level of maturity) and, ultimately, enhance agility.

*Step 7: Conduct the test at regular intervals to monitor progress*

Maintaining agility is not a one-time exercise but, rather, an ongoing process (Sull 2009). Agility must, therefore, be continuously measured and improved within an organization. The test proposed in this chapter can be used to monitor progress over time as part of this improvement process. To this end, the above test should be repeated at regular intervals and the results compared with those previously obtained. Since maturity models can also be used as comparative tools and help organizations benchmark their performance against organizations in the same industry (Netland et al. 2007), leaders of humanitarian organizations could, at this stage, compare their maturity results/progress against similar organizations which have taken the same maturity test.

# Contributions

The contributions of this chapter are two-fold. The first contribution relates to the maturity test itself. In this regard, this chapter proposes an audit tool which is simple and can be implemented rapidly but, nevertheless, covers all important decision making areas related to the building of agility into the organization. Thus, we argue that our model can be used by humanitarian organizations as a roadmap to improve the agility of their logistics operations by leveraging a number of organizational mechanisms. More precisely, the model is expected to provide humanitarian organizations with a performance measurement and decision-making tool that can assist them in:

– evaluating their current practices;
– understanding why the performance of some teams/operations is better than others;
– identifying areas for improvement;
– planning transformations;
– monitoring progress.

The model developed in this chapter is also designed to make the leaders of humanitarian organizations aware that some of the transformations needed to enhance operational agility should be addressed at the organizational level, that is, that agility stems from the organization's own systems, structure and culture and, therefore, needs to be embedded in multiple organizational practices. In other words, the leaders of humanitarian organizations need to go beyond the current perception that agility is limited to operational skills and expertise. Whilst logistics excellence is, undoubtedly, an important requirement, agility is also the result of a complex development process supported by multiple organizational drivers. In this context, leaders become agility facilitators, that is, they create an enabling environment that facilitates field work and rapid adjustments to the multiple disruptions occurring in humanitarian logistics operations.

The second contribution of this chapter relates to the previously mentioned rigour vs. relevance gap that often divides academia from humanitarian practice. Although clear cultural differences between both communities exist, the development of the above model demonstrates that it is possible to establish a connection between rigorous academic research and humanitarian logistics practice, and that academic research can be presented in a way that is more accessible to, and applicable by, practitioners. In doing so, this study echoes Brannick and Coghlan's (2006) argument that research should be designed not only to fit the requirements and purposes of the academic community (i.e. to build theoretical knowledge), but also to meet the needs of the community of practice (i.e. it should be conducted in a way that is relevant to the concerns of the practitioners and useful to address these concerns).

# Limitations and Further Research

Three limitations and opportunities for future research should be considered in relation to this study. Firstly, the test proposed in this chapter is non-normative, that is, it does not provide any insight into the way practices can be improved (Netland and Alfnes 2011). Whilst the 40 key practices presented in Table 20.1 provide details as to how the strategic-level capabilities (being purposeful, action-focused, collaborative and learning-oriented) can be developed within an organization, this study does not explain the ways in which the key practices themselves can be successfully achieved and/or improved. To address this limitation, additional research could explore the role of the previously mentioned three sets of agility drivers, that is, people, processes and technology that are expected to underpin the achievement of the key practices (see L'Hermitte et al. 2015 for further detail).

The second research limitation relates to a critical aspect of the prior research underpinning the development of the maturity model. In this regard, it is important to note that the collection of our quantitative data coincided with an unprecedented level of activity and complexity for the humanitarian community due to the simultaneous occurrence of five crises designated Level 3. On the UN scale, Level 3 is the highest level of emergency and relates to acute and extensive crises requiring an exceptional level of response and resources. The five crises designated Level 3 at the end of 2014 were Central African Republic, Syria, South Sudan, Iraq and the Ebola outbreak (Development Initiatives 2015). In this context, the level of response to our survey was unsurprisingly low and, as indicated in section "Research Background", we received only 59 usable responses. As a consequence, the empirical testing of the 40 key practices and, in particular, the process of identification of those generating the highest levels of variability in operational agility has not produced generalizable results, that is, results that are applicable beyond the limit of the research reported in L'Hermitte et al. (2017). To address this limitation, the 40 key practices listed in Table 20.1 need to be further considered and validated. In particular, future research should investigate which among these practices are the most strongly associated with operational agility (i.e. exhibit the most statistically significant levels of bivariate correlation with operational agility).

Thirdly, the maturity test presented in this chapter has been designed by drawing both on prior academic studies (primarily in the business management discipline) and evidence from our own research. Although this, arguably, supports the model's applicability, the maturity test has not been applied empirically and its practicality remains to be established with a number of humanitarian organizations. In addition to doing so, future research could also use the feedback of these organizations to complete and/or refine the model.

## Concluding Comments

This chapter builds on our previous research that has extended the concept of agility beyond operational expertise and into organizational practice. The organizational mechanisms considered are as diverse as instilling a sense of purpose that guides and focuses action when field workers face turbulent and uncertain circumstances, developing standardized processes and procedures that support swift action without preventing adaptability, shifting authority to the field to support more flexible decisions, expanding the adaptive skills of individuals, enhancing intra/inter-organizational trust and the ability to solve problems collaboratively, as well as building up a learning system that provides field workers with new problem-solving methods and techniques that have been successfully tested by other teams (L'Hermitte et al. 2015; 2016; 2017). In short, our research argues that agility should be built into the organization and that conducting responsive and flexible humanitarian logistics operations depends on the development of four strategic-level capabilities, that is, being purposeful, action-focused, collaborative and learning-oriented.

In order to support the practical implementation of our research and the development of the four above-mentioned capabilities within humanitarian organizations, this chapter presents an easy-to-use diagnostic tool designed for the leaders of humanitarian organizations to quickly obtain an informed assessment of the organization's capacity to be agile. This tool, based on a maturity test, includes 40 practices that support the development of the capabilities. Despite its simplicity, the test is structured and comprehensive, and covers all important organizational mechanisms. Although it is expected that the test will enable the leaders of humanitarian organizations to rapidly and objectively identify areas of excellence and areas of improvement, its usefulness remains to be tested in real life with humanitarian organizations.

In addition to assisting humanitarian organizations in evaluating and enhancing their agility, the development of the maturity model is designed to demonstrate that research can (and should) be made more relevant, practical, easily understandable and readily applicable by practitioners. It is both the researchers' and the practitioners' responsibility to work closely with each other in order to ensure that the focus, content and outcomes of the research relate to the concerns of humanitarian organizations and that research utilization is achieved. Doing so will most certainly contribute to closing the gap between research and the humanitarian logistics practice, and to gaining the trust of practitioners.

# References

Appelo, Jurgen. 2011. *Management 3.0: leading agile developers, developing agile leaders.* Upper Saddle River, NJ: Pearson Education.

Argyris, Chris, and Donald A. Schön. 1974. *Theory in practice: Increasing professional effectiveness.* San Francisco, CA: Jossey-Bass.

Beamon, Benita M., and Burcu Balcik. 2008. "Performance measurement in humanitarian relief chains." *The International Journal of Public Sector Management* 21 (1):4–25.

Besiou, Maria, and Luk N. Van Wassenhove. 2015. "Addressing the challenge of modeling for decision-making in socially responsible operations." *Production and Operations Management* 24 (9):1390–1401.

Bowles, Marcus. 2000. "Organisational agility benchmarking and generic self-assessment tool." Working Futures. Accessed August 31. https://www.researchgate.net/publication/275522967_Organisational_Agility_Benchmarking_and_Generic_Self-Assessment_Tool

Bowles, Marcus. 2011. "eReadiness audit tool." Launceston: University of Tasmania.

Brannick, Teresa, and David Coghlan. 2006. "To know and to do: academics' and practitioners' approaches to management research." *Irish Journal of Management* 26 (2):1–22.

Carnegie Mellon University. 2010. "CMMI for services, version 1.3." Software Engineering Institute. Accessed August 31. http://resources.sei.cmu.edu/library/asset-view.cfm?assetid=9665

Charles, Aurelie, Matthieu Lauras, and Luk Van Wassenhove. 2010. "A model to define and assess the agility of supply chains: building on humanitarian experience." *International Journal of Physical Distribution & Logistics Management* 40 (8/9):722–741.

Chiesa, Vittorio, Paul Coughlan, and Chris A. Voss. 1996. "Development of a technical innovation audit." *Journal of Product Innovation Management* 13 (2):105–136.

Chopra, Sunil, William Lovejoy, and Cadance Yano. 2004. "Five decades of operations management and the prospects ahead." *Management Science* 50 (1):8–14.

Clarke, Paul, and Ben Ramalingam. 2008. "Organisational change in the humanitarian sector." ALNAP. Accessed August 31. http://www.alnap.org/resource/5231.aspx

de Oliveira, Marcos Paulo Valadares, Marcelo Bronzo Ladeira, and Kevin P. McCormack. 2011. "The supply chain process management maturity model – SCPM3." In *Supply chain management – Pathways for research and practice,* edited by Dilek Onkal, 201–218. Rijeka: InTech.

Development Initiatives. 2015. "Global humanitarian assistance report 2015." Global Humanitarian Assistance. Accessed August 31. http://www.globalhumanitarianassistance.org/report/gha-report-2015

Dijkzeul, Dennis, Dorothea Hilhorst, and Peter Walker. 2013. "Introduction: evidence-based action in humanitarian crises." *Disasters* 37:S1–S19.

Dove, Rick. 2001. *Response ability: the language, structure, and culture of the agile enterprise*. New York, NY: John Wiley & Sons.

Ferguson, Julie E. 2005. "Bridging the gap between research and practice." *Knowledge Management for Development Journal* 1 (3):46–54.

Flyvbjerg, Bent. 2006. "Five misunderstandings about case-study research." *Qualitative Inquiry* 12 (2):219–245.

Fraser, Peter, James Moultrie, and Mike Gregory. 2002. "The use of maturity models/grids as a tool in assessing product development capability." Paper presented at the IEEE International Engineering Management Conference, Cambridge, United Kingdom, August 18–20.

Friedman, Victor J. 2001. "Action science: Creating communities of inquiry in communities of practice." In *Handbook of action research: Participative inquiry and practice*, edited by Peter Reason and Hilary Bradbury, 159–170. London: Sage.

Howden, Michael. 2009. "How humanitarian logistics information systems can improve humanitarian supply chains: a view from the field." Paper presented at the 6th International ISCRAM Conference, Gothenburg, Sweden, May 10–13.

Humphrey, Watts S. 1997. *Managing technical people: Innovation, teamwork, and the software process*. Reading, MA: Addison-Wesley.

Jahre, Marianne, and Nathalie Fabbe-Costes. 2015. "How standards and modularity can improve humanitarian supply chain responsiveness: The case of emergency response units." *Journal of Humanitarian Logistics and Supply Chain Management* 5 (3):348–386.

Kovács, Gyöngyi, and Karen M. Spens. 2007. "Humanitarian logistics in disaster relief operations." *International Journal of Physical Distribution & Logistics Management* 37 (2):99–114.

Kovács, Gyöngyi, and Karen M. Spens. 2009. "Identifying challenges in humanitarian logistics." *International Journal of Physical Distribution & Logistics Management* 39 (6):506–528.

Kovács, Gyöngyi, and Karen M. Spens. 2011. "Trends and developments in humanitarian logistics – A gap analysis." *International Journal of Physical Distribution & Logistics Management* 41 (1):32–45.

Kunz, Nathan, and Gerald Reiner. 2012. "A meta-analysis of humanitarian logistics research." *Journal of Humanitarian Logistics and Supply Chain Management* 2 (2):116–147.

L'Hermitte, Cécile, Ben Brooks, Marcus Bowles, and Peter H. Tatham. 2017. "Investigating the strategic antecedents of agility in humanitarian logistics." *Disasters*. Published online in Wiley's Early View.

L'Hermitte, Cécile, Peter H. Tatham, and Marcus Bowles. 2014. "Classifying logistics-relevant disasters: Conceptual model and empirical illustration." *Journal of Humanitarian Logistics and Supply Chain Management* 4 (2):155–178.

L'Hermitte, Cécile, Marcus Bowles, Peter H. Tatham, and Ben Brooks. 2015. "An integrated approach to agility in humanitarian logistics." *Journal of Humanitarian Logistics and Supply Chain Management* 5 (2):209–233.

L'Hermitte, Cécile, Peter H. Tatham, Marcus Bowles, and Ben Brooks. 2016. "Developing organisational capabilities to support agility in humanitarian logistics: an exploratory study." *Journal of Humanitarian Logistics and Supply Chain Management* 6 (1):72–99.

Lind, Douglas A., William G. Marchal, and Samuel A. Wathen. 2015. *Statistical techniques in business and economics.* New York, NY: McGraw-Hill.

Lockamy, Archie, and Kevin P. McCormack. 2004. "The development of a supply chain management process maturity model using the concepts of business process orientation." *Supply Chain Management: An International Journal* 9 (4):272–278.

Logistics Manager. 2014. "Revealed: all the awards winners." Accessed August 31. http://www.logisticsmanager.com/2014/11/22827-revealed-all-the-awards-winners/

Long, Douglas C., and Donald F. Wood. 1995. "The logistics of famine relief." *Journal of Business Logistics* 16 (1):213–229.

Maon, François, Adam Lindgreen, and Joëlle Vanhamme. 2009. "Developing supply chains in disaster relief operations through cross-sector socially oriented collaborations: A theoretical model." *Supply Chain Management: An International Journal* 14 (2):149–164.

McLachlin, Ron, and Richard C. Larson. 2011. "Building humanitarian supply chain relationships: lessons from leading practitioners." *Journal of Humanitarian Logistics and Supply Chain Management* 1 (1):32–49.

Netland, Torbjørn H., and Erlend Alfnes. 2011. "Proposing a quick best practice maturity test for supply chain operations." *Measuring Business Excellence* 15 (1):66–76.

Netland, Torbjørn H., Erlend Alfnes, and Håkon Fauske. 2007. "How mature is your supply chain? A supply chain maturity assessment test." Paper presented at the 14th International EurOMA Conference: Managing operations in an expanding Europe, Ankara, Turkey, June 17–20.

Oloruntoba, Richard, and Richard Gray. 2006. "Humanitarian aid: an agile supply chain?" *Supply Chain Management* 11 (2):115–120.

Overstreet, Robert E., Dianne Hall, Joe B. Hanna, and R. Kelly Rainer. 2011. "Research in humanitarian logistics." *Journal of Humanitarian Logistics and Supply Chain Management* 1 (2):114–131.

Panda, Abinash, and Rajen K. Gupta. 2014. "Making academic research more relevant: A few suggestions." *IIMB Management Review* 26 (3):156–169.

Pedraza-Martinez, Alfonso J., Orla Stapleton, and Luk N. Van Wassenhove. 2013. "On the use of evidence in humanitarian logistics research." *Disasters* 37 (1):S51–S67.

Perkins, Caroline. 2012. "Organisational change management maturity." Change Management Institute. Accessed August 31. https://www.change-management-institute.com/sites/default/files/CMI%20White%20Paper,%20Change%20Agility%20-%20Feb%202012.pdf

Piaget, Jean. 1971. "The theory of stages in cognitive development." In *Measurement and Piaget*, edited by Donald Ross Green, Marguerite P. Ford and George B. Flamer, 1–11. New York, NY: McGraw-Hill.

Ramalingam, Ben, Kim Scriven, and Conor Foley. 2009. "Innovations in international humanitarian action." ANALP. Accessed August 31. http://www.alnap.org/resource/5664.aspx

Schön, Donald A. 1983. *The reflective practitioner: How professionals think in action.* London: Temple Smith.

Schön, Donald A. 1987. *Educating the reflective practitioner.* San Francisco, CA: Jossey-Bass.

Schweigert, Tomas, Detlef Vohwinkel, Morten Korsaa, Risto Nevalainen, and Miklos Biro. 2014. "Agile maturity model: Analysing agile maturity characteristics from the SPICE perspective." *Journal of Software: Evolution and Process* 26 (5):513–520.

Shapiro, Debra L., Bradley L. Kirkman, and Hugh G. Courtney. 2007. "Perceived causes and solutions of the translation problem in management research." *The Academy of Management Journal* 50 (2):249–266.

Sharifi, H., and Z. Zhang. 2001. "Agile manufacturing in practice: application of a methodology." *International Journal of Operations & Production Management* 21 (5/6):772–794.

Sodhi, ManMohan S., and Christopher S. Tang. 2008. "The OR/MS ecosystem: strengths, weaknesses, opportunities, and threats." *Operations Research* 56 (2):267–277.

Sue, Valerie M., and Lois A. Ritter. 2007. *Conducting online surveys.* Thousand Oaks, CA: Sage Publications.

Sull, Donald N. 2009. *The upside of turbulence: Seizing opportunity in an uncertain world.* New York, NY: Harper Collins.

Survey Monkey. 2016. "Sample size calculator." Accessed August 31. https://www.surveymonkey.com/mp/sample-size-calculator/

Teece, David J., and Gary Pisano. 1994. "The dynamic capabilities of firms: An introduction." *Industrial and Corporate Change* 3 (3):537–556.

Teece, David J., Gary Pisano, and Amy Shuen. 1997. "Dynamic capabilities and strategic management." *Strategic Management Journal* 18 (7):509–533.

Thomas, Kenneth W., and Walter G. Tymon. 1982. "Necessary properties of relevant research: lessons from recent criticisms of the organizational sciences." *The Academy of Management Review* 7 (3):345–352.

Tomasini, Rolando, and Luk Van Wassenhove. 2009. *Humanitarian logistics.* Basingstoke: Palgrave Macmillan.

USAID. 2015a. "Diagnosing supply chain maturity: Supply Chain Compass tool helps three countries." United States Agency of International Development. Accessed August 31. http://deliver.jsi.com/dlvr_content/resources/allpubs/logis ticsbriefs/DiagSCMatu.pdf

USAID. 2015b. "Supply Chain Compass – Question list." United States Agency of International Development. Accessed August 31. http://deliver.jsi.com/dlvr_con tent/images/imgtopics/imgscessentials/Supply%20Chain%20Compass% 20Questions.pdf

USAID. 2016. "Supply Chain Compass." United States Agency of International Development. Accessed August 31. https://scc.deliver.jsi.com/home

Van de Ven, Andrew H., and E. Paul Johnson 2006. "Knowledge for theory and practice." *The Academy of Management Review* 31 (4):802–821.

Van Wassenhove, Luk N. 2006. "Humanitarian aid logistics: Supply chain management in high gear." *The Journal of the Operational Research Society* 57 (5):475–489.

Wendler, Roy. 2014. "Development of the organizational agility maturity model." Paper presented at the Federated Conference on Computer Science and Information Systems, Warsaw, Poland, September 7–10.

WFP. 2009. "Closing the learning loop – Harvesting lessons from evaluations." World Food Programme. Accessed August 31. http://documents.wfp.org/stel lent/groups/public/documents/reports/wfp225420.pdf

WFP. 2016. "Year in review 2015." World Food Programme. Accessed August 31. https://www.wfp.org/content/wfp-year-review-2015

WFP Logistics. 2015. "WFP Logistics in 2014." World Food Programme. Accessed August 31. http://www.wfp.org/logistics/blog/how-did-wfp-logistics-rise-chal lenges-2014

Whiting, Michael C., and Beatriz E. Ayala-Öström. 2009. "Advocacy to promote logistics in humanitarian aid." *Management Research News* 32 (11):1081–1089.

Yusuf, Y.Y., M. Sarhadi, and A. Gunasekaran. 1999. "Agile manufacturing: The drivers, concepts and attributes." *International Journal of Production Economics* 62 (1–2):33–43.

# Part VI

Conceptual, Future

# 21

# The Evolutions of Humanitarian-Private Partnerships: Collaborative Frameworks Under Review

Rolando M. Tomasini

## Introduction

In 2015, the UN Global Compact (UNGC) celebrated 15 years of its creation, after being proposed by UN Secretary General Kofi Annan at the 1999 World Economic Forum in front of an audience of business leaders as a call for shared values. This anniversary marked the biggest and most comprehensive effort done by the United Nations to coordinate interaction with the private sector to influence business practices by translating UN objectives into business principles. The uphill was steep for the UNGC team upon its official launch in 2000 with 44 companies. They assumed the mandate to work with companies towards more responsible business practices that could positively influence society and contribute to its challenges globally. It took them at least five initial years to bridge the cross-sectoral cultural gap through arduous dialogue with the private sector about not only the issues, but the legitimacy of the UN in this dialogue. The commitment from the UN was solid and persistent with both Secretary General Kofi Annan and Ban-Ki Moon supporting proactively with their leadership.

Upon retiring from his role as the UNGC Executive Director, George Kell, a UN career diplomat, handed over a remarkable successful organization. UNGC enrolled during his time 12,000 organizations in 170 countries

R.M. Tomasini (✉)
United Nations Office for Project Services, Copenhagen, Denmark
e-mail: rmtomasini@gmail.com

© The Author(s) 2018      **627**
G. Kovács et al. (eds.), *The Palgrave Handbook of Humanitarian Logistics and Supply Chain Management*, https://doi.org/10.1057/978-1-137-59099-2_21

and significant contributions on their mandate in the area of corporate practice, operating environment, and worldviews. The baton was passed on to Lise Kingo, a leading corporate sustainability private sector executive who could support the cross-sectoral dialogue with her business understanding and acumen. Looking back at his experience Kell summarized three forces that fuelled the corporate sustainability movement since the Conference in Rio+20 in 2012: "the power of transparency, an increasing recognition that externalities must be accounted for, and growing understanding of the opportunities associated with problem solving" (The United Nations Global Compact 2015).

The UNGC is not alone in this area of humanitarian-private collaboration. On the contrary their success is reinforced and based on the many other interdependent initiatives, forum, and organizations that have been launched through the same period with significant influence on the corporate sustainability agenda.

Looking at this significant and important trend, the question is not about how successful these initiatives have been, nor what opportunities remain. These two questions have been largely addressed by a myriad of reports that measure their impact, identify the gaps, and highlight the evolution of the needs over time. The question here is focusing on how has cross-sector partnerships evolved as a collaborative framework for the latter to function, and what have we learned from that process?

## Methodology

The content for this article has been collected by reviewing from the United Nations sets of policies and resolutions all documents related to the private sector engagement and business partnerships for the period of 2000 to 2015. Many of these documents make reference to prior milestone agreements that were then revisited for a wider understanding. Similar efforts were done in looking at third party documents on the same topic from relevant entities within and outside the United Nations System such as the policies of individual United Nations agencies (UNICEF, UNHCR, UNFPA, etc), and the OECD. The United Nations content was then compared with the development strategy documents emerging from the list of the major development donors who have adapted their policies to include and promote more private sector engagement the Nordic countries, and the United Kingdom. Further data has been collected from the speeches of high level officials of all the entities mentioned here above in public forum focussing on the role of private sector in development and private sector partnerships. Similar review of the speeches has been done for dignitaries participating at high level events with a particular focus on ministers of foreign affairs. Additional information for triangulation has also been used from extensive dialogue and consultations with practitioners in the different agencies responsible for private sector relations, trade commissions, and ministries.

The data collected has been classified in different categories: policy, recommendations, and case studies. Policy documents have been read and analysed to understand the regulatory framework they provide for the sectors. More importantly, they have been analysed in terms of who do they impact and how when it comes of the topic. Based on the latter, a hierarchy of the policies has been established defined by the scope of their impact. Some policies are global, while others are subsets of global policies adapted to regional or national level. Recommendations have been sub-classified depending on the author as some are drafted by international organizations, while others are drafted from the perspective of the private sector or non-governmental actors. While case studies are not explicitly cited in the content, they have been reviewed as support of the arguments presented here. Finally, the content collected has been reviewed in chronological order in highlight evolutions and trends in the sector on the particular subject. This has allowed to define the cause-effect link between the policies and the actions in the sectors leading to the analysis and conclusions presented in the article.

## Two Sectors, Two Cultures, Two Modus Operandi

If we focus on the 15-year period that the UN invested in bridging the two sectors through the UN Global Compact, one would notice a significant evolution in the types of partnerships and collaborative models that were established among the two sectors. Looking at the types and models of partnerships that emerged during this period a clear trend shows a shift from actors based partnerships towards a more network based approach. In the actor based, partnerships were established between two or more organizations that developed a suitable arrangement that was in line with their objectives to contribute to a specific set of development goals. In the network based approach, partnerships are established around a set of well-defined development objectives that set the direction of the agenda for multiple stakeholders from different sectors to convene and join forces towards joint action. Another significant shift has been how public sector has moved away from being a contractor to becoming a more integrated partner in development.

Historically, development organizations have looked at the private sector merely as a market actor whose primary role has been to act as a supplier. While supplying to development programs demands some alignment on their operating principles and values, such alignment has not been a pre-requisite for the private sector to exist outside the development arena. As we gained more transparency and greater shareholder pressure has been placed on corporations. Thus the markets have become more informed and more demanding of private sector actors and their social and environmental impact and performance. The rise of corporate social responsibility and progress on the sustainable development dialogue has structured and helped to capture best practices and guidelines that the private sector has had to integrate to bridge the gap between them and the public sector. At the same time, the development sector has been equally scrutinized by the public for their performance and impact while addressing today's pressing development issues. These evolutions have shifted the relationship between the develop-ment organizations and the private sector to move their discussion from traditional procurement solutions towards an interaction that is focussed on a more adaptable, agile, and aligned collaboration. This initially trans-lated into setting up longer term agreements within the procurement framework, but also to engage in a wider conversation about co-investment and co-development of solutions in the context of partnerships.

The initial challenge for these wider conversations was the absence of a partnership regulatory framework that would be aligned with the financial rules and regulations of most public organizations. There was also the issue of assessment and mitigation of the risks inherent in developing closer relation-ships with private sector organizations that are not consistently accountable to operate and contribute to the same principles and value of a development organization. In other words, the questions of: how do we select and formalize an agreement with a private sector partner that does not compromise or interfere with the procurement policies? And, how do we make sure that we are not exposing the development mandate and license to operate to undesir-able risks inherent in a profit-driven company?

As a result, the first partnerships we witnessed over the above cited 15-year period are very cautious and exploratory. They were designed and developed with significant support from the highest leadership levels of both sectors and mobilized substantial resources to be anchored and embedded in the orga-nizations that led them. These partnerships were under a lot of pressure to perform given the level of investment they required, and while they raised a lot of inspirational awareness for others around them, they had little flexibility and room to integrate more partners around the issues they addressed. While lessons were being developed on how to work together, the private sector contribution outside of the procurement framework was more focussed on philanthropic initiatives, sponsorships, and cause-related marketing.

As experience developed, and lessons were learned, the focus shifted from the actors to the issues, and on how to integrate the network of actors around an issue or event. Thus, we see fewer partnerships between a set of organizations, and instead broader collaborations on specific issues that required cross-sector and multi-stakeholder collaboration like the Global Fund, the StopTB, Cities Alliance, Water Supply and Sanitation Collaborative Council, etc. This opened the door for more companies to be involved, but most importantly to use the partnerships as a more inclusive platform where companies can interact with their development partner while also engaging under the same umbrella with other entities such as community groups, non-governmental organizations, academia, different levels of society, and donors. Through this cross-sectoral and multi-stakeholder collaboration the regulatory frameworks have evolved to become more inclusive and agile in facilitating different roles for different players at various points on the value chain. For example, a partnership may focus on capturing best practices about a development issue through extensive consultation with community actors, non-governmental organizations, academia, and industry players. The needs identified may highlight specifications for procurement or problems that need innovation and co-development for more sustainable solutions. The same partnership may provide advisory services on the same topic to ministries and social society on how to design and implement projects related to their focus. The same partnership may be involved in the monitoring and evaluation of projects in their area. In each of these stages they may be able to pull the different members of the partnership as they are needed as long as it does not compromise transparency or lead to any conflict of interest.

Collaboration among the two sectors still has many areas of improvement that could lead to higher impact and efficiencies. There are still questions about the most effective and appropriate mechanism to de-risk private sector investment in development and emergency areas? How to integrate innovation, especially from SME, into international public procurement mechanisms? How to develop and stimulate market dynamics in fragile states? How to attract foreign capital and investment while protecting local players and economy in certain areas? How to manage the risks that humanitarian and development organizations assume when working with a private partner? How to solidly align the private sector partners towards the Sustainable

Development Goals (SDGs)? What are the new models of public-private partnerships we should be considering, and when? And the list goes on.

However, the important point to highlight is not the limitation of our knowledge and capacity at this point on these issues, but rather the mechanisms we have in place to address them. For starter, the UNGC defined a set of ten principles as operational considerations in the areas of human rights, labour, environment, and anti-corruption. Their implementation has become even more concrete on the UN side with the provisions of a set of "Guidelines on a principled approach to the cooperation between the United Nations and the business sector" (UN-Business Action Hub 2015). These guidelines were revised in 2009, from their original in 2000, as a result of the General Assembly resolution 68/234 supported by the member states as means to implement the 2030 Sustainable Development Agenda. Undeniably, the most important guiding light that we have today for this are the 17 SDGs that confederate the different sectors, across all regions to invest and act towards a common set of interdependent goals. The SDGs are owned by each country, and they concern the private sector as much as they concern public and international institutions. Leaders are communicating on them as an opportunity to engage in broader agendas, while companies are inspired by them to define and where to position their corporate citizenships.

## Agenda 2030: SDGs

The definition of the SDG presents a paradigm shift that, unlike its predecessors, places a great emphasis on the national governments to own them and proactively invest in their implementation. The SDG concern and impact everyone. They are not exclusive to developing nations, nor to the development actors. They are interconnected leading to project design and implementation that consider and contribute multiple objectives. For example, a new rural primary care facility considers several SDG. Foremost it considers goal 3 on good health and wellbeing primarily, but can have tight links to clean water and sanitation (SDG 6), to decent work and economic growth (SDG 8).

Take as well as an example the strong links related to climate action (SDG 13). The World Health Organization under the health and climate mandate have been requested solicited by the ministries of the members states under the General Assembly resolution 61.19 to address both issues in unison. They have been requested to (1) raise awareness (2) provide evidence and monitor progress (3) support implementation, and not surprisingly (4) build partnerships that support implementation. The third and fourth points are nearly impossible to achieve without a cross-sector dialogue that integrates private sector, not a supplier, but rather as a source of expertise, capacity to innovate, and potential to promote economic inclusion when it is guided to build local capacity, especially with a gender balance focus.

An extension of these examples could be interpreted as well from issues where a mandate is less well defined such as roads and accessibility. The issues of health and climate are inevitably related to the latter given that on one hand roads and accessibility to facilities is quintessential for communities to benefit from health infrastructure and at the same time, roads can lead to greater air pollution which is the leading risk factor to non-communicable diseases. Again, here is an issue that demands significant investment not only from an infrastructure angle. The cost of the roads is merely the cost of the asset. The total cost of the road should consider the maintenance and all the components of the benefits and impact such facility would have in the neighbouring communities. A real solution for cases like this demands research and innovation with a cross-sectoral dialogue among the different constituencies. The result from this dialogue could be new and more environmentally friendly materials from local sources and mainte-nance model that stimulates local economic growth and employment.

Clearly, this type of integrated and comprehensive approach where cross-sector actors interact closely to develop a systemic solution to a development need calls for new models of interaction. Thus SDG 17 aims to revitalize global partnerships for sustainable development is an essential component of the solutions. Through this goal, the principled and value driven collabora-tion are the keys to unlock the solutions and the need to go from millions of dollars of interventions to the trillions that are required to meet the ambi-tions of the 2030 Agenda. This goal acknowledges the need for long-term investments in sustainable energy, infrastructure, transport and communica-tions technologies for developing countries under the guidance of the public sector. Achieving this target demands the public sector from those countries to be ready to attract the investments from these private sector players, and to develop their own capacity to implement these solutions with transparency, and with the necessary technical and financial oversight mechanisms.

## Conclusions

The support that the member states have provided towards the implementa-tion of the SDGs and the cross-sector partnerships is further developed and noticed today in the updated drafts of the development strategies of most OECD DAC donors and the national plans of their recipients. While development aid remains constant in figures, the allocation of resources has been repurposed by many donor countries to focus on how to leverage their contribution to promote partnerships and innovations from their private sector towards the development agenda. As a result, ministries are collaborating to develop funding instruments such as grants and loans to private companies that can implement solutions in development. They are revising their collaboration with development banks and domestic funds to promote, de-risk, and fund innovation for initiatives that contribute to development agendas. This is extremely helpful to support the expansion and investment that some of these companies require in order to become an active player in areas of the world where they are not used to work, to adapt their product and services to those settings, mitigate the financial risks they assume in their new investments, and offset any losses from the learning curve in their new settings.

Thus, the trend will continue for partnerships to emerge according to the needs with cross-sectoral networks developing around them. Response towards these needs will challenge our current policies and guide the development of new ones that will support more collaborative models that extend beyond the traditional funding mechanisms we have today and the public procurement framework. This shall lead, as defined by the member so the Addis Ababa Conference on Finance for Development, into revised public and international regulatory frameworks where cross-sector dialogue can be sustained to define solutions, identify funding, and channels returns on investment in ways that do not compromise neither the principles of public fund management, nor the UN values and humanitarian principles. In other words, to partner it with equal access to all potential parties, in a transparent and auditable manner, fairly and competitively, with integrity and accountability.

Already, during the recent Women Deliver Conference and the World Humanitarian Summit in Istanbul, several of these initiatives were launched to facilitate the role and contribution of the private sector in development. In the area of disaster relief the Connecting Business Initiative, was committed as a coordination mechanism for private sectors contributions which could take the form of pre-positioning supplier, meeting humanitarian needs, providing resources, knowledge, and expertise to disaster prevention. Similar initiatives have emerged in connectivity, health, climate change, etc.

While the trend seems to be solid towards these network based partnerships, and the figures promise substantial financial support, the question of value alignment, efficiency and impact will only be answered by the test of time through undefined methodologies that will become the innovation of our generation. Much research about public-private partnerships set up in the 1980s and 1990s remains inconclusive about the methodologies for measuring the social and economic impact of these political decisions. A lot these partnerships were used and mere financing mechanisms to postpone national debt domestic infrastructure projects. Thus the experience from the past in the partnership model is very different in that SDG are more holistic and extend beyond the financial models of the past. Moreover, it will be interesting to see in a few years if this forthcoming experience will either contribute to our understanding of the methodologies for measuring their impact, and hopefully to the solution of the development problems they are designed to address. The challenge and urgency defined in Agenda 2030 is as big and the opportunity to work together. What is clear and encouraging today is that never in our history has political and cross-sectoral willingness and support been so concerted and committed towards the same goal, SDGs, with such clear targets.

# References

UN-Business Action Hub. 2015. "Guidelines on a principled approach to the cooperation between the United Nations and the business sector". Accessed August 20th 2016. https://business.un.org/en/documents/5292

The United Nations Global Compact. 2015. "Impact: Transforming Business, Changing the World". Accessed August 20th 2016. https://www.unglobalcom pact.org/library/1331

# 22

# Review of Empirical Studies in Humanitarian Supply Chain Management: Methodological Considerations, Recent Trends and Future Directions

Lijo John

## Introduction

Humanitarian supply chain management (HSCM) encompasses a set of processes and systems aimed at mobilizing resources such as people, machinery, etc., collecting information and focussing on helping people affected by a disaster. HSCM includes a variety of activities such as procurement, transportation, tracking, warehousing, and delivery of aid material (Van Wassenhove 2006). Logistics forms the core of the humanitarian activities for three major reasons. First, it serves as a bridge and helps in connecting preparedness and response phases, procurement and distribution of aid, and forms a chain of information flow between agency headquarters and field (Balcik et al. 2010). Second, logistics activities form nearly 80% of the entire HSCM operations and it's efficiency plays a crucial role in the effectiveness of humanitarian operations (Carroll and Neu 2009). Third, logistics operations often generate large volumes of data which is instrumental for drawing plans in preparedness phases (Rodriguez et al. 2012).

Though academic interest in the emergency management is evident for more than five decades, the disaster management as a field of study emerged only after 1980s (Altay and Green 2006). Studies in disaster management

L. John (✉)
Indian Institute of Management Kozhikode (IIMK), Kozhikode, Kerala, India
e-mail: lijoj06fpm@iimk.ac.in

© The Author(s) 2018

**637**

G. Kovács et al. (eds.), *The Palgrave Handbook of Humanitarian Logistics and Supply Chain Management*, https://doi.org/10.1057/978-1-137-59099-2_22

mainly focussed on isolated issues such as search and rescue, location of distribution centres, vehicle routing, etc. Post 2005, the term "humanitarian logistics" has been used widely in comparison to "disaster management" (Galindo and Batta 2013). However, definition of disaster management is unclear and often disagreed on. For the purpose of this paper, we choose the definition suggested by Lettieri, et al. (2009). They define disaster management as "the body of policy and administrative decisions, the operational activities, the actors and technologies that pertain to the various stages of a disaster at all levels."

Noteworthy, literature reviews addressing the humanitarian logistics are Altay and Green (2006), Kovács and Spens (2007), Lettieri et al. (2009), Simpson and Hancock (2009), and Galindo and Batta (2013). Altay and Green (2006) review the OR/MS applications in disaster operations management published between 1980 and 2004 in operations and non-operations management journal. Galindo and Batta (2013) carry forward Altay and Green (2006) work and review publications from 2005 to 2010. Kovács and Spens (2007) review the academic and practitioner journals and propose a framework distinguishing between actors, phases, and logistical processes of disaster relief. Lettieri et al. (2009) review of the literature on disaster management published between 1980 and 2006, focusing on a thematic analysis of disaster management from a conceptual level. Simpson and Hancock (2009) review operations research applications in emergency management since 1970s. Other than these reviews, specific topics in the HSCM research have also received attention for literature reviews. Kovács and Tatham (2009) review the performance of the HSCM from a gender specific dimension. Dorasamy et al. (2013) reviewed the nature of research conducted in the knowledge management systems used in disaster support between 1990 and 2010. Heaslip (2013) reviewed the role of service operations in HSCM. In recent years, the researchers have also reviewed methodological considerations in HSCM research, such as logistic models (Ozdamar and Ertem 2015), game theory (Muggy and Stamm 2014) and economic cost (Kousky 2014). Appendix 1 summarizes the major reviews in HSCM.

The previous literature reviews have not attempted to synthesize the empirical methodological considerations in the HSCM. Since HSCM as a research area has started to receive much interest in the recent past, empirical methodologies have started to receive prominence. It warrants a closer look at the research methodologies commonly used in the HSCM research and track the evolution of the area from an empirical methodological perspective. This chapter aims to address the following question: what is the nature of empirical methodological considerations used in the HSCM research? What are the areas which have not received adequate academic enquiries? And what should be the future direction for research in HSCM. This study summarizes the existing literature in HSCM from a methodological perspective and presents useful classification of the academic research which could be used as lens by academicians and practitioners for future research in the HSCM.

The rest of the paper is organized as follows. The second section discusses certain key concepts and definitions used in disaster management literature. Furthermore, sections "Review Methodology" and "Results" discuss the methodology used for review and results of the analysis. Section "Methodological Classification" provides the results of the methodological classification in HSCM and in section "Discussion and Future Research", we provide future research directions.

# Definition of Key Concepts

Operating conditions of HSCM is very different from its commercial counterpart. Varied objectives and mechanisms drive HSCM with extreme uncertainty and dynamic operating environment offering unique management challenges (Day et al. 2012). Some of the issues that make HSCM unique are absence of a strict chain of command, actors operating as loosely coupled systems, life and death vs. profit and loss as operating philosophy, lack of coherence and congeniality among the supply chain actors, independent donor behaviour with varied mandates, high levels of uncertainty, shifting overall priorities etc. (Kovács and Spens 2007).

The literature does not clearly demarcate between humanitarian logistics (HL) and the humanitarian supply chain (HSC) (Kovács and Tatham, 2010). Thomas and Kopczak (2005) defined humanitarian logistics emphasizing on activities for efficient flow of information and material:

> The process of planning, implementing and controlling the efficient, cost-effective flow and storage of goods and materials, as well as related information, from the point of origin to the point of consumption for the purpose of alleviating the suffering of vulnerable people. (Thomas and Kopczak 2005)

Thomas and Kopczak (2005) fail to capture the synergistic impact of intra and inter-organizational practices on the overall humanitarian operations. HL was defined by Thomas and Mizushima (2005) as "the process of planning, implementing and controlling the effective, cost-efficient flow and storage of goods and materials as well as related information, from the point of origin to the point of consumption for the purpose of meeting the end beneficiary's requirements." Although there are strong elements of SCM implied in this definition, the humanitarian logistics is more tactical/operational oriented. It is a system that comes into its own once the disaster has occurred. For the purpose of this chapter, the above definition is being adopted. This definition provides a holistic view of the humanitarian logistics and establishes that humanitarian operations are not restricted to post disaster scenarios but a continuum, which starts before a disaster and continues after it.

Lee and Zbinden (2003) categorize activities in disaster management into three phases viz, pre-disaster preparedness phase, post-disaster response phase and recovery/rehabilitation phase as shown in Fig. 22.1.

The preparedness phase of the HSCM focuses on pre-positioning of stocks at critical places, getting into long term agreements with aid suppliers, logistics partnerships, preparation of contingency stock, and training volunteers. These decisions are usually made based on the historic profile of the disasters, geographical location and demographic location. Effectiveness of preparedness phase defines responsiveness of relief activities (Oloruntoba and Gray 2009). In the response phase, demand and stock availability (including on stand-by at supplier end and pre-positioned at warehouses) is reconciled to identify initial response capability. The damage assessment and demand estimation is the central activity. Log of balance stock and incoming donations is used for last mile distribution. In the recovery phase the focus shifts to long term rehabilitation of affected people. Effectiveness of preparedness phases is analysed and responsiveness of the response phase operations is also evaluated. The loss and damage is registered for compensations and claims (Kovács and Spens 2007). The recovery and rehabilitation phase aims at re-establishing local economy with

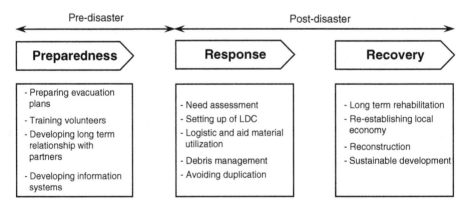

**Fig. 22.1** Stages of disaster management

sustainable development, reconstructing local infrastructure, and formulating long term rehabilitation plans (Thomas and Kopczak 2005).

# Review Methodology

Review process aims at creating a foundation for the advancement and facilitating theory development within the area under consideration. The review helps in discovering new areas for research and might as well indicate saturation of certain others. A three-stage process was used for this review, modified from methods employed by Tranfield et al. (2003):

- *Material collection*: Selection and defining the scope of the review process.
- *Category selection*: General aspects like author affiliation, year of publication, journal, etc., and specific aspects of the articles are selected in stage one.
- *Material classification and evaluation*: Analysing the meta-information and identifying emergent characteristics.

## Material Collection

Though humanitarian research is often published in practitioner journals (Beamon and Kotleba 2006) this review is restricted to the articles published in peer-reviewed academic journals since academic journals are the highest form of communication within academic community (Gunasekharan and Ngai 2005). The articles for review was selected through a systematic keyword searches methodology. The keyword strings were created for running queries in several journal databases.

The keywords used for selection were various alternatives of "humanitarian supply chain" from the literature. As discussed previously, similar usages of keywords across the literature facilitated usage of alternatives for material selection, "Humanitarian" was replaced by "disaster" or "emergency" or "relief". "Supply chain", "chain" and "logistics" were used interchangeably with "management". A total of 12 combinations of keywords were created using Boolean relationships. Examples of search terms included "humanitarian supply chain management", "relief chain management," or "emergency logistics management". Multiple keywords, such as "disaster" AND "supply chain", "relief" AND "logistics", or "humanitarian" AND "logistics" was searched for in the title and abstract. To gather the bibliography several databases were utilized such as science direct, emerald insight, SCOPUS, IEEE Xplore, Taylor and Francis, EBSCOhost and Wiley online. This review considers research articles published between 1995 and 2015 in peer-reviewed journals. The timeline for the review was selected to identify the impact of the Indian Ocean tsunami on the HSCM research. Van Wassenhove (2006) had mentioned the role Indian Ocean tsunami played in focusing the attention of academician and practitioners towards HSCM. Thus, the study wanted to compare the nature of studies pre-Indian Ocean tsunami and post-Indian Ocean tsunami.

## Category Selection

The articles were classified based on bibliographic categories and research based categories. The classification categories used for the review of selected articles were year of publication, author affiliation, methodology used, disaster types and operational stage and research type. The bibliographic categories include year and author affiliation. The research categories include the operational stage of the research, disaster focussed in the study, research type and the methodology used. These categories were selected to identify the nature of empirical studies on HSCM.

### Author Affiliation

The affiliations were named "international" if the authors represented collaborative research were they were from different continents. If the authors were form the North America, we have marked it as "USA and Canada" as almost all the publications were from USA except for a few exceptions. For authors from other continents we have used markers "Europe", "Asia", "Africa and Middle East", and "Australia and Oceania" depending upon their affiliation.

### Operational Stage

Lee and Zbinden (2003) categorize humanitarian operation into three categories: pre disaster preparedness phase, post-disaster response phase, and post-disaster rehabilitation phase. However, it is not possible to have a water tight compartmentalization of the humanitarian processes, yet from a research point of view, one needs to address a specific question. In this regard, we have categorized the research based on the main focus of the paper. For example, a paper addressing search and rescue operation is categorized as response operation, whereas rebuilding is categorized as a relief/rehabilitation operation. Research papers addressing more than one phase of the disaster management has been categorized as "multiple" while classifying. For example, research papers focussing on the performance measurement of the disaster management operations is categorized as "multiple".

## Disaster Type

Nature of the disaster type addressed in the research forms the basis of this categorization. We have categorized them as "natural" (floods, earth-quakes, cyclones, etc.), "man-made" (accidents, terrorist attacks, civil wars, etc.), "humanitarian" or "all types" if no specific disaster type is being defined. "Humanitarian" disasters are complex in nature and they might be a combination of the multiple individual disasters. For instance, the large earthquake in a country might trigger a mass exodus of people leading to large number of internally displaced people creating a refugee crisis.

## Research Type

Wacker (1998) classifies the research in operations management from a theory building perspective into two major categories: viz. analytical (formal) research and empirical research. The formal research primarily employs a deductive approach whereas the empirical studies use primarily an inductive approach. Since the focus of this study is purely on the empirical studies in HSCM, only the classification of the empirical studies proposed by Wacker (1998) is being used here. This classification scheme helps in classifying the selected papers based on the nature of theory building exercise undertaken in each study within the realm of empirical methodologies.

Empirical research methodology uses the data from the external organizations to test the hypothesized relationships. The empirical research is again classified into three major sub-groups: viz. empirical experimental research (EER), empirical statistical research (ESR), and empirical case study research (ECR). EER focuses on the careful manipulations of the variables and relationships to identify the effect of the one variable on the other. These studies focus on drawing out causalities of the relationships. This type of research requires a closed environment for the validity of the assumptions. ESR is used to empirically verify the theoretical relationships developed based on the observation from the real world using structured or unstructured data collected through interviews, field visits, survey instruments, etc. ECR is used to develop relationships within a limited set of data points. Primarily the sample size is kept small but with a large number of variables to identify new empirical relationships. ECR studies include field studies, action research etc. ECR does not focus as much on the generalizability as much as the relationship building with the domain of the case under consideration (Meredith et al. 1989).

## Methodology

The empirical research is classified based on the primary methodology used in the research, such as action research, case study, filed studies (includes group interviews, Delphi method, panel discussion, focus groups, structured and semi-structured interviews, etc.) statistical analysis (use of

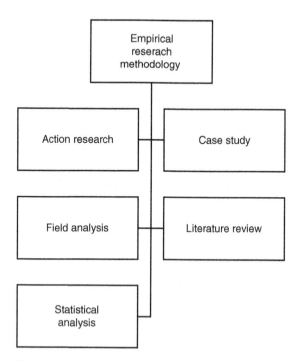

**Fig. 22.2**  Classification schema for the literature review

econometric models on either primary or secondary data). The studies focussing on theory building and proposing frameworks are included in this review as empirical studies in HSCM. Previous literature reviews in HSCM are also included in this review. Figure 22.2 summarizes the classification schema used in this study.

# Results

A total of 142 articles were collected by structured search method as described in section "Review Methodology". These articles were classified based on attributes for each article such as methodology, operational stage, disaster type, and research type. This section provides a discussion on the summary of the articles reviewed.

## Year of Publication and Author Affiliation

As shown in Fig. 22.3, the first decade of the review window, i.e., between 1995 and 2005, not many publications on humanitarian logistics can be found. However, post 2005, the number of publications have significantly increased. This surge can be attributed to the Indian Ocean tsunami (2004) leading to a widespread damage across many Asian countries.

Figure 22.4 summarizes the author's affiliation of the reviewed articles. Unlike as observed by two previous studies (Altay and Green 2006 and Galindo and Batta 2013) reviewing analytical studies, Europe contributes a major part (41%) of the total empirical research in the field of humanitarian

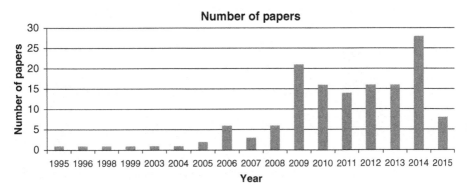

**Fig. 22.3** Number of publications

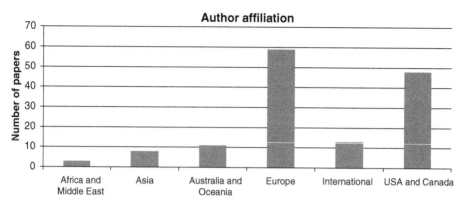

**Fig. 22.4** Author affiliation

logistics. USA and Canada comes second with about 34% of the total publications whereas authors with "International" and Asian affiliation contribute about 9% and 5% of total publications, respectively.

## Operational Stage

About half (49%) of the papers address multiple stages of humanitarian logistics. Furthermore, nearly quarter (26%) of the total articles focussed on issues relating to response stage of the humanitarian logistics. Only

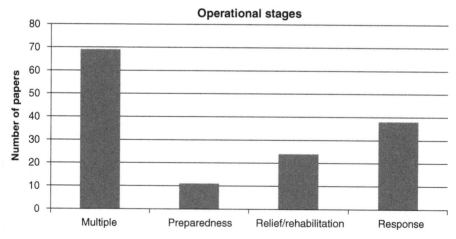

**Fig. 22.5** Disaster operational stage

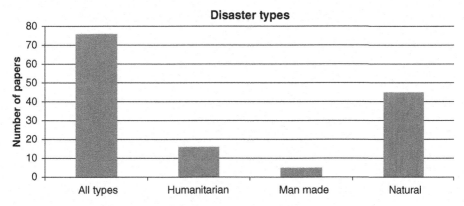

**Fig. 22.6**  Types of disasters studied

7% of the research papers dealt with the preparedness issues whereas about 14% of the papers focus on the relief/rehabilitation phase of the humanitarian operations. The classification of the papers is shown in Fig. 22.5

## Disaster Type

Nearly 31% of the papers are based on the natural disasters whereas 54% of the papers do not specify any particular type of disaster and take a more generic view of the entire process. Only a meagre 11% and 3% of studies focus on humanitarian and man-made issues, respectively. Other than few handful studies, man-made disasters, and humanitarian disasters are not much looked into (Fig. 22.6).

# Methodological Classification

Figure 22.7 also shows the trend of the research in humanitarian logistics. The empirical studies have still not gained traction with the academic community even after multiple authors have argued for the role empirical studies towards theory building in HSCM (Kovács and Spens 2007; Kovács and Tatham 2009; Richey 2009; Tatham and Houghton 2011).

The humanitarian studies, has been traditionally based on the empirical research as shown in Fig. 22.7. In this section, we analyse the nature of

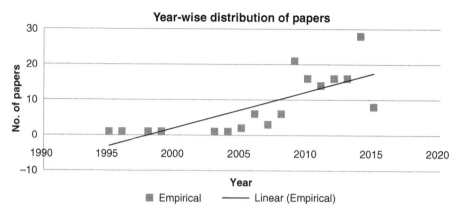

**Fig. 22.7** Trend of empirical studies in HSCM research

methodologies used in the empirical research in humanitarian logistics studies, based on the operational phases, methodologies, disaster types, and research types. Furthermore, a temporal classification of the studies based on the case studies used in the empirical research is considered for two reasons. First, the case studies are the most commonly used empirical methodology, and second, to the identify the cases that have acted as the context for the HSCM studies.

## Operational Phases

The humanitarian logistics operations can be sectored into three main operational phase: preparedness phase, response phase and relief/rehabilitation phase. Those studies which focus on more than one phase are classified as "multiple". Table 22.1 summarizes the distribution of various methodologies in empirical research according to the operational phase within which the studies are anchored.

The primary observation from Table 22.1 indicates that the empirical research in HSCM focuses more on multiple phase issues (Fig. 22.2). Nearly half (49%) of the studies using empirical research methodologies focus on the issues not restricted to any single phase of the HSCM operation. Comparing to the review of OR/MS studies in HSCM published by Altay and Green (2006) and Galindo and Batta (2013, there is in stark difference compared to the overall distribution of the studies across the phases of HSCM operations. Response phase issues studied using the empirical research methodologies account to 27% of the total studies whereas, relief/

**Table 22.1** Distribution of empirical studies based on the operational phases

| Methodology | 1995 | 1996 | 1998 | 1999 | 2003 | 2004 | 2005 | 2006 | 2007 | 2008 | 2009 | 2010 | 2011 | 2012 | 2013 | 2014 | 2015 | Grand Total |
|---|---|---|---|---|---|---|---|---|---|---|---|---|---|---|---|---|---|---|
| **Multiple** | 1 | | | | 1 | 1 | 1 | 2 | 1 | 1 | 9 | 7 | 5 | 7 | 11 | 16 | 6 | 69 |
| Case study | 1 | | | | | | | | | | | | | 1 | 2 | 5 | 2 | 11 |
| Conceptual | | | | | | 1 | 1 | 2 | | 1 | 5 | 5 | 2 | 4 | 3 | 5 | | 29 |
| Field studies | | | | | 1 | | | | | | 2 | 1 | 2 | 1 | 3 | 1 | 1 | 12 |
| Literature review | | | | | | | | | 1 | | 1 | | 1 | | 3 | 5 | | 12 |
| Statistical analysis | | | | | | | | | | | 1 | 1 | | 1 | | | 3 | 6 |
| **Preparedness** | | | | | | | | | | 1 | 1 | 2 | 2 | 1 | | 2 | 2 | 11 |
| Case study | | | | | | | | | | | | 1 | 1 | | | 1 | 1 | 4 |
| Conceptual | | | | | | | | | | 1 | 1 | | | 1 | | | 1 | 4 |
| Field studies | | | | | | | | | | | | 1 | 1 | | | | | 2 |
| Statistical analysis | | | | | | | | | | | | | | | | 1 | | 1 |
| **Relief/rehabilitation** | | | | 1 | | | | 1 | 1 | 4 | 5 | 1 | 1 | 4 | 3 | 3 | | 24 |
| Case study | | | | | | | | 1 | 1 | | | | | | | | | 2 |
| Conceptual | | | | | | | | | | 4 | 2 | 1 | 1 | | | | | 8 |
| Field studies | | | | 1 | | | | | | | 3 | | | 1 | 3 | | | 8 |
| Statistical analysis | | | | | | | | | | | | | | 3 | | 3 | | 6 |
| **Response** | | 1 | 1 | | | | 1 | 3 | 1 | | 6 | 6 | 6 | 4 | 2 | 7 | | 38 |
| Action research | | | | | | | | | | | | | 1 | | | | | 1 |
| Case study | | 1 | 1 | | | | | 1 | 1 | | 2 | 1 | | | | 1 | | 8 |
| Conceptual | | | | | | | | 2 | | | 3 | 2 | 1 | 1 | 1 | | | 10 |
| Field studies | | | | | | | 1 | | | | 1 | 2 | 2 | 2 | | 2 | | 10 |
| Statistical analysis | | | | | | | | | | | | 1 | 2 | 1 | 1 | 3 | | 8 |
| **Grand total** | 1 | 1 | 1 | 1 | 1 | 1 | 2 | 6 | 3 | 6 | 21 | 16 | 14 | 16 | 16 | 28 | 8 | 142 |

**Table 22.2** Methodological distribution of empirical studies

| Methodology | 1995 | 1996 | 1998 | 1999 | 2003 | 2004 | 2005 | 2006 | 2007 | 2008 | 2009 | 2010 | 2011 | 2012 | 2013 | 2014 | 2015 | Grand Total |
|---|---|---|---|---|---|---|---|---|---|---|---|---|---|---|---|---|---|---|
| Action research | | | | | | | | | | | | | 1 | | | | | 1 |
| Case study | 1 | | 1 | | | | | 1 | | | 3 | 2 | 2 | 2 | 3 | 6 | 4 | 25 |
| Conceptual | | | | | | 1 | 1 | 4 | 1 | 6 | 10 | 8 | 4 | 3 | 3 | 8 | 2 | 51 |
| Field studies | | 1 | | 1 | 1 | | 1 | 1 | 1 | | 5 | 4 | 5 | 7 | 1 | 3 | 1 | 32 |
| Literature review | | | | | | | | | 1 | | 1 | | 1 | 1 | 3 | 5 | | 12 |
| Statistical analysis | | | | | | | | | | | 2 | 2 | 1 | 3 | 6 | 6 | 1 | 21 |
| **Grand total** | 1 | 1 | 1 | 1 | 1 | 1 | 2 | 6 | 3 | 6 | 21 | 16 | 14 | 16 | 16 | 28 | 8 | 142 |

rehabilitation phase studies and preparedness phase studies account for 17% and 8% of the studies, respectively. Table 22.2 shows the year-wise distribution of use of empirical methodologies in HSCM research. Table 22.2 shows that conceptual studies which use empirical methodologies are most common studies.

From Table 22.1, under the multiple phase studies in HSCM, the conceptual studies are the most common ones. These studies either focus on developing frameworks and models for operationalizing various humanitarian initiatives (Stephenson 2005; Poulton et al. 2006; Alexander et al. 2006; Caroll and Neu 2009; Chandes and Pache 2010) or explores various humanitarian challenges from a multiple phase perspective (Oloruntoba and Gray 2006; Smirnov et al. 2007; Regnier et al. 2008; Jahre et al. 2009; Otham et al. 2014). Multiple phase studies started to gain momentum post 2008 and have seen a steady increase since then. The field studies account for only 17% of the total multiple phase empirical studies in HSCM and case studies and studies employing statistical analysis account for 16% and 9%, respectively.

Empirical studies focusing on the response phase of the HSCM operations shows a similar trend as the multiple phase research. The conceptual studies (Poulton et al. 2006; Alexander et al. 2006; Seybolt 2009; Kovács et al. 2012) and field based studies (Moore 1996; Oloruntoba 2005; Guven and Ergen 2011; Merminod et al. 2014; Holguin-Veras et al. 2014) have dominated the response phase studies as well with both accounting for about 26% of them individually. Studies employing statistical analysis and case study methodology each account for about 22% of studies. Only one study (Yates and Paquette 2011) use action research as the principal methodology in response phase study for identifying the impact of social media in responding to a disaster. The empirical studies in HSCM in preparedness phase and relief/rehabilitation phase account for 8% and 17% of the studies, respectively. The principal methodologies used in these phases of research include case study methodology, conceptual studies, field studies and statistical analysis. The year-wise distribution is summarized in Table 22.1.

## Disaster Types

The year-wise distribution of the empirical methodologies according to the types of disaster focus is being summarized in Table 22.3. Table 22.3 shows that more than half (54%) of the studies employing empirical methodologies

**Table 22.3** Methodological distribution of empirical studies based on disaster types

| Methodology | 1995 | 1996 | 1998 | 1999 | 2003 | 2004 | 2005 | 2006 | 2007 | 2008 | 2009 | 2010 | 2011 | 2012 | 2013 | 2014 | 2015 | Grand Total |
|---|---|---|---|---|---|---|---|---|---|---|---|---|---|---|---|---|---|---|
| **All types** | | | | | | 1 | 1 | 3 | 1 | 4 | 10 | 10 | 8 | 6 | 10 | 15 | 7 | 76 |
| Case study | | | | | | | | | | | 1 | 1 | 2 | 1 | | 3 | 2 | 10 |
| Conceptual | | | | | | 1 | 1 | 3 | | 4 | 6 | 8 | 2 | 2 | 2 | 3 | 2 | 34 |
| Field studies | | | | | | | | | | | 1 | | 2 | 1 | | 1 | 2 | 7 |
| Literature review | | | | | | | | | 1 | | 1 | 1 | 1 | | 3 | 5 | | 12 |
| Statistical analysis | | | | | | | | | | | 1 | | 1 | 2 | 5 | 3 | 1 | 13 |
| **Humanitarian** | 1 | | | | | | | | | 1 | 8 | 1 | 1 | 1 | 2 | 1 | | 16 |
| Case study | 1 | | | | | | | | | | 2 | | | 1 | 1 | | | 5 |
| Conceptual | | | | | | | | | | | 4 | | 1 | | 1 | 1 | | 7 |
| Field studies | | | | | | | | | | 1 | 2 | 1 | | | | | | 4 |
| **Man made** | | 1 | 1 | | | | | | | | | | 2 | 1 | | | | 5 |
| Case study | | | 1 | | | | | | | | | | 1 | | | | | 2 |
| Conceptual | | | | | | | | | | | | | 1 | | | | | 1 |
| Field studies | | 1 | | | | | | | | | | | | | | | | 1 |
| Statistical analysis | | | | | | | | | | | | | | 1 | | | | 1 |
| **Natural** | | | | 1 | 1 | | 1 | 3 | 2 | 1 | 3 | 5 | 3 | 8 | 4 | 12 | 1 | 45 |
| Action research | | | | 1 | | | | | | | | | | | | | | 1 |
| Case study | | | | | | | 1 | 1 | | | | 1 | 1 | | 2 | 2 | | 8 |
| Conceptual | | | | | | | | 1 | 1 | 1 | | 1 | 1 | 2 | | 2 | | 9 |
| Field studies | | | | | 1 | | | 1 | 1 | | 3 | 1 | 1 | 5 | 1 | 5 | 1 | 20 |
| Statistical analysis | | | | | | | | | | | | 2 | | 1 | 1 | 3 | | 7 |
| **Grand total** | 1 | 1 | 1 | 1 | 1 | 1 | 2 | 6 | 3 | 6 | 21 | 16 | 14 | 16 | 16 | 28 | 8 | 142 |

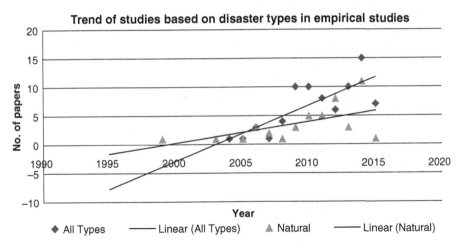

**Fig. 22.8** Trend of studies based on disaster types in empirical studies

take a generic view of disasters, while 32% of papers focus specifically on the natural disasters. Humanitarian disasters and manmade disasters account for 11% and 4% of the studies, respectively.

The empirical research has focused less on natural disasters. This can be explained by the methodological classification in the empirical research with respect to the disaster types. Most of the empirical studies in HSCM research which take a generic view of disaster use conceptual modelling as the primary methodology. These studies aim towards theory building (Jahre et al. 2009; Glenn Richey 2009) or conceptual exploration (Hristidis et al. 2010; Scholten et al. 2010; Geale 2011a; Haavisto and Kovács 2014). Figure 22.8 shows the trend of distribution of the papers based on the disaster type. It can be observed that the empirical studies taking a generic view on the disaster has received greater attention post 2005, whereas the prior to 2005, the empirical studies preferred anchoring their exploration based on the natural disasters. This also indicates that the research in HSCM is evolving towards the general theory for disaster management. This trend towards the general theory for the HSCM shows the evolution of the area (Meredith et al. 1989).

## Research Type

The classification of the empirical studies in HSCM based on Wacker (1998) research types is summarized in Table 22.4. ECR is the most common type

Table 22.4 Methodological distribution of empirical studies based on research types

| Research types | 1995 | 1996 | 1998 | 1999 | 2003 | 2004 | 2005 | 2006 | 2007 | 2008 | 2009 | 2010 | 2011 | 2012 | 2013 | 2014 | 2015 |
|---|---|---|---|---|---|---|---|---|---|---|---|---|---|---|---|---|---|
| **Empirical Case study** | 1 | 1 | 1 | 1 | 1 | 1 | 2 | 6 | 3 | 6 | 19 | 11 | 10 | 11 | 10 | 22 | 7 |
| Action research | | | | | | | | | | | | | 1 | | | | |
| Case study | 1 | | 1 | | | | | 1 | | | 3 | 2 | 2 | 2 | 3 | 6 | 4 |
| Conceptual | | | | | 1 | 1 | | 4 | | 6 | 10 | 6 | 4 | 3 | 3 | 8 | 2 |
| Field studies | | 1 | | 1 | | | 1 | 1 | 1 | | 5 | 3 | 2 | 5 | 1 | 3 | 1 |
| Literature review | | | | | 1 | | 1 | | 1 | | 1 | | | | 3 | 5 | |
| **Empirical experimental** | | | | | | | | | | | | | | | | | |
| Conceptual | | | | | | | | | | | | 1 | 1 | | 1 | | |
| Statistical analysis | | | | | | | | | | | | 1 | 1 | 1 | | | |
| **Empirical statistical** | | | | | | | | | | | 2 | 4 | 3 | 5 | 5 | 6 | 1 |
| Conceptual | | | | | | | | | | | | 1 | | | | | |
| Field studies | | | | | | | | | | | | 1 | 3 | 2 | | | |
| Statistical analysis | | | | | | | | | | | 2 | 2 | | 3 | 5 | 6 | 1 |

of theory building exercise in HSCM research. ECR accounts for nearly 80% of the total research output. ESR accounts for the rest 18% of the research and EER account for a meagre 2% of the studies. Table 22.4 summarizes the distribution of the research types in HSCM empirical studies. As observed previously, majority of ECR anchored on conceptual arguments either based on multiple cases (Schulz and Blecken 2010; Thevenaz and Resodihardjo 2010; Martinez et al. 2011; Mazurana et al. 2013; Merminod et al. 2014; Tatham et al. 2015) or develop theory based on insights from various sources and published reports on one or more disaster incident (Perry 2007; Caroll and Neu 2009). ESR has employed various statistical methodologies to identify relationships between the disaster impact and its quantification. ESR study the macro-economic impact of the disaster (Noy 2009), need for international aid in relief and rehabilitation (Fink and Radaelli 2011), volume and nature of calls in a disaster scenario (McLay et al. 2012), relationship between the aid and disaster democracy (Kalyvitis and Vlachaki 2012), impact of public-private partnership in disaster relief operations (Swanson and Smith 2013). Most commonly used statistical analysis methodology is regression. Only three studies have been experimental in nature while being classified as the EER. Hristidis et al. (2010) explored the nature of data management and analysis carried out during a disaster situation while Kumar and Havey (2013) explored the nature and functioning of a decision support system in both pre-disaster and post-disaster scenario. These two studies focused on multiple stages in the HSCM operations. Huber et al. (2011) focused on evaluating the performance measurement systems during the response phase of the humanitarian logistics activities.

## Cases in Empirical Studies

The case studies in HSCM research are a source of rich data and provide opportunities to explore the interaction between multiple factors. The very nature of the HSCM research warrants more empirical case based approaches to understand the machinery of HSCM operations. To gather insights into the cases that have been used in the HSCM research, the study tabulates a temporal distribution of the cases in Table 22.5. Table 22.5 also indicates the major disasters (which have resulted in the death of at least 200 people or injured at least 1000) that have occurred in during the time frame (1995–2015) of our review. The data for this was collected from EM-DAT.

**Table 22.5** Distribution of case studies used in empirical research

| Major Disaster between 1995 and 2015 / Cases | 1995 | 1996 | 1997 | 1998 Hurricane Mitch, Central America | 1999 Western Turkey earthquake; Odisha super cyclone | 2000 | 2001 | 2002 | 2003 South eastern Iran earthquake | 2004 Indian Ocean tsunami | 2005 U.S. Gulf Coast Hurricane Katrina; Northern Pakistan earthquake | 2006 | 2007 | 2008 Sichuan Earthquake, China | 2009 | 2010 Haitian Earthquake | 2011 Tohoku Earthquake, Japan | 2012 Cyclone Sandy, USA | 2013 Typhoon Haiyan, Philippines; Pakistan earthquake | 2014 Pakistan Floods | 2015 Nepal earthquake, Chennai Floods, India |
|---|---|---|---|---|---|---|---|---|---|---|---|---|---|---|---|---|---|---|---|---|---|
| Afghanistan | | | | | | | | | | | | | | | 1 | | | | | | |
| Africa | | | | | | | | | | | | | | | 1 | | | | | | |
| Chad | | | | | | | | | | | | | | | | | | | 1 | | |
| Cyclone Larry, Australia | | | | | | | | | | | | | | | | 1 | | | | | |
| Darfur, Sudan | | | | | | | | | | | | | | | | | | 1 | | | |
| Ethiopia | | | | | | | | | | | | | | | 1 | | | | | | |
| Fiji | | | | | | | | | | | | | | | 1 | | | | | | |
| Haitian Earthquake | | | | | | | | | | | | | | | | | 1 | 2 | | 1 | |
| Humanitarian Organization | | | | | | | | | | | | | | | | | | | | 1 | |
| Hurricane Georges, Dominican Republic | | | | | 1 | | | | | | | | | | | | | | | | |
| Hurricane Katrina | | | | | | | | | | | | | | | | | | | | 1 | |
| India | | | | | | | | | 1 | | | | | | | | | | | | |
| Indian Ocean tsunami | | | | | | | | | | | 1 | 1 | | | | | | | | | |

| | | | | | | | | |
|---|---|---|---|---|---|---|---|---|
| Lagos, Nigeria | | | | | | 1 | | 1 |
| Lake Nyos Disaster, Cameroon | | | | | 1 | 1 | | |
| Liberia and sierra Leone | 1 | | | | | | | |
| Malawi refugee crisis | 1 | | | | | 1 | | 1 |
| Mozambique Cholera outbreak | | | 1 | | | 1 | | |
| Mumbai, India | | | | | | 1 | | |
| Odisha Super cyclone, India | | | 1 | | | 1 | | |
| Pakistan Earthquake | | | | | 1 | | | |
| Turkey | | | | 1 | | | | |
| Uttaranchal, India | | | | | | | | |
| Voluntary Organizations Active in Disaster (VOAD) El Paso, Texas | | | | | | | 1 | |
| Yogyakarta Earthquake, Japan | | | | | 1 | | | |

From Table 22.5, shows that most of the major disasters have not been considered as a candidate for the case studies in last two decades. Haitian earthquake (Yates and Paquette 2011; Holguin-Veras et al. 2012; Coles et al. 2012; Altay and Labonte 2014) and Indian Ocean tsunami (Oloruntoba 2005; Clasen et al. 2006; Scharffscher 2011; Athukorala 2012) are most commonly used events as cases for evaluation. Other events which have drawn attention of the researchers were not major events in particular.

## Discussion and Future Research

The review brought out various themes in the research carried out in HSCM. These themes mostly revolve around multiple stage issues. The complexity of the humanitarian operations requires strategic alignment between various stages. The literature shows that majority of research focus on multiple phases of disaster management operations than single phase studies. These results are in direct contradictions to previous methodological reviews (Altay and Green 2006; Galindo and Batta 2013) anchored in analytical reviews. One of the major findings of this review is that there is a stark difference in the nature of problems studied using analytical methodologies and empirical methodologies. This shows a serious limitation of the disaster management research anchored in the analytical studies which fails to transcend operational phase boundaries. Figure 22.9 outlines the timeline of the major activities carried out in HSCM according to the operational phases.

The limitations of single phase research are the restricting assumptions made while defining the system. The localized focus of the research question oblivious to multiple phase extensions of the problem tends to produce a suboptimal solution in a localized domain. These modelling approaches fail to address the complexities associated with multiple phases and changing nature of the problem across the phases. The simplifying assumptions fail to capture the complexity associated with the problem. The second challenge with single phase research is the inability of the models to capture the changing nature of operational issues across the timeline. This can be observed in the nature of the supply chain itself. During the initial stages, when the focus of the relief operations is on saving lives of affected people, the supply chain needs to be responsive. However, as the time passes and the relief operations stabilizes and the focus shifts towards recovery and the supply chain needs to transform itself to an efficient supply chain (Oloruntoba and Gray 2009). The change in the nature of supply chain

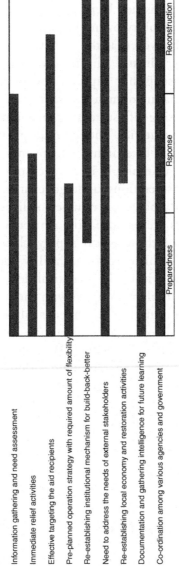

**Fig. 22.9** Timeline of disaster relief issues

is slow rather than an abrupt transformation. Majority of studies focussing on issues like inventory management, vehicle routing, facility location, performance measurement, etc. tend to take a minimalistic view of this transformation and focus on individual stages of disaster relief operations. For example, inventory studies in disaster management mostly focus on post-disaster response phase issues. Demand profile in the response stage is stochastic with a high variability owing to poor need assessment and the quality of information. However, as the operations stabilize, information becomes reliable and deterministic. This transformation of demand profile in the post-disaster phase is not captured by piece-wise optimization approach. Similarly, the nature of materials requirement undergoes change with initial stages requiring life-sustaining materials whereas the later stages need rehabilitation material. Though multiple item inventory models are studied, the nature of these items remains more or less similar. The challenge lies in modelling multiple item inventory models with varied characteristics. Cost considerations undergo changes as well. Response stage functions are mostly based on number of lives saved, whereas the rehabilitation phase costs are based on the efficiency of the relief operations. The exploration of the classical supply chain problems such as inventory management, vehicle routing, facility locations, scheduling, etc. is primarily anchored within the analytical domain. However, while the complexity of these problems coupled with the restrictive assumption used in model formulation in HSCM renders analytical solutions of little practical significance. This offers an opportunity to explore these issues from an empirical perspective. Modelling the inter-relationships between the factors affecting the various operational decisions, use of econometric models for predictions, use of secondary data to model the impact of the disasters are few direction where empirical approaches could be used to overcome the methodological challenges associated with analytical modelling.

## Future Research

### Response and Rehabilitation Phase

One of the major gaps in the humanitarian literature is the lack of academic research in conjunction with the humanitarian agencies. Even though the survey indicates a large number of cases studies in various setting, majority of studies are not carried out in association with any humanitarian organization.

Another area which requires immediate attention from the research is on relief/rehabilitation phase. Previous reviews (Lettieri et al. 2009; Galindo and Batta 2013) have also made similar observations. There are very few studies that focus on the economic continuity and infrastructure rebuilding in the affected areas. One of the ways to re-establish the economic activities in the affected area is by focussing on the business continuity. More research needs to be carried out in understanding and re-establishing the disrupted business supply chains, production of goods, recovery time frames for the affected community, infrastructure redesigns, etc. From a methodological point of view, the nature of challenge often presented in the recovery and rehabilitation phases are complex with multiple stakeholders with often conflicting mandates working together. Though this complexity does not seem to be unique for recovery and rehabilitation stage, the lack of urgency associated with the decision making often leads to lesser utility of analytical models in this stage. The empirical studies, especially those based on the secondary data can be used for the identifying macroeconomic consequences of the recovery strategies used in this stage.

The empirical studies using primary data and statistical analysis can be used for understanding the needs of the affected community at large. Often seen as an opportunity to build-back-better in post disaster, the empirical methodologies especially case studies and field studies can be used for the gaining first-hand information regarding the affected community. Moreover, the nature of impact of the disaster on the community also needs to be studied. The impact of the external aid on the local political regimes has not been studied well in literature. Though studies have pointed out the negative impact of the external aid on the affected communities in general, further enquires are required to understand impact of external aid on infrastructure building, education aid, health care financing and environmental impact. An aggregate analysis of the representative impact of the aid through empirical enquires remains open and requires much refinement. Studies anchored in rehabilitation phase require further enquiries into improvements in housing, transportation, and nature of collaborative efforts between communities based organizations and private sector organizations. Furthermore, there is a need to explore the public-private partnership for effective rehabilitation of the affected communities. Frameworks for partnerships between the affected communities and private sectors towards preparing against disaster vulnerabilities and rehabilitation needs to be prepared for cross-learning opportunities.

**Multiple Phase Research**

The complex and multidisciplinary nature of HSCM demands synergetic associations between various domains. There is a need to model a combined procurement and transportation system linking both preparedness and response phases. Another area of multi-phases and multi-disciplinary research in HSCM would be to explore the epidemic progression post disaster. These models could be combined with supply chain models (multi-echelon, multi-commodity, multi-period, multi-vehicle approaches, etc.) as well. The forecast model extending across phases to capture the nature of variation of the demand across the phases needs to be explored. These forecast models could be used to build in more visibility across the supply chain for both suppliers and customers.

Often the complexity associated with the multiple stakeholder multiple phase issues becomes difficult to be solved using the analytical methodologies With issues in HSCM like coordination challenges that extend throughout the phases of HSCM and yet have received very little academic investigation (Balcik et al. 2010), empirical studies can be used to glean a better understanding of the problem. With a large number of stakeholder, a stakeholder analysis into the changing perceptions and characteristic of the stakeholder will help gain better understanding of the complex challenges in coordination. Further studies are required to explore the inter-relationships between various factors that affect coordination in the complex environment of the HSCM. More studies are required to explore the relationships between multiple stakeholders in the system. Furthermore, quantification of the benefit due to coordination should be explored to explore option for incentivizing the stakeholders to coordinate among them. Cross-functional, inter-agency collaboration and the role of practitioners should also be considered.

# Conclusion

In this paper we have presented a review of empirical studies in HSCM literature from 1995–2015. The articles for the review was collated through a systematic keywords based search and were further classified based on author affiliation, year of publication, research type, operational phase, methodological considerations and the nature of the problem studied. We have identified that there is a between the practitioner requirements and the academic research. This suggests the need for a practitioner oriented research in humanitarian logistics area.

We have also discussed research gaps in the literature and classified the gaps according to the various phases of research. However, the nature of the topic warrants more multiple phase research which has also been discussed. At a broad level, HSCM requires further collaboration between practitioners and academicians. Further research is required to improve coordination between various stakeholders in HSCM, use of robust technologies for HSCM operations, multiple phase studies and developing theoretical foundation for HSCM operations.

# Appendix 1: Summary of literature reviews in HSCM

| Criteria | Scope | Database used | Keywords | Review Period | Classification of papers? | If yes, which categories? | Findings | Proposed research areas |
|---|---|---|---|---|---|---|---|---|
| **Altay and Green (2006)** | OR/MS literature in disaster operations management | ISI Web of Science IFORMS search engine Business Source Premier Cambridge Scientific Abstracts IDS Compendenx Engineering Village 2 Scirus Econbase Civil Engineering Database Scitation SciFinder | Disaster emergency catastrophe extreme event disastrous catastrophic | 1980–2004 | Yes | Phase of disaster research methodology research contribution cause of disaster publication period problem scenario | Mathematical programming is most frequently used method system dynamics, constraint programming and soft OR techniques are underused | Do more research on reconstruction phase, Develop mitigation tools, Develop theory on preparation, response and reconstruction phases, Use new methodologies such as system dynamics, fuzzy systems, soft OR more multi-agency research considering political |
| **Kovács and Spens (2007)** | Literature on humanitarian logistics | Several journal databases | Humanitarian AND logistics humanitarian aid AND supply chains disaster relief AND logistics disaster relief AND supply chains emergency AND | Not specified | No | | Literature focuses on the preparation phase with little focus on immediate response phase, Insufficient mitigation phase studies to | Do more research on response and reconstruction phases, Do more research on planning and execution of operations in disaster relief, Do more research on links and |

(continued)

| Criteria | Scope | Database used | Keywords | Review Period | Classification of papers? | If yes, which categories? | Findings | Proposed research areas |
|---|---|---|---|---|---|---|---|---|
| | | | logistics emergency AND supply chain | | | | address man-made disasters, | similarities between humanitarian logistics and business logistics |
| **Natarajarathinam et al. (2009)** | Literature of supply chain management (SCM) in times of crisis | ProQuest ABI/ Inform EBSCO Science Direct | Crisis risks disaster uncertainty emergency disruption catastrophe crisis management risk management disastrous catastrophic | Pre-1990 to 2008 | Yes | Source of crisis scale of crisis phase of crisis management research methodology type of respondent to crisis | Increase in number of publications in the last years, Increase of number of paper focusing on several phases of disaster management, More research on mitigation and preparation phases, Few research on the recovery phases, Limited empirical, Many analytical research using OR techniques applied research | Do more research on reconstruction phase, Develop scales for level of crisis management, Do more research on robustness and resilience of supply chains, Do more case studies and empirical research, Do more research on supply chain management crisis arising from internal sources |
| **Letteri et al. 2009** | Systematic literature review of Disaster Management | Systematic Review the Social Science Citation Index (SSCI | Disasters, Risk management, Defence sector | 1980–2006 | Yes | Reference, authors, year of publication, journal name, methodology, | Need for a holistic theory in disaster management, Major contributions from US and Canada, | Performance management and knowledge management, organizational issues, meta- |

(continued)

**Appendix** (continued)

| Criteria | Scope | Database used | Keywords | Review Period | Classification of papers? | If yes, which categories? | Findings | Proposed research areas |
|---|---|---|---|---|---|---|---|---|
| | | | | | | country of association | Major studies are process based, lack of studies on learning | organizations, network theory |
| Pettit and Beresford (2009) | Literature about critical success factors in the commercial context | Not specified | Not specified | Not specified | No | | Critical success factors from commercial context are equally important in the humanitarian aid context, Cultural elements and political constraints play an important role in HSCM, Effectiveness of a humanitarian supply chains is determined by structural or cultural factors | Test the critical success factors proposed in the study through qualitative research in the context of humanitarian aid |
| Overstreet et al. 2011 | Framework for research in HSCM | EBSCOHOST, ABI/ Informs, Elsevier, and Google Scholar | Supply chain management, Humanitarian logistics, Disaster relief, Research | Not specified | No | | Research in HSCM and HL is still at infancy, | Organization's personnel, equipment/infrastructure, transportation, information technology/communication, and |

*(continued)*

| Criteria | Scope | Database used | Keywords | Review Period | Classification of papers? | If yes, which categories? | Findings | Proposed research areas |
|---|---|---|---|---|---|---|---|---|
| | | | | | | | | inventory management as they relate to the humanitarian logistics. |
| **Kunz and Reiner (2012)** | Identify the most frequently studied situational factors in the humanitarian research | Business Source Complete, Science Direct, ABI/INFORM Global and Web of Science | Logistics, supply chain, humanitarian and relief | 2010–2011 | Yes | Context of operations, Speed of start, Cause of disaster, Phase of disaster management, Research methodology and Situational factor | Governmental, socio-economic, infrastructural and environmental are the major situational factors under which the major types of research has been done. | Slow onset disasters and continuous aid process is being neglected in the research, More research to focus on the man-made disasters as well with focus on the reconstruction phase of the disaster management, Need for empirical methodologies in the research. |
| **Galindo and Batta (2013)** | OR/MS literature in disaster operations management from 2005–2010 | ISI's Web of Science, Business Source Complete, Compendex Engineering Village 2, Scirus, Emerald, JSTOR, Scitation and Google Scholar | Disaster | 2005–2010 | Yes | Phase of disaster research methodology research contribution cause of disaster publication period problem scenario | Mathematical programming is the most frequently used method with conceptual analysis and combined methodologies gaining importance. Game theory, constrained programming and soft OR are still the under used | Coordination analysis using cluster based approaches, Introduction of technology application based studies, using statistical analysis tools for evaluating the DOM problems, in-depth exploration of soft OR methodologies |

*(continued)*

**Appendix** (continued)

| Criteria | Scope | Database used | Review Period | Keywords | Classification of papers? | If yes, which categories? | Findings | Proposed research areas |
|---|---|---|---|---|---|---|---|---|
| **Abidi et al. 2014** | Humanitarian supply chain performance | EBSCOHOST, ABI/ Informs, Elsevier, and Google Scholar | 1970–2013 | Performance measurement, Performance management, Humanitarian logistics, Humanitarian supply chains, KPI | Yes | Descriptive, theoretical lens, sampling, purpose, context, definitional | Performance models not empirically tested, relationships between the factor and PM not easily verifiable, PM are defined at organizational and process level only, most studies include only internal performance indicators | Need for common measurement framework, need to integrate PM to planning stages, use of IT for PM, impact of stakeholders in PM, |
| **Leiras et al. (2014)** | Humanitarian Logistics | Not specified | Not specified | Humanitarian logistics, Humanitarian supply chain | Yes | General information, disaster types, disaster life cycle, research method, problem type, optimization type, decision level, stake holder perspective, coordination perspective | Preparation and response studies are more widespread than recovery phases, few studies linking theory and practice, slow onset disaster are not addressed, productivity and efficiency studies are not focused, | Hierarchical planning could be a suitable way to explore impact of politics, Predominance of work focused on the strategic decision and need to extend the analysis to the other decision levels Need to learn from business logistics, need to focus on coordination studies |

# References

Abidi, H., de Leeuw, S., & Klumpp, M. (2014). Humanitarian supply chain performance management: A systematic literature review. *Supply Chain Management: An International Journal, 19*(5/6), 592–608.

Alexander, B., Chan-Halbrendt, C., & Salim, W. (2006). Sustainable livelihood considerations for disaster risk management: Implications for implementation of the government of Indonesia tsunami recovery plan. *Disaster Prevention and Management: An International Journal, 15*(1), 31–50.

Altay, N., & Green, W. G. (2006). OR/MS research in disaster operations management. *European Journal of Operational Research, 175*(1), 475–493.

Altay, N., & Labonte, M. (2014). Challenges in humanitarian information management and exchange: Evidence from Haiti. *Disasters, 38*(s1), S50–S72.

Athukorala, P. C. (2012). Indian Ocean tsunami: Disaster, generosity and recovery. *Asian Economic Journal, 26*(3), 211–231.

Balcik, B., Beamon, B. M., Krejci, C. C., Muramatsu, K. M., & Ramirez, M. (2010). Coordination in humanitarian relief chains: Practices, challenges and opportunities. *International Journal of Production Economics, 126*(1), 22–34.

Beamon, B. M., & Kotleba, S. A. (2006). Inventory management support systems for emergency humanitarian relief operations in South Sudan. *The International Journal of Logistics Management, 17*(2), 187–212.

Carroll, A., & Neu, J. (2009). Volatility, unpredictability and asymmetry: An organizing framework for humanitarian logistics operations?. *Management Research News, 32*(11), 1024–1037.

Chandes, J., & Paché, G. (2010). Investigating humanitarian logistics issues: From operations management to strategic action. *Journal of Manufacturing Technology Management, 21*(3), 320–340.

Clasen, T., Smith, L., Albert, J., Bastable, A., & Fesselet, J. F. (2006). The drinking water response to the Indian Ocean tsunami, including the role of household water treatment. *Disaster Prevention and Management: An International Journal, 15*(1), 190–201.

Coles, J. B., Zhuang, J., & Yates, J. (2012). Case study in disaster relief: A descriptive analysis of agency partnerships in the aftermath of the January 12th, 2010 Haitian earthquake. *Socio-Economic Planning Sciences, 46*(1), 67–77.

Day, J. M., Melnyk, S. A., Larson, P. D., Davis, E. W., & Whybark, D. C. (2012). Humanitarian and disaster relief supply chains: A matter of life and death. *Journal of Supply Chain Management, 48*(2), 21–36.

Dorasamy, M., Raman, M., & Kaliannan, M. (2013). Knowledge management systems in support of disasters management: A two decade review. *Technological Forecasting and Social Change, 80*(9), 1834–1853.

Fink, G., & Redaelli, S. (2011). Determinants of international emergency aid—humanitarian need only?. *World Development, 39*(5), 741–757.

Galindo, G., & Batta, R. (2013). Review of recent developments in OR/MS research in disaster operations management. *European Journal of Operational Research, 230*(2), 201–211.

Geale, D. (2011a). North American Foot-And-Mouth Disease Vaccine Bank (NAFMDVB) for cross border livestock health FMD exercise, available at: www.cblhconference.com/pdf/2011-pres-NAFMDVB_CBLHC-fnl.pdf (accessed March 2, 2017).

Glenn Richey Jr, R. (2009). The supply chain crisis and disaster pyramid: A theoretical framework for understanding preparedness and recovery. *International Journal of Physical Distribution & Logistics Management, 39*(7), 619–628.

Gunasekaran, A., & Ngai, E. W. (2005). Build-to-order supply chain management: A literature review and framework for development. *Journal of Operations Management, 23*(5), 423–451.

Guven, G., & Ergen, E. (2011). Identification of local information items needed during search and rescue following an earthquake. *Disaster Prevention and Management: An International Journal, 20*(5), 458–472.

Haavisto, I., & Kovács, G. (2014). Perspectives on sustainability in humanitarian supply chains. *Disaster Prevention and Management, 23*(5), 610–631.

Heaslip, G. (2013). "Services operations management and humanitarian logistics", Journal of Humanitarian Logistics and Supply Chain Management, 3(1), 37–51.

Holguín-Veras, J., Jaller, M., Van Wassenhove, L. N., Pérez, N., & Wachtendorf, T. (2012). On the unique features of post-disaster humanitarian logistics. *Journal of Operations Management, 30*(7), 494–506.

Holguín-Veras, J., Taniguchi, E., Jaller, M., Aros-Vera, F., Ferreira, F., & Thompson, R. G. (2014). The Tohoku disasters: Chief lessons concerning the post disaster humanitarian logistics response and policy implications. *Transportation Research Part A: Policy and Practice, 69,* 86–104.

Hristidis, V., Chen, S. C., Li, T., Luis, S., & Deng, Y. (2010). Survey of data management and analysis in disaster situations. *Journal of Systems and Software, 83*(10), 1701–1714.

Huber, M., Van Boven, L., McGraw, A. P., & Johnson-Graham, L. (2011). Whom to help? Immediacy bias in judgments and decisions about humanitarian aid. *Organizational Behavior and Human Decision Processes, 115*(2), 283–293.

Jahre, M., Jensen, L. M., & Listou, T. (2009). Theory development in humanitarian logistics: A framework and three cases. *Management Research News, 32*(11), 1008–1023.

Kalyvitis, S., & Vlachaki, I. (2012). When does more aid imply less democracy? An empirical examination. *European Journal of Political Economy, 28*(1), 132–146.

Kousky, C. (2014). Informing climate adaptation: A review of the economic costs of natural disasters. *Energy Economics, 46,* 576–592.

Kovács, G., & Spens, K. M. (2007). Humanitarian logistics in disaster relief operations. *International Journal of Physical Distribution & Logistics Management, 37*(2), 99–114.

Kovács, G., & Tatham, P. (2009). Humanitarian logistics performance in the light of gender. *International Journal of Productivity and Performance Management, 58*(2), 174–187.

Kovács, G., & Tatham, P. (2010). What is special about a humanitarian logistician? A survey of logistic skills and performance. *In Supply Chain Forum: An International Journal. 11*(3), 32–41.

Kovács, G., Tatham, P., & Larson, P. D. (2012). What skills are needed to be a humanitarian logistician?. *Journal of Business Logistics, 33*(3), 245–258.

Kunz, N., & Reiner, G. (2012). A meta-analysis of humanitarian logistics research. *Journal of Humanitarian Logistics and Supply Chain Management, 2*(2), 116–147.

Kumar, S., & Havey, T. (2013). Before and after disaster strikes: A relief supply chain decision support framework. *International Journal of Production Economics, 145*(2), 613–629.

Lee, H. W., & Zbinden, M. (2003). Marrying logistics and technology for effective relief. *Forced Migration Review, 18*(3), 34–35.

Leiras, A., de Brito Jr, I., Queiroz Peres, E., Rejane Bertazzo, T., & Tsugunobu Yoshida Yoshizaki, H. (2014). Literature review of humanitarian logistics research: trends and challenges. *Journal of Humanitarian Logistics and Supply Chain Management, 4*(1), 95–130.

Lettieri, E., Masella, C., & Radaelli, G. (2009). Disaster management: Findings from a systematic review. *Disaster Prevention and Management: An International Journal, 18*(2), 117–136.

Martinez, A. J. P., Stapleton, O., & Van Wassenhove, L. N. (2011). Field vehicle fleet management in humanitarian operations: A case-based approach. *Journal of Operations Management, 29*(5), 404–421.

Mazurana, D., Benelli, P., & Walker, P. (2013). How sex-and age-disaggregated data and gender and generational analyses can improve humanitarian response. *Disasters, 37*(s1), S68–S82.

McLay, L. A., Boone, E. L., & Brooks, J. P. (2012). Analyzing the volume and nature of emergency medical calls during severe weather events using regression methodologies. *Socio-Economic Planning Sciences, 46*(1), 55–66.

Meredith, J. R., Raturi, A., Amoako-Gyampah, K., & Kaplan, B. (1989). Alternative research paradigms in operations. *Journal of Operations Management, 8*(4), 297–326.

Merminod, N., Nollet, J., & Pache, G. (2014). Streamlining humanitarian and peacekeeping supply chains: Anticipation capability for higher responsiveness. *Society and Business Review, 9*(1), 4–22.

Moore, G. H. (1996). My practical experience in emergency management. *Disaster Prevention and Management: An International Journal, 5*(4), 23–27.

Muggy, L., & L. Heier Stamm, J. (2014). Game theory applications in humanitarian operations: A review. *Journal of Humanitarian Logistics and Supply Chain Management, 4*(1), 4–23.

Natarajarathinam, M., Capar, I. and Narayanan, A. (2009). Managing supply chains in times of crisis: a review of literature and insights, *International Journal of Physical Distribution & Logistics Management, 39*(7), 535–573.

Noy, I. (2009). The macroeconomic consequences of disasters. *Journal of Development Economics, 88*(2), 221–231.

Oloruntoba, R. (2005). A wave of destruction and the waves of relief: Issues, challenges and strategies. *Disaster Prevention and Management: An International Journal, 14*(4), 506–521.

Oloruntoba, R., & Gray, R. (2006). Humanitarian aid: An agile supply chain? *Supply Chain Management: An International Journal, 11*(2), 115–120.

Oloruntoba, R., & Gray, R. (2009). Customer service in emergency relief chains. *International Journal of Physical Distribution & Logistics Management, 39*(6), 486–505.

Othman, S. H., Beydoun, G., & Sugumaran, V. (2014). Development and validation of a Disaster Management Metamodel (DMM). *Information Processing & Management, 50*(2), 235–271.

Overstreet, R. E., Hall, D., Hanna, J. B., & Kelly Rainer Jr, R. (2011). Research in humanitarian logistics. *Journal of Humanitarian Logistics and Supply Chain Management, 1*(2), 114–131.

Özdamar, L., & Ertem, M. A. (2015). Models, solutions and enabling technologies in humanitarian logistics. *European Journal of Operational Research, 244*(1), 55–65.

Perry, M. (2007). Natural disaster management planning: A study of logistics managers responding to the tsunami. *International Journal of Physical Distribution & Logistics Management, 37*(5), 409–433.

Pettit, Stephen, and Anthony Beresford. "Critical success factors in the context of humanitarian aid supply chains." International Journal of Physical Distribution and Logistics Management 39, no. 6 (2009): 450–468.

Poulton, C., Kydd, J., Wiggins, S., & Dorward, A. (2006). State intervention for food price stabilization in Africa: Can it work?. *Food Policy, 31*(4), 342–356.

Régnier, P., Neri, B., Scuteri, S., & Miniati, S. (2008). From emergency relief to livelihood recovery: Lessons learned from post-tsunami experiences in Indonesia and India. *Disaster Prevention and Management: An International Journal, 17*(3), 410–430.

Rodríguez, J. T., Vitoriano, B., & Montero, J. (2012). A general methodology for data-based rule building and its application to natural disaster management. *Computers & Operations Research, 39*(4), 863–873.

Scharffscher, K. S. (2011). Disempowerment through disconnection: Local women's disaster response and international relief in post-tsunami Batticaloa. *Disaster Prevention and Management: An International Journal, 20*(1), 63–81.

Scholten, K., Sharkey Scott, P., & Fynes, B. (2010). (Le) agility in humanitarian aid (NGO) supply chains. *International Journal of Physical Distribution & Logistics Management*, *40*(8/9), 623–635.

Schulz, S. F., & Blecken, A. (2010). Horizontal cooperation in disaster relief logistics: Benefits and impediments. *International Journal of Physical Distribution & Logistics Management*, *40*(8/9), 636–656.

Seybolt, T. B. (2009). Harmonizing the humanitarian aid network: Adaptive change in a complex system. *International Studies Quarterly*, *53*(4), 1027–1050.

Simpson, N. C., & Hancock, P. G. (2009). Fifty years of operational research and emergency response. *Journal of the Operational Research Society*, *60*(1), S126–S139.

Smirnov, A., Levashova, T., Pashkin, M., Shilov, N., & Komarova, A. (2007). Disaster response based on production network management tasks. *Management Research News*, *30*(11), 829–842.

Stephenson Jr, M. (2005). Making humanitarian relief networks more effective: Operational coordination, trust and sense making. *Disasters*, *29*(4), 337–350.

Swanson, R. D., & Smith, R. J. (2013). A Path to a Public–Private Partnership: Commercial Logistics Concepts Applied to Disaster Response. *Journal of Business Logistics*, *34*(4), 335–346.

Tatham, P., & Houghton, L. (2011). The wicked problem of humanitarian logistics and disaster relief aid. *Journal of Humanitarian Logistics and Supply Chain Management*, *1*(1), 15–31.

Tatham, P., Loy, J., & Peretti, U. (2015). Three dimensional printing–a key tool for the humanitarian logistician?. *Journal of Humanitarian Logistics and Supply Chain Management*, *5*(2), 188–208.

Thevenaz, C., & Resodihardjo, S. L. (2010). All the best laid plans…conditions impeding proper emergency response. *International Journal of Production Economics*, *126*(1), 7–21.

Thomas, A. S. (2005). Kopczak. *LR, From logistics to supply chain management: The path forward in the humanitarian sector*. Fritz Institute.

Thomas, A., & Mizushima, M. (2005). Logistics training: Necessity or luxury. *Forced Migration Review*, *22*(22), 60–61.

Tranfield, D., Denyer, D., & Smart, P. (2003). Towards a methodology for developing evidence-informed management knowledge by means of systematic review. *British Journal of Management*, *14*(3), 207–222.

Van Wassenhove, L. N. (2006). Humanitarian aid logistics: Supply chain management in high gear. *Journal of the Operational Research Society*, *57*(5), 475–489.

Wacker, J. G. (1998). A definition of theory: Research guidelines for different theory-building research methods in operations management. *Journal of operations management*, *16*(4), 361–385.

Yates, D., & Paquette, S. (2011). Emergency knowledge management and social media technologies: A case study of the 2010 Haitian earthquake. *International Journal of Information Management*, *31*(1), 6–13.

# 23

# Four Theories for Research in Humanitarian Logistics

## Richard Oloruntoba

## Introduction

Humanitarian crises and the logistical activities that enable response to them are increasingly common and global in nature (Day et al. 2012; Vega and Roussat 2015). Since the 2004 Asian Tsunami response and the 2005 response to Hurricane Katrina, the world has witnessed several devastating natural and human-made disasters. For example, Typhoon Haiyan in 2013, the Ebola pandemic in parts of West Africa in 2014, Super Typhoon Yolanda in Tacloban 2014, Nepal earthquake in 2015 and the ongoing refugee crisis accompanying the wars in Syria, Yemen, north-eastern Nigeria, Iraq and Afghanistan (Kamradt-Scott 2016; Oloruntoba and Banomyong 2016). Not surprisingly, academic publications on humanitarian operations (HO), logistics and supply chains have grown concomitantly (Kovács and Spens 2007, 2009, 2011; Holguin-Veras et al. 2012; Vega and Roussat 2015; Oloruntoba and Kovács 2015). However, in spite of growth in academic publications, some authors such as Jahre et al. (2009), Richey Jr (2009) and Tabaklar et al. (2015) have argued that attention to, and use of academic theories in HO, humanitarian logistics (HL) and humanitarian supply chain (HSC) research is limited. Anecdotal evidence further suggests that some HL manuscripts are being rejected by editors in influential

R. Oloruntoba (✉)
Newcastle Business School, The University of Newcastle, Callaghan, Australia
e-mail: Richard.Oloruntoba@newcastle.edu.au

© The Author(s) 2018      **675**
G. Kovács et al. (eds.), *The Palgrave Handbook of Humanitarian Logistics and Supply Chain Management*, https://doi.org/10.1057/978-1-137-59099-2_23

management journals in part because there have been a lack of the explicit use of theory and insufficient theoretical contribution.

Such dearth of deployment of theory may be as a result of the HL area of research being practical, applied and based on the "real world" where practical relevance of research implications for practitioners is of high priority (Tatham and Houghton 2011; EJOR 2016, p. 1; Pedraza-Martinez and Van Wassenhove 2016). Furthermore, limited use of theory in HL research may be as a result of research in the area being "new" and being only recently embraced by researchers as a genuine logistics and supply chain management (SCM) discipline. It may also be as a result of many publications being largely practitioner-oriented as evidenced in several literature reviews of the field (e.g. Kunz and Reiner 2012; Overstreet et al. 2011, p; Kovács and Spens 2011, 2009, 2007). Limited deployment and use of theory may also be as a result of the difficulty in gaining access to areas of crises, and difficulty in collecting empirical data in areas that are often in developing countries or areas in conflict (Oloruntoba 2016).

Regardless of the reasons for a dearth of theory-driven research in HL manuscripts that are submitted for review without mention of theory are often desk-rejected (Hazen 2016; Connelly et al. 2013). Interestingly, some manuscripts do make meaningful contributions to theory, but the authors do not explicitly discuss the theory (Hazen 2016; Connelly et al. 2013). Sometimes, authors mention a theory in the front-end of a manuscript as the reason for undertaking their study, but fail to explain any meaningful contribution that their research has made to the mentioned theory (Chicksand et al. 2012; Hazen 2016). Authors need to not just mention theory or use theory as a basis for the research, but instead clearly show how and where their research contributes to building or extending theory (Hazen 2016; Halldorsson et al. 2015; Choi and Wacker 2011). In some cases, bringing in and testing theory from other disciplines might represent a theoretical contribution (Karatas-Cetin and Denktas-Sakar 2013).

Deploying and using theory whether from within or outside the discipline will also enable a deeper scholarly understanding of the HL phenomenon being studied as well as where the adopted theory or theories fall short in explaining HL and SCM phenomena (Tabaklar et al. 2015; Apte et al. 2016; Moshtari 2016; Pedraza-Martinez and Van Wassenhove 2016). This will help scholars to show how the theory can be extended or modified to adequately explain HL phenomena. This is the principal motivation for this research, and it is important for HL scholars because it defines the problem in a way that demonstrates practical relevance to HL practitioners and scholars. Additionally, Karatas-Cetin and Denktas-Sakar (2013) showed a strong link between the use and deployment of theory in discipline-related research and the growth and prosperity of the discipline. As a result, research in HL needs to be rooted in theory, and contribute to enhancing our understanding of theory and practice.

Thus, this chapter advocates the use of theory in addition to the solid anchoring of HL research in empirical reality. The chapter argues that the deployment and use of theoretical frameworks will increase the practical relevance and theoretical value of research in the discipline. As Whetton (1989, 493) argued: "theoretical insights come from demonstrating how the addition of a new variable significantly alters our understanding of the phenomena by reorganizing our causal maps". Application of a theory in HL research provides a foundation for developing valuable and important research questions (RQs), creating ideas that explain, describe and predict as well as exploring relationships between concepts and other disciplines (Hambrick 2007).

Application of two or more theories to a concept within the field of HL, and each theory with its own unique set of assumptions will potentially help generate even deeper, more useful insights as well as new lines of interesting research. Such deployment of multiple theories would help expand our framework of understanding how to structure key empirical issues in the field of HL such as organization, risk, operations, logistics, sourcing, strategy, inventory, economics, donor behaviour and intra and inter-organizational relationships, coordination and capacity building and so forth (Oloruntoba 2016).

Furthermore, theories deserve attention because of: the fundamental nature of HO and the environment in which humanitarian action takes place—the uncertainty as regards for example not being certain whether donors will fund the next round of HO, where the funds will come from, where the next theatre of HOs will be, or what the needs of the beneficiaries will be. Also, the myriad of organizations, actors and stakeholders involved, each with its own unique incentive and perspective (e.g. suppliers, carriers, military, programme partners, for-profits and others); and the broad spectrum of types of humanitarian assistance ranging from emergency disaster relief to longer term developmental assistance. In addition, the broad range of organizational functions, processes and activities involved such as raising funds from donors and being accountable to donors (and beneficiaries), procurement, transportation, community participation and last mile distribution of relief or other assistance calls for deployment of theory (see Oloruntoba and Kovács 2015 for a full and more recent discussion of developments in these humanitarian activities and processes).

Lastly, the increasingly global and international social, economic and political dimension of HO, HL and HSC deserves the use of theory. For example, a recent report by the United Nations Office for the Coordination of Humanitarian Affairs (UNOCHA) indicated that more than US$19 billion was raised in donations in 2015, but humanitarian needs were much higher. Also, official development assistance alone accounted for US $103.7 billion in 2007, not including private donors (OECD 2008).

When disaster strikes or conflict erupts, large numbers of people often have to move, or be moved out of disaster and conflict areas to safer zones such as internally displaced persons (IDP) camps, refugee camps, temporary transit centres or tracing centres (Oloruntoba and Banomyong 2016; UNHCR 2015; Gustavsson 2003; Harrell-Bond 2002; Black 1998). The wars in Syria, Iraq, Libya, Yemen and Afghanistan, and the current on-going refugee crisis has had significant political ramification for the European Union as we are seeing in debates about new borders in the Schengen zone and the potential for Brexit (Oloruntoba and Banomyong 2016; Hampshire 2015; Weber 2015). Forced migration as a result of conflict has also had similar ramification for the politics and policy responses of Australia as regards the mandatory detention of men, women and children in offshore migration detention centres in the Pacific Islands of Nauru, Manus and Papua New Guinea (the so-called boat people) (Essex 2016; Fleay et al. 2016; Huho and Napitupulu 2016). Complex international humanitarian crises such as this put a lot of strain on the international humanitarian system and are ripe for a range of analyses using a range of theories such as management and organizational theories and theoretical frameworks.

Hence, the objectives of this chapter are to: (1) provide a brief overview of theories that have been deployed in research in HL; and (2) initially suggest three broad categories of theories that may be relevant and useful for consideration by scholars undertaking research in HL. The contribution of this chapter is to trigger interest in the development of theory in the field as well as consideration of theories from organizational and business management and other disciplines that can be valuably deployed in research in HL.

The chapter also generates novel ways of thinking about HL research while the field is still growing rapidly and helps structure and make coherent the various streams of work in the body of knowledge The chapter does this by examining the concept of HL within the context of theory (for example internationalization theory) which could be of value for extending research in the field in interesting ways into the future, especially for international and global HL.

Lastly, the chapter provides a broad foundation for theorizing about HL research and sets the stage for future research. The rest of this chapter is structured as follows: section "The Value of Theory" briefly provides an overview of the value of theories in academic research and the value and relevance of management and organizational theories in the context of HL. section "Summary Overview of Previous Theory-Development" provides a brief overview of some previous theory-driven research in the field, while section "Four Theories for Consideration" analyses one potentially useful theory, the internationalization that can be considered by scholars in the field. In section "Summary and Conclusion", the chapter is summarized and some implications presented.

# The Value of Theory

The value of theories in academic research has been well documented as evidenced in the opening quote of this chapter (Wright 2015; Schmenner and Swink 1998; Kerlinger 1986). Also, leading academic journals in the management and organization field tend to publish papers based on a rigorously applied theoretical framework. In any field of scientific research, researchers must try to systematically develop theory or gather empirical data to test the accuracy of theories as well as revise them when the data suggests (Wright 2015). Good theory is practical precisely because "…it advances knowledge in a scientific discipline, guides research toward crucial questions, and enlightens the profession of management" (Wright 2015; Van de Ven 1989, 486).

The application of theories enables a deeper understanding of a concept. It also enables an in-depth investigation of the implications of a theory for the concept being researched. Using theory in research enables scholars to build, extend, test or refute theories. The use of theory in academic research allows scholars to describe a subject, or concept in detail, explain its significance, position it within the appropriate body of work and field of study, identify its managerial and policy implications for managers and predict how it affects, and is affected by related phenomena and ideas (Kerlinger 1986). Furthermore, applying theory provides a basis for exploring relationships between constructs, and creating research ideas, and it allows scholars to describe a concept in detail, explain its significance, position it within the field of research, identify its managerial implications and predict how it affects and is in turn affected by associated ideas, and phenomena (Connolly et al. 2013; Hitt 2011; Shook et al. 2009; Mentzer et al. 2004). Lastly, the theory adopted in a study determines the method and research techniques deployed to investigate the phenomenon being studied (Karatas-Cetin and Denktas-Sakar 2013).

# Summary Overview of Previous Theory-Development

One of the early theory development attempts in HL research is Jahre et al. (2009). These scholars developed a framework matrix with three dimensions for theoretical development of research within HSCs. The matrix they developed combined the concepts of (1) organizational networks, (2) organizational coordination and (3) organizational structure. Networks can either be permanent or temporary such as humanitarian organizations having long-term suppliers, or suddenly having to work together with completely new partner organizations on the field. Coordination occurs vertically among all levels of the supply chain as well as horizontally among other humanitarian organizations (Jahre et al. 2009). Though the framework matrix is valuable, no specific theory was explicitly mentioned as guiding this work.

However, Richey (2009) seems to be the first to utilize explicitly stated theories to guide his work. Richey (2009) developed a disaster recovery pyramid using four explicitly stated theoretical perspectives: (1) the resource-based view of the firm, (2) communications theory, (3) competing values theory and (4) relationship management theory. He also explicitly stated that this was the first and only attempt to theoretically support research in HL (p. 619).

Nonetheless, Oloruntoba and Gray (2006), another early work applied the theoretical concept of "agility" with its origins in manufacturing and commercial supply chain contexts to the context of HO and HSCs. Studies on agility in the context have since advanced (e.g. Oloruntoba and Kovács 2015; Dubey and Gunasekaran 2016; L'Hermitte et al. 2016). Tatham and Kovács (2010) also applied the concept of "swift trust", a concept originally developed by Mayerson et al. (1996) to the rapid formation of trust in temporary organizations involved in a range of HO.

The most recent HO management theory development work includes Holguín-Veras et al. (2016) and Sodhi (2016). Holguín-Veras et al. (2016) argue for the use of appropriate objective functions in modeling response to beneficiaries in the immediate aftermath of a disaster. These scholars focus on how to design an estimation process for Deprivation Cost Functions (DCF) using contingent valuation method and econometric tools to obtain a DCF for drinkable water in Colombia. Sodhi (2016) used linear regression, structural equation modeling and time series analysis to study the impact of the pre-disaster number of hazards and vulnerability and consequent disaster impact and the economy. Sodhi (2016) finds evidence of a positive loop comprising the economy, population vulnerability and disaster impact, given a constant exogenous hazard rate. Sodhi (2016) suggest that long-term measures aimed at disaster mitigation, economic prosperity and resilience should be analysed concurrently rather than sequentially as commonly studied in research in HL. Therefore, taking into account the interplay between long-term development and short-term disaster response and as such being more strategic. Despite these laudable attempts at theory development, it may be argued that the theoretical underpinnings of HO, HL and HSCM research as regards organization and management theory remain less developed relative to routine commercially oriented SCM.

# Four Theories for Consideration

## Organizational and Management Theories

In this section, the chapter explores the subject of HL research using the lens of one organizational and management theory—the internationalization theory. Organizational and management theories may be broadly classified as (1) endogenous to an organization, (2) exogenous to an organization or (3) a combination of endogenous and exogenous (Hoskisson et al. 1999). For example, internationalization theory from the International Business literature (IB) often begins its exploration of organizational phenomena by considering organization-level concepts such as a wide range of organizational characteristics that determine when, where and why organizations expand overseas. Conversely, other theories such as institutional theory and social network theory often begin a discussion of organizational outcomes by highlighting the influence of outside forces and the outside environment that is beyond each manager's control. For instance, the focus of institutional theory is laws and regulations, and cognitive-cultural and normative pressures that act upon organizations in national and international foreign environments. Social network theory is generally about the influence of partnering organizations such as suppliers and partners to which a focal organization is connected. Examples of combined endogenous and exogenous organization and management theory include the organizational economics and resource dependence theory (RDT). These are mid-range theories that have a combined focus on the two aspects of internal and external influence. Hence, these latter theories often consider individual and firm-level characteristics, but the theories describe them in terms of the broader context—as a nexus of contracts, or a portfolio of dependencies.

First, this chapter aims to capture four theories from those that emphasize environmental influences where incidentally not much scholarly work has been done in HL. For example, work on international and global supply chains, intercultural and social contexts and procurement and other transactions. Second, the chapter also sought to analyse theories that are sufficiently diverse with respect to their origins. In this respect, the internationalization captures perspectives that have filled varying roles within research in the management of international organizations, employees and managers. The chapter utilizes this diversity of thought to lay a conceptual foundation for subsequent theoretically robust explorations of HL.

## The Theory of Internationalization

The theory of internationalization addresses the issue of why some organizations pursue foreign direct investment (FDI) and other organizations do not. Scholars such as Dunning (2003) and Bucklin have incorporated various extensions into the basic internationalization decision. For example, value maximization and cost minimization. Buckley and Casson (1976) are often credited with a sub-component of internationalization theory, the theory of the multinational corporation (MNC). The key assumption is that the costs of doing business abroad results in a competitive disadvantage for an MNC as a result of additional costs incurred by the organization (i.e. the liability of foreignness) (Parkhe 2003; Hymer 1976). For instance, costs associated with geographic distances in international HL increases transportation and distribution costs. Managers must make complex decisions owing to warehousing cost trade-offs due to increased order cycles and lead times (Meixell and Gargeya 2005). Extra costs may also arise for international HO as a result of exposure to different and new languages, customs, values, cultures and non-Western practices as well as from beneficiary, or host country environment such as poor infrastructure, nationalist policies, supplier availability or non-availability and quality as well as perceptions of illegitimacy of foreign owned or foreign operated organizations (Asmussen et al. 2009).

The theory of internationalization in the HL context draws attention to the range of costs and other barriers (e.g. cultural) that must be overcome by humanitarian organizations and their global and international supply chains (Wenji et al. 2015; Kabra and Ramesh 2015). Humanitarian organizations implementing a global or international supply chain face costs associated with their unfamiliarity with the local environment (Calhoun 2002). Effectiveness of logistics and business processes, for example, material planning, scheduling, demand forecasting and needs assessment could be diminished as humanitarian practitioners wrestle with exposure to new and different languages, practices and cultures. Costs may also arise from more macro aspects of the recipient country environment, such as nationalism, (inferior) infrastructure or low levels of legitimacy for foreign organizations (Asmussen et al. 2009). For instance, often, Western organizations sometimes need to overcome negative perceptions about them that are deep seated in a recipient country's national memory.

The home country itself may impose costs that influence global and international HSC decisions (Oloruntoba and Gray 2002, 2003). For instance, there may be restrictions on where to source relief goods and where not to source often with preferred suppliers/countries pre-identified. There is also the issue of tied aid where specific suppliers from a limited number of specified countries supply pre-specified goods in kind with little regard to what is actually needed in a humanitarian crisis. Similarly, there may be home country tax incentives associated with establishing global and international developmental assistance supply chains in some countries thus nullifying open market mechanisms and efficient competitive bidding (e.g. EU, NAFTA). As humanitarian organizations focus on reducing logistics and SCM costs and overall project costs, internationalization theory draws attention to potentially competing costs that must be overcome if humanitarian organizations are to be efficient and more effective from their humanitarian endeavours as they need to give an account to their donors (Zaheer 1995).

The internationalization theory perspective brings with it a significant body of knowledge that could considerably inform global and international HL and SCM research. For instance, there is a wealth of research exploring the international experience of top managers of international organizations, prior international alliances and partnerships and organizational size and structure (Hitt et al. 2006). Such factors may be important determinants of global and international procurement and supply chain relationships that could interact with efficiency-based factors to influence partnering decisions.

The internationalization perspective also differentiates between the (1) scope and (2) scale of international diversification of an organization. In the internationalization perspective, scope describes the range of countries, regions or people/cultural groups with which a HSC and distribution chain is engaged (Anderson and Coughlan 1987) while scale is the extent to which an organization's suppliers and buyers/customers extend across international borders.

Lastly, the internationalization theory perspective offers a valuable set of ideas about how globalizing and internationalizing the HSC could affect overall performance. For instance, after learning about their new/foreign environments and gaining access to knowledge and local/cultural expertise, is longer term repetitive HSCs such as development or reconstruction supply chains likely to experience performance gains, how? However, would such supply chains encounter a threshold, where the costs of logistical involvement and coordination in several countries exceed the benefits of increased access to knowledge and local/cultural expertise and resources (Hitt et al. 1997).

## Social Exchange Theory

Another theory that may be of value in HL research but not often deployed is a behavioural theory often referred to as social exchange theory (Biggart and Delbridge 2004; Cropanzano and Mitchell 2005; Coleman 1986; Ekeh 1974; Emerson 1976). The key tenets of social exchange relate to (1) subjective perceptions of the value of resources being exchanged, or passed from one party to another, (2) obligations and expectations that might often emerge regarding those exchanges of resources and (3) development and maintenance of often-complex political and social relationships resulting from recurring exchanges (Biggart and Delbridge 2004; Cropanzano and Mitchell 2005; Coleman 1986; Ekeh 1974; Emerson 1976). For example, we might consider relationships in the context of international humanitarian assistance. This often involves humanitarian organizations in a rich donor country and a relatively poorer recipient country in which HL operations involve shipment of relief and other valuable goods and services from the donor country in the developed world to the poorer, more vulnerable country (e.g. Haiti after the 2010 earthquake, Philippines after the 2014 Cyclone, Nepal after the 2014 earthquake).

Such tenets align with the (a) exchange of specialized knowledge and other resources, (b) development of commitment and trust and (c) inculcation and appreciation of relational norms and firm competencies by incumbents such as the managers of HO from foreign international relief/aid agencies, and potential successors such as national governments and local partners and NGOs who take over humanitarian projects and associated logistics when the foreign responders depart. This may be after the emergency phase of an event is over or when a project comes to the end of its natural life (Dyck et al. 2002). For instance, the international response to Ebola in parts of West Africa has ended and the last of foreign helpers departed Guinea, Liberia and Sierra Leone. However, local experts have taken over and are continuing monitoring and surveillance of the Ebola virus (Dyke et al. 2002).

Also, other stakeholders such as impacted communities, local public health agencies are integral to the succession process. Put more directly, social exchange theory allows us to discuss the social structures that define, condition and constrain succession processes in HO while retaining the ability to fully incorporate motives and agency. Such succession and handing over can occur in non-international humanitarian action as well as within countries and regions such as after Hurricane Katrina when the City of New Orleans and the State of Louisiana had to take over on departure of helpers from other states (Dyck et al. 2002).

Turner (2003, p. 322) noted that because actors can be individual people or collective actors such as groups, organizations, corporations or nations, the micro-macro problem of connecting people to structure is obviated. Thus, by employing a social exchange theoretical perspective, we integrate current knowledge on succession in a theoretical model relevant to HL, humanitarian organizations and general management scholars.

In addition, a social exchange perspective offers a conceptual foundation for examining exchange relationships across various groups of actors, governments, specialists (such as logisticians, public health officials, military, nutritionists) and other stakeholders during the various phases of a succession process. Behaviour and sociology scholars have proposed multiphase models and suggested that the transition consists of three phases (e.g. Cabrera-Suárez et al. 2001; Dyck et al. 2002), four phases (e.g. Cadieux et al. 2002) or more phases (e.g. Chrisman et al. 2009; Sharma et al. 2003). However, while the specifics vary, each model generally aligns with Le Breton-Miller et al. (2004) three-phase seminal model of succession transition. In Phase 1 of Le Breton-Miller et al. (2004) model, rules and criteria are established for the process of handing over (transition) and communicated, potential successors are identified and a succession plan is created. The skills, abilities, responsibilities of potential successors are assessed, gaps/inadequacies identified and training provided for development in Phase 2. In Phase 3 formal power/authority transfer and handover occurs with the incumbent stepping down and the chosen successor assuming the role of top manager.

Social exchanges may be categorized based on the actors involved in an exchange such as (a) exchanges involving entities or stakeholders within or outside the context of exchanges (b) other stakeholders or (c) exchanges between successors and incumbents (Ekeh 1974; Emerson 1976). Social exchanges and interactions may occur at daily or weekly meetings, for example, between incumbents (foreign humanitarian organizations and NGOs) and local stakeholders such as local partners and national governments as well as local experts across boundaries.

While social exchange has often been viewed from a simplified dyadic perspective, in this chapter we tend to agree with Biggart and Delbridge (2004) who suggest that actors exist at various levels in an exchange system. Interpersonal and inter-organizational ties leading to the development of social capital, social networks and shared identities among exchange-group members begin one interaction at a time, one individual to another. However, with repeated exchanges among members of the group comes an accumulation of obligations, trust and expectations that constitute the exchange patterns quite similar to those identified as social networks in social network theory (Biggart and Delbridge 2004).

Furthermore, in addition to observable network structures, repeated interactions also influence the types and extent of shared schemata characterized by common vision, common understanding, common knowledge and some form of group solidarity. Such shared schemas serve as a frame of reference for future exchanges within members of an exchange group (Granovetter 1985). Over time, these schemas may be passed on to new group members. Hence, it is the ability of a social exchange perspective to address the big picture of the networks of social interactions at the market and nonmarket levels, over time and across various levels, that leads us to advocate for its utility as an overarching, unifying theoretical architecture that connects extant and future research in humanitarian project transitions, transitioning, succession and handover.

An exchange perspective also provides a ready means to study the mechanics of such relationships and to understand how valuable resources such as knowledge (for instance epidemiological expertise) are transferred from foreign responders to local national experts (and beneficiaries). Social exchange theory helps scholars extract insights and offer directions for future research by examining exchanges and exchange relationships between multiple stakeholders across the succession process. This provides a platform to develop new approaches and insights into fundamental succession questions at the end of humanitarian action/projects or at the end of disaster management phases such as emergency relief, reconstruction and rebuilding. Handler (1991) argued that a successful and effective succession process depends on the level of understanding and mutual respect between incumbent and successor, grounded in support, trust, communication and mutual learning. Perceptions of mutual obligation and competence should begin prior to handover. Indeed, Brockhaus (2004) also noted that the quality of the incumbent–successor relationship is critical to an effective succession. Thus, a social exchange perspective may offer a way to organize succession knowledge in the management of humanitarian projects, operations and HL.

## Transaction Cost and Organizational Economics Theory

Transaction costs are the total direct and indirect expenses of carrying out an exchange between organizations in the marketplace or a transfer of resources within an individual organization whether or not its branches are in different countries (Williamson 1975, 1981, 1985). Transaction cost economics is premised on the fact that costs created within market and non-market exchanges are influenced by several important variables such as asset specificity (Williamson 1975, 1981); bounded rationality (Williamson 1975, 81); contract specificity (Williamson 1975, 81); contract effectiveness (Shou et al. 2016); trust (Whipple et al. 2013) and agency (Jensen and Meckling 1976).

Asset specificity arises when an exchange partner has invested in resources that are of limited or no value in other exchange contexts (Williamson 1975, 1981). Asset specificity is a term related to the inter-party relationships of a transaction. It is usually defined as the extent to which the investments made to support a particular transaction have a higher value to that transaction than they would have if they were redeployed for any other purpose.

There are various forms of asset specificity. These include: (1) Physical-Asset Specificity. For instance, the Ebola specific equipment deployed during the recent Ebola epidemic of 2014 may no longer be of value unless there is another outbreak at which such equipment can be re-used. Thus, in this example, the value of an asset can perish; (2) Site Specificity. Site specificity occurs when investments in productive assets are made in close physical proximity to each other. Geographical proximity of assets for different stages of production reduces inventory, transportation and sometimes processing costs. For instance, the United Nations humanitarian clusters/depots in Dubai, Nairobi Kenya, Brindisi (Italy) are major logistical sites and (3) Human-Asset Specificity refers to the accumulation of knowledge and expertise that is specific to one partner or one partnership. For instance as regards exclusive proprietary ownership of nutritional wet feeding of malnourished infants or specialized knowledge of the logistics of humanitarian relief by such organizations as Atlas Logistique in France or the Fritz Institute in San Francisco (McGuinness 1994).

Bounded rationality arises when partner organizations do intend to make rational decisions, but limited human information processing and interpretation abilities make complete rationality impossible. This may also relate to cognitive block and cognitive dissonance where there is a tendency for individual managers to seek consistency among their cognitions (i.e. beliefs, opinions) (Cooper 2007; Festinger 1957). Hence, key decisions are taken under conditions of uncertainty.

Contract specificity explains how exchange partners, who are unable to stipulate all of the potential inputs and outputs of an exchange relationship in advance, rely on explicit contracts to govern the exchange. For example contracts of carriage, warehousing or supply. The transaction cost and organizational economics perspective suggests that organizations make sourcing decisions by combining the factors above to determine the optimal economic merit of each transaction (Hobbs 1996; Williamson 2008). However, in a global or international context, aggregated transaction costs at a systemic level forces an organization (for instance, World Vision International or Catholic Relief Services) to take on a new set of complexities if it is to manage a nexus of sourcing decisions as well as other logistics-related decisions.

Bounded rationality for instance is affected not only by the limited cognitive capability of individual managers and decision makers but also by the context in which decisions will be made as the rules of the game and governance may not be clearly understood (uncertainty) and are not held constant, perhaps, due to different cultures or different institutions. Property rights may be less secure and legal systems may operate differently (Williamson 2008). Hence, assessing transaction costs across national boundaries involves a host of complications that make the task less predictable, and this is important because humanitarian organizations must be seen to be efficient with the use of donor funds and must do more with less.

Sometimes, unforeseen events in a foreign country may impact humanitarian organizations in several ways. Managers with a broad understanding of such global and international complexities and a cosmopolitan view of the world may be in a better position to limit the adverse effects of bounded rationality and more accurately assess cross-border transaction costs. A manager who has worked in, lived in, or travelled to the target countries has a more comprehensive understanding of the peculiarities, costs and risks of operating in each culture and may be in a better position to evaluate the full extent of transaction costs in each country.

Contracting and procurement of goods and services overseas adds additional complexities when it occurs across national boundaries. HL and supply chain relationships often take place and unfold in multi-context, complex interactions (Hitt et al. 2000). Such interactions demand that partner organizations share tacit knowledge and hard-to-codify assets. Hence, confidence that one's partner organization will cooperate in a trustworthy fashion is essential for the relationship to succeed and operate efficiently (Sinkovics et al. 2011).

Scholars in the transaction cost and organizational economics perspective generally argue that formal contract-based governance (i.e. contract specificity) may be reduced as confident positive expectations about a partner's behaviour, or trust, increases (Dyer 1997; Langfield-Smith and Smith 2003). Trust, however, is more difficult to develop across disparate cultures as individual decision makers may have different conceptualizations of efficiency, time and deadlines as a function of their different national cultures. Cultural differences could lead to poor exchanges that make it difficult for trust to develop.

Also worthy of mention in contracting and procurement is the agency problem (Zsidisin and Ellram 2003; Dalton et al. 2007). The agency problem is how there is potentially divergent interests and information asymmetry principals and their agents such as major government donors and humanitarian NGOs, or humanitarian agencies as buyers and vendors of relief goods as sellers/suppliers. Thus, there may be presence of moral hazard, and opportunism on the part of agents by making decisions that serve their own interests rather than the interest of the principal (Dalton et al. 2007).

Agency theory can be applied in HL and supply chain research where there is significant donor funding. This is a neglected area of research in HL despite donor funding being an important input into the supply chain (Zsidisin and Ellram 2003). In this example, humanitarian organizations are agents of the major donors. In this context, monitoring costs incurred by the principal to ensure the agent is not acting opportunistically are often exacerbated by working in different time zones, geographic distance and a range of other environmental uncertainties (Parkhe 2003). Compliance and monitoring costs include administration of various accountability reports such as beneficiary lists that are regularly sent by humanitarian organizations to their donors.

Likewise for humanitarian organizations operating in a foreign country, the choice of agents such as truck drivers, warehouse providers and providers of other logistics services exposes humanitarian organizations to the risk of opportunism. Adopting agency theory as a theoretical lens in global and international logistics and SCM focus on how to manage cross-border buyer-supplier relationships, the problems that might arise and the steps that humanitarian organizations could take to prevent and mitigate those problems.

The transaction cost and organizational economics theoretical tradition has for a long time been a foundational theory for scholarly investigations of commercial (for profit) supply chains, and it may be valuable for scholars working in a global or international humanitarian context (Williamson 2008). This theory has a significant history of investigating the relationship between trust and controls in inter-organizational contracting (Srinivasan et al. 2011; Puranam and Vanneste 2009). Researchers in HL and SCM might need to focus on trust and controls between culturally distant organizations within a supply chain or within a specific humanitarian project.

Scholars of HL might also investigate issues of bounded rationality within HL and supply chains. Such a study might explore how managerial decisions about exchange partners can become less optimal or less efficient in a global or international environment when the information they need to process becomes overly complex. Also, scholars may consider research that compares HSCs that adopt specific assets that do not readily transfer between countries (for instance, assets that are tied to a specific context, language or culture) compared with humanitarian supply chains that adopt more generic assets. The former could gain efficiencies, at the expense of flexibility however. Also, researchers may consider short-term transactional "arm's length" procurement of emergency relief materials as opposed to adopting collaborative, long-term sourcing strategies that could require months, or even years, to break even on the initial investment. However, the latter approach is concerned with long-term value maximization.

## Resource Dependence Theory

Power is at the heart of RDT, and power has its genesis in maintaining control of vital resources (Pfeffer and Salancik 1978; Medcof 2001). Organizations establish relationships with others to acquire those vital resources when lack the necessary resources to accomplish their objectives without recourse to external assistance. When organizations establish relationships with others they lose some element of control over their own destiny and, as a result, they often seek to change such relationships to minimize external dependencies (Pfeffer and Salancik 1978; Medcof 2001). RDT combines the organization's social context with its managerial actions. It describes how organizations may seek strategies to enhance autonomy and control resources on which others are dependent (Hillman et al. 2009).

An important aspect of international SCM within international HO is the decision to go it alone in a foreign country if the humanitarian organization is big enough and has all the resources it needs within its subsidiaries. The humanitarian organization may however choose to buy resources in aid receiving countries, or form an alliance or partnership with a local supplier or partner to provide a needed resource in the foreign country (Parkhe 2011). RDT introduces the possibility that these decisions may be informed as much by power as by issues of cost minimization, control, access to impacted communities, local legitimacy and access to local knowledge and culture. For resources that are critical to humanitarian organizations in their foreign operations for which there are few places from which to source, the supplier or partner has significant power which suggests that the humanitarian organization will attempt to either make it in-house if possible, or seek other means of reducing its dependence on such a supplier or partner (Casciaro and Piskorski 2005; Parkhe 2011).

Nevertheless, for this supply chain decision rising globalization seems to have increased the number of sources, potential suppliers and potential partners such as local partner NGOs for a large number of resources often needed by humanitarian organizations to be effective in their operations overseas. For example, the number of developing country NGOs in long-term partnerships with developed country humanitarian organizations has grown tremendously (Banks et al. 2015; Gatrell 2016; Shaw and Swatuk 1994). Many developing country NGOs are present in countries such as India, Nigeria, Congo, South Sudan and most have access to computers and the Internet as well as all the information they need to be good partners to the big multinational humanitarian organizations. As more of such NGOs and other types of suppliers and partners provide more resources, humanitarian organizations may be less likely to decide to create needed resources in-house. This partly explains why large humanitarian organizations outsourced nearly $20 million in business to a range of African suppliers and partners in 2014 (Munovi 2015; Gill and McNeil 2015).

RDT draws attention to a paradox that organizations face in the make, buy or build a partnership decision for global HO. In one sense, humanitarian organizations' need to reduce their dependencies on other organizations to reduce risk, in the other sense, bringing the resource in-house or going it all alone adds another dimension of risk and difficulty. While supply chain decisions are often based mainly on economic decisions, RDT sheds light on some potential problems. Hence, humanitarian organizations should not want to be overly dependent on one NGO or partner because a more diverse pool of supply chain and other partners will help reduce supply chain risk and the risk of opportunism by partners. Further, Krugman (1997) describes the range of resource dependencies. For example, dependence on another organization, partner, institution or country.

Researchers of humanitarian organizations and allied supply chains will find RDT of value. Hence, they may need to incorporate RDT into their theorizing as they explore international supply chains and the inter-organizational relationships within them. RDT will help extend research from issues of cost reduction to that of relative power, control and autonomy among partnering organizations. Furthermore, Pfeffer (1987) suggests that efforts to control external dependencies might result in unintended consequences such as new patterns of dependence. For example, how extensive international outsourcing holds the potential of reducing operational dependencies but simultaneously introduces possible problems of coordination, information sharing, and knowledge spillover. Hence, scholars might examine the different forms of supply chain and organizational interdependencies, temporal conditions of supply relationships and inter-organizational dependencies across varied humanitarian organizations, HSCs, institutional and national contexts.

## Discussion

The four theories described and their relevance to HL and SCM research are meant to trigger ideas and inspire scholars in the field of HL. Scholars are meant to consider how they might explore the phenomenon of logistics and SCM for humanitarian aid in new ways. We argue in this chapter that analysis of HL through the lens of one or more academic theories enlarges the cognitive schemata through which the scholarly HL and supply chain community makes sense of the phenomenon being researched. The four theories suggested are only a starting point which should change the way we seek for answers and truths in research as well as encourage us to consider the RQs that we ask.

Like the field of SCM as a whole (Carter et al. 2015), theory development in HL and supply chains can be said to be in infancy (see Richey 2009; Oloruntoba and Gray 2009; Kunz and Reiner 2012; Tabaklar et al. 2015), the theories required to adequately understand and describe HL and SCM is in the process of being developed (e.g. Jahre et al. 2009; Richey Jr 2009; Pedraza-Martinez and Van Wassenhove 2016). However, it is noteworthy that some scholars have begun to apply theory in the field of HL and SCM research (e.g. Tatham and Kovács 2010; Tabaklar et al. 2015). However, there remains enormous opportunity to build on these initial suggestions as each of these four theories could be used as the foundation for empirical investigations of HL and SCM and to explore the theories in different types of humanitarian organizations based on their supply chain structure and institutional contexts.

## Combining Theories

As earlier discussed, a strategy for scholars to add value to their research and concurrently avoid desk rejection would be to mix and combine many theoretical perspectives to enhance the possible insights about HL and SCM. A HL and SCM study that combines internationalization theory, organization economics, social exchange theory and RDT should be interesting.

The key to internationalization theory is the liability of foreignness that describes costs incurred by organizations when they do business abroad. Adding how humanitarian organizations might establish potential sourcing relationships in countries with different liabilities of foreignness such as different geographic and cultural distances from the home country or different host country institutional contexts. Van den Waeyenberg and Hens (2012) in their seminal paper argued that inclusion and collaboration with local partners and stakeholders in foreign market contexts are a necessity as a result of institutional voids, and institutional distance limits transferability of business models from developed-country contexts to developing-country contexts.

Adding internationalization theory to this formula could help describe how organizations might overcome liabilities of foreignness in their global and international supply chains. Also, if HO are not going well in one country, can this leave open the possibility of leaving in favour of where liabilities are less? Internationalization theory could offer insights and be used to inform HL and SCM research in this regard.

## Contrasting Theories

Although combining theories to yield complementary perspectives on HL and supply chain should yield fruitful insights, more interesting questions might arise from investigating competing theoretical perspectives. For example, interesting contradictions may arise when concurrently examining the global and international HSC through the frame of transaction-cost and organizational economics and social exchange theory. In organizational economics, global sourcing decisions often follow a prescribed formula, describing a precise point at which humanitarian organizations should engage in contracts to accomplish specific goals. Social exchange theory, however, would suggest that an organization will make social exchanges that align with social, normative, cognitive and regulative norms, which may not always be the most economically efficient.

In structuring their global and international supply chain relationships, humanitarian organizations might find themselves under competing influences from legitimacy-minded institutions as well as efficiency-minded principals such as donors. Contradictions might arise with the parallel exploration of competitive advantage as organizations survive and prosper by outmanoeuvring rivals in search of resources. This includes humanitarian organizations that must compete for funding and positive global media coverage and influence. Hence, the managers of such large humanitarian organizations must make global supply chain decisions with a view towards minimizing dependence on others and maximizing their power relative to their competitors. However, on the contrary, as they expand their global and international supply chains outwards, they could deliberately increase their dependency on others but at the same time becoming more powerful actors in the network. Hence, scholars may want to investigate such co-evolution as humanitarian organizations develop their global and international supply chains.

## Extending Theories: Potential Extensions

Contrasting or combining theories may serve as a valuable means of advancing knowledge; however, scholars can also contribute to what is known about HL by extending theories to bridge gaps that may exist in various areas. For instance, scholars might seek to know how multiple levels or echelons of the HSC could affect our conceptual examination as well as existing models of HSCs. Often, HSCs are conceptualized very simply as donors (a type of supplier), suppliers of humanitarian goods to humanitarian organizations and beneficiaries often conceptualized as customers (e.g. Oloruntoba and Gray 2006, 2009). One way to investigate how multiple levels or echelons of the HSC could affect our conceptual examination would be to embrace a broader emphasis on the multiple tiers of production (i.e. where value is added in the supply chain) and distribution within the supply chain (i.e. to end users /beneficiaries or to extended delivery points).

Many studies in HSCs focus on and explain decisions surrounding just one tier or echelon of the HSC (e.g. sourcing) without considering the second-order implications for other tiers within the same supply chain. Another option could be to examine several HSCs that pass through a single humanitarian agency or organization. Thus, raising new questions about how a humanitarian organization might manage its portfolio of supply chains and how management decisions about one supply chain might affect others in which the humanitarian organization is engaged.

As scholarly research on HL and HSCSCM develops and matures into the future, the community of scholars in this area may be able to develop more comprehensive and sophisticated understandings of HL and supply chain phenomena by applying multiple level analyses and perspectives. Another strategy to extend theoretical exploration of HL and supply chains may be to conceptualize them as a tool or means to an end rather than as an end in themselves. Kovács and Spens (2007) and Oloruntoba and Gray (2006) outlined the notion of humanitarian competitive advantage, competition for donor funds and competition for positive publicity amongst large multi-national humanitarian organizations, though, we often seem to assume that humanitarian organizations do not "compete" because they are not for profits. Such an approach of seeing competitive humanitarian organizations demands far more from existing theoretical perspectives (e.g. swift trust proposed by Tatham and Kovács 2010, agility discussed by Oloruntoba and Gray 2006; Dubey and Gunasekaran 2016; L'Hermitte et al. 2014; Naim and Gosling 2011; Balcik and Beamon 2008) insofar as it shifts the emphasis from managerial decisions about a component of the HSC to outcomes from the level of individual humanitarian organizations that might have been affected by the end-to-end supply chain. Hence, as medium- or long-term HSCs engage one another in competition, for example, for donor funding across several disparate geographically distributed countries, it becomes more important for theoretical investigations to include how such supply chains interact and how individual humanitarian organizations use them to gain competitive advantage.

Furthermore, theory development in HSC research would benefit from more incisive integration of time (or phase of disaster management) into the studies and relationships of interest. For example, it may be valuable to consider how time might be aggregated at levels beyond the conventional emergency relief, rebuilding and reconstruction phases) such that time or phase becomes more conceptually meaningful rather than simplistically and empirically expedient. For example, phases often exist together or overlap. Related to the process of aggregation is how long a particular phase/time lasts in humanitarian response.

Scholars may also discover greater diversity in the rates of change of phases operating in different institutional and cultural contexts. For instance, Nepal after the 2014 earthquake seems to be stuck somewhere in between the emergency phase and the rebuilding phase. Emergency phase is over but the rebuilding, rehabilitation and resettlement/development phase is yet to begin after more than 2 years similar to Haiti after its 2010 earthquake. Hence, scholars may need to focus more on discontinuous non-linear change of phase hence the significance of studies on frequency, rhythm, cycles and interruptions. Whetten (1989) explained how to do this. For comprehensiveness, a developed theory is required to explain when concepts or constructs would be applicable. This limits the hypotheses and/or propositions generated from conceptual models and non-empirical conceptual papers of which much of the published work in HL and supply chains is based. In the following section specific possible extensions to the four suggested theories are discussed.

## Possible Extensions: Internationalization Theory

There are several possible extensions to the theory of internationalization in the context of HL and SCM research. However, two are discussed for brevity. Example studies might investigate:

### (a) Organizational and Entrepreneurial Culture Within Humanitarian Organizations

Some organizations are more entrepreneurial than others, and this applies to humanitarian organizations as well as commercial organizations. More entrepreneurial humanitarian organizations have expanded their supply chains and operations into several developing countries. This is often because their organizational cultures provide strong incentives for individual staff innovation and discovery. For instance, such entrepreneurial organizations promote and provide incentives for freedom of association of their staff members with any others. They promote and provide incentives for exploration of in particular, non-Western cultures by their staff members as well as freedom of travel. As a result, such humanitarian organizations have over the years developed expertise in and detailed knowledge of many aspects of several developing countries. For example, they have developed intimate knowledge of logistics processes, infrastructure, customs as well as institutional and regulatory environments of aid receiving countries in developing areas of the world. As a result of such cultural and institutional expertise and within the context of internationalization theory, it therefore becomes more efficient and more valuable for such organizations to apply their cultural expertise and knowledge simultaneously in all aid receiving countries to which such expertise is relevant. For instance, they may apply the same or similar logistics technology and operating processes in several different aid receiving countries. Hence, such an extension to the theory of internationalization demonstrates the importance of superior cultural and logistical knowledge and entrepreneurship to the organization.

## Supply Chain and Facility Network Considerations

While internationalization theory is a general theory of the boundaries of the firm, another area of possible extension of the theory that can prove particularly valuable is research that deepens understanding of the growth and scale of the supply chain and facility network of humanitarian organizations as well as logistical and supply chain network considerations. An international HSC may be thought of as a collection of facilities linked by flows of services and goods. Each facility has a location, and each location is in a particular country. The types of network facilities typically identified include the head office typically in a developed country where the focus is often on regulators, fundraising and donor relations (Oloruntoba and Gray 2002, 2003). The head office also often has its range of profit seeking suppliers and warehouses.

Another aspect of the facility network is the field office which is typically in a developing country. This also often has its own range of suppliers, sourcing nodes, warehouses, depots and extended distribution points that often stretch from the field in aid receiving developing countries to the head office in developed countries. These head office and field office facilities, together with the linkages and flows between them and component parts make up a complex value chain or more accurately value network. Aid beneficiaries and institutions such as central or local government in aid receiving countries also belong in these value chains. While coordination between different humanitarian organizations in humanitarian response has been well addressed in the literature (e.g. Balcik et al. 2010; Jahre and Jensen 2010; Chandes and Pache 2010), the concept of coordination—within facilities and networks, and between facilities and networks of the value chains of the same humanitarian organization has received minimal attention and is ripe for exploration as an extension of internationalization theory. Likewise, network comparisons of similar sized humanitarian organizations would extend the theory of internationalization in HL and SCM research.

## Possible Extensions: Social Exchange Theory

There are also several possible extensions to social exchange theory in the context of HL and SCM research. However two are discussed for brevity. Example studies might investigate:

# Antecedents and Consequences of Social Exchange Theory

The fundamental premise of social exchange theory relate to the subjective perceptions of the value of resources being exchanged, or passed from one party to another, obligations and expectations that might often emerge regarding those exchanges of resources and development and maintenance of relationships resulting from recurring exchanges. Possible investigations to extend the theory might focus on antecedents and consequences of exchanges and relationships between humanitarian organizations and their local partners in developing countries. For example, researchers might ask the following questions:

(1) What antecedents are necessary and sufficient within a humanitarian organization and a local partner to assure successful and effective exchanges and relationships between the humanitarian organization and its local partner? How do such antecedents influence humanitarian organizational and logistical outcomes in aid receiving countries? In other words, what role does pre-existing internal conditions of humanitarian organizations and their partners play in successful partnering and collaboration especially in the area of logistics?

(2) What are the reciprocation processes between a humanitarian organization and its local partners? International humanitarian organizations are often portrayed as "leaders" of HO and collaborations, and overall controllers of HSCs, while their local partners are portrayed as "followers" who take expert instructions from overseas experts. The way partners reciprocate decisions and actions of humanitarian organizations and vice versa though valuable are yet to be addressed. Thus studies of leader-member logistics groupings and the role that each party plays is important. This is particularly important given the multi-actor context of HO and the many HSC participants, many of whom are based in recipient country organizations (e.g. transport and warehouse service providers and their personnel). Additionally, studies of reciprocation processes in social exchanges should add richness needed to enhance understanding of leader–member relationships within logistics service provision and HSCs and shed more light on leader–member relationships amongst logistics personnel as logistics and supply chain activities are undertaken in a broader social context.

# Possible Extensions: Transaction Cost and Organizational Economics Theory

Transaction cost theory is premised on costs created within market and non-market exchanges being influenced by variables such as asset specificity, bounded rationality, contract specificity, contract effectiveness, trust and agency. Similar to internationalization theory and social exchange theory, there are many possible extensions to transaction cost and organizational economics theory in the context of HL and SCM research. Example studies might investigate topical issues such as opportunism and opportunistic behaviour in HSCs.

Disaster risk is a function of hazard, exposure and vulnerability (United Nations Office for Disaster Risk Reduction 2015), and it is the interaction of these elements that results in many humanitarian crises. Such risk is often expressed as the probability of deaths, injury or loss of infrastructure for a specific period of time. Thus, suggesting that disasters are often the result of the human condition (Natural Hazards Science 2016). However, other researchers describe disasters as manifestations of unresolved development problems. Hence, disasters are not a normal natural phenomenon as the term "natural disaster" conveys. Human beings play a major role (Natural Hazards Science 2016). Thus natural hazards such as Hurricanes and Cyclones or floods impact each community or country differently.

Countries, regions, people groups and individuals are uniquely affected mostly based on pre-existing vulnerability (Natural Hazards Science 2016). For instance, many researchers seem to agree that there are particular vulnerabilities that affect the poorest of the poor and the most marginalized communities in all parts of the world (Natural Hazards Science 2016). Haiti for example has many aspects of its risk and vulnerability profile in its colonial history (Oliver-Smith et al. 2016). The structural and social injustice that we witnessed in Haiti during the 2010 earthquake (i.e. 222,750 deaths, 300,000 injuries, 1.5 million displaced people and more than 3 million affected), and again during the 2016 Hurricane Matthew (so far over 1000 dead despite early warnings) has been multiplied and exacerbated by recent trends in international economics (Australian Broadcasting Corporation 2016). For example, little of the US$13.5 billion pledged by the international community after the 2010 earthquake ever made it to Haiti's people or into its economy (Knox 2015). Most of it (94%) went to private suppliers, vendors and contractors as well as donor nations' own military and civilian entities, international NGOS, and UN agencies—a classic case of opportunism in HSCs.

Investigations have shown that many international opportunistic actors of predatory capitalism rushed to secure quick and easy profits in the wake of the earthquake calamity (Knox 2015). This has helped to preclude any serious attempts to rebuild Haiti after the earthquake, build community resilience or address disaster risk as local stakeholders were completely sidelined in the lucrative business of helping Haiti.

Under the guise of goodwill and solidarity, many foreign businesses embrace and exploit this failed model often characterized by: tied aid; donations of goods in kind that often do not meet requirements of impacted people; over-pricing and supply of low quality goods; pledges of funds that go unfulfilled and a short-term transactional approach that does not deliver long-lasting benefits to affected communities. This opportunistic humanitarian model simply reinforces underlying vulnerability and makes a mockery of building back better and increasing community resilience. Hence, the presence of opportunism in logistics, procurement and supply chains for humanitarian aid is ripe for investigation by researchers as an extension to transaction cost and organizational economics theory.

## Possible Extensions: Resource Dependence Theory

RDT characterizes an organization as an open system, dependent on contingencies in the external environment (Pfeffer and Salancik 1978), and to understand the behaviour of an organization you must understand the context of that behaviour—in other words, you must possess a systems view of the ecology of the organization (Hillman et al. 2009). RDT is also premised on the influence of external factors on how organizations behave and how managers act to reduce environmental uncertainty and dependence. At the centre of such actions is the concept of power which often means control over vital resources (Ulrich and Barney 1984).

Also, RDT argues that organizations will often attempt to reduce others' power over them, and often attempt to increase their own power over others. In summary, the RDT argues that: (1) organizations are not autonomous, but are rather constrained by a network of interdependencies with other organizations (e.g. supply chains and networks); (2) that the basic unit for understanding inter-organizational relationships and society are organizations; (3) organizational interdependence when combined with environmental uncertainty as regards what the actions of those organizations with which the organization is interdependent often results in the reality that organizational survival and continued success are never certain and (4) as a result, organizations and their managers take actions to manage external interdependencies in spite of such actions producing new patterns of dependence and interdependence and (5) such patterns of dependence and interdependence produce intra-organizational and inter-organizational power which in turn influences organizational behaviour (Hillman et al. 2009).

Two areas that seem ripe for exploration in the HL and SCM context are (a) how humanitarian organizations manage their dependences with their key donors, and (b) how humanitarian organizations manage mergers and take-overs of other humanitarian organizations and consolidation of their logistics and supply chain systems as a survival mechanism.

*Donors*

Pfeffer and Salancik (1978) argued that because organizations are often not able to reduce interdependence on other organizations and uncertainty within their networks and the larger social system including governments, organizations undertake other means to reduce such interdependence and uncertainty. Pfeffer and Salancik (1978) argued that the organization, through a range of political mechanisms, seeks to create for itself an environment that is better for its interests. Hence, such organizations may use political means to alter the condition of the external economic environment (Pfeffer and Salancik 1978). They may try to influence government regulations to produce a more favourable environment. In the HSC context, Oloruntoba and Gray (2009) argue that governmental and other types of donors fund the activities of humanitarian organizations and indeed fund HSCs in cash or in goods in kind, and as such, donors may be construed as bona fide parts of the HSC structure either as "suppliers" supplying cash and goods, or as "customers" to whom humanitarian organizations must satisfy and give account for donor funding not to cease.

*Mergers*

RDT offers an externally focused perspective of why organizations acquire other organizations (Haleblian et al. 2009). Pfeffer (1976) suggests three reasons why organizations may engage in mergers and acquisition (1) to reduce competition by absorbing a key competitor, (2) to manage interdependences with sources of input and supplies or purchasers of output (customers) by absorbing them and (3) to diversify operations and as a result lessen their dependence on the current organizations with which they make exchanges.

In the past few years, many humanitarian NGOs have merged to broaden their operations to survive in an increasingly competitive aid market. For instance, in August 2013, Save the Children and Merlin International merged. Before that, in 2010, Danish humanitarian NGO Mellemfolkeligt Samvirke merged with ActionAid International. In fact, mergers and acquisitions between humanitarian organizations are not new. As far back as 1942,

International Rescue Committee was born out of a merger between International Relief Association and Emergency Rescue Committee. Though fewer than commercial sector mergers, they are becoming more frequent as donor funding and global economic power dwindles. This is a an area ripe for exploration and potential RQs include: What magnitude of dependency predicts the likelihood of mergers and acquisitions in the humanitarian sector and how would this impact existing supply and facility network structure of humanitarian organizations? How does power imbalance and mutual dependence influence mergers? Within HSCs and supply partnerships how do humanitarian organizations assess and manage supplier selection and long-term partner complementarity?

## Managerial Implications

The application of multiple theories to the issue of HL and SCM offers practical observations. Each published journal article often conveys vastly different understandings of the same HL and supply chain phenomena based upon the perspective from which the authors investigated it. Each perspective by itself provides important information that contributes to the whole, but is also, by itself, incomplete. By drawing attention to the richness of use of a range of theoretical perspectives and investigating how together they might depict the phenomenon, our article offers a valuable description of the phenomenon that can help humanitarian practitioners to comprehend the many motivations that exist and the many issues that arise in HL and HSCs.

Global attention seems to be shifting towards emerging markets, developing countries and so-called bottom of pyramid countries where many humanitarian crises occur (George et al. 2016; Walsh 2015). Additionally, competition in many spheres and industries has triggered the globalization of demand and supply sources (e.g. George et al. 2016; Walsh 2015; Fawcett and Waller 2015). As humanitarian organizations, their managers and donors move forwards with embracing the more inevitable globalization of HSCs; leveraging the theories suggested herein could help practitioners to understand the gaps between what could be and what is at the moment in the management of their logistics and supply chain activities.

Important global events have highlighted the increasing requirement that practitioners cannot be content with allowing their HSCs to react to events or just go along with events without pre-determined goals and aims. For instance the development of Muslim humanitarian organizations and Islamic approaches to humanitarianism which calls for further empirical investigations and theoretical exploration.

Furthermore the development and use of cash relief and the increasing of incorporation of community members into key decisions regarding humanitarian assistance and distribution of humanitarian assistance. Managers who understand and have planned for such developments are better placed to survive and prosper their humanitarian organizations than those who have not sufficiently accounted for evolving and arising complexities in global humanitarian practice. HL and SCM is widely known to be the basis of successful and effective humanitarian assistance (Thomas 2003). However, theory driven and systematic investigations will be needed to assess the scope and depth to which the theories described in this chapter describe future possible options and current practice.

## Summary and Conclusion

The overarching goal of this chapter is to generate preliminary ideas and inspire scholars to consider adopting and deploying theory in their work. The chapter suggested four theories for the exploration of the phenomenon of HL, HO and HSC management in novel ways. The chapter suggested four valuable theories for possible adoption by researchers and demonstrated how they can be deployed. The theories suggested are: internationalization theory; social exchange theory; transaction cost and organization economics and RDT. These four theories should change and extend the types of RQs asked in research in HL, HO and HSCs as well as the way scholars search for findings. The author hopes that this has been accomplished in a basic way.

Thomas Friedman (2005) suggested that a history of the world written in 2025 would likely point to flattening of the globe as the most crucial development of our time. A massive shift of both potential markets and the available workforce from developed to emerging markets is placing new demands on supply chain managers. Many of the rules of the past no longer apply as managers attempt to navigate cultural differences, geographic distances, language barriers, political uncertainty, currency exchanges, new technologies and multiple time zones in their supply chain. As new rules take shape and the academic community attempts to make sense of them, we believe that the four theories discussed in this article will provide a potent theoretical foundation for exploring ideas, explaining relationships and understanding the phenomenon of global SCM.

# References

Anderson, E. and Coughlan, A.T. (1987). International market entry and expansion via independent or integrated channels of distribution. *Journal of Marketing*, Vol. 51, pp. 71–82.

Apte, A., Gonçalves, P. and Yoho, K. (2016). Capabilities and competencies in humanitarian operations. *Journal of Humanitarian Logistics and Supply Chain Management*, Vol. 6, No. 2, pp. 240–258.

Asmussen, C.G., Pedersen, T. and Dhanaraj, C. (2009). Host country environment and subsidiary competence: Extending the diamond network model. *Journal of International Business*.

Australian Broadcasting Corporation. (2016). Hurricane Matthew: Rising rivers could cause more death and destruction as deteriorating storm moves out to sea. http://www.abc.net.au/news/2016-10-10/hurricane-matthew-makes-its-exit-to-sea/7917250. 12 October 2016.

Balcik, B. and Beamon, B.M. (2008). Facility location in humanitarian relief. *International Journal of Logistics Research and Applications*, Vol. 11, No. 2, pp. 101–121.

Balcik, B., Beamon, B.M., Krejci, C.C., Muramatsu, K.M. and Ramirez, M. (2010). Coordination in humanitarian relief chains: Practices, challenges and opportunities. *International Journal of Production Economics*, Vol. 126, No. 1, pp. 22–34.

Banks, N., Hulme, D. and Edwards, M. (2015). NGOs, states, and donors revisited: Still too close for comfort?. *World Development*, Vol. 66, pp. 707–718.

Biggart, N.W. and Delbridge, R. (2004). Systems of exchange. *Academy of Management Review*, Vol. 29, pp. 28–49.

Black, R. (1998). Putting refugees in camps. *Forced Migration Review*, Vol. 2 (August), pp. 4–7.

Brockhaus, R.H. (2004). Family business succession: Suggestions for future research. *Family Business Review*, Vol. 17, No. 2, pp. 165–177.

Buckley P. and Casson M. (1976). The future of the multinational enterprise. New York: Holmes and Meier Publishers.

Cabrera-Suárez, K., De Saá-Pérez, P., and García-Almeida, D. (2001). The succession process from a resource and knowledge-based view of the family firm. *Family Business Review*, Vol. 14, No. 1, pp. 37–46.

Cadieux, L., Lorrain, J. and Hugron, P. (2002). Succession in women-owned businesses: A case study. *Family Business Review*, Vol. 15, pp. 17–30.

Calhoun, M.A. (2002). Unpacking liability of foreignness: identifying culturally driven external and internal sources of liability for the foreign subsidiary. *Journal of International Management*, Vol. 8, No. 3, pp. 301–321.

Carter, C.R., Rogers, D.S. and Choi, T.Y. (2015). Toward the theory of the supply chain. *Journal of Supply Chain Management*, Vol. 51, No. 2, pp. 89–97.

Casciaro, T. and Piskorski M.J. (2005). Power imbalance, mutual dependence, and constraint absorption: A closer look at resource dependence theory. *Administrative Science Quarterly*, Vol. 50, No. 2, pp. 167–199.

Chandes, J. and Paché, G. (2010). Investigating humanitarian logistics issues: From operations management to strategic action. *Journal of Manufacturing Technology Management*, Vol. 21, No. 3, pp. 320–340

Chicksand, D., Watson, G., Walker, H., Radnor, Z. and Johnson, R. (2012). Theoretical perspectives in purchasing and supply chain management: An analysis of the literature. *Supply Chain Management: An International Journal*, Vol. 17, No. 4, pp. 454–472.

Choi, T. and Wacker, J. (2011). Theory building in the OM/SCM field: Pointing to the future by looking at the past. *Journal of Supply Chain Management*, Vol. 47, No. 2, pp. 8–11.

Chrisman, J.J., Chua, J.H., Sharma, P. and Yoder, T.R. (2009). Guiding family business succession through the succession process: A step-by-step guide for CPA advisors. *CPA Journal*, Vol. 79, pp. 48–51.

Coleman, J. (1986). Social theory, social research, and a theory of action. *American Journal of Sociology*, Vol. 91, pp. 1309–1335.

Connelly, B.L., Kitchen, D.J. and Hult, G.T.M. (2013). Global supply chain management: Toward a theoretically driven research agenda. *Global Strategy Journal*, Vol. 3, No. 3, pp. 227–243.

Cooper, J. (2007). Cognitive dissonance: 50 years of a classic theory. London: Sage Publications.

Cropanzano, R. and Mitchell, M.S. (2005). Social exchange theory: An interdisciplinary review. *Journal of Management*, Vol. 31, No. 6, pp. 874–900.

Dalton, D.R., Hitt, M.A., Certo, S.T. and Dalton, C.M. (2007). 1 The Fundamental Agency Problem and Its Mitigation: Independence, Equity, and the Market for Corporate Control. *The Academy of Management Annals*, Vol. 1, No. 1, pp. 1–64.

Day, J.M., Melnyk, S.A. Larson, P.D., Davis, E.W. and Whybark, D.C. (2012). Humanitarian and disaster relief supply chains: A matter of life and death. *Journal of Supply Chain Management*, Vol. 48, No. 2, pp. 21–36.

Dubey, R. and Gunasekaran, A. (2016). The sustainable humanitarian supply chain design: Agility, adaptability and alignment. *International Journal of Logistics Research and Applications*, Vol. 19, No. 1, pp. 62–82.

Dunning, J.H. (2003). Some antecedents of internationalization theory. *Journal of International Business Studies*, Vol. 34, No. 2, pp. 108–115.

Dyck, B., Mauws, M., Starke, F.A. and Mischke, G.A. (2002). Passing the baton: The importance of sequence, timing, technique and communication in executive succession. *Journal of Business Venturing*, Vol. 17, pp. 143–162.

Dyer, J.H. (1997). Effective interfirm collaboration: how firms minimize transaction costs and maximize transaction value. *Strategic Management Journal*, Vol. 18, No. 7, pp. 535–556.

EJOR (2016). Call for papers: OR Applied to Humanitarian Operations. *European Journal of Operational Research*, https://www.journals.elsevier.com/european-journal-of-operationalresearch/call-for-papers/call-for-papers-or-applied-to-humanitarian-operations (accessed 25 Feb 2017)

Ekeh, P.P. (1974). Social exchange theory: The two traditions. Cambridge, MA: Harvard University Press.

Emerson, R. M. (1976). Social exchange theory. *Annual Review of Sociology*, Vol. 2, No. 1, pp. 335–362.

Essex, R. (2016). Torture, healthcare and Australian immigration detention. *Journal of Medical Ethics*, pp. medethics-2016.http://jme.bmj.com/content/early/2016/02/22/medethics-2016-103387.extract. Accessed 28 May 2016.

Fawcett, S.E. and Waller, M.A. (2015). Designing the supply chain for success at the bottom of the pyramid. *Journal of Business Logistics*, Vol. 36, No. 3, pp. 233–239.

Festinger, L. (1957). A theory of cognitive dissonance. Stanford, CA: Stanford University Press.

Fleay, C., Cokley, J., Dodd, A., Briskman, L. and Schwartz, L. (2016). Missing the boat: Australia and asylum seeker deterrence messaging. *International Migration*, online first. http://onlinelibrary.wiley.com/doi/10.1111/imig.12241/pdf. 28 May 2016.

Friedman, T. (2005). *The world is flat: A brief history of the globalized world in the 21st century*. London: Allen Lane, England pp. 393–395.

Gatrell, P. (2016). The world-wide web of humanitarianism: NGOs and population displacement in the third quarter of the twentieth century. *European Review of History: Revue européenne d'histoire*, Vol. 23, No. 1–2, pp. 101–115.

George, G., Corbishley, C., Khayesi, J.N., Haas, M.R. and Tihanyi, L. (2016). Bringing Africa in: Promising directions for management research. *Academy of Management Journal*, Vol. 59, No. 2, pp. 377–393.

Gil, J.C.S. and McNeil, S. (2015). Supply chain outsourcing in response to manmade and natural disasters in Colombia, a humanitarian logistics perspective. *Procedia Engineering*, Vol. 107, pp. 110–121.

Granovetter, M. (1985). Economic action and social structure: The problem of embeddedness. *American Journal of Sociology*, Vol. 91, pp. 481–510.

Gustavsson, L. (2003). Humanitarian logistics: Context and challenges. *Forced Migration Review*, Vol. 18, No. 6, pp. 6–8.

Halldórsson, A., Hsuan, J. and Kotzab, H. (2015). Complementary theories to supply chain management revisited – from borrowing theories to theorizing. *Supply Chain Management: An International Journal*, Vol. 20, No. 6, pp. 574–586.

Haleblian, J., Devers, C.E., McNamara, G., Carpenter, M.A. and Davison, R.B. (2009). Taking stock of what we know about mergers and acquisitions: A review and research agenda. *Journal of Management*, Vol. 35, pp. 469–502.

Hambrick, D. (2007). The field of management's devotion to theory: Too much of a good thing? *Academy of Management Journal*, Vol. 50, pp. 1345–1352.

Hampshire, J. (2015). Europe's migration crisis. *Political Insight*, Vol. 6, No. 3, pp. 8–11.

Handler, W.C. (1991). Key interpersonal relationships of next-generation family members in family firms. *Journal of Small Business Management*, Vol. 29, No. 3, p. 21.

Harrell-Bond, B. (2002). Can humanitarian work with refugees be humane?. *Human rights quarterly*, Vol. 24, No. 1, pp. 51–85.

Hazen, B.T. (2016). Editorial: 'Overcoming basic barriers to publishing research.' *The International Journal of Logistics Management*, Vol. 27, No. 1.

Hillman, A.J., Withers, M.C. and Collins, B.J. (2009). Resource dependence theory: A review. *Journal of Management*, Vol. 35, No. 6, pp. 1404–1427.

Hitt, M.A. (2011). Relevance of strategic management theory and research for supply chain management. *Journal of Supply Chain Management*, Vol. 47, No. 1, pp. 9–13.

Hitt, M.A., Dacin, M.T., Levitas, E., Arregle, J.L. and Borza, A. (2000). Partner selection in emerging and developed market contexts: resource-based and organizational learning perspectives. *Academy of Management Journal*, Vol. 43, No. 3, pp. 449–467.

Hitt, M.A., Hoskisson, R.E. and Kim, H. (1997). International diversification: effects on innovation and firm performance in product-diversified firms. *Academy of Management Journal*, Vol. 40, No. 4, pp. 767–798.

Hitt M.A., Tihanyi, L., Miller, T., and Connelly, B.L. (2006). International diversification: antecedents, outcomes, and moderators. *Journal of Management*, Vol. 32, No. 6, pp. 831–867.

Hobbs, J.E. (1996). A transaction cost approach to supply chain management. *Supply Chain Management: An International Journal*, Vol. 1, No. 2, pp. 15–27.

Holguín-Veras, J., Jallerb, M., van Wassenhove, L., Pérez, N. and Wachtendorfe, T. (2012). On the unique features of post-disaster humanitarian logistics. *Journal of Operations Management*, Vol. 30 Nos. 7/8, pp. 494–506.

Holguín-Veras, J., Amaya-Leal, J., Cantillo, V., Van Wassenhove, L.N., Aros-Vera, F. and Jaller, M. (2016). Econometric estimation of deprivation cost functions: A contingent valuation experiment. *Journal of Operations Management*, Vol. 45, pp. 44–56.

Hoskisson, R.E., Hitt, M.A., Wan, W.P. and Yiu, D. (1999). Theory and research in strategic management: swings of a pendulum. *Journal of Management*, Vol. 25, No. 3, pp. 417–456.

Hugo, G. and Napitupulu, C.J. (2016). Boats, borders and ballot boxes: Asylum seekers on Australia's Northern Shore. In Van der Velde, M and Van Naerssen, T. (Eds.), *Mobility and migration choices: Thresholds to crossing borders*. Abingdon, Oxon OX14 4RN England: Routledge, p. 213.

Hymer, S.H. (1976). *The international operations of national firms*. MIT Press: Cambridge, MA.

Jahre, M. and Jensen, L.M. (2010). Coordination in humanitarian logistics through clusters. *International Journal of Physical Distribution & Logistics Management*, Vol. 40, No. 8/9, pp. 657–674.

Jahre, M., Jensen, L.M. and Listou, T. (2009). Theory development in humanitarian logistics: A framework and three cases. *Management Research News*, Vol. 32, No. 11, pp. 1008–1023.

Jensen, M.C. and Meckling, W.H. (1976). Theory of the firm: Managerial behavior, agency costs and ownership structure. *Journal of Financial Economics*, Vol. 3, pp. 305–360.

Kabra, G. and Ramesh, A. (2015). Analyzing drivers and barriers of coordination in humanitarian supply chain management under fuzzy environment. *Benchmarking: An International Journal*, Vol. 22, No. 4, pp. 559–587.

Kamradt-Scott, A. (2016). WHO's to blame? The World Health Organization and the 2014 Ebola outbreak in West Africa. *Third World Quarterly*, Vol. 37, No. 3, pp. 401–418.

Karatas-Cetin, C. and Denktas-Sakar, G. (2013). Logistics research beyond 2000: Theory, method and relevance. *Asian Journal of Shipping and Logistics*, Vol. 29, No. 2, pp. 125–144.

Kerlinger, J.C. (1986). *Fundamentals of behavioral research*. Holt, Rinehart, and Winston: Orlando, FL.

Knox, R. (2015). 5 Years after Haiti's Earthquake, Where Did the $13.5 Billion Go? 12 January 2015. http://www.npr.org/sections/goatsandsoda/2015/01/12/376138864/5-years-after-haiti-s-earthquake-why-aren-t-things-better. Accessed 12 October 2016.

Kovács, G. and Spens, K. (2007). Humanitarian logistics in disaster relief operations. *International Journal of Physical Distribution and Logistics Management*, Vol. 37, No. 2, pp. 99–114.

Kovács, G. and Spens, K. (2009). Identifying challenges in humanitarian logistics. *International Journal of Physical Distribution and Logistics Management*, Vol. 39, No. 6, pp. 506–528.

Kovács, G. and Spens, K. (2011). Trends and developments in humanitarian logistics – a gap analysis. *International Journal of Physical Distribution and Logistics Management*, Vol. 41, No. 1, pp. 32–34.

Krugman, P.R. (1997). Pop Internationalism. Cambridge, MA: MIT Press.

Kunz, N. and Reiner, G. (2012). A meta-analysis of humanitarian logistics research. *Journal of Humanitarian Logistics and Supply Chain Management*, Vol. 2, No. 2, pp. 116–147.

Langfield-Smith, K. and Smith, D. (2003). Management control systems and trust in outsourcing relationships. *Management Accounting Research*, Vol. 14, No. 3, pp. 281–307.

Le Breton-Miller, I., Miller, D. and Steier, L.P. (2004). Toward an integrative model of effective FOB succession. *Entrepreneurship Theory and Practice*, Vol. 28, pp. 305–328.

L'Hermitte, C., Tatham, P.H. and Bowles, M. (2014). Classifying logistics relevant disasters: Conceptual model and empirical investigation. *Journal of Humanitarian Logistics and Supply Chain Management*, Vol. 4, No. 2, pp. 155–178.

L'Hermitte, C., Tatham, P., Brooks, B. and Bowles, M. (2016). Supply chain agility in humanitarian protracted operations. *Journal of Humanitarian Logistics and Supply Chain Management*, Vol. 6, No. 2, pp. 173–201.

McGuinness, T. (1994). Markets and managerial hierarchies. In Thompson G. et al. (Eds.), Markets, hierarchies and networks. London, England: Sage, pp. 66–81.

Medcof, J.W. (2001). Resource-based strategy and managerial power in networks of internationally dispersed technology units. *Strategic Management Journal*, Vol. 22, No. 11, pp. 999–1012.

Meixell M.J., Gargeya V.B. (2005). Global supply chain design: A literature review and critique. *Transportation Research*, Vol. 41, No. 6, pp. 531–550.

Mentzer, J.T., Min, S. and Bobbitt, L.M. (2004). Toward a unified theory of logistics. *International Journal of Physical Distribution and Logistics Management*, Vol. 34, Nos. 7/8, pp. 606–627.

Meyerson, D., Weick, K.E. and Kramer, R.M. (1996). Swift trust and temporary groups. *Trust in Organizations: Frontiers of Theory and Research*, Vol. 166, p. 195.

Moshtari, M. (2016). Inter-organizational fit, relationship management capability, and collaborative performance within a humanitarian setting. *Production and Operations Management*, Vol. 25, No. 9, pp. 1542–1557.

Munovi, N.K. (2015). Logistics outsourcing and performance of humanitarian Organisations in Kenya (Doctoral dissertation, University of Nairobi).

Naim, M.M. and Gosling, J. (2011). On leanness, agility and leagile supply chains. *International Journal of Production Economics*, Vol. 131, No. 1, pp. 342–354.

Natural Hazards Science. (2016). Oxford Research encyclopaedia. http://naturalha zardscience.oxfordre.com/view/10.1093/acrefore/9780199389407.001.0001/acrefore-9780199389407-e-25. Accessed 12 October 2016.

OECD (2008). Development aid at its highest level ever in 2008, Organisation for Economic Cooperation and Development. OECD Website: http://www.oecd.org/dac/stats/developmentaidatitshighestleveleverin2008.htm (accessed 26 Feb 2017)

Oliver-Smith, A., Alcántara-Ayala, I., Burton, I., and Lavell, A. (2016). Forensic Investigations of Disasters: A conceptual framework and guide to research (IRDR FORIN Publication No.2). Beijing: Integrated Research on Disaster Risk.

Oloruntoba, R. (2016). Boko Haram: Challenges and techniques of distributing aid in security challenged environments. In Kovács, G and Haavisto, I (Eds.), Supply Chain Management for Humanitarians: Tools for Practice. Kogan Page.

Oloruntoba, R. and Banomyong, R. (2016). Logistics and SCM in the context of relief for refugees and internally displaced persons IDPs. *Special Issue Call for Papers From Journal of Humanitarian Logistics and Supply Chain Management*. Emerald Group Publishing. http://www.emeraldgrouppublishing.com/products/journals/call_for_papers.htm?id=6790. Accessed 25 Feb 2017.

Oloruntoba, R. and Gray, R. (2002). Logistics for humanitarian aid: A survey of aid organisations. In Proceedings of the Logistics Research Network 7th Annual Conference, Technology Innovation Centre, Birmingham (pp. 4–6). September.

Oloruntoba, R. and Gray, R. (2003). Humanitarian aid organisations and logistics. UK: The Institute of Logistics and Transport Corby and the Institute of Marine Studies, University of Plymouth. ISBN: 1-904564-01-1.

Oloruntoba, R. and Gray, R. (2006). Humanitarian aid: An agile supply chain? *Supply Chain Management: An International Journal*, Vol. 11, No. 2, pp. 115–120.

Oloruntoba, R. and Gray, R. (2009). Customer service in emergency relief chains. *International Journal of Physical Distribution & Logistics Management*, Vol. 39, No. 6, pp. 486–505.

Oloruntoba, R. and Kovács, G. (2015). A commentary on agility in humanitarian aid supply chains. *Supply Chain Management: An International Journal*, Vol. 20, No. 6, pp. 708–716.

Overstreet, R.E., Hall, D., Hanna, J.B. and Kelly Rainer Jr, R. (2011). Research in humanitarian logistics. *Journal of Humanitarian Logistics and Supply Chain Management*, Vol. 1, No. 2, pp. 114–131.

Parkhe, A (2003). Institutional environments, institutional change, and international alliances. *Journal of International Management*, Vol. 9, No. 3, pp. 305–316.

Parkhe, A. (2011). Form follows function? Interorganizational networks as a strategic imperative for global strategies. *Global Strategy Journal*, Vol. 1, No. 2, pp. 86–89.

Pedraza-Martinez, A.J. and Van Wassenhove, L.N (2016). Empirically grounded research in humanitarian operations management: The way forward. *Journal of Operations Management*, Vol. 45, pp. 1–10.

Pfeffer, J. (1976). Beyond management and the worker: The institutional function of management. *Academy of Management Review*, Vol. 1, pp. 36–46.

Pfeffer, J. (1987). A resource dependence perspective on intercorporate relations. In *Intercorporate Relations: The Structural Analysis of Business* (eds) Mizruchi, M.S. and Schwartz, M. pp. 25–55. Cambridge University Press.

Pfeffer, J. and Salancik, G.R. (1978). *The External Control of Organizations: A Resource Dependence Approach*. NY: Harper and Row Publishers.

Puranam, P. and Vanneste, B.S. (2009). Trust and governance: Untangling a tangled web. *Academy of Management Review*, Vol. 34, No. 1, pp. 11–31.

Richey Jr, G. (2009). The supply chain crisis and disaster pyramid: A theoretical framework for understanding preparedness and recovery. *International Journal of Physical Distribution and Logistics Management*, Vol. 39, No. 7, pp. 619–628.

Schmenner, R.W. and Swink, M.L. (1998). On theory in operations management. *Journal of Operations Management*, Vol. 17, No. 1, pp. 97–113.

Sharma, P., Chrisman, J.J. and Chua, J.H. (2003). Succession planning as planned behavior: Some empirical results. *Family Business Review*, Vol. 16, pp. 1–16.

Shaw, T. M. and Swatuk, L. A. (Eds.) (1994). *The South at the End of the Twentieth Century: Rethinking the Political Economy of Foreign Policy in Africa, Asia, the Caribbean and Latin America. International Political Economic Series*. New York: St Martins Press Inc.

Shook, C.L., Adams, G.L. and Ketchen, D.J. (2009). Towards a 'theoretical toolbox' for strategic sourcing. *Supply Chain Management: An International Journal*, Vol. 14, No. 1, pp. 3–10.

Shou, Z., Zheng, X.V. and Zhu, W. (2016). Contract ineffectiveness in emerging markets: An institutional theory perspective. *Journal of Operations Management*, Vol. 46, pp. 38–54.

Sinkovics, R.R., Zagelmeyer, S. and Kusstatscher, V. (2011). Between merger and syndrome: The intermediary role of emotions in four cross-border M&As. *International Business Review*, Vol. 20, No. 1, pp. 27–47.

Sodhi, M.S. (2016). Natural disasters, the economy and population vulnerability as a vicious cycle with exogenous hazards. *Journal of Operations Management*, Vol. 45, pp. 101–113.

Srinivasan, M., Mukherjee, D. and Gaur, A.S. (2011). Buyer–supplier partnership quality and supply chain performance: Moderating role of risks, and environmental uncertainty. *European Management Journal*, Vol. 29, No. 4, pp. 260–271.

Tabaklar, T., Halldórsson, Á., Kovács, G. and Spens, K. (2015). Borrowing theories in humanitarian supply chain management. *Journal of Humanitarian Logistics and Supply Chain Management*, Vol. 5, No. 3, pp. 281–299.

Tatham, P. and Houghton, L. (2011). The wicked problem of humanitarian logistics and disaster relief aid. *Journal of Humanitarian Logistics and Supply Chain Management*, Vol. 1, No.1, pp. 15–31.

Tatham, P. and Kovács, G. (2010). The application of "swift trust" to humanitarian logistics. *International Journal of Production Economics*, Vol. 126, No. 1, pp. 35–45.

Thomas, A. (2003). Humanitarian logistics: enabling disaster response. *The Fritz Institute*. Available: http://www.fritzinstitute.org/pdfs/whitepaper/enablingdisasterresponse.pdf. Accessed 20 December 2016.

Turner, J. (2003). *The Structure of Sociological Theory*. Belmont, CA: Wadsworth.

Ulrich, D. and Barney, J.B. (1984). Perspectives in organizations: Resource dependence, efficiency, and population. *Academy of Management Review*, Vol. 9, No. 3, pp. 471–481.

UNHCR. (2015). World at War: Global Trends Forced Displacement in 2014. http://unhcr.org/556725e69.html. 28 May 2016.

United Nations Office for Disaster Risk Reduction. (2015). Proposed Updated Terminology on Disaster Risk Reduction: A Technical Review (August). http://www.preventionweb.net/files/45462_backgoundpaperonterminologyaugust20.pdf. Accessed 12 October 2016.

Van de Ven, A.H. (1989) Nothing is quite so practical as a good theory. *Academy of Management Review*, Vol. 14, pp. 486–489.

Van den Waeyenberg and Hens, L. (2012). Overcoming institutional distance: Expansion to base-of-thepyramid markets. *Journal of Business Research*, Vol. 65, No. 12, pp. 1692–1699.

Vega, D. and Roussat, C. (2015). Humanitarian logistics: The role of logistics service providers. *International Journal of Physical Distribution & Logistics Management*, Vol. 45, No. 4, pp. 352–375.

Walsh, J.P. (2015). Organization and Management Scholarship in and for Africa… and the World. *The Academy of Management Perspectives*, Vol. 29, No. 1, pp. 1–6.

Weber, L. (2015). Rethinking border control for a globalizing world: A preferred future. Abingdon and New York: Routledge.

Wenji, Z., Turale, S., Stone, T.E. and Petrini, M.A (2015). Chinese nurses' relief experiences following two earthquakes: Implications for disaster education and policy development. *Nurse Education in Practice*, Vol. 15, No. 1, pp. 75–81.

Whetton, D.A. (1989). What constitutes a theoretical contribution? *Academy of Management Review*, Vol. 14, pp. 490–495.

Whipple, J.M., Griffis, S.E. and Daugherty, P.J. (2013). Conceptualizations of trust: Can we trust them?. *Journal of Business Logistics*, Vol. 34, No. 2, pp. 117–130.

Williamson, O.E. (1975). Markets and hierarchies: Analysis and antitrust implications. New York, NY: Free Press.

Williamson, O.E. (1981). The economics of organization: The transaction cost approach. *American Journal of Sociology*, Vol. 87, No. 3, pp. 548–575.

Williamson, O.E. (1985). The economic institutions of capitalism. New York, NY: Free Press.

Williamson, O.E. (2008). Outsourcing: Transaction cost economics and supply chain management. *Journal of Supply Chain Management*, Vol. 44, No. 2, pp. 5–16.

Wright, P.M. (2015). Rethinking "Contribution". *Journal of Management*, Vol. 41, No. 3, pp. 765–768.

Zaheer, S. (1995). Overcoming the liability of foreignness. *Academy of Management Journal*, Vol. 38, No. 2, pp. 341–363.

Zsidisin, G.A. and Ellram, L.M. (2003). An agency theory investigation of supply risk management. *Journal of Supply Chain Management*, Vol. 39, No. 2, pp. 15–27.

# 24

# From Aid to Resilience: How to Bridge Disaster Resilience and Humanitarian Supply Chain Management Research

Eija Meriläinen

## Introduction

Disasters are studied within a variety of academic research streams and with a plethora of different foci. The research presented in this book chapter is navigating the terrains between disaster resilience and humanitarian logistics and supply chain management (HLSCM) disciplines. Bridging the two domains connects the top-down managerial view of the aiding organizations to the bottom-up view of the communities affected by a disaster. However, as the two streams of literature frame the disaster phenomena differently and build on different paradigms, conducting interdisciplinary research is not straight forward. The researcher should not only be aware of the underlying paradigmatic assumptions of the bodies of knowledge but should also be able to reflect on where she or he stands with respect to the paradigms. The two paradigms clash and set differing expectations on how the research should be carried out. Recognizing the philosophical foundations of different fields of science and the scientist is important, but it is the method where the paradigms culminate. Different fields of research expect different scoping, sampling, data collection, analysis, and write-up.

Both disaster resilience and HLSCM aim at implications, either implicitly or explicitly: something needs to be done about disasters and human

E. Meriläinen (✉)
Hanken School of Economics, Helsinki, Finland
e-mail: eija.merilainen@hanken.fi

G. Kovács et al. (eds.), *The Palgrave Handbook of Humanitarian Logistics and Supply Chain Management*, https://doi.org/10.1057/978-1-137-59099-2_24

**713**

suffering. Disaster resilience and HLSCM literatures carry an urgency that is spelled out or coded in between the lines. HLSCM scholars and practitioners study honing disaster relief supply chains and operations to better save lives and provide aid to people affected by disasters. Meanwhile resilience scholars and practitioners aim at contributing to policies or frameworks that would support local capacities to respond to, recover from, and prepare for disasters. The focus in HLSCM is on the organizations, whereas disaster resilience literature discusses the affected populations. Where HLSCM adopts a shorter-term, managerial perspective, disaster resilience gazes into the long-term policies. Furthermore, where HLSCM often views the phenomenon top-down, from the point of view on an organization that is managed and is "managing the disaster," disaster resilience gives voice to the bottom-up perspective, the people whose lives have been affected by the disaster. Through combining HLSCM and disaster resilience a researcher can better connect the short-term pragmatic actions with the long-term view on the community. Studying the instrument of aid from the point of view of the long-term resilience of a community is important.

Bridging the understanding between disaster relief supply chains and disaster resilience literature is becoming increasingly topical for two reasons. Firstly, as NGO-provided aid is becoming a more substantial part of the overall disaster relief, the implications of these organizations' current focus on the immediate response phase needs to be better understood with respect to the long-term resilience of the communities. Secondly, as NGOs are increasingly connected to single individual donors and the power over aid efforts is hence not democratically exercised in the local communities, the implications need to be understood (Curtis 2016; Martens and Seitz 2015). If resources are channeled to the communities through an external instrument with a focused power-structure disconnected from the communities, instead of it being owned by the communities, the long-term effectiveness of the disaster relief aid needs to be well-understood.

While HLSCM and disaster resilience share a similar conceptual landscape with disasters at the heart of both fields, they origin from different springs. How the research in each discipline is conducted and written, as well as what gets studied is still bound to the roots and paradigms of the discipline. This book chapter discusses the different philosophical paradigms underlying disaster resilience and disaster relief supply chain management research, bridging the two. The chapter ends with discussing the methods of the author's research carried out in Valparaíso, Chile, in 2015. The purpose of the case part is to highlight how the differing paradigms – held by the researcher and given by the different research streams – manifested and lived throughout the research process. The focus is on how both the research method applied and the disaster resilience literature brought bottom-up perspective into the research domain of HLSCM. The tone and richness of the language used in the chapter give away my (the author's) research paradigmatic positioning, especially toward the end of the chapter.

## Disaster Resilience and Relief

Disasters are complex phenomena reaping destruction exposing and accentuating the inequality and disharmony that exists in the social structures in the *status quo*. While a hazard might not be caused by human activity – such as an asteroid hitting the Earth – a disaster is a process that evolves in the human communities and societies (Cupples and Glynn 2014; UNISDR 2009). Hazard may be of natural origin, but as Smith (2006) argues, there is "no such thing as a natural disaster." Categorization of disasters into slow on-set and sudden-onset disasters, as well as natural and man-made disasters can frame a variety of disaster-related phenomena, potentially helping to outline appropriate responses (Van Wassenhove 2006). However, the damage that a hazard reaps in a community or society defies simple characterizations and evolves over a long period of time, and framing a disaster through a hazard-related stencil oversimplifies the phenomenon.

While the terms "hazard" and "disaster" are sometimes used interchangeably, within this book chapter the term "disaster" is used to discuss a complex social phenomenon, rather than drawing the focus on the characteristics of a hazard. For example, the aftermath of an earthquake does not fall equally on people within an earthquake-prone region, but is shaped by the reality in which it evolves. When in the aftermath of a hazard people lose their homes, access to clean water and food, and are not able to regain these it is often not only a question of a hazard cutting access to these resources, but a question of inequality and restricted access that exists within and across the communities and societies in the stable state.

There are a variety of practitioner and research domains that study how the lives of people and their environment are affected by disasters. Resilience, vulnerability, sustainability (climate change), adaptation, and disaster risk reduction (DRR) are all both practitioner and academic labels under which hazards, disasters, and global environmental change are addressed (Cutter et al. 2008; Alexander 2013; Smit and Wandel 2006), While disasters are often considered exceptions rather than the rule, climate change is slowly becoming the rule of exceptions. It is worsening the status quo of societies, as well as increasing the likelihood and magnitude of hazards.

While this book chapter will not discuss climate change to a great extent, Kelman et al. (2015, p. 21) argue that the global policy community should move beyond vulnerability and resilience, and put an end to "tribalism and separation in order to work together to achieve common goals for humanity." In the paper they refer to how the year 2015 that saw three separate, yet topically highly related policy processes on the international level advancing their separate ways. The Millennium Development Goals gave way for broader Sustainable Development Goals, UNISDR's (2005) Hyogo Framework for national and communal resilience building turned into Sendai Framework for DRR (UNISDR 2015) and the world leaders met in Paris to pledge to keep the global average temperature increase below 2 degree Celsius (United Nations 2015a, b). While the UN efforts are commonly lauded, they are sometimes considered detached from the ground.

Researchers can play a role in uniting the different fronts of Earth saving efforts. Aiming for a silo-hopping, easily accessible and understandable, yet rooted interdisciplinary research could be seen as one way to go about it (Ledford 2015). Trying to bridge different domains of research is one of the challenges for the today's social scientist navigating in an info glut. A researcher can no longer cite the canonical pieces from one sub-field and be confident she or he has addressed *the* discussion (Luker 2008). One may have addressed *a* discussion, but one may not know if it is the (only) relevant one. Knowing one's intellectual home fields and how they relate to another is not straightforward. This book chapter discusses interdisciplinary disaster research that combines "disaster resilience" and "humanitarian logistics and supply chain management." Through studying the paradigms underlying each "home field" the chapter highlights the difference between the streams and describes how the interdisciplinary research was carried out with respect to the paradigmatic differences.

## Vulnerability and Resilience

Discussing "vulnerability" is one way for research to address and understand the unequal effect of disasters on people. Cutter et al. (2008) argue that vulnerability consists of people's exposure to risk, as well as of systemic sensitivities that determine the extent of harm that falls on people and places. The concept of vulnerability is often brought up to highlight how different demographic groups are affected by disasters differently. Factors such as socioeconomic status, gender, ethnicity, and education are few of the factors brought up in the discussion on vulnerability, to explain how people's lives evolve in the turmoil of disasters (e.g., Cutter et al. 2003; Yarnal 2007). While the concept of vulnerability can be helpful, it should be noted that vulnerabilities are a result of the shape of the surrounding reality, the socio-politico-economic-environmental system. Observing the vulnerabilities of the people can draw the focus from the cause to the effect, ignoring the agency of the people affected within the system they are embedded in.

The aftermath of Hurricane Katrina proved to be anything but equal and discussion on race and class, and differing vulnerabilities rose to the fore (Yarnal 2007; Elliot and Pais 2006). For example, Elliot and Pais (2006) found out that in the aftermath of the hurricane an "average" black worker in New Orleans had seven times greater likelihood than a white worker to have lost his or her job. However, the people worst affected were not lacking agency, as the media portrayals may have suggested. The media painted a picture where predominantly White middle class had evacuated from the city, while others had failed to do so (Elliot and Pais 2006; Stephens et al. 2009). Yet, as Stephens et al. (2009) found out in their research, the observers failed to acknowledge the agency of those who stayed and faced the disaster, and regarded them negatively as passive.

One way to highlight the agency of those affected by, or expected to be affected by, a disaster is to discuss disaster resilience instead of vulnerability. Vulnerability and resilience can be considered both as overlapping concepts, as well as labels at opposing ends of a spectrum (Cutter et al. 2008; Wilson 2012). The concept of resilience is often traced back to ecology, where it refers to the idea of a community recovering, or bouncing back, after a shock (Alexander 2013; Holling 1973). Resilience has become a buzzword also in the policy discussions – many governmental entities support the idea of communities themselves being prepared for facing disasters, and different kinds of resilience assessment tools are popping up, both in the academic literature as well as among practitioners and policy-makers (e.g., Singh-Peterson et al. 2014; Cutter et al. 2008; UNISDR 2005).

Disaster resilience is discussed on many levels of abstraction, from nation state levels to local community levels, and with respect to different kinds of institutions (Wilson 2012; Wilson 2013; Manyena 2014). The concept of "community" often sneaks into the discussions over disaster resilience and relief, but is often left vague. It can be considered to refer to the people or place, even if the idea of a unified community especially in populated and fragmented urban contexts is anything but clear or bounded (IFRC 2014; Harrison et al. 2003). Yet there is a lure and justification to discuss the people as resilient and capable communities where power resides, rather than individual victims. Hence the idea of community resilience that emphasizes people's potential to face disasters without external intervention is at the same time empowering, as it is contradicting: if a disaster is understood as a disruption calling for external intervention and balancing in the unequal system, does not advocating resilience mean pushing aside the idea of actually addressing the structural components of disaster and the underlying inequality?

While resilience hints at giving agency to those affected, it can be criticized also for being just an excuse for leaving the dispossessed as they are, continuing "business as usual" (Diprose 2014). And, if one hopes to truly address disasters, business cannot go on as usual. The neoliberal policies have contributed to the polarization of wealth and power, and climate change has become the global ticking time bomb of our age (Harvey 2005; Klein 2015). The shards are already flying. The rural population is shifting toward cities and the urban population is growing (United Nations 2014). Meanwhile, urbanization has led to growth in informal neighborhoods where the living conditions are harsh and disaster preparedness is low (IFRC 2010). At the same time, climate change is also linked to causing major hazards, such as large tornadoes or fire storms. Both the rural and urban populations are at risk. If the structural issues are not addressed, nor the effects globally and regionally balanced out, disasters remain unaddressed. Despite the good intentions, resilience alone is but a feel-good concept and an excuse.

## Humanitarian Logistics and Supply Chain Management

While resilience refers to how the preparedness for, the response to and recovery from disasters comes from within the disaster-affected communities, disaster relief studies the topic from the point of view of organizations external to the affected communities. Humanitarian logistics (and supply chain management) is one of the labels under which the provision of humanitarian aid through supply networks and using operations management approaches is studied (Kovács and Spens 2007; Maon et al. 2009; Altay and Green 2006; Fawcett and Fawcett 2013; Day et al. 2012). This field of research draws often from commercial supply chain management and operations management literatures. The carrying idea of HLSCM was to bridge knowledge between the commercial sector and the humanitarian one, to make the supply chains providing humanitarian assistance better and more effective, and potentially to teach adaptiveness to commercial businesses

(Van Wassenhove 2006). Often the focus is on individual organizations providing aid (e.g., McLachlin et al. 2009). However, collaboration and coordination between aid providers are increasingly highlighted in the humanitarian context, and the focus is moving beyond an individual organization (Balcik et al. 2010; McLachlin and Larson 2011).

Global humanitarian system has grown out of separated altruistic efforts (ALNAP 2015). While ALNAP paints the communities at the heart of the humanitarian system, major members noted in this system are international NGOs, UN humanitarian agencies, national NGOs, humanitarian arms of regional intergovernmental organizations, host governments, donors, and the International Red Cross and Red Crescent Movement. The system has grown remarkably in size, and the NGO's efforts have become an integral part of the global disaster relief. While the amount of humanitarian aid provided has increased significantly and there have been improvements in the humanitarian system, according to ALNAP's report, these improvements have been instrumental (ALNAP 2015). The field of HLSCM continues to focus on improving the operations providing aid, yet there is a further need to understand not only the effectiveness of the supply chains providing relief aid but also the effectiveness of the provided aid to the communities affected in the long term. This is where disaster resilience comes in.

## Philosophical Paradigms in Disaster-Related Research

Ontology, epistemology and methodology are concepts of philosophy of science. When you lay awake at night and think about everything that possibly exists and try to understand the realm of reality, you are tapping into the ontological questions. When, on the other hand, you have come to some faltering conviction on what there is, but start doubting yourself and asking yourself "But how do I know that? Through my senses? Through knowledge of others? Through asking this question?" you have advanced into the domain of epistemology. You might also have a headache. Methods, finally, consists of the variety of ways and tools with which one can try to poke at the reality.

Depending on your eagerness for philosophical pondering, you may (not) find these questions thrilling. And even if you do, provided that you are researching a narrow slice of a phenomenon with urgent real-life manifestations – such as disasters – you might not find these questions a top priority to your work. You might think twice about spending your time questioning the solidity and shape of the scientific ground that one stands on. The human suffering associated with disasters creates a sense of urgency for not only the practitioners but also to the academics, to find solutions rather than exploring the foundations of knowledge.

Yet, academic researchers should be the ones to study phenomena thoroughly. This means taking different angles to a phenomenon through a variety of theoretical lenses and with different methodological tools. Not one researcher or research group can master all the research methods or theories available, but they should aim to connect their niche understanding of a phenomenon to the current and past understanding of that phenomenon. Theories, methods, and whole bodies of knowledge carry along with them a set of ontological and epistemological assumptions about what is and how one may know it. A good researcher not only knows the tip of an iceberg and builds their snow-man on it but also is at very least aware of what lies beneath the surface. The merit of academic writing should not be its incomprehensibility from the perspective of the layman and the practitioner, but its rootedness. So while a researcher cannot master all the possible ways to perceive a reality or poke at it at once, it is good to keep an eye on what one's own field of research assumes of reality and what a researcher herself assumes of it.

Paradigmatic differences exist both between different topics of research, as well as within them. The differences are visible in the academic outputs of research. Articles about the same topic stemming from different paradigms are published in different journals, build on different social theories and apply different methods. While the "methods" or "methodology" section of academic papers offers a space where the ontological, epistemological, and methodological orientation of the research can be spelled out, given the very limited space of academic articles, the authors often cut out their way of framing the phenomenon and rather focus on what they see as the "beef" of the paper. Yet generally, the implicit or explicit paradigm choice made, have an effect on what was studied and how. This is also reflected in how the research is written.

While interdisciplinary research is gaining ground, cross-pollination is still in its infancy. While it can be argued that rigorous research relies on well-built paradigms and jumping too much across silos can make the research muddier, it has its plusses too. As the societies have dived deeper into specialization, people rarely speak across the silos. Knowledge without communication across silos cannot build harmony and understanding. This calls, together with a currently evolving climate disaster, for researchers to cooperate with each other. Yet the collaboration may also tease out the underlying paradigmatic clashes (Ledfordt 2015). These assumptions may also come under discussion when a researcher decides to go against the current and adopts a different standpoint to a phenomenon than scholars that she or he builds upon or resides next to. If one is combining two or more streams of research, one might end up going against at least one current. To protect against drowning, it helps if you have clarified for yourself the philosophical assumptions that you build upon and/or the stream of literature that you primarily will contribute to. This way you both know yourself as a researcher, but also address both the thought of your mentors as well as of your audience.

## Underlying Research Paradigms

We, the researchers, are not as special as we would sometimes like to think. Our thoughts are nurtured by the discourses we swim in and our words echo the tides of time and place (Foucault 2012; Burr 1995). Hence the philosophical paradigms underlying our research are also unlikely to be truly "ours": they reflect our background, the research community we belong to and the research question at hand. Philosophy of science tends to slice the philosophical paradigms often into ontological, epistemological, and methods layers. The use of terminology differs between the fields of research. While the terms "methodology" and "method" are sometimes used similarly, here the word "method" is employed to accentuate the practice of carrying out research.

While the ontological, epistemological, and methods layers can be discussed separately, when they are piled up for the purposes of conducting research, they tend to get entangled. The methods chosen to carry out a research are influenced by what you assume about the nature of reality with respect to a particular phenomenon, and the other way around. Even if you try to layer your own cake out of finely carved, separate ontological, epistemological, and methods-related layers, the cake might end up looking much like the other cakes in your intellectual surroundings. This does not mean you should not make a cake. As a fan of all cakes, I reckon you get more out of eating a cake when you can relate to the effort of making one. Furthermore, when you know what went into the cake in the first place you can either eat it with a confidence in its quality or with a context-related reservation.

What, then, are the different ontological, epistemological, and methods paradigms and how does one know that one is part of one?

It would be easier to explain one layered understanding of the reality, than to examine and compare the layers of one cake with those of other cakes. That implies building on a pre-selected philosophical research orientation. Yet many efforts to define and look at the layers exist. One of them is provided by Burrell and Morgan (1979). They spread social scientists' approaches to ontology, epistemology, human nature, and methodology on a scale from subjective to objective.

- With respect to ontology, the scale goes from subjective *nominalism* to objective *realism.* In nominalism the reality is built from the labels and concepts without which it would not exist. Meanwhile, in realism an external reality exists, even if it can be perceived with the help of ideas.
- Epistemologies, on the other hand stretch from *anti-positivism* on the subjective side to the *positivism* on the objective side of the spectrum. According to Burrell and Morgan (1979) positivism is essentially based on approaches prevalent in natural sciences and it aims at explaining and predicting the happenings of the social world. On the contrary, anti-positivism rejects the observer standpoint, arguing that *understanding* a phenomenon calls for participative and relativist approach to knowledge creation.
- Furthermore, on the subjectivist side of the scale human nature is seen "*voluntaristic*" drawing a focus on people's agency, where the objectivist side is dominated by *determinism.*
- Methodology-wise, Burrell and Morgan separate between subjective, *ideographic* approaches and objectivist, *nomothetic* approaches. Ideographic approach favors obtaining first-hand knowledge on the research topic, nomothetic approach highlights protocol and systematic ways of conducting research.

Many social scientists implicitly or explicitly highlight the distinction between social and natural sciences, between humans and their "background." Some argue that while objectivism and generalizations may give results in the realm of natural sciences, they are not appropriate as such when studying people and their interactions, where subjectivism and interpretivism is called for. Yet this separation of a human from the rest of reality is itself artificial, along with the modernist idea that people and nature could be instrumentalized with the rational tools of scientific thought (Smith 2012; Alvesson and Deetz 2006). Postmodernist intellectual movement came to reject Enlightenment's and modernism's heritage of trying to aim at unveiling part of the true reality through using reason (Burr 1995; Alvesson and Deetz 2006).

Social constructivism is one approach to doing research in social sciences that grew in the domain of social psychology, building heavily on the postmodernism. While social constructionists lay a heavy emphasis on discourses, social constructionism is not merely manifested in language, but also reflected in other aspects of human culture such as buildings (Burr 1995). Where organizational studies have often had a positivistic tone to them, other social scientists, such as ethnographers studying anthropology, have a more constructivist orientation (Mir 2011).

Within disaster studies, realist and positivist research might assume an independent, external reality where a disaster evolves. A researcher holding this stance to disasters might seek to provide ways for mapping or "managing" the disaster from a top-down perspective: finding out the cause-and-effect relations and suggesting the actions that lead to desired outcomes that are measurable. If the researcher were, furthermore, a determinist, the will of the people affected by the disaster would be irrelevant to the "truth." The research conducted by a heavily objectivist researcher is likely to be systematic and aiming for rigor of the method.

A nominalist, anti-positivist research on disaster studies might assume that there is no clear-cut reality where a clear-cut disaster evolves. What a disaster is and to whom, or how it is framed, is a matter of stand-points, of conflicting narratives. What we call a disaster is a social phenomenon, rather than a natural one. The people affected by the disaster have agency, as do the ones involved in organizations providing aid. The methods chosen by a subjectivist researcher would emphasize understanding gained through first-hand knowledge over a systematic method.

Both the subjectivist and the objectivist perspectives can be found within the fields of disaster studies. This is discussed to a greater detail in the following part of the chapter. The Fig. 24.1 describes how the phenomenon can be approached differently, from bottom-up or top-down, but neither perspective is necessarily right or wrong. However, the differing approaches bring out different sides of a phenomenon. Whether we see a forest or a tree is not a question of right or wrong, but of where our research wants to draw the focus to.

While navigating the different layers of subjectivist-objectivist continuum can be helpful, the questioning the philosophical foundations of science can go deeper, drilling to the very foundation of "science." A major issue with Academic research and education is that it continues to carry a Eurocentric and Americanized aura with Greek temple pillars hovering along the impression. The bodies of knowledge that lie beneath its marble steps are generally built by and for "Western," white men. For example, the early social scientists went out to "indigenous" communities to observe them and write

**Fig. 24.1** The format of truth?

about them. These biased accounts not only disregarded the view of the people being studied but also the "knowledge" gained from the biased accounts was sometimes then both the justification, as well as result, of the oppression that ensued (Smith 2012; Fanon 2005).

Furthermore, the academic research that assumes the existence of one reality to be studied can distance it from indigenous communities and other-than-modernist audiences. Blaser (2014) argues that research is not only dealing with one (re)animated world but also a variety of different ontologies that go deep beyond "culture." He stresses the message brought up by various indigenous philosophers and intellectuals, writing that stories are not merely accounts of what is "out there," but "they partake in the variably successful performance of that which they narrate" (Blaser 2014, p. 54). Addressing the heterogeneity of ontologies in the context of Academic research remains a great challenge.

If the purpose of the disaster-related research is indeed geared toward aiding the people affected by disasters, a researcher needs to understand the context within which the research is carried out, as well as at least the defining brush strokes of inequality and privilege that exist in the very pattern of our social reality and that are specific to the context to be studied. If a researcher is studying a disaster in a society or community that she or he is not part of, one might inadvertently end up echoing oppression and inequality, even if that is the thing you have a great intent of critiquing. And even if the research would circulate the right themes, it might stand separate from the practice and echo solidarity in just words. In her book *Muddying the Waters* Nagar (2014, p. 2) writes about "ever-evolving journeys that confront and embrace the messiness of solidarity and responsibility." She argues for muddying the binary between research and activism and emphasizes the role of radical vulnerability – with intellectual and emotional openness to critique – in building politically engaged alliance work that not only advances the research but also the cause.

## Paradigms Behind SCM Research

HLSCM is one of the fields studying disaster relief. In his field-framing memorial lecture paper, Van Wassenhove (2006) argues that private sector logistics should be applied in the humanitarian aid context to improve the performance of disaster logistics. While the suitability of applying for-profit supply chain practices in the not-for-profit context of disaster relief is debated, the proponents of the supply chain management view to disaster relief operations see it as a tool to more effective disaster relief also in the interrupted disaster context (McLachlin et al. 2009, Van Wassenhove 2006). The differences in emphases between the commercial and humanitarian sectors stem not only from the interrupted environment but also from other issues, such as:

- Status quo disrupted
- In humanitarian supply chains the end-user is a "beneficiary" instead of a customer, and organizations represent the customer (Oloruntoba and Gray 2009; Haavisto and Kovács 2014)
- Measuring performance in monetary terms may not be appropriate, yet the supply chain perspective calls for performance measurement, for example, in the form of scorecard (McLachlin et al. 2009)
- Coordination and collaboration is called for, yet building relationships between different humanitarian actors is difficult (Balcik et al. 2010; McLachlin and Larson 2011)
- The organizations should respect the humanitarian principles of humanity, impartiality, neutrality, and independence (OCHA 2011)

Despite these differences, authors in HLSCM often build upon the conventional supply chain management and logistics literature and exploring these underlying assumptions is important. The "management" in supply chain management gives away the connection to, or aspirations toward, management and organizational studies (Mentzer et al. 2001). Logistics and supply chain management are conventionally concerned with managing activities entities and actors, along with flows of information, material, and funds. When things work "well," humans execute the system without bringing "human" errors. Technological tools, such as enterprise resource planning (ERP) systems, are there to make things "smoother." In supply chain management human needs are communicated in the form of demand that is supplied to. The origin of the need and the source of supply are often disconnected, and might cause moral decoupling (Eriksson et al. 2013).

The "management" adds a positivist ring to the field at the offset. While supply chain management along with its predecessor, sibling, and/or subcategory logistics often have a pragmatic flair, Fawcett and Waller (2011) argue that theory is relevant to supply chain research and is not at odds with its relevancy to practice. Research questions in SCM may for example seek to improve the efficiency or effectiveness of a company through seeking the correlations and causations of supply chain management actions and the following results. The aim of the research is often connected to providing top-down managerial implications to an organization. While measuring of processes is common, when people are interviewed, their views are often reflected against how the organization is expected to behave, not in terms of the people's sense making. Managerial or expert views may carry more weight than those of the row employees, that are resources of the organization, rather than its leaders.

Methodology-wise, Spens and Kovács (2006) found out, published research in logistics to be "hypothetico-deductive, with a strong emphasis on using survey methods," while they saw inductive and abductive research gaining ground as well. Case studies are one label under which qualitative research is carried out in the domain of management research. While the management sciences are increasingly welcoming to alternative and critical ways of conducting research – see, for example, Mir's (2011) account on blurring the boundaries of ethnography and case analysis in researching multinational corporations – the positivist case study setup is also visible in HLSCM. Subjectivity is stripped away from the research conducted: for example, through aiming for construct validity, internal validity, external validity, and reliability (Yin 2013) or through having a sample of cases between which one can conduct a cross-case comparison (Eisenhardt

1989). Yet, as Dyer and Wilkins (1991) argue that case studies should go in depth to generate better theory, and the way down deep is through better stories, rather than better constructs.

## Paradigms Behind Disaster Resilience Research

Resilience is discussed under a number of disciplines. It can refer to anything from an organization's ability to withstand competition on a market place to the survival of microbe communities in a petri dish after being disturbed "from the outside." Disaster resilience, on the other hand, is a term closely related to DRR. These streams of literature discuss how human communities face disasters and recover from them. While the concept of resilience conveys the grass-roots, bottom-up, approach and empowerment, disaster resilience and DRR discussions often drift to devising top-down policies. There the priority shifts from the people affected to the people devising the schemes for the people affected.

While the existence and usefulness of the concept "community" can be debated, of the researchers that discussed disaster-related resilience and referred to a "community resilience" tend to be the ones who saw the affected as assemblages with agency, as subjects and not merely as objects. Different scientific communities understand disaster resilience differently and tackle the research process with different methods. Two articles that discuss "community resilience" highlight my understanding of "community resilience" within disaster resilience. Furthermore, they highlight two different approaches to conducting research within "community resilience."

One of the framing articles on "community resilience" was written by Norris et al. (2008) and titled "Community Resilience as a Metaphor, Theory, Set of Capacities, and Strategy for Disaster Readiness." This conceptual article built on literature review and covered many aspects of community resilience – beyond what one would potentially expect from an article published in a journal of community psychology. In 2011 some of the authors behind the 2008 paper came out with an article "Exploring Community Resilience in Workforce Communities of First Responders Serving Katrina Survivors" (Wyche et al. 2011). The paper builds on survey, focus groups, and key informant interviews. The paper uses a qualitative data analysis, building on grounded theory approach with an iterative coding scheme. Clear themes emerge and these themes raise the discussion of the paper, leading finally to implications both to research, policy, and practice. While the paper draws on data of the "community," the paper ends up providing a top-down overview.

Another example of a "community resilience" article is one by Barrios (2014) titled "'Here, I'm not at ease': anthropological perspectives on community resilience". The article "reviews the contributions the anthropological literature and the ethnographic case studies of two post-Hurricane Mitch housing reconstruction sites make to the theorizing of community and resilience in post-disaster reconstruction" (Barrios 2014; p. 330). The methods section describes the paper as an ethnographic narrative built on a survey of 230 households, combined with 40 ethnographic interviews and more than 100 informal conversations. (Barrios 2014) The use of "ethnographic interviews" and the "informal conversations," instead of, for example, "formal and structured interviews" convey a more anti-positivist perspective to research, where the researcher is there to understand and convey understanding of the phenomenon through learning from the "community," instead of providing facts about the community.

While the Barrios' (2014) paper builds on similar notions of community resilience as Norris et al. (2008) and includes a discussion on social capital, the article clearly discusses disasters – and is published in journal titled *Disasters*. The paper's main contribution is the skillful narrative that takes a person through the issues of disaster reconstruction in a particular community, and it is supported by statistical data on the communities discussed. The paper concludes with practical recommendations to researchers, NGOs, and government officials, as well as highlights how communities are not static. Yet where the Wyche et al. (2011) paper's contributions were structured themes upon which conversation was build, this paper's merit is weaved in between the lines.

## Disaster Relief and Resilience

A variety of paradigms and methods are employed within the streams of disaster resilience and community resilience research. What many of these streams of research have in common is their effort in trying to bring out the perspective, voice, and concerns of the community affected by the disaster. Even if the narrative in some cases leads to top-down managerial or policy implications backed by statistical analysis and generalizations, disaster resilience lays a heavier emphasis on bottom-up approaches than disaster relief studies provided by HLSCM. The perspective of HLSCM is a more managerial one and the discussions being had are more pragmatic.

While the context of international long-term development aid projects differs from that of the disaster relief operations, some of the same critical discussions are being had in both spheres. A big question relates to how the aid provided by external organizations is connected to the long-term well-being and resilience of the communities, and some new research addresses this question in the disaster relief context. In their research conducted after the 2009 tsunami in American Samoa, Binder and Baker (2016) discuss how outside aid, provided with a loose understanding of the local culture and practices, was at places miss-aligned and contributed to the disharmony in the aftermath of the tsunami. Binder and Baker further argue that while the people needed help, they were not helpless (2016).

Similarly, Kayser et al. (2008) that studied the connection of disaster relief efforts to local resilience after the South Indian tsunami of 2004, point out that disaster relief research and practice building on understanding of one cultural context may not be applicable in another. Kayser et al. (2008) conclude that while some basic needs may be universal after a disaster, the resources provided should support the communities and individuals affected. While Kayser et al. (2008) highlight their argument with cultural typologies, such as dividing between Western versus non-Western, and individualistic versus collectivistic perspectives, they recognize that subcategories exist.

In disaster relief context resilience is not only characteristic of the affected but also of the organizations providing aid. Day (2014) argues that in disaster relief it is the collective resilience of a disaster relief supply network that leads to reliable aid provision. While the complex adaptive supply network perspective adopted by Day (2014) takes a more holistic view on the disaster relief supply network and its resilience, the demand seen from the side of the affected is rather a part of the environment, than the supply network.

## Methods of a Case Study in Disaster-Related Research

Acknowledging the multitude of different orientations to perceiving and studying the nature of reality can help a researcher see the limitations and merits of one's own approach. Looking at ontologies and epistemologies can put one's understanding about understanding into a perspective. Yet, the label one gives oneself is irrelevant if it does not come to life in the methodology of one's research. While the label might end up shaping one's intent and thus action, action gives the blessing to the label. For example, even if I described myself as an anti-positivist, post-colonialist, feminist researcher, this label is from my perspective less important than how I actually conduct the research I engage in.

Methodology is context-specific, depending on the fields of research contributed to, key pieces of literature built on, research questions chosen, the collaborating authors of a research project from the local university, the access to data, and variety of other factors. Between the two fields of HLSCM and disaster resilience, a world of alternative research methods exists: from surveys to ethnographies, from quantitative to qualitative research. In this part of the chapter, I use the field research conducted by myself and my colleagues in Valparaíso, Chile, in 2014 as a case of what different methodological choices made. The chapter brings out few of the ways in which the paradigmatic clashes underlying my research came to life. If this book chapter has so far appeared to be one of those preaching about unattainable academic standards, this chapter hopefully eases some of that pressure by accentuating how research is an evolving, iterative process.

## A Wicked Mess

I went to Chile for a 1-year research visit. I had drafted a research proposal for my research in Chile a year before going there. Also the research collaboration with a local university was established early on. I had in mind studying the "27F," an earthquake that struck Chile in 2010. I had previously lived briefly in Christchurch, a few years after the city was struck by devastating earthquakes in 2010 and 2011, and I was curious to understand the dynamics of the same "natural" disaster in different societal contexts. Also my professional background also shaped my initial approach. I started out my thesis as an SCM practitioner aiming to be an SCM scholar in the context of disasters.

I had an assumption that empowering local people through a focus on businesses would be a great way to empower the affected communities in the aftermath of a disaster. I saw businesses as representatives of the community, approaching the phenomenon from top-down: I already had the organization in mind, I only needed to know its impact on the community, not vise-versa. I set out to study the involvement of local businesses in disaster relief and reconstruction supply networks. I had in mind to conduct a case study with a focal company. Even if I saw a case study as inductive, I was interested in testing my hypothesis about the applicability of the "universal" supply chain instrument in the new social and societal context. Hence my idea was to build the case study on rigorous, structured interviews.

Yet, as I learned more about disasters through a multitude of academic streams of literature, through books and movies, through songs and news coverage, my mind started to change. The narrative of disasters became far from clear. Causation and correlation ran away from one another, nature and human became entangled, supply chains shifted shapes from power hierarchies to institutions to streams of material. And most of all, I became humbled in front of other cultural contexts and aware of not understanding the history of disasters. This became particularly clear when the focus of my study shifted from the 2010 earthquake to the Valparaíso fire of 2014. The fire erupted in a town next to the city of my up-coming research visit, while I was still in my home country. My collaborator and I agreed that for the purposes of data collection we could study this sudden-onset disaster instead of the earthquake.

As I followed the Chilean and international news coverage on something that I thought I was supposed to become an "expert" on or have a say in as a researcher, I got woozy on the knees and wanted to call the whole thing off. While part of me had acknowledged the complex nature of disasters, the HLSCM literature had given me a slightly naïve perspective to disasters. In the commercial context I had seen SCM as the instrument to match market demand with the supply. I had assumed that in the disaster relief SCM the difference was just semantics, and matching humanitarian need with supply was not all that different from the commercial side. However, as I started seeing disasters more as social and societal wounds with long histories and a multitude of narratives, the managerial perspective to need-supply matching seemed to only scratch the surface. If HLSCM was an instrument in responding to a disaster, how would the instrument work toward healing the deeper, long-term wounds? To better understand the view of the communities, I hung on to disaster resilience literature. Without realizing it, the ontology and epistemology of the researcher in me had taken many steps toward the subjectivist direction. In my eyes also HLSCM had gained more shades between the positivist blacks and whites.

The humbling continued during my whole stay in Chile, where I had the great chance of meeting wonderful people who shared with me their disaster narratives. Sometimes this happened in formal interview situations or on "field visits," while at other times the encounters and other learning experiences took place in the stream of the everyday. For example, when buying fresh vegetables from the market or bread and avocado from the corner store, I realized for myself that my original idea of studying the local businesses through supply chain management lens would have drawn the focus on the bigger enterprises operating locally. This would not have met my real aim of empowerment of the people in the affected neighborhoods. While my friend with a Chilean history had hinted at that already earlier, it had been hard for me to *cachar*[1] prior to living there.

The wonderfully outlined research of mine with a focal company had turned into a bunch of narratives from the sides of organizations and the "community" that did not fit together and raised more questions than they answered. Furthermore, the fact that I kept learning daily about the local everyday kept me constantly on my toes: if I keep forgetting where to put the toilet paper in the bathroom, how can I expect to have anything to say about how disasters should be managed? I was in a turmoil of shaky philosophical orientations, where full-blown social constructivism seemed like the only way to progress in my research process, even if it at the same time questioned the whole idea of having social scientists. In the end, my interviews were semi-structured, some leaning toward open-ended. I had field notes from field visits, pictures and videos of the city, its reconstruction and nature. I continued to walk the hills of the city. Yet I believe I learned most about disaster-related phenomena also during my "free time," in informal settings. For example, upon hearing what I study, people would tell me stories about their experiences with disasters, the relation of disasters to everyday life and interpretations of what ought to be done.

Also my own narrative, of disasters and myself, was changing. Coming from a global periphery, I had lived under a false inherent conviction of my own objectivity in the global system. While I had acknowledged subjectivity of research, I had not thoroughly gone through the subjectivity of my own sensemaking before the "field" research in Chile. As I found myself weaving together other people's narratives of a disaster, I realized I had to go through my own loom and its compatibility with the narratives I was facing. While through the reflexive process I came to know my own narratives and identities better, what stroke me most as a researcher was in which ways the "Western" academic heritage followed me around and how much I represented it. When communicating of my research I often used English (instead of Spanish or my native Finnish) and referred to academic theories that may not have reflected even my own sense-making processes in my own cultural context. The access to data that I had – or did not have – was rarely related to who I thought I was, but what I was perceived as representing as a researcher. Despite who I thought I had been, I was walking around with the aura of Western Academia and leveraging its power.

---

[1] Get it.

Also my former SCM practitioner experiences started haunting me: the expectations of the global business environment had never made sense in the light of the ontology I had grown into. Yet I had been able to buy the basic assumptions without much questioning when working as a practitioner, and was also bringing some of these same assumptions into my research.

The mess of and distinction between private narratives and "organizational" narratives became vital also in my research process, as I was trying to make sense of the Valparaíso fire both from the point of view of the aiding organizations, as well as the community. While the data came in many forms and from many sources, one many of those formally interviewed were both representing an organization, as well as part of the affected community. Through the interviews I was able to hear both people's views on the disaster as private people, as well as from the point of view of the organization they were presenting.

This was extremely interesting and provided valuable insight, but it also made dealing with the "data" more complex. It was understood that people did not want their private, more informal opinions and sensemaking to be connected to organizational "truths." The interviewees were given chances to comment on the transcripts of the recorded interviews and no quotes would be taken without their permission. Furthermore, the narratives were weaved together, instead of being used separately in ways that could expose individual views. While this provided anonymity and a more coherent view on the phenomenon, at the same time it brought back the issue about the looms of the researcher: is it the community talking, bottom-up, or is it the researcher claiming to speak for a greater community? Are the respondents aware of what type of research they are contributing to, when the focus is not clearly on the organizations, nor on the community, but in between?

## Some Sense of Clarity

While throughout the data collection I was overwhelmed by a sense of humility and felt that I knew absolutely nothing about anyone else's world, and no one narrative would ever exist, when I finally got distance from the phenomenon, a narrative started forming. Through adopting an oscillating stand-point to my data through a set of theories, concepts and methods I was able to start weaving together the different strands of information. I hoarded literature to make my standpoint seem more secure. I read more on disaster resilience literature, political philosophical theories and paired these up with the supply chain management perspective. Not everything fitted together perfectly, but through reflecting my data against my philosophical stand-point "pile" of cake I was able to see how what I had learned formed a narrative that I believed was worth writing.

While I drew from the disaster resilience literature and was truly interested in community empowerment, I realized that neither the formal interviews conducted with different organizations, nor the informal encounters that took place, gave me the entitlement to speak for the people affected. In many ways I was looking at the phenomenon top-down, as a foreigner, and primarily through the lenses of the organizations providing aid, rather than those to be aided. Even if what I saw through my lenses would not have been same as what the organizations saw, I could not in this case wiggle out of that point of view and speak the narrative of the "resilient" communities.

Through adopting an oscillating stand-point I did not at first abandon social constructivism and highly subjective, interpretivist approach. Yet, as I started putting the pieces of the narrative together and pulling then toward the bodies of knowledge, my words started carrying more universal claims with respect to the phenomenon. The narrative was further broken to a few academic articles: one paper with a heavier focus on the "bottom-up" perspective of disaster resilience, and another from the managerial "top-down" perspective. Yet both pieces of literature navigated the same interface, between the network of aid providers and the community affected.

Throughout the research process, my understanding of "my" ontology and epistemology evolved and I became more conscious of this evolution. While my peripheral ontology bred by my background was often clashing with the academic bodies of knowledge, as a researcher I was operating in their sphere of influence and my thinking was directed by the dominant narratives, even if I tried to wriggle away from their grasp and see different ontologies. I was not able to consolidate all the ontological clashes, yet for a fleeting moment I was able to pin down what the reality was for me as a social scientist, and how the epistemology and methods of my research aligned with that.

As a human living on the planet Earth – and hoping to continue living on it for some time still – in my reality I saw a magnificent rock floating through space, covered in beautiful greens and blues. Yet something gray was growing on its surface. The social scientist in me saw also a cloth, almost transparent, on top of the big round rock. The cloth was weaved with stories. It may not have been the only cloth, but it is the one I could see. There were thick strands of narratives crisscrossing the cloth as well as countless delicate ones all around it. Some – not all – of the big, thick, narratives were entangled with the ugly gray growing on the rock and eating the green and blue.

When I was doing research, I was pulling the cloth from one corner, seeing how it folds differently depending on where I pulled and whether I pulled the dominant narrative or not. Pulling a dominant narrative was easy. One tug lifted a cloth in visible way that was easy to describe. But a dominant narrative was just one of the narratives. It may have also been connected to nasty gray stuff. So I wanted to be careful and tried pulling gently here and there, following the different folds of the cloth. Finally, as a researcher I was expected to contribute, and I started laying my own teeny tiny stiches on the cloth. How and where I pulled, tugged, and stitched the cloth was my methodology as a social scientist.[2]

## Conclusion

The chapter began by introducing two fields of research that study disasters are being prepared for, responded to and recovered from. Where the field of HLSCM focuses on how organizations providing aid could organize their operations and supply chains, the disaster resilience literature can bring out the view and agency of the people affected by a disaster. Through drawing from the two fields of research, bottom-up and top-down perspectives on disaster-related research could be bridged. This would broaden the perspective of aid provision from the shorter term managerial implications to long-term community perspective, as well as policy implications.

Yet conducting interdisciplinary research is not straightforward. Different streams of literature flow from different springs, build on different theories and philosophical foundations. The ontological and epistemological assumptions may lay buried in the history of the field, but still continue to influence how the research in the field is conducted. Different fields of research expect different scoping, sampling, data collection, analysis, and write-up. While silos are being broken, much of the effort of academics is about preaching to the choir, a pre-existing scientific community, and conventions are held. A researcher navigating between two or more fields benefits from understanding the underlining paradigmatic differences, shuffling between them and searching for balance.

The chapter went through the ontological, epistemological, and methods paradigms underlying disaster resilience and HLSCM research from the

---

[2] In this metaphor, bottom-up view would consist of stitching together a narrative building on the delicate strands of narratives, whereas a top-down view would follow along the seams of the dominant narratives.

researcher's angle to the two fields. As the paradigms and their clashes culminate in the method, in the end of this book chapter methods of the author's field research process were described through a narrative. The different paradigms were present throughout the journey and were interacting even in the final "outputs." The method chosen could be simplistically titled as an inductive case study or an ethnography. Yet instead of providing a label, the purpose of the case was to provide insight into how the research process and methodological stance evolved and how the understanding developed through different paradigmatic perspectives. The case highlights how the ontology, epistemology, and methods of the research did not layer up in a perfect manner. The real research process was not straightforward execution of a conviction, but a process of weaving and reflecting on the loom.

# References

Alexander, D. E. 2013. "Resilience and Disaster Risk Reduction: An Etymological Journey." *Natural Hazards and Earth System Sciences* 13 (November): 2707–16. doi:10.5194/nhess-13-2707-2013.

ALNAP. 2015. "State Of The Humanitarian System Report 2015." Accessed October 8. http://www.alnap.org/resource/21036.aspx.

Altay, Nezih, and Walter G. Green III. 2006. "OR/MS Research in Disaster Operations Management." *European Journal of Operational Research* 175 (1): 475–93. doi:10.1016/j.ejor.2005.05.016.

Alvesson, Mats, and Stanley A. Deetz. 2006. "Critical Theory and Postmodernism Approaches to Organizational Studies." In *The SAGE Handbook of Organization Studies*, 255–83. 1 Oliver's Yard, 55 City Road, London EC1Y 1SP United Kingdom: SAGE Publications Ltd. http://sk.sagepub.com/reference/hdbk_org studies2ed/n8.xml.

Balcik, Burcu, Benita M. Beamon, Caroline C. Krejci, Kyle M. Muramatsu, and Magaly Ramirez. 2010. "Coordination in Humanitarian Relief Chains: Practices, Challenges and Opportunities." *International Journal of Production Economics*, Improving Disaster Supply Chain Management – Key supply chain factors for humanitarian relief, 126 (1): 22–34. doi:10.1016/j.ijpe.2009.09.008.

Barrios, Roberto E. 2014. "'Here, I'm Not at Ease': Anthropological Perspectives on Community Resilience." *Disasters* 38 (2): 329–50. doi:10.1111/disa.12044.

Binder, Sherri Brokopp, and Charlene K. Baker. 2016. "Culture, Local Capacity, and Outside Aid: A Community Perspective on Disaster Response after the 2009 Tsunami in American Sāmoa." *Disasters*, May, n/a – n/a. doi:10.1111/disa.12203.

Blaser, Mario. 2014. "Ontology and Indigeneity: On the Political Ontology of Heterogeneous Assemblages." *Cultural Geographies* 21 (1): 49–58. doi:10.1177/1474474012462534.

Burr, Vivien. 1995. *An Introduction to Social Constructionism.* New York: Routledge.

Burrell, Gibson, and Gareth Morgan. 1979. *Sociological Paradigms and Organizational Analysis.* London: Heinemann.

Cupples, Julie, and Kevin Glynn. 2014. "The Mediation and Remediation of Disaster: Hurricanes Katrina and Felix In/and the New Media Environment." *Antipode* 46 (2): 359–81. doi:10.1111/anti.12060.

Curtis, Mark. 2016. "Gated Development – Is the Gates Foundation Always a Force for Good?" *Global Justice Now.* January 20. http://www.globaljustice.org.uk/resources/gated-development-gates-foundation-always-force-good.

Cutter, Susan L., Bryan J. Boruff, and W. Lynn Shirley. 2003. "Social Vulnerability to Environmental Hazards*." *Social Science Quarterly* 84 (2): 242–61. doi:10.1111/1540-6237.8402002.

Cutter, Susan L., Lindsey Barnes, Melissa Berry, Christopher Burton, Elijah Evans, Eric Tate, and Jennifer Webb. 2008. "A Place-Based Model for Understanding Community Resilience to Natural Disasters." *Global Environmental Change*, Local evidence on vulnerabilities and adaptations to global environmental change, 18 (4): 598–606. doi:10.1016/j.gloenvcha.2008.07.013.

Day, Jamison M. 2014. "Fostering Emergent Resilience: The Complex Adaptive Supply Network of Disaster Relief." *International Journal of Production Research* 52 (7): 1970–88. doi:10.1080/00207543.2013.787496.

Day, Jamison M., Steven A. Melnyk, Paul D. Larson, Edward W. Davis, and D. Clay Whybark. 2012. "Humanitarian and Disaster Relief Supply Chains: A Matter of Life and Death." *Journal of Supply Chain Management* 48 (2): 21–36. doi:10.1111/j.1745-493X.2012.03267.x.

Diprose, Kristina. 2014. "Resilience Is Futile: The Cultivation of Resilience Is Not an Answer to Austerity and Poverty." *Soundings: A Journal of Politics and Culture* 58 (1): 44–56.

Dyer, W. Gibb, and Alan L. Wilkins. 1991. "Better Stories, Not Better Constructs, To Generate Better Theory: A Rejoinder to Eisenhardt." *Academy of Management Review* 16 (3): 613–19. doi:10.5465/AMR.1991.4279492.

Eisenhardt, Kathleen M. 1989. "Building Theories from Case Study Research." *Academy of Management Review* 14 (4): 532–50. doi:10.5465/AMR.1989.4308385.

Elliott, James R., and Jeremy Pais. 2006. "Race, Class, and Hurricane Katrina: Social Differences in Human Responses to Disaster." *Social Science Research*, Katrina in New Orleans/Special Issue on Contemporary Research on the Family, 35 (2): 295–321. doi:10.1016/j.ssresearch.2006.02.003.

Eriksson, David, Per Hilletofth, and Olli-Pekka Hilmola. 2013. "Linking Moral Disengagement to Supply Chain Practices." *World Review of Intermodal Transportation Research* 4 (2–3): 207–25. doi:10.1504/WRITR.2013.058987.

Fanon, F., Sartre, J.-P., and Bhabha, H. K. (2005). *The Wretched of the Earth.* (R. Philcox, Trans.) (Reprint edition). New York: Grove Press.

Fawcett, Amydee M., and Stanley E. Fawcett. 2013. "Benchmarking the State of Humanitarian Aid and Disaster Relief: A Systems Design Perspective and Research Agenda." *Benchmarking: An International Journal* 20 (5): 661–92. doi:10.1108/BIJ-07-2011-0053.

Fawcett, Stanley E., and Matthew A. Waller. 2011. "Making Sense Out of Chaos: Why Theory Is Relevant to Supply Chain Research." *Journal of Business Logistics* 32 (1): 1–5. doi:10.1111/j.2158-1592.2011.01000.x.

Foucault, Michel. 2012. *The Archaeology of Knowledge.* New York: Knopf Doubleday Publishing Group.

Haavisto, Ira, and Gyöngyi Kovács. 2014. "Perspectives on Sustainability in Humanitarian Supply Chains." *Disaster Prevention and Management: An International Journal* 23 (5): 610–31. doi:10.1108/DPM-10-2013-0192.

Harrison, Philip, Marie Huchzermeyer, and Mzwanele Mayekiso. 2003. *Confronting Fragmentation: Housing and Urban Development in a Democratising Society.* Lansdowne: University of Cape Town Press, Juta and Company Ltd.

Harvey, David. 2005. *A Brief History of Neoliberalism.* Oxford: Oxford University Press.

Holling, C. S. 1973. "Resilience and Stability of Ecological Systems." *Annual Review of Ecology and Systematics* 4 (1): 1–23. doi:10.1146/annurev.es.04.110173.000245.

IFRC (International Federation of Red Cross and Red Crescent Societies). 2010. "World Disasters Report 2010: Focus on Urban Risk."

IFRC (International Federation of Red Cross and Red Crescent Societies). 2014. "World Disasters Report 2014: Focus on Culture and Risk." Geneva, Switzerland: International Federation of Red Cross and Red Crescent Societies.

Kayser, Karen, Leslie Wind, and R. Ashok Shankar. 2008. "Disaster Relief Within a Collectivistic Context: Supporting Resilience After the Tsunami in South India." *Journal of Social Service Research* 34 (3): 87–98.

Kelman, Ilan, J.C. Gaillard, and Jessica Mercer. 2015. "Climate Change's Role in Disaster Risk Reduction's Future: Beyond Vulnerability and Resilience." *International Journal of Disaster Risk Science* 6 (1): 21–27. doi:10.1007/s13753-015-0038-5.

Klein, Naomi. 2015. *This Changes Everything: Capitalism vs. The Climate.* Reprint edition. New York: Simon & Schuster.

Kovács, Gyöngyi, and Karen M. Spens. 2007. "Humanitarian Logistics in Disaster Relief Operations." *International Journal of Physical Distribution & Logistics Management* 37 (2): 99–114. doi:10.1108/09600030710734820.

Ledford, Heidi. 2015. "How to Solve the World's Biggest Problems." *Nature* 525 (7569): 308–11. doi:10.1038/525308a.

Luker, Kristin. 2008. *Salsa Dancing into the Social Sciences: Research in an Age of Info-Glut.* USA: Harvard University Press.

Manyena, Siambabala Bernard. 2014. "Disaster Resilience: A Question of 'multiple Faces' and 'multiple Spaces'?" *International Journal of Disaster Risk Reduction* 8 (June): 1–9. doi:10.1016/j.ijdrr.2013.12.010.

Maon, François, Lindgreen, Adam, and Vanhamme, Joëlle. 2009. "Developing Supply Chains in Disaster Relief Operations through Cross-sector Socially Oriented Collaborations: A Theoretical Model." *Supply Chain Management: An International Journal* 14 (2): 149–64. doi:10.1108/13598540910942019.

Martens, Jens, and Karolin Seitz. 2015. "Philanthropic Power and Development Who Shapes the Agenda?" Bischöfliches Hilfswerk MISEREOR.

McLachlin, R., and P.D. Larson. 2011. "Building Humanitarian Supply Chain Relationships: Lessons from Leading Practitioners." *Journal of Humanitarian Logistics and Supply Chain Management* 1 (1): 32–49. doi:10.1108/20426741111122402.

McLachlin, Ron, Paul D. Larson, and Soaleh Khan. 2009. "Not-for-Profit Supply Chains in Interrupted Environments: The Case of a Faith-Based Humanitarian Relief Organisation." *Management Research News* 32 (11): 1050–64. doi:http://dx.doi.org/10.1108/01409170910998282.

Mentzer, John T., William DeWitt, James S. Keebler, Soonhong Min, and et al. 2001. "Defining Supply Chain Management." *Journal of Business Logistics* 22 (2): 1–26.

Mir, Raza. 2011. Blurring the Boundaries Between Case Analysis and Ethnography: Reflections on A Hybrid Approach to Researching Multinational Corporations. In R. Marschan-Piekkari & C. Welch (Eds.), *Rethinking the Case Study in International Business and Management Research*, 301–322. Edward Elgar Publishing.

Nagar, Richa. 2014. *Muddying the Waters: Coauthoring Feminisms across Scholarship and Activism.* 1st edition. Champaign: University of Illinois Press.

Norris, Fran H., Susan P. Stevens, Betty Pfefferbaum, Karen F. Wyche, and Rose L. Pfefferbaum. 2008. "Community Resilience as a Metaphor, Theory, Set of Capacities, and Strategy for Disaster Readiness." *American Journal of Community Psychology* 41 (1–2): 127–50. doi:10.1007/s10464-007-9156-6.

OCHA. 2011. "Humanitarian Principles |OCHA." http://www.unocha.org/about-us/publications/humanitarian-principles.

Richard Oloruntoba, and Richard Gray. 2009. "Customer Service in Emergency Relief Chains." *International Journal of Physical Distribution & Logistics Management* 39 (6): 486–505. doi:10.1108/09600030910985839.

Singh-Peterson, Lila, Paul Salmon, Natassia Goode, and John Gallina. 2014. "Translation and Evaluation of the Baseline Resilience Indicators for Communities on the Sunshine Coast, Queensland Australia." *International Journal of Disaster Risk Reduction* 10, Part A (0): 116–26. http://www.sciencedirect.com/science/article/pii/S2212420914000570#.

Smit, Barry, and Johanna Wandel. 2006. "Adaptation, Adaptive Capacity and Vulnerability." *Global Environmental Change*, Resilience, Vulnerability, and Adaptation: A Cross-Cutting Theme of the International Human Dimensions

Programme on Global Environmental Change Resilience, Vulnerability, and Adaptation: A Cross-Cutting Theme of the International Human Dimensions Programme on Global Environmental Change, 16 (3): 282–92. doi:10.1016/j. gloenvcha.2006.03.008.

Smith. 2006. "There's No Such Thing as a Natural Disaster." *Understanding Katrina: Perspectives from the Social Sciences.* http://understandingkatrina.ssrc. org/Smith.

Smith, Linda Tuhiwai. 2012. *Decolonizing Methodologies.* 2nd edition. London & New York: Zed Books.

Spens, Karen M., and Gyöngyi Kovács. 2006. "A Content Analysis of Research Approaches in Logistics Research." *International Journal of Physical Distribution & Logistics Management* 36 (5): 374–90. doi:http://dx.doi.org/10.1108/ 09600030610676259.

Stephens, Nicole M., MarYam G. Hamedani, Hazel Rose Markus, Hilary B. Bergsieker, and Liyam Eloul. 2009. "Why Did They 'Choose' to Stay? Perspectives of Hurricane Katrina Observers and Survivors." *Psychological Science* 20 (7): 878–86. doi:10.1111/j.1467-9280.2009.02386.x.

UNISDR (United Nations International Strategy for Disaster Risk Reduction). 2005. "Hyogo Framework for 2005–2015: Building the Resilience of Nations and Communities to Disasters." http://www.unisdr.org/2005/wcdr/intergover/ official-doc/L-docs/Hyogo-framework-for-action-english.pdf.

UNISDR (United Nations International Strategy for Disaster Risk Reduction). 2009. "Terminology on Disaster Risk Reduction." http://www.unisdr.org/files/ 7817_UNISDRTerminologyEnglish.pdf.

UNISDR (United Nations International Strategy for Disaster Risk Reduction). 2015. "Sendai Framework for Disaster Risk Reduction 2015–2030." United Nations.

United Nations. 2014. "World Urbanization Prospects: 2014 Revision."

United Nations. 2015a. "ADOPTION OF THE PARIS AGREEMENT." https:// unfccc.int/resource/docs/2015/cop21/eng/l09r01.pdf.

United Nations. 2015b. "A/RES/70/1 – Transforming Our World: The 2030 Agenda for Sustainable Development."

Van Wassenhove, L. N. 2006. "Humanitarian Aid Logistics: Supply Chain Management in High Gear." *Journal of the Operational Research Society* 57 (5): 475–89. doi:10.1057/palgrave.jors.2602125.

Wilson, Geoff A. 2012. "Community Resilience, Globalization, and Transitional Pathways of Decision-Making." *Geoforum*, Themed issue: Spatialities of Ageing, 43 (6): 1218–31. doi:10.1016/j.geoforum.2012.03.008.

Wilson, Geoff A. 2013. "Community Resilience, Policy Corridors and the Policy Challenge." *Land Use Policy*, Themed Issue 1-Guest Editor Romy Greiner Themed Issue 2- Guest Editor Davide Viaggi, 31 (March): 298–310. doi:10.1016/j.landusepol.2012.07.011.

Wyche, Karen Fraser, Rose L. Pfefferbaum, Betty Pfefferbaum, Fran H. Norris, Deborah Wisnieski, and Hayden Younger. 2011. "Exploring Community

Resilience in Workforce Communities of First Responders Serving Katrina Survivors." *American Journal of Orthopsychiatry* 81 (1): 18–30. doi:http://dx. doi.org/10.1111/j.1939-0025.2010.01068.x.

Yarnal, Brent. 2007. "Vulnerability and All That Jazz: Addressing Vulnerability in New Orleans after Hurricane Katrina." *Technology in Society*, Perspectives on Hurricane Katrina, 29 (2): 249–55. doi:10.1016/j.techsoc.2007.01.011.

Yin, Robert K. 2013. *Case Study Research: Design and Methods*. 5th edition. Los Angeles: SAGE Publications, Inc.

# Index

© The Author(s) 2018                                                    **743**
G. Kovács et al. (eds.), *The Palgrave Handbook of Humanitarian Logistics
and Supply Chain Management*, https://doi.org/10.1057/978-1-137-59099-2

CPSIA information can be obtained
at www.ICGtesting.com
Printed in the USA
BVOW06*0829261017
498722BV00001B/4/P